Caldera® OpenLinux

INSTALLATION AND CONFIGURATION HANDBOOK

Gary Wilson

Caldera® OpenLinux Installation and Configuration Handbook

International Standard Book Number: 0-7897-2105-8

Library of Congress Catalog Card Number: 99-62401

Printed in the United States of America

First Printing: September 1999

01   00   99   4   3   2   1

Trademarks

Warning and Disclaimer

EXECUTIVE EDITOR
Jeff Koch

ACQUISITIONS EDITOR
Gretchen Ganser

DEVELOPMENT EDITOR
Hugh Vandivier

TECHNICAL EDITORS
Eric Richardson
Kurt Wall

MANAGING EDITOR
Lisa Wilson

PROJECT EDITOR
Natalie Harris

COPY EDITORS
JoAnna Kremer
Matt Wooden

INDEXER
Diane Brenner

PROOFREADER
Billy Fields

SOFTWARE DEVELOPMENT SPECIALIST
Michael Hunter

INTERIOR DESIGN
Anne Jones

COVER DESIGN
Maureen McCarty

LAYOUT TECHNICIAN
Timothy Osborn

Contents at a Glance

Table of Contents

III Configuring Hardware

8 Installing and Configuring Printers 233

27 Installing and Configuring Mail Services   529

28 Installing and Configuring an FTP Server   535

29 Overview of Network Security   543

Appendixes

About the Author

Gary Wilson is the Director of Computer Services for a medial research center at Columbia University's School of Physicians and Surgeons. He has worked on computers for the last 25 years and has worked as a trainer and training consultant for 10 years, publishing several articles, Internet-posted essays, and training manuals in Word Perfect, Corel Draw, PageMaker, and Ventura Publisher. Gary has worked with Linux since 1995 and has experience in setting up, maintaining, and integrating systems on computer networks and teaching new users how to use Linux.

Dedication

I would like to dedicate this book to Lallan Schoenstein, who showed me the meaning of laissez les bons temps rouler.

Acknowledgments

Book credits should run on and on, like the credits at the end of a movie. That can't really be done, even if that many people should get recognition. There is a long list of people involved who make the whole production possible.

Special recognition should go to Gretchen Ganser, who made this book happen.

Many others at Que should also be recognized. Development Editor Hugh Vandivier, in particular, made many improvements to the manuscript. The Technical Editors—Kurt Wall, the author of *Linux Programming Unleashed*, and Eric C. Richardson—made invaluable improvements.

This book never would have happened if it weren't for Caldera Systems and their first-rate Linux distribution. Also, of course, hundreds, probably thousands, have made the Linux operating system and open source software a reality: Linus Torvalds (Linux), Alan Cox (maintainer of the Linux kernel), and Donald Becker (Linux's networking code); Richard Stallman (GNU and Free Software Foundation); Andrew Tridgell, Jeremy Allison, Luke Kenneth Casson Leighton, and all the members of the Samba Team; Larry Wall (Perl); Brian Behlendorf (Apache); John Ousterhout (Tcl/Tk); Guido van Rossum (Python); John Gilmore (the GNU project/Cygnus Solutions); Paul Vixie (Bind); Eric Allman (Sendmail); and Eric Raymond (Open Source Initiative). It is impossible to list everyone, but I am grateful to them all and offer my apologies to all I have not listed.

The OpenLinux users' mail list deserves its own recognition. Participants such as Eric Ratcliffe, David Bandel, and many more unselfishly give their time to help others whenever they have a problem. The OpenLinux users list is possibly the highest quality discussion list I've ever seen on the Internet.

Many others have helped me bring this book to a finish, including George Balassi, who seems to know something about everything related to computers; Charles Petzold, who knows everything you'd ever want to know about computer code; and Deirdre Stapp, who is a very good teacher. Thanks to my colleagues at Columbia University's Sergievsky Center, especially Victor Moran, who had to shoulder an extra load for me.

Tell Us What You Think!

As the reader of this book, *you* are our most important critic and commentator. We value your opinion and want to know what we're doing right, what we could do better, what areas you'd like to see us publish in, and any other words of wisdom you're willing to pass our way.

As the Associate Publisher for Que, I welcome your comments. You can fax, email, or write me directly to let me know what you did or didn't like about this book—as well as what we can do to make our books stronger.

Please note that I cannot help you with technical problems related to the topic of this book, and that due to the high volume of mail I receive, I might not be able to reply to every message.

When you write, please be sure to include this book's title and author as well as your name and phone or fax number. I will carefully review your comments and share them with the author and editors who worked on the book.

Fax: 317.581.4663

Email: opsys@mcp.com

Mail: Associate Publisher
          Que
          201 West 103rd Street
          Indianapolis, IN 46290 USA

Introduction

Linux is one of the most versatile computer operating systems available today. It has the capability of performing functions usually found only on high-priced computer systems, yet the cost for a Linux system is considerably lower.

The secret to Linux's success is that it can run on or use just about any computer hardware out there and it is compatible with practically any other system available. Never before has such a friendly and compatible computer operating system been able to get along with just about any combination of hardware you can throw at it.

Ask someone who works on one of those high-end systems about Linux and you will often find they envy what you can do with your Linux computer. Not only can your Linux computer do what their computers are doing, it can use common, easy to get hardware like Jaz drives and CD-ROM writers that they can only dream about.

That's part of the secret to Linux's success as an operating system. A low price is nice, but it's not enough to ensure success. The system has to be able to do what you need.

Open Source Software

Open is the key word to the Linux operating system. It is so important that this distribution of Linux is called *Open*Linux.

Perhaps you already know why open source software is considered by many computer professionals to be the best choice possible. In that case, you may not need to know why Linux is one of the most reliable computer operating systems available today.

On the other hand, maybe you bought this book because you want to know more about a "free" operating system. Then you might want to know what free really means.

Linux is free. That is true. However, it doesn't mean that there is no cost involved. Often, there is a price to be paid, but it's usually quite low and reasonable.

When it is said that Linux is free, it means free from stifling restrictions. The license covering the Linux kernel and many of the utilities and programming tools that come with it was established by the Free Software Foundation. This is the GNU General Public License, also called GPL or copyleft (like many things in Linux, a play on the word copyright). The terms of the license are included in Appendix C, "The GNU General Public License," of this book.

Under the terms of this license, Linux may be freely distributed by anyone, anywhere, at any time. No restrictions. But it is not shareware, freeware, or public domain software. Linus Torvalds and others who have contributed to its development retain the copyright to the Linux source code. But the code is available to study, improve, give away, or sell, as long as nothing is done that would restrict any of these rights.

The Free Software Foundation was initiated by Richard Stallman, a brilliant computer programmer at the Massachusetts Institute of Technology who found that copyrights and patents were getting in the way of software development. The GNU General Public License gives people the freedom to develop, copy, learn from, change, and improve software without fear of legal entanglements.

The majority of OpenLinux users will probably never look at the source code or attempt to modify it in any way. Few people even know how to tinker with the computer's operating system. Moreover, even if you knew how to work with the source code, it is unlikely you would be spending your time modifying the operating system—unless you are a member of the Linux development team. It is an involved process that takes a great deal of time and effort.

So you might wonder, what does it really matter?

Originally, all software was open source. That is, anyone who wanted it had access to the source code for the computer programs.

From the very beginning, computer code was shared by everyone. Progress depended on making sure that any developer working on a computer system had access to whatever code had already been written. There was no reason to rewrite what had been done by others. Computer programmers could take the best of what had already been developed and build on it. Shared code was the foundation for all computer development. It worked so well, computers have practically taken over the world.

Limiting access to code is a recent development. Many top software developers believe that this blocks progress. Open source licensing is designed to protect the foundations of computer software development and to keep it open and free from restrictions.

Open source development is based on a time-tested model. Open source uses the peer review process at the heart of the scientific method. Following this trusted scientific model, open source software must stand up to the most demanding scrutiny. This is different than what is used in closed source development, where testing is often limited so that "secrets" are not revealed. Open source software goes through a rigorous review that ensures that only the best survives.

Scientists publish their results for others to examine, verify, and use. When open source software is published, it is widely examined and verified. Sloppy or inefficient code is quickly dismissed. New ideas can be added just as quickly. Changes can be added based on suggestions by reviewers. In fact, open source code testing and development is more comprehensive and effective than is possible in the closed environment imposed during the development of proprietary software systems and applications.

"Given a sufficient number of eyeballs," says the president of the Open Source Initiative, Eric S. Raymond, "all bugs are shallow." Open source software makes it easier to correct bugs. And open source distribution makes it very difficult to hide defects or computer viruses in the software. It is difficult, if not impossible, for developers of open source software to hide defects. The peer review system eliminates the factor of people with a vested interest in a product being put in the position of also being responsible for testing the software's capabilities and then verifying its usability.

With the development of a global Internet, Linux software development has become worldwide. Some of the most highly skilled computer professionals around the world from Pakistan and India to Mexico and South Africa are now working on developing open source software 24 hours a day.

It is one of the greatest collective development projects ever seen. Many open source development groups such as the Samba team, which designed the award-winning software that integrates Linux and Windows computers, are working together even though they are in many different countries.

In fact, open source applications are the foundation of the Internet. The success of the Internet is proof enough of the stability and robustness of open source systems and applications.

Take the example of just one open source application: TCP/IP. TCP/IP is the communication protocol used by computers to "talk" to each other over the Internet. It is the core network protocol found in OpenLinux.

TCP/IP was first designed in the 1970s. Its purpose was to allow dissimilar computers to talk to each other. It worked. As the Internet grew from its modest beginning, users helped to improve TCP/IP and developed it so that today it is found on virtually all workstations, mini-computers, and mainframes.

As a result of years of unrestricted open source distribution and the contribution of many users, TCP/IP is the most widely used network protocol in the world. It is so successful that Microsoft has adopted TCP/IP as the primary network protocol for its Windows NT system even though it has its own proprietary network protocols.

There are many other open source success stories. Samba is the open source program that connects Linux and UNIX computers with Windows computers. It is so successful that SGI distributes it with some of its graphics computers and *Windows NT Systems* magazine gave it a top award for its excellence in Windows networking.

The Apache Web server that is included with OpenLinux is another open source application. This is the most popular Web server available, with over 50% of the market worldwide. Its popularity isn't just because it is "free" software. It is because open source development has allowed Apache to become the best Web server product available. It is so predominant in its field that both IBM and Apple have chosen it as the default Web server on some of their commercial platforms.

In fact, the entire Internet is an open source success story.

More information on open source software can be found at these Web sites:

- The Free Software Foundation at www.fsf.org
- The Open Source Initiative at www.opensource.org

Caldera OpenLinux

Caldera OpenLinux combines the Linux kernel and hundreds of applications and utilities. I use the terms *Linux* and *OpenLinux* in this book. *Linux* refers to the operating system in general, whereas *OpenLinux* refers to the specific distribution prepared by Caldera Systems.

See "What Is Caldera OpenLinux" in Chapter 1, "Preparing to Install OpenLinux" for more information.

Caldera OpenLinux couples the ease of installation and ease of use of a Windows-based system with the advanced sophistication of a UNIX-like operating system. And OpenLinux comes with professional office applications—word processing and spreadsheets—that are the most commonly sought by computer users. Using Linux has never been easier.

While OpenLinux is a remarkable high-end system, it is no more difficult to install and maintain than Microsoft's Windows NT operating system.

OpenLinux adds hundreds of computer applications, including Corel WordPerfect, the StarOffice suite (StarWriter, StarCalc, and StarOffice Presentation), and Netscape Communicator. But there is much more.

OpenLinux includes a full set of network applications including TCP/IP, the Internet protocol, and PPP for dial-up connections to the Internet. Other Internet programs include the Apache Web server as well as telnet, FTP, and email applications.

OpenLinux also has graphics programs including GIMP, an image processor similar to Photoshop, and Paint. It has games, multimedia, and a long list of utilities.

This book takes you through the entire installation process and the different options that are available in OpenLinux. It covers many configuration options, and it shows you some of the most common ways OpenLinux computer systems are used.

This is a hands-on book about Caldera OpenLinux. It's for anyone who has to set up OpenLinux and get it working.

After you've spent some time working in OpenLinux, you too will discover why thousands of highly skilled computer professionals are freely giving their time and energy to develop the Linux operating system.

Who Should Use This Book

This book is designed for users who need to install, configure, and run OpenLinux. For beginning users of OpenLinux, step-by-step instructions guide you through the procedures involved in installation. You do not have to be familiar with UNIX user commands to use this book or OpenLinux, but the more you do learn about the Linux operating system, the more you will be able to do.

Information in this book goes beyond just the operating system. It explains many of the details involved in choosing and setting up the hardware for your system and decodes technical jargon.

For those who are new to Linux, this book is also a good general resource for learning about the operating system.

For experienced Linux users, this book puts into one place the installation and configuration procedures for the most commonly used features of OpenLinux.

For advanced users, this book can serve as a basic system administrator's manual. It covers everything that a system administrator needs to know to keep an OpenLinux system running.

Who Should Not Use This Book

OpenLinux is a complex system. No book can cover everything, or should attempt to.

This book only touches on programming in Linux. The same is true for configuring and customizing the kernel.

You can get a network server up and running based on what is in this book, but for full-production systems, I recommend specialized books on specific networking systems and protocols. Fortunately, many good resources are already available for these advanced topics.

If you are new to computers, installing and configuring OpenLinux is not a good place to begin. It would only be a frustrating experience that might leave you hating your computer and unhappy with OpenLinux. For real beginners, I strongly recommend that you get a computer with OpenLinux already installed— several major computer manufacturers sell them. If you already own a computer, find someone who can install OpenLinux on it for you. This is what almost all Microsoft Windows and Mac OS users do. Then you can spend your time learning how to use the system.

Linux User Groups (LUGs) are organized in every state in the United States and 68 countries around the world. They can be an excellent resource for information about Linux and help with installation. A database of LUGs can be found on the Web at `www.linux.com/lug/`.

The list of vendors selling computers with Linux already installed is rapidly expanding. Caldera Systems can direct you to distributors who sell systems with OpenLinux already installed. Contact Caldera Systems at 1-888-GO-LINUX, or (801) 765-4888. Linux Online maintains a list of vendors selling computers with Linux already installed. The list covers 20 countries around the world and lists hundreds of vendors from Dell to Cobalt Networks, including many local businesses. The Web page is at `www.linux.org/vendors/systems.html`.

How to Use This Book

This book is designed to give you a thorough understanding of how to use OpenLinux. Pore through its pages. It's not necessary to start at the beginning and work your way through to the end. If you already have OpenLinux installed, you can skip those chapters.

This book is for both new users and those with experience on Linux computers. You can use each part of the book on its own.

For example, if you have used Linux but are new to the K Desktop Environment (KDE), you'll find a complete guide to KDE beginning in Chapter 3, "Configuring the KDE Desktop." Spend just an hour studying this chapter, and you will learn the tricks that will make you a master of KDE.

You can use the other chapters on hardware and applications in the same way.

The book is divided into five parts and six appendixes.

Part I: Installing OpenLinux

Part 1 covers how to prepare your computer for installation and the installation procedure.

- Chapter 1, "Preparing to Install OpenLinux," explains what you need to know before you start to install OpenLinux. Before you can install OpenLinux, you need to know how you want to use your computer and what hardware you have. You need to consider these and other issues to ensure success.

- Chapter 2. "Installing the Operating System," takes you step by step through the installation of the operating system software from the Caldera OpenLinux CD-ROM that's included with this book. OpenLinux includes a special edition of Partition Magic that helps you divide your computer's hard drive between Windows and OpenLinux. The chapter covers partitioning the hard drive, setting up a computer with both Windows and OpenLinux or just OpenLinux, video card and monitor configuration, and network configuration.

Part II: Configuring and Customizing OpenLinux

- Chapter 3, "Configuring the KDE Desktop," is a detailed introduction of the KDE desktop. Here's where the look and feel of what you see on your computer monitor is defined. You can make your computer look like a Macintosh or a Windows computer, or you don't have to make any changes.

- Chapter 4, "Using the KDE Desktop," shows how to use the many robust KDE utilities that come with OpenLinux, including the file manager, the Kedit text editor, Kmail email, the Kppp Internet dialer, and Kfind.

- Chapter 5, "Configuring Your System with COAS," instructs you on the use of the Caldera Open Administration System (COAS). Linux is a versatile operating system for home and commercial users, but many Linux users have found it difficult to administer. COAS is an improved way to administer Linux systems.

- Chapter 6, "Understanding and Using the OpenLinux File System," is a road map for the OpenLinux file system. If you have a road map, there is no need to get lost when working in OpenLinux. This is an explanation of what you will find on your OpenLinux computer.

- Chapter 7, "Using the Character Mode Terminal," explains why sometimes the best way to do something in OpenLinux is to use the character mode terminal. Almost every computer system now uses a Windows or Macintosh-style interface, as does OpenLinux, but at times you might want to use a character mode terminal. Here is how to do that.

Part III: Configuring Hardware

- Chapter 8, "Installing and Configuring Printers," instructs you on installing and configuring printers.

- Chapter 9, "Installing and Configuring a Backup System," is about choosing a backup media. There are many choices of where to store your backup. Tape backups may be slow, but they are reliable and have a good track record. Tape is also the lowest cost backup medium available per megabyte. Here is how to choose a tape system and a look at two alternatives: writing to a compact disc and using high-capacity removable disks like the Jaz disk. This chapter also provides a guide to installing and configuring a backup system using BRU 2000 and a backup strategy that the world's top computer systems administrators have used for years.

- Chapter 10, "Installing Sound," is about installing sound support in OpenLinux.

- Chapter 11, "Configuring File System and Performance," covers configuring your OpenLinux system for maximum performance. It shows you how to obtain information about your system, how to check and fix disk problems, how to monitor what is happening on your computer, and how to improve performance.

- Chapter 12, "Using Zip and Jaz Drives," explains how to use removable zip and Jaz disks on your OpenLinux system. This chapter also shows how to format disks, how to use disks formatted for Windows, and how to make the drives accessible to all users.

- Chapter 13, "Writing to CD-ROMs," tells you how to burn your own CD-ROM on an OpenLinux computer.

- Chapter 14, "Connecting to PalmPilots," shows you how to connect to PalmPilot using Kpilot, which come with the KDE desktop.

Part IV: Running Applications

- Chapter 15, "Installing and Configuring Commercial Applications," explains how to set up and run the commercial applications that are included with the boxed edition of OpenLinux. This includes an introduction to configuring and running WordPerfect on OpenLinux. WordPerfect is one of the best word processing programs available on any kind of computer system. OpenLinux includes the personal edition of WordPerfect 8.

   The chapter also covers installing and configuring StarOffice, which is a complete office suite that includes word processing, spreadsheet, and presentation software. Finally, the ApplixWare Office Suite is introduced. Installing and using the trial version is explained.

- Chapter 16, Running Windows Applications," introduces Wine and VMware, two programs that you can use to run Windows applications on your Linux system.

- Chapter 17, Configuring and Running Netscape Communicator," introduces configuring and running Netscape Communicator. Netscape Communicator is the standard Web browser on OpenLinux. Netscape also can be used for email and for reading Usenet news.

- Chapter 18, "Configuring and Running GIMP," introduces configuring and running GIMP. The GNU Image Manipulation Program Graphic image editor is like the popular Macintosh and Windows program Photoshop. It is used for creating new images or for editing existing images. It can also be used for photo retouching.

- Chapter 19, "Overview of Programming in OpenLinux," introduces the computer languages, compilers, and tools included with Linux.

Part V: Configuring OpenLinux Network Servers

- Chapter 20, Installing and Configuring a Windows Network," details installing and configuring a Windows network on OpenLinux. One of the great success stories of open source software is Samba. Running on an OpenLinux server, Samba looks like Windows NT to Windows 95/98 computers on the network. It does everything NT does, and many systems administrators think it does it better. While millions of Linux Web servers proved OpenLinux's viability and reliability, Samba on OpenLinux has been a secret success story. Offices around the world have Linux servers running Samba and only a handful of key operators know the secret.

- Chapter 21, " Installing and Configuring Novell Network Services," introduces installing and configuring Novell network services on OpenLinux. This chapter explains both how to connect an OpenLinux workstation to a Novell network server and how to set up an OpenLinux server to provide basic Novell file and print services.

- Chapter 22, "Installing and Configuring NFS," explains the Network Files System (NFS), which is used to share files between different Linux or UNIX computers.

- Chapter 23, "Installing and Configuring AppleTalk," introduces connecting Macintosh computers to your OpenLinux network server.

- Chapter 24, "Installing and Configuring a Dial-In and Fax Server," describes how to let users call into your system. An OpenLinux server can be set up to accept incoming calls or faxes.

- Chapter 25, "Installing and Configuring a Firewall," illustrates an OpenLinux firewall. A firewall has become popular as a frontline of defense against computer break-ins. While nothing is foolproof, firewalls give a network a high level of security. This is a full discussion of the hardware needed and the steps involved in installing and configuring a firewall server.

- Chapter 26, "Installing and Configuring the Apache Web Server," introduces building a OpenLinux-based Web site. Apache is the number one Web server software in the world, and, like Linux, it is a free, open source system. Here's what you'll need to configure to get your Web server up and running.

- Chapter 27, "Installing and Configuring Mail Services," provides you with the necessary information for setting up a mail server. OpenLinux comes with a full range of mail services.

■ Chapter 28, "Installing and Configuring an FTP Server," is about installing and configuring an FTP server. The File Transfer Protocol predates the World Wide Web. But it hasn't gone away. That's because it's still the best way to move files from one computer to another. This chapter covers the steps necessary to configure an FTP server and how to secure anonymous FTP (where anyone can connect to your server to get a copy of a file you have made available).

■ Chapter 29, "Overview of Network Security," provides an overview of network security, complete with an explanation of the basic steps you need to take to secure your OpenLinux computer.

Appendixes

■ Appendix A, "Installation OpenLinux Using LISA," is a step-by-step explanation of installing OpenLinux using LISA. This is the alternative, nongraphical installation procedure for OpenLinux.

■ Appendix B, "XFree86 Configuration," explains XFree86 configuration. This is the version of the X Windows graphical operating environment used by OpenLinux.

■ Appendix C, "The GNU General Public License," is the GNU General Public License. This is the software license covering the Linux operating system.

■ Appendix D, "Finding Help," has information on how you can find help with OpenLinux and the Linux operating system and additional information about Linux.

■ Appendix E, "Hardware Compatibility List," is the OpenLinux hardware compatibility list. It is a list of CD-ROM drives, network cards, disk drives, mouse devices, and video cards supported by the version of OpenLinux included with this book.

Conventions Used in This Book

You should know about some conventions when using this book, especially if you've never used a UNIX-like operating system before.

Case matters in Linux. Whereas on some other operating systems it does not matter whether you type in uppercase or lowercase, it does matter in Linux. For this reason, Linux sees *run*, *Run*, *RUN*, and *rUn* as four different commands. This is not just true for commands; it is true for filenames, file directories, or anything else you can find on a Linux computer.

Therefore, if a command or filename is specified, you will have to type exactly what appears in the book. Linux commands appear in text in a special `monospaced font`. Commands you type are displayed in **boldface type** so that they are clearly distinguishable.

A sample command is

Type **df -h** and press Enter.

Ctrl+C means that you hold down the Ctrl key and press the lowercase letter *c*.

New terms appear in *italic*.

With the mouse, *click* means to press the left mouse button once, *double-click* means to press the left mouse button quickly two times, and *right-click* means click the right mouse button once. This, of course, assumes that you are right-handed.

Throughout the book, you'll find Notes, Tips, and Warnings that are set off visually:

N O T E This paragraph has additional information that should be considered.

 TIP This paragraph suggests an additional information for a given task.

CAUTION

This paragraph notes dangers involved in a given procedure.

Installing OpenLinux

1

Preparing to Install OpenLinux

What Is Caldera OpenLinux?

For someone new to Linux, getting started can sometimes be confusing. Linux is a free system, but it's not easy to get it for free. In fact, the best way to get Linux is to buy it on a CD-ROM. Lucky for you such a CD is included for free with this book.

OpenLinux is more than just the Linux operating system. It is a comprehensive collection of software tools and applications put together in what is called a *distribution*. A distribution is assembled by experienced Linux professionals who work hard to make all the different components work together. You could do the same thing yourself and get everything for free.

That's not a real option for most Linux users. Even if you have the skill to put together your own Linux collection, it is hard to match the quality of the Linux distributions available today. Besides, choosing a good distribution can save you months of work.

Many good Linux distributions are available, and each one is put together to meet certain requirements. Each distribution has its own "personality" because each is tailored to meet requirements determined by the company building the distribution.

OpenLinux is designed by a highly respected team with years of experience with Linux and business network systems. Caldera calls it "Linux for business" because its designers have assembled it with the tools and applications that people in the business environment most commonly seek. That's its "personality."

OpenLinux was the first Linux distribution to be self-hosting. That means that everything included with the system can be rebuilt just using what comes with OpenLinux. You don't need anything external to duplicate everything found in OpenLinux. This is an engineering concept used on all bulletproof systems.

Don't get the wrong idea. Saying that this is a "Linux for business" doesn't mean that you can't use it elsewhere. In fact, OpenLinux is a good choice for almost any environment including home computers and school systems.

Deciding How You Want to Use OpenLinux

Before you can install OpenLinux, you need to know how you want to use it on your computer.

You can use OpenLinux for setting up a personal workstation in a manner similar to Windows NT Workstation. You can use it as a word processing system in an office or for just about any other task required on a business computer system. You can also set up OpenLinux on your personal computer at home, keeping track of phone numbers and addresses, connecting you to the Internet, and printing out your budget plans. OpenLinux is best known for its server strengths. You can set up OpenLinux as a single server handling both the internal needs (intranet) and the external needs (Internet) of a small- or medium-sized office. You can also make OpenLinux part of an enterprise-wide system. In that case, you might set up an

OpenLinux server to handle one primary task as part of a larger network. Regardless, you can fine-tune each OpenLinux server for a particular task such as storing user files or handling email.

Using OpenLinux Workstation

OpenLinux is designed out of the box to be a workstation system. This means that if you follow all the default settings, when the installation is finished the computer will start up and run in a way that is similar to Windows NT Workstation with a full set of applications from word processors to spreadsheets. It will also include some network services.

If you are already comfortable working on a Windows computer, you will have little trouble with OpenLinux. For many people, office applications and connecting to the Internet are the primary reasons for using their computer. OpenLinux has both, and all its Internet capabilities were built in from the beginning, not added on later.

The K desktop environment is equal to the graphical windowing systems found on high-end UNIX workstations. It is similar to the CDE desktop environment used on many UNIX workstations. KDE has the ease of use of a Windows-based computer.

OpenLinux workstation includes Corel WordPerfect, one of the most advanced word processing programs on any system, and also includes the complete StarOffice suite, which integrates a word processor, a spreadsheet, and a presentation graphics program.

OpenLinux workstation can be used for more than just word processing and spreadsheets. It has personal information managers, graphics programs, databases, 3Com Palm organizer support, music players, and much more. There are also hundreds of games available in OpenLinux.

OpenLinux workstations are already widely used in offices and schools around the world. In fact, their use is expanding faster than any other workstation system available.

Using OpenLinux Server

OpenLinux comes equipped with proven, extensible server software. The Linux operating system has shown its capabilities with the key role it has played on the Internet.

An OpenLinux computer can be a single file server for the many network needs of an office or home network, or it can be used as a server connected to other servers in a larger network.

OpenLinux can be used as:

- Windows network client and server
- Novell network client and server
- NFS client and server

- AppleTalk network server
- PPP dial-in server
- Network firewall
- Web server
- Mail server
- File transfer (FTP) server

If you plan to use OpenLinux as a network server, you will need to find out the specific hardware requirements for the network. Network servers typically use Ethernet or modems (or both) for connections to other computers.

Determining how the server will be used is necessary for deciding what hardware configuration it should have. For example, a network firewall might not need a big disk drive, but it will need a lot of memory. On the other hand, most file servers need hard disk space, particularly for users' ever-expanding storage needs. For this, you will want to get the biggest and most reliable hard drives available within your budget.

Before you purchase a network server, do your best to make sure that it has everything you need. In my years as a network systems administrator, I have never had a network server that didn't need to have something added to it as needs changed or expanded. This is not difficult to do when it is planned and done on a schedule with an orderly shutdown.

It is another thing altogether to set up a new server and, after putting it into production, find out that it doesn't have the right hardware to do the job. I once worked on setting up an email server for a couple of hundred users. A small test group tested and used the new server before it was put into full production. After about two weeks, I started getting complaints that users couldn't get their email. After working with many users and eliminating complaints from those whose problems were not related to the server, I found that there were times the response of the server could become unacceptably slow.

The problem, it turned out, was that the server needed more memory—a lot more memory to respond properly during peak demand. The new email server used IMAP instead of POP3. IMAP gives users greater flexibility, but it also uses more memory per user. The server was built on the basis of what was needed for the previous POP3 mail server, not what would be needed for an IMAP server.

See Chapter 27, "Installing and Configuring Mail Services" for an explanation of IMAP and POP3.

Needless to say, taking down the new mail server to add more memory had to be done in off-hours on an emergency basis. This is not what you want to do.

What You Need (Minimum Hardware)

You can run OpenLinux on almost any computer system now available. The Linux kernel was built to run without a lot of overhead. It is an efficient, even elegant, operating system.

Linux has been appearing on computer networks because a network engineer can expand the system by taking a computer slated to be thrown out and put it to work with Linux. In this way, Linux servers have been quietly added to many enterprise computer networks.

When users saw how efficient and reliable Linux was on these older computers, the word began to spread.

That was my own experience. The capability to use an old Intel 386 computer as a server got me started using Linux. The research center where I work depends on grants from foundations and the government. Budgets are always tight, so money is not always available to purchase additional equipment.

I discovered that by putting Linux on old, unused computers, I could expand the network without breaking the budget. Our first Linux computer used an early version of Caldera's Linux distribution. It served a small workgroup for a new project at the center. Nobody knew that anything different was going on. I was finally "found out" by a UNIX expert from another department. He was working on the project and wanted to know how this workgroup was doing things that, as far as he knew, could only be done on expensive UNIX systems. And he knew we didn't have one of those. He was impressed that we were able to do with this old computer what he was doing on a system that cost at least 10 times as much.

Here's the minimum hardware you'll need for installing OpenLinux:

- Pentium, Pentium II, Pentium III, or compatible CPU
- 32 megabytes of RAM
- 3.5-inch floppy drive
- CD-ROM drive
- 1 gigabyte hard drive:
    - Small installation takes 160 megabytes.
    - Standard installation takes 300 megabytes system.
    - Standard installation plus WordPerfect, StarOffice, BRU, and Netscape Communicator takes 780 megabytes.
    - Full installation takes 1.2 gigabytes.
- A mouse (three-button mouse recommended) and a 4 megabyte video card (8 megabytes recommended)
- SVGA monitor
- For networking you also need an Ethernet card or a modem

N O T E It is possible to install OpenLinux on a computer that does not meet all of these specifications. For nonstandard setup information, see Appendix A, "Installing OpenLinux Using LISA." ▪

What You Need (Optimum Hardware)

No one wants to start installing OpenLinux only to have it fail to work. Most of the time the problem comes from attempting to use hardware that isn't supported.

OpenLinux has a strong reputation for not failing, but the weak point is the hardware. Most Linux "failures" are really hardware failures. For success in using Linux in business, or at home, it is necessary to get the right hardware. This may seem obvious, but too many problems come from making the wrong hardware choices.

Hardware problems can happen whether you are installing a version of Windows or a version of Linux. Most users never have to confront this problem because they buy a computer with Windows already installed. At the company that assembled the computer, someone made sure the hardware had software drivers that worked reliably with the operating system.

Macintosh and UNIX systems minimize such problems by strictly limiting what users can add to the system. The strength, and weakness, of Intel-based computers and their compatibles is that they are open systems that can accept a variety of optional equipment.

Just as with a Windows-based system, on a Linux-based system you can minimize your problems by being conservative in your choice of hardware. No matter what hardware you have in your computer though, you will need to make sure that Linux supports it.

Before you buy a new computer or new components, check the hardware compatibility list for OpenLinux. See Appendix E, "Hardware Compatibility List," for a complete list of the hardware supported by the version of OpenLinux on the CD-ROM included with this book. If the hardware you want to use is not on the list, you can look at the information on the Caldera Systems Web site at www.calderasystems.com for an up-to-date list.

New hardware is constantly being added to the support list, but if the version of OpenLinux you have does not support the new hardware , you will have to get the version that includes the needed support. If you are adding a new component to an existing OpenLinux system, sometimes you can add the necessary software driver module without reinstalling the system software. This is an advanced task that requires experience with Linux.

See Chapter 5 "Configuring Your System with COAS," which introduces the procedure for adding software driver modules.

Getting the optimal hardware depends on how you want to use your OpenLinux computer. Here are some guidelines on hardware components that can help you make the best choice.

CPUs and System Boards

Linux works with Intel's 386, 486, Pentium, Pentium II, and Pentium III processors, as well as the comparable CPUs from AMD and Cyrix.

Any new system being sold today is fully adequate to run OpenLinux as a personal workstation. Even the most inexpensive Pentium now being sold has good performance. Sometimes these basic systems can even be used as a server depending on how the server will be used. However, most servers require that you get the most powerful CPU your budget can afford.

Almost all system boards and CPUs being sold today are reliable and high quality. The differences between brands on the market are not in their system boards or CPUs. Those are all practically the same. Some high-end computers that use specialized system boards and processors are the exception. The differences in brands come with the peripherals they use, the video systems, hard drives, and all the other components that are added on.

One thing to consider is expandability—what systems engineers call *scalability*. Can cards be added to the system board? Some systems come with no available slots for adding cards. Also, check for the maximum amount of memory the system board can use. Sometimes you discover that you have to add memory later, and you don't want to find out then that the system can't be expanded. In addition, some system boards come with all the memory slots filled with smaller chip sets. These require that you completely replace the existing memory when you want to expand the memory, rather than just adding additional memory chip sets to the system.

SMP

OpenLinux takes full advantage of the power of symmetrical multiprocessing (SMP). SMP is a special kind of architecture for network server system boards that allows more than one CPU to be installed on the board. Each separate CPU chip can execute processes at the same time. OpenLinux can support as many as 16 processors, producing remarkable performance. SMP requires a multiple or dual processor system board. The most advanced boards have a separate cache for each processor.

You should consider SMP if you want to use OpenLinux on a client/server network. On a client/server network, a client workstation (for example, an OpenLinux, Windows, or Macintosh workstation) sends a request to an application server. The application server (for example, a server running a database) processes the request and sends the results back to the client workstation.

At each request, the application server is processing the data. This can become a bottleneck that ties up the CPU. Using SMP improves performance because multiple CPUs share the processing.

System Bus

A *bus* is a mechanism for communicating between the system board and hardware that has been added, such as a network card or video card. OpenLinux works with all primary bus types:

- ISA
- EISA
- VLB
- PCI
- PCMCIA
- AGP

For computers being sold today, PCI is the bus usually found in desktop computers, and PCMCIA is the bus used on notebook computers.

AGP (Accelerated Graphics Port) is a new bus type for high-speed video acceleration on Pentium II and Pentium III computers. The AGP bus is limited to video cards. AGP video cards are designed primarily for rendering graphics for games and do not provide any noticeable speed improvement for regular computer use. OpenLinux supports some AGP cards. If your computer has an AGP video card, you will want to make sure it is a model that OpenLinux already supports. If not, commercial drivers might be available.

See Chapter 2 "Installing the Operating System" for more information on video drivers.

Some peripheral cards—particularly modems and sound cards—have a feature called *plug and play*. These cards are designed to work with Windows 95 or Windows 98. They do not work with older Windows or DOS systems or with Windows NT. OpenLinux has limited support for plug and play. Avoid any plug-and-play cards if you don't want trouble.

Plug-and-play cards are intended to simplify adding peripheral cards to computer systems. On the original Intel-based systems running DOS, you needed to know about I/O addresses, IRQs, DMA channels, and memory regions in order to install additional devices on the system. These are the hardware paths that are used for communications between the peripheral device and the computer system.

Plug-and-play cards are assigned an IRQ and DMA channel at boot time by the system BIOS. In standard cards that do not support plug and play, this information is assigned to the card with jumpers on the card or with installation software provided by the card's manufacturer. Many peripheral cards have small pins sticking out from the board, often lined up in rows. If you connect a pair of pins with a jumper, that closes a connection between the pins. This is how settings are configured on the card. The documents that come with the card will show what the pins are for. For example, a modem card might have a set of pins for COM1, COM2, COM3, and COM4. A jumper on the pair of pins for COM2 would mean that the modem would be set to use COM2. Setting jumpers requires that you know what settings the other components in your computer use so that you don't set two components to use the same settings, which would create a conflict that would make them both unusable.

Plug-and-play poses a problem because the IRQ or DMA channel assigned to the card can change every time the computer is booted or rebooted. In fact, the IRQ or DMA channel will most likely change if you add any hardware to your computer. Even Windows 95 or Windows 98 sometimes can't find a card that has been reassigned, especially if the reassignment has created a conflict that the BIOS doesn't know about. For greatest reliability and stability on your OpenLinux computer, it is best to stay away from plug and play.

A bus type found on some of the newest computers is USB, or Universal Serial Bus. USB is a serial connection for computers that is *hot-pluggable:* you can connect or disconnect a device from a USB port without turning off your computer. A single port can support as many as 127 devices in a chain connection. The version of OpenLinux that is included with this book has only experimental support for USB. The experimental drivers are not reliable. USB support is still under development, with a more reliable driver expected sometime in mid-1999, and a fully developed driver by the end of the year.

Memory

Linux is efficient in its use of memory, especially when compared to operating systems like Windows NT. It is even possible to set up a Linux computer with only 2 megabytes of RAM (random access memory), though it would constantly be swapping to the hard drive. The true minimum needed for Linux is 4 megabytes of RAM.

RAM used to be high-priced, but that is no longer the case. You should get as much RAM as you can afford. A minimum of 16 megabytes of RAM is needed to run the X Window clone that is used by OpenLinux, XFree86. To get full use from your computer, I recommend that you have at least 32 megabytes of memory. This is the same recommendation that is made for computers running Windows 98.

Generally, if you have to choose between more memory or a faster CPU, you should opt for more memory. Nothing improves overall computer performance better than adding memory.

RAM comes in several different varieties, such as SDRAM and EDO. Any memory type works with OpenLinux.

OpenLinux supports as much as 4 gigabytes of RAM, but if you plan to use more than 1 gigabyte, you will need to install extra cache memory, or the system's overall performance will become sluggish.

Disk Drives

Almost any standard disk drive available today works with OpenLinux. Most problems come with the new, high-speed, "ultra-wide" controller cards. Driver modules for the newest controller cards are sometimes not available.

When choosing a hard drive, get the biggest drive you can afford. You can never have enough drive space. It is almost a law of science that no matter how much drive space you have, it is never enough.

Hard drives don't vary greatly between the major brands. If you find that you have a bad hard drive, it's likely all the hard drives in that particular batch will have a problem. Difficulties that produce unexpected failure are usually introduced at the point of manufacture. So if you have to replace a drive that prematurely failed, check its time and place of manufacture and try to get a replacement that has a different time or place.

The hard drive controller can make a difference in your computer's performance. There are two types of hard drive controllers: IDE and SCSI. These controllers are also used to connect to CD-ROM drives and floppy drives.

If the computer will be a file server—that is, it will be used primarily to store and retrieve user files—get the fastest controller your budget can afford. The speed of the controller is the biggest single factor in the performance of a file server.

IDE Controllers

IDE (Integrated Device Electronics) connectors are standard on almost all PC systems. *EIDE* refers to an "enhanced" IDE controller that is used with the newer high-capacity hard drives. Ultra Direct Memory Access (UMDA) drives are a new generation of high-speed EIDE drives. Most UDMA drives are fully EIDE backward compatible and will work with EIDE controllers.

IDE connectors are found either on the system board or on a peripheral card. A ribbon cable joins these connectors to the IDE drive. The controller is on the drive itself. That is why it is necessary to set jumpers on IDE drives. Jumpers are used to disable the controller on secondary IDE drives so that the controller on the primary drive controls both drives on the "IDE channel." On some of the newest systems, you can do this in the BIOS configuration screen, eliminating the need to set the jumpers.

IDE drives are reliable and inexpensive. OpenLinux is configured to support as many as four IDE hard drives. There is almost never a problem with installing OpenLinux on an IDE hard drive. The only problems come from installing both Linux and Windows onto multiple-gigabyte IDE drives, and that's not really a problem, if it is done right.

Sometimes users think that the IDE drives are faster than SCSI drives because IDE controllers often respond faster than SCSI controllers. IDE controllers don't have all the extra capabilities found on SCSI controllers. This gives IDE controllers less overhead so that they can act on a request more quickly. IDE controllers work through your computer's CPU, which means that when it is accessing the disk the CPU isn't doing anything else. This isn't a problem on a single-user system, though you sometimes notice how everything slows down when you are reading or writing a big file to the disk.

SCSI Controllers

SCSI (Small Computer Systems Interface) devices are standard equipment for most network servers, as well as all UNIX and Macintosh systems. However, manufacturers label several different SCSI standards as well as nonstandard implementations as SCSI. Generally, OpenLinux works with any of the SCSI controllers from the major manufacturers. If you have a SCSI controller in your computer, you should make sure that OpenLinux supports the specific controller you have. Check out the compatibility guide in Appendix E.

If you follow any of the Linux discussion groups on the Internet, you will notice that problems installing onto new SCSI drives are a frequent complaint. Usually the problem can be traced to someone using a SCSI controller that doesn't have a Linux driver module available. Because no error message displays that explains this to the user or that tells the user how to get driver updates, many new users just complain that Linux "doesn't work."

So why would anyone bother with getting a SCSI controller? Because SCSI controllers are "smart." When you access a SCSI hard drive, the controller handles everything itself. The CPU doesn't get involved. This means that the system isn't tied up during disk reads or writes. There is no noticeable delay in other functions on the computer when the disk is being accessed. This is particularly important on network servers. In fact, because of SCSI's "smarts," SCSI drives are faster than IDE drives on multiple-user systems: that is, systems that have multiple users accessing the computer at the same time. (This does not refer to multiple-user computers that have more than one user who each access the same computer at different times.)

SCSI drives also support as many as seven devices, with Wide SCSI able to support as many as 15 devices. This is important on heavily used systems that can easily have more than four drives and any number of peripherals such as CD-ROM drives, Jaz drives, and more. System boards often support only three or four additional PCI cards, so making one of those cards a SCSI card means that you can add at least seven devices to that one board. You cannot do this with an IDE connector.

Using a SCSI controller for adding devices has another advantage. The system board has only a limited number of IRQs and I/O ports, and when you start adding devices, you can quickly fill them all. Adding devices to a SCSI chain doesn't do this because the entire device chain uses the controller's IRQ and I/O port.

One of the major concerns on server systems is *fault tolerance:* that is, the server's capability to continue functioning if some piece of hardware should fail. The most common components to fail on servers are hard drives and power supplies.

Computers designed to be network servers may have built-in redundancies such as multiple power supplies and hard drives. This often includes hot swapping, which means that they have connectors and fasteners that allow the removal and replacement of a defective part without powering down the computer.

Redundant Array of Inexpensive Drives (RAID) offers redundancy against disk drive failure. OpenLinux supports both software and hardware RAID.

RAID can also improve disk drive performance and capacity. Stripingdoes this. A *stripe* is a contiguous sequence of disk blocks. Multiple hard disks appear as one disk. The resulting disk partition is not only the size of all the disks combined, it is much faster because the drives are accessed in parallel.

Software RAID works with either IDE or SCSI controllers and any combination of disks.

Hardware RAID controllers are the most sophisticated, powerful, and expensive SCSI controllers. They allow PC servers to handle mass storage media in much the same way as mainframe computers do. This allows much faster access to data as well as fault tolerance. Software RAID is not nearly as flexible or fast as hardware RAID, but software RAID is considerably cheaper.

SCSI controllers and drives in general cost more. Most individual users on a single-user workstation probably have no reason to pay a premium for SCSI. On any heavily used system with frequent reads/writes from the hard disk whether for a database, bookkeeping, or document management, the improved performance of SCSI can be worth the extra cost. All server systems should be run only from SCSI drives.

Monitors and Video Cards

Linux can be installed on a computer with almost any video system: monochrome, CGA, EGA, VGA, and SVGA. But to install OpenLinux, you will need an SVGA, or Super VGA, video system.

OpenLinux defaults to running an X Windows system. If you want to install OpenLinux as a non-Windows computer or use an older video system, you will need to follow the installation procedures detailed in Appendix A.

The standard installation of OpenLinux uses the XFree86 X window server. When OpenLinux is installed and running, the resolution you will get will be similar to what you would have on the same computer with Windows 95/98 or Windows NT.

You should check the hardware compatibility list to make sure that OpenLinux supports your video card. Most video cards on the market are supported. Usually the newest cutting-edge video cards do not yet have drivers available because no manufacturer writes Linux video drivers. Independent developers write all the drivers.

If you have the latest AGP video card, XFree86 may not yet support it. Also, 3D video capability is only used by video games that support it. You'll have to get special drivers for 3D video, the main source is commercial vendors and the drivers can be quite pricey. 2D video is the default mode used almost universally on all computer systems.

Video memory is an important consideration. More memory means more colors and higher resolution. A video card with 2 megabytes of memory is limited to a 16-bit color palette of about 65,000 colors at a resolution of 640 pixels by 480 pixels. A 4 megabyte video card can display a 24-bit color palette with about 16 million colors, also known as true color. It supports a resolution of 800 pixels by 600 pixels or 1,024 pixels by 768 pixels. An 8 megabyte video card can display a true color palette at a resolution of 1,600 pixels by 1,200 pixels and usually supports a faster refresh rate.

Performance is also improved by adding memory, but the amount of video memory is not what determines the speed of the video card. The type of memory on the card determines that. The more expensive cards generally use fast video RAM.

Monitors are usually described by their size and dot pitch. The diagonal distance across the tube determines the size. The "standard" monitor is 15 inches, and sizes go up from there. *Dot pitch* refers to the resolution on the screen, and a larger dot pitch means that small fonts and graphics details are fuzzy. Your monitor should have a dot pitch of .28 or smaller. To avoid screen flicker, make sure the monitor has a refresh rate of 75Hz or better.

Look at the controls on the monitor: Some monitors have only one or two controls and can't be properly adjusted. In addition, the monitor should not be interlaced. Interlacing reduces the cost of production by using a technique that refreshes only half the horizontal lines on the screen at a time. This slows down the actual refresh rate and creates a noticeable screen flicker.

CD-ROM Drives

OpenLinux works with almost any CD-ROM drive available, whether it is an IDE type or a SCSI type. Any speed drive works, though some of the newest fast CD-ROM drives are reported to be flaky on Linux computers.

As with a lot of hardware, sometimes it is a better choice to get a CD-ROM drive that's not the newest type. A CD-ROM drive that has been around awhile will give you the most reliable performance. The problem is not with Linux. The problem is that new hardware is often rushed to market before all the bugs have been worked out.

CD-ROM disc formats can sometimes be an issue in Linux. The standard data CD format is called *High Sierra* or *ISO9660*. In addition, the data on the CD is written in a unique format. Therefore, each CD has two formats, one that indicates that it is a data CD (and not a musical or other kind of CD) and one that defines how the data is written on the CD. The Linux/ UNIX format for CDs is called *Rock Ridge,* which saves the data in a format that preserves long file names and links. OpenLinux 2.2 can also recognize the *Joliet* format for long file names on Windows CDs. In addition, OpenLinux can read the formats for earlier versions of Windows and DOS CDs. If you have an earlier version of OpenLinux or a different Linux distribution, you may not be able to read some of the non-Linux CD formats.

Most CD-ROM drives have a headphone jack so that you can play audio CDs even if you don't have a sound card on your system. You can also connect CD-ROMs drives to a sound card for playing music through attached speakers.

The new DVD drives work like a CD-ROM drive on OpenLinux, but you won't be able to play DVD videos on OpenLinux.

Network Access

Network controller cards and modems handle network and Internet connections. OpenLinux supports Ethernet, frame relay, and token-ring network cards.

Ethernet   Ethernet is the most common hardware used in office networks. A standard Ethernet network controller card operates at 10 megabytes per second. It gives excellent performance and dominates network systems worldwide. Many new cards support the Fast Ethernet standard of 100 megabytes per second. Fast Ethernet adapters are usually just a couple of dollars more, and most will work on 10MBps Ethernet networks. The speed of the network hubs determines the speed of the network—10Mbps or 100Mbps. Fast Ethernet hubs and switches are considerably more expensive than standard Ethernet hubs and switches, so they are not as widely installed.

Look for an Ethernet adapter that uses *bus mastering*. With bus mastering, a controller connected to an expansion bus (usually a PCI slot) can communicate directly with other devices on the system without going through the CPU. Bus mastering improves performance of the device because requests don't have to be diverted through the CPU. For example, a bus mastering Ethernet adapter is much faster because network requests go directly to the adapter. The card is in charge of the expansion bus and doesn't require the intervention of the CPU.

Modems   OpenLinux can connect to the Internet by modem using the PPP protocol. It supports both internal modems and external modems connected to the serial port. OpenLinux supports almost every type of modem available.

The only modems that cause problems are the "winmodems," designed to be used on Windows 95/98 computers. Only a few of these modems work on Windows NT systems. These internal modems are also known as controllerless modems and generally cost quite a bit less. They rely on the system's CPU and require special Windows-only software to run.

The new V.90 protocol has introduced modems that produce respectable performance. Unlike prices for most other computer components, modem prices are not an indicator of performance quality. Check with your service provider for modem recommendations. Getting a modem that best matches the ISP's system can make a noticeable difference in performance.

All new modems include faxing capability that can be used in OpenLinux.

There is no exact formula for deciding between an internal and external modem. Internal modems work just like external modems and don't take up any extra space on the desktop. External modems require a serial port and power connection, but many internal modems are plug and play and don't work properly with Linux. External modems don't have this problem and have the added benefit of a series of lights that can help when trying to figure out modem problems.

For dial-in servers, special multiple-port modem devices handle more than four connections. OpenLinux can support more than four serial ports and includes drivers for the multiple-port cards.

Mouse Devices

OpenLinux works with almost any mouse, trackball, or touch pad. The most common mouse connection is through the serial port. If your mouse uses a bus port, OpenLinux assumes it is using IRQ 5. If you have a PS/2 mouse, OpenLinux assumes it is at IRQ 12.

There are advantages to using a three-button mouse. The third button is used for a number of functions in X Window, such as cutting and pasting. To do this with a two-button mouse, you'll have to modify the default setup so that you can emulate the third button by pressing both buttons at the same time.

Backup Devices

Tape backup systems are standard on most servers. Tape systems are reliable, and many have the capacity to handle the multiple-gigabyte drives that are standard today. Any tape drive that works from a SCSI connection should work with OpenLinux.

DAT (Digital Audio Tape) driveshave multiple-gigabyte capacities and have a good record for reliability and longevity. Tapes are also the best choice for long-term storage.

Floppy tape drives and parallel-port tape drives are also supported. These are useful for backing up personal files, but most do not have the capacity to handle full system backups without making multiple tape changes.

Nontape backup systems are popular because they usually offer faster access, but they are all much more expensive. Iomega Zip and Jaz drives are popular but should not be considered for long-term storage. The disks are prone to mechanical failure, especially if mishandled. Writeable CDs are useful for backups. The disks are not easily breakable and are usable for many years, though long-term reliability is unknown. CDs are much faster to read than tapes, but they take a long time to create, even with the newer, faster writers.

Laptop Computers

OpenLinux can be installed on most laptop computers being sold today. Just make sure that it has enough memory and hard drive space as well as a CD-ROM drive. Generally, laptop computers run X Window at 800 by 600 pixels. Check for video driver compatibility if you need more colors and a higher resolution.

See the section on video installation in Chapter 2 for more information.

See Appendix D for laptop compatibility information.

Installing the Operating System

Installing OpenLinux on a Windows Computer

You have several different options for installing OpenLinux. One of them is to put it on a computer that is already running Microsoft Windows. Why would you do that? Maybe you have heard about Linux, and you just want to try it out before completely turning your computer over to a new operating system. Maybe you need software that runs only in Windows. Or maybe you just like to have two different systems on your computer. Hey, that's just fine, too.

- If you are not installing OpenLinux on a Windows computer you can jump ahead to Beginning Installation.
- If you are upgrading from an earlier version, you should read the section on upgrading before you go any further even if you are installing onto a computer that will also be running Windows.
- If you have Windows on your computer but you have a free disk drive that will hold OpenLinux or you already partitioned your drive before you installed Windows, you don't need to do any further preparation, and you can skip the section on partitioning.
- If your Windows computer is full and you do not have enough free disk space, repartitioning with fips or PartitionMagic will not be able to create a space big enough to install OpenLinux. The minimum amount of free space necessary is 250 megabytes, but the standard installation with the full office software programs really needs at least 1 gigabyte of space.
- If you have a video card that is not listed as a supported card, installation through Windows and Lizard will not correctly configure the graphics. I recommended that you use the LISA installation.

  See Appendix E, "Hardware Compatibility List," for a list of supported video cards.

  See Appendix A, "Installation OpenLinux Using LISA," for information on LISA installation.
- If you are installing OpenLinux on a notebook computer that cannot boot from the CD-ROM drive, you should use the LISA installation. Windows and Lizard installation from a disk do not correctly detect PCMCIA cards even if they have been properly inserted before installation begins.

For Windows users, you can use the fips program on the OpenLinux CD included with this book to create a Linux partition using the free space on your hard drive without damaging yours Windows system. If you bought the boxed version of OpenLinux with three disks, you can use PartitionMagic CE that is included on the Windows Tools and Commercial Packages CD to do the same thing.

If you have the boxed edition of OpenLinux 2.3, you can insert the OpenLinux Windows Tools and Commercial Packages CD, which starts up just like a CD with a Windows program on it. But beware, *you cannot install OpenLinux as a Windows program*. Instead, OpenLinux has a Windows-based presentation that offers

■ Creation of installation floppy disks

■ Access to OpenLinux-related documents

■ The Caldera Edition of PartitionMagic and BootMagic (if you bought the commercial package from Caldera Systems)

To begin in Windows, insert the OpenLinux Windows Tools & Commercial Packages CD. The screen shown in 2.1 should appear. If it doesn't, double-click on My Computer and then double-click on the OpenLinux CD icon.

Part
I
Ch
2

FIGURE 2.1
The opening screen for Windows installation of OpenLinux.

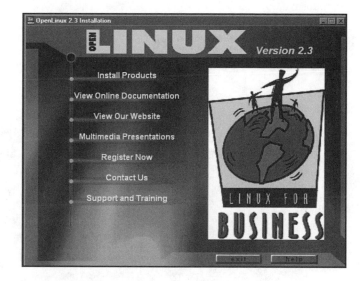

The primary step that you'll be taking here is to install the Caldera Systems products on the CD. If you want, before you begin that process, you can look at the other choices.

Besides installation, the other features on the CD are

■ **View Online Documentation—** This choice opens your default Web browser and opens a Web page from the CD with links to documents that are included on the OpenLinux CD, including a full collection of How-To items from the Linux Documentation Project, Caldera's own answers to Frequently Asked Questions, and a list of products and services available from Caldera Systems. The Web page it opens in on the CD and can be found at \col\doc\index.html.

■ **View Our Website—**If you are connected to the Internet, clicking on this will start up your Web browser and take you to Caldera System's home page (www.calderasystems.com).

- **Multimedia Presentations**—In this selection, you can choose to see a short video advertisement for Caldera's OpenLinux. The second selection is an AVI video tutorial for installation.

- **Register Now** —If you haven't registered your copy of OpenLinux, you can do it here. This is necessary if you want to get the free support offered for new installations. This is a Web-based registration and requires that you have an Internet connection to work.

- **Contact Us**—Selecting this choice displays a page with the address, phone number, email, and Web addresses for Caldera Systems.

- **Support and Training**—This choice displays a page with a short description of services and programs available from Caldera Systems and a phone number to call for more information.

Installing Windows-based Software

The first step you want to take is to choose to Install Products. This opens the screen shown in Figure 2.2.

FIGURE 2.2
Installation of
OpenLinux Windows
software begins here.

There are two ways to proceed. The first choice is to install PartitionMagic CE. Choose this option if you do not have a Linux partition already created on your system. This choice uses PartitionMagic to create a Linux partition on your system and then begins the OpenLinux installation.

If your system already has a Linux partition, the second option starts the Linux installation using the loadlin program.

Using PartitionMagic

The boxed edition of OpenLinux includes a special edition of PartitionMagic, which is a program from a company called PowerQuest that helps you divide your computer's hard drive between Windows and OpenLinux. *Partitioning* is the process of dividing a single hard disk for multiple uses. It is similar to putting up fences in an open field. Like a corral to divide the horses from the cows, you can create partitions that set up separate spaces for Windows and Linux.

Part
I
Ch
2

Using fips to create a Linux partition on a Windows computer

If you don't have Partition Magic, you can use the fips program that is on the OpenLinux CD included with this book to create a Linux partition on your Windows system. *Fips* is a program that you can use to split the hard disk safely without destroying anything on the disk. It works with Windows 95, Windows 98, Windows NT (FAT formatted disks), or DOS formatted disks. It does not work with Windows NT NTFS formatted disks. The name *fips* stands for *First nondestructive Interactive Partition Splitting* program. The program is on the OpenLinux CD in the /col/tools/fips directory.

Before you use fips, you should fully read the fips.doc file found in the fips directory. Be sure to check out the cautions and restrictions on what won't work. Also make sure you have a backup of your system. Whereas fips is known for its safety and reliability, it is possible for an accident to cause the loss of everything on your hard drive.

The first step in using fips is to defragment your hard drive. Use the defrag program included with Windows or any similar utility and set it for optimum defragmentation. Windows NT does not include a defragmentation program, and you will need to get one such as the Speedisk program included with Norton Utilities. Then run a thorough scandisk check to look for any bad blocks on your disk.

The fips program runs from DOS. Create a bootable floppy disk and copy restorrb.exe, fips.exe, and errors.txt from the /col/tools/fips directory onto the floppy. Boot from the floppy disk and then start the fips program by typing **fips** at the A:> prompt. If you are using a floppy created on a Windows 95 or later system, fips starts with a warning (see figure 2.3). You can proceed.

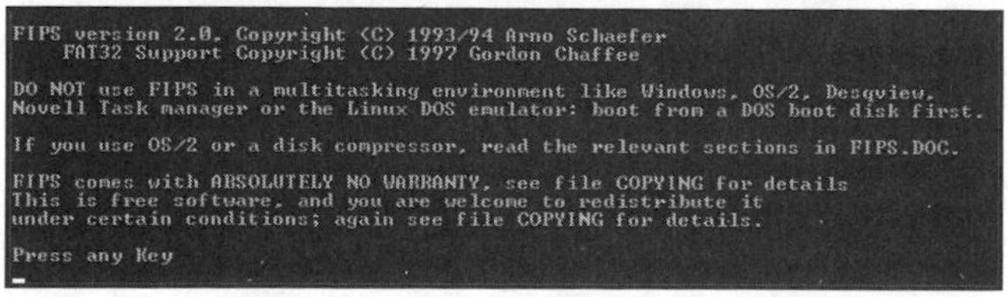

FIGURE 2.3
The Fips warning
screen.

```
FIPS version 2.0, Copyright (C) 1993/94 Arno Schaefer
   FAT32 Support Copyright (C) 1997 Gordon Chaffee

DO NOT use FIPS in a multitasking environment like Windows, OS/2, Desqview,
Novell Task manager or the Linux DOS emulator; boot from a DOS boot disk first.

If you use OS/2 or a disk compressor, read the relevant sections in FIPS.DOC.

FIPS comes with ABSOLUTELY NO WARRANTY, see file COPYING for details
This is free software, and you are welcome to redistribute it
under certain conditions; again see file COPYING for details.

Press any Key
```

If you boot from a floppy created on a Windows 95 or 98 system, the fips program opens with a warning. You can proceed anyway.

continues

continued

Fips then detects your hard drive and whether you have more than one and asks which one you want to repartition. The hard drive is then read, and a partition table is displayed. The important figure on the table is the last column MB, the number of megabytes for each of the four possible partitions on the hard disk.

If you have more than one partition on the hard disk, you will be asked to indicate which one you want to split. Enter the start cylinder for the new partition. Make sure that the new Linux partition starts on a cylinder below the 1,024th cylinder, or you will not be able to boot into Linux. The 1,024th cylinder is were IDE ends and EIDE (Enhanced IDE) begins.

Use the cursor keys to increase or decrease the cylinder the size of the new partition. Make sure that you make it big enough for what you want to install. The standard installation takes 500 MB for system software and packages. You'll want even more space than that. When you have the size you want, press Enter to continue.

Exit fips and restart the computer. You are now ready to proceed with the installation of OpenLinux on your new partition.

Before you run PartitionMagic, you should take two steps. First, run a virus check, particularly on the master boot record of your hard drive. PartitionMagic is going to make changes in the MBR and might not work properly if there's a virus hidden there.

After you've checked for viruses and cleaned anything found, defragment your hard disk. This moves all the files scattered around your disk and puts them together in one area on your disk. This enables PartitionMagic to give you the maximum possible free space for OpenLinux.

To defragment your hard disk in Windows 95/98, click the Start button, choose Programs, Accessories, System Tools, Disk Defragmenter. Choose the disk drive that you want to defragment and click OK. You should see a progress meter like the one in Figure 2.4.

FIGURE 2.4
The Windows disk
defragmention progress
meter.

Leave the computer alone until defragmentation is finished. If you use the computer for anything while it is defragmenting, the process has to keep restarting. Defragmentation can take some time depending on how big your hard disk is and how fragmented it has become. Defragmenting is something that needs to be done regularly on a Windows computer. If you are running Windows NT, a disk defragmentation utility is not included with the operating system. You will need to get one like the optimizer included with the Norton Utilities for Windows NT.

Once the disk is ready, you can install PartitionMagic and create a Linux partition.

Installing PartitionMagic

The next step is to install the Caldera Edition of PartitionMagic. Start the installation program is from the OpenLinux Windows Tools & Commercial Packages CD. Click on the Install Partition Magic CE option (as shown in Figure 2.2).

You should then see the screen shown in Figure 2.5.

Part

I

Ch

2

FIGURE 2.5
The startup screen to install PartitionMagic.

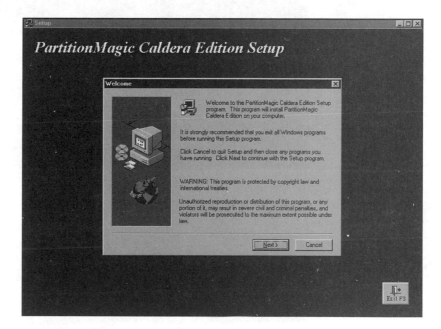

Click Next to begin installation. The destination directory is displayed. The default destination directory for PartitionMagic is in the Program Files directory. You can leave it there or choose another directory if you prefer.

Click Next, and the program group for PartitionMagic is displayed. When you click on Next, the installation is completed. The final screen is shown in Figure 2.6.

When you reach the final screen, you will be given a choice to finish. By clicking on Finish, you are actually starting the PartitionMagic software. At this point, nothing has been changed on your computer. You have only set up the software. After you click on Finish, you will see a warning message like the one in Figure 2.7.

FIGURE 2.6
The final screen for installation of PartitionMagic.

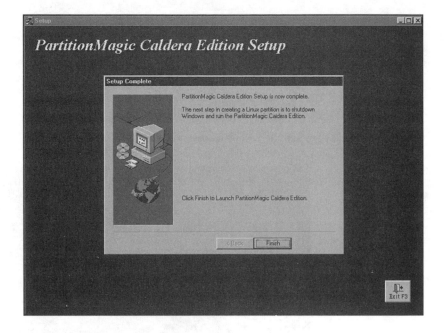

FIGURE 2.7
A warning message. You must remove the CD-ROM before creating a Linux partition with PartitionMagic.

Remove the CD and click OK to proceed. If you are installing PartitionMagic on a Windows NT computer, you need to create a boot disk for PartitionMagic. Follow the simple onscreen instructions. You are prompted to insert a blank floppy disk and then a boot disk is created.

Creating a Linux Partition

The When your system reboots, the Caldera Edition of PartitionMagic automatically starts. The screen display for this edition is different from what you would see with the full commercial edition. This reflects that this limited edition does not have all the capabilities of the full version, but it will do a good job of making space on your Windows computer for OpenLinux.

There are two sections of the screen where you need to make choices. On the left side, in the area labeled Drive Info for Selected Partition, it shows which disk drive will be changed. This should show the disk drive that has Windows installed on it.

If you want to install OpenLinux on a different drive, you should click Select Partition. You can then indicate which disk drive or partition on a drive you want to use for OpenLinux.

On the right side of the screen is a section labeled Linux partition size. In this section, you have four choices. If one of the choices is not possible (for example if your disk drive doesn't have enough free space), those choices will be grayed out.

The choices are

- **300 MB**—This is the smallest size PartitionMagic lets you create. It is big enough for only a minimal install of OpenLinux.

- **800 MB**—This choice creates a space big enough for the standard OpenLinux installation. It creates a partition that is practical for an OpenLinux workstation.

- **1640 MB**—This creates a partition big enough to install all of the OpenLinux packages as well as all of the commercial applications including WordPerfect, StarOffice, Applix Office, and BRU.

- **Maximum free space**—If you want OpenLinux to be your primary workstation operating system, this would be the best choice. It makes all free space available for OpenLinux and leaves a 100MB space for a swap partition. This is only good if you expect to make limited use of Windows. It does not leave enough space for you to add any additional software to your Windows partition.

The results of your two choices—the disk drive to use and the amount of space for OpenLinux—is shown in the area labeled Size Info for Selected Partition.

This area shows the total size of your disk partition, the amount of space used by Windows files, and the amount of free space on the partition. The two columns show the size before you've resized with PartitionMagic and what the results would be after resizing.

When you've made your choices, click OK, and the Linux partition is created.

Now you've created a partition where OpenLinux can be installed. The next step is to install the operating system. Insert the OpenLinux CD into the CD-ROM drive and reboot the computer. Lizard, the Linux installation Wizard, begins.

NOTE If you've created a Linux partition with PartitionMagic, two essential steps come next:
- First, install the OpenLinux operating system
- Second, install BootMagic ■

First you have to install OpenLinux, but when you restart the computer, it will come up in Windows and you won't see OpenLinux. You have to install BootMagic to access OpenLinux.

See the section "Setting Up BootMagic" for instructions on installing BootMagic.

Upgrading from an Earlier Version

OpenLinux 2.3 includes a tool for updating version 2.2 systems. If you have OpenLinux 2.2 already installed, look at the UPDATE.txt file on the OpenLinux CD for more details. The update script will work only on unmodified 2.2 systems. If you've customized your system or upgraded any of the system software, the update script will probably refuse to run. In that case, you can update by selecting individual software packages on the 2.3 disk and installing them on your system.

Updating from OpenLinux 2.2

The update script is a convenient way to go from version 2.2 to 2.3. Before running the update script, make sure that you have a complete backup of your system. Then log in as the root user and mount the OpenLinux 2.3 CD.

Copy the "update-2.3.000.0.tgz" file to the root directory (/) of your system (not "/root"). Extract the contents of the archive using the command **tar zxvf update-2.3.000.0.tgz.** (If you are not using the CD included with this book, you should check and make sure that is the name of the update script on your CD.) This installs the update script.

Make sure all users are logged off the system and enter single-user maintenance mode. To do this, enter the command:

`/sbin/telinit 1`

To make a test run, enter the command:

`/sbin/update.col — test`

If the test does not indicate any problems, run the update script by entering the command:

`/sbin/update.col`

When the update is finished, you will be prompted to reboot the system. If you aren't prompted to reboot, enter the command:

`/sbin/reboot`

No direct upgrade is possible from OpenLinux 1.3 and earlier versions. The 2.3 Linux kernel requires a completely new installation. This is true for all Linux distributions. Major changes in the Linux kernel were introduced in version 2.2, which is why a complete reinstallation is required. But you can simplify the upgrade so that you can save as much of your current system as possible.

Here's the way to do it with a minimum of disruption.

1. Make a complete backup of your system. This is a safety measure and ensures that you can go back to a working system in case there are any unforeseen complications. If you have BRU, a backup utility included with earlier versions of OpenLinux, you can use it to back up your system. Any backup files created this way are compatible with the version of BRU that's included with OpenLinux 2.2.

See Chapter 9, "Installing and Configuring a Backup System," to find out more about backups.

2. Make a separate backup of files that will be restored on the new system. This includes

   - The /home directories where all the user files are found
   - The /etc configuration files that you've customized
   - The /opt files from installed software packages
   - The /usr/local files that have been added
   - /var configuration files
   - /usr/local or any other directories or files that you want to have on the new system

3. Install the OpenLinux operating system. If you have any of these directories on its own partition (such as the /home directory), you might be able to run the setup and not reformat those partitions. Look at the section in installation on custom partitions. If that is the case, your files will be there after installation.

4. Restore whatever files are needed from backup.

One word of warning: Configuration files can change as new versions of the operating system and software packages are introduced. Be careful when restoring configuration files. In fact, make sure you back up the new configuration files before you overwrite them with the files from your old system. Some old configuration files won't work on the new system or have features that are only available with new-style configuration files. Also some software packages may not work properly after being restored from backup. These packages may need to be reinstalled to work properly.

Installing OpenLinux

If you created an OpenLinux partition using PartitionMagic, the installation program takes you directly to the first installation screen. You can skip this next section and go directly to the first screen.

Otherwise, if you are not continuing from the OpenLinux Windows partition and installation program, you have three ways to start installation of OpenLinux:

- **Start from Windows**—In Windows, insert the OpenLinux CD and click on Install Products. Choose Launch Linux Install (as shown in Figure 2.8). This will copy some installation software onto your hard drive, then restart the computer in DOS mode and then begin installation.

- **Boot from the OpenLinux CD**—If you have a bootable CD-ROM drive and if it is enabled in your system's BIOS, you can insert the OpenLinux CD into the CD-ROM drive and reboot the computer.

- **Boot from an OpenLinux Installation floppy disk**—If you do not have a bootable CD-ROM drive, you will need to boot from an installation floppy disk.

FIGURE 2.8

To start OpenLinux installation from Windows, click on Launch Linux Install.

To create the floppy disks needed for installation, you will need two blank disks, label one Install and the other Modules.

The procedure runs as follows:

1. Insert blank floppy disk (the one labeled Install).
2. In Windows, insert the OpenLinux CD, select Install Products, and choose Create Floppy Install Disks In the next window that opens, select Create Lizard Install Diskette.
3. A DOS window opens, type in the drive letter for the blank disk.
4. An installation disk is then created.
5. Repeat the same steps for a Modules disk, but choose Create Lizard Modules Diskette.

Insert the OpenLinux CD in the CD-ROM drive and, if needed, the installation floppy disk. Restart the computer.

The First Screen

The first screen that opens is shown in Figure 2.9. For new users, a lot of messages go by that won't mean much. There's no need to worry about what any of them say. Messages that say None or Skipped don't mean that the installation won't work.

This is an initial probe of your computer's hardware. Many steps are involved in installation, and the messages here might be useful for getting technical support, but otherwise they have no meaning for the steps you'll be taking during installation. You can just ignore whatever they say.

FIGURE 2.9
The system startup
screen. Installation
begins with a probe of
your system.

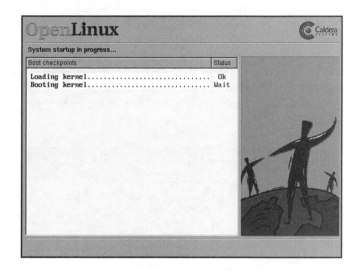

The screen display does show you that something is happening, and that's a good thing because this part can take a few minutes and sometimes seem to hang. But wait, it's just probing your system, and on some computers this can take a while. One of the probes being done during this time is a search for the OpenLinux installation source. If a CD-ROM drive is found, it is assumed that this will be the source. If no CD-ROM drive is found, a search is made for a network server that may have the installation files. If neither is found, you will be prompted to enter the information.

Selecting Mouse and Language

The next screen begins the configuration process. You have to make several choices before the actual installation can begin. The first is to choose a language to be used for installation. This is for installation only and does not determine the language that will be used after installation. That is set during keyboard setup later in the installation process.

If you move the mouse when the screen first displays, you may experience a delay. Make sure you move the mouse slowly the first time you try to use it. That's because Lizard is attempting to detect your mouse type. Ignore the slight delay, if there is one, and continue with the installation.

You can set up OpenLinux 2.3 in one of four languages: English, German, French, and Italian. Because mouse selection is not until the next screen, you may have to use the keyboard to make this selection if your mouse is not responding.

Use the up- and down-arrow keys to move between the different languages. Press the Tab key to move to the Next button. Press the Enter key to move to the Mouse setup screen.

The next step is to set up the mouse (see Figure 2.10). This is the only chance you'll have during setup to get your mouse working correctly. Spend some time here and make sure you have everything set exactly as you want it. Even though you can continue through setup without a mouse by using the keyboard, it is a good idea to get the setup done right before you continue because you'll need the mouse in OpenLinux. This setup screen is the easiest mouse configuration screen you'll find in any Linux setup, including OpenLinux after it has been installed.

FIGURE 2.10
The mouse setup screen. This is the only chance you'll have during setup to get your mouse working properly.

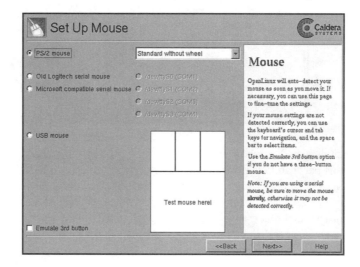

Your mouse was probably automatically detected during the language selection screen. The movement initiates autodetection. If you move the mouse and the mouse pointer moves, it was detected. If not, you will need to use the keyboard—the Tab and up- and down-arrow keys—to change the settings.

CAUTION

Do not select the wrong type or you might not be able to use your mouse. If you accidentally select the wrong type and can't get the system to respond to the keyboard or mouse, you will need to reboot the system and start the setup again.

Four basic mouse types are presented

- PS/2 mouse
- Old Logitech serial mouse
- Microsoft compatible serial mouse
- USB mouse

If the correct mouse is not detected, select the one that you have on your system. For serial mouse devices, make sure that the correct serial port is selected. The display shows the serial ports with the Linux name and the common Windows name for the same port is shown next to it as COM1, COM2, and so on.

There is a test spot on the screen where you can test the mouse buttons for proper response.

Also on this screen is a drop-down list of mouse types. This enables you to refine the mouse configuration further. The choices include the following:

- Standard without wheel
- MouseManPlus
- IntelliMouse
- ThinkingMouse
- GlidePoint
- NetMouse
- NetScroll

Choosing the correct configuration makes it possible to use all the features available for your mouse. If you want to configure a two-button mouse to emulate a three-button mouse, select that option. The third button is used for copy-and-paste operations in Linux.

 TIP You can change the mouse, keyboard, and video settings after installation by running the lizardx tool from the KDE desktop. You can start this by typing in the command **lizardx** in a terminal window or from the COAS launcher on the KDE Application Launcher. Select X-Server to start lizardx.

Configuring the Keyboard, Video Card, and Monitor

Next, you will configure the keyboard, video card, and monitor on your computer.

> **CAUTION**
>
> Make sure your video card is supported by OpenLinux, or you might run into problems here.

The first step is to select a keyboard. Keyboard selection includes choosing a model and language layout.

The default keyboard layout is the older Generic 101-key PC. This works for almost any keyboard, but most keyboards shipped with new computers are the 104-key style keyboards. If you choose the 101-key option and you have a 104-style keyboard, you won't be able to use some of the keys on your keyboard. You can also select a couple of other specific models of keyboards.

The language layout is based on standard keyboard settings for those languages. There is a one-line test field below that where you can try typing characters if you want to make sure that all the needed characters are supported by your choice.

Selecting a Video Card   In the next step, you are shown the video card type that Lizard has detected on your system (shown in Figure 2.11). In most cases, you will not need to change the card type shown. In fact, I recommend that in those cases where what is shown is wrong, don't change it here. You should continue with the installation and reconfigure later using the XF86Setup program.

TIP   Some of the most recent high-end video cards are are not correctly configured. If you have one of these cards, you have to install using LISA.

See Appendix A for instructions on how to install with LISA.

FIGURE 2.11
The select video card screen. The Lizard installation program detects your video card.

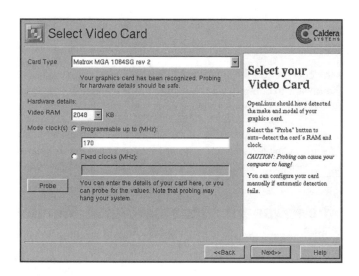

You should refine the initial probe, which is basic. By clicking on the Probe button, the video card's capabilities are detected. The probe looks at the amount of video memory on the card and the clock speeds supported.

When you run the probe, it gives you a warning that the screen will be blanked for five seconds. Click on Probe to continue. There is no danger to your video system in running this probe and no need to worry about the momentary screen blankout. After the probe completes, check to make sure that the video memory is correct. Sometimes this isn't properly detected. If it is wrong, manually enter the amount of RAM on your video card. When that's ready, click OK to continue.

CAUTION

I need to emphasize that you must make sure you have a video card that OpenLinux supports. Check the hardware compatibility list. If your video card is not supported, the installation might continue but the system will not start properly, if at all, when installation is completed.

See Appendix E for a list of compatible hardware.

Selecting a Monitor   The next screen is for selecting your monitor (shown in Figure 2.12). Some 1,700 different monitors are listed, and even then you won't find them all. This is why the top of the list contains a set of typical monitor settings.

Part

I

Ch

2

FIGURE 2.12
Select a monitor. The monitor selection determines the resolution capabilities for your system.

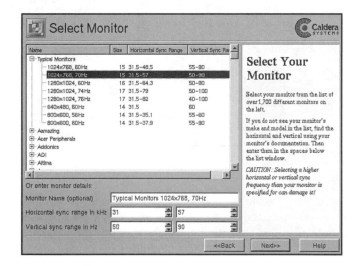

This setting is important to get right. It determines the resolution that is displayed on your system. Get it wrong, and the display may be unreadable.

CAUTION

Be warned: if you put in a capability that exceeds what your monitor can actually handle, you risk doing permanent damage to the monitor.

If you do not see your monitor listed, you have two choices. You can leave the default choice that the Lizard installation program detected, or, if you have the documents that came with the monitor, you can enter the horizontal and vertical refresh rates (sync range) in the appropriate boxes on the screen. Put in only the numbers given by the manufacturer. If you don't know, don't guess: use the default.

Selecting a Video Mode   Selecting the video mode (see Figure 2.13) is the only place where I've seen problems in setting up OpenLinux. So many possibilities are available, and the setup program even offers to test every possibility shown, but you do that at your own risk. I wouldn't recommend it.

FIGURE 2.13
Select a video mode. Proceed cautiously if you decide to change the video mode.

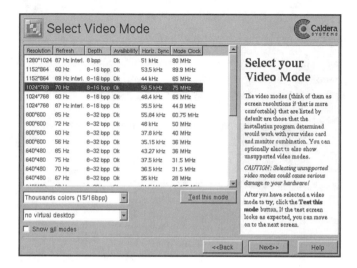

Some of the settings on this screen are

- **Resolution**—The numbers refer to pixel dots on the screen. The higher the numbers on the resolution, the smaller the dots appear on the screen. This means type appears smaller, but more fits on the screen. The standard setting used on Windows computers doing word processing is 800×600. Graphics workstations are usually set for the highest number available.

- **Refresh**— Higher numbers are better. It means less eyestrain and less screen flicker. Only high-end monitors can really support the high refresh rates. If you don't have one of those monitors, choose a median refresh rate.

- **Depth**— The number of colors available. The more colors displayed, the more video memory is required. Sometimes you have to make a trade-off between resolution and color depth. If you need high resolution, you may have to settle for fewer colors. Or, if you need 16 million colors, you may have to settle on a lower resolution.

If you want to see more than just the modes that your monitor will support, click on the box that says Show All Modes.

If you choose to test a mode, the screen blanks out and then open a test screen. This screen stays on for about 10 seconds and then returns to the Select Video Mode screen.

CAUTION

That is not always what happens, though. Testing can be unpredictable. On some machines, for example, the system hangs on a gray screen rather than go to a test screen. Usually you can use the Ctrl+Alt+Backspace key combination to get back to the installation screen.

Testing an unsupported mode can freeze the monitor system altogether, and only a reboot will bring it back to life. Unsupported modes can include those listed as OK under Availability. That's because it may seem to be supported, but the hardware driver may not properly support that mode.

If you have trouble here, you have three options:

- **Choose the defaults**— One way to proceed is to accept the defaults selected by the Lizard installation program. This usually creates a working system, though it might not be optimized to the maximum number of colors or resolution. You could try adjusting it later using lizardx or the XF86Setup programs. If you choose the defaults and they are unworkable, when you restart the system, OpenLinux will attempt to open in X Window mode (runlevel 5), but after several minutes if that fails it will open in character-terminal mode (runlevel 3). You could then configure using the XF86Setup program.

- **Get a commercial driver**—Usually the newest, state-of-the-art video cards don't have a Linux video driver that is supported by XFree86, the windowing server in OpenLinux. You can obtain drivers from commercial vendors who can provide drivers for most of the new video cards and often have added capabilities for high-end graphics acceleration. In that case, you use the default installation, and after the install, you install the commercial video driver. Two of the most popular commercial video drivers are AcceleratedX and MetroX. The Web site for Accelerated X is at www.xig.com; MetroX is at www.metrolink.com.

- **LISA installation**—If you are using a video card that isn't supported or you want to use a commercial video driver, you might want to use the LISA installation. This gives you more options on video configuration.

Selecting Where to Install OpenLinux

Clicking Next takes you to the screen labeled Installation target. The next step is selecting the partition in which to install OpenLinux (see Figure 2.14).

NOTE Do not get confused by the different ways the word *partition* is used. A partition can be a section of a hard disk or the whole disk. Windows-based PCs work with these kind of partitions, but the partitions are called by drive letters: C, D, E. They can each be a part of the hard disk or the entire disk, depending on how the disk was set up.

FIGURE 2.14

The installation target screen. Select where to install OpenLinux.

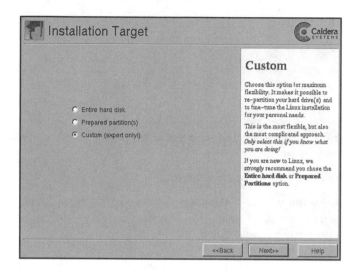

That's why you can divide a single hard disk into two partitions and have Windows installed on one partition and OpenLinux on the other. Each partition is seen as being separate from the other, and anything that happens to one partition won't affect the other partition. In fact, unless there is a total failure by the hard drive itself, the fact that partitions function separately is used to build greater reliability into the system. For an explanation, see the section on custom partitions later in this chapter.

You have three choices available here:

- Entire Harddisk
- Prepared Partition(s)
- Custom (Expert Only!)

Lizard does a probe of all your hard disks. If it does not find a Linux partition, it will select Entire Harddisk. If it finds a Linux partition, such as the one created by PartitionMagic, Prepared Partition(s) is selected. You can continue with the choice that was made, or you can choose Custom (Expert Only!). If you choose Custom, you must know what you are doing or you could end up with an unusable system. This is, as it says on the screen, a choice for experts only.

What follows is an explanation of each choice.

Entire Harddisk　If a Linux partition has not been defined already, the entire hard disk will be formatted for OpenLinux. This is a good choice for a computer that is an OpenLinux workstation. A swap partition is also defined automatically. This setup choice is similar to the way that Windows NT Workstation is set up. If you choose this option and click Next, you will be prompted to choose which disk drive on your system to use (see Figure 2.15). IDE drives are named /dev/hda, /dev/hdb, /dev/hdc, and so on. SCSI disk drives are named /dev/sda, /dev/sdb, and so on. When you've selected the drive and continue with the rest of the setup, the entire disk will be formatted and anything that was on the disk will be lost. If you have something on the disk that needs to be saved, you should back it up before starting the installation procedure.

Part
I
Ch
2

FIGURE 2.15
The select hard disk screen. If you choose Entire hard disk, you will be asked to select the disk.

Prepared Partition(s)   If you've created a Linux partition with PartitionMagic or with one of the other utilities for doing this such as fips, this is the choice that will be selected. If you've set up your system with PartitionMagic, you should make this choice. A swap partition also is defined automatically. This setup creates a system that is easily switchable between OpenLinux and Windows.

The next screen, shown in Figure 2.16, defines the partition to use for your OpenLinux installation. If you have more than one Linux partitions on your system, they are displayed here. Confirm that the correct partition is selected and then click on Next to continue.

Custom (Expert Only!)   If you are setting up a single-user workstation, you probably don't need to do custom partitioning. But for servers, you should consider custom partitioning. What's at issue is both performance and data security.

Although a server can be set up with either of the other two choices, for maximum performance, flexibility, and security, you'll want to do a custom setup. That said, be very careful doing this. This is not something to be attempted by beginners. If you are not familiar with Linux partitioning and you want to use custom partitions, you should try to get expert help for this step.

FIGURE 2.16
Select the root partition where OpenLinux will be installed.

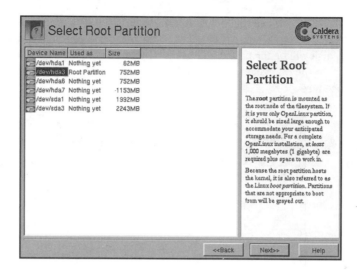

Custom Partitions Explained   How to partition your system is a hot topic among Linux pros. Many good partitioning strategies are out there, and you should find out as much as you can about the different possibilities. Only you can decide what works best for your system.

This explanation does not cover setting up disk mirroring, striping, or any other kind of hardware or software RAID. That is a specialized topic that can sometimes require that you rebuild the kernel, depending on what you need. It is never done during the initial setup and installation.

See Chapter 11, "Configuring File System and Performance," for an introduction to RAID with OpenLinux and performance tuning your system.

To custom partition your OpenLinux system, you must understand the directory structure.

See Chapter 6, "Understanding and Using the OpenLinux File System" for a reference on directory structure.

Disk partition strategies are based on controlling storage space and separating user space from system space. There are many reasons for doing this, and security is one of them.

I had a system that a cracker broke into. The break-in was quickly discovered, and the computer was taken offline before any real damage was done. Because the system files were in their own partition and the user files were in another partition, I had a quick and easy solution for bringing the system back online.

There was no need to go through the system files and find out whether anything had been changed. The system partition could simply be reformatted and the system files reinstalled. It took maybe an hour, but that is much less time than can be spent culling through system logs and files looking for evidence of unwanted changes and Trojan Horse programs. And it gives you a setup that you know is clean. The user files didn't have to be touched during reinstallation and they were easily checked.

Having separate partitions is not only useful for disaster recovery, it can also be useful for controlling the use of disk space. You can think of partitioning as putting up fences. Each area has its own space that has been defined by how it will be used.

Deciding how you want to divide the partitions on your system seems to be as much art as science. This is the part that always seems to generate lively discussions. Whatever you do, realize that you are going to have to live with your decision, so choose carefully. It's no easy matter making a change after the system is up and running. That's one reason why you should approach this subject cautiously.

Part
I
Ch
2

First, you'll need to know how you intend to use the computer. A firewall or router probably doesn't need any fancy partitioning, and you should skip custom partitioning. A file server, print server, Web server, mail server, or probably any other kind of server, on the other hand, needs to be partitioned carefully so that its growing needs can be met without choking the whole system.

After you've decided how the system will be used, you'll have to decide how to allocate space. For this, you'll need to understand how the different directories on OpenLinux are used. Finally, after the space has been allocated and the partitions defined, you will need to assign the mount points for each partition. Assigning mount points is explained in the next section "Steps Involved in Custom Partitioning."

Table 2.1 provides a short definition of some of the Linux directories and their space considerations. If you are not experienced in partitioning Linux systems, these definitions provide an introductory explanation only. You should not make any final decisions based on this information alone. You should get expert advice.

Table 2.1 Linux Directories

Directory	Description
/	The root partition. Everything resides under the root partition. This and a swap partition are the only necessary partitions. Some strategies call for putting a tight limit on the root partition, but that should only be done by someone who really knows what he is doing. It can easily lead to disaster if not carefully planned with full knowledge of the whole system.
/home	This is where all the user files go. On a file server, this is usually the biggest partition. It is even a good idea to put this partition on its own disk drive. It can speed up system performance because accessing user files is then handled separately from program files.
/usr	This is where the OpenLinux system files are located. It can be anywhere from a couple of hundred megabytes to over a gigabyte, depending on what you've installed. This directory needs to be big and have extra space in case you need to install additional software packages. The only software not found in this directory is some of the commercial packages, which are found in the /opt directory.

continues

Table 2.1	Continued
Directory	**Description**
/usr/local	Linux old-timers use this directory for installing software packages that aren't included in the standard installation. If you want, you can set this up as a separate partition. Then, if you have to reinstall your system files and this is on its own partition, you won't have to format this partition, and you'll be able to save those special files without reinstalling them. Some Linux pros have started to use the /opt directory for these special software packages because it is also needed for commercial software.
/var	You should take two areas of /var into consideration during partitioning: the log files and the spool files. OpenLinux writes all of its system logs into the /var/log directory. Heavily used systems can create large log files. Also printing and mail services make extensive use of /var/spool. If they don't have enough space, the system will choke. On heavily used systems and busy mail servers, it is a good idea to give /var its own partition.
/tmp	The temp partition is for temporary files. If you've enabled disk quotas, the /tmp directory gets heavy use. On busy systems, it's a good idea to put /tmp on its own partition. Putting /tmp on its own partition is the only way to control its growth. On busy systems, the /tmp directory expands rapidly. If its not on its own partition, it can fill up the root partition, which is where it is located. On a single user system, there is no reason to put /tmp on a separate partition.
/opt	Most commercial software is installed into the /opt directory. By putting /opt on its own partition, you may not have to reinstall the software if the system files have to be reinstalled and reconfigured.

You should never put /etc, /bin, or /dev on its own partition.

Steps Involved in Custom Partitioning

After selecting custom partitioning, OpenLinux displays a list of the devices on your system (see Figure 2.17).

The Lizard custom partitioning tool is one of the easiest to use partitioning tools available for Linux. It is generally the best and easiest way to do custom partitioning.

The table that is displayed shows the disk devices installed on your system, the start and end cylinders, size, system type, and mount point. It also indicates whether the partition is bootable and whether it will be formatted as part of the installation process.

The root partition must be formatted as part of the installation of OpenLinux. Any other partition may or may not be formatted, depending on your choice. If you need to install onto a system partition without formatting root, you will have to use the LISA installation (see Appendix A).

FIGURE 2.17
The partition hard disk screen. A display of your hard disks and how they have been partitioned.

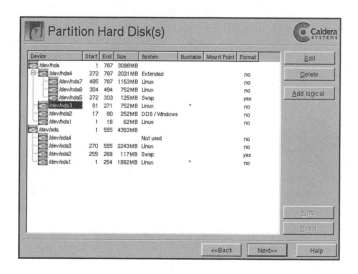

The display table shows the devices using their Linux name, /dev/hda for the first IDE disk drive, /dev/hdb for the second, and so on. SCSI drives are named /dev/sda, and so on.

Each disk drive can have as many as four primary partitions. The numbers 1 through 4 designate these. The first primary partition on the first IDE drive would be named /dev/hda1. If you need more than four partitions on a drive, you'll need to create logical partitions. Each primary partition can be divided into logical partitions.

On my workstation, I have a 4 gigabyte IDE hard disk. Windows is installed on the first primary partition. It's designated as /dev/hda1, and it takes up 1 gigabyte. Then, on /dev/hda2 I've put a swap partition. It's 64 megabytes, because that's how much memory I have on my computer. You should create a swap partition that is the size of your computer's memory.

On my workstation, I've installed OpenLinux on /dev/hda3, but I wanted to divide my partitions and not have one big partition. Therefore, I created logical partitions in /dev/hda3. The numbers for logical partitions start at five no matter whether you have one or four primary partitions, so I have three logical partitions in /dev/hda3. They are named /dev/hda5, /dev/hda6, and /dev/hda7.

When you create a primary or logical partition, you must indicate where the partition starts and where it ends. These numbers correspond to the cylinders on the hard drive. Because it's not really possible to think in terms of cylinders when figuring out disk space, the Lizard partitioning tool displays the total size in megabytes after you've entered start and end numbers. You can adjust the numbers until you get just the size you want.

The other setting in defining the partition is the System type. Your choices are Linux, Swap, and Windows. After you've created your swap partitions, you'll probably only need to create Linux partitions. These are partitions for anything you'll be doing in Linux.

Next to System type is a selection button for Bootable. This is already activated for the bootable partition on your system, and you probably won't need to change it here. Finally, there is a box for selecting formatting. If this is the / root partition, you will not be given a choice. It will automatically be selected for formatting. For any other partition, you can choose to format. If the partition has never been formatted, then you must format it to make it useable.

Next to Bootable is a place for designating the mount point. Every partition must have a mount point, or it will not be available for use on the system. The mount point is the directory on the file system where you will access the partition. The minimum installation has just the / root mount point. You have to designate at least one partition as the / root mount point. You then have six other choices. Those choices are explained in Table 2.1. Or select <other> to create your own custom mount point.

After you've configured the partitions and their mount points, write down the information in a log book or system administrator's book where you can find it. You may need this information again, and if you ever have to reinstall anything, you will have to know how all the partitions were used. You'll need a full partition map. If you ever have to reinstall, all the mounting information is lost, and you must reenter it by hand. There are no shortcuts for custom partitioning.

Maintain a Logbook

A logbook can be one of the most important tools you have for maintaining your Linux computer. Make a record of the installation, what options were used, how the drive is partitioned, and how the hardware is configured. Make sure to update the log with every change you make.

Then when an emergency arises, you can obtain the information you need quickly. Whether you have to install new hardware or reinstall some or all of the software, having a record makes it easier to get back to where you were when the problem occurred. Relying on your memory, especially in an emergency situation, is a bad idea.

Don't depend on writing notes on scraps of paper or sticky notes, either. You should get a bound notebook and keep entries in chronological order.

Every Linux professional I know swears by their logbook and has a story about how it rescued them from certain disaster.

Once you've completely defined the partitions, click the Next button.

Formatting the Partitions No matter how you've chosen to partition your system, using the entire disk, the prepared partition, or the custom partition method, the next step is to format the partitions. You must format the root partition and a swap partition before you can proceed.

Be careful here. Take a close look at the screen, shown Figure 2.18. Make sure that the partitions to be formatted are the ones you want formatted. After a partition has been formatted, you cannot recover anything that was on the partition before. *You cannot undo formatting,* so proceed with caution.

FIGURE 2.18
The formatting screen. Check this screen carefully before starting to format your disks.

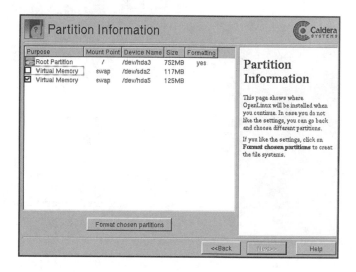

On the bottom of the screen toward the center, is a button that says Format Chosen Partitions. Clicking that button starts the formatting. You must do this to continue with installation. A message on the screen appears beside the partitions indicating that formatting is taking place. When it is finished, the message says Done. After formatting is completed, you can click Next to continue installation.

Selecting and Installing Software

Selecting the software packages to install is next. The packages are the "tools" of OpenLinux. These are the programs that carry out every task for the operation of the computer. The OpenLinux CD contains hundreds of these software packages.

The standard recommended installation is probably the right choice for most users setting up a workstation. In addition to the standard installation, five special customized installation options are available: Business Workstation, Development Workstation, Home Computer, Network Server, and Web Server. For limited systems—that old computer you're saving from the graveyard—the minimal installation may be the best choice because hard drive space is limited.

FIGURE 2.19
Select the packages to be installed.

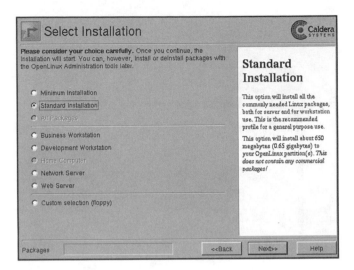

Here's what's in the different options (see Figure 2.19):

- **Minimum Installation**—This option installs about 170 megabytes of files on your system. It installs only what is needed to have a working system, but not most of the software that users expect to find on their computer system.

- **Standard Installation**—This option installs all the packages needed for setting up OpenLinux as either a workstation or a server. It installs about 650 megabytes of files.

- **All Packages**—This option installs everything on the OpenLinux CD onto your system. It takes up as much 1.4 gigabytes of space.

- **Business Workstation**—All the packages commonly found on a business computer, including text processing applications as well as security and network connectivity. It installs about 500 megabytes of files.

- **Development Workstation**—Similar to the Standard Installation plus packages for software development including compilers and interpreters for many programming languages including C, C++, Fortran, Java, Perl, Python, and Tcl/Tk, also other tools used for programming. It installs about 680 megabytes of files.

- **Home Computer**—Similar to the Business Workstation with packages for creating documents plus games and PPP modem dialup software. Also includes Web browsers, mail clients, and other Internet tools. It installs about 840 megabytes of files.

- **Network Server**—This option installs only those packages needed for a general-purpose server. It includes software for a file server, Samba, mail, FTP, DNS, and other network servers. It does not include X Windows or the KDE desktop and installs only about 250 megabytes of files.

- **Web Server**—Similar to the network server, this option installs the Apache Web server package and other software needed for a Web server. It does not include X Windows or the KDE desktop and installs only about 200 megabytes of files.
- **Custom selection (floppy)**—Lets you install a custom set of files defined from a list from a floppy disk. The list must be in the file /etc/pkgs.sel on the floppy disk. Sample package lists for creating this file are found in the /col/data directory on the OpenLinux CD. Copy a sample file and edit it to create your own custom installation.

NOTE If you don't have enough space for any one of the options, that option will be grayed out to show that it's not available. One reason to stick with the recommended installation, even if you have lots of hard drive space, is because it's so easy to add something later on. This way your system won't become bloated. ■

After selecting the packages, select Next. The installation of the OpenLinux software will begin immediately. While the software is being installed, you can continue to configure sound and the network setup. The response of the computer may be significantly slowed down while the package installation continues. This is not something to worry about because most of the system resources are being devoted to the installation. A bar is displayed across the bottom of the screen that indicates the progress of the software package installation in percentage terms.

Sound Card Detection

While the packages are being installed, if a sound card was detected on your system ,the drivers are automatically loaded. The next screen lets you test the sound card (see Figure 2.20).

FIGURE 2.20
Test your sound card to make sure it is working correctly.

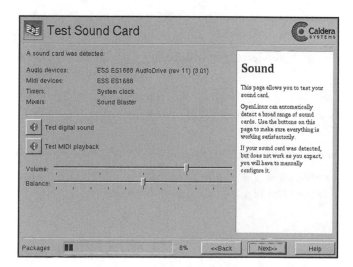

The top part of the screen shows what sound card was detected. You may want to write down this information, if you don't already have it. It can help you later if you need to adjust your sound settings or you want to install a new sound driver.

When you click on the test digital sound button, you should hear music playing. You can adjust the volume and balance using the sliders below the buttons.

Clicking on the MIDI playback should also start music playing.

If the tests fail, you can manually configure the sound card after the OpenLinux installation is completed.

See Chapter 10 on installing and configuring sound.

N O T E Sound card installation is a new feature in OpenLinux 2.3. It still has some bugs. Sound cards are not always correctly detected or sometimes are detected but are not configured correctly. There are even times when OpenLinux doesn't correctly detect the sound card and the Test Sound Card window is blank. If you have problems, just continue with the installation. You can configure sound later following the instructions found in Chapter 10. This chapter includes information on how to get the top-quality OSS sound driver. ▪

First User Setup

After you've tested the sound card, you must define two users. First, you are prompted to enter a password for root. Root is the superuser who can do absolutely anything on the system. This is a special user account that is not meant for everyday use. It is reserved for system administration and installing software.

The root password should be at least five characters long. There are many considerations involved in selecting a password.

See Chapter 30, "Overview of Network Security," for an introduction to an approach for selecting passwords.

The next screen is labeled Set Login Name(s) (see Figure 2.21). It is mislabeled. You can really only add one user at this time. To add more users, use COAS after installation is complete.

See Chapter 5, "Configuring Your System with COAS," for more details.

The screen shows a sample real name of Caldera Systems OpenLinux User. Do not use this name. Put in the name of a user, often your own name.

CAUTION

Do not use the sample login name of col. This is sample text only. Using this name could create a security hole on your system and should be avoided.

FIGURE 2.21
Set login name. You create your first user account here.

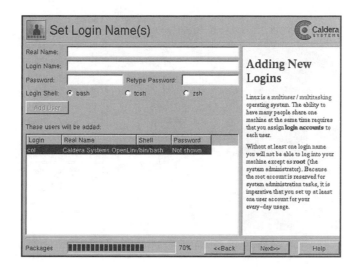

Part

I

Ch

2

The login name you choose should not be longer than eight characters. After you've entered a password and typed it a second time to confirm spelling, the Add User button will no longer be grayed out. You have to click the Add User button to continue.

Though it appears that you can add additional users at this point, this does not work. Only the first user added here shows up on the system's user list after installation is complete.

Configuring Network Options

If your system will be on an Ethernet network, the next step is to set up networking. This section is not about accessing the Internet or setting up a modem connection. This is strictly for setup of a TCP/IP-based local network.

You do not need to set up Ethernet configuration information if:

- You're not on a local area network and your only network connection is by modem to your office or an ISP. That does not require this network setup.
- You are on a local area network, but all setup is handled by a DHCP server. A Dynamic Host Configuration Protocol server assigns configuration information to your computer.

If you don't need to set up any Ethernet networking configuration, click the No Ethernet button (see Figure 2.22).

If your network has a DHCP server, click the Ethernet Configured Using DHCP radio button.

If you are on a network, click the third radio button, Ethernet Configured Statically. If Lizard detected an Ethernet network card in your system, this button will automatically be chosen and some configuration information may be automatically entered.

FIGURE 2.22
Set up networking. This
is used to configure an
Ethernet network.

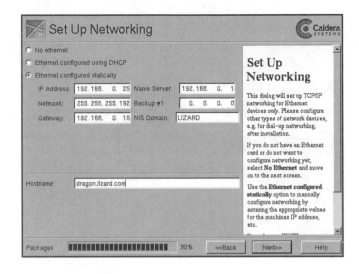

CAUTION

Don't assume that the configuration information that was detected is correct. In fact, much of it may be wrong. Check every number. If any number here is wrong, your network connection won't work.

If you don't know the answers, you will have to get them from your system administrator. Make sure each field is filled in correctly:

- **IP Address**—This is the Internet address assigned to your computer. Get the information from the network system administrator. Don't make up a number. It would make your computer unusable on the network and could also wreak havoc for others on the network.

- **Netmask**—This is the network mask that is used internally by your machine to determine what type of network it is on. Get the netmask from your system administrator.

- **Gateway**— This is your computer's route to the outside world. Get this information from your network system administrator.

- **Name server**— This is the computer on your network that turns human-readable names like www.yahoo.com into IP number addresses that computers can understand.

- **Backup #1**— Often there is a secondary name server that can be accessed if the primary name server doesn't respond.

- **NIS domain**— If your network uses NIS, get the domain information from your network system administrator. If not, just leave the setting blank.

You should also fill in the hostname. If the computer is not on a network, the hostname will be localhost. The hostname is recorded with the IP address in the network system records.

Don't make up a hostname, but you can usually choose a name and have that named assigned to your computer. Get the information from your network system administrator. The hostname is the name of your computer and the full domain name for the network your computer is connected to. A typical hostname might be `hal.calderasystems.com`. This says that it is the computer named hal at calderasystems.com.

Installing the Linux Loader

The next screen installs the *Linux Loader* (*LILO*). LILO is a Linux boot manager that starts Linux and can be set up to start any other operating system on your computer.

The screen lists all bootable partitions (see Figure 2.23). The list shows the partitions, using the Linux name such as /dev/hda1, the file system type, and the label. The label is what you type to choose that operating system on bootup.

FIGURE 2.23
Use LILO to start Linux or Windows on the same computer.

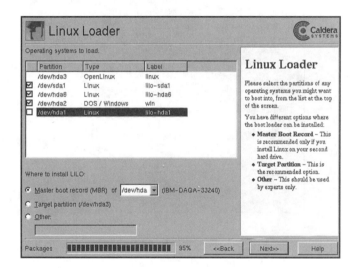

Select the partition that will be the default operating system when you start your computer. This is the system that starts after 30 seconds if you make no selection.

Below that, indicate where you want to install LILO. The choices are

■ **Master boot record (MBR)**— This is the recommended choice if you do not plan to use BootMagic (included with PartitionMagic on the boxed edition of OpenLinux). Also choose this option if you have installed OpenLinux on its own hard drive (if Linux is the only operating system on your computer and you won't be using Windows or if Linux is installed on a second hard drive).

■ **Target partition**— This option puts LILO on the OpenLinux partition and is the recommended choice if you are using Boot Magic.

■ **Other**— This is the expert level option for those who want to put LILO in another location.

If you are unsure what to choose, accept the default choice that Lizard selected. The default choice is based on an analysis of the system.

Setting up a Time Zone

The last step for installation is to choose a time zone (see Figure 2.24).

FIGURE 2.24
Select a time zone. You can use the map or use the drop-down list.

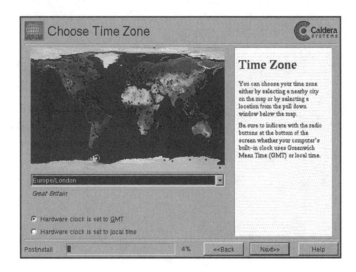

Selecting a time zone is fairly straightforward. A big color map is shown, and you can point to the area on the map that is close to where you are. That chooses a time zone.

You also can select from a drop-down list that is shown directly below the map.

At the bottom of the screen are two choices to indicate a setting for the computer's hardware clock. The Internet uses Greenwich Mean Time (GMT or UTC), which is the first choice, but the BIOS on most PC system boards uses local time. This can mean that using GMT time for OpenLinux may run into system conflicts. Your best choice is to use Local Time.

If your computer has both OpenLinux and Windows or DOS installed on it, you must choose Local Time. Otherwise, time settings will never be right when you switch operating systems because those other operating systems only recognize local time.

If you complete the time setting and the software packages have not yet finished installing, a Tetris-like game is displayed for your entertainment. You can play the game or do something else until the installation finishes. When it reaches that point you must click the Finish button.

The installation disk will be locked until the system restarts, but once it restarts you should remove the disk.

N O T E After you've finished the installation of OpenLinux, make sure you remove the CD. If you don't take out the CD and if you have a bootable CD drive, the next time you start up your computer it will start the installation process instead of starting the system on your drive. ▓

When you click on the Finish button, the system restarts in OpenLinux. This is not a full rebooting of the system. It is a soft boot. If you used PartitionMagic to divide your hard drive between Windows and OpenLinux, wait until the system login screen comes up and then choose Shutdown. You have to do a full shutdown and start up in Windows in order to install BootMagic.

Don't worry about what is being displayed on the screen during the first start of the system after an installation. The display might read that the modules are failing to load, but this is not the case. The modules are being loaded, but at the same time the module database is being created. The next time everything should appear to be normal.

If you used PartitionMagic, you have one more step before you are finished.

Setting Up BootMagic

If you have the boxed edition of OpenLinux, you can use BootMagic if you want to share your computer between Windows and OpenLinux. If you used PartitionMagic, after you've installed OpenLinux, your computer will go directly to Windows the next time you start it up. You won't have an option to start OpenLinux.

To get that option, you'll need BootMagic, but don't install BootMagic until you've installed OpenLinux, or it won't work.

To install BootMagic you need to be in Windows. Insert the Windows Tools & Commercial Packages CD. Choose the Install Products option. In the next window, select Install Boot Magic.

This installs the BootMagic program on your system. You also can create a BootMagic emergency boot floppy disk at this time.

When the installation is complete, the BootMagic configuration program is started. It shows your Windows partition and marks it as the default. If the Linux partition is not shown on the list, click Add and select the Linux partition. The Startup Delay setting is the amount of time to wait before starting the default choice. If you plan on using OpenLinux as your primary workstation operating system, you should change the default in BootMagic to Linux.

Click Save/Exit when you are done and then restart the system. When the computer starts up, you can choose between Linux and Windows. ●

Configuring and Customizing OpenLinux

Configuring the KDE Desktop

You can configure the K Desktop Environment (KDE) just the way you want it. Here's where you define the look and feel of what you see on the computer monitor. You can make your computer look like a Macintosh or a Windows 95/98 computer, or you can leave it the way it comes, looking like a high-end OpenLinux workstation.

If you've heard about windows managers in Linux, KDE includes a windows manager, KWM, but it is much more than just a manager. It's an integrated windows environment.

See The K Window Manager at the end of this chapter for more information on KWM.

KDE provides a common interface for all the software applications you'll be using in OpenLinux. That means that OpenLinux has both the kind of Linux platform preferred by computer professionals and scientists with the friendly interface expected by most everyday computer users.

KDE is a total graphical environment. That means it has

- A windows manager
- A file manager
- A help system
- A configuration system
- Many tools and utilities
- Plus dozens of applications from a mail reader to a drawing program

KDE is free software according to the GNU General Public License. All KDE libraries are available under the LGPL, making commercial software development for the KDE desktop possible, all KDE applications are licensed under the GPL.

Starting OpenLinux

After you've completed the initial OpenLinux setup, you will have a fully operating computer. Here are some tips on starting your computer so that you won't run into trouble.

The OpenLinux system is started by a program called *LILO*, or *LInux LOader*. You'll see a prompt that says something such as LILO boot:. The way the boot prompt appears varies depending on how you installed OpenLinux, and if you use BootMagic.

If you are using BootMagic, a BootMagic screen appears where you can choose to start either Windows or OpenLinux. If you choose OpenLinux, a prompt appears that looks something like this:

```
LILO
Φboot:
```

If you don't have BootMagic, a Caldera Systems screen will be displayed, with a Φboot: prompt at the bottom of the screen.

Normally, you'll do nothing when you see the boot: prompt, and the startup procedures will begin. This will take you directly into the K login screen. For normal startups, you can then proceed to log in.

Nevertheless, you have some important options when you see the LILO boot prompt. Knowing about these options can help you, particularly if you have a problem on your system and need to get in through a backdoor.

LILO Options

When LILO starts, at the boot: prompt you can type in commands that can change the way OpenLinux starts. For example, if you aren't using BootMagic, LILO can be configured to start DOS or Windows.

At the LILO boot prompt on an unmodified, standard OpenLinux installation, the program assumes that you will be starting Linux. Therefore, you can either type the word **linux** or wait a few seconds and the word is automatically entered—though you won't see it—and OpenLinux starts up.

You can add options after the word **linux**. This is one of the tricks of Linux pros. You can force OpenLinux to start up in a nongraphical terminal mode, or you can even force it to start in single-user mode, which is used for certain kinds of system maintenance, hard disk repairs, and emergencies.

For example, entering **linux 3** at the boot: prompt tells OpenLinux to start in the nongraphical terminal mode. This can be useful if you are having problems with your graphical video setup.

The number **3** refers to runlevel 3. A *runlevel* is just a way of indicating how the system should be run, which parts of the system should be started after the kernel is loaded, and so on. OpenLinux follows the UNIX System V standard. There is nothing similar on Windows or Macintosh systems.

When you select a runlevel, the system reads the configuration files for that runlevel and initiates them. In fact, when you shut down you are simply changing the runlevel from 5, if you are in the KDE windowing environment, to 6, which begins the shutdown scripts.

There are seven runlevels, and OpenLinux uses six of them:

- 0—Halt the system
- 1—Single-user mode
- 2—Multiple-user mode, without network support
- 3—Multiple-user mode, with network support

- 4—Not used
- 5—KDE windowing environment
- 6—Shut down and reboot the system

LILO Error Codes

Sometimes, when a problem occurs, LILO seems to stop after only partly starting. When this happens, where LILO stops can tell you what the problem is. Each letter of the word LILO is displayed on the screen after a step in the startup procedure is completed. Reading the letter code can give you a clue as to where any problems are:

- **Nothing**—If no letters are displayed, either LILO isn't properly installed, or the LILO boot sector isn't active.
- **L**—Indicates that LILO has started but that the disk drive has failed to respond.
- **LI**—Indicates that LILO has successfully loaded and the disk drive has responded, but a configuration error has occurred. This error can be fixed on some systems by adding a line to the /etc/lilo.conf file. With a text editor, under the line that says read-only line in the default entry, add the word linear on a line by itself.
- **LIL**—Indicates that LILO has reached the second stage of loading, but a disk media failure has occurred.
- **LIL?**—Indicates that LILO has reached the second stage of loading, but it was loaded at the wrong address. This error is usually caused by a configuration mismatch.
- **LIL-**—The descriptor table is bad.

If the problem is not a bad hard disk, fixing it probably requires booting from an emergency floppy disk and reconfiguring and/or reinstalling LILO. Most of the configuration problems come from the way multiple-gigabyte hard disks are mapped.

Starting OpenLinux

Normally, once you install OpenLinux, it just starts up. You don't need to enter any special commands. The startup looks somewhat similar to what you might see on Windows NT or Macintosh systems. Stuff flashes by that you can ignore for the most part, but you'll notice one big difference after the startup procedure has finished.

On Windows and Macintosh systems, you can have the system set up so that the user never has to login to the system unless the computer is used on a network. On Linux systems, you always have to log in before you can use your computer.

Logging In   At the login prompt, enter your username.

> **CAUTION**
>
> Only log in as root if you are doing system administration work.

After you've entered your login name, enter your password, and click Go.

This takes you to the KDE desktop. OpenLinux 2.3 uses the KDE desktop environment version 1.1.1.

The first time you log in, you'll see the KDE configuration wizard (as shown in Figure 3.1). You'll know it's the wizard because there is an actual Wizard displayed in the window. This wizard is always available, so if you decide you don't want to make any changes the first time you start you can always use it later.

Part

II

Ch

3

FIGURE 3.1
The first time you log in, you'll see the KDE configuration wizard.

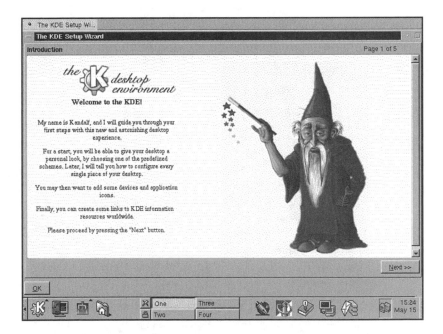

The KDE configuration wizard takes you through some configuration options. You might want to look through the different wizard screens to see some of the options available. But all of the changes the wizard offers to make at this point can be done later.

After the initial introductory screen, clicking the Next button opens the Theme selection screen (as shown in Figure 3.2). Four different themes are displayed: KDE, Windows, MacOS, and BeOS. These are color and display themes. They change the look onscreen, but they do not make the system work like the other operating systems. No matter what theme you choose, you will be working in OpenLinux, and the computer will work like a Linux computer, not like one of the other systems.

FIGURE 3.2

The KDE Setup Wizard theme offers a choice between the KDE default and Windows, MacOS, and BeOS themes.

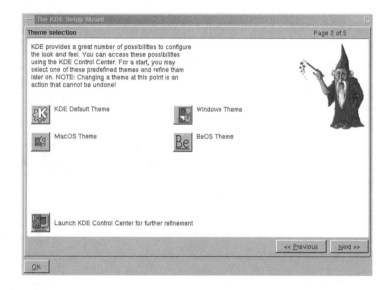

The next screen offers to create drive icons on your desktop (as shown in Figure 3.3). This puts icons on the desktop that let you access the floppy and CD-ROM drives from the KDE desktop without having to mount them first.

N O T E Throughout this book, I've used the KDE theme. If you've chosen another theme, your screens will not only look different, but you will find that the location of the taskbar, the panel, and other tools will be different. ■

The next screen offers to put a printer icon on your desktop (as shown in Figure 3.4). If you have a printer on your system or have access to a network printer, you'll want to have the printer icon on your desktop. A single click on the printer icon does it. There is no visible response, but the icon appears on your desktop, and you see it when you exit the wizard.

FIGURE 3.3
The KDE Setup Wizard
can configure drives
on your desktop.

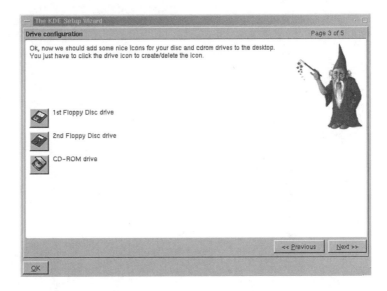

FIGURE 3.4
The KDE Setup Wizard
can add a printer icon
on your deskktop.

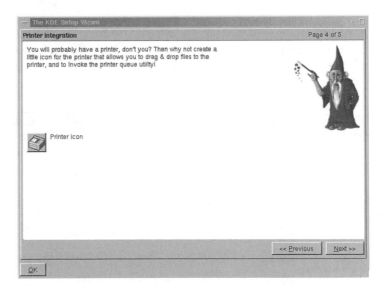

The final screen puts icons on your desktop that link to the Caldera Systems Web site as well as several different KDE Web sites (as shown in Figure 3.5). If you want easy links to any of those sites, you should choose them here. Finally, click OK to finish the KDE configuration wizard.

Part
II

Ch
3

FIGURE 3.5
The KDE Setup Wizard can add links to the KDE and Caldera Systems Web sites.

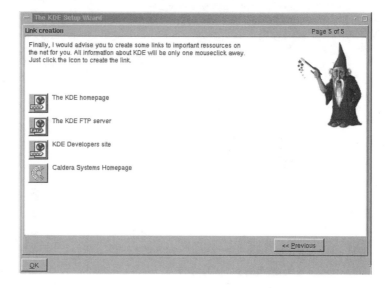

Introduction to the KDE Desktop

The KDE desktop (shown in Figure 3.6) has a familiar look. It is easy to use for anyone who has worked on a Windows or Macintosh system. There are many similarities but there are also differences.

FIGURE 3.6
The KDE desktop.

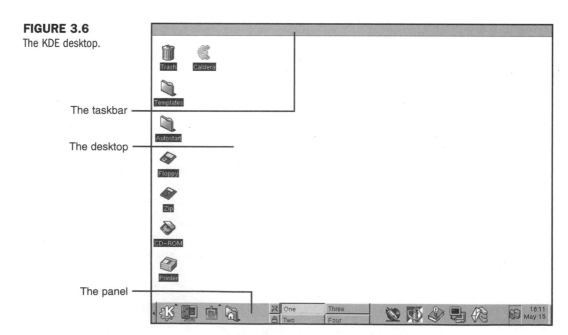

The desktop is divided into three areas:

- The taskbar across the top of the screen.
- The panel across the bottom of the screen.
- The desktop area where icons are located.

The Taskbar

Across the top of the screen is the taskbar. Every time you open an application, a button for that application is put on the taskbar. This is similar to the taskbar on Windows systems and works in the same manner. At any time, clicking on the button in the taskbar brings that application to the top on your screen. Clicking on the taskbar button with the right mouse button shows a list of options. You can change the look of the taskbar in the KPanel configuration tool. There are settings for the taskbar, which you can hide and place on different sides of the screen.

Right-click on a blank area on the KPanel across the bottom of the screen. The Panel configuration tab contains settings for the taskbar. The choices are to hide the bar, put it across the top of the screen (the default), across the bottom of the screen, or make it a button on the top left of the screen.

The Panel

The panel goes across the bottom of the screen. It is used to launch applications and also has pop-up menus that offer access to other applications and tools. Figure 3.7 labels each feature, and Table 3.1 tells a little more about them.

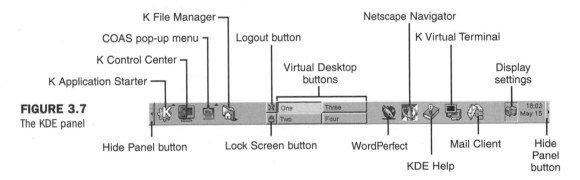

FIGURE 3.7
The KDE panel

Table 3.1   Features on the KDE Panel

Button	Description
K Application Starter	A pop-up menu that opens a menu of OpenLinux applications and utilities. The keyboard shortcut to access the Application Starter is Alt+F1.
KDE Control Center	Used to adjust the many of the KDE settings.
COAS pop-up menu	The Caldera Open Administration System is used for many system administration tasks.
KFM	The K File Manager is a powerful utility used for copying, moving, and deleting files, and much more. The little house shape on the icon indicates that it will open in your home directory.
Logout button	The Logout button will exit the K desktop and return you to the login screen. It does not shut down the system. That you can do from the login screen by choosing the Shutdown button.
Lock screen button	This will display whatever screensaver you have selected and lock access to the screen until your password has been entered.
Virtual desktop buttons	Each button represents a virtual desktop, which lets you reduce screen confusion by running application on different desktops. Opens to desktop number One when first started. The default number of virtual desktops is four, but the number can be changed. To add desktops, right-click on a blank area on the KPanel across the bottom of the screen. In the KPanel Configuration select the Desktops tab. Move the slider marked Visible to the right to add desktops. They are added in two's. You can have up to eight virtual desktops.
KDE help	A browseable introduction to the fundamentals of the KDE desktop.
KVT	The K virtual terminal enables you to run programs from a terminal command prompt.
Display settings configuration tool	Use to change the screen colors, screensaver, and other settings.

Other icons on the panel represent applications like WordPerfect and Netscape Communicator. On the right end is a clock showing the time and date.

On either end of the panel is a Hide Panel button. Clicking on either of these buttons hides the panel so that you have more space available on your desktop. When the panel is hidden, clicking on the same button puts the panel back across the bottom of the screen. You can also configure it to hide itself automatically until you click on the button.

The panel is easy to change. To configure settings on the panel, click the right mouse button on a blank area on the panel and select Configure. You can also click on the K Application Starter and go to Panel. In Panel, select Configure.

The KPanel Configuration screen has many options (seen in Figure 3.8). The location section lets you place the panel on any side of the screen: top, left, bottom (the default), or right. The style section makes it appear bigger or smaller. The taskbar section changes the location of the taskbar from top to bottom, or as a button on the top left of the screen. The hidden option completely removes the taskbar from the screen.

FIGURE 3.8
The KPanel
Configuration window.
The panel is easy to
change.

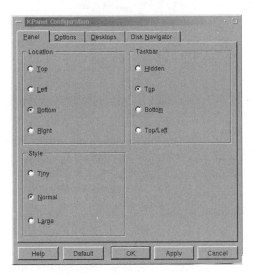

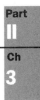

The Options Tab   You can set many options for the panel, as seen in Figure 3.9.

Menu Tooltips   You can turn the Tooltips—the text labels that appear when you hover your mouse over a button—on or off. You can also adjust the time before the tips are shown from a small delay to a long delay.

See the section titled Modifying buttons in the Panel later in this chapter.

Visuals   Visual settings start with options to hide the panel and the taskbar. If you choose to hide either one, you can set the delay time before each is hidden and the speed that is used for hiding. If you hide either, moving the mouse pointer over the area of the screen where they are normally displayed will make either reappear.

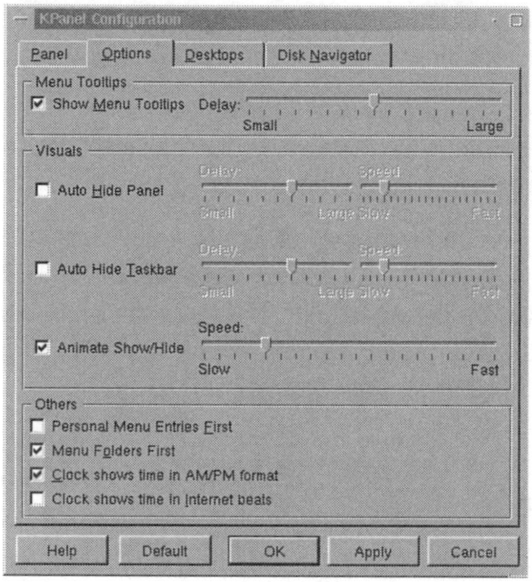

FIGURE 3.9

The panel options include controlling the Tooltips and auto-hiding the panel or taskbar.

If you enable the Animate Show/Hide feature, the panel or taskbar shrinks or expands as it disappears or reappears.

Others   Other settings start with the option to change the order of the entries of the K Application Launcher. If you select Personal Menu Entries First, applications you've added to the Application Launcher are listed as the primary entries. All the other application will be listed in a separate submenu called Default. The standard setting is Menu Folders First.

Use the clock settings to change the clock from a 24-hour setting to a 12-hour AM and PM display.

You'll also see a new option to show the time in Internet beats. This is a new time standard developed by the Swatch company in cooperation with Nicholas Negroponte, the founder and director of the Massachusetts Instititue of Technology's Media Laboratory. The idea is to have one time without time zones or geographical borders.

Internet time is based on Swatch Beats, a unit of measurement that divides the day into 1,000 beats, beginning at the meridian in Biel, Switzerland (you guessed it: Swatch headquarters). The time is then shown in beat numbers in the format @610, which would be 610 Internet time. The Swatch company includes Internet time capabilities in its products, primarily watches, and also has PC, Macintosh, and Palm Pilot programs for converting Internet time to your local time. No Linux converter is available. For more information look at their Web site at www.swatch.com.

The Desktops Tab   The Desktops tab (seen in Figure 3.10) defines the available virtual desktops.

FIGURE 3.10
The panel desktops
configuration tab is
used to add virtual
desktops.

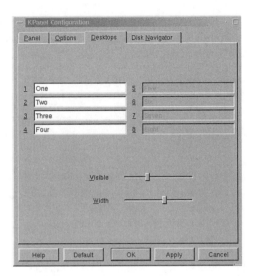

You can change the names of the virtual desktops from the defaults of One, Two, and so on to anything you wish (projects, themes, and so on). Move the slider named Visible left or right to add or subtract the number of virtual desktops two at a time. You can also adjust the size of the virtual desktop buttons on the panel by moving the width slider.

The Disk Navigator Tab   The fourth tab in the Panel Configuration (seen in Figure 3.11) is for adjusting the look of the Disk Navigator.

FIGURE 3.11
The panel Disk
Navigator configuration
choices.

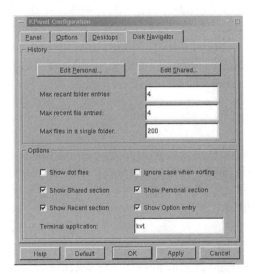

The Disk Navigator is a utility that can be started from the KPanel to navigate through the file system. he Shared section shows resources shared by all users including CD-ROM, removable disks, and so on. The Personal section displays the user's home directory.

To change these settings, click on Edit Personal or Edit Shared, whichever you want to change. The K File Manager is started, showing the entries for the section you are editing.

To add an entry, from the File menu under New select the entry type you are adding: Folder, File System Device, FTP URL, Mime Type, Application, Internet Address (URL), or World Wide Web URL.

The recommended method is to create a URL entry. For example, to create a link to start WordPerfect, select Internet Address (URL) and click on OK. That creates a link icon named URL. Right-click on the URL icon and select Properties. Change the File Name from URL.kdelnk to WordPerfect.kdelnk. On the URL tab, enter:

```
/opt/wp8/wpbin/xwp
```

Then click on the icon below the entry box, select the WordPerfect icon or any icon that you'd like to use. Close the KFM window and click on OK when you are finished with the configuration options. This should restart the KPanel and will put the additional entries in place under either Shared or Personal, depending on what you changed.

You can change other settings here to display the number of recent folders and recent file entries as well as the maximum number of files to display in a folder.

You can click the option to show files that start with a dot: These are configuration files that are normally hidden from display. You can also click an option to hide any section of the Disk Navigator. Normally names of files, folders, and other items are sorted with uppercase names displayed first in alphabetical order followed by lowercase names. One option ignores case when sorting.

Modifying buttons in the Panel   You can add buttons for your favorite applications to the panel. Click on the K Application Starter and on the pop-up menu find Panel. It's near the bottom of the list. From the pop-out menu, select Add Application and the menu of installed applications is shown. Select the application you want to add. An icon is automatically placed on the panel.

Pointing the mouse at the new button displays Tooltips for the new button. These are short descriptions of what application the button launches. You can easily change the Tooltip by right-clicking the panel button and selecting Properties. Click the Application tab and put text for the ToolTip in the Comment field.

If the change doesn't appear right away, you may need to restart the panel. Right-click on a blank area on the Panel and select Restart.

You can remove buttons by right-clicking on them and selecting Remove.

To move a button, right-click on it and select Move. You can then move it along the panel to the location where you want it to appear. Click again on the right mouse button to place it. Be careful, moving buttons can have unexpected results, even making some buttons disappear or move to other areas of the panel.

TIP On some screens, those at a resolution of 800×600 or less, the clock might not appear. Changing the panel's configuration style to Tiny makes the clock appear.

You can edit the pop-up menus on the panel to add or remove programs. To do this, click the K Application Starter and on the pop-up menu find Panel. On Panel, select Edit Menus.

The first time the Menu Editor opens, it shows the Application Starter menu on the right side and a box that says EMPTY on the left side.

If you want to add or delete items from the Application Starter, click the item on the menu that is shown. After the item is highlighted, right-click on it, and a list of options is shown.

Options include changing the item, moving it, or deleting it. You can also add items to the menu by selecting New (see Figure 3.12).

Part

II

Ch

3

FIGURE 3.12
Applications can be added or removed from the Application Launcher using the Menu Editor.

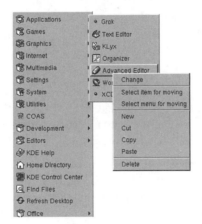

In Figure 3.13, the EMPTY item appears on the top of the menu list so that you can create your own personal pop-up menu. If you want to create your own menu, you'll want to give it a name. Under options on the menu line select Change Menuname and enter a name for your personal menu.

You can add items from the Application Starter menu on the right of the screen by selecting the item and right-clicking the mouse. Choose Copy, select your personal menu, right-click, and choose Paste. You can also drag items and drop them from the Application Starter menu to your personal menu.

FIGURE 3.13

Choose EMPTY to add
your own personal
pop-up menu.

You are not limited to the applications and utilities on the Application Starter menu. You can add any of the hundreds of applications on your system. This requires creating a KDE link file. Right-click on your personal menu and select New. The K Menu Editor opens with a panel that shows all the settings needed to create the link file. You need to indicate the file type, name, icon, and more. If you are sure about any of the settings, you can find an explanation in the Menu Editor Help menu.

The Desktop

The desktop is the area in the center of the screen. Three icons are placed on the desktop by default: Trash, Templates, and Autostart. You can add your own icons if you want. The Trash icon is for deleting files, much like the Recycle Bin on Windows or the Trash can on a Macintosh. I explain the Autostart folder later in this chapter.

The Templates folder contains sample files that you can use to create new icons on the desktop. There are six samples for device, FTP, Mime, Program, URL, and WWW types. These are the same templates that are available when you right-click the mouse on an empty area of the desktop under the New pop-out menu.

The desktop is also where your working programs are displayed.

The KDE desktop is configured with four virtual desktops, though you can change these if you want. Virtual desktops make your life easier when using Linux's multitasking capabilities. You can start working on one desktop, get everything started, then push that desktop aside, and start working on something new on a second desktop. You can start word processing on one desktop, start a spreadsheet on another, and a presentation program on a third desktop.

Then you don't need to minimize and maximize and click around between programs, just switch to the desktop for the program you need.

These are called *virtual desktops* because they aren't really on a separate system. The capabilities are limited to what you can run on your system with the amount of memory and disk space you have available.

Configuring the KDE Desktop

You can use the KDE desktop to place icons for frequently used programs. You can also put icons on the desktop for easy "mounting" of floppy disks, CD-ROMs, or Zip disks.

You can change the look of the KDE desktop with the Display Settings panel (see Figure 3.14). Start this utility from the Display Settings button on the lower-right side of the Panel next to the clock. An alternative is to click on a blank area of the desktop with the right mouse button and select Display Properties.

Part
II
Ch
3

FIGURE 3.14
The Display Settings panel lets you change the look of your desktop.

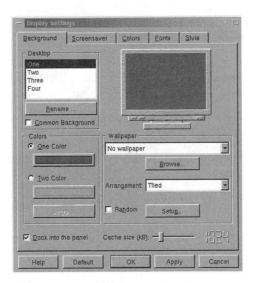

The Display Settings has many options as I describe in the following sections.

Background Tab

The Background tab has settings for the colors of each of the virtual desktops. You can set a color for each desktop or click on Common Background to have the same background in all of your desktops. A preview monitor shows your current selection.

Color options let you choose a single color background, or you can blend two colors to create a background. If you do this, click on Setup, and you are given three options to define the way the blend is handled: Blend from top to bottom, from the right side to the left, or use a pattern.

> **CAUTION**
>
> Make sure you have lots of video memory before you use this option. Adding a blend uses a considerable amount of display memory and can slow down screen writes.

Another option is to use *wallpaper,* which is a graphic image placed on top of the background color that does not replace the color. KDE comes with many predefined images, or you can add your own if you know how to create jpeg graphics. Changing the arrangement of the graphic can further modify the look. You have a range of options from tiling to scaled. Try them out to see the different effects.

> **CAUTION**
>
> Adding wallpaper can also slow down the display because it takes additional video memory.

If you check the Random box, the selected wallpaper randomly displays on the background. Click on Setup to define which images to include in the random display.

The Dock into the panel option puts an icon on the bottom right end of the panel next to the clock, making it easy to call up the display settings quickly.

Use the Cache size slider to adjust video cache. If your screen response seems sluggish, you can try making adjustment here. Add cache only if your video card has lots of memory.

Screensaver Tab

Choose from dozens of screensavers (shown in Figure 3.15). You'll even find screensavers that are familiar to Windows users: Morph3D and Pipes. The Screen of Death screensaver can be fun. I find myself changing screensavers every month or two. My current favorite is Attraction, which I've modified in the Setup to display Tails with Glow turned on. All of the screensavers have custom settings, click on Setup to see the options.

The time delay sets how long your computer should be idle before the screensaver starts. You can enable password protection so that when this option is turned on, a password is required to return to the desktop after the screensaver has started. The Priority slider sets the processing priority relative to other processes on your system. If you are running processes that take a long time and the screensaver is likely to come on, make sure to set the screensaver priority to Low or your other processes will be slowed down. A low priority, however, will make some of the more animated screensavers appear very sluggish.

Part

II

Ch

3

FIGURE 3.15

You can set and modify your screensaver from the Screensaver tab of Display Settings dialog box.

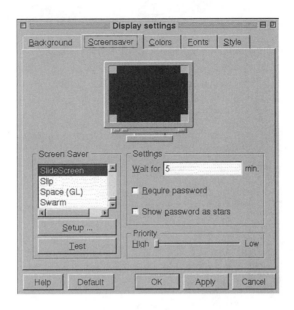

In the sample screen that shows a small display of your screensaver choice, you'll see a gray box in each corner of the screen. Click on one of those gray boxes and you are given a choice of three settings: Ignore, Save Screen, and Lock Screen. These are settings for what will happen when you leave the mouse pointer in the corner for more than 5 seconds.

You can set each corner to one of the three settings. The default setting is Ignore. The Save screen setting means that the screensaver will come on (thus, "saving" the screen from possible burn-in). The Lock setting means that the screensaver will come on and access to the screen is locked until your password is entered.

Colors Tab

A dozen color schemes are predefined for the KDE desktop. Besides the default KDE color scheme, some predefined color schemes are similar to those used by Windows 95, MacOS, BeOS and other computer systems. Choose a color scheme that works for you. Many theories circulate about which color scheme works best. If you've never changed color schemes, now might be a good time to try it. You might be surprised about how much of a difference it can make in your work. Studies show that color schemes affect more than just legibility. They also affect the way you respond to your computer in general. Choose a color scheme that you find friendly. You can also make up your own color scheme. The Widget color selection lets you set colors for each element of the desktop. You must select each separate part of the display that you want to change and set a color that you want. To use the new color settings, click Apply. If you've created your own color scheme, be sure to save it.

Fonts Tab

This defines the display fonts used by the desktop. If the display on your system doesn't look right, sometimes you just need to change the default font being used for display. The default font is Helvetica, but other choices are installed with the default setup:

- Charter
- Lucida
- Lucida Bright
- New Century Schoolbook
- Symbol
- Times
- Utopia

Lucida is a modern font with a casual flair that is a good choice to replace Helvetica. The other fonts can be harder to read. You shouldn't used Symbol for this at all because it's all Greek letters. The fixed font setting uses the standard fixed font. This is the most readable of the fixed fonts available on the default setup.

Style Tab

The Style tab provides three options. If you are used to working in Windows, you'll want to select the Draw widget in the style of Windows 95. This is the default setting. Check boxes and other items like that on the screen are then displayed the way they are on Windows 95; otherwise, the style used is the UNIX-standard Motif style.

You can change the display to act more like a Macintosh, putting the menu bar at the top of the screen. Put a check in the box by that option to enable it.

You should select the option to apply fonts and colors to non-KDE apps for most operations. With this on, the KDE look and feel is applied to non-KDE applications. This option sometimes has difficulties displaying the screen font properly. If you open a non-KDE application and the font for menu items looks wrong, you should go back to the Display Settings and try different Font settings.

Adding Devices and Applications to the Desktop

Devices and applications can have easy-to-access icons on the desktop. Desktop icons for disk drives and the CD-ROM drive are particularly useful. These icons simplify mounting and unmounting disks.

You can add a device or application icon by right-clicking in a blank area on the desktop. A list of options is shown, see Figure 3.16. Select new and you are given the following choices:

- Folder
- File System Device
- FTP URL
- Mime Type
- Application
- Internet Address (URL)
- World Wide Web URL

FIGURE 3.16
Adding a new device or application icon.

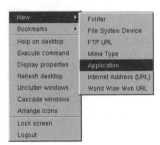

As you can see, desktop icons can be created to represent everything from files on your system to sites on the Web. What follows are the steps to add the CD-ROM device to your desktop. You can follow the same steps, with appropriate modifications, to add other devices like the Floppy drive and Zip or Jaz drives.

1. To add a CD-ROM drive icon to the desktop, select New, File System Device. This starts the process of creating a KDE link file.
2. A dialog box opens with a space for a New File System Device name. A sample name is shown saying Device.kdelnk. Click on OK, and a Device icon is put on the desktop.
3. Right-click on the newly created icon and select Properties. In the File Name box change Device.kdelnk to CD-ROM.kdelnk. Change only the word *Device*. Do not change the extension *.kdelnk*, which tells the K window manager that this is a special type of file. The name you put here is the name that is displayed under the icon on the desktop. Typical names are *Floppy, CD-ROM, Zip, Jaz,* or the names of other devices on your system.

4. The Permissions tab lets you change the file permissions for the device link. For a CD-ROM, all of the permissions should say Read. There should be no Write, Exec, or Special permissions because the standard CD-ROM drive is a read-only device.

5. The Device tab is where you enter the information on the device. This requires some knowledge of the devices on your system. To find the necessary information on the devices for this setup, you can use a text editor and open the fstab file in the /etc directory.

6. Find the line in the fstab file for your device. You can tell the correct line because the mount point has a familiar name such as *floppy* or *cdrom*. The fstab line begins with the device name, which is what you'll enter on the top line under Device. For the CD-ROM drive, on my system, the fstab file shows that the device is /dev/hdc. Enter that information under Device. The default Mount Point for the CD-ROM is /mnt/cdrom.

   Because the file system for the device is already defined in the fstab configuration file, you can leave the file system as default.

7. If you click the button named Mounted Icon, you can select from a collection of icons for an icon to be displayed when the disk in mounted. Click the Unmounted Icon button to choose an icon to be displayed when the disk has been dismounted.

That's all there is to it. Now you can mount a CD by inserting a disk into the CD-ROM drive and clicking the new icon you've created. To dismount a CD, right-click on the icon and choose unmount.

You have an alternate way of setting up the CD-ROM and floppy disk icons on the desktop. The K Wizard uses the automount feature for its setup by defining the device for the CD-ROM as /auto/cdrom and for the floppy as /auto/floppy. Using automount you can insert and remove disks without issuing a mount or unmount command. The automounter detects when a disk is present or has been removed so that you don't have to do that. To access automounted disks, you need to use the icons on the desktop.

You can configure the automount feature in OpenLinux in the /etc/am.d/conf file. See the manual page for amd for more details.

Configuring the KDE Control Center

The Control Center is where you change all the KDE desktop settings. Start the KDE Control Center (shown in Figure 3.17) by clicking the Control Center button on the panel. It's right next to the K Application Starter button.

If you are logged in as root, you can change a number of settings, including the look of the initial login screen. Here are the different settings in the Control Center and how to use them.

Applications

These settings control how each application is displayed. The most important setting to change is the Login Manager. Make sure you are logged in as root and then make the recommended changes.

FIGURE 3.17
The KDE Control Center. You can adjust all of KDE's settings in the Control Center.

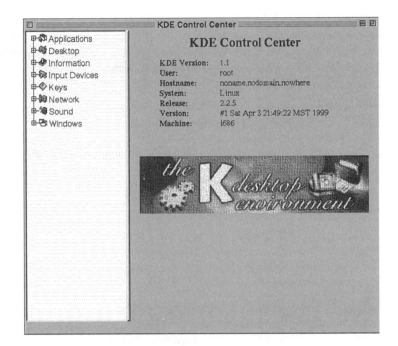

Login Manager   The default Login Manager user settings need to be changed. The default shows a list of all users on the login screen. In most businesses, this is considered a serious security flaw. It makes user names known to nonusers. Click the Users tab and uncheck the box by the Show Users setting. The other settings concern the appearance of the login screen. You can create your own custom login screen, replace the Caldera Systems logo with your own company logo and make other changes to the appearance of the login screen. To change the logo, click on the Appearance tab, click on the KDM logo, and select your logo. You can indicate the full path and name of the logo. You must have a copy of your own logo on the computer to do this.

File Manager   The settings here change the look of the file manager by selecting the fonts and colors. The default fonts are small with Helvetica for the standard font and Courier for the fixed font. Bigger sizes are not always more readable because they can make the font display too big to fit into the allocated space. If you want to try a different standard font, choose Lucida, it has a casual, modern flair to it without loosing legibility.

Part

II

Ch

3

Colors on the File Manager are treated like colors in a Web browser. In addition to a background color and text color, there are colors for URL links. Through check boxes you can change the cursor when it hovers over a link, underline all links, and force the File Manager to use your chosen color even it you are viewing a Web page with the color definitions changed.

The Other tab settings let you activate the Allow per-URL settings option. When you enable this option, you can save individualized View settings while using the File Manager for each URL that you open, whether it is a disk directory on your system or a Web page on the Internet. With a URL open, go to View and choose the settings you want. These are the settings for window size and what menu options are shown or hidden in the window.

If you use the tree view in the File Manager, you have the option here to enable the Tree view follows navigation option. This means when you click on directories in the right part of the screen, directories displayed on the tree list on the left side of the screen, even if you leave the directory. This makes it faster to go back to directories you've previously opened, but it adds to the "clutter" of the tree.

Web Browser   The K File Manager has built-in Web browsing capabilities. Like any Web browser, configuration settings control the way it looks and operates.

If you have a network firewall, you may have a proxy server that you go through for access to the Internet. For KFM to access the Internet through a proxy server, the proxy settings have to be enabled and the ports indicated. If you don't know the proxy information, obtain it from your network administrator.

The HTTP tab has language settings. Some Web sites have document pages in multiple languages. You can specify your language preferences in the Accept languages box. The list is in the order of preference. Use the standard two-letter language abbreviation. *En* is for English, *es* for Spanish, *fr* for French, *de* for German, and so on.

For example, say you've designated English and Spanish here, and you visit a Web site that is primarily in French. It also has alternate pages set up in Spanish but not English. Thus the Spanish pages—and not the French pages—would be displayed as your preferred choice.

The Accept Character Sets lets you designate character sets. The default English-language character sets are utf8, us-ascii, and iso-8859-1. Put an asterisk * here to accept any character set.

If you are having trouble opening a Web site and continually get an Open With message when you try to access it from KFM, try checking the Assume HTML box. Some Web servers don't send a response that KFM recognizes as HTML, and so it doesn't know how to open them. Try forcing KFM to treat all accesses as HTML and see if that fixes it. Don't enable this unless you are having a problem because not all accesses are HTML.

The User Agent tab sets the identity of the Web browser. Netscape Navigator has the User Agent name of Mozilla. The KFM User Agent name is Konqueror (after the navigator and the explorer comes the conqueror.) Web sites that read the User Agent information use this option and send pages that are optimized to the specific browser. You can change the User Agent information if you want to force those Web sites to send pages in a format meant for a different browser. If you do that, however, the pages may not be readable.

The Cookies tab settings let you enable or disable cookies. Some Web sites you've visited place cookies, or small files, on your system that identify you. Cookies save user information, login names, and other personal information. They cannot have any information you haven't already provided to the specified Web site. A Web site can't use cookies to obtain information from your computer system. Mostly they are helpful because you won't have to reenter information every time you visit the Web site. Uncheck the Enable Cookies to turn off this feature.

> **CAUTION**
>
> Some users think that this increases personal security on the Web. That's not the case, and if you disable cookies for this reason, you may have a false sense of security. Cookies cannot contain any information you haven't already given to a Web site. If you are concerned about security, be cautious about information you give to the Web sites you are visiting.

Part
II
Ch
3

The default cookies setting is to enable cookies, with a policy of asking the user what to do when a cookie is being received from a Web site.

Console   The Konsole settings show possible color schemes for this character-mode terminal that accessed through the utilities section of the Application Launcher. This configuration panel is still under development. If you want to change the colors or other parts of the Konsole configuration, open the program and change the settings there.

See the section on Konsole in Chapter 4 for more information on changing the settings in Konsole.

Panel   The settings for the K Panel can be adjusted here. The options displayed here are the same settings described in the section on the K Panel configuration.

Desktop

The many different settings for the desktop can all be adjusted here. The display settings can be changed for the:

- Background
- Borders
- Colors
- Fonts
- Desktop Icons
- Language
- Screensaver
- Style

Adding KDE themes

A new feature in KDE is *themes*, which change the overall look of the KDE desktop. At first, just a few themes were included with KDE, but now dozens of themes have been developed.

Themes can make your system look like another operating system such as a Macintosh or a Windows computer, or they can make your system look like the control panel of a space voyager.

To handle all of these developing themes, a theme manager has been developed. Be warned, though, the themes and the theme manager are still only at an experimental level. Some themes can misbehave and crash your system; others don't completely uninstall and permanently change features on your desktop.

If you want to experiment with themes, the theme manager and over 60 themes are included on the OpenLinux 2.3 disk. The themes selected for the disk are the ones considered to be the most stable. You can find the files in the /col/contrib/RPMS directory. Just remember that anything found in the /contrib directory isn't supported by Caldera Systems as part of OpenLinux.

The first step to installing themes is to install the theme manager. Insert the OpenLinux CD and click on the CD icon on the desktop. Click on col to open the directory and then click on contrib. In the contrib directory, click on RPMS. Find the file named kthememgr-0.8-3.i386.rpm. Click on the file, and the Kpackage utility starts. Click on install to install the theme manager.

After you've installed the theme manager, install any of the themes you want to try out. All of the KDE theme files start with the name *kdetheme*.

The theme manager runs from the KDE Control Center under Desktop. Selecting Theme Manager displays a list of themes that have been installed on your system. Click on the name of theme to see a sample display of the theme. To use a theme, click on Apply, but remember, sometimes changing to a new theme can't be fully undone.

Information

Here's where you can find out many of the details of your system. The information section details are all displayed using technical names that may be unfamiliar to new users, but this can be essential information for getting technical support for your system. For Linux professionals this is a quick and easy way to find most of the essential system information.

Information is provided on:

- Devices
- DMA Channels
- Interrupts
- I/O Ports
- Memory
- Partitions
- PCI
- Processor
- SCSI

■ Samba Status

■ Sound

■ X server

Input Devices

The Input Devices control panel lets you change the settings on the keyboard and mouse. If you need to have the KDE Desktop work properly with any of the possible international keyboard styles, make sure that the keyboard is correctly installed here. For left-handed users, the setting to change to a left-handed mouse is found in Input Devices under the Mouse settings.

Keys

Part
II

Ch

3

You can remap the keyboard shortcuts in the Keys section. Shortcuts initiate an action by an application and can be used in place of the mouse. The K Window Manager uses the global keys for switching between windows and desktops, opening and closing windows, and similar functions. KDE uses the standard keys in applications for cutting, copying, pasting, and similar functions. Most of these shortcut keys are the same as those used in Windows 95.

You cannot remove the current and KDE default shortcut settings, and you cannot save changes to them. You can, if you want, create your own keyboard shortcut scheme and save that. To use a newly created scheme, click on Apply.

Network

The network section is not used for network settings.

See Chapter 5, "Configuring Your System with COAS," for network settings.

Sound

The sound section is not for configuring your sound card. This section is for assigning sounds to system events.

See Chapter 10 to configure sound.

Windows

Change the look of the windows on the K desktop. There are several settings in this section, including extensive customization possibilities for how the mouse responds. One setting here you might want to change is on the section for the title bar. KDE defaults to what is called Title animation. This means that if the title of a window is too long to fit on the title bar, the title will be scrolled back and forth so that you can read the whole title. To turn this feature off, go to the Title animation setting and move the control slider to 0. That will stop the animation.

If you make any changes in the Control Center, you must click Apply or the changes won't be made.

Configuring the K File Manager

One of the most powerful features of KDE is the file manager (KFM). It can do just about everything. With something so useful and powerful, you'll want to know how to customize it to work just the way you want.

The K File Manager has many similarities to file managers on Windows or Macintosh computers. What makes the KFM file manager unique is that it is truly an Internet file manager.

You can use the K File Manager in the same way whether you are accessing files on your computer or files over the Internet. It has built-in Web browser and FTP capabilities.

You open files on your own system by selecting the directory and clicking the file icon. You open files on the Internet by opening the Uniform Resource Locator (URL) for the file. The URL is a way to point to a file on another computer on the network (see Figure 3.18).

You can start the K File Manager by clicking the KFM button in the panel. The icon is a folder with a small house shape on it. This opens the File Manager in your home directory.

The KFM window has menus, a navigation tool bar, and a location field that shows file names, paths, and URLs.

FIGURE 3.18
A Web page opened in the K File Manager.

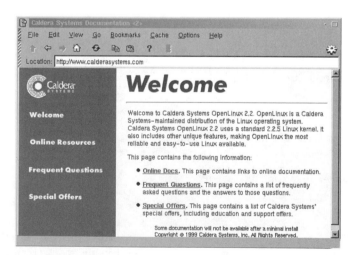

The navigation toolbar has buttons for moving between directories and handling files (shown in Table 3.2).

Table 3.2   The File Manager Toolbar

Button	Description
Up	Moves up one directory, or folder.
Back	Moves back to the previous location.
Forward	If you moved back, the Forward button is no longer be grayed out and you can move forward.
Home	Moves to your home directory.
Reload	Reloads the directory display. Sometimes necessary to see changes you've made.
Copy	Copies files.
Paste	Pastes copied files into a new location.
Help	Opens the K File Manager Handbook.
Stop	Stops a process before it finishes.

Some of the tasks that can be handled by KFM include the following.

Opening a Folder or Directory

Directories, also called folders, contain all the files on your system.

To open a folder, do a single-click. To open a folder in a new window, right-click the folder. To select a folder without opening it, hold down the Control key while you click it.

Opening a File or Application

Files are opened in much the same way as folders.

To open a file to see its contents, a single-click opens the file in the application that is associated with the file. If the necessary application isn't open, KFM starts it. If KFM doesn't know what application is associated with the file, it prompts you to enter the application's name. A click on the Browse button shows a list of applications that KFM knows about.

To open an application, click the application's icon.

To select a file or application without opening it, hold down the Control key while you click on the filename or icon.

To view a graphics file, right-click on the file's icon and select Image-viewer from the pop-up menu.

Tree View

To change the view of KFM to a tree view, click the View menu and select Tree View. This is similar to the look of the Windows Explorer file Manager. It makes it easier to move between all the many different directories.

Part
II

Ch
3

Bookmarks

KFM can keep a set of bookmarks that are similar to the bookmarks or favorites found in popular Web browsers. This makes it simple to move quickly to file locations that you frequently access.

To add a bookmark to KFM, move to the directory you want to add. Then, on the Bookmark menu select Add Bookmark. Once you've added a bookmark, it is available in KFM and from the menu list that is displayed when you right-click on the blank area on the desktop.

View or Change File Properties

To view the properties of a file or application, right-click on the file icon in KFM. Select Properties from the pop-up menu. File permissions are displayed. If you are the owner of the file or are logged in as root, you will be able to change the file permissions and ownership properties.

Add a Subdirectory

To add a subdirectory, click the File menu and choose New. Select Folder and type the name for the new folder.

Open a Web Location

To open a Web site, click the File menu and choose Open Location. Type the full URL of the Web site, such as `http://www.calderasystems.com`.

Start an FTP Session

To open an FTP file transfer, click the File menu and choose Open Location. Type the full URL of the Web site, such as `ftp://ftp.calderasystems.com`. This is for "anonymous" FTP sessions. If you need to specify a login name, enter the location this way:

`ftp://username@ftp.calderasystems.com`

Of course, this is just an example. Instead of username, you should type your login name for the FTP server to which you are connecting. Instead of `ftp.calderasystems.com`, you should type the name of the FTP server to which you are connecting. When you enter the information this way, after you've connected to the FTP server you are prompted to enter your password.

The Autostart Folder

KDE has an Autostart folder. This is like the startup folder found on Windows 95/98 or the Autostart folder found on a Macintosh.

Any program or file placed in the Autostart folder starts up automatically after you've logged in.

To put something in the Autostart folder, open a KFM window and navigate to the directory with the file or application you want. Click and drag the file or application to the Autostart folder on the desktop. A menu appears that gives you a choice to copy, move, or link the file to the Autostart folder. Choose Link.

The K Window Manager

Behind the KDE desktop is the K Window Manager, which is the program that controls how everything is displayed. KWM is completely integrated into KDE.

Most of the settings in the Control Center are settings for KWM. For longtime Linux users who want to configure KWM by editing a configuration file, the kwmrc configuration file is located in the ~/.kde/share/config directory.

KWM is what is called a *second generation* window manager. It was developed with a modern GUI toolkit for its widgets (buttons, menus, list boxes, and so on) instead of proprietary code.

Several keyboard shortcuts are standard to KWM and are highlighted in Table 3.3.

Table 3.3   K Window Manager Shortcut Keys

Key Combination	What it does
Alt+Esc or Ctrl+Esc	Opens the Current Session task manager for switching sessions or logging out.
Alt+Tab and Alt+Shift+Tab	Changes windows in the current desktop.
Ctrl+Tab and Ctrl+Shift+Tab	Switches between virtual desktops.
Alt+F2	Opens a miniature command-line window.
Alt+F3	Opens the window operation menu.
Alt+F4	Closes the current window
Ctrl+F[1...8]	Switches to virtual desktop number 1 to 8.
Ctrl+Alt+Esc	Destroy mode: The cursor becomes a pirate symbol. Put the pirate symbol over a window you want to force to close and click.

Getting Help

Help is available almost anywhere you are in the KDE desktop. The general help system is available by clicking the Help button on the lower-right side of the K Panel. KDE help files are all Web-style html documents and moving through them is just like moving through Web

Part
II

Ch
3

pages. In addition, every KDE application has specific help that is available by clicking the Help menu item on the right end of the menu.

Shutting Down

Just as with a Windows 95 or Macintosh computer, you should never just turn off your computer or press the Reset button. If you do, it usually causes a problem. Because OpenLinux is a *multitasking* system, you can cause additional problems by doing this. Some files are kept open, and tasks are taking place that no user will know about unless he has done a thorough probe of the system.

Shutting down properly is similar to the procedures you use on a Windows or Macintosh computer.

From the KDE desktop, click the K icon in the lower left corner of the screen and choose Logout. This takes you back to the login prompt.

At the login prompt, click the Shutdown button. You'll see a list of choices. Choose either Shutdown or Shutdown and Restart. When the System halted message appears, you can turn off the computer.

An alternative way to shutdown is from a terminal window on the KDE desktop. Open a terminal window, if you don't already have one open, at the prompt enter the following command:

```
telinit 6
```

This initiates the run level 6 scripts, which close down the system.

Shutting Down in an Emergency   Sometimes you find that a problem has occurred and you can't exit the KDE desktop and return to the login prompt. You can't run the telinit command unless you are root. If you can't become root and you can find no way to shut down the computer except by turning it off, try to issue the sync command before you do anything else. You can run this command from any terminal prompt. The sync command forces Linux to write everything in memory to disk.

## CHAPTER 4

Using the KDE Desktop Applications

The KDE desktop user interface is more than a window manager. Many different window managers are available for Linux, and a window manager only controls the actions of windows and starts programs. KDE has much more.

KDE includes a file manager with an integrated Web browser (described in the previous chapter) and a full set of applications. There is even a KOffice set of applications in development for word processing, spreadsheets, and presentations. KDE is Internet-aware, meaning that, for example, you can start the editor and open a file over the Internet, whether it is a Web document or a text file on a network server.

OpenLinux 2.3 includes a full set of KDE applications. New applications are regularly added to KDE. Watch the KDE Web site at www.kde.org if you want to stay on top of the latest developments.

Following in this chapter are introductions to some of the most commonly used KDE applications.

The Kedit Text Editor

Kedit (shown in Figure 4.1) is a basic text editor. Plain text files are used everywhere in OpenLinux. Kedit is the default text editor for the KDE desktop.

You can use Kedit for many of the editing tasks that experienced Linux users have been doing with the vi or pico text editors. Kedit is not meant to replace the more powerful XEmacs or Emacs editors, but it is designed to be a simple, easy-to-learn, and easy-to-use text editor.

FIGURE 4.1
Kedit, the default text editor.

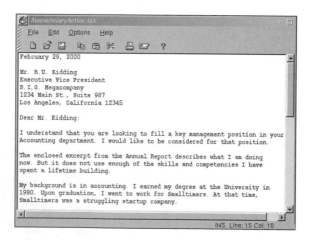

To start Kedit, click on the K Application Launcher (the big K on the lower left corner of the screen). From the pop-up menu, highlight Applications. In Applications, select Text Editor. (The Advanced Editor selection is Kwrite, a programmer's editor that I cover in the next section.)

Kedit has all the standard features found in most text editors. OpenLinux system administrators use Kedit in place of editors such as vi that have been the traditional editors used for system maintenance. Kedit has some of the same features and capabilities as vi and can easily replace it for those who prefer a graphical text editor that makes full use of the mouse. It does not have syntax highlighting or any of the other features used by programmers that are found in vi. For a programmer's editor, see the next section on Kwrite.

You can drag and drop files from the desktop or from a K File Manager window onto Kedit to edit the files. Many files are automatically associated with Kedit and open in Kedit if you click on them in the K File Manager.

You can open multiple documents at once. From the File menu, choose New Window to start an additional document. You can use the new window to start a new document or open one that already exists. To move text between two open documents, highlight the text you want, select copy from the Edit menu—or click on the copy icon—select the second document, and put the cursor where you want to place the text. Click on the Paste icon or select Paste from the Edit menu. The text from the first document appears in the second document.

You can edit text in Kedit with the standard highlight, copy, and paste features. Icons to cut, copy, and paste are shown on the toolbar just below the menu line (see Figure 4.1).

Part

II

Ch

4

Cutting and Pasting with a Mouse in KDE

You can copy and paste text in Kedit, or any KDE application, by dragging the mouse cursor and selecting any text on the screen. Highlighting the text automatically places it in the KDE Clipboard. There is no extra step needed to put text in the Clipboard. Put the mouse cursor in the location where you want to paste the text and press both mouse buttons at the same time. Alternatively, you can press the middle button of a three-button mouse, but this works only if your mouse is set up for three-button emulation. If your mouse is not set up for three-button emulation, see the instructions on how to do this in Appendix B, "XFree86 Configuration."

Kedit has only a few configuration options. Kedit does not support multiple fonts or even different sizes of the same font in a document. For that kind of document formatting, you need a full word processing program. You can change the default font type, style, and size under the Options menu.

If the text in the editing screen is going off the screen, go to Options and select Kedit Options. Check Word Wrap to stop text from extending beyond the frame. The other Kedit options are to turn on word wrap when your text reaches the edge of the window and to automatically create backup copies of any files edited. The mail command setting sets the commands for sending files you have open in the editor. This uses the standard Linux mail command and the default setting is

```
mail -s "%s" "%s"
```

The first %s is the subject line of the mail message. The second %s is the To address of the mail.

The other options that can be changed are the spell checker. Kedit uses the KSpell spelling checker. The standard encoding is 7-Bit/ASCII. Change it to Latin1 if you use accented characters such as the Spanish ñ

Kedit supports opening and editing files across the Internet. To open a file across the Internet, select Open URL from the File menu. Enter the information for the file on an Internet server, either a Web server or an FTP server. The information might be something like this:

```
ftp://ftp.mycompany.com/pub/myfile.txt
```

Of course, you need to put in the real name of the ftp site and the file to be opened, but this would open the file. From there, you can edit it and when you are done, select Save URL from the File menu. For more information on accessing files across the Internet from the KDE desktop, see the section "File Manager," in Chapter 3, "Configuring the KDE Desktop."

You can directly email a text file in Kedit. Select Mail from the File menu. A dialog box opens where you can enter the email address and a Subject line for the email. The file is mailed as the body of the message, not as an attachment. This only works, of course, if you are connected to the Internet and have email set up on your Linux computer. If you need to set up your home computer to connect to the Internet, see the section later in this chapter on Kppp. If your computer is on an office network but you don't have access to the Internet or email, see your network systems administrator in order to get connected.

You can print any open file in Kedit. Under the File menu, select Print. The default is to Print directly using lpr. This is the standard way to print in OpenLinux.

Kwrite, a Programmer's Editor

Kwrite is a text editor that's been optimized for programmers' use. It has code syntax highlighting for C, Java, HTML, Python, Perl, and other programming languages, but it's also good for just about any text editing job. Figure 4.2 shows an HTML document open in Kwrite. The HTML code stands out from the regular text with color highlighting, though you can't see this in a black-and-white figure.

FIGURE 4.2
Kwrite, a programmer's
text editor.

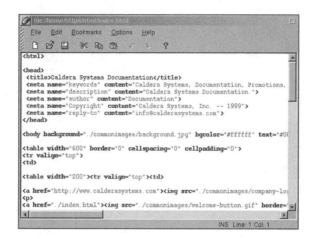

To start Kwrite, click on the K Application Launcher. From the pop-up menu, highlight
Applications. In Applications, select Advanced Editor.

Syntax highlighting is set under Options. Select Set Highlight. You can choose from the following:

- Normal
- C
- C++
- Java
- HTML
- Bash
- Modula 2
- Ada
- Python
- Perl

Most of the other features in Kwrite are similar to those found in Kedit. You can also use it to
open and edit files across the Internet, but you cannot use it to email a file directly.

You can use bookmarks to open frequently used files quickly. Open a file you want to bookmark and select Add Bookmark from the Bookmarks menu.

One difference from Kedit is that you can't print or mail with Kwrite. If you need to print a
document that you are editing in Kwrite or mail the text, you can copy and paste the text into
Kedit and then print or mail the text. You can also paste it into any other editor that can be
used to print or any mail program for sending the text by email. Any text file created in Kwrite
can be imported into any other editor or mail program.

Using Kjots to Take Notes

Kjots is designed to enable you to take short sets of notes and organize them.

To start Kjots, click on the K Application Launcher. From the pop-up menu, highlight Utilities. In Utilities select Kjots. A window similar to that in Figure 4.3 appears.

FIGURE 4.3

Notes are organized as books in Kjots.

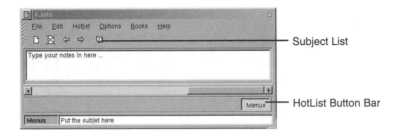

Kjots uses *books* to organize notes. Each set of notes is called a book. To start a note, select New Book from the file menu.

You must give each book a name. These names must be valid filenames and cannot contain characters that aren't allowed in normal filenames.

Each page in a book can have a *subject*. The subject is displayed in the status bar in the bottom of the Kjots window. If the subject is blank, you can enter one by clicking in the blank area and typing a subject name.

To add a new page, go to the Edit menu and select New Page.

To find a page on a specific subject, you can see a list of all the subjects in the currently open book. Click on the Subject List icon (a book), which is located just below the Options menu (as shown in Figure 4.4). Clicking on the subject displays the page. Double clicking on the subject displays the page and closes the subject list.

The hotlist feature enables you to define up to eight books to be included on a button bar that appears just above the subject window. The hotlist button bar makes it easy to move between the most frequently used books.

Kjots has few options to be configured. Under the Options menu are two choices, Config and Config Keys. The Config option sets up the K File Manager as the default Web browser used by Kjots when you open a Web page from inside the program. The Fonts option lets you change the default font used by Kjot.

Config Keys lets you change the default keyboard shortcuts for Kjots. Some of the most commonly used keyboard shortcuts are shown in Table 4.1.

FIGURE 4.4
Kjots with the Kjots
subject list.

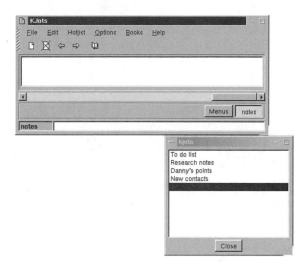

Table 4.1   Kjots Keyboard Shortcuts

To	Use These Keys
Save	Ctrl+S
Cut marked text, put on clipboard	Ctrl+X
Copy marked text to the clipboard	Ctrl+C
Paste text from the clipboard	Ctrl+V
Create a new book	Ctrl+N
Add a new page	Ctrl+A
Go to previous page	Ctrl+J
Go to next page	Ctrl+K
Show subject list window	Ctrl+L
Copy selection to subject line	Ctrl+Y

Part

II

Ch

4

Using Knotes for Sticky Notes

Knotes resemble the familiar brightly colored sticky notes found on your desk, but these appear on your computer screen. Knotes is a full-featured application with many options.

To start Knotes, click on the K Application Launcher. From the pop-up menu, highlight Utilities. In Utilities, select Knotes.

When you first start Knotes, a bright yellow notepad appears (as shown in Figure 4.5). You can begin typing any message you want.

FIGURE 4.5
Knotes resemble the
familiar sticky notes on
your desk.

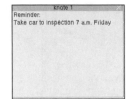

To do more than type in a message, you need to access the Knote pop-up menu. Put the mouse pointer into the Knote and right-click. The menu options include the following:

- A list of all the notes you've created.
- Insert Date, which inserts the current date and time.

Operations include the following:

- **Clear**
- **New Note**—To create a new note.
- **Delete Note**—To delete the current note. A deleted note cannot be undeleted or recovered in any way.
- **Rename Note**—To change the name of the note.
- **Alarm**—To have Knotes sound a time alarm, select this option. A dialog box opens and enables you to set the time and date for the alarm. When the alarm time comes, you hear three beeps, a notice of the alarm appears, and the note associated with the alarm comes to the top of your screen.
- **Calendar**—To insert the current month's calendar into a Knote. This uses the Linux `cal` command.
- **Mail Note**—You can mail notes by selecting Operations from the pop-up menu and clicking on Mail. In the Mail dialog box, you have to enter the full email address and a subject for the mailed note.
- **Print Note**—All notes can be printed.
- **Save notes**
- **Help**—Brings up the Knotes Handbook.
- **Options**—You can change the look of every note with the Options item. Options include putting a 3D frame on the note, turning on or off the auto-indent feature, changing the note font, and choosing a different color. You can change each note individually. Also, under Options, you can choose to change the defaults on all these settings.
- **Sticky**—Makes the note appear on all your desktops. Be careful about making a note sticky. Some users find sticky notes can get to be annoying.
- **To desktop**—Puts a note on one of your virtual desktops.

You can drag and drop files from the desktop and put them in a note.

You can move notes anywhere on the desktop by holding down the left mouse button while pointing to the note and then moving the mouse. To resize a note, use the Alt key while holding down the right mouse button. Moving the mouse resizes the note.

You can close a Knote by clicking on the X in the upper right corner of the note. If all your Knotes have been closed, start Knotes again from the Application Starter. The last note used is displayed. Right-click for the pop-up menu, and a list of all the notes you've saved appears. Table 4.2 lists ways to operate various Knotes functions from the keyboard.

Table 4.2   Knotes Keyboard Shortcuts

To	Use these keys
Cut marked text, put on clipboard	Ctrl+X
Copy marked text to the clipboard	Ctrl+C
Paste text from the clipboard	Ctrl+V
Move cursor to line beginning	Ctrl+A
Move cursor to end of line	Ctrl+E
Move cursor left one character	Ctrl+B
Move cursor right one character	Ctrl+F
Move cursor up one line	Ctrl+P
Move cursor down one line	Ctrl+N
Delete a character to the right	Ctrl+D
Delete a character to the left	Ctrl+H
Delete to the end of the line	Ctrl+K

Part

II

Ch

4

The Konsole Terminal Window

When you need to use a character-based terminal in the KDE desktop, you can do it with the Konsole. You can use it to access your own computer or for telnet access to other computers.

Konsole is similar to other terminal emulators, such as the K Virtual Terminal that launches when you click on the Terminal button on the K Panel across the bottom of the screen. You can use either one in pretty much the same way.

To start the Konsole, Click on the K Application Launcher. From the pop-up menu, highlight Utilities. In Utilities select Konsole.

When a new Konsole terminal window opens (as shown in Figure 4.6), it is the standard 80 characters wide by 24 rows down. This emulates the size of a standard character-mode terminal.

FIGURE 4.6

Konsole is a terminal emulator with features that you can configure easily.

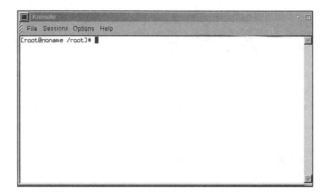

At the prompt, you can type in commands. If you have text open in another file or have another Konsole open, you can copy text to the command line. Highlight the text you want to copy, and then move the mouse pointer to the command line in the Konsole window. Click on the center mouse button or on both buttons of a two-button mouse (if you've set it up to emulate 3 buttons). The text is pasted on the command line.

You can use Konsole for telnet sessions connecting to other Linux computers. Enter the command telnet at the prompt, followed by the name or IP address of the computer you are connecting to.

Menu options in Konsole include changing between a Linux Console, Midnight Commander, and a Bash Shell from the File menu.

The Options menu enables you to define the look of Konsole. You can show or hide the menu bar. You can turn scrollbars on or off. The default setting for the Backspace key is to delete, but that can be turned off.

You can customize the font and size of the terminal window to what you need.

Konsole also has several preset schemes for how the Konsole window is displayed. Besides the default look and a Linux terminal look, other schemes include the following:

- Black type on a light yellow background
- Black type on a white background
- Circuit, white type on a circuit board pattern background
- Green type on a black background
- Black type on a Paper patterned background
- Linux colors, the colors used by a Linux character-mode terminal
- System colors, the KDE color scheme you've chosen
- VIM colors, the color scheme used by the vi text editor. VIM is the Vi IMproved editor that is included with OpenLinux

- White type on a Black background
- Xterm colors, which are Black type on a white background by default

You can save any changes you make to be the defaults the next time you start Konsole. To save the changes, under the Options menu select Save Options.

Kfind to Find Stuff on Your System

If you've heard that finding anything on an OpenLinux computer was complicated and requires knowledge of "grep," you are talking to someone who's never seen Kfind.

Kfind is a powerful search utility that can be used on even a big and complex Linux system. Kfind does not require you to know more than the name or even part of a name of the file you are searching for. It navigates the complicated directory structure and searches your whole system.

To start Kfind, click on the K Application Launcher. From the pop-up menu select Find Files. A window appears as shown in Figure 4.7.

Start Search   Stop Search

FIGURE 4.7
Kfind finds files that are "out there somewhere."

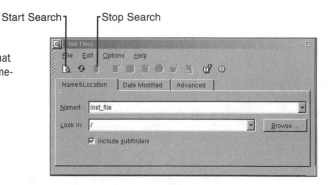

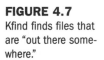

Part
II

Ch

4

To start a simple search, click on the Named field and type in all or part of the name of a file. You can use wildcards such as the asterisk (*) or question mark (?). The Look in field tells Kfind where to search. Use the Browse button to look on your hard drive for a specific directory, or use the /root indicator to indicate a search of the whole system, including all mounted drive partitions. Whole system searches can take some time. Below Look in: is a check box for Include subfolders, which you can check on or off.

The Start Search button (as seen in Figure 4.7) is an icon on the toolbar below the word File on the menu bar. A keyboard shortcut to start the search is the Ctrl+F key combination. To stop a search before it is finished, click on the Stoplight icon.

From the list of files found (an example of which appears in Figure 4.8), you can get information on a file by highlighting the filename and clicking on the Properties icon (as shown in Figure 4.8). It shows you the name of the file, the last time it was accessed, and the ownership and permissions for the file.

FIGURE 4.8
Kfind lists the files it found. You can open the files from this list.

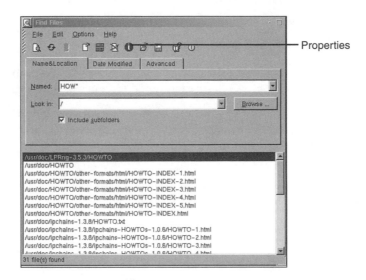

Properties

If you double-click on a filename, it opens the file. If necessary, you get a dialog box asking what application to use to open the file. If the filename is a directory, double-clicking opens the K File Manager with the contents of the directory displayed.

If you highlight a filename in the list, you can click on the Delete button to delete the file.

You can restrict File searches by the date they were modified. First, fill in the Named field and the Look in field as you would in a simple search. Then, select the Date Modified tab (shown in Figure 4.9), which is between the Name & Location tab and the Advanced tab.

The default search is for all files. You can restrict the Date Modified to a range of dates between a starting date and an ending date. You can also restrict it to one or more months, or even to the number of previous days.

Advanced searches are started the same way as are simple searches. You have to enter something in the Named field, and be sure to also set the Look in field. Advanced searches can include date restrictions if you indicate a date restriction on the Date Modified tab.

FIGURE 4.9
Kfind searches can be restricted to the date the files were modified.

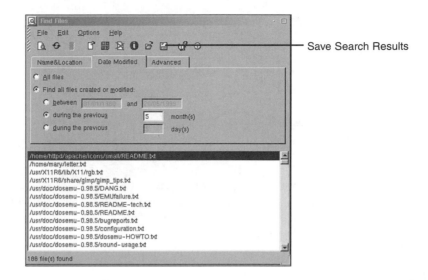

Save Search Results

Advanced search options enable you to restrict searches by the type of file. Some of the types that can be searched for include

- Folders
- Symbolic links
- Executable files
- Postscript documents
- Fonts
- RPM packages
- Graphic images
- Programming source code

Advanced searches can also search for text inside a file or document. You still must fill in the Named field on the Name & Location tab, and you want to again be sure to set the Look in field. Searching for text in a file can include date restrictions if you indicate a date restriction on the Date Modified tab.

In the space next to the line that says Containing Text, in the Advanced tab (shown in Figure 4.10), type in the text you want to search for.

You can save the results of a search by clicking on the Save Search Results icon (shown in Figure 4.8).

Part
II

Ch
4

FIGURE 4.10
Advanced search options let you find text in a file.

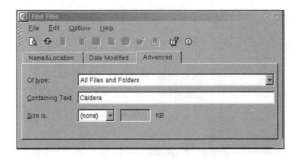

Remember, after you've made changes in any of the advanced search areas, those changes stay there until you remove them or change them again. Sometimes, when a search doesn't appear to be working properly, one of the advanced settings hasn't been correctly updated for the new search, and has settings for the previous search.

The K Address Book

The K Address Book is a basic contact organizer. It is easy to access and quick to use.

To start the K Address Book, click on the K Application Launcher. From the pop-up menu, highlight Utilities. In Utilities, select Address Book.

Each entry you make in the Address Book is displayed like a card file, one at a time (as shown in Figure 4.11). Every new entry or change is automatically saved.

FIGURE 4.11
The K Address Book can keep all your contact information.

You can create a new listing from the Edit menu. Click Add Entry. Enter any of the information fields you need. In addition to the name and address, the Contact tab enables you to enter email addresses and talk addresses. If this information is entered, the Address Book makes it easy to email or talk to a person using the talk program. Talk is a little like the popular Internet Chat but is older and not as frequently used. It was last updated in 1991.

The talk program runs on a Linux character mode terminal. If you are connected to a network and you want to try it out, open a terminal window and enter the command **talk** **user@host**. Replace *user@host* with the name and machine hostname or IP address of someone who is also running the talk program. The screen is divided into two parts, with incoming messages appearing on the top of the screen, and messages you type appearing on the bottom of the screen.

To enter an email address, click on the Edit email addresses button. A new address is started by pressing the X button, typing the email address into the entry field, and finally clicking OK. Talk addresses are entered in the same way.

After you have completed a contact entry(shown in Figure 4.12) and you click OK, the new entry is automatically saved in the Address Book database.

FIGURE 4.12
Add contact information to any Address Book entry.

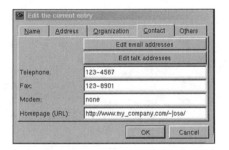

You can print the Address Book or export it into an HTML Web page. To export it as a Web page, go to Export on the File menu and select HTML table. A window opens with two frames. On the left is a list of the Possible Values already defined in the Address Book. Select the values you want to include in your Web page table and click on the right arrow button to include it in the Selected Values frame. When you've selected the values you want to include, click on OK. A window opens where you name the HTML file that will be created. Be sure to put **.html** at the end of the filename so that you can read it in any Web browser.

You can search the Address Book in any of the Address Book fields. On the icon bar across the bottom of the Address Book, select the Search icon (binoculars). In the window that pops up, choose a field to search from the drop-down menu. In the line below that, enter the text that you want to search for, and click on OK to start the search.

The KOrganizer Personal Organizer

The KOrganizer is a Personal Information Manager. It is a calendar, a scheduler, a To-do list, an Address Book, and more. It is similar to programs such as the Lotus Organizer or Microsoft Outlook.

KOrganizer uses the *vCalendar* format. This is an open standard format that enables different programs and devices to share appointment and calendar information openly. Some Windows-based programs export to the vCalendar format, though none use it as their standard format. Microsoft's Outlook 98 and later Outlook programs can import vCalendar files, which means that you can synchronize Outlook with your KOrganizer.

You can use KOrganizer with the KPilot program to synchronize information with a 3Com PalmPilot. To see how to do that, see Chapter 14, "Connecting to PalmPilots."

To start the KOrganizer, click on the K Application Launcher. From the pop-up menu, highlight Applications. In Applications, select Organizer.

When you start KOrganizer, the opening window shows a menu bar, a toolbar, a month calendar, a To-do list, and an appointment calendar (as shown in Figure 4.13).

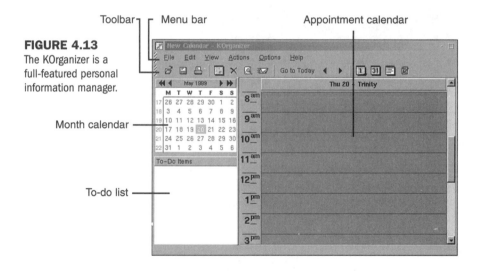

FIGURE 4.13
The KOrganizer is a full-featured personal information manager.

The first time you use KOrganizer, configure the Options settings. On the menu bar, select Options and click on Edit Options. A window appears similar to what's shown in Figure 4.14.

The KOrganizer Configuration Options include the following:

■ **Personal**—In Personal options, enter your name and email address. The Additional line is unused and can be ignored. You can also select whether to autosave the appointment calendar and whether to confirm deletions from the appointment calendar and the To-do list. If you want, you can select a country and have that country's national holidays added to your calendar.

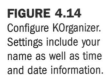

FIGURE 4.14
Configure KOrganizer. Settings include your name as well as time and date information.

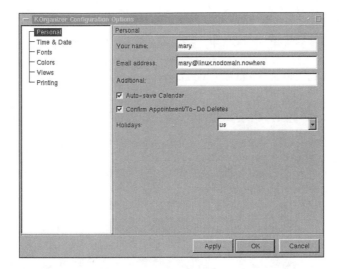

- **Time & Date**—The Time Zone is based on UTC (GMT) time, which is established in Greenwich, England. If you are on the East Coast in the United States, the time zone is -0500 for Daylight Savings Time and -0400 for the rest of the year. You probably won't have to change what is already there. The Time Format is either a 24-hour clock or a 12-hour AM/PM clock. The Default Appointment Time is the time automatically entered whenever you create a new appointment. The Alarm Time determines how much time before a scheduled event passes before the alarm sounds. If the Week Starts on Monday is not checked, the week starts on Sunday.

- **Fonts**—The fonts for the To-do list, the schedule, the monthly calendar, and the time bar can be changed if you want.

- **Colors**—KOrganizer defaults to using the system colors. If you want to use different colors, you can change everything from the background and text colors to the color used when a calendar date is selected.

- **Views**—The Views settings enables you to set the time the Day Begins in the appointment calendar. The default setting is 8 a.m. The *hour size in schedule view* option lets you set how wide the display will be for each hour when you view a daily or weekly schedule. The wider your monitor, the wider you can make this view. By default, the *show events that recur daily in Date Navigator* option is checked. With that option enabled, the Date Navigator (the small monthly calendar that you can click on a day to see the day's schedule) will show dates with recurring events in bold and a different color.

- **Printing**—The Printing settings enables you to select the default printer for KOrganizer and the default paper size.

Part
II

Ch
4

Adding Appointments

The quick way to add appointments is to choose the day of the appointment on the small monthly calendar. Then on the appointment calendar find the time of the appointment. Double-click on the time and then you can type in the appointment information.

Quick appointments added this way can later be edited by highlighting the appointment and right-clicking or by selecting Edit Appointment from the Actions menu.

The other way to add an appointment is to select New Appointment from the Actions menu. You'll see a dialog box similar to that in Figure 4.15. This has more flexibility than the quick method, which you cannot use to adjust the time or, for that matter, any other details about an appointment except its description.

FIGURE 4.15
Using the appointment calendar in KOrganizer.

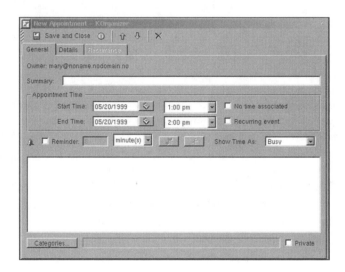

When adding a new appointment in KOrganizer you can set three areas: General, Details, and Recurrence.

General Appointment Settings   On the General tab, you can make the following settings:

- **Summary**—This is the text seen in the appointment calendar. Type in something that enables you to quickly identify what the appointment is about, who it is with, or anything else that you can easily recognize and understand.

- **Start and End Times**—Set the date and time the appointment begins and ends. Clicking the calendar icon next to the date field opens a monthly calendar that you can use to select a date.

- **No time associated**—If you check No time associated, the time fields disappear, and only the date can be set. This is good for all-day events or for general reminders.

- **Recurring event**—If you check Recurring event, the date fields disappear and only the time can be set. The Recurrence tab becomes active, and you can set the frequency of the recurring event.

- **Reminder**—Check Reminder, and you can enter the number of minutes before a scheduled event that the reminder alarm goes off. Click on the music note to select a sound to play with the alarm. Click on the running person to select a program to start with the alarm.

- **Show Time As**—This function isn't used right now, but will be implemented in a future version as a part of a group calendar feature, that enables you to indicate to the group whether a time is busy or free.

- **Description**—The description text entry box is where you can type notes to be displayed with the reminder alarm.

- **Categories**—Appointments can be assigned to one or more categories. This is used as a reminder. If one of the available categories isn't what you want, you can create your own category by typing it into the entry box next to New Category.

- **Private**—Private is not a feature in use by this version of KOrganizer, but it will be used as part of group scheduling in a future version.

Appointment Details Settings   On the Details tab, you can make the following settings:

- **Attendee Information**—This is a list of attendees for the appointment. It can be a single individual or a whole list for a scheduled meeting. If you use the K Address Book, you can fill in the attendee list by clicking on the Address button, and then choosing a name from the Address Book. The name and email address appears in the appropriate fields. After the name is chosen, check the Role, Status, and Request Response fields. Then click on Add.

- **Categories**—These are the same categories defined in the General tab.

Settings for Recurring Events   On the Recurrence tab, you can make the following settings:

- **Appointment Time**—This displays the time set in the General tab. If you change the time here, it also changes in the General tab.

- **Recurrence Rule**—Set the frequency of the recurring event. Settings are very flexible and can be daily, weekly, monthly, or yearly. Within each time span, there are further settings.

- **Recurrence Range**—An recurring event must have a beginning date, but it does not have to have an ending date. If you choose, you can enter an ending day and time, or indicate that the event ends after a certain number of occurrences.

- **Exceptions**—Any rule can have an exception. Set any exceptions you have to a recurring event such as holidays, anniversaries, and so on.

Adding To-Do Items

To add items to the To-Do Items list follow these steps:

1. Right-click in the To-Do box.
2. Select New To-Do.
3. Double-click on the new To-Do Item.
4. Type in a description of the To-Do Item.

After you have entered a To-Do Item, you can right-click on the item and select Edit To-Do. In the Edit To-Do window there are two tabs: General and Details (as shown in Figure 4.16).

FIGURE 4.16
Editing window for To-Do Items in KOrganizer.

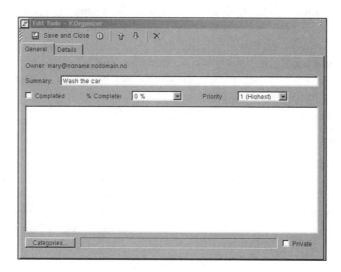

In the General tab, you can make the following settings:

- **Summary**—The short description that appears on the To-Do Items list.
- **Completed**—Check if the item has been completed, but you want to keep it displayed in the list anyway.
- **% Completed**—If the task is partially done, you can indicate a percent completed.
- **Priority**—Indicate a task's priority, with one being highest and five lowest. Tasks cannot be sorted by priority in this version.
- **Notes**—You can add informational notes to any task item.
- **Categories**—Each task can be assigned to a category. This can be used as a reminder. If one of the available categories isn't what you want, you can create your own category by typing it into the entry box next to New Category.

The Details tab matches the Details tab used for Appointments. See the section on adding appointments for an explanation of the different categories in the Details tab.

Changing the View

You can change the display of the KOrganizer from View in the Menu bar.

The different view options are

- **List view**—This shows appointments and events in a list, one item per line. Items associated with an alarm have a bell at the beginning of the line. Recurring events have a circling-arrow icon. Placing the mouse pointer over this icon displays information on the frequency of the recurring event. This view is good for seeing a whole day at a time, especially if you have many appointments.

- **Day view**—This is the default view in KOrganizer. Each hour of the day is shown, with a summary of any appointments.

- **Work Week**—This displays a Monday through Friday view, showing a box with the first few words of the summary for each appointment.

- **Week**—This is similar to the Work Week view but shows the full seven days of the week.

- **Month**—This view fills the full KOrganizer window with a month calendar. The display indicates where there are appointments but cannot display the full summary of the appointment. You can change the display by a week, month, or year by clicking the up and down icons on the right edge of the month view calendar.

- **To-Do List**—The To-Do List view fills the full KOrganizer window with the To-Do List.

Part

II

Ch

4

Using Kppp to Connect to the Internet

Dialing into an Internet service provider from a OpenLinux computer has never been easier. The Kppp utility connects to an Internet Service Provider (ISP).

Home computers and small office networks usually connect to the Internet through a modem connection: They dial in rather than having a full-time dedicated connection that doesn't have to be dialed.

Dial-up Internet connections use *PPP*, the point-to-point protocol. PPP has replaced *SLIP*, the Serial Line Internet Protocol, which you still sometimes see mentioned in documents about dial-up connections to the Internet. PPP is more stable and has error checking features not found in SLIP. SLIP is an older protocol that is no longer commonly used, though you may find an ISP or two that still supports both protocols. A few universities and colleges have not yet upgraded to the PPP protocol. If you need to make a SLIP connection, you won't be able to use Kppp. Instead, you can use the dip program on OpenLinux for making SLIP connections. Use the info pages on your computer for information on setting up dip. To see the info pages, open a terminal window and enter the command **info dip**.

PPP is designed to enable you to use TCP/IP over a modem connection. *TCP/IP* is the Internet Protocol already set up on your computer. TCP/IP is built into all OpenLinux systems.

When you connect to the Internet using PPP, you are seen as part of your ISP's network. Typically, when you connect, you are dynamically assigned an IP address for that session. There are also dial-up accounts where you have an assigned IP address.

The setup of Kppp is the same whether you are using an internal or external modem, and you don't have to change anything special if you are using an on-demand ISDN modem.

On-demand ISDN modems use a serial connection on your system, and the dialup is handled in the same way that dialups are handled by analog modems. Full-time ISDN routers do not require a dialup and do not need Kppp. The setup of full-time dedicated ISDN—or other full-time dedicated connections such as DSL, Cablemodems, Frame-Relay, and T1 connections—is usually handled by the ISP, and your system sees the full-time connection as a part of the network.

How to Use and Configure Kppp

The setup of Kppp involves just a few steps and requires no special knowledge of networking protocols or chat scripts, but you need to know some things before you start. For instance,

- The kind of analog or ISDN modem on your system.
- The serial port used (ttyS0 is COM1, ttyS1 is COM2, ttyS2 is COM3, ttyS4 is COM4).
- The user login name and password for your ISP account.
- The phone number you connect to for Internet service.
- DNS servers for your ISP.

To start Kppp, click on the K Application Launcher. From the pop-up menu, highlight Internet. In Internet, select Kppp. A dialog box similar to the one shown in Figure 4.17 appears.

FIGURE 4.17
Kppp, the Internet dialer.

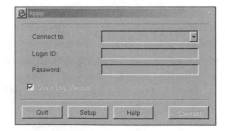

The first time you start Kppp, you need to setup an account. Click on the Setup button, and the Kppp Configuration Panel opens (see Figure 4.18).

FIGURE 4.18
The Kppp
Configuration Panel.

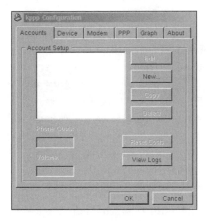

There are six tabs: Accounts, Device, Modem, PPP, Graph, and About. Start in the Accounts tab.

In the Accounts tab, click on New. The New Account panel opens (see Figure 4.19). The tabs in this panel are: Dial, IP, DNS, Gateway, Login Script, and Accounting. If you've ever setup a dialup account on a Windows or Macintosh computer, most of this should look familiar. The settings are done in about the same way.

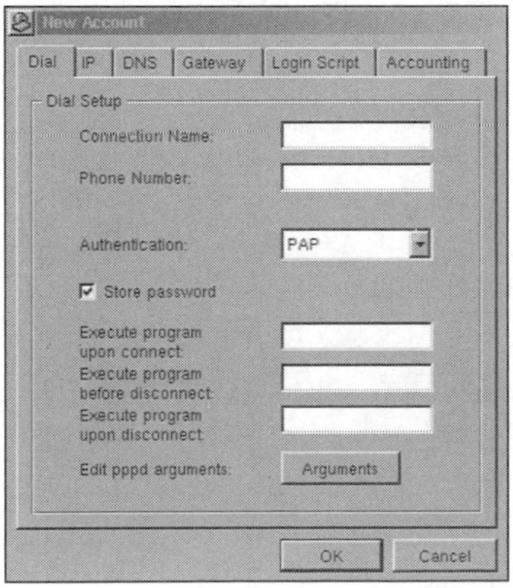

FIGURE 4.19
Setting up a new
Internet account.

Part
II

Ch
4

The steps for setting up a new account are outlined in the following sections.

Dial Setup   From the Dial tab, configure the following:

- **Connection name**—Enter a name for this account; usually the name of the ISP you are using.
- **Phone number**—The phone number you dial to connect to the ISP. If you need to dial a special number—such as 9 for an outside line—put it here. If your ISP has multiple phone numbers, you can add them here by separating the numbers with a colon (:). If the first number is busy or fails, the next number is dialed.
- **Authentication**—This is the method used to verify your username and password on connection. The usual setting is PAP, the Password Authentication Protocol. Many universities, however, still use the older Script-based or Terminal-based methods.
- **Store password**—You can check this box to save your password on your computer. A warning, though—the password is saved as plain, easily readable text.

The IP Setup   From the IP tab (see Figure 4.20), configure the following:

- **Dynamic IP Address**—Most dialup connections use a dynamic IP address: The IP address is assigned on connection from a pool of IP addresses assigned to the ISP. Each time you connect, you can get a different IP address.
- **Static IP Address**—This is a dedicated IP address. If you have an account with an assigned IP address, you need to get the IP address and Subnet Mask from your ISP.
- **Auto-configure hostname from this IP**—Check this if you want Kppp to change your computer's domain and hostname temporarily to the one assigned dynamically by your ISP. Normally, you can leave this unchecked.

FIGURE 4.20
IP setup for a new account.

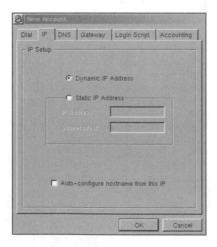

DNS Setup   From the DNS tab (see Figure 4.21), configure the following:

- **Domain Name**—You can enter the domain name of your ISP. This means your computer's hostname is changed while you are connected to match a network machine name for your ISP. When the connection is closed, the computer's original hostname is restored. If left blank, no changes are made in your computer's hostname.

- **DNS IP Address**—Enter the DNS number supplied by your ISP, and click the Add button. Remember to click Add, or the setting won't be made. The Domain Name Server converts Internet names that people understand such as isp.com into IP numbers that computers understand. An ISP might have up to three DNS numbers. The numbers entered here are temporarily inserted into resolv.conf in the /etc directory while Kppp is connected.

- **Disable existing DNS Servers during Connection**—Usually, there is no reason to check this option. If your computer is connected to a network that has its own DNS Server, and the Kppp connection is having trouble, try checking this option.

FIGURE 4.21
DNS setup for a new account.

Part
II

Ch
4

Gateway Setup   From the Gateway tab (see Figure 4.22), configure the following:

- **Default Gateway**—In most cases, check Default Gateway, which makes your computer act as the gateway between you and your ISP. If you need to specify another computer as the gateway, check Static Gateway and enter the Gateway IP Address.

Login Script Setup   From the Login Script tab (see Figure 4.23), configure the following:

- **Edit Script**—This is usually left blank. Only ISPs that use nonstandard logins or have high-lcvel security measures might need to have a customized login script. The settings follow standard PPP chat scripts.

FIGURE 4.22
Gateway setup for a
new account.

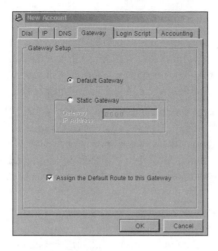

FIGURE 4.23
Login Script setup for a
new account.

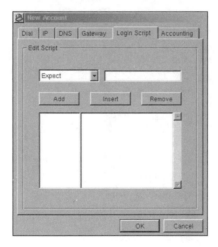

Accounting Setup   From the Accounting tab (see Figure 4.24), configure the following:

■ **Enable accounting**—If you select Enable accounting, click on a country in the list.
Click on the plus sign (+) to see a list of telecom systems to use for tracking usage
costs base on that system. There is no accounting setting for the United States, where
ISPs don't usually charge by time units.

■ **Volume accounting**—You can turn on volume accounting to keep track of the volume
of data being sent and received.

FIGURE 4.24
Accounting setup for a new account.

Configuring Your Modem

After you've set up your account information, you'll need to setup the modem.

Device Setup   Two parts of the Kppp Configuration panel are for setting up your modem: the Device tab and the Modem tab. Start with the Device tab (shown in Figure 4.25):

- **Modem Device**—Set this to the serial port used by your modem (ttyS0 is COM1, ttyS1 is COM2, and so on). If you have an internal ISDN card with AT command emulation, select one of the ttyI0, ttyI1, or other such devices.

- **Flow Control**—This option sets how the serial port and modem talk to each other. The default is CRTSCTS, which is hardware flow control. Don't change this unless you know what you are doing.

- **Line Termination**—This sets how AT commands are sent to the modem. The default setting is CR/LF. If your modem doesn't respond, you can try changing this setting, but it is rarely the reason for problems.

- **Connection Speed**—For most modems, the speed needs to be set to 115,200. If you have an older modem of 28.8 Kbps or less, set this to 57,600.

- **Use Lock File**—A lock file prevents other programs from accessing the modem while it is connected to the ISP. The default setting is checked on.

- **Modem Timeout**—This sets how long to wait for a connection when dialing. It is usually set at 60 seconds.

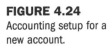

FIGURE 4.25
The Device
Configuration Panel.

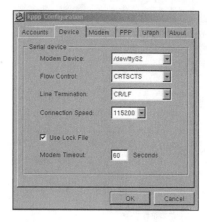

The Modem Configuration Panel After the Device has been set, select the Modem tab (seen in Figure 4.26). Configure the following options:

FIGURE 4.26
The Modem
Configuration Panel.

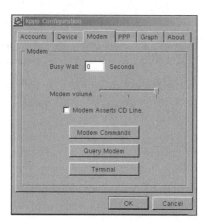

- **Busy Wait**—This option sets the number of seconds to wait before redial if the number was busy. The default is 0 seconds and should not be changed unless necessary.

- **Modem volume**—This sets the volume of the modem speaker when dialing.

- **Modem Asserts CD Line**—This sets how Kppp detects a modem that's not responding. It's normally not checked.

- **Modem Commands**—This button sets the AT commands for your modem. If your modem uses nonstandard AT commands, you can make changes here.

- **Query Modem**—Pressing this button sends a series of AT commands to the modem. It's a quick way to see whether you've chosen the right device.

- **Terminal**—This activates a built-in terminal program, such as the Linux program minicom or Hyperterminal in Windows, and is useful for testing AT commands on your modem.

The PPP Configuration Panel

When the modem has been configured, click on the PPP tab in the Kppp Configuration panel (see Figure 4.27). This defines what happens during a PPP connection. Configure the following options:

FIGURE 4.27
The PPP Configuration Panel.

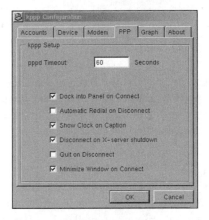

- **pppd Timeout**—This option determines how long to wait (in seconds) after dialing to see if a PPP connection has been made.

- **Dock into Panel on Connect**—After a connection has been made, the Kppp window is minimized and becomes an icon on the K Panel.

- **Automatic Redial on Disconnect**—If a connection gets lost and this is checked on, Kppp automatically tries to reconnect.

- **Show Clock on Caption**—If you've turned on Dock into Panel on Connect when Kppp is shown as an icon on the K Panel, the icon shows a clock that displays the time connected.

- **Disconnect on X-server Shutdown**—If Kppp is connected when you close KDE, the connection is closed.

- **Quit on Disconnect**—This setting closes Kppp when you disconnect.

- **Minimize Window on Connect**—This option puts Kppp in the taskbar rather than on the K Panel after a connection has been established.

That's it. Click OK and the new account is set up.

Connecting to the Internet

After setting up the Kppp account, you are ready to connect to the Internet.

The dialup window shows the account you are dialing in the Connect To field (see Figure 4.28). If you have more than one account, you can select the one you want by clicking on the arrow.

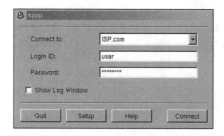

The first time, you'll need to enter your Login ID and Password and then click on Connect. If you check on Show Log Window, you'll be capable of watching the connection and login. When you are connected, the Kppp connection window disappears. After you've connected, you can start Netscape Communicator or other Internet tools and begin to use the Internet.

Using Kmail for Email

One of the most popular reasons for being on the Internet is email. OpenLinux comes equipped with two Windows-based email programs: Kmail and Netscape Messenger.

Kmail has all the basic email functions. In addition, it can support more than one POP email account, for those with more than one. It does not support IMAP accounts. Netscape Messenger supports only one POP account, though it supports multiple IMAP accounts. Most email accounts use POP mail. For more information on using Netscape Messenger for Email, see Chapter 17, "Configuring and Running Netscape Communicator."

To start Kmail, click on the Email icon on the K Panel across the bottom of your screen. Alternatively, click on the K Application Launcher. From the pop-up menu, highlight Internet. In Internet select Mail Client.

The first time you use Kmail, you need to set up your account information (see Figure 4.29).

The settings panel contains six tabs: Identity, Network, Appearance, Composer, Misc, and PGP. To start using Kmail, you only need to set up your identity and your account (network).

FIGURE 4.29
Set up your user
account information in
Kmail.

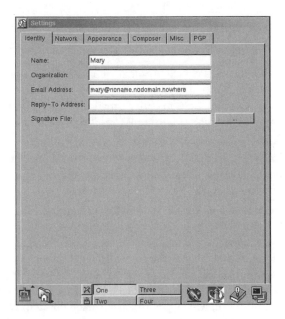

Setting Your Identity

On the Identity tab, set up the following information:

- **Name**—This is the name that identifies you on your email.
- **Organization**—Like name, if filled in, the organization name is sent as part of your identification in your email.
- **Email Address**—The email address should already be filled in. It's based on your user account on your OpenLinux system. If you use a different email address, change the default address that's there.
- **Reply-To Address**—This is usually set to be the same as the Email address.
- **Signature File**—Enter the location of a signature file. If you skip this, Kmail asks you for your signature file every time you compose a new message. A *signature file* is a plain text file that usually consists of a couple of lines of text that include your name, email address, company name, and maybe a phone number.

Part
II

Ch
4

Setting Your Email Account

On the Network tab (Figure 4.30), set up your email account information:

■ **Sending Mail**—You have a choice of Sendmail or SMTP for sending mail. If you choose Sendmail, make sure it is properly set up on your computer. Usually, you use SMTP to forward your messages to either a mail server on your network or to an ISP's server. Enter the server name (for example, **mail.*isp*.com**) and leave the port number at 25.

■ **Incoming Mail**—In incoming mail, you need to set up at least one account so that you can receive mail. When you select Add, you are given a choice of Local Mail or POP3. Most mail accounts are POP3.

■ **Configure Account**—After you've selected an account type, the Configure Account window opens. On a POP account, the Name field is not for your name, but for the name you want to know the account by, such as your ISP's name. Login is the user name for the account. Password is the password for the account. Host is the mail server (for example, mail.*isp*.com) that you obtain from your ISP or system administrator. The Port should say 110. The three check boxes are to Delete mail from server after it has been retrieved, which is normally checked on. Retrieve all mail from server must be checked on. If you have a full-time connection to the mail server, you can Enable interval mail checking, which periodically checks the server for new mail. Leave the Store new mail in account setting at inbox.

FIGURE 4.30
The Network tab is used to set up your Email services.

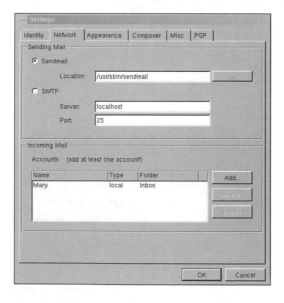

Setting Kmail's Appearance

On the Appearance tab, set the look of text in Kmail:

- **Fonts**—You can change the font used for text in the Message Body and in the Message List. The default setting is 12 point Helvetica. To change the font, click on the ... button.

- **Layout**—Check Long Folder List to make the frame that displays the folder list go down the full length of the left side of the Kmail window.

Setting Your Email Composer

On the Composer tab (see Figure 4.31), set up options for the Email message editor. The display shows the special character codes recognized by the Email Composer: %D for date, %S for subject, %F for sender, and %% for percent sign:

- **Phrases**—These are the fields that are automatically generated with every Email message. The Reply To Sender field is the text that appears before the sender's text in an Email reply. The Reply To All is the text that appears before the sender's text in a reply to all recipients of the message. Forward is the text that appears at the top of every forwarded message.

- **Appearance**—Set the options for adding signatures, which is defined in the Identity tab, and signing messages with a PGP encrypted signature. Word wrap sets how long each line will be in your messages. The default setting is 80, the full width of a typewritten page. You can also select to use a monospaced font.

- **When sending mail**—Set this option to have your mail sent immediately when you click the Send button or hold all messages in the outbox to be sent later when you select the Send Queued command from the File menu. You can also set how a message is encoded when it is sent. Allow 8-bit sends messages as 8-bit ASCII, which sends accented characters as they appear on the screen. Many mail systems do not support 8-bit ASCII and cannot properly handle messages sent this way. The default setting is MIME compliant (Quoted printable), which encodes accented characters with MIME encoding and treats the message as an attachment so that it can be read on any mail system.

Misc Settings

On the Misc tab, set actions on exit and on checking for mail:

- **Folders**—Check Empty Trash on Exit to clear the trash folder when you quit Kmail. Check Send Mail in Outbox Folder on Check to send all mail in the outbox folder whenever you check your email.

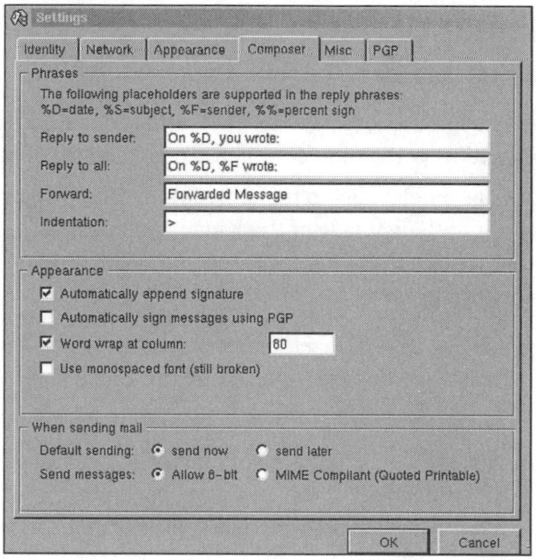

FIGURE 4.31
On the Composer tab you can set the options for creating an Email message.

Setting PGP Security

On the PGP tab, set up secure Email signatures:

■ **Identity**—Kmail can properly interface with PGP or GNU Privacy Guard if you provide the correct user identity. This is used to encrypt your messages when you choose encryption by clicking on the key icon in the Message Composer.

■ **Options**—The two PGP options are to save the secure passphrase so that you don't have to type it in every time. If your computer is completely secure, you might want to enable this. The second option is to also encrypt all message copies that are sent to yourself.

You are now ready to send and receive email.

Using Kmail to Read Email

When you open Kmail, you'll see the mail reader window with a list of mail folders in one frame, a list of messages in another frame, and the text of any selected message in the third frame.

The first step to read mail is to check for mail.

To check for mail, choose the File menu and select either Check Mail or Check Mail In. Check Mail checks for mail in all your email accounts. Check Mail In enables you to specify which account to check. Another way to check for new mail is to click on the icon of an envelope with a ? on top. This works just like Check Mail.

As Kmail retrieves mail, it adds new messages to your inbox. To read your messages, you need to select your inbox.

In the mail reader view (shown in Figure 4.32), the inbox is in the upper left frame of the Kmail window. This frame displays all your folders. The default folders and their functions are as follows:

FIGURE 4.32
Use Kmail to read your Email.

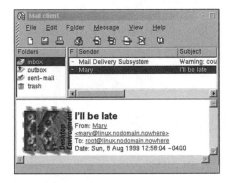

- **Inbox**—Receives all new mail.
- **Outbox**—Stores mail until you've sent it.
- **Sent-mail**—Contains copies of messages sent.
- **Trash**—Holds deleted messages until you've exited Kmail.

To keep your email organized, you can create new folders by choosing Folder from the Menu and selecting Create. You can create as many folders as you want.

When you select a folder in the folder frame, a list of email message headers is shown in the headers frame on the upper right side of the Kmail window. To read a message, select the header, and the content of the message appears in the lower Message frame.

When you are reading a message, you have all the standard options to Reply, Reply to all, Forward, or Delete the message. These options are available from Menu choices, or from icons in the toolbar.

Using Kmail to Send Email

To create an email message, choose File from the Menu and select New Composer. You can also select the Compose New Message icon, which looks like a letter page, on the icon bar. A mail composer window opens, ready for a new message (shown in Figure 4.33).

Part

II

Ch

4

FIGURE 4.33
Use the Kmail composer to write new messages.

Be sure to put an email address in the To field, and also include a Subject.

After typing the message, you can click on the envelope icon to send the message or choose the File menu and select Send. If you want to attach a file, you can click on the Paper clip icon to attach a file, or select the Attach menu item.

Using the Kmail Address Book   When sending email in Kmail, you can use the program's rudimentary address book to store regularly used email addresses. Kmail cannot automatically access addresses in other address books such at the K Address Book. The Kmail Address Book is just a simple list of Email addresses that you can save for use in Kmail only. From the File menu, select Addressbook or click on the Addressbook icon on the toolbar.

Address Book entries are simple, one line email addresses. Addresses can be added to the Address Book from the mail reader window by right-clicking on an email address in the To or From fields and selecting Add to Addressbook.

Using KBiff to Find Out if You Have Email

KBiff is the program that pops up a notice when 'email arrives. This is a very handy utility if you have a full-time connection to the Internet. KBiff polls your mail server and notifies you whenever you have a new email message.

To setup KBiff, click on the K Application Launcher. From the pop-up menu, highlight Internet. In Internet, select Biff. A dialog box appears similar to the one in Figure 4.34.

Kbiff is designed to work with the standard Linux mailboxes. When you first open the program, a default profile is displayed that is set up for this. If you use Kmail, you don't have to change anything—just start using Kbiff for mail notification.

FIGURE 4.34
Kbiff tells you when
you have new email.

The General preference tab settings are

- **Poll**—This is the frequency of polling. The default setting of 60 needs to be changed to at least 600, or once every five minutes. If several users are polling a mail server more frequently than once every five minutes, it is possible to flood the system with too many requests.

- **Mail client**—By default, the mail client is Kmail. If you use Netscape Messenger for your email, change this to netscape –mail.

In the New Mail preference settings tab, a beep sounds when new mail arrives if System Beep is checked by default. You can change this by using either Run Command or Play Sound. If you have a sound file in the .wav format, use the Play Sound option and indicate the full pathname for the file. If you want a sound to play that is in the .au format, use the Run Command option and enter a command like

```
cat newmail.au > /dev/audio
```

This command then runs on the arrival of any new mail, and the sound file is sent to the audio device, which plays the sound.

Check Notify to have a window pop up when new mail arrives. The window shows the name of the mailbox and the number of new emails. Do not turn this setting on if you receive frequent email.

The **Mailbox** settings tab (shown in Figure 4.35) enables you to define one or more mail accounts to poll:

- **Protocol**—This option sets the protocol for the mailbox. Choices include Linux mbox, qmail's maildir, POP3, and IMAP4. The "file" protocol is not a protocol, but can be used to monitor changes to a file.

Part
II

Ch

4

■ **Mailbox**—Leave this with the default settings. It is grayed out if you selected POP3 as the protocol.

■ **Server**—For POP3 and IMAP4, enter the name or IP address of the server.

■ **User**—For POP3 and IMAP4, enter the user name for the account.

■ **Password**—For POP3 and IMAP4, enter the password for the account.

After defining the default account, you can add additional accounts by clicking on the Mailbox icon below the list of accounts.

FIGURE 4.35
Setting mailboxes in the Kbiff setup. Click on the mailbox icon in the lower left corner of the Kbiff window to add a new account

When Kbiff is active, it displays an icon at the right end of the K Panel next to the clock (Figure 4.36). The icon changes depending on whether you have no mail in your inbox, or you have old or new mail. Right-clicking on the icon pops up a menu that enables you to go back into the setup window, check for new mail, open your mail reader, or exit Kbiff.

FIGURE 4.36
The Kbiff icon shows that new mail is waiting.

 Kbiff

Playing Music CDs with Kscd

Playing music CDs on OpenLinux is easy. The first step is to make sure your sound card is properly set up. If you aren't sure, see Chapter 10, "Installing and Configuring Sound."

To start the Kscd CD player, click on the K Application Launcher. From the pop-up menu, highlight Multimedia. In Multimedia, select CD Player.

The CD Player is displayed in Figure 4.37 and contains the following options:

- **The control panel**—The buttons on the right side are used to Play, Stop, or Pause the CD. There are also buttons for Previous Track, Next Track, Skip forward or backward, and Continuous play. The style of the buttons matches any standard CD player.

- **The eject button**—The eject button pops the CD drive open.

N O T E This button might not respond. On some systems, the CD player must be closed to eject a CD, which is then done manually. Also, most older CD-ROM drivers do not support software eject. ■

- **Status display**—The status display is similar to that found on most CD players. Clicking on the Compact Disc button toggles the display between the default elapsed play time, the amount of time remaining for the current track, the total elapsed time, and the total remaining time.

- **The configuration panel**—The button that looks like a hammer and screwdriver opens the configuration panel. This opens to the Compact Disc Database setup.

If Your CD-ROM Player Doesn't Respond

If your CD-ROM player is not responding and you are sure the sound card is working, look at the KSCD options tab. If it says that the device name is /dev/cdrom, this isn't the actual device name. It is a name that's usually set as a link shortcut to your actual drive. You'll need to create the link for the player program. To find the device name of your CD-ROM drive, look in the fstab file in the /etc directory and find the line that for /mnt/cdrom. At the beginning of that line is the device name for the CD-ROM drive. Then, in a terminal window, enter the command:

```
ln -s /dev/hdc /dev/cdrom
```

This example uses a CD-ROM drive at /dev/hdc; use the correct device name for your system.

Part

II

Ch

4

- **CDDB**—This button opens the CDDB, the Compact Disc Data Base editor panel. CDDB lets you automatically identify each CD you play from a database on the Internet onto your computer. The artist and title appear in the display screen, and the name of each track is displayed in the drop-down list below the display screen. For more information on use of CDDB, check out the CDDB Web site at www.cddb.com.

- **Information button**—Click on this button if you want the CD player to start a search of the Internet for information about the artist. This option does not work unless you are already connected to the Internet.

- **Close button**—This button closes the CD player.

- **Volume control**—Move the slider to the right to increase volume and to the left to reduce volume.

- **Track selector**—Click on this button, and you can choose an individual track to play from the list of available tracks.

- **Randomizer**—This button makes the CD player play tracks in a random order.

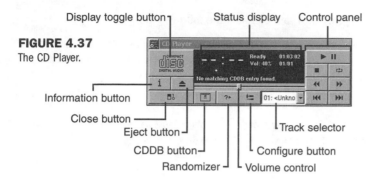

Display toggle button ⌐   Status display   Control panel

FIGURE 4.37
The CD Player.

Information button

Close button ———

Eject button ⌐

CDDB button ⌐

Randomizer ⌐ └ Volume control

└ Configure button

└ Track selector

Using Kview to View a Graphic Image

You can use Kview (shown in Figure 4.38) to view graphics in many different formats. It gives you a quick and easy way to see the graphics and make basic changes to graphics files. It is not an image editor. You can use Kpaint for basic image editing, or for more sophisticated graphics manipulation, you can use GIMP, which is described in Chapter 18, "Configuring and Running GIMP."

To start Kview, click on the K Application Launcher. From the pop-up menu, highlight Graphics. In Graphics, select Image Viewer.

FIGURE 4.38
Viewing a graphic image with Kview.

You can use Kview to view most of the popular graphic formats. It supports gif and jpeg images used on the Web, as well as many Windows and UNIX standard formats, including eps.

When you start the program, it opens with an empty window. You can then use the K File Manager to drag and drop an image onto the viewer to see the graphic, or you can go to the File menu and select Open to load a graphic.

While viewing a graphic, you can change its size and rotation, even flipping the view of the graphic. You can make an image brighter or darker by using the Filter tools.

You can even use Kview to create a slide show. Load multiple images into Kview. Load them one at a time by choosing the File menu and selecting Open. After you have all the images open, choose the Images menu and select Slideshow. To change the image manually, go to the Images menu and select Next or Previous. If you select Slideshow, each image is displayed one after the other until you stop it. You can set the delay time between images under the Edit menu in Preferences.

Using Kpaint to Edit Graphics

Kpaint (shown in Figure 4.39) is a basic image editor similar to the Windows Paint program.

CAUTION

Be warned before you start that Kpaint does not have an Undo function, so proceed cautiously before making any changes on your images.

Part

II

Ch

4

For more sophisticated graphics manipulation use GIMP, described in Chapter 18.

To start Kpaint, click on the K Application Launcher. From the pop-up menu, highlight Graphics. In Graphics, select Paint.

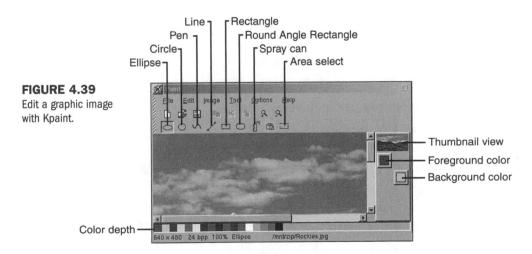

FIGURE 4.39
Edit a graphic image with Kpaint.

Kpaint has some basic image manipulation tools as well as some drawing tools.

To work on an image that's already been created or scanned in, choose the File menu and select Open. The file formats that can be opened include gif, jpeg, bmp, pnm, xbm, and xpm.

When you open an image in Kpaint, the size of the window won't change to fit the graphic, but a thumbnail view of the entire image is shown on the right panel in the Kpaint window (see Figure 4.39).

Some of the imaging conversion tools in Kpaint include

- **Change format**—You can convert the format of any image that you've opened in Kpaint by choosing the File menu and selecting Image Format. From the list of formats, choose the one you want. The list matches the list of formats that can be opened. After you've chosen the new format, you have to Save the file in the new format, or it won't be changed.
- **Resize an image**—To resize an image, choose the Image menu and select Resize. The current image size is displayed on the bottom line of the Kpaint window. Enter a new size, in pixels, in the width and height fields.
- **Change color depth**—The number of colors displayed in the image can be changed by changing the color depth. The current color depth is displayed on the bottom line of the Kpaint window. From the Image menu, select Change Color Depth. You can select a color depth in bits: 1 (black and white), 4 (16 colors), 8 (256 colors), 15 (32k colors), 16 (64k colors), 24 (16.7 million colors, or True Color), or 32 (16.7 millions colors, or True Color). There is no difference in color depth with 24 bit or 32 bit. 32-bit color is usually used for 3D rendering.

Some of the image drawing tools in Kpaint include

- An Ellipse drawing tool
- A Circle drawing tool
- A freehand Pen
- A Line drawing tool
- A Rectangle drawing tool
- A Round Angle rectangle drawing tool
- A Spray Can for spraying colors on a drawing
- A Text tool for adding text to a graphic
- An Area Select tool to select areas of the graphics to be cut or copied and pasted

Kpaint displays the foreground and background drawing colors on the right panel under the thumbnail. To change either one, click on the color square and choose a new color from either the predefined system colors or make your own color from the color palette.

Playing Games

OpenLinux ships with hundreds of computer games. There are card games, board games, and arcade games. The games included in the standard installation of OpenLinux include

- Abalone (a board strategy game)
- Asteroids (an arcade game)
- KBlackBox (a board strategy game)
- Gnu-Lactic Konquest (a multiple-player strategy game)
- Mahjongg (the well-known tile game)
- Minesweeper (the classic minesweeper game)
- Patience (nine kinds of solitaire from Klondike to Freecell)
- Poker (a card game)
- Reversi (a board strategy game)
- SameGame (a board strategy game, like the version on the Macintosh)
- Shisen-Sho (a tile game)
- Sirtet (a Tetris-like game)
- Smiletris (a Tetris-like game with smiley-faces)
- Snake Race (an arcade-type game)
- Sokoban (a board game from Japan)
- XBoard (the excellent GNU chess game)

All of these games can be found on the Games menu in the K Application Launcher pop-up menu.

Using Kpackage to Manage Your Software

Why do you need Kpackage, the software package installation and removal program? After all, OpenLinux seems to have just about everything already loaded into it.

You might find you need it anyway. Kpackage is the easiest way to handle software applications for Linux.

To start Kpackage, click on the K Application Launcher. From the pop-up menu, highlight Utilities. In Utilities, select Kpackage.

When Kpackage opens (as shown in Figure 4.40), it checks the RPM database for a complete list of everything installed on your system. It then opens a window with two panes. On the left pane is a list of all the software installed on the system, organized by groups. The right pane displays details about any package you've highlighted on the left pane. The details include all the package properties, such as the full name, version, and packager. There is also a list of files associated with the package.

FIGURE 4.40
Kpackage makes
installing and unin-
stalling software an
easy task.

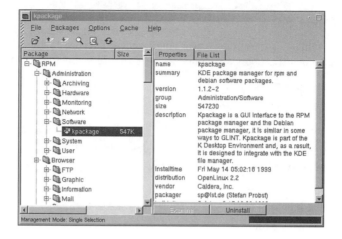

Searching for an Installed Package

To search your system to see whether a package is already installed or to find out the version or other information about an installed package, choose the File menu and select Find Package.

Check the Sub string box if you want to enter only part of the package name. You can click on Find repeatedly to see multiple packages that contain the same name string you entered.

Installing New Software Packages

To install new packages, make sure the Kpackage program is open. Then use the K File Manager to locate the new package to be installed. This is usually from a CD-ROM disk. For example, if you did a standard installation, many packages aren't installed from the OpenLinux CD. The other packages are found on the CD in the /Packages/RPMS directory.

Find the package you want to install and select it by holding down the Ctrl key while clicking with the mouse button. Hold down the left mouse button and drag the file icon onto the Kpackage program. An installation window appears (see Figure 4.41).

In the left pane of the Installation window are the options Upgrade, Replace Files, Replace Packages, Check Dependencies, and Test. Usually, you don't need to change the choices Kpackage makes.

On the right pane is the Properties description of the software package. Clicking on the File List tab displays a list of the all the files that are to be installed, and the location to which they are to be installed.

Instead of using drag and drop, you can install a software package by choosing the File menu and selecting Open. You then need to navigate to the location of the package to be installed. After the package has been selected, you are shown the same Installation window.

FIGURE 4.41
The Kpackage installation window.

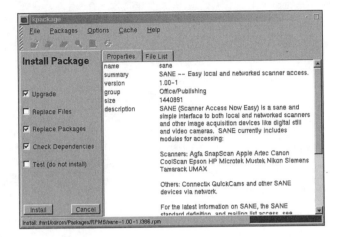

Uninstalling Software Packages

To remove any software package, open Kpackage and find the software application you want
to remove. You can use the Find Package search. When the name of the file is highlighted on
the right pane in the Properties tab, an Uninstall option appears on the bottom line of the
pane. Uninstalling removes all the files. Only a completely new installation can restore a package that's been uninstalled.

Part

II

Ch

4

Configuring Your System with COAS

Easy-to-Use Administration Tools

The Caldera Open Administration System (COAS) is designed to make configuring your system easier. COAS was first released with OpenLinux version 2.2 upgrades. The version of COAS included with OpenLinux 2.3 is significantly improved over that first release. If you have OpenLinux 2.2, you'll want to make sure that you upgrade to this version of COAS.

Managing and administering a Linux system can be a complex task. For many features in Linux, there aren't any administration tools at all.

You can use COAS to configure user accounts, printers, system services, module drivers, and network information. Any other system configuration such as networking with Samba, NFS or Netatalk, PPP dial-up settings, mail and news, and many other settings mostly have to be handled by editing configuration files or, with Samba, using a separate administration system. The free version of Sendmail that comes with Linux is probably the most complex program you'd ever have to configure, yet it is all done manually with a text editor.

Unified administration systems are available for many other operating systems. Linux users can expect a good administration system. That's what Caldera intends COAS to become, and although it's not there yet, it has made a reasonable beginning.

COAS includes several key tools, and more are under development. As additional administration tools become available, you can add them to the system if you want them because COAS is modular. You can install administration modules, called CLAMs, into the system, and you can update them or remove them without recompiling. They are distributed in RPM package format and adding them is as simple as adding any other RPM package.

COAS is designed to have two levels of online help general help for the task and specific, context-sensitive help on each input field. However, many of the tools in the first release do not include help files.

The COAS design includes built-in checks for syntax correctness and consistency to reduce errors in configuration. This is an important feature because mistyping or entering information in the wrong sequence often causes configuration errors.

Because OpenLinux is used worldwide, COAS user interfacesare internationalized so that translations for different languages are available for menus, dialog boxes, and online help. Although it was designed for internationalization, the first release does not make use of this feature.

COAS does not change the format or location of configuration data on the OpenLinux system. COAS works with the standard Linux configuration files so that if changes are made the traditional way—by using a text editor, for example—COAS sees the changes. The same is true the other way: If you've changed a configuration file in COAS, you can open the file in a text editor and the COAS changes are there.

The source code for COAS has been released under the GNU Public License.

Configuring the mouse, keyboard, and video

The Lizard tool for configuring the mouse, keyboard, and video card is included with OpenLinux 2.3. You can access it through the COAS section of the Application Menu. Select X-Server. Alternately, you can open a terminal window and enter the command `lizardx` to start the X-Server configuration tool. Figure 5.1 shows the opening screen.

FIGURE 5.1
The X-Server configuration tool starts with setting up the mouse.

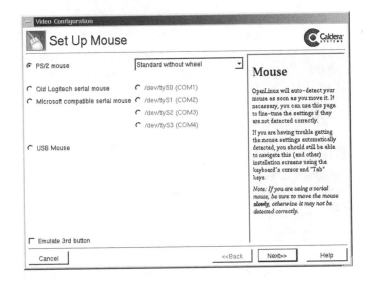

This tool is particularly useful if you need to change your video settings or if you have installed a new video card on your system.

The settings are the same as those described in Chapter 2 on installing OpenLinux. After setting up the mouse, keyboard setup options are displayed. That's followed by video card selection, monitor selection, and finally the video mode.

Part

II

Ch

5

Starting COAS

You can start COAS in several ways. The best way to access COAS's full capabilities is to open a terminal window and enter the following command:

`coastool`

If you are not logged in as root, you are prompted for the root password. This opens up access to all the COAS modules, called *CLAMs* (seen in Figure 5.2), that are installed on your system. CLAMs are Caldera Linux Administration Modules. (They started calling them CLAMs and then later figured out a meaning to match the letters!).

FIGURE 5.2
The COAS administration panel. CLAMs are the COAS modules.

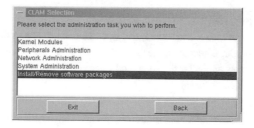

You can also start COAS from the K Panel by clicking on the COAS icon. A pop-up menu showing all the COAS modules on your system is displayed. You can select the module you want to change, but when you are finished, COAS closes. You can only work on one CLAM at a time this way.

Loading and Unloading Kernel Modules

Kernel modules are the Linux hardware drivers for disk drives, printers, sound cards, networks, and so on. Selecting Kernel Modules opens the Kernel Modules panel (seen in Figure 5.3).

FIGURE 5.3
The Kernel Modules panel.

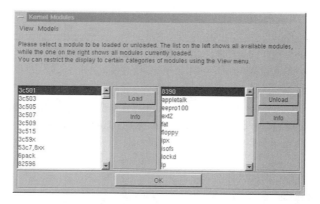

The panel shows two panes. On the left side is a list of all the available modules. On the right side is a list of the modules that are actually loaded on your system. Both lists are in alphabetical order.

You can go to any module, single-click to highlight it, and then click on the Info button. Details on the driver are displayed, including a description and its status.

If you want to install a driver on your system, highlight the module name on the left pane and click Load. If the driver needs additional configuration information, a window pops up, listing fields that need to be filled in. For example, loading the sb module for Sound Blaster emulation opens the panel shown in Figure 5.4.

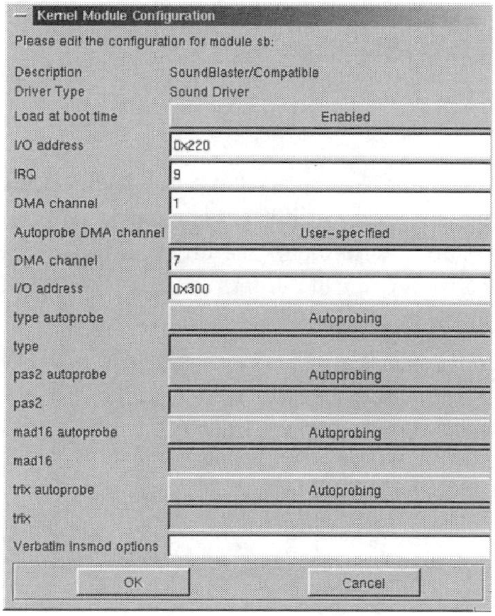

FIGURE 5.4
Configuring the kernel sound module.

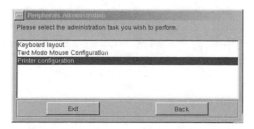

To install the sound module properly, you need to know configuration information such as the *I/O address* (a unique memory location used by the device) and the *IRQ* (an interrupt request line for getting the computer processor's attention, a number from 0 to 15). Also, you might need to load other modules.

Almost any module you install will require some kind of configuration information. If you are unsure about the configuration, do not load the module.

The changes are made in the Modules default file, and the configuration parameters are put into the options folder. You system is then configured to load the selected modules the next time the systems starts up.

Peripherals Administration

The Peripherals Administration panel, shown in Figure 5.5, is used to configure the keyboard layout, the text-mode mouse, and the printer. The Printer Configuration panel is the most important tool here.

FIGURE 5.5
The Peripherals Administration panel.

Part
II
Ch
5

When you are finished using this panel, click on the back button to go to other COAS modules. Clicking on exit exits COAS altogether.

Keyboard Configuration

This panel adjusts the keyboard map, which is a keyboard layout designed to meet the needs of the different alphabets that are used by different languages. This configuration tool does not work with the KDE Desktop Environment (see Figure 5.6). To change the keyboard map on the KDE desktop, use the KDE Control Center.

FIGURE 5.6
You must perform keyboard configuration for the KDE desktop from the KDE Control Center.

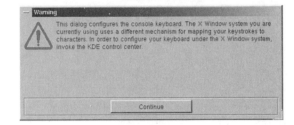

Mouse Configuration

The mouse settings panel is for mouse use in a character-mode terminal. Be careful when making any changes here (see the warning displayed in Figure 5.7). Changing these settings can make it impossible for you to use your mouse in the KDE desktop.

FIGURE 5.7
A warning about changing the mouse settings.

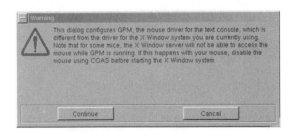

The General Purpose Mouse driver was created for using a mouse on a terminal that doesn't have X Windows or any other kind of graphical interface. If you need to use a mouse on such a nongraphical, character-mode terminal, the GPM driver must be properly configured. The GPM Mouse Configuration panel is shown in Figure 5.8. Make sure that the Model and Device File settings are correctly configured. Select Start at boot time if you need a mouse while working in a character-mode terminal. This does not change the settings for the KDE desktop. However, loading the GPM driver can make your mouse unusable on the KDE desktop.

FIGURE 5.8
The GPM Mouse
Configuration panel.

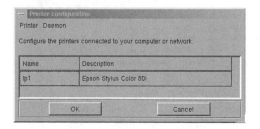

Printer Configuration

You can use the Printer Configuration panel, shown in Figure 5.9, to handle your printer
setup; you can add, edit, or delete a printer setup, and you can start and stop the lpd printer
daemon. This process runs in the background and watches for print jobs. When the daemon
sees a print job, it sends the job to the proper destination.

FIGURE 5.9
The Printer
Configuration panel.

Part

II

Ch

5

The Printer menu offers Edit, Add, and Remove. If you select Add, a list of printer models is
shown. These are the most commonly used printers. If your printer is not on the list, choose
one that is similar.

TIP   Try a printer that is from the same manufacturer. Manufacturers often use the same or similar drivers
for many of their printers. Also, your printer may have PCL or Postscript emulation. If it has PCL emulation, try a Hewlett-Packard Laserjet driver. If your printer has Postscript emulation, try the generic
Postscript printer.

A single click selects a printer model. The next screen asks for a *logical name* for the printer.
This is the name you want to use to identify the printer. The default name of the first printer
is lp1. That's a short and easy to remember name, but if you have several printers, it might
not be so easy to remember what the difference is between lp1 and lp8. Usually, you want to
give your printer a name that identifies it either by make and model, such as Epson850; by a
location such as Accounting; or by some other name that is easily identifiable, such as the
name of the person using the printer (for example, Ricky).

After choosing a name, you'll see settings for the default paper size, the Device (that's the printer port; lp0 is the same as Windows lpt1, the first parallel port), and the speed. The speed setting is for serial connections, which are rarely used. You can ignore this if you are using a parallel port.

When you save, the changes are saved to the printcap file in the /etc directory. The lpd print daemon is then stopped and restarted so that the new printer is immediately available.

There is a special print driver for printing to printers that are not connected to your computer. These printers are called *remote printers*. Toward the end of the list of printer models is a listing that says Generic remote printer. If you are printing to a network printer, you'll need to use this printer model rather than the model of the printer to which you are printing. If you choose this printer, you are not prompted for a default paper size and so on. Instead, you are asked to enter the Remote host—the network name or IP address of the print server that handles the remote printer and the print queue for the printer. If you don't know this information, you'll need to obtain it from your system administrator.

After a printer has been installed, you can edit and modify the settings (see Figure 5.10). If the initial setup needs to be refined, you can do it here.

FIGURE 5.10
The Printer Attributes panel.

Setting up printers in Linux can sometimes be difficult. See Chapter 8, "Installing and Configuring Printers," for more details.

Network Administration Configuration

You can handle some of the network configuration settings in the Network Administration panel (seen in Figure 5.11), including the network settings that are determined during the initial installation.

FIGURE 5.11
The Network
Administration panel.

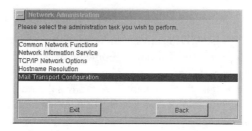

Common Network Functions

The Common Network Settings are for your network card. You can adjust the device name and IP address, netmask, broadcast address, default gateway, and other settings here (see Figure 5.12).

FIGURE 5.12
The Ethernet Interface
Configuration panel.

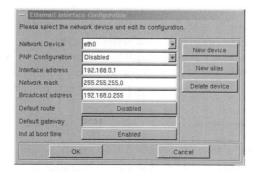

Network Information Service

If you are using the Network Information Service to manage a number of UNIX computers, you can maintain the NIS client and Server setup configuration here. You make entries for the NIS Domain Name and for starting the NIS client on boot. If you receive an error message while trying to load NIS in COAS, it is probably because of an error in the nis.conf file in the /etc directory. Edit that file and remove the line that has only the single word *broadcast* on it.

TCP/IP Network Options

You can enable and disable networking and IP forwarding. Disabling networking here means that you are turning off all possible network connections. Do not disable networking unless you know what you are doing because many services and functions in Linux depend on networking, even if you aren't directly connected to a network.

IP forwarding is a technique used to access the Internet through a firewall. For more information on IP forwarding, see Chapter 25, "Installing and Configuring a Firewall."

Part

II

Ch

5

Hostname Resolution

Domain Name Service (DNS) is used to convert understandable names to IP numbers. Domain names are the *dot-com* names that have become familiar Internet jargon. When you are on the Internet and you want to connect to a Web site, for example the CNN Web site, you use a name, www.cnn.com. The domain names are really substitutes for the IP address of the computer you are connecting to. Because a string of numbers can be more difficult to remember than words, the use of domain names has become the most common way to connect over the Internet (though you have to admit some of the domain names are also difficult to remember).

Computers don't know how to deal with the names; they want the numbers. DNS servers can tell your computer what number to use for the domain name you've requested. Therefore, you have to tell your computer what DNS server to use when it needs to convert a domain name into an IP address number.

Hostname resolution can be roughly translated as "How is the computer supposed to find the IP address of a domain name (host)?" The settings here include adding, modifying, or removing DNS servers. Two check boxes let you enable features that try to prevent address spoofing and let you know when spoofs are attempted. You really have no reason to turn off this feature. DNS spoofing is a trick used by crackers to assign a domain name to a false address, or vice versa. It makes their activities appear as if they are coming from your computer.

Mail Transport Configuration

Under normal circumstances, the Mail Transport Configuration panel is left to its default settings. This means that the fields are left blank.

> **CAUTION**
>
> Do not change any of these settings unless you know what you are doing. These settings are for your Mail Transport Agent (MTA), usually Sendmail, and are not for setting your email client software.

If all mail sent from your computer should appear to be coming from a different computer, put the setting in the Visible Domain field. This might be used, for example, if your computer's host name is mary.my_company.com but you want all mail to appear to come from just my_company.com, you'd enter that setting here. The default setting is blank, meaning that all mail sent will be identified as coming from your computer.

If your mail is not sent directly from your computer, but is sent to a relay system, you need to identify the Mail Relay Host. If you don't know whether you are using a relay server, ask your network administrator or ISP. If you use a relay server, you'll need to identify the protocol used for relay. The Transport Method setting can be either uucp or smtp. The most common setting is smtp. Check boxes indicate whether the relay server is an Internet Hub or a Local Hub. If you don't know, ask your network administrator or ISP. The default setting for Mail Relay Host is blank, which means that your computer directly handles sending and receiving mail.

System Administration

System administration (see Figure 5.13) includes the most common task on any multiple-user Linux system: Account Administration. This section handles adding new users and updating or deleting user accounts.

FIGURE 5.13
The System
Administration panel.

User Account Administration

Linux user accounts are designed to protect the security of the system, while at the same time giving users private storage of their data. User accounts and group accounts can be created for single user access or for shared group access.

Access rights are based on group assignments and user IDs for files and directories. All these tasks are handled in the User Account Administration, shown in Figure 5.14.

FIGURE 5.14
The User Accounts
panel.

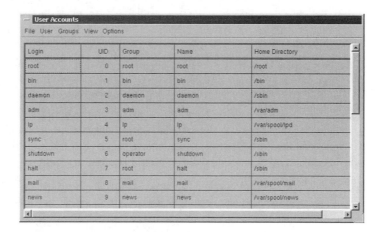

On the menu are four options: File, Actions, View, and Options.

File When all changes and updates have been completed, you exit the User Account tool by selecting File and then clicking Exit.

User   The Actions menu includes the following items:

- **Edit user**—Click on a login name in the list of accounts shown below the Menu line. Then click on Edit user to modify the account information. The options that are available for modification are Full Name, Login shell, password, and Home directory. There is a button to enable or disable logins for the account. The Shadow information button opens a window that contains settings to control password expiration. See Figure 5.15.

FIGURE 5.15
You can modify user accounts by selecting Edit Users on the Actions menu.

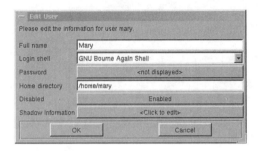

- **Create user**—Clicking Create user opens a window with a space for entering the new user login name. After you've entered a name, a window opens with fields for the new user's Full name, the user ID (UID), the group ID, Login shell, password, and home directory. Logins can be enabled or disabled, and the Shadow Information button opens a window for setting password expiration information. The user ID and group ID are automatically entered using the next available number in the user and group ID sequences. Unless you have a special reason, don't change the numbers that are automatically displayed.

- **Delete user**—Highlight a user login name on the list of accounts and click Delete user to remove a user account. Watch carefully and make sure that the user account you intend to delete is shown as the account that will be deleted. Once you've confirmed that you want to delete the account, you are given the option to remove the user's home directory. This can eliminate an unused directory, but any files that are in the directory cannot be recovered once you've removed the home directory. Make sure there is nothing that needs to be saved in the directory before approving its removal.

Groups   The Groups menu manages groups. Groups are used to assemble users who have files that they need to share. For example, a sales group would have files that they would share among themselves.

The Groups menu has options to create a group, delete a group, rename a group, merge groups, and manage group membership. Select a group on the left panel and the members of the group are displayed in the right panel. To add or remove users from a group, use the Group Membership management option (shown in Figure 5.16).

FIGURE 5.16
Add or remove group
members using the
Group Membership
tool.

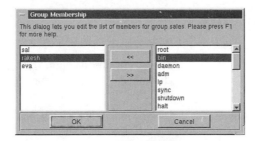

View   The view menu enables you to choose between seeing a list of all users, including system user IDs such as shutdown, mail and users, and regular users. Selecting regular users limits the display to standard user accounts.

Options   You can modify the default preferences by clicking Preferences. You can adjust the beginning user ID number, group assignment policy (the default is that each user is assigned their own unique group identity), the default shell, default password lifetime, and the location of the home directories. Normally, none of the defaults need to be changed.

The Disable shadow passwords option enables you to disable this password security feature. Normally you don't do this.

The Enable NIS lookups option, if clicked on, changes to disable NIS lookups.

Enable/Disable System Services

System services are activated when your system starts up. You can use this tool to see which services are starting on your system. A check mark means that the service is started on system bootup; no check mark means that it isn't started. See Figure 5.17.

FIGURE 5.17
The Enable/Disable
System Services
panel.

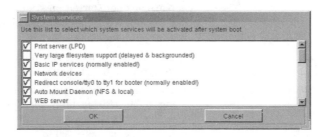

Table 5.1 shows the standard systems found here.

Table 5.1   Standard System Services

Service	Description
Printer server	The line printer daemon (LPD). See Chapter 8 on "Installing and Configuring Printers" for more information.
Very large file system support	Checks and mounts hard disks bigger than 4 gigabytes in background.
Basic IP services	Starts network services listed in /etc/inetd.conf.
Network devices	Starts up networking.
Redirect console	Sets terminal for display of bootup messages.
Auto Mount Daemon	A daemon automatically automounts and unmounts file systems. If the file system is unmounted and a user attempts to access it, it will be automatically remounted.
Web server	Starts the Apache Web server.
Batch server	Runs commands at scheduled times. Used to run system-intensive commands during off-peak hours or run backups at set intervals.
DHCP and BOOTP server	Starts DHCP and BOOTP services for remote assignment of a network address to your system.
GPM Console mouse driver	Starts the mouse driver for non-Windows systems.
Novell Internet Package Exchange	(IPX) networking Starts Novell network support.
IPX RIP/SAP daemon	Starts Novell network services on your system.
Mail Transfer Agent	Starts the mail server.
BSD remote user info daemon	Starts a server that lists all the users on the system. Normally not started on systems with full connections to the Internet because of its potential to be abused by crackers.
rwall daemon	Starts a server that can send messages to users logged onto the system.
BSD remote who daemon	Starts a server that can find out who is currently logged into the system. Normally not started on systems with full connections to the Internet because of its potential to be abused by crackers.
NIS client	Used to connect to an NIS server. The Network Information System centrally manages computers on a UNIX network.
Remote kernel statistics server	Starts a server that collects performance statistics from the kernel. Use the rup command to see the statistics on your system.

Service	Description
Samba SMB server processes	Starts Windows networking on your system. See Chapter 20, "Installing and Configuring a Windows Network with Samba."
Logout daemon	Sets login time restrictions. This daemon is part of the shadow password package. Time and port restrictions are defined in the /etc/porttime configuration file. The system ports are scanned periodically and users are checked against the table of permitted users in porttime. If the user is not specifically permitted on the port at the specified time, the connection will be terminated.
System loggers	Starts various logs of your system.
Cron daemon	Starts the cron scheduler. See Chapter 6, "Understanding and Using the OpenLinux File System."
Network Time Protocol Client/Server	Starts the xntp Network Time Protocol client and server. Synchronizes time on your system with an NTP server on the Internet.

N O T E Many NTP servers are synchronized to the atomic clock at the U.S. Naval Observatory. See the WWW Time Synchronization Server at www.eecis.udel.edu/~ntp/. Normally you would set your server to connect to a secondary server that is synchronized to a primary server like the Naval Observatory atomic clock. Set what the Internet time server your system is to use in the /etc/ntp.conf configuration file. ■

Mounting and Unmounting Disk Drives

On Linux, every disk—from a floppy disk to a zip disk to a hard disk—must be mounted. When OpenLinux was installed, at least one hard disk was mounted at the top root / level of the directory tree.

The File System administration tool, shown in Figure 5.18, displays the disks on your computer and shows where they are mounted on the directory tree (the *mount point*). This tool works with the /mnt/fstab configuration file.

This is one way to mount disks on the system. It has the advantage of showing you all the available disks and many of the mounting options; however, it still requires that you know the file system type of the disk to be mounted—it can't be autodetected here—and you need to know the directory at which the disk is to be mounted. If the directory doesn't already exist, you have to exit the File System administration tool and create the directory before using the mounting tool.

FIGURE 5.18

The File System panel.

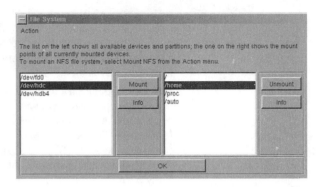

Selecting one of the disks listed on the left panel and clicking Info shows the Linux device name for the disk drive, the directory where it is mounted, the file system type (ext2 is the default Linux type), and any mounting options that have been defined for the disk.

A disk that is shown in the list on the left can be mounted. Just select the disk from the list and click Mount. A panel opens, where you can indicate the system settings for mounting the disk. The Device name is displayed.

The Directory setting indicates the directory in which the disk is to be mounted. This directory must already exist in order for you to mount a disk. The default directory for the CD-ROM drive is /mnt/cdrom. For the floppy disk drive it is /mnt/floppy.

The File System Type setting has to be entered manually if it is not already displayed. Following are some of the more common types:

- **ext2**—Standard Linux
- **iso9660**—CD-ROM
- **minix**—Used for UNIX disks
- **msdos**—DOS disks
- **nfs**—Access to directories on other computers on the network
- **proc**—Process administration
- **swap**—Swap partitions or files
- **vfat**—Windows 95 with long filename support
- **ntfs**—Windows NT file system, read-only support

Clicking on the Options setting button opens a checklist of file system options for the disk drive. The options are

- **Don't mount at boot time**—Enable or disable the automatic mounting of the disk at boot time. Hard disks are usually mounted at boot time; removable disks such as CD-ROMs and floppy disks are usually not mounted on startup.
- **Mount read-only**—File systems can be mounted either with read/write access (rw) or with read-only access (ro). CD-ROMs must be mounted read-only.

- **Any user can mount**—The default setting is that only root can mount disks, but removable disks such as CD-ROMs and floppy disks need to be set so that all users can mount and dismount them.

- **No set-uid binaries**—Generally, execution of programs is allowed, but special programs called *suid programs* are started under the owner or the group of the file rather than under the ID of the logged-in user. The option called No set-uid binaries is usually checked for removable disks, and not checked for hard disks.

- **No /dev files**—This option needs to be checked for all removable disks such as CD-ROMs.

- **No Rockridge extensions**—The standard CD-ROM ISO9660 format restricts filenames to the MS-DOS style of 8+3 characters. The Rockridge extensions allow support for longer filenames plus information about file ownership, and so on.

You can also unmount mounted devices by selecting the directory in which the device is mounted on the right panel and clicking Unmount. Clicking the info button shows the name of the device that is mounted, the name of the directory, the file system type, and the options that have been defined for the device.

System Hostname

You can modify the system hostname by selecting System hostname in the System Administration task list.

System Resource Information

Do you need to know information about your computer system—the kind of processor, its speed, or the processor cache size? The System Resource Information display, shown in Figure 5.19, contains all the essential system information about your computer's CPU.

FIGURE 5.19
The System Resource Information panel.

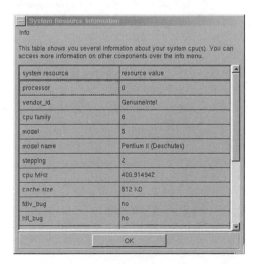

You can obtain other information by clicking Info on the menu line. You can find the following information here:

- **Block devices**—This is a list of the disks and disk-related devices that are registered on your system.

- **Character devices**— This is a list of devices, such as the keyboard, printer, sound, and so on, that are registered on your system.

- **Interrupts**— This is a list of the IRQs on your system and the device that is using the interrupt. This also shows whether an IRQ is being shared, which can be useful for finding interrupt conflicts.

- **System load average**— This is a table that shows the system's load average over three different time periods: one minute, five minutes, and 15 minutes. It also shows the number of currently running processes, the overall number of tasks, and the process ID of the most recent process.

- **I/O ports**— This is a list of I/O ports registered on your system. It shows the start and end addresses, as well as the device that is associated with the port.

- **DMA**— A list of activated DMA channels and the device associated with the channel.

System Clock

You can use this tool to set the current time and the time zone. The time must be entered manually, and in the following format: Day of the week, Date, Month, Year, HH:MM:SS. Following is an example: Wed 18 Aug 1999 17:32:47.

Installing and Removing Software Packages

All the software installed on your OpenLinux system is part of a package. The packages contain all the files necessary to run the software, plus configuration files, information about file locations, and how much disk space the package requires.

When a package is installed, a record is made in the package database. The COAS Install/Remove software package panel opens with a display of the installed package database (see Figure 5.20).

FIGURE 5.20
The Install/Remove
software packages
panel.

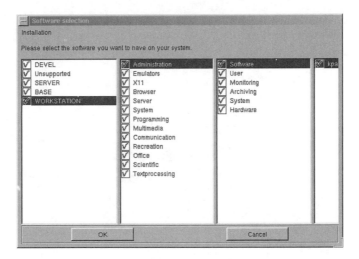

The database is organized by groups and types of software. To uninstall a package, remove the check mark by the package. A blue check mark indicates that the package is installed. No check mark indicates that the package is not installed. A blue check mark on a group or type indicates that all the packages in the group are installed. A green check mark indicates that some of the available packages are not installed.

To install a package, click the menu line Installation, and then select source. Enter the source information for the location of the software package you want to install.

The COAS software installer is still a work in progress and does not have all the features and flexibility that are available in the Kpackage program. You will generally use Kpackage for installing and uninstalling software. See Chapter 4, "Using the KDE Desktops Applications."

Part

II

Ch

5

Understanding and Using the OpenLinux File System

In this chapter

OpenLinux File System Directories

If you have a road map, there's no reason to get lost when you are working in OpenLinux. Following is an explanation of the directories that are found in OpenLinux. Some are easy to figure out and understand; others only a computer programmer can fully understand.

The Linux file system consists of thousands of files. Certain rules have been established concerning which files are typically stored in each of the different standard directories. These rules are summarized in a document called the *File System Hierarchy Standard*, or *FHS*. You can find this document on the FHS Web homepage at www.pathname.com/fhs/.

New users sometimes have a problem finding files, particularly if they don't understand the standard locations for files. Following is an orientation to the file hierarchy structure. First, Table 6.1 contains a short description of the standard file system, followed by sections that include a more detailed explanation of each directory.

Table 6.1   The Standard File System

Directory	What It Contains
/	The root file system
/bin	Programs for startup
/boot	Files for booting up the system (LILO)
/dev	Devices (hard drives, CD-ROMs, and so on)
/etc	System configuration
/home	User home directories
/lib	Shared libraries
/lost+found	Recovered files after file system
/mnt	For mounting devices
/opt	Applications added to the system (Netscape, for example)
/proc	Process information, not a real file system
/root	Home directory for system administrator
/sbin	System programs used for startup and system admin
/tmp	Temporary file space
/usr	Primary collection of program files
/var	Variable data (logs, print and mail spool, and so on)

In addition to the standard file system directories, OpenLinux has these directories:

- **/NetWare**—For accessing Novell NetWare network services. Only exists if you've installed Caldera Systems NetWare services package
- **/auto**—Automount directory. Uses the amd program to automount devices. Default settings are for two floppy drives and a CD-ROM drive. Accessed as /auto/floppy, /auto/floppyz, /auto/cdrom.
- **/bru**—Directory for the Backup and Restore Utility program

- **/initd**—An initial ram disk started by the boot loader to facilitate system startup
- **/install**—Directory used by the installation process

The /root System

The Linux file system hierarchy is commonly referred to as a *tree structure*. The root partition is the top level of the tree, and all the directories branch from it.

The directories can all be on different disk drives or partitions, but because the disk partitions are mounted into the directory tree, the users do not need to know which files are on which disk drive. They only need to know the location of the file on the directory tree.

> **N O T E** The root file system is accessible only to those who log in as the superuser (root) because everything is accessible from the /root system. Restricting access to only the superuser is necessary for system security and to protect user files on a multiple-user system. ■

When the system starts up, the first file system that is mounted is the /root file system. The information about the root system is included in the Linux kernel, but the kernel doesn't know about the rest of the file system. That information is found on the root partition.

If the root system can't be mounted, Linux cannot run. Errors on the root system are a bigger problem than errors on other parts of the file system because they can prevent Linux from starting.

If your system crashes or is not properly shut down, the root system can become corrupted. Because a corrupted system is unstable, Linux automatically checks the partitions on startup after a crash or improper shutdown. The check can take awhile—anywhere from a few minutes to more than half an hour, depending on the size of your drive and the speed of your system.

With serious crashes, you might need to boot from an emergency floppy in order to fix the root file system. See the section later in this chapter that discusses booting in an emergency.

In the event of a serious system error, you can usually mount the partition as read-only and save any data that wasn't backed up.

There's no reason to worry that any serious risk is involved here. Even in serious crashes, data files are rarely lost. The Linux ext2 file system is very reliable and has good built-in protection for data files.

Part
II

Ch
6

/bin Programs for Startup

This directory has basic Linux command files for system startup, and for most of the commonly used commands. Anything in /bin can be executed by all users. All the programs that are used only by the system administrator—the root superuser—are located in /sbin for system startup, and in /usr/sbin for other system administration programs.

Although the name /bin might imply that everything in the directory is binary, this is not the case. The executable commands in /bin include binary files, symbolic links, and shell scripts.

/boot Files for Booting up the System

The /boot directory contains the LILO boot manager files and the boot kernel, which can also be stored in the /root directory as vmlinuz.

This directory also contains a map file with sector information about the location of the kernel. LILO needs the map file because the file system isn't loaded at boot time.

/dev Devices (Hard Drives, CD-ROMs, and so on)

The /dev directory contains all the device files. Almost all the hardware on your system is accessed through the device files. This is an essential directory that must never be removed.

There are two types of devices: *block oriented* and *character oriented*. Block oriented devices include hard disks, floppy disks, and CD-ROMs. Character oriented devices include the keyboard, the printer port, and the modem port.

Table 6.2 explains some of the device names found in the /dev directory.

NOTE The devices are defined in "Linux Allocated Devices," a document maintained by H. Peter Anvin. The devices.txt document can be found on your system in the /usr/src/linux-2.2.10/Documentation directory. ■

Table 6.2 /dev directory Device Names

Name	Description
kbd	Keyboard device
Any device name ending with bm	Bus mouse drivers
Any device name ending with cd	CD-ROM drives
Any device name starting with fd	Floppy disk drives
Any device name starting with hd	IDE disk drives
Any device name starting with lp	Parallel printer interface (such as lpt1, lpt2, and so on in Windows)
port	I/O access port
Any device name starting with sd	SCSI drives
Any device name starting with scd	SCSI CD-ROM drives
Any device name starting with ttyS	Serial interfaces (such as com1, com2, and so on in Windows)

/etc System Configuration

The /etc directory contains the configuration files for the whole system. These files control everything from system startup to network access. Some of the various configuration files that are found in /etc are described later in this chapter.

/home User Home Directories

The /home directory is the directory in which users can save their files. Users are generally restricted from saving files anywhere else on the system. The only exception is the root user. The root user has a home directory called /root because the user home directory is often on a separate disk partition, but root can probably work even if that partition is not accessible for some reason.

Putting the /home directory on its own disk partition prevents users from filling up the entire system with files, which can virtually shut down the system.

Users do not usually have to refer to their home directory by the full path name of /home/ username because when they are logged in, the Linux system automatically puts the user in their home directory.

/lib Shared Libraries

The /lib directory is for shared libraries that are needed for system startup. All other shared libraries can be found in the /usr directory.

/mnt for Mounting Devices

The /mnt directory is the location for mounting removable media such as floppy disks, CD-ROMs, and Zip disks. It is also where NFS-mounted network directories are located. Avoid mounting these systems anywhere else because doing so goes against the FHS rules.

/opt Additional Software Applications

The /opt directory is used for installation of larger programs, usually commercial software. It is the default location for Netscape Communicator, Corel WordPerfect, and StarOffice. Each software package is located in its own directory under /opt. These are *optional* add-on applications; therefore, the directory is named *opt*.

/proc Process Information

The /proc directory is not a real file system. It contains subdirectories for all the running processes. Because it's not really a file system, it doesn't take up any space on the hard drive, and when the computer is shut down it disappears. The name *proc* is short for processes.

Programs that show network statistics usually use the /proc files. One of those programs is the ps command.

/root Home Directory for System Administrator

The system administrator, called the *superuser* or *root*, has a special home directory. It is separate from the user home directories and needs to always be kept on the same partition as the /root directory so that the superuser can log in and have access even if no other partitions are mounted.

/sbin System Programs Used for Startup and System Administration

The /sbin directory contains all the programs that are used for system startup before the /usr file system is mounted. It also contains programs used only by the system administrator. Everything in /sbin can only be executed by root.

The programs in /sbin include the init program, which is used for system startup, and the file system maintenance and repair programs: fdisk, fsck, and mkfs. The network programs ifconfig and route, which initialize the network on startup, are also in this directory.

/tmp Temporary File Space

In the /tmp directory, programs can create temporary files. Check this directory regularly because a full /tmp directory can fill up the whole system drive if it is not on a separate partition.

/usr Primary Collection of Program Files

On a Linux system, the /usr directory takes up the most disk space, aside from user files. This is where almost all the Linux programs are installed.

There are many directories within the /usr directory. Some of the primary directories are described in the following sections.

The /usr/X11R6 Directory   This is where the X Window system files are installed. The name refers to Release 6 of the X Window system. The X Window system on OpenLinux is the Xfree86 server.

The /usr/bin Directory   The /usr/bin directory is the primary program directory on OpenLinux. The main exception is commercial software, which is all installed in the /opt directory.

The /usr/include Directory   The /usr/include directory contains the C library header files.

The /usr/lib Directory   The /usr/lib directory contains the library and object files that are necessary for programming, including the programs used by the GNU C compiler gcc and various other programming languages.

The /usr/local Directory   The /usr/local directory is where files that are not included as part of the standard Linux distribution are usually installed.

The /usr/sbin Directory   The /usr/sbin contains executable programs that are used only by root. System administration programs, network daemons, and servers are found in this directory.

The /usr/src Directory   The /usr/src directory holds the source code files for Linux.

The /var Variable Data Directory

The /var directory has several directories that contain variable data, which means that the data is constantly changing. Following are some of the directories found in /var:

- **log**— System log files and directories for individual logs for the Web server, list server, and so on.
- **nis**—The Network Information System client data.
- **spool**— Spool directories for printing and mail. These spool directories can become quite large.

Configuration Files

Almost everything in OpenLinux is configured with a file found in the /etc directory. This makes configuration easy to maintain. Contrast this with the Windows registry, which is poorly documented and difficult to fix. The following sections describe some of the key configuration files found in /etc and what you need to know about them.

System Startup

When the system is first booted up, the kernel is loaded into memory and starts running. Then the device drivers are initialized. Finally, when the kernel and device drivers are loaded, the init program runs. Init starts the system daemons and other software that are specified in the configuration files.

Daemons are programs that are activated at system startup and then wait in the background until called into action. The name comes from Greek mythology: daemons were guardian spirits. In Microsoft Windows, System Agents perform the same function as Linux daemons. The daemon processes commonly started by Linux include the print spooler (lpd), the Web server (apache), the mail handler (sendmail) the automounter (amd), system loggers, a task scheduler (cron), and various network services.

Linux operates at several run levels. The default run level in OpenLinux is 5, which is the setting for starting up in X Window. Run level 3 is used for a character-mode console. The different run levels are explained in the section on LILO options in Chapter 3, "Configuring the KDE Desktop."

The init program reads the /etc/inittab configuration file, which defines what needs to be started for each different run level.

The standard OpenLinux inittab file looks like this:

```
#
# inittab       This file describes how the INIT process should set up
#               the system in a certain run level.
#
# Author:       Miquel van Smoorenburg, <miquels@drinkel.nl.mugnet.org>
#               Modified for RHS Linux by Marc Ewing and Donnie Barnes
#               Modified for COL by Raymund Will
#

# The runlevels used by COL are:
#   0 - halt (Do NOT set initdefault to this)
#   1 - Single user mode (including initialization of network interfaces,
#       if you do have networking)
#   2 - Multiuser, (without NFS-Server and some such)
#       (basically the same as 3, if you do not have networking)
#   3 - Full multiuser mode
#   4 - unused
#       (should be equal to 3, for now)
#   5 - X11
#   6 - reboot (Do NOT set initdefault to this)
#
# Default runlevel.
id:5:initdefault:

# System initialization.
s0::sysinit:/bin/bash -c 'C=/sbin/booterd; [ -x $C ] && $C'
si::sysinit:/bin/bash -c 'C=/etc/rc.d/rc.modules; [ -x $C ] && $C default'
s2::sysinit:/bin/bash -c 'C=/etc/rc.d/rc.serial; [ -x $C ] && $C'
bw::bootwait:/etc/rc.d/rc.boot

# What to do in single-user mode.
~1:S:wait:/etc/rc.d/rc 1
~~:S:wait:/sbin/sulogin
```

```
l0:0:wait:/etc/rc.d/rc 0
l1:1:wait:/etc/rc.d/rc 1
l2:2:wait:/etc/rc.d/rc 2
l3:3:wait:/etc/rc.d/rc 3
l4:4:wait:/etc/rc.d/rc 4
l5:5:wait:/etc/rc.d/rc 5
l6:6:wait:/etc/rc.d/rc 6
# Normally not reached, but fall through in case of emergency.
z6:6:respawn:/sbin/sulogin

# Trap CTRL-ALT-DELETE
ca:12345:ctrlaltdel:/sbin/shutdown -t3 -r now

# Action on special keypress (ALT-UpArrow).
kb::kbrequest:/bin/echo "Keyboard Request—edit /etc/inittab to let this work."

# When our UPS tells us power has failed, assume we have a few minutes
# of power left.  Schedule a shutdown for 2 minutes from now.
# This does, of course, assume you have powerd installed and your
# UPS connected and working correctly.
pf::powerfail:/sbin/shutdown -h +5 "Power Failure; System Shutting Down"

# If battery is fading fast — we hurry...
p1::powerfailnow:/sbin/shutdown -c 2> /dev/null
p2::powerfailnow:/sbin/shutdown -h now "Battery Low..."

# If power was restored before the shutdown kicked in, cancel it.
po:12345:powerokwait:/sbin/shutdown -c "Power Restored; Shutdown Cancelled"
# Run gettys in standard runlevels
1:12345:respawn:/sbin/getty tty1 VC linux
2:2345:respawn:/sbin/getty tty2 VC linux
3:2345:respawn:/sbin/getty tty3 VC linux
4:2345:respawn:/sbin/getty tty4 VC linux
5:2345:respawn:/sbin/getty tty5 VC linux
6:2345:respawn:/sbin/getty tty6 VC linux

# Run kdm in runlevel 5
kdm:5:respawn:/opt/kde/bin/kdm -nodaemon > /var/log/kdm 2>&1
```

It is not necessary to understand all the different settings described in this file, but you will want to know about some of them.

The default line defines the default startup run level. The line says

```
# Default runlevel.
id:5:initdefault:
```

This tells the system to open up in run level 5, which is the X Window system. It also indicates that each entry in the initab file that specifies run level 5 in the second field of the entry (each field is separated by a colon) is to be initialized. Thus, the following line in inittab says that the K Desktop Manager (kdm) is to be initialized when starting up in run level 5:

```
# Run kdm in runlevel 5
kdm:5:respawn:/opt/kde/bin/kdm -nodaemon > /var/log/kdm 2>&1
```

If you want to change from starting up in X Window to starting up in character-terminal mode, change the 5 to a 3 in the default line and restart the system.

When starting up in run level 5, the following entry in inittab says to run the startup script /etc/rc.d/rc 5:

```
l5:5:wait:/etc/rc.d/rc 5
```

This runs all the scripts contained in the directory /etc/rc.d/rc5.d. These include all the necessary system files; printer, network, and mail daemons; and other files needed to operate the system at the chosen run level.

Equivalent scripts are defined for every run level and can be found in directories named for each run level.

The last script that executes in rc5.d is the S98local script, which is a link to the /etc/rc.d/rc.local file. This is where you put any custom startup programs you want to launch at boot time.

rc.local is a standard shell script, so it can be easily customized if you use a text editor and follow the shell script rules. You can add any startup programs you want to run in the rc.local file. For example, if you have a database that is to be started every time the computer starts up, put the startup command line in rc.local.

The standard rc.local file in OpenLinux looks like this:

```
#!/bin/sh

# This script will be executed *after* all the other init scripts.
# You can put your own initialization stuff in here if you don't
# want to do the full Sys V style init stuff.

if [ -r /etc/.issue ]; then
    cat /etc/.issue > /etc/issue
else
    cat << EOI > /etc/issue

Caldera OpenLinux(TM)
Copyright (C) 1996-1998 Caldera, Inc.

EOI
fi

cp -f /etc/issue /etc/issue.net
echo >> /etc/issue
```

The Profile After Startup   After the system has started up and when you log in, the system reads the profile configuration file found in /etc/profile. The system administrator uses this file to set systemwide parameters.

Following is a standard OpenLinux profile file:

```
# /etc/profile
# $Id$
# Minimum system wide initialization of "login"-bourne shells
# Functions and aliases go in $HOME/.bashrc
#[ -e /etc/config.d/D ] && echo "/etc/profile: \$-='$-'" 1>&2
_ETC_PROFILE=1

PATH="/bin:/usr/bin"

umask 022
if [ ! -x /usr/bin/id ]&&[ -z "$USER" -o -z "$UID" ]; then
  echo "/usr/bin/id: no such file!" 1>&2
  echo "  As this program is essential for OpenLinux shell-initialization" 1>&2
  echo "  you'll experience problems later!  Please install 'sh-utils'..." 1>&2
  [ -z "$USER" ] && USER=unknown
  [ -z "$UID" ] && UID=-1
else
  [ -z "$USER" ] && USER=`/usr/bin/id -un`
  [ -z "$UID" ] && UID=`/usr/bin/id -u`
fi

[ -z "$HOST" ] && HOST=`/bin/hostname -f`
[ -z "$HOSTNAME" ] && HOSTNAME=`/bin/hostname -s`
[ -z "$LOGNAME" ] && LOGNAME=$USER

export _ETC_PROFILE PATH USER HOST HOSTNAME LOGNAME
```

Some things that are usually added to the profile file include pathnames for special programs such as databases or environmental variables that are needed by applications that are used by everyone on the system.

Managing Users

Although managing user accounts is better done through COAS, the user account files are actually just configuration files found in the /etc directory.

Every user account is a line in the /etc/passwd file.

Each line has seven fields that are separated by a colon. The format of each line is

```
login-name:password:user-ID:group-ID:full-name:home-directory:shell
```

Table 6.3 explains each field.

Table 6.3   User Account Fields in the /etc/passwd File

Field	Description
login-name	The user's login name.
password	Should show only an x, indicating that shadow passwords are being used. If this default has been modified, an encrypted copy of the user's password is shown. Passwords are never entered here, but rather by using the passwd command.
user-ID	The ID number assigned to the user.
group-ID	The ID number for the group of which the user is a member.
full-name	Usually contains the user's full name, but you can enter any sort of text here.
home-directory	The absolute pathname of the user's home directory.
shell	The absolute pathname of the user's default shell, usually /bin/bash.

Normally, encrypted passwords are stored in the /etc/shadow file because /etc/passwd has to be readable by any user on the system for proper logging in. The /etc/shadow file is readable by only the root superuser.

Every user account has an entry line in the /etc/shadow file.

Each line has nine fields that are separated by a colon. The format of each line is

```
login-name:password:last-modified:min:max:warn:inactive:expire:flag
```

Table 6.4 explains each field.

Table 6.4   User Account Fields in the /etc/passwd File

Field	Description
login-name	The user's login name.
password	Shows an encrypted copy of the user's password.
last-modified	A number that indicates when the password was last modified.
min	The minimum number of days that must elapse before the password can be changed.
max	The maximum number of days before the password must be changed.
warn	The number of days before the password expires to start giving warning.
inactive	The number of grace days after a password has expired before the account is inactivated.
expire	The date on which the password expires. This is a number based on the number of days since January 1, 1970.
flag	Reserved for future use.

Managing File Systems

When the system starts, it looks at the /etc/fstab file for disk partition mounting instructions. This file is also used whenever you mount or unmount a removable disk.

Following is a sample fstab file:

```
/dev/hda5 / ext2 defaults  1  1
/dev/hda2 swap swap defaults  0 0
/dev/hda6 /home ext2 defaults  1  2
/proc /proc proc defaults 0 0
/dev/fd0 /mnt/floppy msdos defaults,user,noauto 0 0
/dev/hdc /mnt/cdrom iso9660 ro,user,noauto 0 0
/dev/hdb4 /mnt/zip vfat defaults,user,noauto 0 0
```

The fstab file has six fields, although only the first four are necessary.

The fields contain

- The device name. For example, in the first line of the sample file, the first device is /dev/hda5, which indicates that it is partition 5 on the first IDE hard disk.
- The directory in which the device is to be mounted, commonly referred to as the *mount point*.
- The file system or device type.
- Mounting options such as read-only.
- If present, a number used to determine when the dump utility, if used, is to back up the file system.
- If present, a number used by the fsck utility to determine the order in which the file systems are checked.

Running Jobs on a Schedule

cron is a system for scheduling and executing tasks on your Linux system. When you start your system, the crond daemon is started; it reads the configuration files in the /etc/crontab and /var/spool/cron directories.

The /etc/crontab file was automatically generated during installation. The standard default file looks like this:

```
SHELL=/bin/bash
PATH=/sbin:/bin:/usr/sbin:/usr/bin
MAILTO=root

# IMPORTANT! All scripts/commands run by cron with root-privileges
# should be written with security in mind!!!
#
# A common problem is related to temporary files residing in world-writable
```

Part
II

Ch
6

```
# directories (esp. /tmp).  As most GNU utilities (at least sort(1)) respect
# a TMPDIR environment variable it should be used!
# To support this, there are some helper functions in the cronloop hierarchy
# (currently /etc/cron.d/lib/functions), namely cronloop_mk_TMPDIR and
# cronloop_rm_TMPDIR, for handling sufficiently(?) uniq temporary directories
# (exemplary usage may be inspected in Daily/50updatedb).

# Run any at jobs every minute (ONLY if 'atd' is NOT running!)
#* * * * * root [ -x /usr/sbin/atrun ] && /usr/sbin/atrun

# run-parts
03   3   1   *   * root [ -x /usr/sbin/cronloop ] && /usr/sbin/cronloop Monthly
04   4   *   *   6 root [ -x /usr/sbin/cronloop ] && /usr/sbin/cronloop Weekly
05   5   *   *   * root [ -x /usr/sbin/cronloop ] && /usr/sbin/cronloop Daily
42   *   *   *   * root [ -x /usr/sbin/cronloop ] && /usr/sbin/cronloop Hourly

# extensions...

# e.g if you want to have locatedb be built by daemon
# (additional provision have to be taken to allow write access to the
database!)
#55   5   *   *   * daemon /etc/cron.d/lib/update-locatedb
```

cron is used for system maintenance—and anything else that needs to be done on a regular schedule. The crontab file format has five fields. They are, in order

1. Minute (possible values are 0–59)
2. Hour (possible values are 0–23)
3. Day of month (possible values are 0–31)
4. Day of week (possible values are 0–7, with Sunday being represented by both 0 and 7; or the first three letters of a day's name)
5. Command (the command to be executed)

In each of the time/date fields, the numbers can be ranges, such as 4–6. Also, an asterisk (*) indicates that the command is to be run in the entire range of the field.

A cronttab file can be created using the following command:

```
crontab -e
```

This opens up a user crontab file in the vi editor. To use the K Editor, first change the EDITOR environment variable:

```
export EDITOR=kedit
```

Then start crontab -e.

All entries in crontab must follow the field format exactly.

You can use cron to run any job that you want to run regularly without having to run it manually yourself. One of the most common uses for cron is to schedule system backups. For example, if you want to do a regular backup of all user files onto a DAT tape that's at /dev/tape (your setup might be different), at 2 a.m. on Monday through Friday, and using the tar command, you enter the following line in crontab:

```
0 2 * * 1-5 /bin/tar czvf  /dev/tape /home
```

This says that at 2 a.m. on Monday through Friday (1–5), tar will copy all files from the /home directory to the device found at /dev/tape.

Managing Logs

Linux generates a number of logs, which you won't find on Windows or Macintosh systems. Logs are very useful for keeping track of what is happening on your system and for finding problems when they come up. Logs can also grow in size, so they are regularly rotated, that is, removed from the system. You can do this manually or you can add it to the crontab schedule.

Linux has two kinds of logs: *system logs* and *application logs*. System logs contain information about what modules are loaded, login attempts, and almost every kind of activity taking place on the system. The standard system log file is /var/log/messages. The standard mail log is /var/log/maillog.

The configuration /etc/syslog.conf defines what is to be logged and where to log it.

Booting up in an Emergency

What do you do if you can't boot your hard drive? You can use your emergency boot disk. Here's how to do it.

The first thing you need to do is obtain the installation floppy disk. If your computer can boot from a CD-ROM, you can use your installation CD. Either of these can be your emergency boot disk.

If you don't have an installation floppy disk and your computer won't boot from the CD, you'll have to create an installation floppy disk.

Creating a Disk on a Windows System

Use the following steps to create the installation floppy disk on a Windows computer:

1. Insert a blank floppy disk.
2. In Windows, click on the Create Install Diskette in the OpenLinux program group.
3. A DOS window opens; type in the drive letter for the blank disk.
4. An installation disk is then created.

Part
II

Ch
6

If you don't have the OpenLinux Windows software installed on the Windows computer, insert the OpenLinux CD into the CD-ROM drive. The installation program starts. If it doesn't, run the SETUP program found in the WINSETUP directory of the CD.

On the main menu, choose Install Products. On the Install Options menu, choose Create Floppy Install Diskettes.

Creating a Disk on a DOS System

Use the following steps to create the installation floppy disk with DOS:

1. Boot the computer in DOS.
2. Insert the OpenLinux CD.
3. Take a formatted floppy disk and put it in the floppy disk drive. This example uses D: as the disk drive for the CD-ROM; you want to use the correct drive letter for your system.
4. At the DOS prompt, type each of the following commands, followed by the Enter key:

```
d:
cd \col\launch\floppy
install
```

This starts the RAWRITE program, which prepares the floppy disk with the installation boot files.

Creating a Disk on a Linux System

You can use the following steps to create a disk from an existing OpenLinux system:

1. Put the OpenLinux CD into the CD-ROM drive.
2. Open a terminal window and mount the OpenLinux CD:

```
mount /mnt/cdrom
```

3. Change to the directory on the CD with the floppy disk installation image:

```
cd /mnt/cdrom/col/launch/floppy
```

Then enter the following command:

```
dd if=install.144 of=/dev/fd0
```

The Emergency Boot Procedure

Now, if you can't boot your computer, you're already prepared with an emergency boot disk. Follow these steps to boot with the emergency disk:

1. Boot from your installation CD or the installation floppy.

2. When you see the `boot:` prompt, enter the following command:

   ```
   boot root=/dev/hda1
   ```

3. Where it says /dev/hda1, put in the partition to which you installed Linux. For example, if you only have OpenLinux on your computer, it is probably /dev/hda1. If you have a workstation that you share with Windows, the OpenLinux partition might be /dev/hda2.

   This boots the system and puts you into OpenLinux with the KDE desktop environment. To boot the system to a character-mode terminal, add the number 3 for run level 3:

   ```
   boot root=/dev/hda1 3
   ```

After booting this way, you are on a working system and can proceed to find the problem. Also, you can safely back up any data files this way.

Part

II

Ch

6

Using the Character Mode Terminal

Why Use a Character Mode Terminal?

Almost every computer system now uses a Windows or Macintosh style interface. Sun Microsystems uses the CDE desktop on the Ultrasparc. OpenLinux, uses the KDE windowing environment. You can do almost everything from the K Desktop. In fact, when I showed a UNIX expert from a big telecommunications company OpenLinux with KDE, he got excited. He hates all that typing and keyboard stuff. He'd heard about Linux, but he hadn't tried it because he thought that using Linux meant going back to the old ways. He hates a character mode terminal that makes you type everything, where you can't use a mouse to point and click, or cut and paste. His hands and wrists ache from years of typing. When he saw the KDE Desktop, he was sold right away. He now uses OpenLinux his computer at home.

For most of what is being done on the computer, including systems administration, windowing is usually a better way to work, but Linux was built on command-line systems tools and utilities. Some tasks still have to be done from a command line on a terminal. You can do this while you are in KDE by opening up a terminal window with kvt, the K virtual terminal. Alternatively, you can start OpenLinux in terminal (console) mode and work directly from the command line.

Understanding the character-mode shell gives you more control over your computer. After all, the KDE Desktop runs on top of the shell, and many of its functions are controlled by—and sometimes limited by—the shell.

In this chapter, you'll find how to work with a character-mode terminal. Remember, however, when you are doing this that Linux is case sensitive. Run, rUn, and RUN are three different things when Linux looks at them.

Bash Basics

Linux uses a *shell* to communicate between the user and the system. A shell is really just another program; it gives you a prompt, takes simple, easy-to-remember commands, and interprets them into computer language.

Linux shells look a lot like DOS, and if you know how to use DOS, you won't have any trouble getting around on a Linux terminal. However, a Linux shell can do much more than DOS, so you'll want to know about all the additional features.

Many shells are available for Linux, but the standard shell is *Bash*, the *Bourne Again Shell*. Because Bash is standard on all Linux distributions, knowing Bash is useful for working on any Linux terminal.

Bash is an enhanced version of the Bourne shell commonly found on UNIX systems. The original Bourne shell found on UNIX systems does not have many of the advanced features found in other shells. The Bash shell developed for Linux adds many of the best features found in the Korn shell and the C shell.

The shell handles executing a program when you enter the appropriate command. The shell also has its own internal set of commands. These commands are often the same no matter which shell you are using, but not all commands work exactly the same way from one shell to the next. Moreover, some commands are unique to a particular shell.

Sometimes you'll need to know what shell you are using. I've had programs fail to install because I wasn't using the shell it expected. This has happened only when I've been working with software that was originally developed for a different UNIX platform.

How Knowing the Shell Solved a Mystery

I'll give you an example where the shell created a problem. I installed a statistical analysis program, following the instructions exactly. It seemed to work, but it kept freezing when I used a certain function. I checked and rechecked everything. Nothing got it to work.

Finally, I had a programmer look at the code for the module I was using. He noticed a line of code issuing a command that doesn't exist on Bash, but is a standard part of the C shell (csh). It was an obscure line of code for something that's not frequently used, but was necessary for the particular function I needed. He patched the code and everything was fixed. The module was originally developed for a different UNIX system that uses the C shell as its standard.

Here's what you'll be using with a Bash shell and how to get the most out of it:

- **Logging in**—The way you login determines what you can and can't do during your session at the terminal.

- **Shell startup files**—You can use Bash startup files to control the working environment.

- **Aliases**—Instead of typing out a lot of commands, you can make a simple alias that does the task.

- **Command history and completion**—After you've typed a command once, you can recall the command, modify it if you want, and run it again. Also, keyboard shortcuts can complete commands and simplify typing.

- **Pipes**—Pipes enable you to string together multiple commands.

- **Redirecting input or output**—You can put the output of one program into a file or send it to another program, which saves you time and retyping.

- **Wild cards**—Wildcards make typing commands easier.

- **Job control**—In Linux, you can run more than one command at a time. This is known as *multitasking*. Commands can be run in the foreground or background. You want to control the jobs, see what is running, and if you need to, start or stop a command.

Logging In

The way you log in determines what you can and can't do during your session at the terminal. Unlike Windows 95/98 or Macintosh systems, Linux is designed to be a multiple-user system. This means that more than one person can be using the computer at the same time (if everyone is connected through a network).

When you installed OpenLinux, you created a superuser called root and also a regular user. If you login as a regular user, you have certain *rights* on the system. These rights are limited to your own files. You cannot make any changes to other users files or to the system files. If you login as root, your rights aren't limited in any way.

Therefore, if you need to do system administration or install new software, you need to login as root. These are the only times you want to login as root. Doing routine work as root is dangerous. It's too easy to make a mistake from which you can't recover.

After you login, you'll see a command prompt. This looks similar to the command prompt on a computer running DOS, but it's very different. Linux has different prompts, depending on how you login. If you login as root the prompt is the # symbol. If you login as a regular user, the prompt is a $ symbol.

The prompts are defined by the Bash shell and vary so that you can see what your rights are right away.

When you want to do the tasks of root, you don't have to log out as a regular user and log back in as root. You can use the su (switch user, not superuser as some think) command. If you enter the command su and press the Enter key, you become the superuser. You can also enter the command su followed by another username to switch to that user, if you know the password. When you switch user to root, the prompt changes from a $ to # so you can see that you have all the privileges of root.

As with almost everything about Linux, you can change the way the prompt is displayed. The PS1 variable can be set to change your prompt. If you want to have your prompt display the phrase "What's next?" just type

```
PS1="What's next?"
```

This is what your command prompt becomes. No more $. This is only a temporary change, though. After you exit the terminal, the prompt resets to the original setting. If you want the prompt changed every time you log in, see the next section on startup files.

There are special character codes for the prompt. For example, if you want to display the username before the $ prompt, you'd type:

```
PS1="\u \$"
```

If your username is Mary, you have a command prompt that looks like this:

```
Mary $
```

To use the time code in a prompt you can type:

```
PS1="\t >"
```

which gives you a prompt that looks like this:

```
14:22:45 >
```

Here are some of the other prompt codes:

- \d—Displays the date.
- \h—Displays the hostname of the computer.
- \w—Displays the current working directory.

You can also combine the codes for multiple effects.

```
PS1="\d (\u) \$"
```

gives a prompt that looks like this, if the username is Mary:

```
Thu Apr 1 (Mary) $
```

Shell Startup Files

You can use Bash startup files to control the working environment, and you can customize Bash to work exactly the way you want it to. New users don't usually change the way Bash works, but after awhile, when you know more about Linux, you might want to take advantage of this feature.

There are a number of different Bash startup files. They are created automatically if they are needed, and you need to know about them only if you want to make custom changes. Here they are, in the order that they are accessed:

- **/etc/profile**—This is the first configuration file, and is set for all users on the system. After reading profile, Bash looks in the user's home directory for the next configuration files.
- **.bash_profile**— This is a Bash configuration file that runs on login.
- **.bash_login**— If it exists, this is the same as .bash_profile. If .bash_profile exists, this file is ignored.
- **.profile**— This is the same as .bash_profile. If either .bash_profile or .bash_login exists, this file is ignored. This is the personal configuration file used by the version of Bash included with OpenLinux. The other two files are not automatically created. This is where you can put your own custom changes for the Bash shell.
- **.bashrc**— This is a Bash shell initialization file that is executed whenever a non-login shell is started. This file is executed, for example, every time you use the su command.

Part
II

Ch
7

Typically, you won't find all these different startup files. On OpenLinux, you'll probably only find the /etc/profile, .profile, and .bashrc files, and you can put all your changes in your own .profile file.

If you want a customized prompt to appear every time you log in, add the appropriate PS1 command line to the .profile file. You can use any text editor to do this. If you're not sure about a text editor, see the later section of this chapter on the vi editor. If you are in the K Desktop, you can do this with Kedit.

If you are going to edit the file, don't forget that it starts with a dot. That's the way Linux hides files. Most Linux programs and commands automatically ignore files starting with a dot. Almost all these are system configuration files.

One of the most common things to add to the .profile file is an *alias*, which I explain in the next section. You can take any alias you create and put it in your own Bash profile so that every time you login, you can use that alias.

A setting that is sometimes changed in your original Bash profile is the PATH variable. The PATH is a list of directories.

When you enter a command, the shell looks through the directories in your PATH to find it. This PATH is set by root in the /etc/profile file and is common for all users. Sometimes you need to add a directory to your own profile. For example, if you want to add a directory from your home directory (called "personal") to your PATH, you add this line to the .profile file:

```
PATH=$PATH:$HOME/personal
```

Using $PATH indicates that you are keeping the current PATH information. $HOME is the standard Bash variable indicating your home directory. Bash has many more variables, a full list of which is on the manual pages. Typing the following command displays a summary of the options:

```
man bash
```

Aliases

Instead of typing out a lot of commands, you can make a simple alias to do the task. Aliases are the short names you give to commands.

If you type the word alias at the command prompt, you see a list of the aliases that have already been set up on your computer. In the standard OpenLinux setup, typing alias shows the following list of predefined aliases. The alias name is display and the command executed by the alias is shown after the equal sign:

- alias h='history'—Executes the history command to display a list of previously entered commands.
- alias j='jobs -l'—Executes the jobs command with the -l parameter to display a list in long format of jobs being run in background.

- `alias l='ls -Fax'`—Executes the `ls` command with the `-Fax` parameter to display a file list showing all files (a), in a multiple-column format (x), and adding / at the end of names of directories (F).

- `alias ll='ls -Alg'`—Executes the `ls` command with the `-Alg` parameter to display a file list showing all files except the . and ..(A), in the long format (l), displaying non-printable characters in filenames as the character ? (q).

- `alias pd='pushd'`—Executes the Bash `pushd` command to add directories to the directory list. The shell can remember directories in this list. The list is displayed with the command `dirs`; `popd` changes back through the directories in the list.

- `alias which='type -path'`—Executes the Bash `type` command to display full directory path information for any command named after you enter the word which, such as **which ls**.

- `alias z='suspend'`—Executes the Bash `suspend` command to stop the execution of a shell until a restart signal is sent.

These commands might not make a lot of sense to you if you are a new user of Linux, but it does show how aliases work.

You can create your own alias very easily. Say you want to make a shortcut for exiting. You can type the following to use x as that shortcut:

`alias x='exit'`

That's a simple alias. Try it and you'll see how easy it is to do (though if you use it, it exits and forces you to log in again). Be careful when you create an alias—if there are spaces on either side of the equal sign, it won't work.

People who are already used to using DOS often create a set of alias shortcuts that assign the familiar DOS command to its Bash equivalent. Here are some examples:

- `alias copy='cp -i'`—Creates a DOS-like `copy` command for copying files using the Bash `cp` command. The `-i` parameter forces the command to get an OK from you before overwriting an existing file.

- `alias rename='mv -i'`—Creates a DOS-like `rename` command to change file names using the Bash `mv` command. The `-i` parameter forces the command to get an OK from you before overwriting an existing file.

- `alias md='mkdir'`—Creates a DOS-like `md` command for creating new directories using the Bash `mkdir` command.

- `alias rd='rmdir'`—Creates a DOS-like `rd` command to delete a directory using the Bash `rmdir` command. Use cautiously because it does not ask for confirmation before deleting the directory.

You'll find a list of DOS commands and their equivalents in Linux later in this chapter.

Part
II

Ch
7

An alias can include command-line arguments—that is, additional information for the command. This is an example:

```
alias cdm='cd /home/mary/myfiles'
```

This creates a shortcut to the directory with Mary's personal files.

If you want the aliases you've created to be available every time you log in, add them to your .profile file.

Command History and Completion

After you've typed a command once, you can recall the command, modify it if you want, and run it again. This is called *command history*.

To go back in history, use the Up Arrow key on your keyboard. This shows you the previous command you typed. Press the Up Arrow key again, and it displays the one before that, and so on. You can use the Down Arrow key to move down the history list.

You can then run the previous command by pressing the Enter key, or you can use the Left Arrow and Right Arrow keys to move along the command line and edit the command. This is useful if you typed in a command but mistyped a letter. Use the Up Arrow key to display the command you mistyped, use the Left Arrow key to move to the mistake, press the Del key to delete the mistake, and use the Ins key to insert one or more characters.

The default size for command history is 500, meaning the number of events kept in the list.

Command completion refers to keyboard shortcuts that can complete commands without all that typing. Sometimes you can type in just part of a command and the Bash shell can do the rest. This is done with the Tab key.

You can do this for any Bash command. For example, if you are in Mary's home directory and want to go to the myfiles directory, type the command as

cd myfiles

To use command completion, you'd type

cd m<Tab key>

The display then shows

```
cd myfiles/
```

You'll have to press the Enter key to execute the command.

Pipes

Pipes enable you to string together a series of commands. This is done with the vertical bar (¦), or pipe character, on your keyboard.

Pipe is short for *pipelines*. You are creating a pipeline between multiple commands, sending the results from one command to the other. The simple form is command1 ¦ command2. A simple pipe follows:

ls -l ¦ less

This starts the file listing command (ls), modified with the -l argument so that it shows the listing in the long format. The results are sent to the less command, which displays the results page by page.

You can combine a number of commands with pipes. Here's an example:

ls -l ¦ grep .txt ¦ lp

This lists all the files in the directory and sends the results to the grep command, which searches the list for any occurrence of characters *.txt*. Then, all lines that have the characters *.txt* in them are sent to the lp command, which prints them.

Redirecting Input or Output

Redirecting input or output refers to changing the location the input comes from or the location where the output goes. Normally, input comes from the keyboard, and output goes to the monitor. This is called *standard input* and *standard output*.

The most common use of redirection is to create a file from output that is normally just displayed on the monitor. The following command redirects output:

ls -l > filelist

Normally, the ls command displays its list of files on the monitor, but use of the > symbol redirects the list to a file called filelist. Useful files can be created this way. You can create a short text file using redirection and the cat command. One of my favorite uses of redirection is when a user wants to have his email forwarded to another email address. A file must be created in the user's home directory called .forward. That file contains the email address to send all mail to. To do this, type the following:

cat > .forward

This opens a file called .forward. Everything you type after that is put into the file. Type the forwarding address, be sure to press the Enter key at the end, and then type Ctrl+D to close the file.

Input redirection isn't as commonly used, but it enables you to run a program that needs keyboard input. You can use the < character to designate a file that the program is to use instead of keyboard input.

Wild Cards

Wildcards make typing commands easier. DOS and Windows users might already be familiar with wildcards. If you are familiar with the DOS command, however, you'll find a difference here.

Because the shell does the interpreting, you can use wildcards anywhere and at any time in Linux, and they always work the same way. In DOS, each program determines whether to accept wildcards and how to interpret them. You never know what you'll get from program to program.

Wildcards enable you to perform a task for a group of files with similar names without having to type in each name individually. Wildcards are technically called *metacharacters*, which means characters that have a special definition by the shell.

The Bash shell supports three wildcards:

- ?
- *
- []

The ? wildcard is used to match a single character in a filename. You might use it, for example, if you have created a series of reports called report1, report2, report3, and report4. If you want to print all the reports, use the ? wildcard as follows:

```
lpr report?
```

The shell expands this command so that all four reports are sent to the printer using the lpr command. However, if you had more reports and the numbers exceeded a single digit, the ? wildcard won't work. If you had a file named report10, it would not be printed. For that, you need to use ?? or the next wildcard.

The * wildcard can match a single character or multiple characters. Thus, typing the following command prints all the files that print using a single ? wildcard plus the file named report10 and any other file that starts with the word *report*

```
lpr report*
```

Both the ? wildcard and the * wildcard can be used anywhere in a filename.

The pair of brackets indicate a list of characters to use as wildcards. For example, if you want to print only some of your files starting with the name report, you can issue the following command:

```
lpr report[4-8]
```

This prints the files named report4, report5, and so on to report8.

Job Control

In Linux, you can run more than one command at a time. This is known as *multitasking*. Commands can be run in the foreground or background. You want to be capable of controlling the jobs, see what is running, and, if you need, to stop or start a command.

Foreground operations are what you see in front of you on the monitor. If you start a process in the foreground, it takes control until it is done. If you are editing a file using the vi editor, for example, you can't be doing anything else as long as you have the file open.

Multitasking is easy to do in the KDE windowing environment—you just open two different terminal windows. But what if you only have access to a single character-mode console? You can still do multitasking by using the capabilities of the Bash shell. You can send the vi editor into the background and start a second process. To do this, you enter the following commands:

```
CTRL-Z
bg
```

The CTRL-Z command suspends the current process, in this example vi. The bg command sends it into background. After you've typed these commands, you'll have the shell prompt back. You can then start another command. To get the process sent to background back to the foreground, type the fg command.

CTRL-Z suspends the process so that you can do something else, but if you want to run a command in background, you can do that by using &.

For example, if you want to find all the files on your system that are named *memo*, you can use the following command:

```
find / -name "memo" > find.memo &
```

The find command searches your entire system, which can take several minutes if you have a big system with lots of files on it. Using the command this way searches the whole system, redirects the output into a file named find.memo, and makes the whole process run in the background by using &. In the meantime, you can do other work.

Basic File Operations

You're looking at the computer terminal, and you have only a prompt in front of you. How do you move around the different directories, copy files, look at what's in the files, and do the rest of what you need to do? The following commands can get you where you're going.

The File System

Linux treats files differently than in DOS, Windows, or the Macintosh operating system. Linux treats everything as a file in a common directory structure. This is called a *tree structure*, with a top *root* level in place, and with *branches* coming off the root level.

Part
II

Ch
7

> **N O T E** Don't be confused by the terminology. Here, *root* does not refer to the superuser. The same word is being used to refer to two completely different things. ▣

The branches are called *directories*. Each directory can have *subdirectories*. Directories are used like folders in a filing cabinet, which is why they are represented by folder icons on the K Desktop.

Files in DOS, Windows, and Macintosh systems are either executable programs or data such as text files created by a word processing program.

In Linux, data and executable programs are files, but so are the hardware components of your computer. The keyboard, monitor, network card, modem, CD-ROM, and any other device on your computer are all treated as files. When you use one of these devices, Linux does it by reading from or writing to one of the device files.

Directories

The root directory, which is referred to with a single slash (/), is the base that holds the other directories. I explained the standard directory structure in Chapter 6, "Understanding and Using the OpenLinux File System."

You can also add other file systems to the directory structure. For example, you can mount the hard drive of another computer on the network onto your computer, and it appears as part of the directory structure. This is commonly used in networks where the hard drives of other computers on a network are mounted on a primary network server. Everyone on the network can then access those other hard drives by changing to the appropriate directory on the primary server.

Directory Terms The directory structure is referred to with certain terms. Here's a short definition of some of the most common directory terms:

- **Home**—Each user has a home directory where he keeps his files. The overall home directory for all users is found in /home, and each user has a subdirectory in /home. A user named Mary, for example, has a home directory named /home/mary.
- **Parent**— The directory above the current working directory.
- **Root**— The top level of the file system. All directories and subdirectories are contained in the root directory. All devices such as disk drives, the mouse, and keyboard are accessed from directories off of the root directory.
- **Subdirectory**— A directory within a directory.
- **Working directory**— The directory you are currently working in.

Accessing Removable Disks, CD-ROMs

Accessing disk drives in Linux is handled by changing to the appropriate directory, but accessing removable media has an extra step.

Because Linux is a multiple-user system, removable media such as floppy disks, Zip and Jaz disks, as well as CD-ROMs have to be mounted before you can access them. This is a safety feature to prevent any file corruption that might happen from opening or closing a removable disk while someone is trying to access it or has a file open.

Mounting and dismounting disks means connecting and disconnecting them from the directory tree. The parts of the directory tree where the disks are connected are called *mount points*.

The standard OpenLinux installation creates mount points for floppy disks and CD-ROMs. These are file subdirectories called floppy and cdrom and are located in the /mnt directory. The configuration information for these mount points is defined in the fstab configuration file in the /etc directory. For more information on fstab and configuration, see Chapter 6.

In the character-mode terminal, you can mount a floppy disk by inserting the disk into the drive and then entering the following command:

```
mount /mnt/floppy
```

This makes the disk available for your use. To mount a CD-ROM, change the word floppy to cdrom. To remove the disk, you must first dismount it by using the umount command. The following dismounts a CD-ROM:

```
umount /mnt/cdrom
```

Sometimes you issue a mount or dismount command and Linux refuses it. Most often, this has to do with permissions. Sometimes the system is set up so that only the superuser can mount disks. In that case, unless you are logged in as root, you won't be capable of making a removable disk available. Permissions can also cause problems when you attempt to dismount a disk and you 'aren't the user that originally mounted the disk. For more information on permissions, see the later section in this chapter on controlling access to files.

Mounting and dismounting disks are the kind of common tasks that can be simplified by using aliases. Following are some sample aliases that can make the task easier:

- alias cdrom="mount -v /mnt/cdrom"
- alias ucdrom="umount -v /mnt/cdrom"
- alias floppy="mount -v /mnt/floppy"
- alias ufloppy="umount -v /mnt/floppy"

With these aliases, you can mount a floppy disk by simply typing the command floppy, and dismount it with the command ufloppy. The -v means *verbose*, which means Linux displays a message telling you what it is doing when it executes the command.

Part

II

Ch

7

Moving Around Directories

With directories as the basic structure, you'll to know how to move around directories. The first command you'll want to know is pwd. It stands for *print working directory*. If you enter the command at your Bash prompt, the result is a display of the directory you are currently in. Because directory structures in Linux can get deep and complex, finding exactly what subdirectory you are in is useful in moving around and working on the system.

You can move from one directory to another using the change working directory command cd. You need to use the exact directory name you want to change to, including the whole directory structure. If you want to go to the personal directory in Mary's home directory, typing **cd personal** won't get you there unless you are already in Mary's home directory. In most cases, you change directories by typing **cd /home/mary/personal**.

If you are in the /home/mary/personal directory, you can use a double dot to move up one level. To do this, you need to know that Linux represents the current working directory with a period, called a single dot and it represents the parent directory with two dots. The following command moves the working directory from /home/mary/personal to /home/mary:

cd ..

N O T E   You must put a space between the cd and the two dots or the command won't work. ■

Another shortcut is to use the tilde symbol. It refers to your home directory. At any point, you can enter the following command, and it moves you to your home directory:

cd ~

You can also use the tilde symbol in other commands as shorthand for your home directory.

Listing Files

The ls command lists all the files in a directory. It is similar to the DOS dir command. In fact, if you are used to using dir in DOS, go ahead and use it. The two commands are similar in Linux.

Typing the command **ls** shows a list of all the files in the current working directory.

Adding a file descriptor to ls limits the listing to files that match the description, as in

ls *.txt

Figure 7.1 shows the output of this command.

FIGURE 7.1

The output of an `ls` `*.txt` command.

Designating a directory lists all the files found in that directory, like so:

`ls /usr/local/bin`

Figure 7.2 shows the output of this command.

FIGURE 7.2

The output of an `ls` `/usr/local/bin` command.

The `ls` command lists files with just their names. Adding the `-l` flag lists files in the long format, with details on file size and also the time and date the file was saved:

`ls -l`

Figure 7.3 shows the output of this command.

FIGURE 7.3

The output of an `ls` `-l` command.

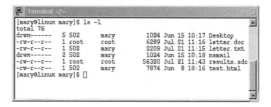

You can use many other flags with `ls`. Some of the most common are the following:

- **-A**—Includes hidden files.
- **-F**—Adds a slash after the filename for directories, an asterisk after executable files, and an at-sign (@) for linked files.
- **-r**—Reverses the order of the file list.
- **-t**—Lists files in order of time modified, latest first, instead of by name.

Viewing File Content

Sometimes you want to see what's contained in a file. The three most common commands used to view files are cat, more, and less.

Viewing a File with *cat* The simplest is the cat command, which is short for *concatenate*. The cat command is designed to concatenate, (join together) multiple files. In this case, you enter cat file1 file2 > file3, which combines the two files to create a third. However, because of the way the command works, you can also use it to display a short file on the monitor.

Typing cat followed by a single filename displays the contents of the file on the monitor. The limitation is that if it is a large file, the contents scroll past faster than you can possibly read them! For a file bigger than a few hundred characters, use either the more or the less commands.

Viewing a File with *more* The more command displays a file's contents a page at a time. The command to see the contents of the Samba configuration file smb.conf is (see Figure 7.4)

more /etc/samba.d/smb.conf

The display is paused until you press the spacebar, which brings up another screen page of data. If you press the Enter key, the display advances by one line. A line at the bottom of the page shows what percentage of the file has been displayed. Pressing the letter q at any time quits the more display.

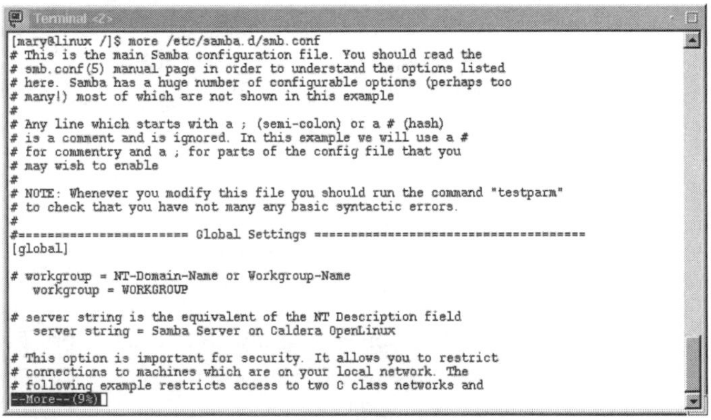

FIGURE 7.4

Using the more command to display the contents of the Samba configuration file smb.conf. The last line of the display indicates that 9 percent of the file has been seen.

Viewing a File with *less* less is a lot like more. more is an old UNIX standard; less was developed by users who wanted additional features.

You start less the same way, and you move from one page to the next by pressing the spacebar. With more, you can move only one direction. With less, if you want to see a previous screen page, you can press the letter b to move back a page. You can also move back or forward a line at a time by using the Up Arrow and Down Arrow keys.

Copying Files

The cp command is similar to the DOS copy command. To copy a file onto a floppy disk, for example, enter the following command (make sure the floppy disk has been mounted, or this won't work):

```
cp report1.txt /mnt/floppy
```

This copies the file named report1.txt onto a mounted floppy disk.

> **CAUTION**
>
> Beware that the cp command does not warn you if it is overwriting a file of the same name.

If you want to be warned about overwriting, add the -i flag:

```
cp -i report1.txt /mnt/floppy
```

A message appears asking overwrite /mnt/floppy/report1.txt? and you have to enter a y to overwrite or an n not to overwrite. Use the -u flag to copy the file as an update, meaning that if a file with the same name already exists, it is overwritten only if the original has an older date.

Moving Files

The mv command moves files to another location or can be used to rename a file in the same location.

The following command moves the file from the current directory to the floppy disk:

```
mv report1.txt /mnt/floppy
mv report1.txt report1.old
```

The following command renames the file to a new name:

```
mv report1.txt report1.old
```

> **CAUTION**
>
> Just like the copy command, the move command does not warn you about overwriting a file. You can use the -i flag to ask for confirmation before overwriting.

Deleting Files

The `rm` command deletes files. Use it cautiously because after you delete a file, you cannot retrieve it. Linux does not have an `undelete` command as does DOS, because of the requirements of a multiple-user system. In Linux, after a file is deleted, its free space is quickly put to use for something else.

If you want to delete a file and be asked for confirmation before deleting, use the `-i` flag. You can simplify that by adding an alias to your .profile so that you are always prompted for confirmation before deleting:

```
alias rm="rm -i"
```

Making Directories

Linux is based on a directory structure, so you'll find that whenever you want to group files together, you'll want to put them in their own directory. The `mkdir` command creates directories. If you know DOS, it also has a `mkdir` command that has a short version, `md`. This is one of the few cases where Linux does not have a shorter command name. You can create an alias called `md` that invokes the `mkdir` command.

Directory names can contain letters, numbers, the period, the hyphen, and underscore characters. Spaces are not permitted. Also forbidden are these characters:

@	#	$	%
^	&	*	(
)	[	]	{
}	'	"	\
/	|	;	<
>	?	!	

Directory names can be up to 256 characters, but anything more than 14 characters can create unwanted complications, especially if your directories are shared with any non-Linux computers.

TIP Remember, spaces are not permitted in directory names. The command `mkdir marys letter` does not create a single directory. It creates two directories: one called marys and the other called letter. If you want a directory like that, you can create a directory called marys_letter. The underscore character is commonly used in place of a word space in directory names.

Deleting Directories

Sometimes, directories need to be removed. The command to remove a directory is `rmdir`, followed by the name of the directory you want to delete.

Directories can only be deleted this way if they are empty. If the directory contains any files, you see an error message saying Directory is not empty. If you get this message and you thought that you had deleted all the files in the directory, check for hidden files. Any file that has a name that begins with a period is considered a hidden file and won't show up with a regular ls file listing. You'll have to do an ls -A to see the hidden files.

CAUTION

Be cautious when using the rmdir command. rmdir can be dangerous because it does not ask you to confirm that you want to delete a directory before it deletes the directory. The command takes immediate effect and is not reversible. There is no second chance like on Microsoft Windows systems.

Linux Commands for DOS Users

If you are familiar with DOS, many Linux commands are similar to what you have previously learned. That's because the DOS operating system was originally patterned on UNIX and borrowed a lot from it. Table 7.1 lists some DOS commands and their Linux equivalents.

Table 7.1   DOS Commands and Their Linux Equivalents

DOS	OpenLinux	Explanation
cd or chdir	cd	Changes working directory
chkdsk	du	Shows disk usage
copy	cp	Copies files
date	date	Used in Linux to set both the time and the date
dir	dir or ls	Lists files in a directory
del	rm	Deletes a file
erase	rm	Deletes a file
format	mke2fs	Formats a file system; must be superuser to use in Linux
md or mkdir	mkdir	Creates a new directory
ren or rename	mv	Renames or moves a file
rmdir	rmdir	Deletes a directory
type	cat	Views a file's contents on the monitor
xcopy	cp -r	Copies files, including directory structure

Part

II

Ch

7

Other OpenLinux Tools, Shortcuts, and Tips

Linux is packed with tools and shortcuts. Many of these aren't covered in the standard Linux documentation. Many times it is assumed that these features are known to the user because Linux pros know them. Following are some of the best of these tools, shortcuts, and tips. As you work in Linux, you will surely discover more.

Switching Terminals

You can switch to a second character-mode terminal using LeftAlt+F2. (This means you must use the Alt key on the left side of the keyboard.) You can then run separate sessions in each terminal. LeftAlt+F3 opens a third terminal, and so on. Under OpenLinux, you can have several terminals open at the same time. These are sometimes called *virtual consoles*. If you are not on a character terminal but are running KDE windowing, Ctrl+Alt+F7 opens the first windows terminal, Ctrl+Alt+F8 opens the second, and Ctrl+Alt+F9 opens a third.

Shutdown and Reboot

The normal way to shut down the system when you are in the character-mode terminal is to use the Ctrl+Alt+Del key combination. This safely shuts down the system and reboots the computer.

Shutdown the Computer Remotely If you are not at the computer's console and can't use the Ctrl+Alt+Del key combination, you can enter the command `reboot`. An alternative is to type the following command:

```
shutdown -h now
```

This brings the system to a halt so that you can turn off the computer. If you are connected remotely, you have to use su to switch to root before you can run this command. It does not restart the computer like `reboot` does. This can be useful if you want to stop the computer and don't want it to restart.

Stop a Program

If you need to stop a program that is running or seems to be frozen, you can kill the process with the Ctrl+C key combination.

Find your Login Name

Type `whoami` to display your username. If you type `who am i`, it gives you your name, host information, and the time you logged in.

Find Who Else Is Logged In

Want to know who else is on the system? Type in **who** for a list of all the users logged into the machine.

Displaying or Changing the Time or Date

Entering the command **date** displays both the date and time. To change either, you must be root. To change the date, enter the command:

date -s *YYMMDD* (year, month, and day)

To change the time enter the command:

date -s *HH:MM:SS* (hours, minutes, seconds—only hours and minutes are required)

> **N O T E** Do not use the time command. It is really a timer and is used to determine how much time it takes for a process to complete. time reports statistics about the amount of user, system, and CPU time used by a process. You can start a program with the timer and then when you exit the program the statistics are displayed. For example, if you open a terminal window and enter the command **time gimp**, the GIMP program is started. When you quit the GIMP program, a display is shown of the amount of user, system, and CPU time was used. ▪

Find What's Running on Your System

Linux calls programs that are running on your system *processes*. You can get a list of processes by entering the following command:

ps a

This displays a list of all processes running. This command is useful when you need to terminate frozen programs by force. The command shows the processes and their identification, PID. You can stop a running process using the kill command with the PID, such as:

```
kill 1797
```

This kills the program with the PID of 1797.

Monitor CPU Usage

Sometimes you need to monitor the running processes. The top command displays a list of all running processes in the order of their share of CPU time. This list is updated every 5 seconds until you terminate the program by pressing the q key. The top program usually runs in its own terminal. It is useful for finding what is using the most resources on your system.

Part
II

Ch
7

Finding Operating System Information

Need to know information on your server's operating system? Enter the command:

```
uname -a
```

This displays the operating system, Linux, plus the version number, date and time the kernel was built, and the computer's processor (for example a Pentium processor shows up as i686).

How Long Has the System Been Running?

Linux users like the fact that the system doesn't need to be rebooted very often. You can find out the length of time your system has been up since the last boot by entering the command `uptime`.

Finding Memory Usage

To display how memory space is used, both RAM and swap space, enter the command `free`. This shows what is being used as well as the amount of free memory.

Finding Disk Usage Information

To get a report that shows information on the disks on your system use the command:

```
df -h
```

The `-h` flag says to put the information in human-readable format. This command shows the size of your disk drives, the amount of space used, and how much is free in megabytes. It also displays the usage in percentage and where the disk is mounted.

Getting File Sizes

Need to know the size of the files in your directory? The command `ls -l` shows you the filename in addition to other information, including the size of your file in bytes.

Getting Directory Sizes

To find out how much space a directory is using, you can use this command:

```
du -bh ¦ more
```

This displays detailed information about disk usage for each subdirectory.

Find what Modules Are Installed

If you need to see which modules are currently installed, you can use this command:

```
cat /proc/modules
```

NOTE Note that files in /proc are not real files. They show information about the active system configuration. ■

See Your User Environment

To see the current user environment including path information, use the command:

```
set ¦ more
```

Show Your Path Information

To see just the current path information use the command:

```
echo $PATH
```

Adding an Environmental Variable

Environment variables are values that are passed to other programs. They can be set at the command line or added to your .profile file if you want them to be there every time you start. The command to create a variable called PRINTER, for example, that sets your default printer to one you've named hp4000, is

```
PRINTER=hp4000
export PRINTER
```

See System Messages

Linux keeps a log of all the system messages. These messages can be useful for finding problems, tracking login attempts, or identifying all those messages that whipped past when the computer started up. To see the whole system message log, enter the command:

```
less /var/log/messages
```

To see specific lines in the log file, you can use the grep command, which can find characters inside files:

```
grep root /var/log/messages ¦ less
```

The preceding command shows a list of all messages in the log that contain the word *root*.

You can use the tail command to see the last ten lines of a file. If you want more or fewer lines, you can add a number. The following command show the last 20 lines of the messages log:

```
tail -20 /var/log/messages
```

Part

II

Ch

7

How and Why to Use File Linking

Linking is used so that you don't have to make multiple copies of the same file. This is more efficient and also saves space while making it easier to work on the system. Because directory and subdirectory names can become quite long, you can make links to shorten them. For example, if you have a shared directory with a file named newreport.txt, instead of typing `/home/shared/projects/projecta/sharedreport.txt` every time you want to access the report, you can create a link like this in your home directory:

```
ln /home/shared/projects/projecta/sharedreport.txt sharedreport.txt
```

This creates a linked file in your directory that points to the actual file. Everyone sharing the file can create similar links so they don't have to type out the full pathname every time they want to get to the rile. Links like this are called *hard links*. They can only point to files and can't cross disk partitions. Symbolic links can cross disks and can point to directories as well as files. For example, for Windows diehards, you can create a symbolic link to your floppy disk drive and call it a: like this:

```
ln -s /mnt/floppy a:
```

If the floppy disk is mounted and you've created the link, type cd a:, and you change to the floppy disk directory.

How to View Web Files on a Character Terminal

You don't have to be running a windowing environment such as KDE in order to view Web files. A very good text-mode browser called *lynx* is installed with OpenLinux. Type in the command lynx, press the Enter key, and it starts. A menu line across the bottom shows what you can access by pressing the highlighted character: H for help, O for options, Q to quit, and so on. The Go command enables you to type in the name of the URL you want to open. No graphics are displayed, but you can read all the text. It's the fastest way to read Web pages you'll ever find.

How to Find Files

You can search for files on your system using the find command. To find a file named report1.txt, search the whole system enter the following command:

```
find / -name report1.txt
```

This command says to search for the file named report1.txt, start the search at the root (/) level, and search through all the directories. The filename can contain wildcards such as * and ?. For a simpler and faster search, enter this command:

```
locate report1.txt
```

However, this only search directories in your PATH.

How to Connect to Another Linux Computer

You can use the telnet protocol to connect to another Linux computer or to many servers on the Internet. The command is `telnet`, followed by either the hostname or the IP address of the machine you are connecting to. You are then prompted for your login name and password. You have to have an account on the other computer to connect by telnet. After connected to another computer by telnet, you can operate on it as if you were sitting at its keyboard. One way you might use telnet is to log in to Linux server from your home computer so that you can access files on your office computer.

How to Transfer Files Between Computers

The file transfer protocol (ftp) is used for copying files between computers. A simple ftp session is started by typing the `ftp` command, followed by either the hostname or IP address of the machine you are connecting to. Some ftp servers are set up to accept anonymous connections. On these systems, use your email address as your password. These are systems set up to share files. You can also use ftp to connect to a computer where you have an account in order to move files to or from that computer. Some typical ftp commands are:

- **binary**—Format needed for transferring non-text files.
- **get**—Use `get` with a filename to transfer a file from a remote computer to the computer you are working on.
- **put**—Use `put` with a filename to send a file to the remote computer.

For a list of possible commands in ftp, type the question mark (?). To get help on a specific command, type the question mark followed by the command, such as:

```
? pwd
```

This displays the message `print working directory on remote machine`. To end an ftp session, type the command `quit`.

How to Add Users

On a character-mode terminal in OpenLinux, use LISA to add users. Enter the command

```
lisa --useradm
```

You can also use the command

```
adduser new_user_login_name
```

You have to be logged in as root to add users. If you use `adduser` rather than LISA, you need to take some extra steps. The `adduser` script creates a login name based on what you typed in, but it puts in a default username and does not create a password for the new user. To put in the user's name, use the following command:

```
chfn new_user_login_name
```

Part
II

Ch
7

This opens the script to change the finger information on the user. You can add the user's full name, and then the program prompts for office and phone numbers, which you can ignore by pressing the Enter key. To create a password for the new account, enter the following command:

passwd *new_user_login_name*

You are prompted to type in the password and then asked to retype it to confirm the spelling. Finally, you need to create the home directory and assign it the proper permissions.

How to Remove Users

You can use LISA to remove user accounts. Enter the command

lisa --useradm

You can also use the command

userdel -r *user_login_name*

userdel deletes the user's account. The -r parameter deletes all files in the user's home directory along with the home directory itself. If a user has files located in other directories, they will have to be searched for and deleted manually.

How to Print

To print a file directly from the command prompt, use the lpr command. This sends the file to your printer without any special formatting. To print a file, enter **lpr** followed by the file-name. This is mostly useful for short text files. To print a copy of the lilo.conf configuration file, for example, enter this command:

lpr /etc/lilo.conf

Printing graphics and text that has been formatted with different fonts, using headlines and other changes in the text, should be handled from a windowing environment. Chapter 8, "Installing and Configuring Printers," covers setting up printer drivers and filters that can handle this.

How to Check and Control the Printer You have to be logged in as root to use the lpc command, which enables you to check the status of the printer, and control some aspects of its use. Type in the command **lpc,** and it prompts you for what action to take. If you have more than one printer, it also prompts for the printer name. Some lpc commands are

- ■ **stop**—Stops the printer.
- ■ **start**—Starts the printer.
- ■ **status**—Displays printer status.
- ■ **quit**—Exits lpc without doing anything.

How to View the Print Queue To view a list of what is in your print queue, use the lpq command. Print jobs are displayed with a job ID and number indicating where the job is in the queue. If the list says active rather than a number, it means that the job is currently printing. Use the job ID when you want to cancel a print job.

How to Cancel a Print Job The lprm command removes a print job from the queue. If you want to cancel a specific print job, you need the job ID—or you can enter **lprm -** to cancel all your print jobs.

> **WARNING**
>
> If you are logged in as root and use lprm -, it cancels everyone's print jobs, not just your own. Most of the time it is unnecessary to cancel *everyone's* print jobs. As a rule, printing problems can be fixed by deleting a particular print job. Besides, canceling all print jobs can cause the loss of someone else's print job that may not be easily recreated.

Command Not Found

This means that the computer can't find the program you've requested. First, check the spelling. Remember that capitalization and spaces between words and characters matter. Sometimes this message means it can't find the program, which might mean that it is not on your PATH. If you know where the program is located—most OpenLinux tools are in /usr/bin—type in the full pathname along with the program name.

Working with Files

Working with files is fundamental on any computer. To get full use of OpenLinux, you need to know about the files on the computer, including ordinary text files, binaries, command text, and executables. You also need to know about file naming.

Naming Files

First, here are some fundamentals about filenames on OpenLinux:

- **Filenames are case sensitive**—Windows or Macintosh users are in the habit of not worrying about uppercase versus lowercase letters. In Linux, case matters. If you use the wrong case, it is the same as using the wrong character.

- **Filenames can be very long**—Filenames, like directory names, can be as long as you want (up to 256 characters). No spaces, though. See the upcoming list for characters that can't be used.

Part

II

Ch

7

■ **Extensions don't matter**—On Windows systems, everything has a three-character extension to identify the file type. A Corel WordPerfect file, for example, ends with the extension .wpd. Executable files must end with the extension .exe or .com. On OpenLinux, extensions don't matter. A file is marked as being executable by its permissions, not its extension, but some common extensions, such as .txt, are used so that other people can quickly identify the file's type. Dots are used in Linux filenames as separator characters to make filenames such as May.payments.report more readable.

■ **Some characters can't be used**—Special characters can't be used in filenames. These include spaces and tabs as well as:

@	#	$	%
^	&	*	(
)	[	]	{
}	'	"	\
/	|	;	<
>	?	!	

File Types

OpenLinux has four different file types: ordinary files, directories, links, and special device files.

■ **Ordinary files**— These are the most common files on an OpenLinux system. They are the files you work with such as text and data files. Binary executable files also fit this category.

■ **Directories**— Directories are files that contain the names of files and subdirectories.

■ **Links**— Links in Linux are similar to shortcuts in Windows or aliases on Mac OS. A link isn't a file but is really a pointer to a file. When you view a list of files, there's a difference between an ordinary file and a linked file. For example, deleting a link does not delete the file it was pointing to.

■ **Special device files**— These are the hardware devices on your computer from your keyboard to the CD-ROM drive. Linux treats all these devices as files.

On Linux, file security defines who can read, write, or execute a file. These are called *permissions* and each file has its own set.

When a file is created, it is owned by the user who created it. Every new file is assigned a default set of permissions. Only the owner of the file and the superuser can change the permissions on the file.

When a new file is created, it is also assigned to the default group of the user that created it. Groups are defined by the system administrator. Each user is assigned to his own group and can then be added to other groups. Typically, groups consist of working groups on the network. For example, the financial department might have a group named finance and the sales department might have a group named sales. To see what groups you belong to, use the groups command.

If you are not using OpenLinux as a server but rather as a single-user workstation, you don't need to worry about groups. The group called users is the primary group that all users belong to by default in OpenLinux.

File Permissions

Access to files (and directories, which are files) is defined by permissions that can be assigned to individual users as well as to groups. This gives a great deal of flexibility in sharing or restricting file access.

Therefore, each file has three separate sets of permissions: one for the owner of the file, another for the group, and one for everyone else. Each of the three are assigned read, write, and execute permission. If you try to read a file but you don't have read permission for that file, you won't be capable of seeing its contents. If you have read permission, you cannot change the file if you don't have write permission.

If you don't have read permission for a directory, you cannot reading its contents, and if you don't have write permission, you cannot change the contents of files in the directory.

To see file permissions, you can use the ls -l command. For example, entering the command **ls -l report1.txt** might produce the following:

```
-rw-r--r--   1 mary      sales       690026 Feb  4 09:40 report1.txt
```

This line contains eight columns of information. The first column, -rw-r-r–, indicates the permissions for the file. The first character in this block is a hyphen, a d, or an l. The hyphen indicates that it is an ordinary file, the d indicates a directory, and the l is for linked files.

This is an ordinary file. The next nine characters show the permissions. The first three indicate the permissions for the owner of the file, the second three indicate the permissions for the group, and the last three indicate the permissions for everyone else.

A hyphen in any of the permissions indicates that the permission is blocked. The three possible permissions are r for reading, w for writing, and x for executing, or running, a program file.

In the preceding example, the user has read and write permission for the file. The file is not executable.

The group has read permission but not write or execution permission. The same is true for everyone else on the system.

The second column, 1, shows the number of links to the file.

Part

II

Ch

7

The third column, mary, shows the username of the owner of the file.

The fourth column, sales, shows the group the file belongs to.

The fifth column, 690026, shows the size of the file in bytes.

The sixth column, Feb 4 09:40, shows the date and time the file was saved.

The last column, report1.txt, shows the filename.

To see the permissions for a directory, use the ls -ld command. For example, to see the permissions on Mary's home directory, enter this command:

```
ls -ld /home/mary
```

Only the owner or the superuser can change the permissions of a file. Most of the Linux system files can only be changed by the superuser.

To change the permissions on a file, use the chmod command. This is for character-terminal use. This process is simplified if you are working in the KDE windowing environment. For more information, see the section on the K File Manager in Chapter 3, "Configuring the KDE Desktop."

For example, to change read permissions on a file named report1.txt using the chmod command, enter this command:

```
chmod a+r report1.txt
```

This indicates to change the permissions so that all users on the system can read the file. To change it back to being readable only by the user, referred to here as the owner of the file, enter this command:

```
chmod a-r report1.txt
```

The command works with a formula. It starts with chmod, then a set of three characters that indicate how the permissions are being changed, followed by the name of the file to be changed.

The middle of the three characters is either a plus or a minus symbol. The plus symbol means to add permission, the minus symbol means to remove permission.

The first character on the left side of the plus or minus is always one of the following:

- **u**—The owner, or user, of the file
- **g**—Group already assigned to the file
- **o**—Other users on the system
- **a**—All the above: user, group, and other

The character after the plus or minus refers to one of the following:

- **r**—Read permission
- **w**—Write permission
- **x**—Execute permission

There is a special extra `chmod` setting that uses the letter `t` to set the sticky bit on a directory. It is seen in the file listings as the last character in the column showing read, write, and execution permissions.

The `t` comes from its formal name of save text mode. If you enter the command `ls -l /` to see the root directory, you see that the /tmp directory has the sticky bit turned on and its permissions are shown as `drwxrwxrwt`.

The sticky bit isn't used too much. Its original purpose was to save a copy of a running program in memory after the program completed. Frequently used programs would have their sticky bit turned on to make them start up faster by never fully closing them. Though the sticky bit is no longer used this way very often because of the great speed of modern computers, sticky bits are now sometimes used for security. After the sticky bit is set on a directory, no one except the owner of the directory or root can move or delete files in the directory, no matter what other permissions exist.

There is a more elaborate way to change permissions for file that uses binary arithmetic. For example, the command to give read permission to a file is

```
chmod +r filename
```

To do this using the binary method you could type

```
chmod 744 filename
```

The first digit, 7, sets the permission level for root. The second digit, 4, sets the permission level for the group owner of the file. The third digit, 4, sets the permissions for the user owner of the file.

The digit is determined by adding up the permissions. No permission is 0. Execute permission is 1. Write permission is 2. Read permission is 4. In the example, 744 gives root read, write, and execute permission (read+write+execute or 4+2+1 equals 7); the group owner gets read permission (4) and the user owner also gets read permission.

For more in-depth information on permissions, you need to get a good Linux systems administration handbook. The one that I like best is *Essential System Administration, 2nd Edition* by AEleen Frisch (ISBN: 1-56592-512-2).

Part

II

Ch

7

Changing Groups, Ownership

The owner of a file or directory can change the group it belongs to. This makes files accessible to a workgroup without making the files world-readable.

To change the group for a file or directory, use the chgrp command. In the example used on file permissions, the file report1.txt was assigned to the group sales. To change the group the file is assigned to, you have to know the exact name of the group to which it is to be assigned.

To change the group for the sample file to the finance group, you can enter the command:

```
chgrp report1.txt finance
```

This gives anyone in the finance group access to the file based on the group permissions for the file.

Sometimes you have to change ownership of a file. A file that has been moved from one account to another, for example, needs to have its ownership changed or it won't be accessible in the new account.

Only the superuser can change ownership. The chown own command needs only the filename and the username of the new owner.

You can also change permissions using the umask command and the binary bit syntax. Get a good book on Linux systems administration to learn more about this and other expert-level file permission issues.

Vi, the Basic Text Editor

Configuration files on OpenLinux are all plain text files. You need a text editor to change these files, and to maintain your system properly, you have to edit at least some of these files.

You'll find the vi text editor on every Linux system, so if you know how to use vi, you'll always have an editor available. And because of its small size, vi is the only editor available for boot or emergency disks.

The vi editor is not a text formatting program. It does not change fonts, adjust margins, or center titles. It is meant for writing and editing configuration files, computer code, and short notes.

The version of the vi editor in OpenLinux is *vim*, the *Vi Improved editor*, which has some enhancements over the original vi editor. The vi editor is part of UNIX history, and as such it has its cheerleaders and its critics. It was the first UNIX editor that was visual. You could see text a full page at a time, and changes to the text were immediately displayed on the screen. Before that, the only text editor available showed only a single line at a time.

Today, the vi editor might seem outmoded and a little crotchety to work with. Other editors that are more visual and work more like modern word processing programs are now available, but for simple text editing, vi is quick, efficient, and it's always available.

The simplest way to start is to enter the command:

`vi filename`

This starts the editor and either opens a file if it exists or creates the file if it is a new filename. The vi editor has three modes: command, command-line, and insert. When you first open a file, the editor starts in command mode.

- **Command mode**—In this mode, simple keystrokes are used to enter commands. For example, pressing the x key does not cause the letter x to be inserted into the document. Pressing the x key invokes the delete command and removes the character under the cursor. In command mode, almost every key executes a command. Uppercase letters are different than lowercase ones. Some commands require a combination of a letter and the Ctrl key. The Up Arrow and Down Arrow keys move the cursor up and down the screen. The Right Arrow and Left Arrow keys move the cursor along the current line on the screen.

- **Command-line mode**— More complex commands require you to change to the command line mode. By pressing the colon key (:), you switch from the capability to move around the screen and enter letter commands to a single command line at the bottom of the screen. To save a file or exit the program, you have to be in command-line mode.

- **Insert mode**— You need to be in command mode and press the *i* or *a* key to enter insert mode. You have to be in insert mode to enter text. To leave insert mode, press the Esc key.

When you open a file in the vi editor, all blank lines are shown with a tilde (~) character.

The following sections outline some of the basic vi operations.

Entering Text

When you open a new file, you must change to insert mode before you can enter text. Move the cursor to the point where you want to enter text. Press the i key to insert text to the left of the cursor. Press the a key to append text to the right of the cursor. Uppercase I and A insert and append at the beginning and end of the current line, respectively. To exit from insert mode press the Esc key.

Correcting Text as You Write

While typing in insert mode, you can use Ctrl+h to delete a letter to the left of the cursor. Ctrl+w deletes the word, and Ctrl+u deletes everything on the line up to the cursor. These commands work only on the line you are on and do not go back up a line.

Part
II

Ch
7

Deleting Text

To delete a single character using command mode, move the cursor until it is over the character you want to delete and press the x key. To delete a word, move the cursor to the first letter of the word and press the d and w keys (one letter after the other) to delete the word. The dd command deletes the line.

The Undo Command

If you are in command mode and make a mistake while deleting a character, word, or line, press the u key immediately after the deletion, and it restores the deleted text.

Searching for Text

Searches are done in the command mode. To start a forward search, use the forward slash key (\). To start a backward search, use the question mark (?). Entering /config and then pressing the Enter key begins a forward search for the word config. To repeat the search, just press / or ?, depending on which direction you want to search.

Saving Files

To save a file, you need to be in command-line mode. Pressing the colon (:) followed by the letter w saves—or writes—the file. To save the file under a different name, use :w *new_filename*. If the file is write-protected, you can overwrite it anyway by using :w!

Save and Quit

To save and quit, use the command-line mode. The command :wq saves the file and quits.

Quitting Without Saving

To quit and disregard any changes to the document, use the command :q!

Midnight Commander

Typing commands on a computer terminal can be tedious. That's why programs are available to simplify tasks and reduce the errors that can come with repeated typing at a command prompt even if you are working on a character-mode terminal. These programs are known as *file managers*.

Midnight Commander is one of the most popular file managers for anyone working on OpenLinux on a character-mode terminal. However, if you are using the KDE Desktop, use the K File Manager, which can do as much and more than Midnight Commander.

Styled on the Norton Commander for DOS systems, MC can move, copy, and delete files and directories. It can also perform many system maintenance tasks. MC is open source software distributed under the same GNU license used by Linux.

Midnight Commander is not included with the standard OpenLinux 2.3 distribution, but you can download the version that was included with OpenLinux 1.3 from Caldera Systems. This version works when you are running a character-mode terminal. It does not work from within the KDE Desktop. You can get it using this ftp command:

```
ftp://ftp.calderasystems.com/pub/OpenLinux/1.3/Packages/RPMS/mc-4.0-1.i386.rpm
```

To install Midnight Commander, change to a directory where you can temporarily put the installation files. You need to be logged in as root to do the installation. Enter the following command:

```
rpm -ivh mc-4.0-1.i386.rpm
```

After the program is installed, you can start it by entering the command **mc**. If you are using Midnight Commander from a terminal window in KDE, start the program with the command mc -x.

You can use a mouse with MC on a character-mode terminal by using the gpm utility. This is a mouse server, and it must be run by root. The program is started with the following command:

```
/usr/bin/gpm -t imps2
```

This is the command for the Microsoft Intellimouse with a wheel using the PS/2 port. If that is not the mouse you are using, using the command gpm -t help for a list of mouse types supported. The common Microsoft-compatible serial mouse is simply designated as ms.

When you start the program (as shown in Figure 7.5), if you move the mouse around, you see the pointer move around the screen. If not—assuming you want to use the mouse—you'll need to figure out why gpm is not working. However, you don't need a mouse to use MC. In fact, it was originally designed to work without a mouse.

FIGURE 7.5
The main screen on Midnight Commander. The center is divided into two window panes.

Menu bar

Hint line

Command line

Function key assignments

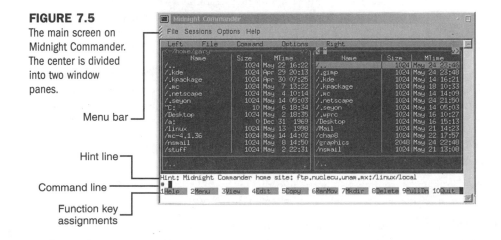

The main screen shows a menu bar across the top. This has drop-down menus. You can access the menu bar using the F9 key or by clicking on it with a mouse.

The bottom three line are a hint line, a command line, and a line showing function key assignments.

In the center of MC is a window with two panes. This is the primary working area. The two panes show two directories at once. One of the two is selected as the current directory. Most file operations such as copying or moving files are done in the current directory. You can switch panes by using the tab key or clicking on the pane you want to use with the mouse.

In the working pane, you can move around using the keyboard or the mouse. You can access commands from the menu or by typing the command at the command line.

Most of the time, MC is used for copying, renaming, deleting, or moving files. It is useful for finding hidden files, and for creating or modifying links. You can use MC to change file permissions and even for deleting those files that were somehow created using characters that weren't supposed to be used in filenames and can't be deleted with the rm command.

You can use MC to view all types of files, even compressed and Web-formatted files. Use the F1 function key for help.

This is just a short introduction to the program. If you start to use it, you will quickly learn that it's the Swiss Army Knife of file managers for working on the character-mode terminal. The manual pages for Midnight Commander are almost a hundred pages, which is some indication of the many features available.

RPM for Installing and Uninstalling Applications

RPM is the Red Hat Package Manager. It's used on many Linux distributions, not just Red Hat or Caldera. If you are using the KDE Desktop, use Kpackage for managing the software packages installed on your system, but if you are working only on a character-mode terminal, you can use RPM from the command line.

A *package* is a complete, fully tested and configured software program. Most RPM packages are available as both compiled binaries and as source code. These are usually found in separate directories named RPMS and SRPMS, the s beginning the second name indicates it is the source code directory.

Not all software is distributed in RPM format, but it is the standard format for software distributed with OpenLinux.

Each RPM file includes compiled software, information on where to put the files during installation, and essential configuration information to run the software.

The RPM software package manager makes maintaining the system easier because it handles installing, uninstalling, and upgrading all software. The RPM database makes it easy to find out what software is installed. You can find out whether a specific program is installed and if it is, what version is installed. Upgrading is handled in a way that protects any customization you have done with your configuration files.

To install an RPM package, you need to know the location of the file. Usually, you either have something you've downloaded off the Internet, or it is a file on a CD-ROM. If you want to add a package from the original OpenLinux CD, you'll find the RPM packages in the directory /Packages/RPMS.

The RPM package manager has five modes of operation: installing, uninstalling, upgrading, querying, and verifying.

Installing

To install a package, enter a command such as the following:

```
rpm -ivh gofigure-1.2.3-1.i386.rpm
```

This installs the Linux kernel package on your system. The `-ivh` means install, in verbose mode (display some information about the package), and show hash marks (#) while installing to indicate the progress.

The RPM package name shows information about the software you are installing. It starts with the software name, gofigure; its version, 1.2.3; the release, 1; and the type of system the software is intended to be used on, i386, which is the designation for Intel and its compatible processors.

During installation, RPM checks first to see whether a package is already installed. If the same package or one that has a higher version number is already installed, it stops the installation process and gives a message that the package is already installed.

Next, it checks for dependencies. Many software packages depend on other software to be installed in order to work. If the other software isn't installed, the dependency check fails, and RPM gives a failed dependency error message.

You can use wildcards with RPM installations. The command `rpm -i gofigure*` installs the gofigure-1.2.3-1.i386.rpm package, but it also installs every other package in the same location that started with the word gofigure. Use wildcards cautiously.

Some other options that you might use during installation are

- **replacepkgs**—If you received an error message that a package is already installed, you can force RPM to install the same or an older package anyway with this option. If you've installed a newer version of a software program but for some reason decide to go back to the older version, use upgrading, which is explained in the next section.
- **replacefiles**— If you try to install a package with a file that's already on the system, you will receive a conflict error message. You can make RPM ignore the conflict and install anyway with this option. It overwrites the file from the other software package.
- **force**— This option forces the installation to ignore all conflicts.

Part
II
Ch
7

> **CAUTION**
>
> Do not use this unless you really know what you are doing. It can cause multiple software failures.

- **nodeps**— Many software packages depend on other packages to be installed. An error message indicates what other package needs to be installed first. This option tells RPM to ignore this error and install anyway.

> **CAUTION**
>
> Usually, packages installed this way don't run correctly, if at all.

Uninstalling

Uninstalling works much like installing. To uninstall a package, you use a command such as this:

```
rpm -ev gofigure-1.2.3-1.i386.rpm
```

This erases the package in verbose mode. A dependency check is also done when uninstalling. If another package depends on the package you are removing, RPM refuses to uninstall it. You can force the package to be removed using the –nodeps option, but that makes the other dependent packages no longer usable.

Upgrading

All software has a regular upgrade cycle where new features are added and old problems and bugs are fixed. Upgrading actually involves removing the old version and installing the new version. The command for upgrading is like this:

```
rpm -Uvh gofigure-1.2.3-1.i386.rpm
```

N O T E Upgrading requires a capital U. If you see a message about a saving a copy of a configuration file to a filename ending with rpmsave, it means that the new version of the software needs a new configuration file. The old configuration file is saved for you in case you need it or want to look at it. ■

You can also use the upgrade mode to go back to an older version of a software package. If for any reason you want to upgrade to an older version, use the –oldpackage option.

Querying

To see all the packages installed on your system, use the following command:

```
rpm -qa ¦ more
```

To find out if a specific software package is installed, the command is like the following:

```
rpm -q WordPerfect
```

The `-qi` option displays complete package information including name, description, release, size, build date, install date, and vendor. The `-ql` option displays a list of files related to the package.

Verifying

Verification compares information about the files installed on your system and the files in the original package. It is used to check for file corruption or missing files. The command used is like the following:

```
rpm -V WordPerfect
```

> **N O T E** Verification requires an uppercase V. The check is made between the files found on the system and a database record made during installation. You do not need to have the original RPM file available to do this check. ■

You can check all installed packages using the `-Va` option.

If you don't want to check against the RPM database—it might be corrupted—you can spell out the full name and path for an RPM package to be used for verification.

If everything verifies properly, nothing is displayed on the screen. If any differences are found, a message appears. The format of the message is a string of eight characters, possibly the letter c indicating that it is a configuration file, and then the filename. In the eight-character string, a dot means that part of the test passed. The following are the possible error codes:

- **5**—Failed the MD5 checksum test
- **S**—Size of the file changed
- **L**—Symbolic link failure
- **T**—Time file was created does not match
- **D**—Device attribute failure
- **U**—User setting failure
- **G**—Group setting failure
- **M**—Mode failure, such as permissions or file type

If you receive any of these failure codes, you probably need to remove or reinstall the package.

Building a Custom Kernel (or Recompiling)

Sometimes you need to rebuild the kernel. Maybe you are updating the system files or you need to add features that have to be included whenever the computer starts up. For example, if you are building a firewall system for a local network, you might need a customized kernel.

Compiling a kernel is a special process, but it can be easily successful. Just make sure you've followed some precautions and give yourself a backdoor in case problems occur.

N O T E You generally do not need to recompile OpenLinux in order to optimize it for your hardware. It is unique among Linux distributions in this respect. It is already lean, with nothing extraneous included in the default installation. OpenLinux makes efficient use of modules. Nothing extra is included in the kernel by default. This means that when you start up the system, a probe is made of the hardware and only the necessary modules are loaded. What you can speed up is the startup process by recompiling to limit the module probe to only the hardware on your system. For example, if you don't have any PCMCIA cards, you can eliminate the probe for them. ■

Most modules—that is, hardware drivers—can be inserted into a running kernel, which eliminates one of the more frequent reasons for building a new kernel on some Linux systems.

That said, reasons still exist why new kernels are compiled, and you have no reason to be afraid of them. No programming knowledge is necessary, and if it's done right, absolutely no risk is involved. If the new kernel doesn't work, the old working kernel is available to run.

Some of the most common reasons to recompile the kernel are

■ Enabling file system quotas

■ Adding power management support for laptops

■ Enabling support for a network firewall

■ Customizing the kernel for a Pentium processor

The first step to take before you can recompile the kernel is to install the kernel sources. Beginning with Version 2.2 of OpenLinux, the sources are no longer automatically installed by default. You need to add the following packages:

■ linux-source-common

■ linux-source-i386

■ glibc-devel

■ ncurses-devel

All four are on the original OpenLinux CD in RPM packages and install easily using RPM or Kpackage.

N O T E Although the process to build a bootable emergency floppy disk is similar, that is not covered here. To build a bootable floppy see the section of creating an emergency boot disk in Chapter 6. ■

There are four steps to building a kernel: configuring the kernel, compiling and installing the kernel, compiling and installing the modules, and configuring LILO and module loading.

Configuring the Kernel

All the work in configuring a kernel is done in the /usr/src/linux directory. In that directory is a configuration file named .config. Do not attempt to edit this file with a text editor—you must use a special configuration program—the make config utility, or one of its variations as explained later in this section. If you've never before compiled the kernel on your computer, this file might not yet exist. If it does, however, make a backup copy (cp .config .config.orig) if you want to be capable of going back to the original working configuration.

When configuring the kernel, you can choose whether to include support for the different parts by selecting yes or no, or you can choose to install many parts of the kernel as modules. Modules can then be loaded as needed using insmod. This lowers the amount of RAM memory required by the kernel.

OpenLinux is configured with loadable modules. This means that it has a very small kernel and only the essential drivers. All other drivers are loaded as modules at startup, and run as if they were compiled into the kernel in the first place. You can build the kernel with all the drivers built in, but this makes for a big kernel that requires more memory.

There are three different ways to access the kernel configuration program:

- **make config**—Runs the configuration program as a long series of questions you must answer. If you want to make a change, or if you made a mistake in any of your answers, you have to start the whole process over from the beginning. There is almost no reason to use this method, which is prone to errors and bad configurations.

- **make menuconfig**—Used if you are in a character-mode terminal. It presents a configuration menu that enables you to choose the different possible options. Help is available throughout on each possible setting.

- **make xconfig**—Used if you want to configure the kernel while in the KDE windowing environment. make xconfig provides the most options for configuring the kernel. If you run make xconfig and you've previously recompiled the kernel and just want to make a modification, you need to click on Load Configuration From File. Enter the name **.config** to load the current configuration. When you save and exit, the new configuration is saved to this file. Help is available throughout on each possible setting.

Many questions arise for kernel configuration, and help is available with every setting, but it does not clarify the choices for a new user. If you are not sure about a setting, don't change the default.

Part

II

Ch

7

In most cases, you might want to change just a couple of things:

- **Processor type and feature**—Look at the processor family option. In this option, you can choose to customize the kernel to a specific processor type. The default choice is i386, which works on any Intel or Intel-compatible processor. The i586 is for any Pentium-class system. The Pentium option is good for all Intel Pentium systems and the AMD K5 and K6. The PPro option is for Pentium II systems. Making a wrong choice renders the system unusable. This is also where you have to go to enable symmetric multiple-processing support. If you have more than one processor, you have to turn on support and recompile the kernel. If you turn this option on and do not have multiple processors, a Pentium computer might continue to work, but will be sluggish. Older computers refuse to work with this option enabled.

- **General setup**— In the general setup configuration, you can turn on Advanced Power Management BIOS support. This is used on laptop computers, but otherwise is not needed.

- **Filesystems**— In the filesystems configuration, you can turn on quota support. This is a good idea on a server system. Enabling quota support enables you to limit the disk space available to users.

- **Networking options**— In the Networking options configuration, you can turn on support for firewalls. A *firewall* is a computer that protects a local area network from the outside world. If your network is connected to the Internet, a firewall is usually a computer through which all connections to the outside world or from the outside world must pass. If you want to use your computer as a firewall, turn on Network firewalls as well as IP firewalling. Be cautious in deciding to set up a firewall computer. Not all systems, even secure ones, have firewalls. Firewalls add an extra point of failure on a network.

Compiling and Installing the Kernel

After you have configured the new kernel, it must be compiled. Compiling takes time and can take many hours on non-Pentium computers. Of course, because Linux is a multitasking system, you can continue to do other work while the new kernel is compiling.

At every step when compiling, make sure to look for error messages when each process stops. One of the most common errors is attempting to build a kernel that is too big. If you receive an error message, you must go back, reconfigure the kernel, and go through each step of the compilation again. Do not skip any of the steps, or you can end up with an unusable kernel.

The first step is to check on dependencies and make sure they are in place. It doesn't usually take very long. This is done with the following command:

```
make dep
```

It's a good idea to next run

```
make clean
```

This is quick and removes unneeded files. The next step is to compile the new kernel. Make sure to spell this properly with a lowercase z and an uppercase I:

```
make zImage
```

This part takes a long time. It builds a compressed kernel, which is why the name begins with a z. The z indicates that gzip compression was used in making the kernel image, just as text or program files compressed with gzip end with gz. One option is to make bzImage. This also uses gzip compression, but uses a different layout and loading algorithm to create a "big zImage." The new kernel is put in the default directory /usr/src/linux/arch/i386/boot/. If make zImage ends without any error messages, the kernel is ready to be installed.

The new kernel is installed by copying the new kernel image file to the /boot directory. When you do this, however, you have to give it a new name. For example, the default boot image file created by OpenLinux 2.2 is named vmlinuz-2.2.5-modular. You don't want to touch that file. It's a perfectly good, working kernel. To install the new kernel, use the following command, giving the file a name that will help identify its features. In this example, the name is used to identify a kernel that has been optimized for the Pentium processor:

```
cp /usr/src/linux/arch/i386/boot/zImage /boot/vmlinuz-2.2.5-pentium
```

The new kernel is now ready for use.

Compiling and Installing the Modules

The next step is to compile the modules. The kernel and modules are compiled to work together. Like everything else in Linux, they are just files. The only way the kernel knows what modules to use is if the kernel and modules have essentially the same name.

If the kernel you are building is the same version as the working kernel, you need to take an extra step in order to protect your working version. If you are building a kernel that is a new version, this step is not necessary.

To preserve the working kernel, you need to move the current modules out of the way because when the modules are compiled, they automatically overwrite the existing modules. You can do this using the move command:

```
mv /lib/modules/2.2.5 /lib/modules/2.2.5-current
```

Now you are ready to compile the modules. Enter the following command:

make modules

If at the end no errors occur, the next step is

```
make modules_install
```

Part
II

Ch

7

Now you have to put the modules in a directory that matches the name of the kernel so that the kernel can find them on startup. To do that, use the following example (this is only an example—be sure to use the proper filenames that you have on your system):

```
mv /lib/modules/2.2.5 /lib/modules/2.2.5-pentium
mv /lib/modules/2.2.5-current /lib/modules/2.2.5
```

Now the new kernel and modules are installed. The last step involves booting the new kernel and configuring the modules to load properly.

Configuring LILO and Module Loading

The last step starts with configuring LILO, the Linux Loader that boots OpenLinux. The LILO configuration file is in the /etc directory and is named lilo.conf. (For more information on LILO and its options, see the section on LILO in Chapter 3, "Configuring the KDE Desktop.") A typical configuration file looks like this:

```
# general section
#
boot = /dev/hda1
install = /boot/boot.b
message = /boot/message
prompt

# wait 5 seconds (50 10ths) for user to select the entry to load
timeout = 50

#
# default entry
#

image = /boot/vmlinuz-2.2.5
        label = linux
        root = /dev/hda1
        read-only
```

The lines in your configuration file might not look exactly like this because there are variations based on your system's hardware and configuration.

The first image entry is the default, and is loaded after the timeout period has passed. The timeout period gives you time to change the boot option before the Linux system starts up. Make a copy of the whole image section, and append it to the bottom of the file.

This is the image entry that you can use to go back to the original working kernel in case any problems occur with the new kernel. The only change that needs to be made on the new entry is to change the label. Change the label to oldlinux. Then, if you want to boot this version of the kernel when the computer starts up, type oldlinux at the boot prompt.

Finally, change the first image section so that the `image=` line points to the new kernel. Nothing else needs to be changed. Here's what the new configuration file looks like using our example (yours will likely look different):

```
# general section
#
boot = /dev/hda1
install = /boot/boot.b
message = /boot/message
prompt

# wait 5 seconds (50 10ths) for user to select the entry to load
timeout = 50

#
# default entry
#

image = /boot/vmlinuz-2.2.5-pentium
        label = linux
        root = /dev/hda1
        read-only

#

image = /boot/vmlinuz-2.2.5
        label = oldlinux
        root = /dev/hda1
        read-only
```

You can then test the new configuration file for errors by entering the command:

```
lilo -v -t
```

Look for error messages and fix any problems. After you've run the test and gotten no errors, you can install the new LILO configuration on the boot sector with the command:

```
lilo -v
```

Now test the new kernel by shutting down and rebooting the computer. When the computer comes back up, you can finish with configuration of the new modules.

Change to the directory:

```
cd /etc/modules/2.2.5
```

This directory name should match the kernel version, so if your kernel version is not 2.2.5, put in the correct number. If you started out with version 2.2.5 and built a new kernel that is version 2.2.6, copy the 2.2.5 directory as follows:

```
cp -R /etc/modules/2.2.5 /etc/modules/2.2.6
```

Part
II

Ch
7

This copies the file that lists the modules to be loaded on startup. If you installed OpenLinux with Lizard, you'll find found files in this directory: .default, .rootfs, default, and rootfs. If you installed using LISA, you'll also find a file that starts with a timestamp and ends with .config.

In the /etc/modules/2.2.5 directory (or whatever version you are working with) are the files for loading modules on startup. When OpenLinux starts, it first looks for the timestamp file, then the hidden file named .default, and finally the default file. Therefore, all you really need is the two files default and rootfs. You can delete the two hidden files and the timestamp files if you want.

In the default file is a list of all the modules to load at boot time. If you have a module that needs to be loaded at boot, you can add it to the list. You have to put in the exact name, without the .o extension.

Some driver modules have settings that need to be passed when they are loaded. This is done by creating a file in the /etc/modules/options/ directory. The name of the file must match the name of the module, without the .o. A typical example of this is the module for a SoundBlaster sound card. For this, you usually install the sb.o module. Then you create and edit a file named /etc/modules/options/sb. In the file sb, put the parameters for your sound card. The typical content is

```
io=0x220 irq=5 dma=5 mpu_io=0x330
```

You are now finished building the new kernel. After you've shut down the kernel and restarted a final time, you will be running with your new kernel and all the necessary modules loaded.

Configuring Hardware

Installing and Configuring Printers

Printing Under OpenLinux

Printing under OpenLinux is different than printing on a Windows or Macintosh computer because OpenLinux is a multiple-user system. This means that even if you are the only user of an OpenLinux workstation, printing to a printer attached to your computer is like printing to a network printer down the hall.

If you think of all Linux printing as network printing, it's not so difficult to understand, but it means that additional steps are involved that might not be necessary on a single-user system.

Handling printing on Linux is no more difficult than setting up printing on a Windows NT or Novell NetWare print server.

The problems usually come from the complex combinations of hardware and software that turn up in some offices. The various printers that use a variety of printer languages from PCL to PostScript to PostScript emulation and the array of software programs from simple word processors to high-end graphics programs can sometimes make working out printing problems difficult.

Usually, though, if your setup is simple, you have a standard printer, such as a Hewlett Packard LaserJet or any Postscript printer, and you use the standard software programs, you won't run into any big problems.

Standard Linux distributions use the *lpr* printing system, which comes from BSD UNIX systems. OpenLinux uses an advanced system, called *LPRng*, that has many enhancements. If you are familiar with the BSD printing system used by most other Linux distributions, you need to know that there are differences between the two systems. Although both appear to work in the same way, there are some key variations. Tricks you might have learned for the standard system might not work the same way in LPRng. To learn more about LPRng, check out the LPRng Web page at www.astart.com/LPRng.html.

Linux printing uses a print spool, where files that are to be printed are stored until they are sent to the printer so that on a multiple-user system, only one print job is trying to access the printer at a time. A series of programs and files are used for managing the print jobs queued up in the print spool:

- The lpd program manages the printing system.
- The lpr program creates print jobs.
- The lpq program allows you to view print jobs in the print queue.
- The lprm program handles deleting print jobs.
- The lpc program can handle printing system:administering.
- Printer configuration is stored in the /etc/printcap file.

Before you install a printer on your OpenLinux system, it's a good idea to check that printer support was initialized on your system. The standard OpenLinux setup includes printer support, but you can check to see what printer port or ports have been set up on your system.

To see which port was initialized on startup, you can use the dmesg command, which will display the bootup messages. Open a character-mode terminal such as Konsole and, at the command prompt, type the following:

```
dmesg | less
```

Scroll through the bootup messages until you find a line that starts with lp (indicated by the arrow in the example in Figure 8.1). The lp devices are the parallel ports on your system. Parallel ports are also sometimes called printer ports because that is their primary use.

On Linux, lp0 is the equivalent of LPT1 on Windows systems, lp1 is LPT2, and lp2 is LPT3.

FIGURE 8.1

Displaying the bootup messages shows the printer ports that are installed on your system.

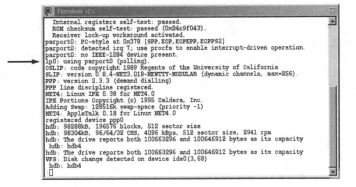

Figure 8.1 shows some typical output from the bootup messages, including a line that says

```
lp0: using parport 0 (polling)
```

This indicates that the kernel initialized parallel port 1 (lp0) on startup. This is the port that is ready for use for printing. You will need this information to install a printer on your system.

You can find additional information on your printer setup in the bootup messages. Look for lines that start with parport. These lines give information about the parallel port, including the port's capabilities, the interrupt (IRQ) it is using, and possibly the name of a printer detected on the port.

Installing a Printer

Only the superuser can install a printer on OpenLinux. You can log in as root, or log in as a regular user and use the su command to become the superuser for this task. Open a terminal window and enter the command:

```
su -
```

Adding the hyphen means that not only will you be logged in as root, but the environment variables including the path and the home directory are changed from your user settings to the superuser settings.

There are two ways to install a printer in OpenLinux. One is to use the Caldera system administration tool COAS; the other is to use LISA.

> **CAUTION**
>
> You can use either COAS or LISA to install printers, but you can't use both. If you start using COAS, use only COAS to install or modify printer settings. If you use LISA, stick to LISA.
>
> The problem is with the way LISA works. LISA keeps its own hidden database of the system configuration and does not work with the actual system configuration files. That means that if you've made a change to a configuration file and not used LISA to do it, LISA does not know about the change. Then, if you use LISA to make a change, all the configuration information you added outside of LISA is lost because your changes will be overwritten. This is the primary reason to use COAS rather than LISA for system administration tasks.

Using COAS to Install a Printer

To start the COAS printer configuration tool, you can

■ Select the COAS icon on the K Panel, choose Peripherals, and select Printer.

■ From the K Application Launcher, choose COAS, Peripherals, and then select Printer.

■ From a terminal prompt, enter the command coastool; from the CLAM Selection window, choose Peripherals Administration; and in the Peripherals Administration window, select Printer Configuration.

In the Printer Configuration tool, shown in Figure 8.2, you can add, edit, or delete a printer setup. You can also start and stop the lpd printer daemon, which is the process that runs in the background, watches for print jobs, and—when it sees them—sends them to the proper destination.

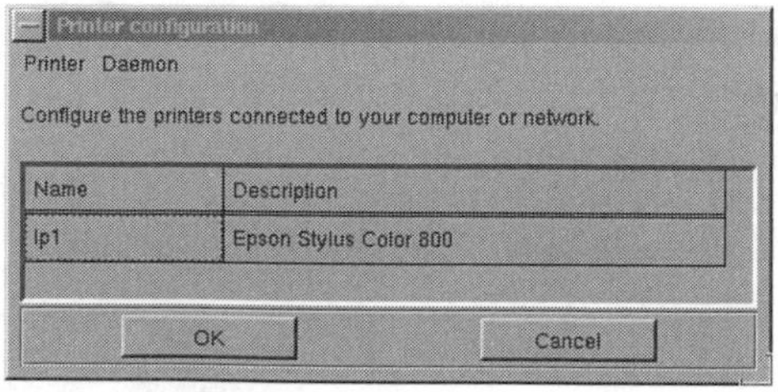

FIGURE 8.2
The Printer Configuration panel.

To install a new printer from the Printer menu, select Add.

The first step is to select a printer model, shown in Figure 8.3. You can choose from about 50 different types. If your printer isn't on the list, pick the model that is the most similar to your printer. A single click selects a printer model.

FIGURE 8.3
Select your printer model, or one that is similar.

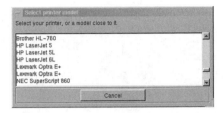

The next screen, shown in Figure 8.4, asks for a *logical name* for the printer. The default name is lp1, and if you have only one printer, you can keep this name. The name helps you identify the printer. If you have several printers on a network that are all of the same type, you might name the printer by its make or model, for example hplaser. If there are many printers of the same kind on your network, naming the printer by its make or model isn't helpful. Instead, give it a name based on the room number or a person who sits close to the printer.

FIGURE 8.4
Give your printer a name that will help you identify where it is located or who uses it.

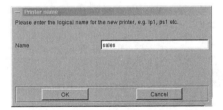

After choosing a name, you'll find settings (see Figure 8.5) for the default paper size, the Device (that's the printer port—lp0 is the same as Windows lpt1, the first parallel port), and the speed. The speed setting is for serial connections, which are rarely used, and is ignored if you are using a parallel port.

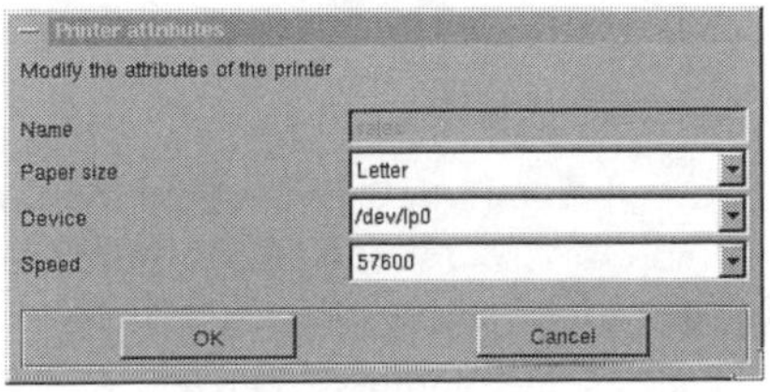

FIGURE 8.5
Set paper size and the printer port in Printer attributes.

The device name is the information that you obtained in a previous step by reading the system messages.

When you save, the changes are saved to the printcap file in the /etc directory. The lpd print daemon is then stopped and restarted so that the new printer is immediately available. Click OK to create the queue, as shown in Figure 8.6.

FIGURE 8.6

The last step is to create the print queue.

There is a special print driver for printing to printers that are not connected to your computer. These are called *remote printers*. In the list of printer models is a model listed as Generic remote printer. If you are printing to a network printer, you need to use this printer model rather than the model of the printer to which you are printing. If you choose this printer, you are not prompted for a default paper size and so on. You are asked to enter the Remote host: the network name or IP address of the print server handling the remote printer and the print queue for the printer, shown in Figure 8.7. If you don't know this information, you need to obtain it from your system administrator.

FIGURE 8.7

Enter the remote host for the printer.

To print to a remote printer on a network, create a Generic remote printer and enter the Remote host name or IP address. After a printer has been installed, you can edit and modify the settings (see Figure 8.8). If the initial setup needs to be refined, it can be done here.

Settings that can be modified here include

- **Type**—The type is the set of predefined printer settings. If you've installed a printer and have used a type that you thought was similar to your printer but it didn't work correctly, you can try changing to a different type here.

- **Resolution**—Standard laser printer resolution is 600x600. Older printers have a resolution of 300x300.

- **Paper size**—This setting is for the default paper size.

- **Device**—The possible printer ports on your system, both parallel ports and serial ports, are displayed.

- **Speed**—This is the speed used for a serial port connection. This is ignored for parallel port connections.

- **2 pages/sheet**—This is used for compressed printing of plain text files. Do not check this for normal printing use.

- **Max. jobsize**—This is normally set to 0 for unlimited, but you can limit the size of the print jobs a queue will accept.

- **Suppress headers**—On most systems you want this checked; otherwise, header pages will appear with every print job.

- **Spool directory**—This option indicates the directory in which print jobs are held until they can be sent to the printer.

- **Send EOF to eject page**—If the last page of a print job isn't coming out on anything that is sent to this printer, check this option to force the last page out.

- **Additional GS options**—Ghostscript is used to convert postscript print jobs to other printer language formats. If you need to add options, you can enter them here.

- **Remote host**—If you set up a printer to print on a network printer, you can modify the remote host setting here.

- **Remote queue**—If you set up a printer to print on a network printer, you can modify the remote queue setting here.

FIGURE 8.8
Modifying the printer setup in the Printer Attributes panel.

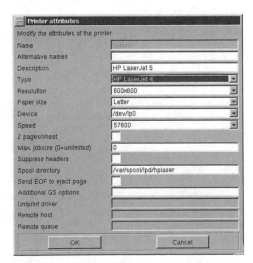

Using LISA to Install a Printer

Although COAS is the preferred way to install printers—it has far more capabilities than LISA—if you are using LISA for system administration, you'll need to install printers with LISA.

To start LISA, open a terminal window using Konsole or Kvt. At the command prompt, enter the following command: lisa

Select System Configuration (see Figure 8.9) and press the Enter key. In the next window, select Hardware Configuration and press Enter. In the Hardware Configuration window, select Configure Printer.

FIGURE 8.9

Starting LISA for printer installation.

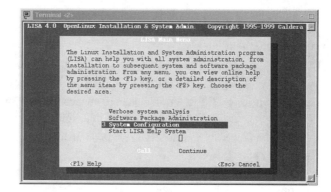

The first step is to select a printer driver.

You can choose from about 50 different types of drivers (see Figure 8.10). If your printer isn't on the list, pick the model that is the most similar to your printer. If you are printing to a printer that's on a network, select Use network printer.

FIGURE 8.10

Select a printer driver.

In the Configure Printer Connection panel, select the port to which your printer is connected. The list shows ports by their common name, followed by the Linux device name, and then the Windows name.

In the Default Printer Resolution panel, choose the resolution for your printer.

In the Default Paper Size panel, select a paper size for your printer.

Your printer is now installed.

The *printcap* File and Print Filters

Whether you installed your printer using COAS or LISA, the configuration information about the printer is saved in the printcap file in the /etc directory.

A printcap file is a plain text code file for controlling the printing system. It contains an entry for each printer setup on your system. A sample printcap entry looks like this:

```
# /etc/printcap
#
# Please don't edit this file directly unless you know what you are doing!

hplaser:\
     :lp=/dev/lp0:\
     :br#57600:\
     :rm=:\
     :rp=:\
     :sd=/var/spool/lpd/hplaser:\
     :mx#0:\
     :sh@:\
     :if=/var/spool/lpd/hplaser/printfilter:
```

Take heed of the warning and do not attempt to edit this file on your own unless you know what you are doing. Colons separate each field of the printcap file, and the backslash at the end of each line indicates that the line is continuing. Each field describes a capability of this printer and uses a two-character code system. Codes that need defined parameters are followed by an equal sign, and then the parameter is entered.

The first field is the name of the printer. Multiple names are separated by a vertical bar.

The lp code designates the device interface that is to be used for printing, the sd code indicates the spool directory, and the sh code indicates that headers should be suppressed.

The documentation for LPRng lists more than 175 possible codes for each printcap printer definition.

Many different printers can be included in the printcap file.

Printer Filters

On Linux systems, PostScript is the default format for print jobs because it can be used on any computer platform. This makes the Linux print files portable to other systems and, unlike most other printer languages, it's easy to view PostScript print files onscreen.

However, Linux is usually installed on PC systems that don't have access to PostScript printers, so filters are used to translate PostScript print files into other printer languages. For this, OpenLinux uses Ghostscript, a filtering program that has drivers for most of the widely used printers.

It's not necessary for you to configure the filters manually. Under normal everyday use, you'll never even know that Ghostscript is being used for you print jobs.

TIP

You can also use Ghostscript manually to convert Postscript format files into other formats. If you have a Postscript file and you want to convert it into another printer language, open a terminal window and change to the directory with the Postscript file.

Then enter the command:

```
gs -sDevice=printer -sOutputFile=new_filename postscript_filename
```

In this command, replace the word *printer* with the printer format you want to convert to. Some of the supported formats are: deskjet, djet500, laserjet, ljet3, ljet4, necp6, bj10e, bj200, and ibmpro.

In the OutputFile, put the name of the new printer file you are creating, and finally enter the name of the Postscript file that is being converted.

After you enter the command, Ghostscript will convert the file and then stop once it is finished. Press the Enter key to continue and at the GS> prompt enter Ctrl+D to finish the process.

Then send your new file to the printer. Use the cp (copy) command to send a copy of the file to the print device:

```
cp new_filename /dev/lp0
```

Change the device name to the device used by your system.

Using Ghostscript this way defaults to a letter-sized page. Ghostscript has many options, including options to change the page size. The Ghostscript man pages have the details.

Configuring LaserJet Printers

OpenLinux includes a tool for configuring HP LaserJet printers on your system.

To start the HP LaserJet Control Panel, click on the K Application Launcher. From the pop-up menu, highlight Utilities. In Utilities, select HP LaserJet Control Panel. The HP LaserJet Control Panel, shown in Figure 8.11, enables you to set additional features in your printer configuration. You can use this tool for any HP LaserJet or compatible printer.

FIGURE 8.11
The KDE HP LaserJet
Control Panel.

The LaserJet tool has four tabs: Paper, Printer, Operations, and Fonts. Table 8.1 provides a brief description of the settings for each tab.

Table 8.1   Ljet Tool Settings

Option	Description
Paper settings	
Format	Defines paper size.
Copies	Indicates the default number of copies to print.
Lines	The number of lines on a page. The default for Letter size paper is 60.
Orientation	Indicates whether the default page is printed as portrait (tall) or landscape (wide).
Miscellaneous	Lets you change the default of autofeed to manual feed.
Printer settings	
Mode	Sets print quality. The default is presentation. Economy uses less toner, but it can make type hard to read and can produce coarse images.
Printer	Lets you select the printer to configure.
Resolution	Sets the printer resolution. Most new printers are 600.
Density	Sets the amount of toner to use when printing. The default of medium probably shouldn't be changed. Higher densities plug up graphics with too much toner.
Resolution Enh	Lets the printer simulate higher printing resolutions using resolution enhancement. The default setting—medium— probably shouldn't be changed.

continues

Table 8.1   Continued

Option	Description
Operations settings	
End of Line Mode	The default setting is UNIX LF. If you are printing files that were created on a Windows computer, you might need to change this to DOS CR+LF to get it to print correctly.
PageProtect	Used for pages with graphics that exceed the size supported by the printer's memory. Auto Page Protection sends the file to the printer in a way that won't overload the printer, and big graphics appear properly on the page even if it exceeds the printer's capabilities.
Powersave Time	If your printer has a Powersave mode, you can set the idle time before entering Powersave here. The default is 15 minutes.
Reset, Eject, Initialize	These buttons send their respective commands to the printer connected to your computer.
Fonts settings	
Language	The default printer language for HP LaserJets is PCL. If your printer is a PostScript printer, you can change this setting to PostScript.
Symbol Set	The default symbol set for HP LaserJets is PC8. Change this only if you know what you are doing.
Font	Uses a number to define the default printer font. The default is 0.
Pitch	Sets how many characters per inch to print using monospaced type. The default is 10.0.
Point Size	The default font size is 12.0

Controlling Printers in KDE

The KDE desktop includes the Klpq program, which combines the lpq, lprm, and lpc commands into one easy-to-use program. Here's a reminder, though: If you want to do more than view what is in a print queue—for example, if you want to change the print job order or delete a print job—you have to have the necessary access permissions. You cannot delete someone else's print job unless you are logged in as root.

To start Klpq, click on the K Application Launcher. From the pop-up menu, highlight Utilities. In Utilities, select Printer Queue. Because OpenLinux uses LPRng, select the LPRng radio button before clicking OK.

Klpq gives you easy access to all the printing utilities used to control print jobs (see Figure 8.12). It doesn't do anything itself. It uses lpq, lprm, and lpc to carry out its tasks.

FIGURE 8.12
Klpq, a program for managing print queues.

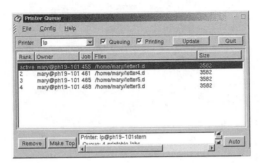

Once Klpq has started, it displays your default print queue. If you have other printers set up on your system, a drop-down list of all the printers that are set up on your system is available in the area next to the Printer listing.

If nothing shows up at all, check the Spooler setup under the Config menu item. Make sure that the system setting is for LPRng.

In the center frame of the Printer Queue window, a list of print jobs appears. Each job is ranked by the order in which it is to print, and the owner of the print job is indicated along with other information (such as the size of the print job).

From the list of print jobs shown, you can highlight a job and, from the bottom bar on the Printer Queue window, you can click on the Make Top button to make the job the next job that is printed. Clicking the Remove button deletes the job from the print queue.

If you receive a message in the message area next to the Make Top button that says This is a privileged command, you are attempting to change a print job that's not yours. To have the right to perform some tasks, you must be logged in as root.

Setting Your Default Printer

If you have multiple printers set up on your system, you might want to specify a default printer. You can do this by defining a PRINTER environment variable.

To set the PRINTER variable, open a terminal window and enter the following command:

```
export PRINTER=hplaser
```

The name *hplaser* in this sample command needs to be changed to the name you used for your printer. This is the command for the bash shell. If you are using another shell, your environment variables are probably set differently.

Printing to a Printer on a Windows Network

If you have Samba set up and running on your computer, you can use it to print from your OpenLinux computer to a shared printer on a Windows network. See Chapter 21, "Installing and Configuring Netware Network Services," for details on Samba.

Create a Samba Printer in *printcap*

You need to edit your printcap file (in the /etc directory) manually to do this because neither COAS nor LISA can create the right kind of entry.

The new entry should look like this:

```
nt-printer:\
     :cm=Laser Printer on NT Server: \
     :sd=/var/spool/lpd/nt-printer: \
     :mx#0: \
     :af=/var/spool/lpd/nt-printer/acct:\
     :lp=/dev/null:\
     :if=/var/spool/lpd/nt-printer/smbprint:
```

The printer name can be any name you choose. For this sample, the name is nt-printer. After editing your printcap file, be sure to stop or start the lpd daemon using the COAS print administration tool. In COAS, choose Peripherals and select Printer. From the Printer Configuration menu, choose Daemon and select Stop. After the daemon has been stopped, select start to restart the print daemon.

Create Spool Directories

You need to create some spool directories that match the new printcap entry. Execute the following command (as root, of course):

```
mkdir /var/spool/lpd/ nt-printer
mkdir /var/spool/lpd/smb/acct
chown daemon.daemon /var/spool/lpd/ nt-printer
chown daemon.daemon /var/spool/lpd/smb/acct
```

Create an smbprint .config File

smbprint needs a configuration file that is located in the spool directory. The file goes in the /var/spool/lpd/nt-printer directory and is called .config.

If you plan to use the printer as the guest user, the entry will look like this:

```
server=SERVERNAME
service=Printer-Service-Name
user=guest
```

Replace *SERVERNAME* with your server's name, and replace *Printer-Service-Name* with the sharename on the print server. To find the printer service name (sharename), run the following command:

```
smbclient -L SERVERNAME
```

This replaces *SERVERNAME* with the Windows machine's *workgroup* name. If everything is set up correctly, you see a list of services offered by the Windows machine, including the sharename of the printer.

If the guest account isn't available, your .config file should look like this:

```
server=SERVERNAME
service=Printer-Service-Name
user=username
password=user-password
```

Create the Print Filters

You need two filters now:

```
/var/spool/lpd/nt-print/filter
/var/spool/lpd/nt-print/smbprint
```

For the smbprint filter, a modified file was prepared by Caldera Systems technical support. Here's a copy of that file. You will need to create this file, name it smbprint, and place it in the /var/spool/lpd/nt-print directory:

```
#!/bin/sh -x
# This script is an input filter for printcap printing on a UNIX
# machine. It
# uses the smbclient program to print the file to the specified
# smb-based
# server and service.
#
# This file was originally altered by hamiltom@ecnz.co.nz (Michael
# Hamilton) so that the server, service, and password can be read from
# a /usr/var/spool/lpd/PRINTNAME/.config file.
#
# This script was further altered by david@caldera.com (David M. Brown)
# to include using an additional filter file $spool_dir/filter meant to
# envoke Ghostscript.

# Debugging log file, change to /dev/null if you like.
#
logfile=/tmp/smb-print.log
# logfile=/dev/null

eval acct_file=$$#
spool_dir=`dirname $acct_file`
config_file=$spool_dir/.config

eval `cat $config_file`
```

```
# Some debugging help, change the >> to > if you want to save space.
echo "server $server, service $service" >> $logfile

(
# NOTE You may wish to add the line `echo translate' if you want
# automatic CR/LF translation when printing.
#       echo translate
        echo "print -"
        cat ¦ $spool_dir/filter
) ¦ /usr/bin/smbclient "\\\$server\$service" $password -U $server -N -P >> $log-
file
        echo "-----" >> $logfile
```

Then you need to create a file named filter and place it in the /var/spool/lpd/nt-print directory. Replace the *DEVICE* and *RESOLUTION* settings with the correct ones for the printer
you to which you will be printing. To see a list of devices supported by Ghostscript, enter the
following command: gs –h.

The Ghostscript filter file should look like this:

```
#!/bin/sh
DEVICE=ljet4
RESOLUTION=600x600
PAPERSIZE=letter
SENDEOF=

if [ "$PAPERSIZE""= "a4" ]; then
     T=A4
else
     T=US
fi

nenscript -T$T -ZB -p- ¦
if [ "$DEVICE""= "PostScript" ]; then
     cat -
else
     gs -q -sDEVICE=$DEVICE \
             -r$RESOLUTION \
             -sPAPERSIZE=$PAPERSIZE \
             -dNOPAUSE \
             -dSAFER \
             -sOutputFile=- -
fi

if [ "$SENDEOF" != "" ]; then
     printf "\004"
fi

exit 0
```

You then need to change the ownership of these files. Enter this command:

```
chown daemon.daemon /var/spool/lpd/nt-printer/
```

You are now ready to start printing.

If you receive errors, try accessing the server to see what services are available. Use the following command:

```
smbclient -L SERVERNAME
```

If it comes back with a hostname error, you might have the wrong server name. The server name isn't the hostname; it is the Windows workgroup name.

If either smbclient or smbprint comes back with an error, you need to check your Samba configuration.

Another common reason for errors is that the Windows machine hasn't been properly setup for print sharing. If no services show up with the following command

```
smbclient -L SERVERNAME
```

the Windows computer needs to be checked.

Installing and Configuring a Backup System

Backing up is one of those things that everyone talks about, but that few actually do! Backups are one of those tasks that nag at you, and never quite seem to get done—unless you've set up a backup policy that's easy to follow. Modern computer systems are amazingly reliable, and data loss due to system failure is infrequent. User-caused data loss, however, continues to be a big problem—and having a backup can be a real lifesaver.

Setting a Backup Policy

Setting a backup policy and a schedule increases the likelihood that you'll do backups. The world's top computer systems administrators have been using a backup strategy for years. It really works.

Start by deciding what data needs to be backed up, the frequency of the backups, and to what media you plan to backup.

When you do backups, you'll use a combination of complete backups, which back up all the files, and incremental backups, which back up only files that have been changed since the last backup.

As a rule, backups are scheduled for the middle of the night. On most systems, this is the time when the fewest files are open because of the small number of users. Also, backing up puts some load on the system, so scheduling it at the least busy time will interfere with fewer users (who might find system response sluggish while a backup is running).

If you are the only user of your OpenLinux computer, you should try to back up the whole system once a week, or at least once a month. If you have critical files, you might want to copy those files onto a removable disk such as a Zip disk or even a floppy disk on a more frequent schedule. Otherwise, you shouldn't need to back up so frequently.

Make sure your backup device is properly set up before you go any further. Most tape backup systems are accurately detected during installation. After startup, open a terminal window and enter this command:

```
dmesg | less
```

Scroll through the listing and look for your tape drive. If it doesn't appear, you may need to load a module driver. See Chapter 5, "Configuring Your System with COAS," on using COAS to load modules. To configure CD writers for backups, see Chapter 13, "Writing to CD-ROMs." If you are using Zip or JAZ disks, see Chapter 12, "Using Zip and Jaz Drives."

If you are running an OpenLinux server, you will need to schedule more regular backups, but that doesn't mean you need to back up everything on a daily basis. Only part of your system needs daily backup.

Here's what you need to back up:

- **User files**—Back up the user files in the /home directory on a daily basis. Do a complete backup of the directory once a week and an incremental backup every day. If you are using a tape backup system, take note of the following backup strategy that professional systems administrators have used for years.

  Using nine tapes, you can have a reliable backup going back over the last year:

Part

III

Ch

9

Tape Number	Used for
Tape 1	First week full backup plus daily incremental backups
Tape 2	Second week full backup plus daily incremental backups
Tape 3	Third week full backup plus daily incremental backups
Tape 4	Fourth week full backup plus daily incremental backups
Tape 5	First monthly full backup
Tape 6	Second monthly full backup
Tape 7	Quarterly full backup
Tape 8	Month 6 full backup
Tape 9	Yearly full backup

  The tapes are rotated so that after week 4, you start again with tape 1. Monthly tapes are rotated. Save the yearly full tape backup and never rotate it. All tapes should be replaced with new tapes yearly.

- **Configuration files**—The configuration files in the /etc and /var directories don't change as frequently as user files, but they need to be backed up on a weekly or monthly basis, depending on how frequently your configuration changes.

- **Program files**—The program files in the /usr and /opt directories rarely change. Do one good backup after installation. You can update the backup if you add any updates. Usually, these program files can be easily restored from the original installation disk, so backups aren't as critical.

Choosing a Backup Medium

There are many choices as to where to store your backup. Tape backups might be slow, but they are reliable and have a long track record that proves their reliability. However, there are other backup media you can use. Two of the more interesting new options are writing to a compact disc and using high-capacity removable disks such as the Jaz disk.

For both capacity and features, though, nothing beats a tape system. Even a single-user system needs more space than a CD or Jaz disk can offer.

TIP Add an extra measure of security to your backups. Take a tip from systems administrators who have long followed the practice of keeping a duplicate copy of their backups at a separate location. This might be a copy of the monthly backup, for example. That way, even if a total disaster occurs at your work site—such as a fire—you have a backup copy of the data that you can use for system recovery.

Following are some possible choices for backup media:

- **Floppy disks**—Floppy disks are still the backup media of choice if you want to make a quick backup of your essential files or take files home or out of town.

- **CD Writers**—As CD writers have become more reliable, the prices have also come down. The disks themselves are very inexpensive. One advantage to this option is that the disks that are created are not easily damaged, so they provide a very reliable backup. Long-term viability is still unknown, although the disks will probably be usable for many years. The technology uses a system of laser burning to create the disk, which is not the way commercial CDs are created. Commercial CDs are pressed and, therefore, sturdier. CD backups can be read on almost any system with a CD-ROM drive. There are two downsides to CD writers: They are very slow, and can only hold up to about 650MB.

- **Rewritable CDs**—More expensive than the CD Writers are the rewritable CD-ROM drives. These are a newer technology, and they work in a way that is similar to the CD writers. However, these disks can be rewritten. These disks are more expensive than the write-once variety. Otherwise, though, everything about them is similar to the CD writer.

- **Jaz and Zip**—Zip drives are very popular and have become standard on many office PCs. Both the drives and disks are inexpensive. The disks hold 100MB of data, are good for quick and portable backups, and are replacing floppy disks in many cases. They can easily hold the bigger files that current software produces, most of which won't fit on a single floppy disk. The company that makes the Zip drive—Iomega— also makes Jaz drive. Jaz disks can hold up to a gigabyte of data, and they use a more advanced technology for better overall performance. The Jaz drive and Jaz disks are more expensive. The drawback to Jaz and Zip disks is that they are easily vulnerable to damage, and neither Jaz nor Zip disks will last as long as your other choices. However, they are very convenient for use over a shorter term. Don't rely on them as the sole backup media for your critical files.

- **Tape drives**—Tape backup devices are standard on most Linux servers. Tapes are incredibly reliable and rarely have errors; furthermore, if properly stored, they'll last longer than almost any other backup media in their price range.

For peer-to-peer workgroup networks and medium-sized networks, the Travan and higher-end digital audio tape (DAT) drives are usually the best choice. These drives adhere to standards and have good capacity. Travan drives can handle up to 8GB of data with compression, which should be enough for small networks of 5–10 PCs. The DAT drives have better overall performance and can hold up to 24GB of data. DAT drives are more expensive than Travan drives, but a 4mm DAT tape costs much less than the Travan QIC cartridges.

- **High-end tapes**—Higher-end tape alternatives can get quite expensive. These drives have greater capacity and higher speed than you can get with Travan or DAT. The three most widely available drive types are the Sony Advanced Intelligent Tape (AIT), Quantum Digital Linear Tape (DLT), and Exabyte Mammoth 8mm drives. Each of these holds a minimum of 20GB of uncompressed data and provides higher sustained transfer rates than either Travan or DAT. If price is no object, the high speed and capacity of these tape systems can make backing up a breeze.

BRU 2000 Backup Utility

BRU 2000, the Backup and Restore Utility included with OpenLinux, can be used to support a wide range of backup strategies, from the simplest to the most sophisticated backups. The version of BRU that is included with the full boxed edition of OpenLinux is the personal edition. A network edition is also available.

The network version of BRU 2000 includes features that are not in the personal edition, such as backup of mounted network partitions. If you want more information on the network edition, you can find it on the BRU Web site at www.estinc.com.

BRU is a backup program that's been used on UNIX systems since 1985. It's a proven and reliable system that is device independent—that is, as long as the device works on your system, BRU can use it for backups. This includes floppy disks—not that you are likely to use BRU in that way—but the point is that it will work with anything.

To start BRU 2000 personal edition, click on the K Application Launcher. From the pop-up menu, highlight Utilities. In Utilities, select BRU-PE Backup Utility. The BRU 2000 opening screen is shown in Figure 9.1.

The first time you use BRU, you'll need to configure the program. Select Configure BRU from the File menu.

There are two tabs in the Configuration Utility (shown in Figure 9.2): Globals and Devices. Following is a list of the settings in the Globals tab:

Part
III

Ch
9

FIGURE 9.1
You can use BRU 2000 to backup anything from a floppy disk to a high-capacity tape drive.

FIGURE 9.2
BRU Configuration Utility.

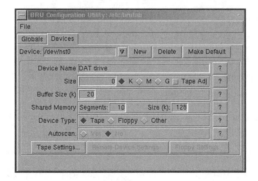

- **Overwrite Protection**—Turn this option on so that BRU asks for confirmation before overwriting a backup. If the backup is older than the number of days indicated in Recycle Days, no confirmation will be requested.

- **Recycle Days**—If you've turned on Overwrite Protection, this parameter defines how old a backup needs to be before BRU will overwrite it without asking for confirmation.

- **Compression Buffer Size**—If you use compression, this is the size of the buffer BRU will use. Bigger sizes mean faster backups but can slow down other operations on the system. The default setting is 500.

- **Maximum Writes Maximum**—This indicates the number of times BRU should write to a tape before it is retired. The default is 1,000.

- **Mount Command and Unmount Command**—These options are reserved for special scripts needed for autoloaders.

Following is a list of the settings in the Devices tab:

- **Device**—To define the device, click on New. Select your device type from the drop-down list. In the Device Node field, type in the device name for your backup device. A SCSI tape, for example, might be /dev/st0. A Travan tape might be /dev/nst0. If your device isn't listed, you will need to configure the brutab file in the /etc directory. Brutab files have already been written for most tape backup systems that are available on the BRU 2000 Web site at www.estinc.com/brutabs.html. Get a copy of the brutab for your tape system, put it in the /etc directory, and then restart the BRU 2000 configuration.

- **Device Name**—Type in any name you want. This is the name you'll see for the device.

- **Size**—The size of the backup device. If you have a 4-gigabyte tape drive, you can put 4 and check the G for 4 gigabytes, or you can put 4000 and check the M for 4000 megabytes. Putting a 0 here means that BRU will write until it gets a write error. On tape systems, checking Tape Adj will automatically adjust tape sizes from what the manufacturer claims is the actual size.

- **Buffer Size**—The BRU buffer size. You can fine-tune this setting to improve performance, but if it is mistuned, performance can seriously deteriorate. The default is 20, which works for all systems. DAT drives sometimes work better with either 16 or 32.

- **Shared Memory**—Shared memory size for use during Double Buffering. If your backup device is on the same computer as the drive being backed up, Double Buffering doesn't make a difference. If you are backing up a remote system, it can improve performance.

- **Device Type**—Make sure this matches your backup device. Settings are Tape, Floppy, or Other.

- **Autoscan**—The default setting is on. This enables an automatic verification of your backup when the backup ends.

- **Settings**—Settings buttons for Tape systems, remote devices, and floppy drives. Default settings usually don't need to be changed.

If you have multiple backup devices—for example, both a tape drive and a JAZ drive—you'll need to set one of them as the default backup device. When configuring the default device, in the Devices tab of the Configuration Utility, click on the Make Default button.

When the configuration is finished, be sure to Save from the File menu, and then exit.

After the backup device has been configured, check to see that it is the device BRU is using. From the File menu, select New Device. Make sure that your backup device shows in the Device field.

To start a backup, click on the backup button, which is the top button on the BRU window. Two panes are opened. On the left is a listing of your home directory, and on the right is the list of what will be backed up (see Figure 9.3).

> **CAUTION**
>
> If your tape drive uses hardware compression, make sure to turn off software compression in BRU. In fact, it's probably a good idea to turn off software compression altogether. There's some risk in using compression on backups. Compressed backups are not as reliable and are more prone to failure during restoration.

FIGURE 9.3
Select files and directories to be backed up by BRU.

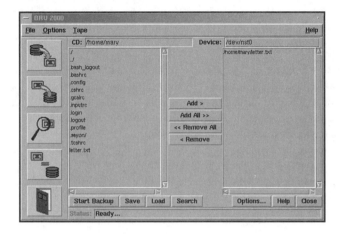

If you click on the Options button, you can set certain options, such as the age of the files to back up and whether to use compression. Compression fits much more, but is also significantly slower.

When you've selected all the files to be backed up, you can click on Start Backup. You are asked to select a name (Archive Label) for the backup. Give it a name that will help you identify the backup later—cryptic names can be frustrating six months later when you are trying to remember what you meant when you wrote them. Keeping a log with the names and fuller descriptions can be useful.

An Archive Requirements window opens, telling you how many files and directories are being backed up, the size of the backup in kilobytes, and the number of disks or tapes that are needed (see Figure 9.4). You can click Continue, or after a pause, the backup begins.

If you want to use BRU to schedule backups, first go through all the steps for a standard backup. After you've selected the files and directories to back up, click on the Save button. Give this backup plan a name that will allow you to quickly identify what it will back up, such as FullHome for a full backup of the /home directory. The names have to be valid Linux file names, without any spaces or nonstandard characters. After you've saved it, BRU offers to open the Scheduler.

FIGURE 9.4
Archive Requirements
shows the size of the
backup.

If you aren't already in the Scheduler, select Scheduler from the File menu to schedule backups.

The backup scheduler (as shown in Figure 9.5) enables you to schedule daily or weekly backups. You can also set the time for the backup to run.

FIGURE 9.5
BRU backup scheduler.

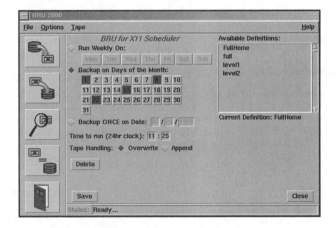

Finally, you can run BRU from a command line. For details, see the man pages by entering the command `man bru`. The 20-page manual displays all the options that are available when you use BRU from the command line. A printed manual is also available, for a price, from the manufacturer. See the BRU Web site for details (`www.estinc.com`).

tar for Backup

The tar (Tape ARchiver) utility is the old reliable way to back up files. It works under almost any conditions. Linux old-timers swear by it.

You might have seen files in Linux that end with .tar. These are files created with the tar utility. tar is used for more than backups—it's also used to put together a bunch of different files into one file for easy distribution. But tar started life as the Tape ARchiver backup utility.

The GNU tar utility included with OpenLinux is easy to use. It includes an option to compress archives, and it supports incremental backups.

tar is a command-line utility. It has no graphical interface. Open a terminal window using Konsole or Kvt. Following is a simple backup command:

```
tar cvf - /home > /tmp/backup.tar
```

This command creates a file in the /tmp directory called backup.tar. The entire contents of the /home directory are in the file.

You can then copy the tar file onto a backup disk such as a CD, Jaz, or tape.

To use compression while using the simple backup, change the command to read

```
tar czvf - /home > /tmp/backup.tgz
```

The .tgz extension indicates that it is a compressed file.

The next example could be used to back up directly to a mounted Jaz drive. However, if you do this, make sure you have enough space:

```
tar czvf /mnt/jaz/backup.tgz - /home
```

For a tape drive, use the device name:

```
tar czvf /dev/st0/backup.tgz - /home
```

If you have a backup that's too big to fit on a single disk or tape, you can use the multiple-volume option. However, if you do that, you can't use compression. When the first disk or tape fills up, tar will prompt you to insert another:

```
tar cvMf /dev/st0/5mar2000.tar - /home
```

To restore a backup using the Jaz disk example, use the following command:

```
tar xzvf /mnt/jaz/5mar2000.tgz /home
```

Table 9.1 lists the primary function parameters for tar.

Table 9.1   tar Primary Function Parameters

Parameter	Description
-A, --catenate, --concatenate	Appends to the end of another tar archive.
-c, --create	Creates a new tar archive.
-d, --diff, --compare	Finds the difference between a tar archive and the files. Used for verification of an archive.
--delete	Deletes files from an archive. Can't be used with tapes.
-r, --append	Appends files to the end of a tar archive.
-t, --list	Lists contents of a tar archive.

Parameter	Description
-u, --update	Appends only files that are newer than the ones already in a tar archive.
-x, --extract, --get	Extracts files from a tar archive.

There are dozens of other optional parameters. The -f parameter used in the examples specifies the file to which you want to send output. The -v is for verbose, which displays messages about what is happening.

Use the u parameter for incremental backups.

tar backups can be scheduled to run regularly on a daily, weekly, monthly, or yearly basis at any time of day using the crontab utility.

Add the appropriate command to the crontab file for root. For example, to perform a nightly backup at 2 a.m. of the /home directory to a SCSI tape drive, add this to root's crontab file:

```
00 02 * * * tar cvf /dev/st0/homefiles.tar - /home
```

For more details on using crontab, see the section on cron in Chapter 6, "Understanding and Using the OpenLinux File System."

cpio for Backup

Another backup method is to use the GNU cpio utility. Like tar, you start this at a command prompt. cpio is more complex to use than tar, but it can be more reliable because if a tar file has a corrupt block somewhere, you can't access the rest of the backup file. With cpio, only the bad block can't be accessed.

cpio copies files into or out of a backup archive. Creating a backup is called the *copy-out mode*. The backup archive that's created has the file and information about its owner, timestamp, and access permissions.

cpio requires a list of files that it is supposed to back up. One of the easiest ways to create a list is to use the ls (list) command. For example, to back up the /home directory to a SCSI tape device, enter this command:

```
ls /home ¦ cpio -o > /dev/st0
```

You can also use the find command. It has many additional options that you can use to narrow down the files being archived. For example, the following command archives all the files modified in the last 24 hours:

```
find /home -mtime 1 -type f -print ¦ cpio -o > /dev/st0
```

The copy-in mode extracts files from the backup archive. The following command would restore all the files from either of the two backup examples above:

```
cpio -i < /dev/st0
```

You can schedule cpio backups to run regularly on a daily, weekly, monthly, or yearly basis at any time of day using the crontab utility.

Add the appropriate command to the crontab file for root. For example, to perform a nightly backup at 2 a.m. of the /home directory to a SCSI tape drive add this to root's crontab file:

```
00 02 * * * ls /home ¦ cpio -o > /dev/st0
```

For more details on using crontab, see the section on cron in Chapter 6.

Installing and Configuring Sound

Installing Sound

OpenLinux supports most of the popular sound cards. It uses the free version of the OSS sound driver. The sound drivers in OpenLinux are "business audio" drivers that provide support for digital audio sampling and playback. Features like Advanced Wave Effect (AWE) for improved sound over the Internet and other multimedia technologies are not fully supported, if supported at all.

OpenLinux 2.3 uses modular sound support: Configuration is handled by inserting the proper module driver. This allows ISA PnP (Plug and Play) sound cards to be configured easily. For most users, sound will be properly set up during installation. Some cards, like SoundBlaster Live!, will not be fully set up even if they are detected. This and other cards need special drivers.

If your sound card was not properly set up during installation, you can try to install the Linux sound drivers manually. For the SoundBlaster Live! card, a section later in this chapter shows where you can download the driver from the Internet. Your other option is to install the commercial OSS sound drivers, as explained later in this chapter.

In most cases, SoundBlaster and SoundBlaster-compatible cards work using the basic installation routine. The 16-bit sound cards described as SoundBlaster compatible are really only compatible with the 8-bit SoundBlaster Pro. They typically have a 16-bit mode that is not compatible with the SoundBlaster 16 and not compatible with the OpenLinux sound driver.

Hannu Savolainen wrote the free Linux sound drivers. The support Web page for the sound drivers is www.linux.org.uk/OSS/.

You'll need to be logged in as root to install the sound drivers. To install sound support in OpenLinux, start the COAS system administration tool for the kernel (shown in Figure 10.1).

FIGURE 10.1
The COAS Kernel Modules configuration panel.

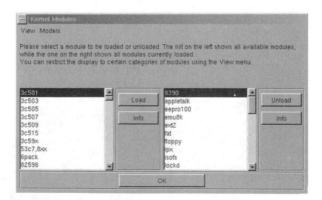

You can start COAS in three ways:

- Select the COAS icon on the K Panel, choose Kernel
- From the K Application Launcher, choose COAS, then Kernel
- From a terminal prompt, enter the command coastool, from the CLAM Selection window choose Kernel Modules

In the Kernel Modules panel, load these modules:

```
uart401
sound
sb
```

The sb module is the standard SoundBlaster and SoundBlaster-compatible driver. When you load, the module a configuration panel is opened. The default settings for the SoundBlaster sound card are shown in Figure 10.2. If your sound card has different settings for the IRQ, DMA channels, or I/O port address, enter them here. Click on OK. COAS will configure your system to load the newly selected modules on startup.

FIGURE 10.2
The SoundBlaster module configuration panel.

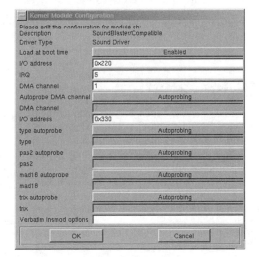

Part
III

Ch
10

TIP A bug in COAS causes problems loading the sb sound driver on some systems. Caldera Systems technical support says this failure occurs "because one or more of the required modules are already loaded." The message continues, "We are working on a fix for COAS. In the meantime, to work around the issue select the sb module and load it a second time."

The SoundBlaster AWE 64 is a plug-and-play card and requires a configuration file in the /etc directory as well as its own drivers. Follow this procedure:

1. Create a configuration file by entering the command pnpdump > /etc/isapnp.conf. Now, when you restart your system, the SoundBlaster AWE 64 is recognized. Make sure that you restart your system before going to Step 2.

2. Load the sb module in the COAS Kernel Modules panel. COAS prompts you that uart401 has to be loaded as well and then loads it.

3. Load the opl3 module.

4. Load the awe_wave module.

SoundBlaster Live! Drivers

Creative Labs has hired a team of programmers that specializes in writing Linux drivers. They have produced a binary driver for the SoundBlaster Live! sound card. This is one of the most expensive sound cards on the market. If you want top quality sound, you might be willing to pay the price.

To get the SoundBlaster Live! driver, go to the Creative Labs Linux Web page at developer.soundblaster.com/linux/. There, you'll find a link to the driver along with other Linux-related links. If you have another Creative Labs sound card, you might want to check this site as well. It has several useful links related to sound and video on Linux.

Follow the installation instructions included with the driver file that you download from Creative Labs.

Testing Your Sound Installation

Once you've installed the sound drivers, check their status. Enter the command:

```
cat /dev/sndstat
```

This will display a detailed listing of your sound devices. If you don't see anything, your sound drivers haven't been installed properly. Figure 10.3 shows a sample output screen.

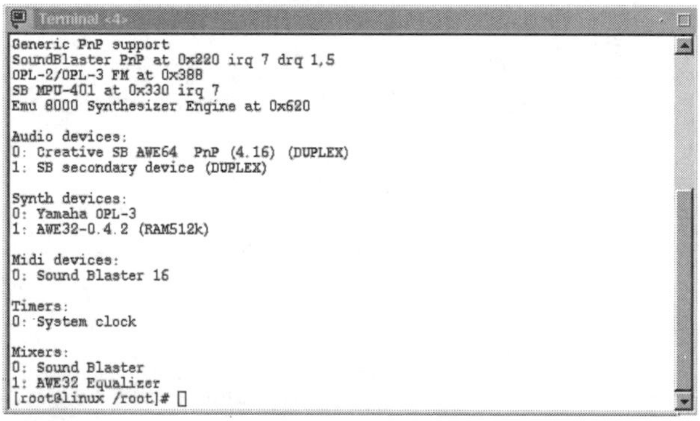

FIGURE 10.3
A list showing the installed sound devices.

```
Terminal <4>
Generic PnP support
SoundBlaster PnP at 0x220 irq 7 drq 1,5
OPL-2/OPL-3 FM at 0x388
SB MPU-401 at 0x330 irq 7
Emu 8000 Synthesizer Engine at 0x620

Audio devices:
0: Creative SB AWE64 PnP (4.16) (DUPLEX)
1: SB secondary device (DUPLEX)

Synth devices:
0: Yamaha OPL-3
1: AWE32-0.4.2 (RAM512k)

Midi devices:
0: Sound Blaster 16

Timers:
0: System clock

Mixers:
0: Sound Blaster
1: AWE32 Equalizer
[root@linux /root]#
```

If you see the message "No such file or directory," the device files weren't created, and you'll have to reinstall the drivers. "No such device" means that sound driver is not loaded. Go through the installation procedure again.

When the device is loaded correctly, you can test the sound setup. To test standard PC sounds you'll need AU or WAV audio files. *AU* is a Sun Microsystems format that is universally recognized by all computer systems, but AU quality is rather poor. *WAV* is the native sound format for Windows. WAV format is much better quality, but the files are much bigger, though not as big as MP3 files. WAV is the format generally used for sounds on Linux.

You can search your system for files by using the K Find Files tool and searching for *.au and *.wav. The standard KDE desktop setup includes some WAV sound files that are designed to be associated with actions like opening windows and shutting down. If they are on your computer, you can use them for testing your setup.

If you need to get sample sound files, you can find WAV sound samples at the Wave Events Web site at www.waveevents.com. A Web site with a good selection of free sound samples in AU and MP3 format is the Novepulse MultiMedia Web site at www.novepulse.com.

Next, do a quick check using one of the sound files. This example will use one of the sound files that is installed with the KDE desktop. If you don't have the file, you'll need to get a sound sample file to do this check. You should use only AU or WAV sounds for the check.

You'll send the sound file to the sound device. It won't sound pretty, but it's just a crude way to test that sound is set up. Enter the command:

```
cat /opt/kde/share/sounds/ktalkd.wav >/dev/dsp
cat /opt/kde/share/sounds/ktalkd.wav >/dev/audio
```

The reason for the two lines is to test two different devices on the sound card. /dev/dsp does the analog to digital conversion, and /dev/audio does the digital to analog conversion. You can substitute any WAV or AU file for this test. Make sure to put in the proper name for your sound file. Don't worry about the sound quality. This is not a proper sound player, but it is only a way to test the sound.

If all this works, you can use the command-line MP3 player included with OpenLinux to get a better idea of the quality of the sound. You'll need an MP3 file to do this test. The Novepulse Web site has some good, small MP3 sample sounds. The command to test your sound with MP3 is

```
mpg123 filename.mp3
```

N O T E   If you don't know about MP3, there's a section about it later in this chapter. ▓

Be sure to put in the proper filename for your MP3 file.

If everything is working OK, open the Sound Mixer Panel under Multimedia on the K Application Launcher. Use KMix to control volume and sound balance, see Figure 10.4.

FIGURE 10.4
The Sound Mixer Panel controls balance and volume for all the sound devices on your system.

Then try playing a CD. Open the CD player on your computer and insert a music CD. Start the CD Player. It is also under Multimedia on the K Application Launcher. Click on the play button to start playing the CD, see Figure 10.5.

FIGURE 10.5
The CD player supports CDDB, the CD Database.

 TIP

If you receive an error message indicating it couldn't find the CD-ROM drive, you need to create a link to the CD-ROM for the player program. You'll need to know the device name of your CD-ROM drive. To find the device name of your CD-ROM drive, look in the fstab file in the /etc directory and find the line that for /mnt/cdrom. At the beginning of that line is the device name for the CD-ROM drive. Then, in a terminal window, enter the command:

```
ln -s /dev/hdc /dev/cdrom
```

This is an example using a CD-ROM drive at /dev/hdc; use the correct device name for your system.

The controls on the CD player are designed to resemble what you'd find on a regular CD player. One feature, though, isn't on regular CD players: *CDDB*, the CD Database system.

If you set up and use CDDB, you'll always have easy access to full information about your CDs because that information is automatically downloaded over the Internet onto your computer when you start the CD. The artist and title appear in the display screen, and the name of each track is displayed in the drop-down list below the display screen.

CDDB is a free service. For more information on use of CDDB, check out the CDDB Web site at www.cddb.com.

To set up CDDB in the CD player, click on the Configure KSCD button in the middle of the buttons across the bottom of the player. It's the button with a hammer/screwdriver symbol on it. If you want to use this feature, make sure that Enable Remote CDDB is checked on (see Figure 10.6).

The only entry that is necessary is the default entry for the CDDB Internet site. The entry should read www.cddb.com cddbp 8880 -. If you have other CD databases you want to use, add them here.

The next time you play a CD, if you are connected to the Internet, the database will be checked and the information about your CD will be displayed.

FIGURE 10.6
When setting up CDDB, make sure the Enable Remote CDDB is checked on.

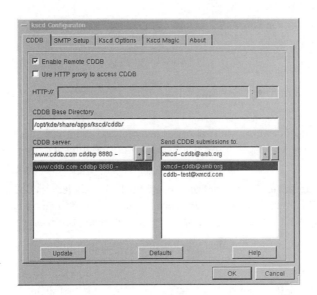

Make Your OpenLinux PC a Boombox with MP3

MP3 is the hottest thing in the world of music. It is a file format easily distributed on the Internet that produces sound of CD quality.

MP3 is short for *MPEG-1 Layer 3*, a technology invented in 1991 at the Fraunhofer Institute, a German audio research lab. Unlike other compression formats, MP3 files do not lose their quality. That's part of what makes them so popular.

College students first grabbed onto MP3 because of its flexibility—it's easy to create your own playlist—and because the files are small enough to distribute over the Internet. The sound quality is so close to CD sound that PCs were easily turned into virtual boomboxes.

MP3 has spread far beyond the campus. You can now buy an MP3 Walkman-like player and take the music you've downloaded onto your OpenLinux system anywhere you want.

To find out more about MP3, look at the Web site at www.mp3.com. It's also the best Web site to go to when you are looking for free MP3 music files. The site has hundreds, maybe thousands, of free music files.

If you have sound working on your system, you can play MP3 music on your OpenLinux computer without any additional setup. A basic command-line MP3 player is included. The program is mpg123, a fast and free MP3 player. The *123* refers to the program's capability to play Layer 1, 2, and 3 formats.

To play an MP3 music file, simply use the command:

```
mpg123 filename.mp3
```

This will start the music playing.

The limitation with mpg123 is that it doesn't have a playlist and the other features found in graphical MP3 players.

You can get one of the top graphical MP3 players, Xaudio, for only $10. It's shareware, and you can get a free trial version by downloading it off the Internet at www.xaudio.com/ downloads/.

Look for the Linux version and get the binary file that's labeled "statically linked package: xaudio-1.0-5.i386.rpm." The version number may be different if an update has been made available. This is an rpm package that you can install using the K package manager.

Once it's installed, open a terminal window and enter the command:

```
mxaudio
```

The Xaudio player (see Figure 10.7) can play files on your system or files on Internet servers. From the File menu select Open File to play a file that is on your system, select Open URL to play a file from a Web site, or select Open PlayList to use a playlist you've created.

FIGURE 10.7
Turn your PC into a boombox. The Xaudio player can play MP3 music files.

The graphical player is installed in the /usr/bin directory. You can add an icon to the desktop to launch the player from that directory.

The Xaudio player is fully configurable. A help file is included that describes all of its configuration options.

Open Sound Commercial Drivers

A commercial solution is Open Sound System for OpenLinux. Hannu Savolainen, the same person who wrote the free drivers, developed the Open Sound System (OSS).

OSS supports all the advanced features not found in the basic drivers that ship with OpenLinux, and it's easy to install and almost always can autodetect your sound card during installation so that no special knowledge or skills are required.

OSS supports full-streaming audio, speech recognition and generation, computer telephony, Java and other multimedia technologies, as well as synchronized audio capabilities required for desktop video and animation playback.

The driver is only $20 and well worth the price. You can find out more at the Open Sound System Web site at www.opensound.com.

Part
III
Ch
10

There's a demo version of the software available for free download. It only runs for three hours, but it gives you a chance to try out the program.

If you decide to install the demo version, make sure you get the package prepared for Caldera OpenLinux 2.3. The other versions might not work. If you have the boxed edition of OpenLinux, the demo version of the software is on the Windows Tools & Commercial Packages CD.

The installation procedure is simple. Move the installation package you have downloaded to the /tmp directory. At a terminal prompt, in the /tmp directory, enter the command:

```
tar zxvf osslinux*
```

After that you should have three files in the /tmp directory: INSTALL, oss-install, and oss.pkg.

OSS can't be installed if a sound driver is already loaded. If you want to see whether you have a sound driver loaded, enter the following command:

```
cat /dev/sndstat
```

If it displays information about sound drivers, you have a driver installed.

The installation procedure for OSS/Linux automatically unloads and disables the sound driver if it is loaded. You are asked for permission before any existing sound driver is disabled.

Execute the installation program. At the /tmp prompt, enter the following command:

```
./oss-install
```

Make sure you enter the dot followed by a slash.

Use the Tab key to maneuver through the screens.

The default directory to install to is /usr/lib/oss, but the program offers to install the drivers in other directories.

After installation is complete, you can start the driver by entering the command:

```
soundon
```

To stop the driver, use the command:

```
soundoff
```

If you need to change the configuration of the driver first stop the sound driver by using the soundoff command, then enter the command:

```
soundconf
```

Configuring Hardware Performance

In this chapter

Computer users and system administrators are always trying to get more out of their computers without buying more hardware. How can you make your system run faster? It's a question that's been around since the first computer was built.

Optimizing hardware performance is always a compromise between what is possible and what you can afford.

OpenLinux is a well-tuned system right out of the box, so making changes is not something you should do casually. A change that might seem to improve one part of the system can cause a problem in another part.

You can rarely improve hardware performance by copying a set of instructions from a book. This chapter is only an introduction to the process of configuring your hardware for performance. For a full understanding of the process and of what is happening in your system, you should look at a Linux system administrator's manual.

This chapter tells you where to look for possible bottlenecks, how to improve memory performance when you can't add memory, and how to check your hard disk and improve its performance.

System Information

The first step in configuring hardware performance is obtaining information about your system.

You can use the KDE Control Center to find most of the information you need. Although nothing can be changed from this panel, it can give you the kind of details you need to troubleshoot your system.

To launch the KDE Control Center, select the KDE Control Center icon on the K Panel or, from the K Application Launcher, choose KDE Control Center.

Click on Information in the left pane, and a list of 12 information areas is displayed. Click on an information area icon to display its contents in the right pane.

N O T E An alternative way to access the information about your system is to go to Settings from the K Application Launcher, choose Information, and select the specific area of information for which you are looking. ■

This panel has 12 information areas, which I outline in the following sections.

Devices

This page (shown in Figure 11.1) displays information on the available devices, listing them by group. *Character devices* are the device names for keyboards, modems, and so forth. *Block devices* are the device names for floppy disk drives, hard disk drives, and so on. The Miscellaneous devices are for device types that aren't defined as character or block devices. The bus mouse is one device found under miscellaneous. The numbers are not related to the device names in the /dev directory, but instead refer to device types. The information is read from /proc/devices and /proc/misc.

FIGURE 11.1
The KDE Control Center shows device information.

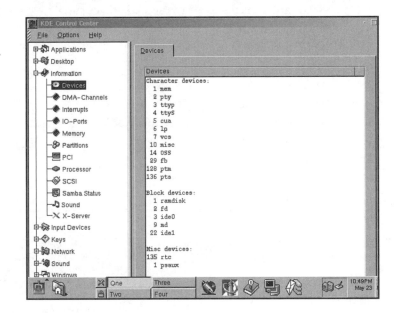

DMA Channels

This page shows which DMA channels are being used. A *DMA channel* is a direct connection that allows a device to transfer data to and from memory without going through the processor. This information is read from /proc/dma.

Interrupts

This page (shown in Figure 11.2) displays which interrupts are being used. An *Interrupt Request Line* (*IRQ*) is used by keyboards, mice, network cards, and so on to send interrupt signals to the processor that the device is ready to send or receive data. There are 16 possible interrupts. Hardware problems are frequently caused by two devices that are attempting to use the same interrupt. This information is read from /proc/interrupts. The standard hardware interrupts are shown in Table 11.1.

Part
III

Ch
11

Table 11.1   Standard PC Hardware Interrupts

IRQ	Description
0	System timer
1	Keyboard
2	Second programmable interrupt controller
3	ttyS1 and ttyS3 (COM 2 and COM 4)
4	ttyS0 and ttyS2 (COM 1 and COM 3)
5	Sound card (sometimes used as second printer port)
6	Floppy disk controller
7	Printer port (lp0)
8	System clock
9	Available
10	Available, sometimes network or video card
11	Available, sometimes network or video card, IRQ holder for PCI steering
12	PS/2-style mouse
13	Numeric coprocessor
14	Primary IDE hard disk controller
15	Secondary IDE hard disk controller

FIGURE 11.2

The KDE Control Center displays interrupts used by devices such as the mouse and network card.

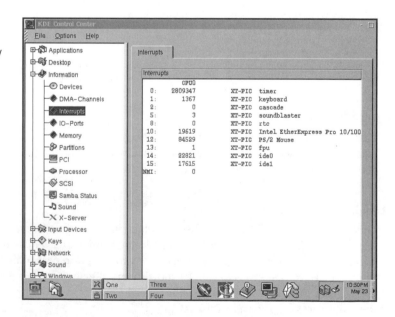

I/O Ports

This page shows I/O port use. *I/O ports* are memory addresses used by the processor for communication with a device that has sent an interrupt signal to the processor. No two devices can share the same I/O port, and system problems can be caused when two devices attempt to do so. This information is read from /proc/ioports

Memory

This page (shown in Figure 11.3) displays current memory use as well as total memory, free memory, shared memory, and buffer memory. It also shows swap memory and how much of it is free. This information is read from /proc/meminfo.

FIGURE 11.3
The KDE Control Center displays memory information.

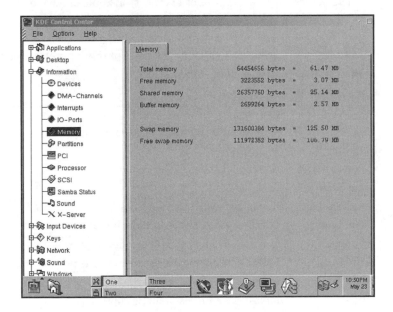

Partitions

This page shows the partitions mounted on your system. Partitions are listed by device name, and the size is shown in blocks. This information is read from /proc/partitions.

PCI

This page shows technical details about PCI (Peripheral Component Interconnect) cards installed on your computer. This information is read from /proc/pci. The PCI bus on the system board is a high speed, 32-bit connector for add-on cards. Network and video cards as well as some sound cards use the PCI bus. If an add-on card in your system isn't using the PCI bus, it is using the ISA (Industry System Architecture) bus, a slower 16-bit connector.

Processor

This page (shown in Figure 11.4) displays the CPU installed in your computer, its speed in MHz, its cache size, and so on. This information is read from /proc/cpuinfo. The contents and field names vary from processor to processor. Some of the most common field names are shown in Table 11.2.

Table 11.2   Definitions of some of the computer processor information fields shown by Procossor information.

Item	Description
processor	CPU number. On single processor systems, this is usually 0. The number is assigned by the manufacturer and has no special meaning.
vendor_id	Manufacturer name
model name	Common name, such as Pentium
cpu MHz	Speed of CPU
cache size	Size of cache memory on CPU
fdiv_bug	Indicates whether the fdiv cpu bug is present
hlt_bug	Indicates whether the hlt cpu bug is present
sep_bug	Indicates whether if the sep cpu bug is present
f00f_bug	Indicates whether the f00f cpu bug is present
fpu	Indicates whether a numeric coprocessor is present
bogomips	Bogus MIPS (Millions of Instructions Processed per Second). A speed measurement tool.

N O T E Bogomips are calculated by timing a short loop during the boot process. The resulting figure cannot accurately compare transfer rates with a different processor. Therefore, it is a bogus measurement that cannot be used for any real speed comparisons. ■

FIGURE 11.4
The KDE Control Center displays CPU information.

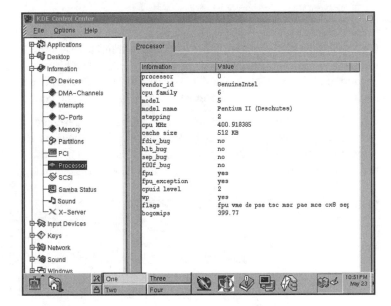

SCSI

This page shows the SCSI devices installed on your computer. Typical SCSI devices are hard drives, CD-ROM drives, and some removable disk drives such as the JAZ drive. Also, most scanners use SCSI connections. This information is read from /proc/scsi/scsi.

Samba Status

This page shows the status of the Samba server running on your computer, as well as details about service use, user and group IDs, and other information about the current use of your server. Information is updated every minute, and is read from the smbstatus utility. For more information on setting up and running a Samba server, see Chapter 20, "Installing and Configuring a Windows Network."

Sound

This page displays information about the sound card installed on your computer and its driver. This information is read from /dev/sndstat.

X Server

This page displays the name, version number, and other details about the X Server on your system. It also shows the dimension in pixels and centimeters, the resolution in dots per inch, and available color depths for your screen.

Managing Processes

On a multiple-user system such as Linux, many different users can be using different programs at the same time. A program can even be started and continue to run in the background after the user who started it logs off. Process management can improve the performance of your computer and take care of problems and conflicts as they develop.

The KDE Task Manager (shown in Figure 11.5) is a tool designed to help you both monitor and manage processes. The KDE Task Manager is also known as *Ktop* and performs the same function as the monitoring program called top. To launch the KDE Task Manager, from the K Application Launcher, go to System, and choose Task Manager.

FIGURE 11.5

The KDE Task Manager shows a list of processes on your system.

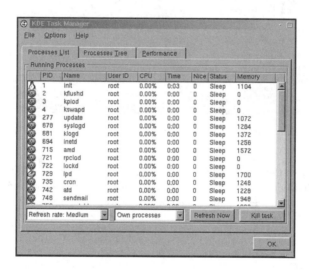

When the Task Manager opens, there are three tab panels: Processes List, Processes Tree, and Performance.

The Processes List tab shows a list of processes that are currently running on your system. The list can be sorted by each column:

- **PID**—The process ID number assigned by the system when the process started.
- **Name**—Program name of the process.
- **User ID**—The login name of the user that started the process.
- **CPU usage**—The percentage of CPU time used by the process.
- **Time running**—The amount of CPU computation time the process has used so far.
- **Nice**—The scheduling priority for the process.
- **Status**—Indicates whether the process is running or sleeping.
- **Memory**—The total amount of memory, in kilobytes, that the process uses.

Two list boxes and two buttons appear across the bottom of the Task Manager Processes List window:

- **Refresh Rate**—How often the process list is updated. Slow, medium, and fast rates are available.

- **Process Filter**—Used to reduce the number of processes displayed. Choices are all, system, user, or your own processes.

- **Refresh Now**—Click this button to force an immediate update of the processes list.

- **Kill Task**—To terminate a process, highlight a process and press this button. Doing so sends a kill signal that shuts down the process.

In addition to the buttons, pointing to a process and right-clicking shows a pop-up menu that enables you to send different signals to the process or change its scheduling priority. A process is *reniced* to change its priority, which determines the amount of CPU time the process receives to do its job. Database sorts and other long-running processes are often reniced so that response time for active users isn't as sluggish. If you are logged in as a regular user, you can only change the priority order of your own processes. To change the priority of all running processes, you have to be logged in as root.

The Processes Tree tab (seen in Figure 11.6) shows the relationships between running processes. A process started by another process is referred to as a *child* process. The tree shows the *parent* and *child* relationships of the processes.

Part

III

Ch

11

FIGURE 11.6

The KDE Task Manager shows a tree of the processes on your system.

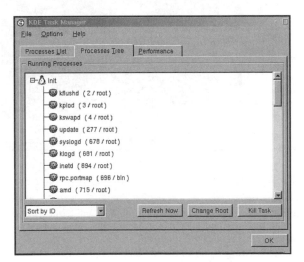

A list box and three buttons appear across the bottom of the Task Manager Processes Tree window:

- **Sort**—Change the sorting order of the child processes. The options are to sort by process ID number (PID), the process Name, or Owner (UID) of the process.

- **Refresh Now**—Click this button to force an immediate update of the processes tree.

- **Change Root**—If you are interested in only a certain subtree, select the parent process and press this button to make the process the root of the tree. Pressing this button with no process selected resets the root to the default setting.

- **Kill Task**—To terminate a process, highlight a process and press this button. Doing so sends a kill signal that shuts down the process.

The Performance tab (seen in Figure 11.7) shows two meters: The top meter is overall processor load, and the bottom meter is total memory used. The red line in the memory usage meter is the separation between physical memory (RAM) and virtual memory (swap space).

FIGURE 11.7
The KDE Task Manager performance meters.

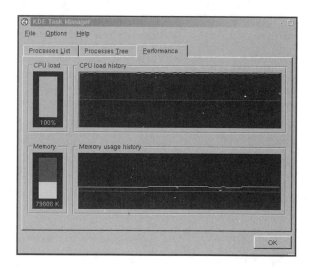

Neither meter is very useful. A built-in disparity in the CPU usage meter shows CPU usage for everything, including the KDE Task Manager. This means that you can't get a true reading of CPU usage this way. The uptime command, explained later in this chapter, is more useful for monitoring CPU usage.

Because Linux uses caching to minimize disk access, the memory meter can't distinguish between good caching and a program that's a memory hog.

Following are some tips on what you can do to configure hardware performance using the KDE Task Manager. Taking these steps can often improve overall system response:

- **Watch for processes that have very high time figures**—These can be processes that have gone into a loop or that have another error. Check with the user who started the process. Usually, you'll need to kill the process.

- **Watch for processes that are consuming a high CPU percentage**—If it is a process that shouldn't be tying up everything else on the system, renice the process to force it to a lower priority or kill the job and restart it during off-peak hours. Of course, don't do that without talking to the person who started the process.

- **Watch for processes that take up lots of memory**—If you don't think that the process should be using so much memory, check the program that is being run. Something might be wrong. Don't renice memory hogs; that won't reduce the amount of memory they are consuming.

- **Don't worry about processes that are sleeping**—Having lots of sleeping processes has no effect on system performance.

Monitoring System Load

Another useful tool for monitoring the system is the uptime command. Open a terminal window and enter the following command:

```
uptime
```

The results will look something like this:

```
10:30am   up 6 days, 145 users, load average: 2.01, 2.41, 2.14
```

This line indicates the current time(how long the system has been running); the number of users; and the load average over the last minute, the last five minutes, and the last 15 minutes. The load average is based on the average number of jobs waiting to run within the given time period.

Run uptime regularly to get a feeling for the typical load average for your system. Then, if the system seems to be slow one day, you can look at the load and see if the sluggishness is being caused by a higher than normal load, which can be temporary and might take care of itself after the heavy process is done.

If you have a single-user workstation, your system load average should never go much over 2. If it regularly does, you probably need to analyze what you are doing. You might be running too many big jobs at the same time, or you might need a more powerful processor to keep up with the workload.

Server loads are different. Any server load that is less than 3 shows that the demand is low. A well-used server will show a load average of around 4 or 5, but any server with a load average that is more than 10 is headed for trouble. If you regularly see a load level that high, you need to take measures as soon as possible to either redistribute the load or to increase the server's capacity.

For a more precise level of monitoring, you can use the monitoring utility called top. Top provides constantly updated information. To start top, open a terminal window and enter the command **top**. A sample top screen is shown in Figure 11.8.

FIGURE 11.8

You can use the top program to monitor system load.

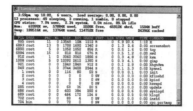

Top gives a constant readout of the system load, while using very few system resources. The first line of the display shows the current time, how long the system has been up, the number of users, and the load average during the last 1, 5, and 15 minutes. You can toggle the load average display off or on by pressing the l key.

The processes line shows the number of processes running at the time of the last update. You can toggle the processes display off or on by pressing the t key.

The CPU States line shows the CPU use time in percentages in user mode, system mode, niced tasks, and idle. You can also toggle the CPU states display off or on by pressing the t key.

The memory line shows the total available memory, the amount of memory used, how much is free, shared memory, and buffered memory. You can toggle the memory display off or on by pressing the m key.

The swap line shows swap space usage, the amount available, and the amount free.

The rest of the display shows the running processes, listed in order of process ID (PID).

Eliminating Daemons

One way to improve the performance of your system is to make sure you aren't running unnecessary processes.

A Linux system is constantly working, whether you are aware of it or not. Many background processes, called *daemons*, are started at bootup time. Some daemons that are loaded by default might not be needed on your system; removing unneeded daemons frees up processing cycles and can improve overall performance. However, depending on which daemons you remove, you might not see a noticeable performance boost because many of these background processes are set to run only during idle times, during off hours, or on demand.

To see the daemons that are being loaded at startup on your system, use the COAS system administrator Systems Services tool. Take one of the following actions to launch this:

- From the COAS icon on the K Panel, choose System and select Daemons.
- From the K Application Launcher, choose COAS, System, and then select Daemons.

From the list of installed daemons (see Figure 11.9), you can select which ones are to launch on startup; uncheck any process that you don't want launched on startup. Following are some of the daemons you might be capable of removing, depending on how you are using your system:

FIGURE 11.9
The COAS System Services tool shows which processes are launched on startup.

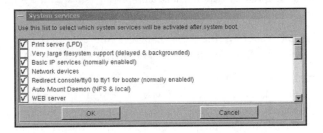

- **Printer server (LPD)**—If you don't have access to a printer, either connected directly to your computer or over a network, you don't need to run the print server daemon.
- **Web server (Apache)**—If you aren't running a Web server on your system, you can disable the daemon.
- **DHCP and BOOTP**—If you aren't using DHCP or BOOTP for managing network IP addresses, you don't need to run this daemon. DHCP and BOOTP are server daemons used to assign network addresses automatically to computers on a local area network. There can be only one DHCP server for any set of network addresses.
- **IPX**—If you aren't connected to a Novell network, you don't need the IPX daemon.
- **Mail Transfer Agent (Sendmail)**—If your computer isn't being used as a mail server, either for your workstation or for a network, you should disable this daemon. In fact, there are many good reasons to disable it. For one thing, Sendmail is unlike other daemons in that it runs frequently and consumes lots of processor cycles. Email programs don't need Sendmail—most email programs use SMTP to transfer mail to a server that is running Sendmail. If you are using OpenLinux on a single-user workstation, it is unlikely that you need Sendmail.
- **The remote user daemons**—The BSD remote user info daemon, rwall daemon, and BSD remote who daemon aren't needed for most purposes and require a fair amount of time when used. If you aren't sure whether you need these daemons, you don't need them.

N O T E You can also manage daemons using LISA. From the command prompt, start LISA and choose System Configuration. Select System Configuration again, and then choose Configure daemon/server autostart. ■

Memory Performance and Swap Space

Memory is as important to your system's performance as the CPU. To perform well, the system must have adequate memory. There's no real substitute for adding memory if you don't have enough.

You can't do a lot to improve the performance of your computer's memory; you either have enough memory or you don't. There's no in-between state that can be tweaked.

When you installed OpenLinux, you created a *swap partition*, a space that is usually twice the size of the amount of memory installed on your computer. This is an area of hard drive space that Linux can use as virtual memory. When the system runs out of memory, it uses the swap space as if it were memory—but swap space is considerably slower than actual memory. Swap space is usually used only on big memory intensive jobs such as high-end graphics editing or database management systems.

A temporary solution to an out-of-memory problem is to create a swap file. This is also good if you have a new program that requires more swap space than was originally installed on your system.

You can have multiple swap spaces and files. Swap files are slower than swap partitions, but you can easily resize or remove them, freeing up their space for other use. Also, when you use swap files, there's no need to reinstall the system. To create a swap file, log in as root.

First, decide how big your swap file will be. Don't make it bigger than 128MB, which is the Linux limit for each individual swap file or partition. Also, you must decide on a name for your swap file.

You'll need to set aside the space for the swap file on the hard drive. To do this, use the dd command. To set aside 64MB of space for a swap file, enter the following command:

```
dd if=/dev/zero of=/swap bs=1024 count=64000
```

The dd (device-to-device copy) utility is being used here to create a blank space. A blank device is read, the if=/dev/zero, and "copied" to create an empty area. The of=/swap parameter defines the swap file's name. This will create a file called /swap that has 64,000 blocks of 1,024 bytes each, for 64MB.

Enter the sync command to make sure that everything is written from memory to the hard disk:

```
sync
```

Next, the file needs to be formatted as a swap file, which is done with the `mkswap` command:

```
mkswap -c /swap 64000
```

The mkswap utility sets up the swap area. The `-c` parameter checks for bad blocks before creating the swap file. The `/swap` parameter is the name of the swap file that is being created and must match the name used with the dd utility. The `64000` parameter is the number of blocks in the swap file and must match the number of blocks created by the dd utility.

To activate the new swap file, use the `swapon` command:

```
swapon /swap
```

Now you have 64MB of extra swap space available on your system.

To deactivate the swap file, enter the `swapoff` command:

```
swapoff /swap
```

If you want the new swap space to be loaded every time you boot up the system, you'll need to add it to the fstab configuration file in the /etc directory.

Open the file in a text editor, and put the following command on its own line:

```
/swap none swap sw
```

This line indicates that the device to be mounted is named /swap. It doesn't have a mount point (none). The file system type is swap, and the options are set to swap.

You can delete a swap file just like any other file, but be sure to turn off the swap file first using the `swapoff` command, and then remove any references to it from the fstab configuration file.

Checking and Fixing Disk Problems

Every time OpenLinux starts up, it checks the file system. You can also check the file system manually. You might want to do this if your system has been up for a long time (and therefore hasn't been checked in a while), or if you think that there might be a problem with one of your disk partitions.

> **CAUTION**
>
> Do not check a mounted disk. Checking a mounted system can lead to unrecoverable damage if any files are open.

Part

III

Ch

11

The fsck command checks the file system. First, unmount the disk you want to check with the umount command (the first *n* of *unmount* is left out of the umount command name). If the root partition needs to be checked, you need to be in single-user, read-only mode. Open a terminal window and enter the command

```
telinit 1
```

This puts you into single-user mode. Enter the root password to log on to the system. Then, remount the root partition in read-only mode:

```
mount -n -o ro,remount /
```

The -n parameter mounts without writing to the /etc/mtab table of mounted devices. This is necessary when mounting read-only. The -o ro parameter mounts with the read-only option. The remount parameter unmounts and then remounts an already-mounted file system. The / parameter indicates that the root file system is being mounted.

You are now ready to continue checking the root partition.

To check a partition, enter the following command:

```
fsck filesystem -f
```

For file system, enter either the device name, such as /dev/hda1, or the directory where the partition is mounted, such as /home.

The -f forces a check, even if the device was cleanly unmounted.

Improving Hard Drive Performance

The hard disk also affects your system's performance, but not in the same way that the CPU and memory do. Hard disk performance is only noticed when you are reading from or writing to the disk.

Following are some tips on how to maximize the performance of your hard disk system. First, I show you some things you can do with your system as it is. Then, if you still need to improve performance, I have added some steps you might want to consider.

Tip #1: Clean Up Your Disk

The first tip might seem obvious: Clean up your disk drive. Delete unneeded files. Move off anything that needs to be saved but won't be used. Eliminate excess directories and reduce the number of subdirectories, if possible.

These suggestions might seem obvious, but you'd be surprised how much junk accumulates on everyone's disks. Freeing up disk space can help the system perform better.

Tip #2: Defragment Your Disk

Fragmentation on Linux systems is not like fragmentation on Windows 95/98 or Windows NT systems. Windows uses the FAT file system. Windows 98 introduced the FAT32 file system, though it is not necessary to convert to FAT32 to run Windows 98. Windows NT can be set up using FAT or an enhanced file system called NTFS. All these file systems handle file storage in essentially the same way.

On any Windows system, fragmentation is a constant problem, and if you don't take care of it, system performance can be eroded.

Linux uses the second extended file system, called ext2, which handles file storage in a completely different way. Linux doesn't have the kinds of problems found on Windows systems, which leads many to think that fragmentation isn't a problem at all—but that's not exactly true.

The following sidebar tells a little story to give you a rough idea of what's going on.

Linux Warehouse Storage System Versus MS Warehouse Storage System

Let's say there are two warehouses where you live. One is called MS Warehouse, and the other is called Linux Warehouse.

First, we'll go inside MS Warehouse. Inside, you see someone very hard at work. He has a palette with a giant crate on it marked YourFile. The warehouse worker takes the crate into the storage area. At the first available opening, the worker stops, opens the crate, and puts as much of the crate's contents into the opening as will fit. The worker then moves on to the next available opening and fills it with as much as it will take. This continues until the YourFile crate is completely stored. If you ever need part of YourFile, the warehouse worker looks at the record and quickly moves to the area in which YourFile is stored and retrieves it. If the whole contents need to be retrieved, the warehouse worker has to go to each section of the warehouse in which the different parts are stored. About once a month, a special team from the Defragmenter department comes in, sifts through the warehouse, and reorders the storage so that every crate has its contents stored in one place rather than scattered around the warehouse.

Now we'll look in the Linux warehouse. Here, the warehouse worker looks at the crate marked YourFile and checks the record of what's already stored. He finds a space that's big enough to hold the whole crate. He moves YourFile to that space and stores it there. If you need to access the YourFile crate, the warehouse worker checks the record, finds it, and retrieves it. The entire contents are right there, so retrieval of the whole thing—or just part of it—doesn't involve any extra steps. This is why some people think that the folks at the Linux Warehouse don't have a Defragmentation team, and it is also why good defragmentation tools aren't available. But a closer look at the Linux Warehouse reveals that as the warehouse gets full, or that sometimes a crate comes in that's bigger than any single available space. Therefore, the crate is divided up, and it will stay divided as long as it's stored there.

The point is that all file systems tend to become fragmented over time. The Linux file system reduces fragmentation, but doesn't eliminate it. However, this is not a problem that comes up on a frequent basis, and for a single-user workstation, it might not be a problem at all.

On busy servers, however, file fragmentation will degrade performance over time.

The best way to defragment Linux is to do a complete backup, reformat the partition, and then restore the files from backup. When the files are restored, they will be written in contiguous blocks: They won't be fragmented. This is a big job and probably isn't necessary for program partitions such as /usr that don't change often, but it can work wonders on a /home partition on a system with a lot of users. The amount of time it will take isn't that much different than the amount of time it takes to defragment a Windows NT server.

If hard disk performance is still not satisfactory, there are some other steps you might want to consider, but any hardware solution that involves upgrading or buying new equipment can be expensive. Be prepared to spend some money if you must have top-level performance.

Tip #3: Upgrade from IDE to SCSI

If your hard disk is an IDE drive, you can obtain better overall performance by upgrading to a SCSI drive. Because the IDE controller must access the CPU, actions that are both CPU-intensive and disk-intensive can become very sluggish. SCSI controllers handle reading and writing without going through the CPU. When the IDE drive is reading or writing, the users might complain about the slowness of the system because the CPU cycles are being tied up by the IDE drive.

Tip #4: Get Faster Controllers, Disks

Standard SCSI controllers cannot read or write data any faster than standard IDE controllers, but some very fast "ultra-wide" SCSI controllers can make a real difference in the speed of reads and writes.

EIDE and UDMA controllers are much faster IDE controllers. The new UDMA controllers can approach the speeds of the fast SCSI controllers, though they are still slower. The top speeds for UDMA controllers are burst speeds; sustained transfer rates are considerably slower. IDE controllers, including UDMA, are built into the drive itself. To get UDMA performance, you don't buy a controller, you buy the drive, which includes the controller.

One aspect of disk drives that is often overlooked is the speed of the disk itself. A disk's speed is given in RPMs, which stands for *revolutions per minute*. Faster RPMs are, well, *faster*. If you have the budget for it, most manufacturers of server systems provide 7,500 and even 10,000 RPM SCSI disks. Standard SCSI and IDE disks provide 3,600 RPMs.

Tip #5: Use Multiple Controllers

IDE and SCSI disks can be chained. An IDE chain is limited to two devices and a standard SCSI chain is limited to seven. Most likely, if you have two or more SCSI disks in your system, they are chained to the same controller. This is fine for most operations—especially if you use your computer as a single-user workstation—but if you have a server, you can improve performance by giving each SCSI drive its own controller. Of course, good controllers can be expensive.

Tip #6: Tune Hard Disk Parameters

You can use the hdparm utility to tune the performances of IDE hard disks. The utility was designed particularly for use with UDMA drives.

By default, Linux uses the safest, but slowest, settings for accessing IDE drives. The default mode does not make use of the faster performance possible with UDMA drives.

You can use the hdparm utility to improve performance significantly by enabling these features:

- **32-bit support**—The default setting is 16-bit.
- **Multisector access**—The default setting is single-sector transfers per interrupt.

CAUTION

Before using a utility like hdparm, make sure your system is fully backed up. Using hdparm to change the IDE parameters can cause a total loss of the data on the drive if something goes wrong. Take care.

Hdparm can show you a great deal of information about your hard disks. Open a terminal window and enter this command for information on the first IDE drive on your system (change the device name to get information on any other IDE drives):

```
hdparm -v /dev/hda
```

The display shows the information obtained from the drive when the system was started, including whether the drive is operating in 16-bit or 32-bit mode (I/O support) and multisector access (multcount). For a more detailed display of information about the disk drive use the -i parameter.

Hdparm can also test drive transfer rates. Enter the command to test the first IDE drive on your system:

```
hdparm -Tt /dev/hda
```

This test measures the direct device reads and the buffer cache reads. The result is an optimistic "best-case" figure.

Part

III

Ch

11

To change the drive settings to enable 32-bit transfers, enter this command:

```
hdparm -c3 /dev/hda
```

The -c3 parameter enables 32-bit support. Use -c0 to disable it. The -c1 parameter also enables 32-bit supportand uses less memory overhead, but it does not work with many drives.

Most new IDE drives support multisector transfers, but the default Linux setting is for single-sector transfers.

> **CAUTION**
>
> Be careful with this setting. On some drives, enabling mutlisector transfers can cause total corruption of the file system. The problems are mostly with older drives.

To enable multisector transfers, enter this command:

```
hdparm -m16 /dev/hda
```

The -m16 parameter enables 16 multisector transfers. A setting of 16 or 32 is optimum for most drives, except those from Western Digital. Western Digital drives have small buffers and performance will significantly drop with any setting over 8. A setting of 4 may be optimal for Western Digital drives.

Enabling multisector access can reduce the load on the CPU by 30 to 50 percent while it can increase data transfer rates by up to 50 percent. To disable multisector transfers use the -m0 parameter.

There are many more options for tweaking hard drives using hdparm. For more detailed information on hdparm, read the hdparm man page:

```
man 8 hdparm
```

Tip #7: Use Software RAID

RAID, Redundant Array of Inexpensive Drives, can also improve disk drive performance and capacity. Linux supports both software RAID and hardware RAID. Software RAID is built into the Linux kernel and costs much less than hardware RAID. The only cost for software RAID is what it costs to buy the disks on your system, but software RAID doesn't give the performance boost of hardware RAID. Hardware RAID uses specially designed hardware to control multiple disks on your system. Hardware RAID can be expensive, but it has an performance improvement to match.

The basic idea of RAID is to combine multiple, small, and inexpensive disk drives into an array of disk drives that gives the same performance level of the single large drives found on mainframe computers. The RAID drive array appears to the computer to be a single drive.

RAID can also use parallel processing. Disk reads and writes take place simultaneously on parallel data paths to the disks in the RAID array.

In 1987, IBM cosponsored a study at the University of California at Berkeley that led to an initial definition of RAID levels. There are now six defined RAID levels, as shown in Table 11.3. OpenLinux supports Levels 0, 1, and 5.

Table 11.3	The different RAID levels
Level	**Description**
RAID 0	Level 0 is data striping only. In level 0, data is split across more than one drive, resulting in higher data throughput. This is the fastest and most efficient form of RAID. However, no data mirroring occurs at this level, so the failure of any disk in the array results in a loss of all data.
RAID 1	Level 1 is full disk mirroring. Two copies of the data are created and maintained on separate disks. A level 1 array tends to be faster on reads and slower on writes compared to a single drive, but if either drive fails, no data is lost. This is the most expensive RAID level because every disk requires a second disk for its mirror. This level provides the best data security.
RAID 2	Level 2 is intended for use with drives that do not have built-in error detection. Because all SCSI drives support built-in error detection, this level is of little use and is outdated. Linux does not use this level.
RAID 3	Level 3 is disk striping with a parity disk. Saving parity information on a separate drive allows recovery from the failure of any single drive. Linux does not support this level.
RAID 4	Level 4 uses large-block striping with a parity disk. The parity information means that data can be recovered if any single drive fails. The performance of a level 4 array is very good for reads. Writes are slower because the parity data must be updated each time. OpenLinux does not enable this level.
RAID 5	Level 5 is similar to level 4, but it distributes parity among the drives. This speeds up disk writing. The cost per megabyte is the same as for level 4. Level 5 provides high speed random performance with a good level of data protection. It is the most widely used RAID system.

Part

III

Ch

11

Software RAID is Level 0. It uses striping to make multiple hard disks appear to be one disk. The result is much faster than any of the single disks would be alone because the drives are accessed in parallel.

Software RAID works with either IDE or SCSI controllers, and with any combination of disks.

Support for software RAID is built into OpenLinux. If you want to see it, enter the following command at a prompt:

```
cat /proc/mdstat
```

The display will look something like this:

```
Personalities :
read_ahead not set
md0 : inactive
md1 : inactive
md2 : inactive
md3 : inactive
```

What you see here is a listing of meta-disk one to meta-disk four. The meta-disks are RAID disks. They can be formatted and mounted just like any other disk, but first they have to be configured and running.

To do that, you will need the raidtools package on the OpenLinux CD in the /col/contrib/RPMS directory. The package includes raidadd, raidrun, raidstop, and some other tools. Setting up software RAID isn"t too difficult. The steps involved include

1. Choosing the disk partitions to combine
2. Creating a mount point
3. Setting up a configuration table
4. Adding the configuration table to the kernel
5. Starting up the meta-disk, formatting it, and mounting it

For complete instructions on installing software RAID, you can start with the Software-RAID How-To that"s included on the OpenLinux CD. Also check out the Linux Software RAID home pages at http://linas.org/linux/raid.html.

Hardware RAID   Hardware RAID controllers are extremely expensive SCSI controllers that cost tens of thousands of dollars at the high end, but they'll make your server respond like a mainframe computer. Hardware RAID should be installed by your computer manufacturer or an authorized dealer. They should handle installation and configuration.

Tip #8: Tweak Kernel Parameters

You can adjust the system kernel parameters to improve performance, sometimes dramatically. Be very careful if you decide to do this. Changes to the system kernel can optimize the system, or they can bring it crashing down.

> **CAUTION**
>
> Never play around with kernel parameters on a system you are using. This must be tested out on a system that no one is using because of the danger of crashing. Set up a test machine and use it to make sure that everything works correctly before putting the system into production.

A detailed document is included with OpenLinux that describes how to tweak the system kernel parameters. You should carefully study this document before you attempt any changes to the system kernel.

You'll find the document on your OpenLinux computer. The file is /usr/src/linux /Documentation/proc.txt.

Tip #9: Tweak Memory Performance

You can also tweak the memory system on Linux. If you get out of memory errors or your system is used for networking, you might want to adjust the memory allocation settings.

Memory is allocated in 4kb pages. Adjusting the "freepages" setting can make a significant improvement in performance. To see the current settings on your system, open a terminal window, and enter the command:

```
cat /proc/sys/vm/freepages
```

You'll get a reading of three numbers, something like:

```
128    256    384
```

These are the minimum free pages, free pages low, and free pages high settings. The values are determined at startup. The minimum setting is double the amount of memory on your system; the low setting is 4 times the amount of memory. The high setting is 6 times the memory on your system.

Free memory never goes below the minimum free pages count.

Swapping (using the disk space allocated to a swap file) begins if the number of free pages falls below the free pages high setting. Intensive swapping starts when the free pages low setting is reached.

Increasing the free pages high setting can sometimes improve overall performance. Try increasing the high setting to 1 MB, or 1024. The echo command adjusts the setting. To increase the free pages high setting to 1 MB, using the sample settings, enter this command:

```
echo "128 256 1024" > /proc/sys/vm/freepages
```

N O T E Test the settings on the system when it is not being used. Make sure to monitor performance both before and after making any adjustments so that you can determine what setting is best for your system. ▪

Part
III

Ch
11

12

Using Zip and Jaz Drives

Zip and Jaz Disks

The Zip drive has almost replaced the floppy drive in many offices. Zip disks can hold 100 megabytes, more than enough space for even the biggest of today's word processing files, spreadsheets, or presentations, and the disks are cheaper per megabyte than floppy disks.

In fact, Zip drives have become so common that I've been sent files on Zip disks by people who just assumed that I'd be able to read them. Luckily, support for Zip drives and their bigger cousins, the 1 gigabyte and 2 gigabyte Jaz drives, is built into OpenLinux.

Zip and Jaz drives are installed either as internal drives, using SCSI, IDE, or ATAPI connections or as external drives using SCSI interfaces. There is also an external Zip drive that uses the printer's parallel port. To use a parallel port Zip drive, involves an extra five minutes of setup time.

How to Setup Zip and Jaz Drives

There's no special software to install for Zip or Jaz disk drives, like on some other systems. The main procedure involved is setting up mounting instructions, as for any other disk drive on your system. Make sure you're logged in as root before you do this setup.

First, you'll need to create a directory where the drive can be mounted. The standard approach is to create a directory named Zip for Zip drives and jaz for Jaz drives. The command for creating the Zip-mounting directory is

```
mkdir /mnt/zip
```

If you are creating a Jaz directory, just substitute the word *jaz* for the word *zip*. If you want all users to be able to read and write to the zip directory, make sure you set the permissions:

```
chmod 666 /mnt/zip
```

For internal Zip and Jaz disk drives, the drive should be automatically recognized during startup. To check that the drive was recognized and to get the proper device name for mounting instructions, you can use the dmesg command. Enter the command:

```
dmesg ¦ grep -i zip
```

This searches the system messages that are generated during startup. It will display the information about your Zip drive. Replace the word *zip* in the command with *jaz* to find the information on your Jaz drive. Figure 12.1 shows a message about finding a Zip drive.

The disk is now accessible at the /mnt/zip directory. The vfat command is for disks that are in Windows 95/98 format. If you want to reformat your disks so that they use the Linux ext2 file system, see the section later in this chapter on formatting disks.

FIGURE 12.1
The Zip drive is seen at startup

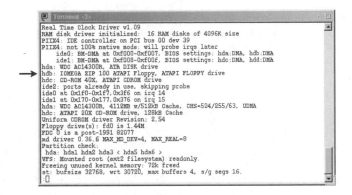

```
Real Time Clock Driver v1.09
RAM disk driver initialized:  16 RAM disks of 4096K size
PIIX4: IDE controller on PCI bus 00 dev 39
PIIX4: not 100% native mode: will probe irqs later
    ide0: BM-DMA at 0xf000-0xf007, BIOS settings: hda:DMA, hdb:DMA
    ide1: BM-DMA at 0xf008-0xf00f, BIOS settings: hdc:DMA, hdd:DMA
hda: WDC AC14300R, ATA DISK drive
hdb: IOMEGA ZIP 100 ATAPI Floppy, ATAPI FLOPPY drive
hdc: CD-ROM 40X, ATAPI CDROM drive
ide2: ports already in use, skipping probe
ide0 at 0x1f0-0x1f7,0x3f6 on irq 14
ide1 at 0x170-0x177,0x376 on irq 15
hda: WDC AC14300R, 4112MB w/512kB Cache, CHS=524/255/63, UDMA
hdc: ATAPI 20X CD-ROM drive, 128kB Cache
Uniform CDROM driver Revision: 2.54
Floppy drive(s): fd0 is 1.44M
FDC 0 is a post-1991 82077
md driver 0.36.6 MAX_MD_DEV=4, MAX_REAL=8
Partition check:
 hda: hda1 hda2 hda3 < hda5 hda6 >
VFS: Mounted root (ext2 filesystem) readonly.
Freeing unused kernel memory: 72k freed
st: bufsize 32768, wrt 30720, max buffers 4, s/g segs 16.
:[]
```

After you've found your Zip or Jaz drive and if it's not a parallel drive, it's ready to use. You'll need to mount it first before you can use it. The `mount` command for the Zip drive found in Figure 12.1 would be

```
mount -t vfat /dev/hdb4 /mnt/zip
```

Reformatting is not necessary, though, and the disks can be used as they come. You can safely save any kind of files you have on your OpenLinux system to the disks.

If you have a parallel port Zip drive, there are extra steps that you'll need to take to use your drive.

First, insert a Zip disk into the drive. Then open the COAS kernel administration tool. From the K Panel, click the COAS icon and select Kernel.

In the Kernel Modules panel, in the right-side pane, is a list of loaded modules. Find the module named lp, select it and click on the Unload button. This removes the parallel port printer module.

Then on the left-side pane, find the ppa module and load it. If you have a Zip Plus parallel drive, load the imm moduleand not ppa.

This also can be done from a command line in a terminal window with this command:

```
rmmod lp
```

That removes the printer module. Then insert the Zip parallel port module:

```
insmod ppa
```

If you have a Zip Plus drive, use `imm` instead of `ppa`.

You can then mount the disk that's in the drive and use it.

Part
III

Ch
12

To simplify mounting and to make the drive easily accessible to all users, you can add the Zip or Jaz drive to the `fstab` table of deviceson your system. Then mounting a disk becomes a simple matter of inserting a disk and entering the command:

```
mount /mnt/zip
```

That's because all of the other information about the device is in the `fstab` table. To enter the drive into the table, use a text editor and open the file fstab in the /etc directory.

On a line by itself, enter a line like this:

```
/dev/hdb4 /mnt/zip vfat defaults,user,noauto
```

Make the changes appropriate for your system, be sure to have the correct device name and mount point. If it is a Jaz drive, the mount point should say `jaz` and not `zip`. The other entries in the line indicate that the disk is formatted for Windows and that all users can mount or unmount disks.

You also can set up an icon on the KDE desktop for accessing the drive that mounts on a single-click and then unmount through a right-click.

You can add a device or application icon by right-clicking in a blank area on the desktop. Choose New and select File System Device.

A dialog box appears with a space for a New File System Device name. Change the device name to Zip.kdelnk or Jaz.kdelnk, whichever you have on your system. Click OK, then right-click on the new Zip or Jaz icon and select Properties. Select the device tab and enter the device name, in this example it is /dev/hdb4. On the next line put the mount point, /mnt/zip. Click the Mounted Icon button and select the appropriate icon to be displayed when a disk is mounted. Click the Unmounted Icon button to choose an icon to be displayed when the disk has been unmounted.

Now you can mount a Zip disk by inserting a disk into the disk drive and clicking the new icon you've created. To dismount a disk, right-click on the icon and choose Unmount.

Printing and Parallel Port Zip Drives

If you have a parallel port Zip drive you can connect a printer through the port on the drive, but you cannot use the drive and print at the same time. To print, you have to remove the Zip driver and restore the printer parallel port driver. In COAS you would remove ppa or imm, whichever you have loaded, and then load the lp module. This also can be done from the command line in a terminal window.

If your printer isn't directly connected to your computer, for example, you use a printer on a network, you don't need to bother with any of this.

If you have a parallel port Zip drive and you don't want to go through loading and unloading modules to use a printer connected your computer, the simplest solution is to install a second parallel port card in your computer. These cost only a few dollars and then there would be no conflict. Attach the Zip drive to the second parallel port and then you can print through the first parallel port while using the Zip drive at the same time.

How to Format Disks

Zip and Jaz disks can be used right out of the box because they are Windows 95 format.

TIP

MacOS formatted Zip and Jaz disks must be reformatted before you can use them. Follow the procedures for converting the disks to ext2 file format.

If you want, you can convert the disks to the Linux ext2 file system format, though that is not necessary to be able to use the disks on your system.

To convert the disks, you need to delete the Windows partition on the disk and then create a Linux partition. This should not be attempted by anyone who is not comfortable with using the fdisk command.

> **CAUTION**
>
> Be careful when using fdisk if you are logged in as root. You could end up erasing your entire system—with no way to get it back. Proceed cautiously when using fdisk as root.

To erase a Zip disk, enter the following command (this example uses the device name /dev/hdb, you should change the device name to match the device name for your drive):

```
fdisk /dev/hdb
```

Use the d (delete) command to delete any existing partitions. Then create a new partition with the n command, make it primary partition number 1, use w to write the partition table to disk, and quit with q.

In fdisk, to get help use the m command. A list of commands is displayed. One other command you might want to use is the p command. This will show the partition table.

After the partition has been created, you need to format with this command:

```
mke2fs /dev/hda1
```

The 1 is the number that you gave this partition in fdisk. Now you can mount the disk:

```
mount -t ext2 /dev/hda1 /mnt/zip
```

If you have the Zip or Jaz drive listed in the fstab table, you'll need to change the line so that the format is shown to be ext2 and not vfat and that the device is using partition 1 and not 4, as in /dev/hda1. Zip and Jaz Windows-formatted disks are formatted on partition 4 rather than 1.

Part

III

Ch

12

Writing to CD-ROMs

Writing to CDs

OpenLinux comes with CD writing software installed as part of the standard setup. If you have one of the supported CD-Recordable (CD-R) drives installed on your computer, you can make full use of it with the X-CD-Roast program.

This version of X-CD-Roast does not work with the CD-ReWritable (CD-RW) drives. CD-RW drives let you erase and reuse disks, but the disks they create aren't readable by all CD players.

Only SCSI CD-R drives can be used with X-CD-Roast. These are also the most reliable CD-R drives available, so it's what you want anyway.

The prices of CD-R drives and their disks are very reasonable. Blank CD-R media cost less per megabyte than floppy disks, Zip disks, or any other writeable media, and they are much more reliable than floppy disks, Zip disks, or JAZ disks.

When you create a recordable CD disk, you use a process called *laser burning*. This is not how store-bought CDs are made; they are pressed from a mold. The recordable CDs are more easily damaged than store-bought CDs, especially by extreme temperatures or sunlight.

Although the disks created this way are different from store-bought CDs, they work just the same way. You can use them in any CD-ROM drive, and any operating system can read them.

You can use X-CD-Roast to write CDs from data on your drive, create new audio CDs, or duplicate audio and data CDs. The disks hold about 74 minutes of audio or 650 megabytes of data.

Because of their flexibility, their support for data and audio formats, and their storage capacity, recordable CDs have become the medium of choice for distribution of data, image storage, multimedia presentations, and training and marketing materials as well as backups of computer files.

The only downside to CD writing is that it can be slow. Some of the newer drives are faster, but even then the writing process can take more than an hour.

Starting X-CD-Roast

X-CD-Roast has everything found in the commercial products sold for other operating systems. It is very reliable and has a very low rate of failure.

For those who want to know the technical side, it's a Tcl/Tk/Tix front-end for mkisofs and cdrecord, the two Linux command-line tools for writing CDs. The home page for X-CD-Roast is www.fh-muenchen.de/home/ze/rz/services/projects/xcdroast/e_overview.html.

Under the default installation, the root user must run X-CD-Roast. This can be changed, but not everyone should do that. You want to be cautious about giving everyone the right to run the program because of the way CD writing works. It creates the possibility that rather than writing to a CD, your system hard drive will be overwritten, and your entire system trashed. When X-CD-Roast is running, it writes to a partition, not a file. Therefore, you can do major damage if you choose the wrong partition.

CAUTION

Any program that must be run as root can open a security hole because it can be exploited to gain root access. On a standalone machine, this isn't really much of a problem because remote users can't access the system. On a networked system, however, this is potentially a real security problem. If your computer is networked, use the following instructions to enable users to use X-CD-Roast without being logged in as root. Then make sure that all users are properly trained so that they don't wipe out your partitions when they are writing CDs.

To enable all users to run X-CD-Roast, you need to be logged in as root. Then enter the following two commands:

```
chown root /usr/X11R6/bin/xcdroast
chmod +s /usr/X11R6/bin/xcdroast
```

You must perform the initial setup of X-CD-Roast as root. To start it, click on the K Application Launcher. From the pop-up menu, highlight Applications. In Applications, select XCDRoast. You see the opening screen, as shown in Figure 13.1.

FIGURE 13.1
X-CD-Roast is part of the standard OpenLinux installation.

Part
III

Ch
13

When you first start the program, it searches for supported devices. If you receive a warning that no generic SCSI support has been found, click Continue anyway. OpenLinux usually loads this module as part of the default setup, and X-CD-Roast does not always properly detect it at this point. Only if your SCSI devices aren't detected later during the setup do you need to go back and check to make sure this module is loaded.

The next window is a warning that there isn't a configuration file. Finally, you'll have to click on a button to accept the disclaimer of responsibility for any problems that you might encounter when using this program.

The first step is to go into setup. Click on the Setup button. In setup (shown in Figure 13.2), you'll see four tabs: CD Setup, HD Setup, Misc., and Defaults.

FIGURE 13.2
X-CD-Roast setup.

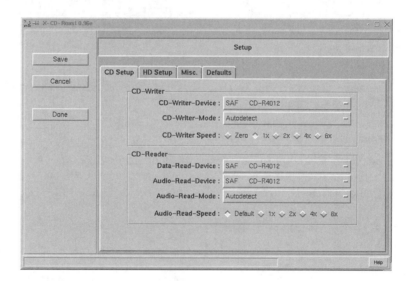

The primary setting to look at here is the CD-Writer Device setting. If your device isn't set properly, or if it's not recognized, you can't write CDs.

In CD Setup, the options are as follows:

- **CD-Writer Device**—The device name for your CD-Recordable drive. This shows the drive detected on startup. This drive must be a SCSI drive.

- **CD-Writer Mode**—This should be left set to Autodetect. All the supported devices will be correctly detected. The only time you might choose a mode here is if you have an unsupported drive and you are choosing a mode that you know works with your drive.

- **CD-Writer Speed**—Set this to the speed that your drive supports. Don't bother trying a speed higher than what your drive supports. In fact, for some drives the speed setting here has to be lower than the speed the manufacturer claims is supported. Some drives only work at Zero speed. If your writes are not successful, try setting a lower speed.

- **Data-Read Device**—This can be the same device as the CD-Writer Device. If you have a second CD-ROM drive, you can put it here. Unlike the recording device, this can be either a SCSI or IDE drive. This is the device used for CD data reading, for example, when creating duplicates of existing CDs.

- **Audio-Read Device**—This is the same device as the CD-Writer Device. It must be a SCSI drive. IDE drives are not supported for this.

- **Audio-Read-Mode**—This is normally set to Autodetect. If you have one of the newer drives that are SCSI-3/mmc-compliant, make this setting SCSI-3/mmc because it won't be correctly autodetected.

- **Audio-Read-Speed**—Normally set to default. This only affects CD-R drives. CD players do not have selectable speed settings, so if your Audio-Read device is not a recordable drive, this setting is ignored. Some devices have to be set at 1x or 2x to work properly.

The next tab, HD Setup (shown in Figure 13.3), should have a pop-up warning from X-CD-Roast: "Doing wrong things here can delete the whole hard disk." You only have access to this tab if you are logged in as root. If it is missing, you aren't logged in as root.

FIGURE 13.3
X-CD-Roast HD setup.

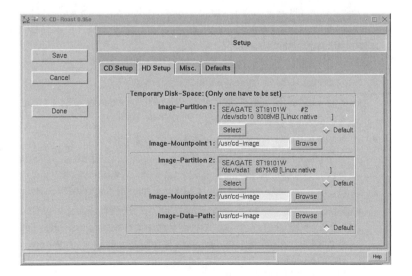

Part
III

Ch
13

The HD setup sets the space in which images are stored on your hard disk during the operation of creating a CD. The image that will eventually be written to the CD is first saved onto the hard disk, and then it is transferred to the CD. The default setting is to use one space on a single partition on your system, but the program gives you the option of designating one, two, or three areas for saving images.

The best way to do this is to create an 800MB partition that will just be used for CD writing. That partition is then mounted and used for only this purpose. It will give you the best, and fastest, results. Everything on that partition will be overwritten any time you write a CD.

Adding a Partition

If you want to add a partition for CD writing, you can either add a new hard disk to your system or change the partition information on your existing system. If you decide to change the partition information on an existing disk drive, make sure to back up everything. Sometimes additional space is available on a hard drive, such as a Windows partition that you are no longer using, but in most cases the entire disk is already allocated. That means that changing the partition information to create a special partition for CD writing will destroy all files on the disk.

The `fdisk` command is used to create or change disk partitions. After you use the `fdisk` utility, you need to create a file system on the partitions using the `mkfs` command.

Run the `fdisk` command only on an unmounted disk. To start `fdisk`, open a terminal window and enter the following command:

```
fdisk disk_drive
```

The disk drive is either an existing disk or a new disk that has been added to the system. The drive name will be something such as /dev/hdb, for a second IDE drive. The command to partition the second IDE drive with `fdisk` is

```
fdisk /dev/hdb
```

Following are the steps to create a partition with `fdisk`:

1. Type **p** to list the current partitions. Note what partitions exist. Typing **m** at any command prompt displays a menu listing of all available commands.

2. Type **n** to create a new partition, and then press Enter.

3. Type **p** to create a primary partition. Type the number of the primary partition you are creating (usually the next available number after any partitions that are already installed). If this is a new, second IDE drive, type **1** here to create the first primary partition, or /dev/hda1.

4. Specify the size of this partition. First, type the cylinder number where the partition starts—this is usually the first number shown in parentheses—and then press Enter. Next, define the size of the partition. You can do this by specifying the size in megabytes. For example, to create an 800MB partition, type **+800M**. `fdisk` automatically marks the new partition with hex code 83 for native Linux.

5. Follow steps 2–4 to create any additional partitions you want on the disk drive.

To save the new partition information, you must write the information to the disk. Type **w** at the command prompt and press Enter. You see a message indicating that the partition table has been modified.

Finally, use `mkfs` to build a file system on the partitions so you can use it. This utility creates an ext2 type file system, the default Linux file system. To make a file system, enter the following command:

```
mkfs /dev/hdb1
```

Of course, change the drive designation from `/dev/hdb1` to match your new partition. Be careful: The `mkfs` utility completely erases all data. Make sure that you indicate the correct drive.

Because most users didn't set up their systems with this in mind, they don't have a special partition that was created just for CD writing. There's no need, though, to go through all the work involved in adding another partition. Instead, you can indicate a data path where the images will be saved. No other data will be overwritten. This is slower, but it works, and it won't overwrite the whole disk partition.

In HD Setup, pick the option that matches your system. If you have a partition created just for CD writing, indicate that in Image Partition 1. If not, set up the Image Data Path. The options are as follows:

- **Image Partition 1**—This is the partition where CD images are saved during the writing process. The partition needs to be at least 800MB in size. This will be a device name such as /dev/sdb1. The default button indicates that this will be used as the default partition. Partition 2 and the Image Data Path are the other two choices for default.

> **CAUTION**
>
> The warning bears repeating. All data on the partition will be erased and overwritten. Be careful what partition you indicate here.

- **Image Mountpoint 1**—This is the directory in which Image Partition 1 will be mounted.
- **Image Partition 2**—Same as Image Partition 1. Use this when you want to designate two different partitions.
- **Image Mountpoint 2**—This is the directory in which Image Partition 2 will be mounted.
- **Image Data Path**—A directory path that indicates where to save an image file. The directory must be on a partition that has enough free space (about 800MB) for the writing operation.

Part
III

Ch
13

The primary setting to look at in the Misc. setup (shown in Figure 13.4) is audio. If you plan to write music CDs, make sure that your sound card is set up in DSP Device for Audio. If it's not, you cannot listen to sound as it is being recorded (this is not generally recommended) or test the audio tracks you've written (which is a good thing to do). In Misc. Setup, the options are as follows:

FIGURE 13.4

X-CD-Roast Misc. setup.

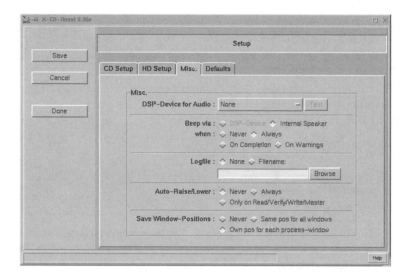

- **DSP Device for Audio**—Indicate your sound card's DSP device. Your sound card needs to play digital data at 44.1 kHz, 16-bit stereo in order for you to listen to audio tracks. If not, or if you don't have a sound card, set this to None. You can still create audio CDs; you just can't listen to them. Use the Test button to check the settings. You should hear a gong sound.

- **Beep via/when**—Choose between your sound card and the computer's internal speaker for beeps. Also choose whether to enable beeps and, if enabled, whether to beep on completion, on warnings, or on both.

- **Logfile**—If you want X-CD-Roast to keep a log, enable it here and give it a filename. If you enable this, make sure that you put it in an existing directory. This logs all the actions you take when using the program.

- **Auto Raise/Lower**—Set whether and when X-CD-Roast is to iconify itself.

- **Save Window Positions**—Set whether X-CD-Roast is to remember the position of its windows.

To start with, you probably want to leave the default settings to the Defaults (seen in Figure 13.5). After you've worked with X-CD-Roast, you'll be able to see whether you need to adjust any of these settings. In Defaults Setup, the options are as follows:

FIGURE 13.5
X-CD-Roast Defaults setup.

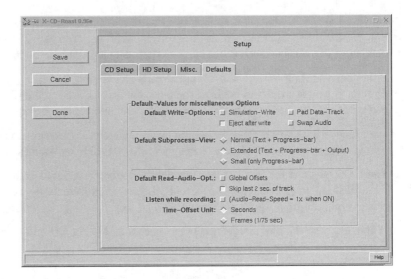

- **Default Write Options—Simulation Write** tests whether your system is fast enough to write without errors. The Default is off. **Pad Data** is used as a workaround for a bug in earlier versions of Linux. This is not needed for OpenLinux 2.3. **Eject after write** auto ejects the disk when writing is done. This should be selected on. **Swap audio** swaps the byte-order of audio-tracks to write. Usually you won't need this option, but if you end up with an audio CD containing only static noise, you can fix that with this option. This is normally off.

- **Default Subprocess View**—Settings for how the Read, Verify, and Write windows are displayed.

- **Default Read Audio Opt.**—**Global offsets** means that all tracks are assigned the same offset. This is normally off. **Skip last 2 sec. of track** skips the two-second pause normally found on audio CDs. This defaults to on.

- **Listen while recording**—If you enable this, all audio tracks are read at single-speed. This requires that the sound device be set in the Misc. setup tab.

- **Time-Offset Unit**—Choose between seconds or frames.

Writing Data to a CD

To write data to a CD with X-CD-Roast, you don't just copy files from one part of the computer onto the CD-R disk. You need to create a Master CD that will be copied onto the CD-R disk.

The Master CD can be a file or several files and directories, up to about 650MB. Once the data for the Master CD has been designated, X-CD-Roast copies it onto the CD-R disk. This

Part

III

Ch

13

copying process is what takes so long because files that you are copying must be converted into the CD-ROM ISO9660 format. The conversion process can take a long time. Duplicating data and audio CDs is much faster because their data is already in the CD-ROM format.

If the files you want to write to a CD are already all together (for example, if it's your home directory), you are ready to begin. If the files you want to write to the CD are not already grouped together, you need to put them together all in one place before proceeding.

I've found that using Jaz disks for setting up the Master CD files works very well, but you can use whatever you want, such as a directory you've set aside on your hard disk.

The ISO9660 standard for CDs does not allow for subdirectories to go below eight levels. If your master data directories go down more than eight subdirectories, the offending directories are moved into a special directory called rr_moved during the writing process.

When you have the files ready for copying, select the Master CD button from the Main Window of X-CD-Roast. Figure 13.6 shows the Master CD window.

FIGURE 13.6
X-CD-Roast Master CD window.

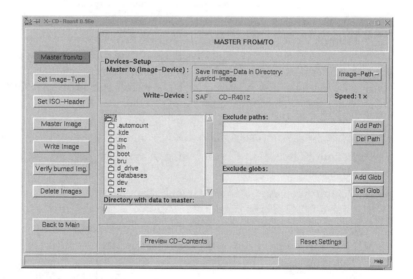

Set the Master from/to

Indicate the location of the data that is to be written to the CD. You can type in the information, such as **/mnt/jaz/master_files**, or you can double-click on the Directory Selection window and find the directory where the files are.

Exclude paths are directories that are not to be included. These have to be the full directory name. For example, if you have a directory called sources that is to be excluded, you don't enter the single word, but rather the pathname /mnt/jaz/master_files/sources.

Exclude globs excludes all files of a certain type. For example, if you put *.tmp here, all files in the master-from directory ending in .tmp are not included for writing to the CD.

The Preview CD Contents button enables you to see what the contents of the CD will look like. This is not always 100% accurate, but it will give a good idea of the final contents.

The Calculate Size button calculates the actual size of the data being written to the CD. This can be useful when you want to see if you can add more to the CD.

Set Image Type

You'll need to define the image type for the CD you'll be creating. The choices follow:

- **UNIX Rock-Ridge**—This is the standard Linux/UNIX format. Good for long filenames that are case sensitive, this properly recognizes file links and Linux file permissions. This is not a good choice for disks that might be read on Windows or DOS computers, which can read the disk but cannot see all the information correctly.

- **Rock-Ridge+Win95/NT**—This is the standard setting that is generally used. It works correctly for both Linux/UNIX systems and Windows systems, and has Joliet support. *Joliet* is the Windows 95/NT CD format that allows long filenames, deeper directory levels, and more than one dot per filename. DOS computers cannot read the long file- names.

- **Win95/NT**—This creates a true Joliet CD for Windows systems. DOS systems cannot read the long filenames. They can be read on Linux systems, but this does not preserve Linux file system information.

- **DOS**—This creates a CD that has only short 8-3 style files names and that can be read by all systems.

- **Custom**—You can create your own CD type.

Click the Save as default button so that the choice you've made is loaded the next time you start X-CD-Roast.

Set ISO9660 Header Strings

This sets the header information on your CD. Enter all fields that you want and leave any you don't want blank. The settings are

- **Volume ID**—This is the disk label name displayed on file listings.

- **Publisher ID**—Name of the publisher of the CD. This can include contact information such as a mailing address and phone number. Maximum of 128 characters.

- **Preparer ID**—Name of the person who prepared the CD. This can include contact information such as a mailing address and phone number. Maximum of 128 characters.

- **Application ID**—Name of any application on the CD. Maximum of 128 characters.

Create the Master Image

The master image sets where the image will be generated. The default setting matches the partition defined in HD setup.

The Calculate Size button shows the exact size of the final CD image. The size is determined by both the data to be written and the requirements of the ISO image type, such as Rock Ridge.

You must create the master image before you can write it to the CD.

Write the Master Image to a CD

This writes the CD image from the master image. The options include Simulation Write, which enables you to test to make sure the image can be written without errors. Eject after write to auto eject when writing is done. Pad Data Track corrects a bug in earlier versions of Linux and is an option that can be ignored on OpenLinux 2.3 systems.

Verify the Burned Image

This checks whether the burned CD matches the master record.

Duplicating a Data CD

To duplicate a data CD, click on the Copy Data CD button in the X-CD-Roast main window.

When you enter the Copy Data CD window (shown in Figure 13.7), a CD Information panel identifies the CD that is in the Data Read device that was set in the X-CD-Roast CD setup. The Image Information panel shows information about the contents of the CD.

FIGURE 13.7
X-CD-Roast Copy Data
CD window.

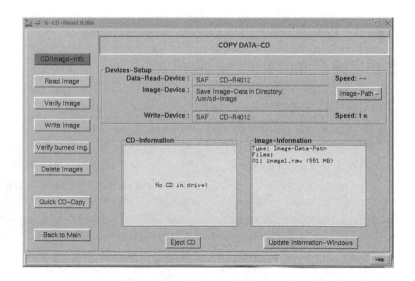

Click the Update Information Windows button every time you put in a new CD to be duplicated.

Duplicating a data CD takes three steps:

1. Read the image:

   ■ **Diskspace Needed for Image**—Displays the size of the image to be copied.

   ■ **Diskspace available**—Shows how much free space is left.

   ■ **Image ISO9660 Label**—Displays the label of the CD being copied.

   You can choose whether to read the image to a file or to the partition. Reading to a partition is faster.

2. Verify the image:

   ■ **Image size**—Shows the size of the image on the CD to be copied.

   ■ **Image ISO9660 Label**—Shows the label of the CD to be copied.

   Verify compares the CD in the drive with the image written to a partition or file.

3. Write the image. This writes the image from your hard drive to the a disk in the CD-R drive. If the CD being duplicated is in the drive, remove it and put in a blank recordable CD:

   ■ **Simulation Write**—Enables you to test the writing without making any changes to the blank CD.

   ■ **Eject After Write**—Ejects the CD when writing is finished.

   ■ **Pad Data Track**—Used as a workaround for a bug in earlier versions of Linux.

   ■ **Verify burned image**—Checks whether the burned CD was written correctly.

Copying Audio to a CD

To duplicate an audio CD, click on the Copy Audio CD button on the X-CD-Roast main window. The Copy Audio CD window opens, as shown in Figure 13.8.

Audio CDs have tracks, and copying of audio is done in a track-at-once mode.

Copying audio is similar to copying data. The tracks are read from the CD to your hard disk, and you can verify the tracks by listening to them. Then you write the tracks to the CD.

Click on the Select/Show Tracks to Read button, and a pop-up window opens. Here you can select or deselect tracks to be copied. You can enter a track title for your own information. In the CD Title field, you can type a name for your new CD.

In the top pane of the pop-up window is a list of the tracks that have been selected, in order. In the lower pane is a list of additional tracks still available on the CD. Click on the Order button.

FIGURE 13.8
X-CD-Roast Copy Audio
CD window.

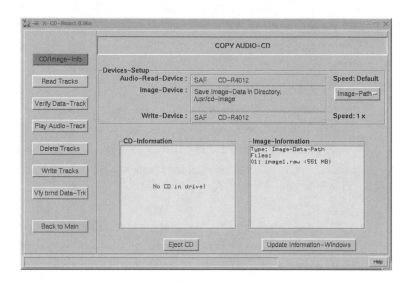

If you choose merging, the tracks are merged so that the two second pause between tracks is eliminated. However, on a CD that is created this way you can't select tracks because it has all been merged into one track.

Following are the options for the Read Tracks button:

- **Track Totals**—Shows the number of tracks on the CD to be copied.
- **Total Length**—Displays the total length of the CD.
- **Tracks Selected**—Shows how many tracks have been selected to be copied.
- **Selected Length**—The length of the tracks selected.
- **Free space**—Shows how much space is left.

Once the tracks have been selected and verified, you can write the CD, if you want. Writing follows almost the same procedure used in copying data CDs.

The display during writing, however, shows the following options:

- **Tracks on HD**—Shows how many tracks have been found on the image partition.
- **Total Length**—Shows the total length of all the tracks on HD.
- **Tracks to write on CD**—Total number of tracks to write.
- **Total CD Size**—Shows how long the final CD will be.

Click on Select/Show Tracks to Write. The display shows the tracks that are to be burned and the order in which they are to be placed on the CD. At this point, you can deselect tracks and change the order. When everything is ready, click Done. Then, to write the CD, click on Start Write Tracks. When the writing is finished, you can check the contents against the original by clicking on the Verify Burned Data Track button.

CD Writing Questions and Answers

Here are some FAQs regarding writing files to a CD.

Q: What is the recording speed of CD-R?

The speed rating of a CD-Recordable drive determines how fast it can record data to blank CD-R media. Speeds such as 1X, 2X, 4X, 6X, and 8X are based on multiples of the original playback speed of first generation CD-ROM players. For a CD-ROM player or CD recorder, a 1X speed is about 150KB per second. Therefore, a 2X recorder records at 300KB per second, and so on.

Q: Does CD-RW make CD-R obsolete?

No. The CD-ReWriteable drives give users more options, but the drives and the rewriteable disks are more expensive. Also, the CD-RW disks are less reflective and therefore not always readable by all CD readers. Because the CD-RW drive can write to the CD-R media, many CD-RW users purchase the inexpensive CD-R disks for regular use and save the much more expensive CD-RW disks for special use. Thus, the CD-R disks will probably always be available.

Q: How long can an unused CD-R disk be kept before it is no longer useable?

Probably about three to five years.

Q: How long is data recorded on a CD-R disk readable?

The CD-R media manufacturers claim longevity from 50 years to over 100 years. That's possible only if the disk is put into special cold storage. If you don't do that, it is probably safe to say that if the CD is kept in the best possible condition and not subjected to extreme heat or light, the data will be readable for five to ten years. According to the National Science Academy, putting a CD in the freezer increases its longevity to 75 years or more. It recommends that you put the disk in a zip-lock bag before you freeze it.

Part
III

Ch
13

Q: What about labeling CD-Rs?

Don't use stick-on labels. If the label is put on wrong—for example, with a bubble or misaligned—the disk might become unusable. Use a water-based felt tip pen. Never use a ball point pen or any other sharp object to label disks.

Q: Is there really any difference between the different brands of blank disks?

All disks are manufactured to the same specifications. There is no significant difference between any of the major brands of disks on the market. Avoid the no-name brand disks—these are often manufactured using shortcuts to reduce costs.

Q: Why are different brands different colors?

The color of the disk is usually determined by the color of the dye used in the recording layer, although some manufacturers add color simply to achieve a certain look. Some disks appear green, some blue, and others yellow or other colors. These visual differences are not important in choosing a disk.

Q: Can I work on another process while a CD is being burned?

The answer is maybe. Word processing or similar programs that do not constantly access the disk won't interfere with CD writing.

Accessing a database, editing a graphic image, or other tasks that make intensive use of the disk drive can interfere with the CD writing process and might leave you with a corrupt CD.

Q: I have only one CD drive on my system. Can I make a copy of another CD without copying the contents onto my hard drive?

Technically, yes, but doing it this way makes it more likely that you'll end up with a corrupt CD. Any errors that occur when reading the original disk make the CD unusable. It is much better to do this on a system with two CD drives or to copy the contents to your hard drive and use the copy to create the CD-R disk.

Q: Can I compress music CDs in order to fit more on a disk?

Instead of writing a true audio CD, convert your audio files into mp3 files. Mp3 has a 1:10 compression ratio. See Chapter 10, "Installing and Configuring Sound," for details on setting up an mp3 player on your system so that you can play your mp3 disks.

Q: Does it matter what speed I use for recording?

No matter what speed you use for recording, the disk you create can be read on a CD reader of any speed. Newer recorders and media are designed for 2X and 4X recording speeds and generally produce better results at those speeds. Older recorders seem to work best at 1X.

Q: Why do I get SCSI timeout errors?

Check your SCSI cables and SCSI termination. If the cables are okay and the SCSI drive is properly terminated, there may be a problem with the controller. If you can, try using a different controller. That's one way to tell if the controller is the problem.

Supported CD-Writers

These CD-Writers are supported by cdrecord-1.6.1, and therefore by this version of X-CD-Roast. Questions about which CD-Writers will be supported in the future should be directed to the author of cdrecord, Joerg Schilling (schilling@fokus.gmd.de).

All Compliant Drives

All SCSI-3/mmc and ATAPI/mmc Compliant Drives

- COMPRO CW-7502
- Dysan CR-622
- Dysan CR-1622
- DynaTec CDM-240J (see Pinnacle RCD-4x4)
- DynaTec CDM-240 (use cdrecord driver=yamaha_cdr100 and report inquiry)
- DynaTec CDM-400 (use cdrecord driver=yamaha_cdr100 and report inquiry)
- Grundig CDR-100
- Hewlett Packard 4020i
- Hewlett Packard 6020i
- HP C4324/C4325 (HP SureStore 4020i/6020i)
- HP 7100
- HP 7110
- HP 7200
- HP 8100
- Hi-Val CD-R (see Pinnacle RCD-4x4)
- JVC XR-W2001 (uses TEAC code—audio not working)
- JVC XR-W2010 (uses TEAC code—audio not working)
- JVC XR-W2020 (uses TEAC code—audio not working)
- Kodak PCD-200 or Kodak PCD-200 Plus
- Kodak PCD-225

Part
III

Ch
13

- Kodak PCD-240
- Kodak PCD-600 (not tested)
- Matsushita CW-7502
- Memorex CR-622
- Memorex CR-1622
- Microboards PlayWrite 2000 (use cdrecord driver=sony_cdu924 and report inquiry)
- Microboards PlayWrite 4000 (use cdrecord driver=yamaha_cdr100 and report inquiry)
- Microboards PlayWrite 4001RW
- MicroNet MasterCD Plus 4x4 (use cdrecord driver=yamaha_cdr100 and report inquiry)
- MicroNet MasterCD Plus 4x6
- Mitsumi CR-2401-TS (not tested)
- Mitsumi CR-2600-TE
- Mitsumi CR-2801
- Mitsumi CR-4801
- Olympus CDS615E
- Olympus CDS620E (use cdrecord driver=sony_cdu924 and report inquiry)
- Olympus CD-R2x6 (use cdrecord driver=sony_cdu924 and report inquiry)
- Optima Dis Kovery 650 CD-R (use cdrecord driver=sony_cdu924 and report inquiry)
- OTI CDRW 965
- Panasonic CW-7502
- Philips CDD 521 (CDD521/02 Revision: 2.06 has bad firmware—seems not to work)
- Philips CDD 521 (upgraded units only: ID: CDD521/10 Revision: 2.07)
- Philips CDD 522
- Philips CDD 2000
- Philips CDD 2600
- Philips CDD 3600
- Philips CDD 3610
- Philips Omniwriter 26
- Philips Omniwriter 26A
- Pinnacle Micro RCD-1000 (see TEAC/JVC): Need to upgrade firmware to 2.35
- Pinnacle Micro RCD-5020 (see TEAC/JVC—audio not working)
- Pinnacle Micro RCD-5040 (see TEAC/JVC—audio not working)
- Pinnacle Micro RCD-4x4

- Pioneer DW-S114X
- Plasmon CDR 4220 (not tested)
- Plasmon RF-4100
- Plasmon RF-4102
- Plasmon CDR 4400 (use cdrecord driver=yamaha_cdr100 and report inquiry)
- Plasmon CDR 480
- Plextor PX-R24CS (use cdrecord driver=ricoh_ro1420c and report inquiry)
- Plextor PX-R412C
- Procom PCDR 4 (use cdrecord driver=yamaha_cdr100 and report inquiry)
- Ricoh RO-1420C
- Ricoh MP-6200
- Ricoh MP-6200I
- Ricoh MP-6201
- Smart & Friendly CD-R1002 (use cdrecord driver=sony_cdu924 and report inquiry)
- Smart & Friendly CD-R1004 (use cdrecord driver=yamaha_cdr100 and report inquiry)
- Smart & Friendly CD-R2004 (use cdrecord driver=sony_cdu924 and report inquiry)
- Smart & Friendly CD-R2006 PLUS
- Smart & Friendly CD-R2006 PRO
- Smart & Friendly CD-R4000 (use cdrecord driver=yamaha_cdr100 and report inquiry)
- Smart & Friendly CD-R4006
- Smart & Friendly CD-R4012
- Smart & Friendly CD-RW226
- Sony CDU920S
- Sony CDU924S
- Sony CDU926S
- Sony CDU928
- Sony CDU940S
- TEAC CD-R50S
- TEAC CD-R55S
- Taiyo Yuden CD-WO EW-50
- Traxdata CDR-4120
- Traxdata CDRW-4260
- Turtle Beach 2040R (use cdrecord driver=ricoh_ro1420c and report inquiry)

- Wearnes CD-R622
- Wearnes CD-R632P
- Yamaha CDR-100
- Yamaha CDR-102
- Yamaha CDR-200
- Yamaha CDR-400 (Firmware revision 1.0d and up otherwise upgrade)
- Yamaha CDR-401
- Yamaha CRW-4001
- Yamaha CRW-2260
- Yamaha CRW-4260

Unsupported Drives

cdrecord will never support the following drives because they are too old:

- JVC XR-W1001
- Pinnacle Micro RCD-202
- Ricoh RS-9200CD

The following drives are currently not supported:

- Creative Labs CDR 4210
- JVC XR-W2001
- JVC XR-W2010
- JVC XR-W2020
- Panasonic CW-7501
- Pinnacle Micro RCD-1000
- Pinnacle Micro RCD-5020
- Pinnacle Micro RCD-5040
- Plasmon CDR-4240
- Ricoh RS-1060C
- Sony CDW-900E

## CHAPTER 14

Connecting to PalmPilots

Using KPilot

3Com's PalmPilot is the most popular handheld computer around. More than two million are currently in use. Not surprisingly, OpenLinux includes a program that works a lot like the Palm Desktop for Windows.

It's called KPilot (shown in Figure 14.1), and it's part of the KDE set of programs. KPilot works with 3Com's Palm Pilot computers.

FIGURE 14.1

KPilot connects your PalmPilot to your OpenLinux computer.

Setting Up KPilot

The first step to setting up KPilot is to create a symbolic link to the serial port used to connect to the Palm computer. KPilot expects to find the Pilot computer at /dev/pilot.

To create the link, enter the following command:

```
ln -s /dev/ttyS0 /dev/pilot
```

This sets the link to ttyS0, which is COM1. Change this to match your serial port. For COM2 use ttyS1, for COM3 use ttyS2, and for COM4 use ttyS3.

You're now ready to start up KPilot.

The first time you start Kpilot, the setup window opens (see Figure 14.2). The device should say /dev/pilot. The speed should be set at 57600. The Pilot User is any name you want. The other settings don't need to be checked.

FIGURE 14.2
The KPilot setup window. Be sure to check the device and speed settings.

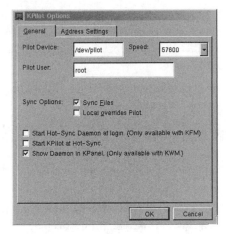

KPilot also comes with two conduits. The email conduit can be set up to check for mail and let you use KPilot as a simple mail program. The other is vCalendar, which synchronizes your Appointment calendar in KOrganizer with KPilot.

The vCalendar conduit does not work properly yet. For updates, look on the KDE home page (www.kde.org) for KPilot downloads.

The email conduit is buggy, and you might want to skip it until it's upgraded. However, if you want to try it, choose Conduit from the menu and select Setup. Select the email mail conduit (popmail_conduit) and click the arrow button to install it. Select the newly installed PopMail conduit and click on the Settings button. The settings are shown in Figure 14.3.

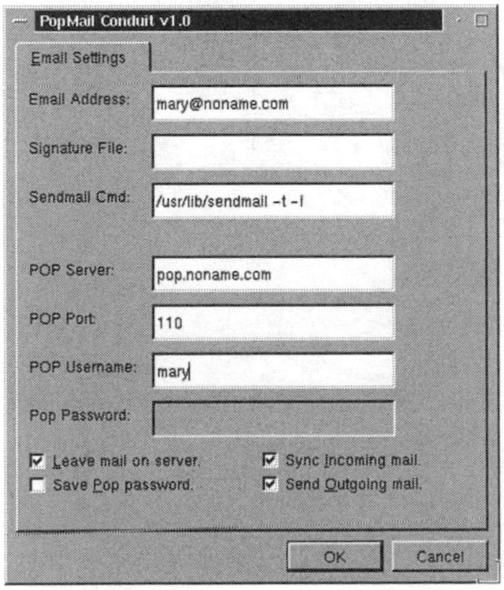

FIGURE 14.3
Set the KPilot email settings if you want to synchronize email with your PalmPilot.

The email address is your email address. The Pop settings are the server, port, and username used to retrieve your email. Sync Incoming Mail and Send Outgoing Mail set whether KPilot is to check for new mail on the POP server and send any pending mail from the PalmPilot when you open the program.

Once you have KPilot set up, you can synchronize with your Pilot computer. To use the email conduit, KPilot must be open during the synchronization; otherwise, it does not matter whether it is open. To synchronize, start the KPilotDaemon from the K Application Launcher in Utilities (it's right under KPilot). When the daemon is started, a familiar double-arrow icon appears in the lower right corner of the K Panel. That means that you can synchronize any time by pressing the Hot Sync button on the Pilot computer while it is docked.

Once KPilot has been synchronized, you can view the memos as well as the address book from your Pilot. There also is a utility for uploading files to your Pilot. You can access the memo and address view, as well as the file installer, from a drop-down panel just below the menu bar.

The Memo Viewer

The memo viewer enables you to view the memos on your Pilot, export them to text files, import new memos to be installed the next time you Hot Sync, or edit existing memos.

The Address Book Viewer

The Address Book viewer (see Figure 14.4) lets you view, import, export, and edit your Pilot Address Book. Any changes you make are updated on your Pilot when you use the Hot Sync.

FIGURE 14.4
The KPilot Address Book viewer includes a Quick List for your frequently used contacts.

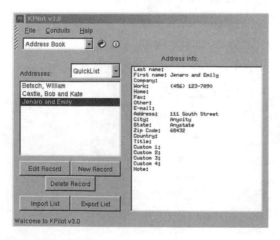

The File Installer

You can use the file installer by dragging and dropping files into the file-list area or by clicking the Add File button to add a file. These files are installed on your PalmPilot during the next Hot Sync if Sync Files is checked in the settings panel. If you choose not to install the files on the PalmPilot, click Clear List to remove any pending files. An internal copy of the file is kept, so you can even drag and drop URLs from the K File Manager's browser.

Alternatively, you can drag and drop files or URLs onto the Hot-Sync Daemon icon on the K Panel. For this to work, however, Sync Files must be checked in the settings panel. The files are then installed the next time you Hot Sync.

Running Applications

## CHAPTER 15

Installing and Configuring Commercial Applications

WordPerfect, One of the Best Word Processors

WordPerfect is one of the best known word processing programs available on any kind of computer system. OpenLinux includes the free personal edition of WordPerfect 8.

WordPerfect is well known as one of the top office applications, and its availability on Linux has put Linux on more desktop systems than any other application that is available.

WordPerfect 8 for Linux is similar to the Windows version. It is the most advanced word processing program available on Linux, and has a wide range of features, including many that aren't found in Microsoft's Word.

WordPerfect's extra features include a font preview when you access the program's pull-down font list. WordPerfect also shows you a list of the most recently used fonts, sizes, and colors in a separate pull-down list. In addition, WordPerfect has a spell-as-you-go and a grammar-as-you-go set of utilities.

WordPerfect has language modules for a half dozen European languages.

WordPerfect uses a Shadow Cursor that enables you to click and type any blank area on a page. For details on using this feature, see the section on editing features later in this chapter.

WordPerfect's Reveal Codes feature is one of its best. You can fix almost every formatting problem using Reveal Codes. This is a feature that Microsoft should have copied long ago—it would save Word users hours of headaches. In Word, there is no way to find hidden formatting problems, and you can be forced to eliminate all formatting or delete a section in order to get rid of a problem such as a paragraph with a funny indent that won't go away. Then you have to reformat the document completely, or at least recreate the problem section.

WordPerfect can read more than 40 different file formats, including Microsoft Word 97 and Word 2000, and can save files into other formats, making it easier to exchange your WordPerfect for Linux documents with others who might not yet be using Linux. This feature is not perfected yet, however, and might not ever work seamlessly. Many issues are involved in document transportability. Although WordPerfect has one of the best implementations available on Linux, it's only about three-quarters of the way there. Most, but not all, formatting is preserved, graphics are not converted, and many times font differences mean that the documents won't exactly match page-for-page. Font conversion is a problem regardless of whether you are moving a document to Word for Windows or WordPerfect for Windows.

If you need to create Web content, WordPerfect includes what it calls Internet Publisher capabilities, which enable you to save your documents as HTML.

WordPerfect 8 for Linux has three different distributions:

- The Personal Edition is free for personal, noncommercial use with registration. It has the full word processor, multiple-language support, and some import/export filters. Some of the advanced features are disabled, including graphic drawing and the ExpressDoc templates. You can get this edition of WordPerfect for free from the Corel Web site at `linux.corel.com/linuxproducts_wp8_download.htm`. If you have the boxed edition of OpenLinux, it is included on the Windows Tools & Commercial Packages CD. If you need the language modules, including dictionaries for Canadian French, Spanish, German, Dutch, Italian, or English variations for Canada, Australia, or the United Kingdom, you can download them from Corel as well.

- A boxed Personal Edition—which adds 130 fonts plus a font installer utility, 90 ExpressDocs, an online manual in PDF format and Adobe Acrobat Reader to read it, an advanced drawing application, more than 5000 clipart images, 200 photos, 187 textures, and additional import/export filters—is also sold.

- The Server Edition includes everything from the Personal Edition plus advanced site license management software, advanced system utilities, and support for the Oracle database engine. It also includes a version of WordPerfect 8 that can be used on Linux systems running in nongraphical terminal mode.

N O T E A WordPerfect Office 2000 suite for Linux that includes WordPerfect 9 is expected in late 1999 or early in the year 2000. Corel says that it will include Linux versions of its office suite programs, including a spreadsheet and a presentation program. ■

To install WordPerfect, download the files or files into a temporary directory and enter the following command for each file you downloaded:

```
tar xvzf filename
```

In place of `filename` put the name of each file you downloaded. Once you've done this, the command to start installation is

```
./Runme
```

If you have the boxed edition of OpenLinux, you can find a WordPerfect RPM package on the Windows Tools & Commercial Packages CD. Insert the CD, and make sure that you are logged in as the root user.

Click on the K Application Launcher and select COAS on the popup menu. Click on Commercial Products. The OpenLinux Commercial Install Page opens. Click on the link to the commercial packages. A list of commercial packages is shown. Click on WordPerfect 8 to install the package.

The first time you run WordPerfect you'll receive a warning that you can use the software for only 90 days without registering (see Figure 15.1). Registration is free and not too difficult. If you plan to use WordPerfect 8, you need to visit the registration Web site at linux.corel.com. You'll have to scroll down the page to find the registration link.

Enter the registration information and submit it. As you might guess, because Corel is giving the software away for free, it's a very busy Web site. It usually takes several tries before a registration goes through. In the meantime, you can start using the software. When you receive the registration number, be sure to save it in a safe place; that way, if you have to reinstall the program for any reason, you won't have to reregister.

FIGURE 15.1
Registration warning. You have 90 days to register the Personal Edition.

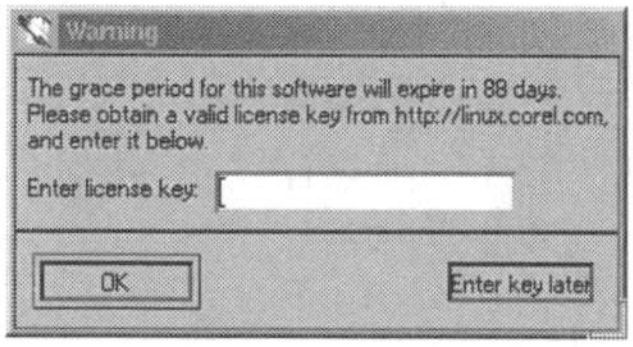

If you've used WordPerfect for Windows, you'll notice right away that the program on Linux opens two windows: a document window and a command window (shown in Figure 15.2). One of the reasons for the command window is to make use of Linux's multiple-user capabilities.

Document window   Command window

FIGURE 15.2
WordPerfect 8 for Linux has a document window and a command window.

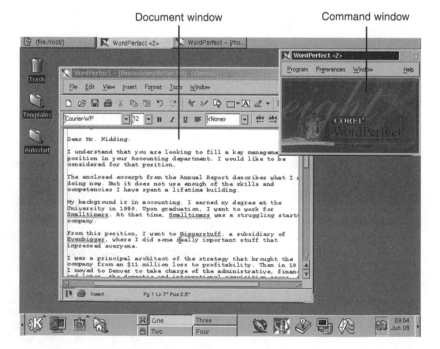

The command window is also used to open previous documents from a list of recently used documents, to set preferences, to manage open windows, and to perform many other tasks. The command window has a Print Manager and a File Manager, and is where the program is shut down when you finish using it.

Set Preferences

Preferences are set in the command window. The Preferences window is shown in Figure 6.3. To open it, click Preferences in the menu bar of the command window. Be careful in making changes to preferences. Sometimes WordPerfect doesn't like having its default settings changed, particularly in the Application Bar. Because the defaults work just fine and make use of all the program's features, there's not really a strong reason to make many changes anyway.

FIGURE 15.3
WordPerfect preferences window.

Display Preferences

In the Display Preferences window, click Document to set default settings for the document window (shown in Figure 15.4). Table 15.1 shows the options you can change.

Table 15.1   Document Display Preferences

Setting	Description
Table Gridlines	Show dashed lines when table lines are turned off.
Graphics	Display or hide graphics in documents.
Blinking Cursor	Enable or disable a blinking cursor.
Hidden Text	Display or hide hidden text.
Comments	Display or hide comments in documents.
Vertical and Horizontal Scroll Bars	Enable or disable scroll bars.
Shadow Cursor	Set color, shape, and actions of shadow cursor.
Measurement	Set measurement units in inches, centimeters, millimeters, or points.

FIGURE 15.4

Set display preferences for documents.

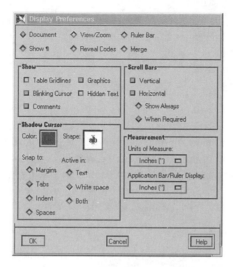

To set the default view and zoom preferences, click View/Zoom in the Display Preferences Window (shown in Figure 15.5).

FIGURE 15.5

Set view and zoom preferences for documents.

The default view can be set to Page, the default setting, which shows the page in a format similar to how it will look when printed. The other choice is Draft, which does not display all the formatting so that the text can be displayed faster.

The default zoom setting is 100%. On 15-inch or smaller monitors that use resolutions of 800x600 or lower, a better setting is 83%.

Click ruler bar to set the way the ruler bar will function (see Figure 15.6).

FIGURE 15.6

Set display prefer-
ences for documents.

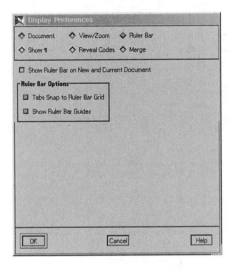

A toggle button enables or disables the ruler bar. There are two options. The first, Tabs Snap to Ruler Bar Grid, enables a "snap" to an invisible tab grid in your document. The grid lines occur every 1/16 of an inch, or every millimeter.

The second option is to Show Ruler Bar Guides. When this is turned on, a dotted vertical line is displayed any time a tab or margin marker is moved.

Click on Show ¶ to show formatting symbols in documents (see in Figure 15.7).

If you enable Show Symbols on New and Current Document, the formatting symbols you select here are displayed. Symbols for Space, Hard Return, Tab, Indent, Center, Flush Right, Soft Hyphen, Advance, and Center Page can be turned on or off with the toggle buttons.

Click Reveal Codes to set the font and formatting used by the Reveal Codes window. The set-tings are shown in Figure 15.8.

The Show Reveal Codes on New and Current Document setting enables or disables showing the Reveal Codes window when any document is opened. You cannot use this to disable the Reveal Codes feature.

FIGURE 15.7

Formatting symbols can be turned on or off as part of the display settings.

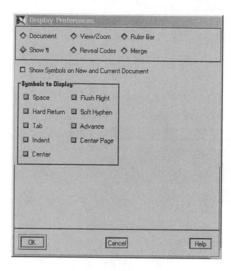

FIGURE 15.8

Set the font and formatting options for the Reveal Codes window.

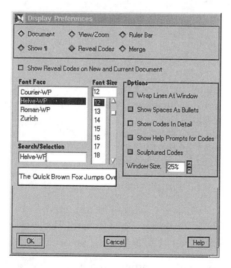

The Options start with Wrap Lines at Window, which prevents the text from going past the current window. Show Spaces as Bullets, Show Codes in Detail, and Show Help Prompts for Codes all mean exactly what they say. Sculptured codes means that the codes are displayed in a 3D-like format. The Window Size sets how much of the document window is taken up by the Reveal Codes window.

Click Merge to set how merge codes will be displayed: as codes, as markers in the text, or hidden.

Environment Preferences

In the Preferences window, click Environment to set default settings for every time you start WordPerfect (shown in Figure 15.9). Table 15.2 shows the options you can change.

FIGURE 15.9
Settings in the
Environment prefer-
ences are used every
time you start the
program.

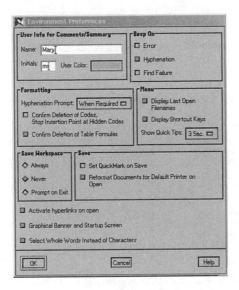

Table 15.2   Environment Preferences

Setting	Description
User Info for comments/Summary	Your username, initials, and a color that will be used for comments and summaries you put in documents.
Beep On	Set when WordPerfect is to beep.
Formatting	Set when to prompt for hyphenation, confirm deletion of code, and confirm deletion of table formulas.
Menu	Display or hide last four opened files, the short-cut keys on menus, and set time delay on Quick Tips.
Save Workspace	Save document window currently on the screen so that you come back to the same document the next time you start WordPerfect.
Save	Save Quickmark puts a bookmark in the document at the current cursor location for a quick return to the mark when a document is reopened. Reformat documents for default printer on open has a default setting of On.
Activate Hypertext	Makes all hypertext links in a document active.
Graphical Banner	Enable or disable the graphic image shown when the program starts.
Select Whole Words instead of Characters	Enable or disable automatic whole-word selection.

Files Preferences

In the display preferences, click Files to set the default location for your document files (shown in Figure 15.10).

FIGURE 15.10

Set file locations for documents.

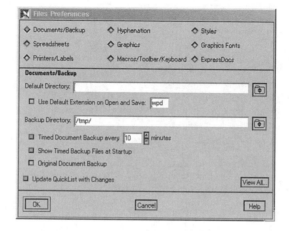

The Files Preferences specify the directories for documents you create, macros, and other files such as spreadsheets. Click each of the categories listed in the top panel to make the settings. Table 15.3 shows the options you can change.

Table 15.3   File Preferences

Setting	Description
Documents/Backup	Directory in which your files are saved, default file extension, and timed backup settings.
Spreadsheets	Directory in which spreadsheet files are saved.
Printers/Labels	Default printer file and label type.
Hyphenation	Directory and filename of supplemental hyphenation file.
Graphics	Directory in which graphics files are saved.
Macros/Toolbar/Keyboard	Directory for macros, Toolbar and keyboard files.
Styles	Directory for style, formatting, definition files.
Graphics Fonts	Directory for Type 1 (PostScript) fonts; only the root user can change this setting.
ExpressDocs	Directory for document templates.

In the display preferences, click Summary to set document search options (shown in Figure 15.11).

FIGURE 15.11
Document Summaries
are used to facilitate
searches.

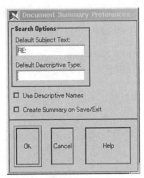

WordPerfect's QuickFinder uses the Document Summaries to organize and quickly locate documents. When you create a document summary, the information is saved as part of the document. By default, Create Summary on Save/Exit is enabled. This automatically creates a document summary. Default subject text and descriptive text for summaries can be indicated here but are commonly left blank.

In the display preferences, click Application Bar to modify the application bar (shown in Figure 15.12). The application bar is the set of icons below the menu line that starts with File.

FIGURE 15.12
You can customize the
application bar to add
or remove features.

The application bar has icons that are shortcuts to frequently used functions. Function icons can be added or removed from the application bar. Changing the application bar can sometimes make WordPerfect unstable.

CAUTION

Unless you have a strong reason to make changes, it is safest just to skip this and leave the defaults. The default settings are based on studies of the most frequently accessed functions and generally represent the best choice anyway.

In the display preferences, click Keyboard to modify the keyboard setting (shown in Figure 15.13).

FIGURE 15.13
You can change the keyboard setting to match earlier versions of WordPerfect.

The default keyboard setting is for WordPerfect for Linux version 8 (_XWP8_). You can change this to earlier versions of WordPerfect for Linux. Or, there are also keyboard definition files for Windows and DOS versions of WordPerfect.

Click Font to modify the font display settings (shown in Figure 15.14).

FIGURE 15.14
Use font preferences to set the display sizes.

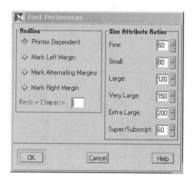

The font preferences set the display sizes used by WordPerfect to display type. The settings are in percentages and are relative to the size of the normal type display. *Redlining*, called *tracking* in MS Word, is a feature that marks all text changes in a document and is used to keep track of additions or deletions in a document. The redline settings are Printer Dependent by default, which is usually shading. You can change this to using a character in the margin to indicate where text has been changed.

Click Convert to modify settings for conversion of imported files (shown in Figure 15.15).

FIGURE 15.15
Conversion preferences specify how files are imported.

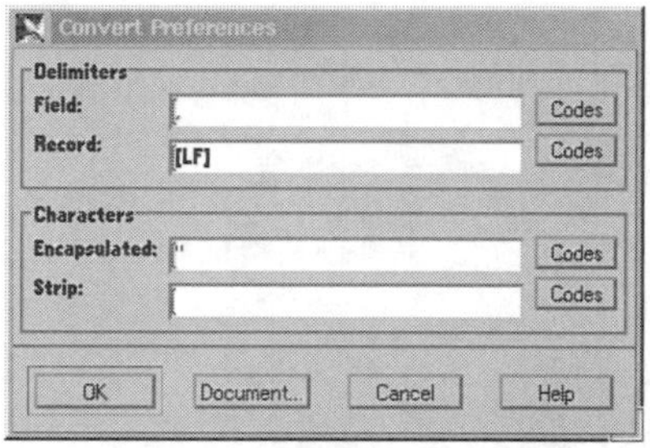

The Convert Preferences set how set field files such as databases and spreadsheets are imported. These are files with fields that are separated by defined characters such as a tab or a comma. Define the separator character in the Field area, and determine how records are separated in the Record area. The Codes button is used to insert the code for special characters such as tab. Encapsulated defines a character that is used to enclose each field. Strip defines characters you want stripped from the file when you import it.

Click Color to set the color scheme for WordPerfect (see Figure 15.16).

FIGURE 15.16
Choose a color scheme or create your own.

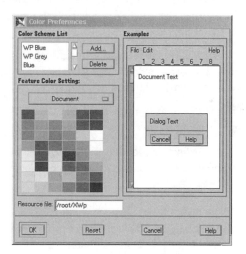

The Color Preferences setting has a half dozen color schemes from which to choose. The default setting is WP Blue. You can choose any one of the other predefined schemes, or you can define your own scheme using the Feature Color Setting panel. To create your own color scheme, choose the different elements of the WordPerfect display by clicking the button that says Document and setting a color for each element, including Document. Any changes you make are shown in the Examples panel.

Click Print to set printing defaults (shown in Figure 15.17).

FIGURE 15.17

Set default printing preferences for quantity and quality.

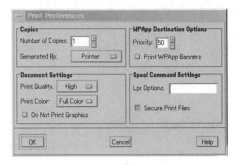

The default printing preferences set the default number of copies to print, the print quality, and the color.

Set up Your Printer

The next step is to set up printing. WordPerfect 8 uses its own printer drivers, not any of the ones set up as part of the standard OpenLinux installation. WordPerfect includes print drivers for hundreds of printers. These are drivers that WordPerfect has developed over many years, and are known to produce some of the best output possible.

This is not the way any other software in OpenLinux prints. Most documents that are created in Linux are either plain text or PostScript format. The Ghostscript program converts complex PostScript documents into non-PostScript printer languages.

To set up printing for WordPerfect, you must make sure that you can print from OpenLinux first. WordPerfect builds on a working printer setup for its printing setup.

WordPerfect includes a Printer Destination tool that is used to set up its printer ports. You must be logged in as root to set up the printer ports. Enter the following command to start the Printer Destination tool:

```
/opt/wp8/shbin10/xwpdest
```

From the Create menu, select Automatic, and WordPerfect printer ports are created for all the printers you have set up and working on your computer. (See Figure 15.18.) When that's done, you can exit the Printer Destination tool.

The next step is started from an open document window in WordPerfect. With a document open, select Print from the File menu. The Print panel opens. See Figure 15.19.

On the top line, click Select. When you first begin, the Available Printers window in the Select Printer panel is blank. Click the Printer Create/Edit button.

FIGURE 15.18
The Printer Destination Program creates WordPerfect printer ports.

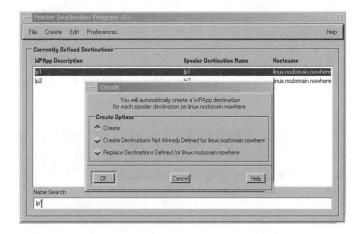

FIGURE 15.19
The WordPerfect Print panel.

In the Printer Create/Edit panel (shown in Figure 15.20), click the Add button. Find your printer in the list of available printer drivers. If your printer isn't listed, find one that is similar. These printer drivers are actually the DOS printer drivers for WordPerfect version 6.

If your printer isn't listed, you can check the WordPerfect Web site for the latest print drivers. You can find the printer drivers at www.corel.com/support/printerdrivers/index.htm. Look for WordPerfect 6 drivers. These are DOS files in an EXE compressed format. After you've downloaded the file, use the unzip tool to decompress the file. For example, the file that includes the latest drivers for the Epson Stylus is named 60DM01.EXE. Enter the following command:

```
unzip 60DM01.EXE
```

This command unzips the file. The unzipped file is named WP60DM01.ALL, but you have to rename this file so that the name is all lowercase. You also have to change the extension so that it has a .us before the .all in the name. The Epson Stylus file, for example, would be named wp60dm01.us.all.

Save the file in the /opt/wp8/shlib10 directory.

After you've selected a driver, click OK. You don't need to change the name of the print driver.

FIGURE 15.20

The WordPerfect Printer Create/Edit panel. After adding a printer, the destination must be set.

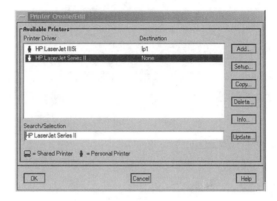

The printer is listed in the Printer Create/Edit panel, but the destination is listed as none. (See Figure 15.20.) With the printer highlighted, click the Setup button.

There are several settings in the Printer Setup panel (shown in Figure 15.21), including the Initial Font, that you need to adjust to fit your needs. Find the Destination button and click it.

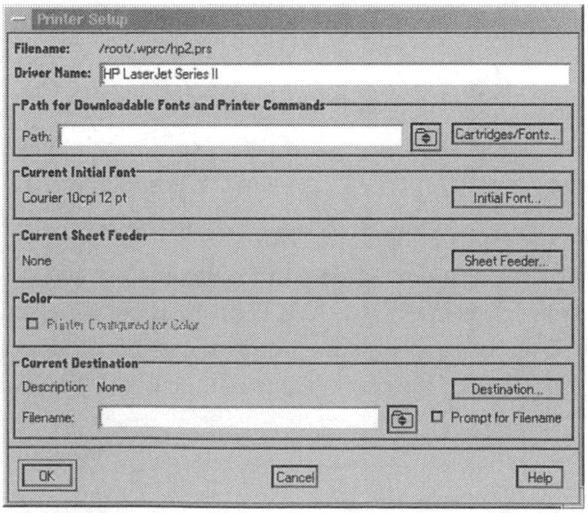

FIGURE 15.21

The WordPerfect Printer Setup panel.

The Select Destination panel (shown in Figure 15.22) sets the printer port that is to be used for this printer. At the top are two settings: WPApp and lpr. WPApp is for the ports that were created with the Printer Destination Program. These are the ports you need to use. The other setting is for the traditional Linux lpr printing.

FIGURE 15.22
Select Destination window for assigning a printer port.

Select your printer port and click OK. The printer is now ready for use.

Fonts in WordPerfect

WordPerfect insists on going its own way with fonts. WordPerfect won't find any fonts you might have set up and added to your KDE desktop because it has its own font rasterizer.

Fonts are stored as a series of outlines that define the look of each character. A font outline is displayed with screen pixels and printed with dots on a laser or ink-jet printer. The process of converting the font outline to a pattern of dots or pixels is called *rasterization*.

If all the work you do is in WordPerfect, using its fonts won't be a problem. If you need to share WordPerfect documents with other applications in Linux, however, this is a problem. The fonts in WordPerfect won't appear in any other applications, and vice versa: Fonts in other applications don't automatically appear in WordPerfect.

The free personal edition of WordPerfect includes some basic fonts that are not top-quality because of licensing issues involved with the high-quality fonts that normally ship with WordPerfect. To get the high-quality fonts, you have to purchase one of the boxed versions of WordPerfect. If you plan to use WordPerfect in an office, you need to do this anyway. The free edition is meant for personal use only—not for commercial use.

With either boxed edition, you get an excellent utility for adding fonts to WordPerfect, in addition to 130 high-quality fonts.

If you want to install additional fonts and you have the font installer utility, copy the font files to the /opt/wp8/shlib10 directory. WordPerfect requires both .pfb and .afm files to install a Type 1 font. To use the font installer, you must be logged in as root. Then start WordPerfect in administrative mode from a terminal window, using the following command:

```
/opt/wp8/wpbin/xwp -admin
```

Open a document, and from the Format menu, select Font. In the Font panel, click the Install Fonts button.

WordPerfect uses standard PostScript Type 1 fonts. Type 1 fonts are widely available and are the standard for all high-end graphics work. Type 1 fonts are available for download on the Internet, as well as for purchase from type foundries such as Adobe, Bitstream, Monotype, and others.

Microsoft's Windows program uses TrueType fonts, and these fonts are easy to find, but they have to be converted to PostScript for use with WordPerfect. There are utilities that will do this for you. Search sites such as www.freshmeat.net for the latest font utilities. Converting TrueType fonts to PostScript using these tools can mean a loss in quality. Most of the conversion utilities cannot completely render all the aspects of a font when converting from TrueType to PostScript. If quality is important to you, stick with real PostScript fonts, at least until better conversion tools become available.

Corel is working on a TrueType conversion tool for WordPerfect that is expected to be included with the commercial version of WordPerfect 9 for Linux. If Corel's success in font management and conversion on other platforms can be used as a guide, its Linux TrueType conversion tool will be worth waiting for.

After you have set up your fonts in WordPerfect, you might want to change the default font for all your documents. Changing the default font in WordPerfect is not a well-documented feature.

The default font is not set in preferences—it's set by the default printer. Open a document and select Print from the File menu.

Next to Current Printer, click the Select button. In the Select Printer panel, click the Printer Create/Edit button. In the Printer Create/Edit panel, click the Setup button. In the Printer Setup panel, find the Current Initial Font section and click the Initial Font button. Select the Initial Font you want to use. It will be the default font for your documents.

Using the WordPerfect Command Window

The WordPerfect command window is used for overall handling of documents (see Figure 15.23).

FIGURE 15.23
The WordPerfect command window.

In the command window help is the PerfectExpert, which is a help facility that you can use for all aspects of creating a document. It sets up a window with help for everything from starting a document to formatting the document and adding visual elements. (See Figure 15.24.)

FIGURE 15.24
The PerfectExpert contains shortcuts to most word processing tasks.

You can use the command window to set all the preferences for how the program will work, and it includes a File Manager for handling your files (see Figure 15.25).

FIGURE 15.25
The WordPerfect File Manager.

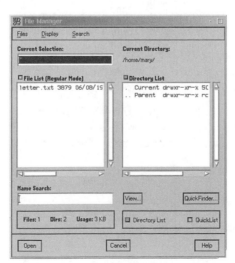

You can use the File Manager to copy, delete, and move your files. It has all the capabilities of a standard file manager.

Right-click on the File Manager window, and you see a pop-up menu with options to move to the top or bottom of the file list or to select all files.

There's also an option for changing the File Manager Setup. You can also access this setup from the Display menu. Several options can be adjusted, including the way files are listed in the File Manager and the startup mode that will be used.

The QuickFinder is a hidden gem in WordPerfect. This handy tool can do any kind of search you need. Put in a filename or part of a name and the directory is searched. There are options for searching your whole system or just particular directories. (See Figure 15.26.)

You can use the Search For option to search the content of files for a particular word or words.

FIGURE 15.26
The QuickFinder is one of the most sophisticated searching tools available on Linux.

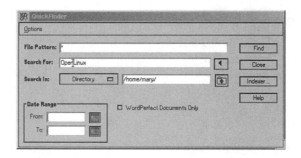

This tool is one of the most sophisticated search tools available for Linux, and is likely to be used for more than just WordPerfect-related tasks. Spend some time with it, and learn how to use it. It can save you hours of work when you know how to use its many features.

The File Pattern field can be a wild card such as the * character, which means any file, or you can limit the files for which to search by an extension such as *.wpd.

The Search For field is the key to QuickFinder's powerful capabilities. Click the icon to the right of the Search For text box, and you'll find that searches can be infinitely refined. On a system with lots of files, you can use this feature to find the most obscure file on your system.

Search For operators including AND, OR, NOT, Followed By, and Group, as well as the ? and * wild cards (for a single character or any characters, respectively). Searches can be limited to the first page of a document, a document summary, or the entire document.

Search words can be flagged to be case sensitive. Multiple search words can be limited by their closeness within a document to a line, a paragraph, a page, and so on.

Using these features, you can search for all files that contain the words *OpenLinux* and *Linas*. In the File Pattern field, put an * to indicate that all files will be searched. In the Search For field, the command looks like this:

```
OpenLinux & Linas/Entire/NoCase/Document
```

You can get all of these settings just by clicking the icon to the right of the text field and clicking the choices you want to make. This command means that the QuickFinder searches for the words *OpenLinux* and *Linas*, looking through the entire document, ignoring upper- and lowercase spellings of the words, and the words must both appear anywhere in the document.

The searches can also be limited to a specific directory or a date range indicating when the file was last saved. One of the features in the command window is the option under the Program menu to open a Remote Window. In a networked environment, with multiple users of OpenLinux, this option enables you to make your WordPerfect available for display on another Linux computer—even if it doesn't have WordPerfect on it. This allows for simple collaborative work on documents across the network.

In WordPerfect, the Remote Window option enables you to share documents without the remote user having to run WordPerfect. From a computer on the network, use an X window to connect with the computer on which WordPerfect is installed. To make the document available, enter the display command to indicate the remote display information for the user who is connected by the remote X window. The command might be something like this:

```
mary:2
```

This indicates that user mary on display 2 has access.

TIP WordPerfect includes supplemental help information for system administrators. To start the WordPerfect Sysadmin Help, open a terminal window and change to the /opt/wp8/wpbin directory. (This is the default directory for OpenLinux 2.3 installations, but if you have WordPerfect installed in a different directory, go to that directory.) Enter the following command:

```
./xwpsahlp
```

A graphical help screen for systems administrators opens.

The command window also has a print queue manager that can handle all your print jobs. You can change print priorities, cancel print jobs, and easily perform all the other tasks of managing printers from the Printer Control panel (shown in Figure 15.27).

FIGURE 15.27
The WordPerfect Printer
Control panel.

File Conversion Capabilities

One of the most sought features of WordPerfect for Linux is its capability to create documents that are compatible with other operating systems and other word processors.

The developers at WordPerfect have always emphasized preserving file format compatibility. Even though they continue to add or enhance functions in WordPerfect, the file format has stayed the same since version 6. Astounding as this might seem, the Linux version creates files that are in the same format as those in the Windows version. Files move back and forth between systems without any losing any formatting. The only problem is that Windows and Macintosh systems use different font metrics, so the fit can vary greatly. The page-by-page fit can be quite different.

File compatibility is not a feature in Microsoft Word, by the way. Word does not even properly preserve formatting between its different versions.

Before WordPerfect for Linux came on the scene, most users of Linux had trouble exchanging documents with Microsoft Office users. There are some other options, but none are completely satisfactory.

WordPerfect's import filters do a good job of importing Word 97 documents, as well as documents of many other formats. Most text formatting is preserved during the conversion process.

Graphics, however, are not converted because of the internal format used by Microsoft Word for graphics in files. WordPerfect for Linux comes with an ample list of import filters:

- AmiPro 1.2–3.0
- Applix Words 4.0
- ASCII text
- FramMaker 3–5
- Interleaf HTML documents
- Interleaf 3.1cx 3.1ps, 4.0cx, 4.0ps, and 5.0
- Island Write 3 and 4
- ISO Latin
- Microsoft Word 4, 5, and 5.5
- Microsoft Word for Windows 2–97
- Rich Text Format (RTF)
- WordPerfect for Macintosh 2 to 3
- WordPerfect for DOS all versions
- WordPerfect for Windows all versions

WordPerfect can also be used to save documents in other formats. The exports formats include the following:

- AmiPro 1.2 through 3.0
- Applix Words 4.0
- ASCII generic word processor
- ASCII text
- FrameMaker 3, 4, and 5
- Interleaf 3–5
- HTML
- ISO Latin text
- Microsoft Word for Windows 2–95
- Postscript
- Rich Text Format
- WordPerfect 4.2–8

WordPerfect's Editing Features

Text editing in WordPerfect will be familiar to anyone who has used a word processing program. All the standard features are available, including change fonts and font sizes, text justification, and so on.

One of the special features is the Shadow Cursor. The Shadow Cursor is used to enter text anywhere in the document, as shown in Figure 15.28. This makes it easier to have a block of text in a document that is unconnected to any other text on the page. Just click anywhere on the page, and you can start typing. The Shadow Cursor changes its look to show how text is aligned when you start typing. A left arrow means left-justified, a right arrow means right-justified, and a double arrow (see Figure 15.28) means the text is centered.

FIGURE 15.28
The shadow cursor, shown here with a double arrow, can be used to place text anywhere on the page.

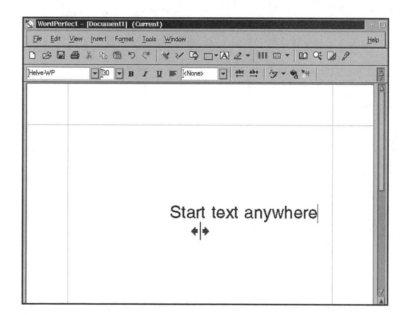

You can start the spelling and grammar tools from the toolbar. There are also spell-as-you-go and grammar-as-you-go features that you can use.

The spell-as-you-go option automatically fixes misspelled words if the dictionary has narrowed options down to only one suggestion. A grammar-as-you-go option does the same thing with grammar. Not everyone considers the spell-as-you-go feature desirable. Spell-as-you-go doesn't warn you when it changes a word. If you don't want that to happen, just turn the feature off. Some people find it helpful, though, because they can speed up their typing by not worrying about how to spell common words. To turn spell-as-you-go on or off, select Proofread from the Tools menu and click Spell-As-You-Go, or click Off.

The grammar checker flags both misspelled words and grammar mistakes with red and blue underlines, respectively. If you right-click on these, you receive either a suggested spelling correction or a grammar tip.

To turn grammar-as-you-go on or off, select Proofread from the Tools menu and click Grammar-As-You-Go, or click Off.

If you turn on grammar-as-you-go, spell-as-you-go is automatically turned off.

Grammar-as-you-go is a popular feature and is commonly turned on. It will not automatically replace words; rather, it gives you a choice to make the change.

WordPerfect 8 has both an undo and a redo. Undo can be used to reverse changes made to text, graphics, or tables. Redo reverses the last undo action. WordPerfect saves a history of all your editing actions in a document so that you can reverse up to the last 300 actions.

The Insert Symbol feature has support for a wide variety of special characters that don't appear on the keyboard (see Figure 15.29). From the menu line, highlight Insert and then select Symbol from the drop-down menu. You can also get the symbols by pressing the Ctrl+W key combination.

FIGURE 15.29

Add special characters to your documents using the Insert Symbol feature.

The symbols can be used to insert any of a number of special characters from about a dozen different character sets. Special character sets include multinational, phonetic, box drawing, typographic symbols, iconic symbols, math and scientific, Greek, Hebrew, Cyrillic, Japanese, and Arabic.

WordPerfect has a sophisticated macro language that you can use to record commands to perform repeated tasks. A macro can be created, for example, to open a file, add a fax cover sheet, and then print the entire document—with the cover sheet—to a printer or a fax modem.

You can create a macro by recording all your steps as you work. You can also write your own macros by learning the macro command language.

Following are the steps to record a macro:

1. Select Macro from the Tools menu and click Record.

2. Type in a name for the macro.

3. Start using the WordPerfect functions you want to include in the macro. When you finish, continue on to step 4.

4. Stop recording the macro by selecting Macro from the Tools menu and clicking Record.

Use the following steps to play a macro:

1. Select Macro from the Tools menu and click Play.

2. Type in the name of the macro you want to play or click the icon next to the Macro Name field and select the macro you want to run.

3. Click Play.

WordPerfect includes more than two dozen predefined macros. These include a macro that adds a large capital letter to the beginning of the paragraph, another that converts normal type into white type on a black background, and a macro that saves all open documents. For information about the included macros and to learn more about creating your own macros, use the online macro manual. To open the manual, select Help and click Macros.

WordPerfect's Graphics Capabilities

Some of the graphics capabilities of WordPerfect are disabled in the free Personal Edition included with OpenLinux. If you need a drawing tool and other graphics-related capabilities, consider getting the boxed version of WordPerfect for Linux.

The program comes from Corel, a company with one of the best drawing programs available for Windows systems: Corel Draw. The drawing tool in the boxed edition has many capabilities.

You can use the Drawing Layer to create drawings directly on top of text. The drawing tools create lines and shapes, as well as adding color, gradient fills, and patterns to drawings. You can rotate and resize graphics within an image box. You can also wrap text on both sides of an image or contour it around odd shapes.

If you are working primarily in word processing, getting WordPerfect's drawing tools can save you time if you frequently add your own graphics. Otherwise, you can use GIMP, which is included with OpenLinux, to create your graphics and then import the files into your WordPerfect documents. See Chapter 18, "Configuring and Running GIMP," for more information.

WordPerfect for Linux can import the following graphics formats:

- BMP
- CGM
- CorelDRAW
- gem
- gif
- HPGL
- jpeg
- MicroGrafx
- pcx
- pict2
- png
- Sun Raster
- Targa
- tiff

You can use WordPerfect's Web publishing capabilities to create HTML documents, complete with hyperlinks and bookmarks. You can also convert Web files directly into Corel WordPerfect format. This makes WordPerfect a handy HTML editor for Linux.

The StarOffice Suite

StarOffice is a complete, Microsoft Office 2000-compatible suite that includes a word processor, database, spreadsheet, presentation, and other software. Version 5.1 of the program is included with OpenLinux 2.3.

StarOffice is a free suite of programs. It is owned by Sun Microsystems and can be downloaded from www.sun.com/staroffice/. Sun offers the option to get the program on a CD for $9.95 plus shipping. Look on the company's Web site for details.

If you have the boxed edition of OpenLinux, you have the StarOffice suite on the Windows Tools & Commercial Applications CD.

Since Sun bought StarOffice, it has made the entire suite of programs available for free for any kind of use, personal or commercial. StarOffice is the first new office suite to be introduced in recent years that has successfully penetrated the market dominated by Microsoft Office. That is, in part, because of its integrated features and cross-platform compatibility in addition to its low price: free!

StarOffice includes just about everything you need for a typical office workstation. It has a Web-enabled word processor (StarWriter), a spreadsheet (StarCalc), a drawing program

(StarDraw), a database (StarBase), and a presentation program (StarImpress). It also has a scheduler (StarSchedule) and email (StarMail) capabilities.

StarOffice is designed to do everything from one place, in contrast to the normal Linux philosophy of using a specialized tool for each task. The advantage for users is a shorter learning process because everything works pretty much the same way in each program in the suite, and you never have to leave the program to do most of your tasks.

Like Microsoft Office, however, you'll have more functions than you'll ever use in a lifetime because not everyone needs to be capable of doing everything. The program is designed to offer a broad range of features for almost every possible use. All the features can sometimes be confusing, and getting to exactly what you want can take many steps. You lose the efficiency of the Linux approach of specialized tools.

In order to maximize the interoperability between the different parts of the suite, StarOffice has its own desktop with its own navigation bars and window manager. This restricts everything to being internally sharable within StarOffice. Open windows within StarOffice have to stay within the program's desktop restrictions. This adds extra overhead to the program's response time and can slow it down somewhat, depending on your system.

Most users, however, will not consider these to be serious limitations. They've been using office suites with even more limitations than those described here, with response times that can encourage frequent coffee breaks.

StarOffice has a very Windows-like feel to it, which has made it very popular among former Windows users who are making the transition to Linux. There's not much to relearn, and because it has all the major components expected in an office suite, it offers a business-class solution for office applications on the Linux workstation.

How to Install StarOffice

The download file for StarOffice version 5.1 is almost 75MB. This can take hours to download. If you choose to do this rather than buy the CD, it can take several tries. If you are using a modem connection, the modem line can be dropped in the middle of a file transfer, requiring you to restart the download process. Even if you have a dedicated access line, such as a T1 connection, the download can get interrupted. If you have successfully downloaded the file, be sure to make a backup copy so that you don't have to do it again.

After you download the file from Sun Microsystems, follow the instructions for installation of the software. If you bought the CD from Sun, use the installation instructions that come with the CD.

If you have the boxed edition of OpenLinux, the StarOffice program is on the Windows Tools & Commercial Applications CD. Insert the CD and make sure that you are logged in as the root user.

Click on the K Application Launcher and select COAS on the popup menu. Click on Commercial Products. The OpenLinux Commercial Install Page opens. Click on the link to the commercial packages. A list of commercial packages on the CD appears. Click on the link for StarOffice. An instruction page opens that gives more details on installation. Click the language you want to install, and Kpackage starts. Click on Install to finish the installation.

Installing the StarOffice Server

If you have StarOffice on a CD, follow the installation instructions that came with the CD.

If you have downloaded StarOffice from the Web, you need to decompress the file.

Open a terminal window and copy the file to a temporary directory. Change to the directory with the copy. For example, you can put the copy in the /tmp directory, and then enter the following command:

```
cd /tmp
```

Then you'll need to untar the file. The following example uses the downloaded version of StarOffice 5.1. The command is

```
tar xvf so51_lnx_01.tar
```

This uncompresses the file and puts everything into a directory named so51inst. Change to the new directory:

```
cd so51inst
```

This is the StarOffice installation directory. You are now ready to install StarOffice.

You need to be logged in as root in order to install the StarOffice server. Although it is possible to install StarOffice as a single user, it's a good idea to install the StarOffice server and use the program that way, no matter whether you are setting up for one user or for several. If you install only the single-user version and you ever need to have a second user on your system, you'll have to install another copy of the whole program for the second user. The installed program takes up more than 150MB, which is why the default installation for OpenLinux is to install the server version.

First, I'll go through the server installation. The instructions for a single-user installation follow later.

Installing the StarOffice Application Server   Make sure that you have read through the previous section on the libcrypt library. If you haven't, go back and make sure that you don't need to update your version of the glibc libraries in order to install StarOffice.

To proceed, from a terminal window, make sure you are in the directory with the StarOffice installation files. In the example with the version 5.1 download, that is the /tmp/so51inst directory. Change to the program setup directory, which on version 5.1 is office51. If you have a different version of StarOffice, enter the correct directory for that version.

To start the setup, enter the following command:

```
./setup /net
```

The first window that opens is the welcome screen. Click on Next to continue.

The next window (shown in Figure 15.30) asks for your registration customer number and key. This is the information you were given after you registered for the free download. Enter the information at this time, and then click Next.

FIGURE 15.30
StarOffice preparing installation window asks for the registration key code.

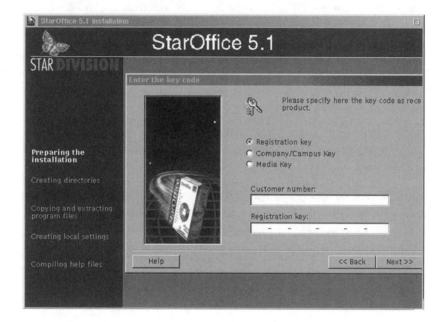

An Important Information window is displayed; it includes an explanation about the glibc libraries. After looking through this information window, click Next. The terms of the license for personal use are displayed. Read the terms, and if you agree, click Accept.

The next step is to choose between Standard, Custom, and Minimum installations. If you choose Custom, you can choose to have StarOffice automatically linked to the KDE Desktop for all users of StarOffice. If you don't need this, choose Standard.

On the next step, watch out for the directory in which the program is installed. StarOffice defaults to installing in the home directory of the user who is installing the program. Because you need to be logged in as root, it says /root/Office51. You want to install into the /opt directory. At the prompt, change the directory name for installation to /opt/Office51. That's the standard location for installing the server edition. Click Next, and it asks for confirmation to create the directory. Click Yes.

If you chose Custom, the next window shows the options that can be installed with StarOffice. Click on the plus sign by Optional Components. Make sure that the KDE integration block is shown in full color. See Figure 15.31. If it isn't in color, it won't be installed. Add any other options that you also need, such as support for other languages. Don't touch the Program Modules. Because everything in StarOffice is designed to work together, unless you know what you are doing, you might remove the functionality of more than just the program you've decided to remove. If you want to remove a program because space is a problem, you should probably not use StarOffice. Find another solution. The program, although it is big by Linux standards, is half the size of comparable Windows programs. It takes up a relatively small space on the computer systems that are now shipping, which all have at least 4GB of hard drive space.

FIGURE 15.31
Select KDE integration in StarOffice.

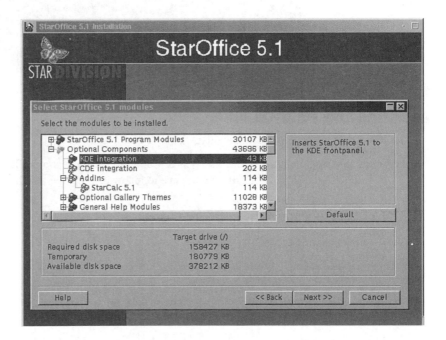

Click the Complete button, and the installation begins. The rest of the installation looks a lot like the installation of a Windows program. See Figure 15.32. It was designed to look this way.

FIGURE 15.32
StarOffice installation screen.

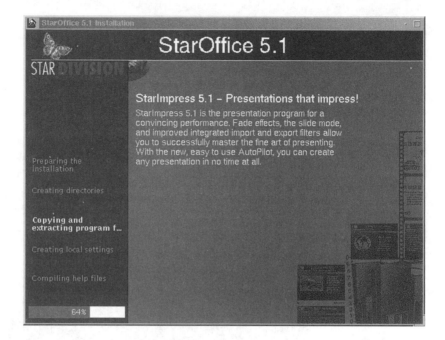

Installing the User Client

First, make sure you are logged in as the user and not as root.

If you installed from the Windows Tools & Commercial Applications CD included with the boxed edition of OpenLinux, the procedure to follow is to open a terminal window and enter the following command:

`/opt/Office50/bin/soffice`

If you downloaded StarOffice version 5.1 or later, open a terminal window and enter the following command:

`/opt/Office51/bin/setup`

Whichever way you are starting, the same installation window that opened when starting the server installation opens now. Click Next.

The registration window opens. If you have the boxed edition, you'll find the media key inside the front cover of the OpenLinux 2.3 manual.

If you downloaded the free version 5.1, enter the customer number and key code for the user. If you don't have one, go to the Star Division Web site at www.stardivision.com and register to get one.

The User Data window opens next. Enter the information that matches the registration key.

The Important Information window opens next. This is the same Important Information window that appeared during the server installation. The License Agreement is shown; if you accept the terms, click Accept.

The Installation Type window offers two options: the Standard Workstation Installation and the Standard Installation (local). See Figure 15.33.

FIGURE 15.33
StarOffice client installation has two options, Standard Workstation and Standard (local).

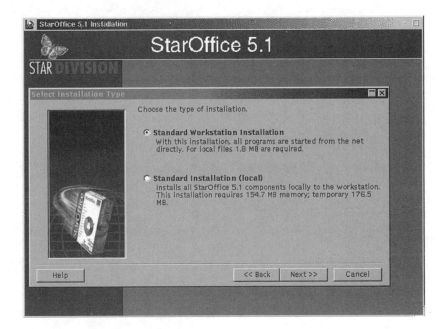

The Standard Workstation is the preferred choice. It installs only the files needed to run the program. The total file space required for this installation is 1.8MB. The local option installs the entire program in the user's home directory and takes up about 155MB. There is no advantage to using this option. Click Next when you've made your choice.

The default directory for installation is the user's home directory. There is no reason to change this. Click Next, and you are prompted with a message that the directory doesn't exist. Click Yes to create the directory. Finally, click the Complete button to finish the installation.

After it's completed, you'll need to log out and back in so that the parts that are integrated with the KDE desktop will be accessible.

Installing a Single-User Version of StarOffice   The procedure for installing a single-user version of StarOffice is the same as for installing the server version, with two differences. First, the command to start installation is `./setup`. Do not include the `/net` parameter. The second difference is that you must install the whole program into your home directory. Unless you are root, you do not have the necessary permissions to install the program anywhere else.

On the K Application Launcher, you'll find a section called Personal. Choose this section, and a pop-out menu offers Setup, SPAdmin, and StarOffice. Click on StarOffice to start the program suite.

StarOffice Configuration

The first time you start StarOffice 5.1, you need to configure the Internet settings. If you don't want to use StarOffice with the Internet options, click Don't use the Internet. See Figure 15.34.

FIGURE 15.34
StarOffice can be used with the Internet, for email, Web browsing, and creating or editing HTML documents. To do this, you need to configure the Internet settings.

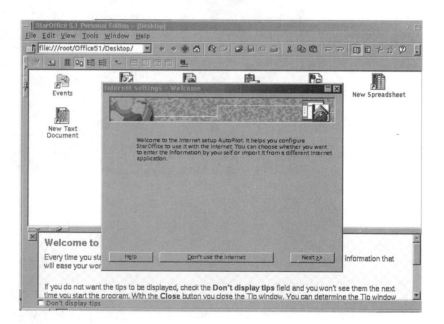

To configure the Internet settings, click Next. For the StarOffice Web browser, the first setting is for a proxy server. If you use a proxy server on your network, put the settings for the proxy server and proxy port here. If you aren't sure whether your system uses a proxy server, ask your network administrator.

The next window is for configuring email settings. You need to enter your email username and password, the POP3 server from which you receive mail, and the SMTP server you use to send mail. Give the configuration its own name.

For Usenet news, the next window needs your account name and the name of your news server.

The StarOffice Desktop

When you start StarOffice, it takes over your desktop. In fact, it works best at the maximum size of your screen. The StarOffice desktop works like a combination of file manager and Web browser. See Figure 15.35.

FIGURE 15.35
Opening StarOffice.

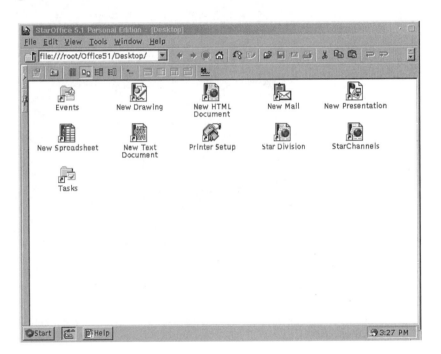

A menu bar across the top shows the file path or Web address of the contents of the desktop main work area. There are also additional bars: a Function Bar, an Object Bar, and a Main Toolbar.

Two additional parts of the StarOffice desktop facilitate your work: the Explorer and the Beamer.

The Explorer The Explorer is active after the initial setup, but hidden on the left margin of the StarOffice desktop. Click the Show arrow, by the menu bar, to see the Explorer window. See Figure 15.36.

FIGURE 15.36
The StarOffice Explorer.

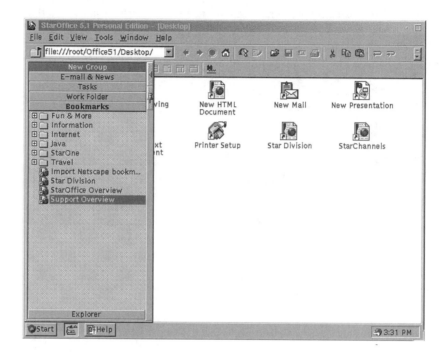

The first time StarOffice is started, there are a number of predefined groups in Explorer:

- **New Group**—Adds additional buttons to the Explorer.
- **Work Folder**—Opens the default folder where your documents are saved. This folder is one of the options you can define.
- **Tasks**—Shows icons for default document styles that can be used to start new documents.
- **Bookmarks**—Set up with several predefined bookmarks for links to favorite files on your system or across the Internet. You can also use this like a bookmark file on a Web browser to add links to favorite Web sites.
- **Explorer**—Opens the Explorer extended file manager tool.

If you are using the Explorer, you'll probably want to activate the Beamer. From the View menu, select Beamer.

The Beamer The Beamer (see Figure 15.37) opens another panel on the StarOffice desktop. It works with the Explorer and makes using the Explorer more efficient.

FIGURE 15.37
StarOffice Beamer
facilitates the use of
the Explorer.

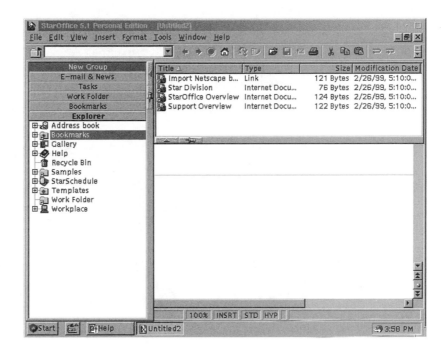

Clicking on a folder in the Explorer displays its contents in the Beamer panel. From the Beamer, you can open a file by double-clicking on it, or you can drag and drop a file onto the desktop work area to open the file. Dragging a file into an open document creates a link to the file.

Configuring Options StarOffice has two overall configuration settings: One is for configuring the toolbar displays, and the other sets the general options for all the programs in the suite. Choose Tools from the Menu bar and select Configuration. See Figure 15.38.

You can change all the toolbars to work the way you want them to. For example, you might want to add a function you frequently use and put it in a place that is easily accessible.

Generally, it's a good idea to leave this alone. Only after working in the program for a while should you consider making any changes in the toolbar configuration. The default setup has been carefully designed for efficient use of the most frequently used options.

The other setting is for General Options. From the Tools menu, select Options. See Figure 15.39.

FIGURE 15.38
StarOffice toolbar con-
figuration.

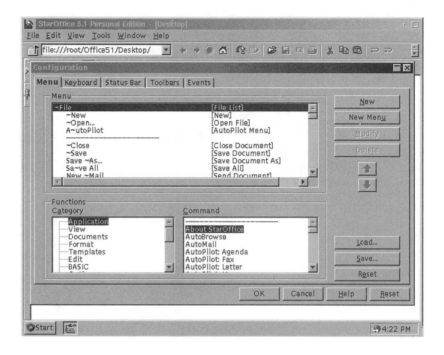

FIGURE 15.39
Setting StarOffice
General Options.

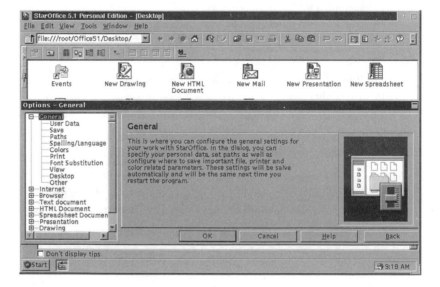

The settings here cover everything in StarOffice:

- **General**—The general settings include your user name and other registration information. You can change this only to a new name that matches a new registration code. Other settings are for automatic saves and backups and file locations, including the Work Folder. You can also change the default language here.

- **Internet**—StarOffice's Internet settings for Web browsing, FTP, and email. You can change the proxy server settings, DNS, and other information for the StarOffice Web browser.

- **Browser**—The browser has several settings, including whether cookies are accepted, the cache size, and Java support.

- **Text document**—Default text document settings include how documents are displayed, the default layout, and fonts.

- **HTML document**—Like the settings for text documents, these are the default settings for any HTML documents you create.

- **Spreadsheet**—Document Global settings for spreadsheets. Options cover what content is displayed and how the input entries are handled.

- **Presentation**—Default settings for presentation documents, including whether to display guides and snap to guide settings.

- **Drawing**—Default settings for drawings, including whether to display guides and snap to guide settings.

- **Picture**—Default settings for StarImage documents.

- **Formula**—Printing format options for printing StarMath formulas.

Configuring Printers and Fonts

If you have already set up printing for OpenLinux, most of the default settings in StarOffice probably don't need to be changed. Because the program comes from Germany, the printer settings default to a European paper size of A4. If you are in North America, you'll probably want to change this setting to letter size. To do this, you need to run the Printer Setup utility.

You can use the Printer Setup utility to add printers as well as to modify your current printer setup. Start the Printer Setup utility from the K Application Launcher in the Personal section where you start StarOffice. Select SPAdmin, the StarOffice Printer Administration tool.

If you want to make changes in the printer setup, you must be logged in as root. If you are not logged in as root, you can open the Printer Administration tool, but you can't make any changes. The Printer Installation administration panel shows what printers are installed and the available printer drivers, and has buttons for adding or modifying printers and fonts. See Figure 15.40.

FIGURE 15.40
StarOffice Printer
Installation.

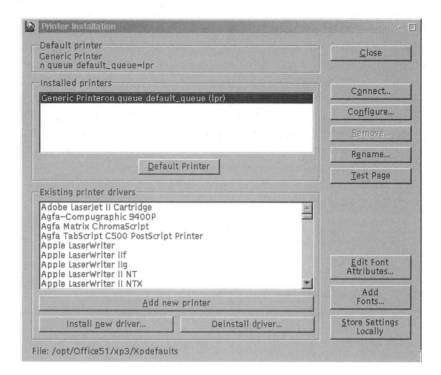

A list of existing printer drivers is shown; these are all PostScript printers. If you have a non-PostScript printer, your print jobs are converted by GhostScript to the non-PostScript format. This is set in your OpenLinux printer setup.

Scroll through the StarOffice printer driver list; if your printer is there, choose it and click the Add new printer button. This enables you to use a printer driver designed for use with your printer in StarOffice.

A downside to StarOffice is that it supports only PostScript printing. Most offices do not have PostScript printers, which means that all printing from StarOffice is slower because everything has to be converted using GhostScript. (PostScript printing in general is slower because everything has to be transformed by a special PostScript RIP in the printer. A *RIP*, raster image processor, is a hardware device in the printer that converts the PostScript outline fonts and images into bitmap dots for printing.)

The lack of HP Laserjet printer support is a real shortcoming with StarOffice.

N O T E You do not have to use a driver designed for your printer in order to print from StarOffice. You can use the default generic printer driver for all printers that have been properly set up as part of OpenLinux. See Chapter 8, "Installing and Configuring Printers," for more information on setting up printers. ■

When you add a printer, a Configure panel opens with choices for printer parameters for paper size, resolution, margins, and so on. Change the defaults if you need to and then click OK. After you've done that, click on the Test Page button to print a test page using the new printer setup. If the page is successful, you can click the Default Printer button to make the new driver your default printer.

StarOffice uses PostScript Type 1 fonts. You can temporarily add fonts by clicking the Add Fonts button and then browsing to a directory in which Type 1 fonts have been installed.

If you want to make additional fonts available to StarOffice permanently but don't want to install them as part of the X server for your KDE desktop, you can add the SAL_FONTPATH variable to your shell startup script. Point it to the directory path for the Type 1 fonts.

The best way to add fonts is to install them in the X server. The default X server for OpenLinux is XFree86. A utility for installing Type 1 fonts into XFree86 is available at ftp://sunsite.unc.edu/pub/Linux/X11/xutils. The name of the utility is type1inst-0.6.1.tar.gz. The README file included with the package explains how to set up and use the font installer.

Other programs also convert TrueType fonts to Type 1. The conversion process, however, produces a font that is of poor quality. This is not a solution for business applications.

StarOffice's Main Programs

StarWriter, StarCalc, StarBase, and StarImpress are similar to Microsoft's Word, Excel, Access, and PowerPoint. Unlike Microsoft Office, where each of these is a separate program, all the StarOffice programs work together in a common environment. This gives you great flexibility because no real barriers exist between a word processing document and a spreadsheet or database.

To make the best use of StarOffice and its integrated programs, a feature called the AutoPilot is included. Rather than starting an individual program to create a new document, you can use the AutoPilot and tell it what kind of document, spreadsheet, or database you want to create. It sets up everything and starts the program you need to do the job.

Following is an overview of some of the most commonly used programs in the StarOffice suite. This will give you an introduction to each program and enough information to get you started. For more in-depth information on StarOffice, several good books have been recently published. A good book for beginners is *Sams Teach Yourself StarOffice 5 for Linux* by Nicholas D. Wells and R. Dean Taylor (ISBN: 0-672-31412-6).

AutoPilot

You can use the AutoPilot feature (shown in Figure 15.41) to simplify all tasks in StarOffice. The AutoPilot makes use of StarOffice templates to create letters, faxes, agendas, memos, and presentations.

FIGURE 15.41

Use AutoPilot to start
new documents.

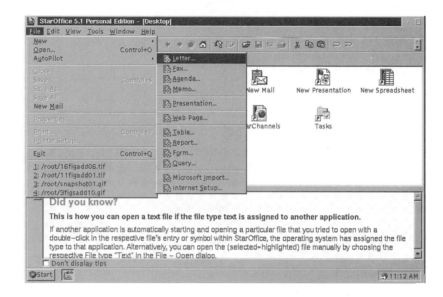

To start AutoPilot, choose the File menu and select AutoPilot. Choose from one of the several predefined settings. These are based on templates for standard documents.

In addition to the AutoPilot, there are many ways to create new or open existing documents in StarOffice. There are icons on the desktop for many tasks. The following sections describe some of the programs in the StarOffice suite and some alternative ways to start the programs, along with brief descriptions.

StarWriter

StarWriter is the word processor in StarOffice. To start StarWriter, choose New from the File Menu and select Text Document. Alternatively, from the Explorer Tasks group, click the Text icon. This opens a new document window. StarWriter has all the standard features found in a word processing program. You'll find most of the settings in the Options settings for StarOffice.

Some settings for StarWriter are available under the Tools menu. One is AutoCorrect feature. On the Tools menu, select AutoCorrect/AutoFormat. These settings are used by other parts of StarOffice that offer autocorrection.

You can add to or delete from the definitions in the Replacement Table. (See Figure 15.42.) This is a handy feature that can be used to correct words you frequently mistype, as well as to create shortcuts for words you regularly use (such as a company name). Other settings in this panel are for exceptions and autoreplacement.

FIGURE 15.42
StarWriter autocorrec-
tion settings.

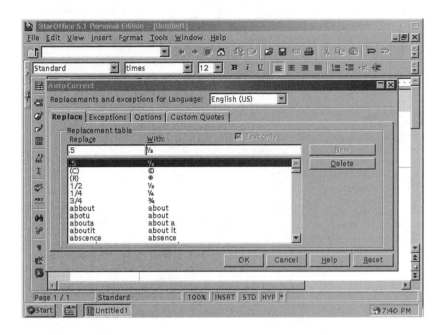

Other settings on the Tools menu include default formats for Outlining and Footnotes.

StarWriter can open a wide variety of documents, including those created in Word 97, and it can save documents in many different formats.

The formats that can be converted by StarWriter include the following:

- ASCII text
- Mac Text
- MS Word for Windows 6.0, 95, and 97
- Rich Text Format (RTF)
- All earlier StarWriter formats

The formats to which StarWriter documents can be saved (converted) include the following:

- ASCII text
- HTML
- Mac Text
- MS Word for Windows 6.0, 95, and 97
- All earlier StarWriter formats

The document conversions are good, but not always complete. Check carefully to make sure that everything has been converted if you are moving documents back and forth between StarOffice and Microsoft Office.

StarWriter has many well-implemented features, including its right-click menus.

StarCalc

StarCalc (shown in Figure 15.43) is the spreadsheet program in StarOffice. To start StarCalc, choose New from the File Menu and select Spreadsheet. Alternatively, from the Explorer Tasks group, click the Spreadsheet icon.

FIGURE 15.43
Use StarCalc for your spreadsheets.

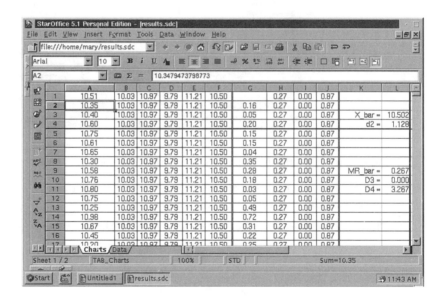

StarCalc has many of the capabilities of spreadsheet programs such as Excel or Lotus 1-2-3.TStarCalc can convert from and to Lotus and MS Excel 4.0, 5.0, 95, and 97 formats.

StarDraw

StarDraw is the drawing program in StarOffice. To start StarDraw, choose New from the File Menu and select Drawing. Alternatively, from the Explorer Tasks group, click the Drawing icon.

StarDraw is a basic vector drawing program. A vector drawing program uses lines, boxes, circles, and ellipses to create images. Objects can be grouped together, and color can be added. This is useful for creating spot graphics in reports or presentations.

StarImage

StarImage (shown in Figure 15.44) is the graphics editing program in StarOffice. To start StarImage, choose New from the File Menu and select Image. Alternatively, from the Explorer Tasks group, click the Image icon.

StarImage is a bitmap image editor. It is similar to GIMP or PhotoShop, but more limited in its capabilities.

FIGURE 15.44
Graphic editing can be done in StarImage.

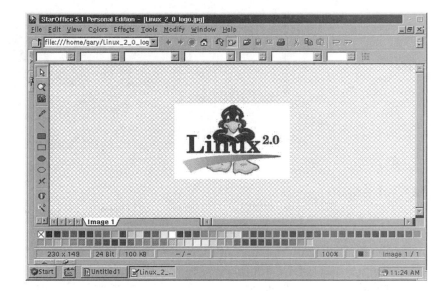

StarImpress

StarImpress is the presentation program in StarOffice. To start StarImpress, choose New from the File Menu and select Presentation. Alternatively, from the Explorer Tasks group, click the Presentation icon.

StarImpress (shown in Figure 15.45)creates slide show presentations. It is similar to Microsoft's PowerPoint or Harvard Graphics.

StarBase

StarBase is the database program in StarOffice. To start StarBase, choose New from the File Menu and select Database. Alternatively, from the Explorer Tasks group, click the Database icon. StarBase uses the dBase format by default and it supports SQL and ODBC. StarBase is suitable for personal databases or some small office needs. It is not a substitute for an industrial-strength database.

FIGURE 15.45
StarImpress can used like PowerPoint to create presentations.

StarSchedule

StarSchedule is the scheduler in StarOffice. It has a task list, calendar, hourly scheduler, and contact address book. The view can be changed from daily to weekly or monthly. To start StarSchedule, double-click the Events icon on the desktop.

StarSchedule also has a direct connection to the PalmPilot. Setup is under Tools. Select PalmPilot Hotsync Configuration. StarSchedule is similar to Microsoft's Outlook or the Lotus Organizer.

StarMail

StarMail is the email client. Click the E-mail & News button in the Explorer to see email. Click on the New Mail icon on the desktop to write a new email message.

To use email, you must have all the email settings completed. To check your email settings, right-click on the blank area of the desktop. Under New are choices for the outbox, POP3, or IMAP accounts.

Other StarOffice Programs

Other StarOffice programs include StarDiscussion for, participation in Usenet-style news groups; an HTML editor, for creating and maintaining Web pages; StarChart, for creating charts; and StarMath, an integrated formula editor.

ApplixWare Office Suite

ApplixWare Office is a comprehensive suite of applications. It includes Applix Words, Spreadsheets, Graphics, Presents, Mail, and HTML Author.

You can download a 30-day trial version of ApplixWare for Linux on the Web at `www.applix.com/applixware/linux/main.cfm`. If you have the boxed edition of OpenLinux, the trial version is included on the Windows Tools & Commercial Applications CD. After 30 days, you must purchase the program if you want to continue using it.

ApplixWare includes a package of programs that is not difficult for any new user to learn, especially anyone who is already familiar with other office programs.

The different applications in ApplixWare are well integrated, making it easy to insert documents from one application into another. The customizable star (*) menu, included on every application's window, includes shortcuts to all of the other applications.

To install the trial version from the Web, you need to uncompress the file using the tar utility. Enter the command:

```
tar xvf applixdemo-v442-x86-glibc-linux.tar
```

The file name may be different if a new version is available. After you've uncompressed the file, follow the instructions that are included in the file for installing the program.

If you have the boxed edition of OpenLinux, ApplixWare is on the Windows Tools & Commercial Applications CD. Insert the CD and make sure that you are logged in as the root user.

Click on the K Application Launcher and select COAS on the popup menu. Click on Commercial Products. The OpenLinux Commercial Install Page opens. Click on the link to the commercial packages. A list of commercial packages on the CD appears. Click on the link for ApplixWare. An instruction page opens that gives more details on installation.

ApplixWare installation has three parts. Before installing the applications, you need to install the menu and help modules. Click the language you want to install and Kpackage opens. Click on Install to finish the installation of the menu and help modules.

Second, install the application software. Click on Software Install, which opens Kpackage. Click on install to finish application software installation.

Finally, you can install the optional components including clip art, documentation, and additional dictionaries and thesauri.

After the installation is complete, ApplixWare appears on the KDE Application Menu the next time you start the KDE Desktop. You can also manually restart the K Panel by right-clicking on the panel and selecting restart.

To start ApplixWare Office, click on the K Application popup menu. Under Office, select Applix.

ApplixWare Configuration

You can configure ApplixWare by accessing the star (*) menu. On the ApplixWare Main Menu (shown in figure 15.46), click on * to access configuration options. Select ApplixWare Preferences.

FIGURE 15.46
Click on the * to access ApplixWare configuration.

Each preference option is explained in the Help menu, which you can access by clicking on the help button in the lower right corner of the window.

In addition, each application has its own preference settings, which you can access by starting the application and then clicking on the *. Preferences are at the bottom of the list.

ApplixWare's Main Programs

You can start the ApplixWare Office programs by clicking on the icons on the Main Menu, or you can click on the * menu and select the program you want to start from the list that is displayed.

Words   ApplixWare's word processor, Applix Words, is similar to WordPerfect or StarWriter. Because Words is incorporated with the other ApplixWare office applications, you can easily integrate documents created in the other applications with Words to create complex and sophisticated reports and other kinds of documents.

The first time you use Words, you can easily convert your existing word processing files to Applix Words format. Choose Import from the File Menu, and select the file you want to use. The conversion happens automatically. Words has import and export filters for all versions of Microsoft Word, including Word 2000, and for all versions of WordPerfect.

You can apply character attributes, align text, undo the previous command, save, print, and more using the clickable icons called *ExpressLine icons*.

No matter what ApplixWare application you have open, you always see the same basic elements: the Title Bar, the Menu Bar, and the row of ExpressLine command icons.

Spreadsheets   Applix Spreadsheets is a full-featured program that is strikingly similar to Microsoft Excel. If you know Excel or Lotus 1-2-3, you shouldn't have any trouble getting started on Spreadsheets.

Spreadsheets has ExpressLine icons for common spreadsheet tasks, including Print Preview, Wrap Text, Protect Cell(s), Create Chart, and others. You can use Applix Spreadsheets to access more than just one spreadsheet at a time using its 3D Sheets Bar.

Spreadsheets not only has the same look at Excel, it uses the same syntax for creating formulas. Of course, the Spreadsheets macros are not written in Microsoft's Visual Basic.

Spreadsheets can import Excel 97 and 2000, Lotus 4, comma-separated values (CSV), ASCII, and others formats. It can export Excel 5.0, Lotus 3, CSV, ASCII, and other formats.

Graphics and Presents   ApplixWare has two graphics programs, Applix Graphics, a graphics editor, and Applix Presents, a presentation program.

Applix Graphics is a simple painting program similar to KPaint or the Windows Paint program. You can use the clip art files included in Graphics and modify them for your needs, or you can draw your own images.

Applix Presents is a top-quality presentation program that supports many of the features made popular by PowerPoint, including animations and slide shows. It can import more than two dozen formats, including PowerPoint 97 and 2000. It can also export into more than a dozen formats, including PowerPoint 97.

HTML Author   ApplixWare includes a Web page editing tool, HTML Author. This is full-featured, WYSIWYG-style HTML editor. It is similar to Netscape Composer, the most popular WYSIWYG HTML editor on Linux, but HTML Author has many more features.

Running Windows Applications

You can run Windows software on OpenLinux with Wine, which is included with the OpenLinux standard installation, or VMware, which you can download from the Web.

Whereas running Windows programs on Linux is not always successful, the latest versions of these programs have produced some impressive results.

One development coming out of the Wine project is Winelib, which allows programs written for Windows to be compiled under Linux and then run as native Linux applications. Corel is using Winelib to port the company's office suite to Linux. Corel has also been making substantial contributions to the Wine project.

VMware is a commercial application that has caused quite a buzz. It is an emulator that runs a virtual Windows environment on Linux. You can use VMware to run almost any Windows application, including Microsoft Office, on your Linux system.

Using Wine

Wine (*Wine Is Not an Emulator*) is an open source project that recreates the Windows APIs as free software. An *API* –(*application program interface*) is a set of routines, protocols, and tools for building software applications. The Wine Web site is at `www.winehq.com`.

OpenLinux includes Wine in the standard installation. It is a free, open source program that you can use to run some unmodified Windows 3.1, Windows 95, and Windows NT software Linux.

Wine has fairly good performance, but Wine does not yet support many Windows applications. You can get more details at the Wine Web site.

Because Wine is already installed on your system, if you also have Windows installed on the same computer, you are almost ready to run a Windows program using Wine.

N O T E You don't have to have Windows installed on your computer to use Wine, but if you don't, it takes extra set up. To run Wine without Windows, see the document no-windows in the /usr/doc/wine-990804 directory for instructions on the steps you'll need to take. ▪

To use Wine, you'll first need to mount the drive where Windows is installed, either by putting an entry into /etc/fstab or by manually mounting it.

With the Windows drive mounted, open a terminal window and enter the `wine` command followed by the filename of the program you want to run. This filename should include the full pathname to the program file.

For example, to run Windows' Solitaire program, enter this command:

```
wine sol
```

If the Windows drive is on your search path, the Solitaire program will run. If not, enter the full pathname such as:

```
wine /mnt/windows/sol.exe
```

The configuration file for Wine is the wine.conf file in the /etc/wine.d directory. The manual page for Wine gives a summary of some of the options available.

VMware Installation

VMware is a virtual machine monitor that allows multiple operating systems to run on your Linux system. VMware requires a Microsoft operating system to run Windows applications. It has very high levels of application compatibility. The Web site for VMware is at www.vmware.com.

You can download a copy of VMware for Linux from the VMware Web site. After you have downloaded the program, you need to purchase a license in order to install and run the program. A 30-day trial license is also available to evaluate the software's capabilities. See the Web site for details.

Once you've downloaded the file, you can install VMware using the following instructions. Make sure you are logged in as root before you install VMware.

1. Use the tar tool to uncompress the file you downloaded:

   ```
   tar zxf vmware-forlinux-102.tar.gz
   ```

   The filename may be different if you've downloaded a different version of the software.

2. Run the installation script. Change to the directory that was just created for the VMware installation program:

   ```
   cd vmware-distrib
   ```

   Then run the script by entering the command:

   ```
   ./install.pl
   ```

3. Install the VMware license. Save the VMware license file in the ~/.vmware directory with the name *license*.

VMware is then installed and ready to run. Change to a directory where you would like to run VMware from and enter the command:

```
vmware
```

This starts the program. The first time you run the program. it starts with the VMware configuration. Choose the Wizard option and answer the questions prompted on the screen.

At each screen, follow the instructions and click on the Next button to proceed to the next screen. You either have to select an option or fill in some information.

After you've answered all the of questions, click on the Finish button, and the wizard saves your new configuration.

The first screen asks what operating system will be installed in the virtual machine. This sets the default values, such as the amount of disk space needed.

The second screen asks about the location of the virtual machine. I recommend that you set up each virtual machine with its own directory. All associated files, like the configuration file and the disk file, are placed in this directory.

The default location is in vmware/*OS* in your home directory, where *OS* depends on the operating system you are installing in the virtual machine. For example, if your are configuring for Windows 98, the default directory is vmware/win98.

The next screen sets the size of the virtual disk that you wish to create. This has to be large enough to hold the guest operating system and all of the software that you intend to install in the virtual machine, with room for data and growth. You cannot increase this size later, so make sure it is big enough.

Next, select whether to let the virtual machine access the CD-ROM drive. If you decide to do this, you must specify the path to that device. This path is set to /dev/cdrom by default. In most cases, you will require access to the CD-ROM drive.

The next screen allows (or disallows) access to the floppy disk drive. Floppy access is usually necessary. The default setting is /dev/fd0.

Next, you set the networking capabilities of the virtual machine. You can configure the virtual machine to operate in a stand-alone mode, or you can network it.

The No Networking option configures the virtual machine to be a stand-alone machine.

The Bridged Networking option configures the virtual machine for connection to the network through a bridge. The bridge forwards packets to and from the virtual machine. The virtual machine looks like a real machine to other machines on the network. If this option is selected, the virtual machine needs to be assigned an IP address.

The Host-only Networking option configures the virtual machine so that it is visible only to the host machine on which it is running. This is useful for sharing files between the virtual machine and the host machine.

Click on the Done button to save the configuration. You can modify the configuration settings any time by using the configuration editor in the Settings menu.

Running Windows Applications on VMware

After you have installed and set up the virtual machine, you need to install a "guest" operating system on the virtual machine.

To do this, insert the CD-ROM for the guest operating system such as Windows 95, 98, or Windows NT. Start the virtual machine and install the guest system on the virtual machine. Follow the installation procedure you would use for installing that version of Windows on any other machine. After you have installed Windows, you can install your Windows applications on the virtual machine.

When you have installed the application, you should be able to click on the application's icon and start the program just as you would on a Windows system.

Part
IV

Ch
16

## CHAPTER 17

Configuring and Running Netscape Communicator

Netscape Communicator, More than a Web Browser

Netscape Communicator (shown in Figure 17.1) is the standard Web browser on OpenLinux, and is the most popular Web browser on Windows and Macintosh systems.

Netscape Communicator is more than just a Web browser, though. It is a whole package of programs for Internet communications.

FIGURE 17.1
Netscape Communicator version 4.61 is installed with OpenLinux 2.3.

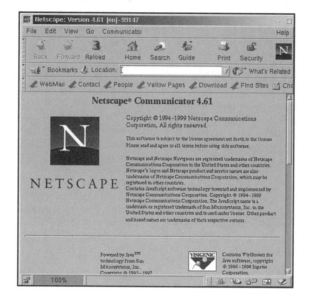

The components of Netscape Communicator 4.61 include the following:

- **Netscape Navigator**—The Web browser
- **Netscape Messenger**—A program for reading, composing, and sending email
- **Netscape Composer**—An HTML editor for creating and publishing Web pages

Netscape has the most full-featured Web browser available on Linux. It includes support for Java applets and JavaScript, as well as several plugins.

The Netscape Messenger is one of the best email client programs available on any platform, with several features aimed at business users. It has full IMAP4 support, which is used on many corporate mail servers. It supports multiple IMAP4 accounts, but it supports only one

POP3 mail account, even though many users have more than one POP3 mail account. If you have multiple POP3 accounts, you can use KMail—which supports multiple POP3 accounts but does not support IMAP4—instead of Messenger. If you want to use KMail, there is a section in Chapter 4, "Using the KDE Desktop Applications," that describes how to use it.

This version of Netscape Communicator is not the open source Web browser that Netscape is developing under the name of Mozilla.

Mozilla is an open-source project based on an early version of the source code for Netscape Communicator 5.0. Alpha versions of the Mozilla browser have been built for Linux and UNIX as well as Windows and Macintosh systems. The alpha version of Mozilla does not include some of the features found in Netscape, but it already has features not found in Netscape, such as support for XML.

The acquisition of Netscape by America Online slowed development until it was made clear that support for Mozilla would continue. The first beta version of that browser is expected to be released in late 1999.

Part
IV

Ch
17

Configuring Netscape Communicator

Netscape Communicator is a standard part of the OpenLinux installation. You'll find an icon on the K Panel for starting the program (see Figure 17.2). You can also start Communicator from the K Application Launcher, from the Internet section.

FIGURE 17.2
Start Netscape
Communicator by
clicking its icon in the
K Panel.

The first time you start it, the Netscape License Agreement displays. Review the agreement and click Accept.

A message is shown (the same message might appear twice), indicating that the disk cache directory for Netscape has been created. The directory is named .Netscape and is used to improve Netscape's performance. This is not an error and, although it is labeled as an error message, it does not require any action on your part. Click OK and proceed to open Netscape Communicator.

By default, Netscape Communicator opens the Navigator window, which is the Web browser—the most commonly used part of Communicator's set of programs.

Before using the Navigator or any of the other Communicator programs, configure the preferences. Under the Edit menu, select preferences. The panel that opens sets preferences for all the components of the Communicator. (See Figure 17.3.)

FIGURE 17.3
Panel for setting preferences in Netscape Communicator.

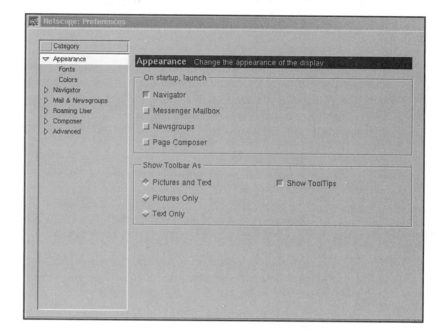

N O T E Some changes to the Communicator preferences do not take place immediately. You have to close the Navigator program and then restart it before the changes take place. ■

On the initial panel, you can change the default program that Communicator launches. The choices are

- Navigator
- Messenger Mailbox
- Newsgroups
- Page Composer

The Newsgroups option uses the Messenger program to read Usenet newsgroups.

The other appearance option in this panel changes the display of the toolbar. The choices are Pictures and Text (default setting), Pictures Only, and Text Only.

Tool Tips, the little help messages that appear when the mouse pointer is paused over an icon or menu choice, can be turned off here by clicking the toggle button next to Show ToolTips.

Under Appearance are options to change the default fonts and colors for Navigator. These settings are for standard HTML pages on the Web, but more and more Web sites use code to override these settings. Designers generally find the default fonts to be no more than functional, and have tried various workarounds to make Web pages more readable.

Communicator can use any font you have installed as part of the KDE desktop, either PostScript Type 1 fonts or TrueType fonts, if you have set up a TrueType font server on your system. Generally it's a good idea to be conservative in your choice of default fonts.

For some purposes, it is necessary to set the Use my default fonts, overriding document-specified fonts option. For some users, this is the only way to make Web pages readable. Well-designed Web sites are readable even with this setting on, although some sites are not accessible if you use this setting.

You can also change default colors for text, background, and links. Colors are also regularly changed by Web designers. Again, though, there are users who need to select the option to always use their own colors.

Click on the triangle next to the Navigator item in the Category panel to open the Navigator preferences panel. (See Figure 17.4.)

Part
IV

Ch
17

FIGURE 17.4
Setting Navigator preferences.

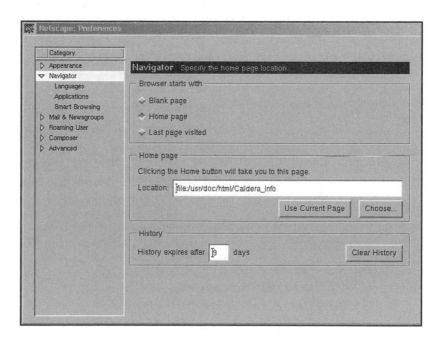

Settings on this panel start with the opening page for the browser. The choices are a blank page, a home page, or the last page visited. If you select home page, the home page is defined in the next section of the panel.

The easiest way to set the home page is to open the page you want to use as the home page, and then open this panel in Preferences and click Use Current Page. You can also type in the URL for the page in the box next to Location, or click the Choose button, which is used to choose a file on your system.

The History setting is for the cache of visited Web sites. The longer the number of days, the more site information is saved. This has advantages and disadvantages. Finding a page in cache speeds up the response of the Navigator, but the cached page can be old. If most of the Web sites you visit update their pages more frequently than once a week, make the cache reflect that so that you don't have to reload pages regularly to make sure that you have the most current page displayed.

You can use the Advanced Preferences setting to fine-tune how often the cached version of a Web page is compared to the source page to see whether the cache file needs to be updated. The choices are every time, once per session, or never. The default setting is once per session.

The Languages setting enables you to make a list of preferred languages. Web pages are sometimes available in more than one language, so adding additional languages here gives you more flexibility. For example, if you placed English, Spanish, and French in your list, and you visited a Web site that was displayed primarily in German but that also had a French version available, Navigator would automatically show you the French version.

Under Applications, you can add helper applications such as Adobe's Acrobat Reader. Acrobat Reader is often used to distribute corporate documents, user manuals, and presentations on the Web. Most government forms are available in PDF format (the format used by Acrobat Reader), including tax forms and passport applications.

You can download Acrobat Reader from Adobe Systems at www.adobe.com. After you have downloaded the program and installed it (following their instructions), you can add it to the Navigator applications. That way, any time you are browsing the Web with Navigator and you click on an Acrobat PDF file, the program automatically starts so that you can read the file.

To add Acrobat Reader after you have installed it, follow these steps:

1. In the Preferences Applications panel, click the New button.
2. Under Description, enter **Acrobat**.
3. For MIME Type, enter **application/pdf**.
4. In the Suffixes field, type **pdf**.
5. Set the Handled By section to Application.
6. In the box next to Application, enter the full path name to start the program:
   `/opt/Acrobat4/bin/acroread %s`
7. Click OK.

In step 6, make sure you use the correct path for where Acrobat is installed on your system. It might be different than what is used here.

For more information on plugins that can be added to Communicator, go to the Plugins Web site at `home.Netscape.com/plugins/`. A limited number of plugins are available for Linux. Two popular plugins that you might want to add are

■ Flash Player for Linux by Macromedia, found at `www.macromedia.com/shockwave/`

■ RealPlayer G2 beta for Linux by RealNetworks, found at `www.real.com/products/player/linux.html`

You'll need to download the programs and follow the instructions to install them. The default location for plugins is the /opt/Netscape/communicator/plugins directory. To see what you have installed, select the Help menu selection at the right end of the toolbar, and then click About Plugins. The installed plugins are listed.

Also, make sure that you add them in the Applications panel, as you did for Acrobat Reader.

Also in the Applications panel is a box in which you can enter the path for a directory that is used as the default directory for downloading. If this is left blank, the downloads go to your current directory. It is a good idea to create a directory named download in your home directory and point to that directory here. That way you can always find your downloads.

The Smart Browsing panel is used for configuring a new feature in version 4.61. This is a feature that Netscape describes as a tool to make Web searching easier. On the right end of the toolbar is a button called What's Related?. At any time when you are browsing the Web, you can click this button for a display of additional Web sites that are related. The limitation to this feature is that the list of related sites is often not available, and when it is, the list is usually limited. Moreover, when you use this button, it sends information about what you are browsing to Netscape without your knowledge. It's not a replacement for using the major search engines such as Yahoo or Excite.

Configuring Netscape Messenger

The Netscape Messenger is both an email program and newsreader for Usenet newsgroups and other news servers that use the same format. The next settings in the Netscape Preferences panel are for Mail & Newsgroups. (See Figure 17.5.)

The Mail & Newsgroups general settings start with how plain quoted text is displayed. This is text inside mail messages that quotes previous messages, and each line starts with a >. The style of this text is italic by default in order to set it apart. You can change the style to plain, bold, or bold italic. The size can be normal, bigger, or smaller.

Part
IV

Ch
17

FIGURE 17.5

Netscape Mail & News
settings.

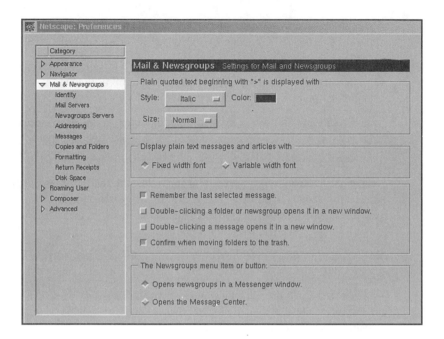

Plain text messages can be displayed using the fix font or the variable width font. You can define these fonts under the Appearance Preferences. The default setting is the fixed width font.

You can customize message handling with the other options. Remember the last selected message opens Messenger at the last message you read. This is the default setting. Double-clicking a folder, newsgroup, or message can be enabled so that it opens in a new window. Confirm when moving folders to the trash is enabled by default.

Usenet newsgroups are read in a Messenger window by default.

Click Identity to set your name, email address, and signature card. A *signature card* is a text file attached to the end of any email message. Usually it is used for adding your full name, an email address, possibly a phone number, and a postal address. Sometimes users also add phrases or quotes. This is usually a file in your home directory named .signature.

Click Mail Servers and enter the information about your mail server. The default setting is for POP3, using your own system as the mail server. If you are not using your own computer as your mail server, delete pop in the Incoming Mail Servers window. Then click Add to set up a new mail server. If you connect to IMAP servers, Messenger accepts multiple listings. If you connect to a POP3 server, you can set only one mail server.

After clicking the Add button (shown in Figure 17.6), enter the server name in the Server Name field. This is a name that you can get from your network administrator or from your Internet Service Provider. Some settings to look at are the toggle button to Remember Password, which means that you don't have to enter your password every time you connect to the mail server. If your computer is secure (meaning that an unauthorized person can't easily come and sit down at the computer and open your mailbox), you might want to click this option. The check for mail frequency is something that should be turned on only by those with a full-time network connection. If you have a dial-up connection, you probably don't want the computer dialing in to check for mail every 10 minutes.

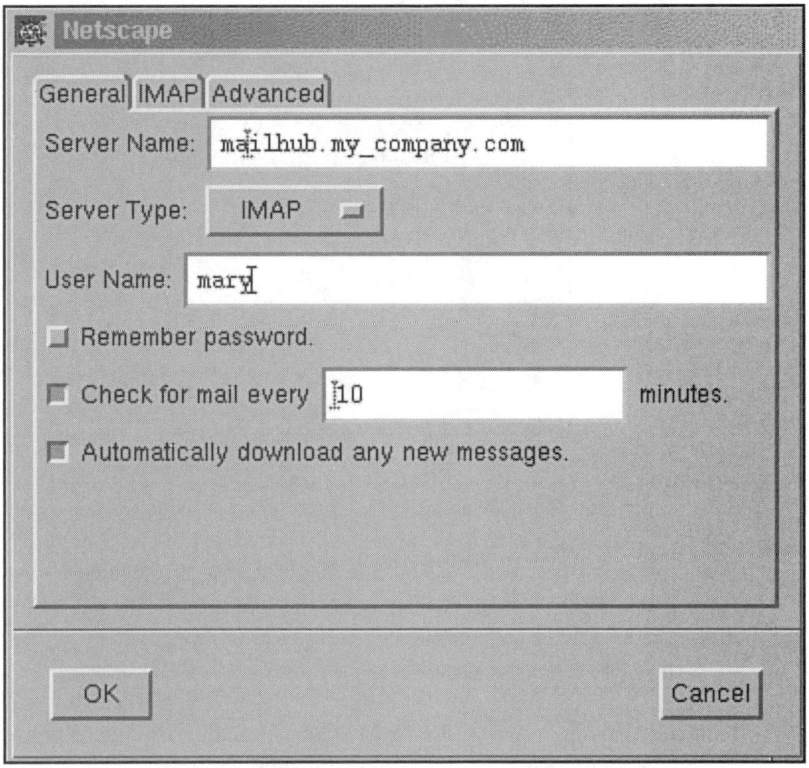

FIGURE 17.6
Add a mail server.

Consider the deleted message settings for IMAP carefully. If you are using IMAP, click on the IMAP tab. In IMAP, the default settings are to flag messages to be deleted, but not to delete them. Flagged messages can be filtered out of the display so that you don't see them, but they are not actually removed from the system. With the default settings, messages are never deleted until you manually do it by choosing from the File menu to Remove Trash or to Compact Folders. You can change this default behavior by selecting Empty Trash on Exit in the IMAP settings, or by selecting the setting to remove the message immediately. (See Figure 17.7.)

FIGURE 17.7
IMAP settings.

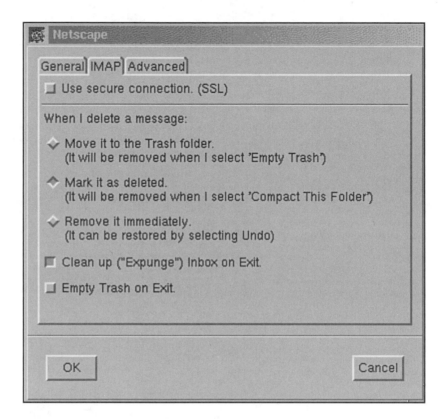

 TIP Poor performance from IMAP accounts can frequently be traced to users who have hundreds of messages that are flagged to be deleted but that are not actually deleted. When you connect, Messenger must load the headers for all the messages, including those flagged to be deleted. If you have not deleted these files, Messenger can take a very long time to load, even with a high-speed connection. Make sure to either manually delete your messages by emptying the trash, or change the default settings so that messages that you've marked for deletion are actually deleted.

You can also obtain the Outgoing Mail Server setting from your network administrator or ISP. This is often the same setting as your Incoming Mail Server.

To set up news reading, click on the Newsgroups Servers, which is for Usenet newsgroups. Tens of thousands of these newsgroups exist, and they cover everything from the most trivial topics to rocket science.

Most businesses do not offer access to Usenet newsgroups, but if you've set up OpenLinux on your home computer, your ISP probably provides access to Usenet. Add a news server in the same way that you added a mail server.

You'll use Messenger to read news and post messages.

Click Addressing to enter settings for addressing messages. Messenger includes an Address Book that you can use to store names, email addresses, and other contact information. When you start to enter an address in the To: field of a new message, Messenger watches for a match in your Address Book and completes the address so that you don't have to type the whole thing.

If your network has a Directory Server, you can change the default to the Directory Server. Directory Servers, also called LDAP servers or address lookup services, are used to look up the email address of someone who is not in your personal address books. If you aren't sure if your network has a Directory Server, ask your network systems administrator.

Click Messages for settings regarding how messages are forwarded. If you've received a message that you want to send to someone else, the default setting is for the forwarded message to be sent as an attachment. Some email systems, however, have problems with attachments. If you find that attachments are a problem, you can change the setting to Quoted or Inline. Quoted puts the message inside your message and puts a special character (the default character is >) in front of every line of the forwarded material to indicate the parts that are being "quoted." Inline puts the message inside your message, below a line that marks the beginning of the message that is being forwarded, without any additional characters or formatting.

Message Wrapping for incoming text is not enabled in the default setting. Enable wrapping if messages regularly go past the message window, making it necessary for you to use the horizontal scroll to read the message.

Outgoing plain text messages are set to wrap at 72 characters. Change this to 60 characters to make it more compatible with other computer systems, particularly older systems.

The 8-bit character settings have two options. The Internet is a 7-bit network. Basically, that's the plain ASCII characters—the ones that are part of the standard English alphabet—and the Arabic numerals. Accented characters or non-Roman alphabets require an 8-bit character set (some even require a 16-bit character set). It is possible to transfer 8-bit characters in messages, but some older mail servers don't know how to handle them. The default Netscape setting is to transfer the message as is. These messages can be properly read by Messenger and most other modern mail readers. If you are having trouble getting messages through, change to Using quoted printable MIME encoding. This requires the recipient to use a MIME-compliant mail reader such as Messenger.

MIME, the Multipurpose Internet Mail Extension, is a specification for enhancing the capabilities of email. MIME provides extensions that allow multiple objects within a single message, character sets other than 7-bit ASCII, multifont messages, and the capability to insert images, audio, video, and multimedia into messages.

Because the MIME standards are still emerging, many mail readers do not have MIME capabilities. A frequent complaint on Internet discussion lists is the use of MIME for messages because it can make messages unreadable by users who have mail readers that don't recognize MIME. Even among MIME-compliant mail readers, the implementations are different. Messages created in Outlook don't always translate properly in Messenger, for example.

It is best not to use MIME unless you know that all your messages are going to people who have mail readers that can handle it.

Click Copies and Folders for settings for copies, drafts, and templates. The default setting is to save a copy of all messages you send in a folder named Sent on your computer.

Formatting is for setting how outgoing messages are formatted. The default setting is to send messages in HTML format. Many users like sending their messages in HTML format because they can change the size and look of the fonts, add images, and use other formatting options. If you are sending to someone who has exactly the same capabilities, this works very nicely; however, most email systems do not support HTML formatting, and using this option to send to someone without this capability makes your message practically unreadable. It's generally a good idea to set this to Use the plain text editor to compose messages. It's not as much fun, but it's more likely to make your messages readable by everyone to whom you are writing.

The Return Receipts settings handle requests for return receipts. You can request return receipts that are sent when someone receives your message, although this does not guarantee that that person is the one who received the message. It only confirms that someone received a message, and it does not guarantee that the message was read. Also, most mail systems do not support this feature because it has no standard, and one might never be agreed upon.

Use the Disk Space settings to keep your email from taking over your hard disk. You can use these settings to prevent messages that are too big from being saved and to compact folders automatically. You want to regularly delete newsgroup messages, or they too can overflow your system.

Roaming User access enables you to connect to Communicator and access your user profile. You must be using IMAP for your email in order to use roaming access. Also, a roaming access server must be maintained on your network so that you can use this feature. Set the server information, whether it is LDAP or HTTP, and define the parts of your user profile that are to be transferred when making a "roaming" access. Ask your network administrator to find out whether roaming access is available on your system.

The Composer settings define defaults for the Netscape HTML editor. The author name setting is used for easily attaching author information to any Web pages created or modified with the Composer. Edited pages are automatically saved every 10 minutes. You can adjust this setting to your preference. There is a default template for any new Web pages created in Composer. You can change this to your own template. External editors define a text editor for editing the HTML source code and an image editor for modifying images placed on Web pages.

The default colors for normal text, link text, active links, and visited links as well as the background color or image can be changed from the defaults.

If the Web pages you edit are to be transferred to another Web server, the process is referred to as *publishing*. The publish preferences include two options that automatically convert links and images in your documents so that they work properly after the pages have been transferred to the Web server. This is a good feature and should be left at its default setting. However, don't rely on this always working properly. Always check your Web pages after you have transferred them to the Web server and make sure the images load properly and the links work correctly. You'll find that sometimes you need to make adjustments.

A default publishing location can also be set.

Many of the Advanced options generally don't need to be changed. The only ones you might want to adjust are the cache settings.

The Advanced general settings enable images to load automatically; enable Java and JavaScript support. Cookies are enabled by default.

Netscape saves Web pages you've accessed in a disk cache so that you can quickly access them again. The disk cache settings define the size of the disk cache and the memory cache as well as the location of the disk cache. Adjusting the size of the cache can sometimes make a dramatic improvement in Netscape's performance.

TIP If you regularly visit only a small number of Web sites, leave the cache settings at the default. If you visit a wide range of Web sites, make your cache smaller or even eliminate it. You might get better response times because Netscape isn't checking your cache before it accesses a new Web site.

If your computer is behind a network firewall that uses a proxy server, you need to make the proxy settings. Get the information that needs to be entered here from your network administrator.

Browsing, Downloading, and Printing

Netscape's Navigator works very much like Navigator does on other platforms (such as Windows). To go to a specific Web site, select Open Page from the File menu, or enter the Web address in the Location box below the toolbar. It's not necessary to put in the `http` or `ftp` indicators: Navigator figures that out for you.

The only difference is in downloading files. On the Linux version of Navigator, if you want to save—that is, download—a file from either an http site or an ftp site, you don't just click on the link. That displays the file rather than saving it. To save a file, hold down the Shift key when you click on the filename.

Netscape Navigator prints Web pages using any printers you have set up on OpenLinux. You don't need any special settings to print. You can start printing by selecting Print from the File menu or by clicking the Printer button on the toolbar.

Using Messenger

You can start the Messenger mail program from the Navigator. With the Navigator open, choose the Communicator menu and select Messenger. The Mail & News program opens. (See Figure 17.8.)

FIGURE 17.8

Netscape Messenger.

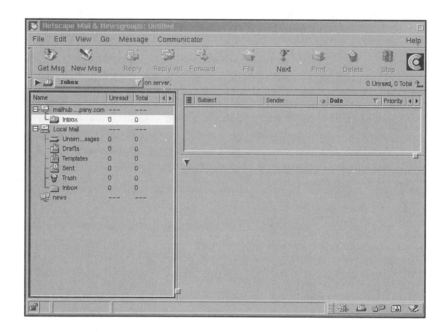

The open window has three panels. Down the left side is a tree showing your mail server, local mail, and news. Next to the tree panel is a panel that shows a list of mail messages. Below that is a panel that displays the contents of any selected message.

When Messenger first opens, it checks your mail server for messages. If you want to check for new messages manually, click the Get Msg button on the toolbar.

You can read messages, delete them, or file them into folders. Create as many folders as you want. To save messages on your own computer, create folders by right-clicking Local Mail and selecting New Folder. If you connect to an IMAP server, you can right-click on your Mail

Server and create folders on the server. These folders are then accessible from any connection you have—on the job, on the road, or at home.

Messages that are received with an attachment have a paperclip icon. Click on the icon; a window opens under the message, showing a file attachment icon and the attachment file's name. If the attachment is in a format that is recognized by Messenger, the icon shows you the format. Double-click the icon, and you are given a choice of opening the file or saving it. The best bet is to save it. Sometimes opening the attachment, even if it is a format that Messenger recognizes, does not work correctly.

In addition to saving messages and their attachments, you can reply to a message or forward it to one or more other email addresses. Click the Reply or Forward buttons. The difference between the two is that if you click the Reply button, the email address of the sender is automatically put in the To: field. (Be careful, though—this is not always detected correctly. Make sure that the message is going to the right person.) When Forwarding, you'll have to enter the To: address.

To send a new message, click the New Msg button. Enter the To: and Subject: information and write your message. You can attach files by clicking the Attach button, which also has a paperclip icon.

Click the Send button to send the message.

If you are writing messages and you are not connected to the Internet, you can choose Send Later from the File menu. This is a handy feature if you have a dial-up connection. That way you can prepare all your email messages before you dial into your service provider. Your messages are then saved in Local Mail under Unsent Messages. When you are connected to the Internet and ready to send your messages, open the Unsent Messages folder and double-click on each message you want to send. When the message opens, click the Send button.

Using the Address Book

You can access the Address Book from the Communicator menu: Select Address Book. The Address Book provides a handy way to keep your frequently used email addresses.

When you start a new message and type in an address in the To: field, Messenger searches the Address Book for matching addresses as you type. Often, only a letter or two is necessary before the address you want is matched.

You can add new addresses by clicking the New Card button.

An easy way to add addresses is to click the From: address field in any message you've received. A window pops up, showing the address that is being added. You can make any adjustments you want and click OK to save the address to your Address Book.

Using the Newsreader

Before you can access Usenet newsgroups, you have to set up your news server in the Communicator Preferences. After your news server has been set, select Newsgroups from the Communicator menu.

The first time you go to Newsgroups, you'll have to download a listing of all the available newsgroups. This can take a long time because more than 40,000 Usenet newsgroups exist. When you have a list of newsgroups, you need to subscribe to a group in order to access the messages in the newsgroup. Right-click on the news server and select Subscribe to Newsgroups.

Select a newsgroup from the displayed list. The easiest way to find a newsgroup is to select the Search tab and enter a word, such as **Linux**, that appears in the name of the newsgroups to which you want to subscribe. Click the Search button; a list appears.

After you have subscribed to the newsgroups, you can read the messages in each group to which you've subscribed, send your own messages to the group, or reply to messages.

Using Netscape's Composer

The Composer (shown in Figure 17.9) is a Web page editor that you can use to create new Web pages or modify existing pages. The settings for the Composer are found under Preferences.

FIGURE 17.9
The OpenLinux default home page, opened for editing in the Netscape Composer.

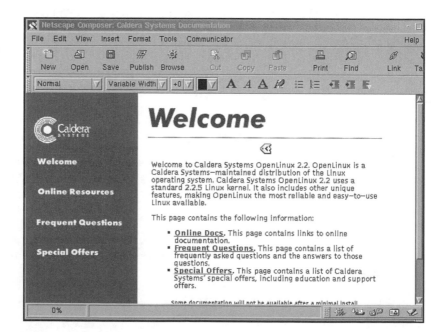

There are just a few settings. You can indicate an Author name, which is then included with every Web page edited in the Composer. You can turn the Autosave feature on and define a default template for new pages.

The External editors settings enable you to indicate a text editor to use. This is set in the field next to HTML source. Many Web page designers directly edit the HTML source code to get precisely the effect they want. Even the best HTML editors have limitations in their capabilities.

The Images field enables you to indicate an image editor to use for any images included on your Web pages.

The Composer is a very good, full-featured HTML editor. Most users do not need anything more than what is available in the Composer. After you've started a new Web page or opened up one that has already been created, you can add and edit text just as you might in a word processor.

To start a new Web page, choose New from the File menu. The primary choices are Blank Page, Page From Template, and Page From Wizard.

Experienced users often use the Blank Page option and build their own pages. If you are connected to the Internet, you can use one of Netscape's predefined templates using the Page From Wizard feature, which takes you through the steps for setting up a basic Web page. Access it by clicking File, New, Page From Wizard.

You can check spelling in the Web document by selecting a word or part of a document; or, you might not select anything, which checks the entire document. Then click on Check Spelling in the Tools menu.

To save a page, select Save from the File menu. To save links and images with a page, use the Publishing Preferences dialog box.

Part

IV

Ch

17

Configuring and Running GIMP

GIMP: More Than Just a Painting Program

GIMP, the *GNU Image Manipulation Program*, is an image editor, similar to the popular Adobe Photoshop or Corel's PhotoPaint, for creating new images or for editing existing images. It is not just a painting program, however. You can also use its advanced scripting features for batch processing of images to apply a standard set of changes quickly to a large number of images.

GIMP was originally created to produce graphics for the Web, and the program certainly shines in that area. Its capabilities have expanded beyond Web graphics. It is a complex program: GUM, the GIMP Users Manual, is almost 600 pages long.

GIMP was written by two college students, Peter Mattis and Spencer Kimball, at the University of California-Berkeley. In addition to GIMP, they also created GTK (GIMP ToolKit), which has become a popular GUI toolkit for programmers creating applications with graphical interfaces.

The strength of GIMP is its modular design. The program itself is fairly basic. The plug-in modules provide all the advanced features. This makes the program very flexible, easy to modify, and easy to update.

The program primarily displays graphics and provides basic image manipulation, and you can use a wide array of plug-ins and add-ons to manipulate the graphics for everything from filtering to special effects.

New plug-ins are constantly being created for GIMP. You can find all the available plug-ins, program updates, and more at the GIMP Web site at www.gimp.org.

GIMP supports many file formats, including the ones shown in Table 18.1.

Table 18.1 Graphic Formats Supported by GIMP

Format	Description
gif	Compuserve's Graphics Interchange Format, recognized by most Web browsers, limited to 256 colors. It supports animation and transparency and has licensing restrictions.
jpeg	Joint Photographic Experts Group, recognized by most Web browsers, supports 16 million colors, and used primarily for photographs.
png	PNG's Not GIF, a versatile format designed to replace GIF.
xpm	X PixMap, standard format for the X Window system.
tiff	Tagged Image File Format, original format used for scanned images.
tga	Truevision File Format, a widely used bitmap file format for 24- and 32-bit truecolor images.
mpeg	Moving Pictures Experts Group, a standard video format.

Format	Description
ps	PostScript, a page description language used to create graphic images.
pdf	Portable Document Format, a format that is readable using Adobe's Acrobat Reader.
pcx	Bitmapped image format, first used by MS-DOS paint programs.
bmp	Windows BitMaP format, used for MS Windows graphics.

It can also read Photoshop psd files, so there are no big problems in moving graphics between GIMP and Photoshop.

GIMP is included in the standard installation of OpenLinux 2.2. The first time you start GIMP, a window opens, prompting you to install the program. This installs the individual user files for each new user. The program itself is already installed.

When the installation begins, a window opens, containing a description of the program and details about what will be installed in your home directory. You can read through this information to learn more about GIMP. Click the Install button to finish the installation.

Adding GIMP Plug-ins

The standard GIMP installation includes more than 125 plug-ins. To see what is installed on your system, look in the /usr/X11R6/lib/gimp/1.0/plug-ins directory.

The list, however, doesn't tell you what all the different plug-ins can do. To get an idea of what each plug-in is used for, check out the Web page maintained by Gunnar Glaeser at www.infotech.tu-chemnitz.de/~nt/marb/glaeser/gimp-plugins/html/index.html. This Web page has samples of the effects of most of the GIMP plug-ins.

If you want to see what other plug-ins are available, look at the GIMP Plug-in Registry at registry.gimp.org. This Web site has a complete list of all available plug-ins, along with descriptions of each one and links for downloading the plug-in.

To add a plug-in, download the plug-in to your system. Then copy the plug-in to the /usr/X11R6/lib/gimp/1.0/plug-ins directory. The next time you start GIMP, the plug-in will automatically be included.

To start GIMP, choose Graphics and select GIMP from the K Application Launcher. After you have installed the individual user files, the GIMP toolbox is opened, along with a Tips window. The tips are shown every time you start GIMP. If you don't want the Tips window to be displayed every time, click on the toggle button next to Show Tip Next Time to stop it from displaying on startup.

When GIMP starts up, only the Toolbox is open. Click on File to start a new graphic or open one that has already been created. Figure 18.1 shows the GIMP toolbox and an opened graphic. The graphic is one of Larry Ewing's Linux Penguins, one of the most widely distributed GIMP-made graphics.

FIGURE 18.1
The GIMP toolbox and a graphic window opened with one of Larry Ewing's Linux penguins.

Setting GIMP Preferences

To configure GIMP's preferences, click on Preferences in the File menu for the configuration options. Figure 18.2 shows the Preferences window.

FIGURE 18.2
Setting GIMP preferences.

The first tab is for display settings. The Image size setting is in pixels and is the default size for a new graphic. The Image type setting allows for either color option—RGB or Black and White. CMYK, the color setting used for commercial printing, is not used for displaying on the monitor. Previews of images can be small, medium, or large.

RGB and CMYK Color Models

Color models are a way of expressing color as numbers that computers can work with. The models enable precise definitions of color and are used for the exchange of color information between computers and people.

The RGB (Red, Green, Blue) model is the color format used on computer monitors, color scanners, and televisions.

The CMYK (Cyan, Magenta, Yellow, and Black) model is the color format used in printing.

The two formats each produce a different part of the color spectrum. Without getting into all the details, the difference between the two is a problem for computer users.

If you only display colors on a computer monitor, you probably never run into this problem; but if you ever want to print the colors you see on your monitor, you'll quickly run into the problem.

A raw conversion of what you see on the monitor (RGB) to a printed page (CMYK) can produce surprising results. The colors on the printed page can be very different from the colors you see on the monitor.

PhotoShop has a CMYK display option that attempts to make the monitor display an image that more closely matches what is printed. However, this doesn't really work, and the image on the screen never really matches the printed image. GIMP doesn't bother to attempt to display images in CMYK format, knowing that the result will be unsatisfactory.

Color management systems are software tools designed to match color between input devices such as scanners, display devices such as monitors, and output devices such as printers. PhotoShop also includes a color management system, which is more advanced that its CMYK display option. You can use the PhotoShop color management system to create fairly accurate color calibration.

For greater precision, graphics professionals use spectrophotometers such as the Colortron, which is available for the Macintosh and Windows operating systems. This hand-held tool reads color information from a monitor, from a printed page, or from any other source. The color management system uses the results of the readings to calibrate the monitor display more precisely. Spectral tools and a color management system are not yet available for Linux systems.

The Interpolation setting defines the process that is used when the image display is zoomed in or out. When an image is enlarged or reduced, pixels are added or deleted in order to display the image. *Interpolation* is the process used to add or delete pixels.

Interpolation involves assigning color values to pixels based on the color values of existing pixels in the image. When you change an image, GIMP looks at the pixels, compares neighboring pixels, assesses their color, and calculates an intermediate color for the new pixels.

Cubic is the slowest—but most precise—method of interpolation. This method averages the values of surrounding pixels and adds that average value to the image to produce smooth tonal gradations.

Linear interpolation averages neighboring pixels but uses a less sophisticated algorithm than cubic. This makes it faster, but the result is that tonal gradations tend to look jagged.

The default interpolation is linear. Most regular GIMP users choose cubic interpolation because of its higher quality. Enable cubic interpolation by clicking on the toggle button.

The Transparency Type sets what is displayed in the transparent background areas of an image where no other image is shown. The default is for Mid-Tone Checks and Large Checks.

The Interface tab has the setting for the levels of undo. The default is 5. Each additional level of undo requires additional disk space, so increase this number only if you have lots of extra disk space.

I recommend that you leave the other settings in this tab unchanged, unless you know what you are doing. The Marching Ants Speed refers to the dots that are displayed around an area that has been selected with one of the selection tools.

The Environment tab has settings for controlling memory usage. The normal settings are optimized for a speedy response by GIMP. If you have a limited amount of memory available, click on the Conservative memory usage; but note that this significantly slows the response time in GIMP.

The Directories tab sets the default directories for GIMP's temp files, swap files, tools, and plug-ins. Generally, you never want to change this unless you have a special need and know what you are doing.

GIMP's Toolbox

The GIMP toolbox contains all the standard graphic tools (see Figure 18.3).

Most tools in the toolbox have options that you can configure by double-clicking on the tool. Double-click on the first tool in the upper left-hand corner, the Rectangular Select Tool (see Figure 18.4). This opens a window that shows the Feather option. You can use the Feather option to make the outside edges of a graphic transparent. The edges of the graphic are also blurred to give the image a "feathered" look.

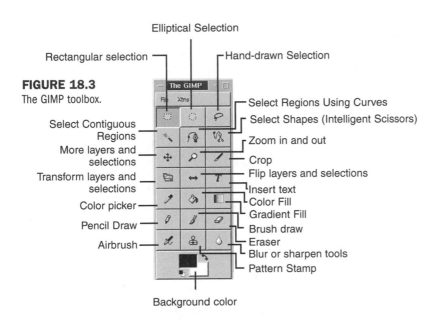

Elliptical Selection

Rectangular selection ─┐ ┌─Hand-drawn Selection

FIGURE 18.3
The GIMP toolbox.

── Select Regions Using Curves

Select Contiguous Regions ──── ┌─ Select Shapes (Intelligent Scissors)

More layers and selections ── ─ Zoom in and out

Transform layers and selections ── ─ Crop

── Flip layers and selections

Color picker ── ─ Insert text

── Color Fill

Pencil Draw ── ── Gradient Fill

── Brush draw

Airbrush ── ── Eraser

── Blur or sharpen tools

── Pattern Stamp

Background color

Part
IV

Ch
18

FIGURE 18.4
Double-click on the Rectangular Select tool to set the Feather option.

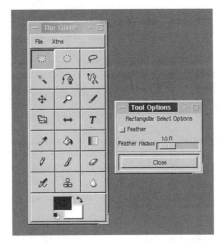

Double-clicking on the other tools shows their options.

Table 18.1 describes each of the toolbox options.

Table 18.1   GIMP Toolbox Tools

Tool	Description
Rectangular selection	Select rectangular or square shapes.
Elliptical selection	Select elliptical or circular shapes.
Hand-Drawn selection	Works like the PhotoShop Lasso; select by freehand drawing.
Select Contiguous Regions	Works like the PhotoShop Magic Wand; select adjacent pixels of similar color.
Select Regions Using Curves	Select using Bézier curves, like the Pentool Paths in PhotoShop.
Select Shapes	Automatically select a shape by defining its edge.
Move layers and selections	Move a selection or layer.
Zoom in and out	Change the view from smaller to larger.
Crop	Crop scanned images to use only a part of the image.
Transform layers and selections	Rotate, scale, shear, or distort a selection or layer.
Flip layers and selections	Mirrors an image horizontally or vertically.
Insert text	Add text to a graphic.
Color Picker	Choose a color from an existing color on the image.
Color Fill	Fill a selected area with current foreground color.
Gradient Fill	Fill a selection with a gradient blend.
Pencil Draw	Line drawing tool.
Brush Draw	Drawing tool with brush effects.
Eraser	Erase part of an image.
Airbrush	Draw with soft, semi-transparent strokes.
Pattern Stamp	Repeat a pattern or part of an image.
Blur or Sharpen tool	Blur or sharpen areas, similar to Smudge in PhotoShop.

GIMP's Right-click Menu

When a graphic is open, a right-click with the mouse pointer over the graphic displays the full menu of options from saving to applying filters and special effects of various kinds (see Figure 18.5).

FIGURE 18.5
The GIMP right-click menu.

You can use the right-click menu to save images and open additional images. You can also use this menu to access the many plug-ins and other advanced features available in GIMP.

To learn more about all the features available in GIMP, see the GIMP User's Manual. GIMP's scripting features, in particular, have many advanced uses. The full user manual for GIMP is on the Web at manual.gimp.org.

For a practical book that shows you graphic arts techniques using GIMP, as well as how to use some of GIMP's many complex features, check out *Sams Teach Yourself GIMP in 24 Hours* by Joshua and Ramona Pruitt (ISBN: 0-672-31509-2).

Part
IV

Ch

18

Overview of Programming in OpenLinux

Linux started life as a programmers' system. Computer programmers discovered that they could work at home using Linux and do pretty much the same thing they were doing on the job. The only difference was that their home PCs were relatively inexpensive and the systems on the job were the kind that accountants list as big budget items.

Given Linux's heritage, OpenLinux is predictably packed with hundreds of programming compilers, interpreters, debuggers, and other programming tools. OpenLinux comes with a C compiler and the Java Development Kit, and it includes several scripting languages such as perl, tcl, python, and gawk.

gcc, the Backbone of Linux

The one necessity for Linux programmers is the GNU C compiler, commonly called *gcc*. OpenLinux uses the Cygnus-modified version, called *egcs*. Linus Torvalds, the originator of Linux, said that the reason he set up Linux under the GNU license was because the system had been built on gcc. In fact, the high quality of gcc is the foundation for Linux's famous stability.

The gcc compiler compiled almost all the packages in OpenLinux. The compiler is used not only for packages written in the C and C++ programming languages but also for those written in Fortran, using the g77 compiler that is a front-end to gcc. There are other front-ends for gcc, as well for other programming languages.

You do not need to be a C programmer or even understand C programming in order to use Linux, but if you *are* a C programmer, you'll find that Linux provides an excellent environment for code development.

A gcc manual is installed with the program on your OpenLinux system. To access the manual, use the GNU info system. The GNU info pages have more detailed information than do the man pages for gcc. From a terminal window, enter the following command:

```
info gcc
```

Use the spacebar to move through the document one page at a time. Use the ? key to display a help screen for the info system. The q key exits the info system.

To start the GNU C compiler, use the gcc command. For example, to compile a program named hello.c, enter the following command:

```
gcc hello.c -o hello
```

The -o option defines the name of the executable file that is created. gcc has many other options. In addition to the options, gcc recognizes files by these extensions:

- .c—C source code files
- .o—Object code files

- **.s**—Assembly code files
- **.C**—C++ files
- **.cpp**—C++ files

gcc generates binary files that are in the ELF format. The *Executable and Linking Format (ELF)* is designed to make maximum use of shared libraries. *Libraries* are collections of files that perform specialized functions. Many functions are used by every program, and rather than writing that function into each and every program, a link to the library file that performs the function is made in the C program.

Libraries can be *static*, *shared*, or *dynamic*. Static libraries are included with the program when it is compiled. When a program is compiled with shared libraries, a link that points to the library is included with the program, but the library itself is not included. A dynamic library is like a shared library, but it is not loaded with the program when it starts up. A dynamic library is loaded only when instructions in the program call for it. A dynamic library can also be instructed to unload.

Shared and dynamic libraries make the C programming code much smaller and more efficient.

Programming in C, C++, and other languages is a complex task. Many excellent books are available on programming in Linux; two of them are listed at the end of this chapter.

Shell Programming

For new users of Linux who want to explore beyond the default setup, one area of programming to explore is the use of shell programming and scripting languages.

You can take care of many tasks using the capabilities that are built into the shell. Shell programs are not as fast as compiled programs and are prone to errors, but if they are kept simple and targeted to one task, they can be quite useful.

These simple shell programs can be a good way to start learning programming techniques. If you've ever written a macro in a word processing program, you already understand how to do shell programming.

Shell programming is usually used in the same way a macro is used. A program is written to automate repetitive tasks or to modify the way something functions on your system. For example, a shell program can be written to create a copy command that asks if it is okay to overwrite an existing file.

Shell programs are really just text files that contain a set of instructions. The file is made executable with the following command:

```
chmod +x shell_program
```

To execute it, type the shell program's filename.

Following is a very simple shell program to create a copy command that asks if it's okay before overwriting:

```
#!/bin/bash
cp -i $1 $2;
```

Save the text file and give it the name *copy*. Then make it executable with the following command:

```
chmod +x copy
```

Put the file in the /usr/local/bin directory, and you can use the new copy command. This shell program is much simpler than most shell scripts. It is meant only to show the procedure for creating a shell program.

If you want to learn about shell programming, many good books are available on the subject. One that can get you started is listed at the end of this chapter.

Scripting programs such as Tcl, perl, Python, and gawk are more powerful than shell programs. In fact, some of the programs included with OpenLinux are really scripts, not compiled programs. The difference with scripts is that they are interpreted rather than compiled, which can make them somewhat slower. However, no rigid line exists between programming languages and scripting languages. Often, scripting languages are the best way to go when you need to create a program.

Scripting languages frequently extend applications by using the scripting program to bind with other applications. This process is called *gluing*. One example of this is COAS, the system administration program included with OpenLinux. COAS is built on the Python scripting language, and it glues together several system administration applications into a common user interface that makes system administration easier and more efficient.

Learning a scripting language can be easier than learning a programming language. You don't have to know about as many topics, and you don't have to worry about memory pointers, include files, shared libraries, and the other things that are required when using a programming language like C.

perl, Tcl, and Python have many similarities, and for many tasks any one is as good as the other. The "script wars" are raging on the Internet over which of these is the "best." There is no clear best choice, although perl is by far the most popular.

awk

awk is a venerable interpreter language. The name comes from the initials of the inventors of the language: Alfred Aho, Peter Weinberger, and Brian Kernighan. The GNU awk is called *gawk*, and it ships with Linux. awk programs look like they are written in the C language, and they have some similarities in structure.

If you are a systems administrator, you might want to look at awk. It is commonly used to analyze logs and generate reports about the system, to analyze directory listings by file size or date, and so on. One of awk's advantages is that it is a fairly simple program that is easy to use. However, everything in awk is included in the perl programming language. If you plan to learn the more complex perl language with its greater range of features, you can probably skip learning awk.

awk works by looking for patterns and then processing the information. It searches through one or more files and checks for records that match a pattern. If awk finds a match, the action defined by the program you wrote is performed.

An awk program uses a structure that defines a pattern or patterns and then the associated action. Actions are enclosed in curly braces and separated by semicolons. The format is

```
pattern {action}
```

awk is designed to work with files that are in a database-like format, divided into fields or cells. When awk scans a line, it breaks it down into fields. Fields are separated by a space or tab character. Fields are numbered by awk beginning at one, and the dollar symbol ($) is used to represent a field.

For instance, the following line in a file

```
dog cat
```

has two fields:

```
$1        dog
$2        cat
```

Field zero ($0) is the entire line.

Following is a simple awk program:

```
{ print $1 }
```

This is only an action, with no pattern. If no pattern is specified, the action is performed on every line in the file.

This action indicates that every line is to be displayed on the terminal (print) and that the first field is to be displayed ($1).

You can use a text editor and create a file named test. In the file, put this simple program:

```
{ print $1 }
```

Then run the program using the following command:

```
awk -f test   /etc/fstab
```

The -f option indicates that awk is to read the program source from the file; in this case, the program file is called test. This simple program displays all the system devices defined in the /etc/fstab file.

Building on this simple example, you can create awk programs that read specified fields on logs, databases, or similar files and take actions with the results.

The Web home page for the awk programming language is at `cm.bell-labs.com/cm/cs/awkbook/index.html`. A good Web site to check for awk resources is the awk knowledge base at `goawk.webjump.com`.

perl

perl, the Practical Extraction and Report Language, was initially designed to take care of system administration tasks. It was initially designed by programmer Larry Wall to replace awk when he couldn't get awk to do everything he needed. After he released it for free on the Internet, perl use quickly spread because of its zippy performance and relative ease of use. perl is now the dominant CGI program for Web pages, and most Web forms are processed through perl scripts.

In fact, perl is often thought of as *the* CGI program. *CGI,* the *Common Gateway Interface,* is a standard for running applications on Web servers. A plain HTML document is a text file that can't do more than display text or graphics. CGI programs are used for forms, shopping carts, and most of the other dynamic features of a Web site. A CGI program can be written in any language that can be executed on the system, though special requirements make the program accessible to Web users.

Many of the dynamic effects seen on Web pages are really perl scripts. The `slashdot.org` Web site is an example of the power of perl. Every page on the site is built by a perl script rather than traditional HTML, giving the site's developers great flexibility in creating dynamic content for their pages. This means that the content of the Web site's pages are always changing and are never static.

One reason perl is the most popular scripting language is because it has a remarkably low incidence of faults, far lower than that found even in commercial products.

perl is a highly evolved language that can be quite complex. Its speedy performance is achieved through the use of efficient code that new users might find to be dense. This shouldn't put off beginners. There are more perl resources available than there are for any other scripting language. Not only are there an abundance of books, but you can find many perl resources on the Internet. You'll also find an abundance of top-notch perl programs, libraries, and routines that are available for free on the Internet to help you get started.

perl is one of the most portable programming environments available. In fact, there are more systems on which perl can be run than there are systems that support Java, a programming language designed for portability.

A simple perl program is one found in many perl tutorials that use it to demonstrate how perl can store user input and return it on command. It's the "What's your name" program.

Try it out yourself. In a text editor, create a new file and call it *name*. Put the following text in the file:

```
#!/usr/bin/perl
print "What is your name? ";
$name = <STDIN>;
chomp ($name);
print "Hello, $name!\n";
```

Make the program executable at a command line:

```
chmod +x name
```

Then run the program:

```
./name
```

The first line of the program "prints" the text string `"What is your name?"` to the monitor. The second line assigns the value `$name` to whatever you type on the keyboard, the standard input device. The `chomp` command removes the new line character at the end of the keyboard input that is added when you press the Enter key. The final line "prints" the text string to the monitor using the `$name` value, ending it with a new line character `\n` (like pressing the Enter key on the keyboard).

You can build graphical applications in perl using the Tk toolkit that was developed for the Tcl scripting language.

If you are unsure which scripting language to use, I'd recommend you try perl. It *is* the most popular scripting language, with the most resources and widest availability of experienced programmers.

The primary perl Web site is at `www.perl.com`. You can learn more there about perl and Perl/Tk for graphical applications.

Tcl

Tcl (pronounced *tickle*), the Tool Command Language, is an open source scripting language and a C library. The *Tk* (pronounced *tee-kay*), ToolKit, extension is used to interface with X Windows so that you can build graphical programs without a lot of coding. It is also popular for building graphical front-ends to databases.

Tcl and Tk were designed by John Ousterhout of the University of California, Berkeley. The Tcl source code is open, and Tcl/Tk can be used freely in any application, even commercial applications. Tcl is the second most popular scripting language after perl.

One reason for the popularity of Tcl is Tk, which provides a fairly high-level, easy-to-use interface to the window system. If you have done shell programming or any other kind of programming, you can learn enough to write Tcl programs in a few hours.

Tcl is used primarily to "glue" together other languages and programs.

The graphical shell for Tcl/Tk is *wish*, the windowing shell. With wish you can create graphical applications. For example, the X-CD-Roast application included with OpenLinux is written in Tcl/Tk. The Tcl/Tk part of the application provides a graphical interface to the cdrecord program, a nongraphical program for writing CDs.

You can create a simple script to see how a Tcl/Tk graphical interface is created. In a text editor, create a file named *hello*; in the file, enter the following text:

```
#!/usr/bin/wish
button .hello -text "Hello Linux World!" -command {puts "Hello"}
pack .hello -padx 10 -pady 10
```

Make sure that the path to wish is the same on your system. If it is not, adjust the line to indicate the proper path to wish. Save the file and make it executable on a command line:

```
chmod +x hello
```

Then run the program by entering the following command:

```
./hello
```

The result should look like Figure 19.1.

FIGURE 19.1
A simple Hello World graphical display using Tcl/Tk.

Tcl's strength—and its weakness—is its simplicity, making it the easiest to learn of the scripting languages. This simplicity, however, is also the reason its performance can be sluggish, especially on complex tasks.

The Tcl/Tk Web site is at www.scriptics.com. This site contains the latest versions of the software as well as links to tutorials for beginners and many resources for Tcl/Tk.

Python

Python is an object-oriented scripting language developed by Guido van Rossum. The name comes from one of van Rossum's favorite television shows, "Monty Python's Flying Circus," but Python is no joke. Like the other scripting languages, Python is freely available software.

Python is the most structured of the scripting languages. One of the strengths of Python is that its code is easy to read. Also, you can break down Python coding into pieces, work on them independently, and then easily assemble them into the final program.

Python's performance is comparable to that of perl. It is commonly used for CGI programming on the Web, small database reports, and system administration.

Python scales well and can be used for bigger jobs as well as smaller tasks. An example of a "bigger job" using Python is the Ultraseek Server software. Ultraseek Server is Infoseek's commercial search engine product that can run on Linux servers as well as other platforms. Most of the program is written in Python, with over 11,000 lines of Python code. The user interface is built on Python-scripted HTML templates with over 17,000 lines of Python code. You can try it out on the python.org search page at
www.python.org/search/search_web.html.

The following simple Python script shows how easy it is to read the code. In a text editor, create a new file named *add*. In the file, put the following text:

```
#!/usr/bin/python
base = 1
end = 0
print 'Enter a number to add'
print 'To subtract enter a negative number'
print 'Enter 0 to end the program'
while base != 0 :
    print 'Current total:',end
    base = input('Number? ')
    end = end + base
print 'Total = ',end
```

After you've saved the file, make it executable in a command line:

```
chmod +x add
```

Then execute the program:

```
./add
```

This program defines two variables, base and end. The print lines define strings of text to be displayed on the monitor. The rest of the script says that as long as the input doesn't equal zero, add the sum, display it, and wait for additional input. If the number 0 is input, the program ends and a total is displayed.

As you can see from the sample program, Python code does not have semicolons at the end of every line of code like you find in perl or C and Java programs. Also, curly braces don't enclose blocks of statements.

The plainness of Python is intentional. The idea is that you have less to remember about Python coding syntax, and therefore it is easier for infrequent or casual users to make use of it.

You can build graphical applications in Python using the Tk toolkit that was developed for the Tcl scripting language. For more information on this and on Python in general, look at the Python Web site at www.python.org.

Finding Out More

If you want to find out more about shell programming, there are many books on the subject. One is *Sams Teach Yourself Shell Programming in 24 Hours* by Sriranga Veeraraghavan (ISBN: 0-672-31481-9).

There are more good books about perl than any of the other scripting languages. The authoritative guide to perl programming is the book co-authored by Larry Wall, the creator of perl, and commonly called "The Camel Book" because of the camel illustration on its cover:

- *Programming Perl, 2nd Edition* by Larry Wall, Tom Christiansen, and Randal L. Schwartz (ISBN 1-56592-149-6).

If you're interested in learning Tcl, check out *Effective Tcl/Tk Programming* by Mark Harrison and Michael J. McLennan (ISBN: 0-201-63474-0).

Tcl and the Tk Toolkit (ISBN 0-201-6333-7) is considered to be the classic book on the subject even though it was published in 1994. It's written by John Ousterhout, who created Tcl.

There are a few books dedicated to Python. The best of them is *Internet Programming with Python* by Aaron Watters, Guido van Rossum, and James C. Ahlstrom (ISBN 1-558-51484-8).

If you are interested in Linux programming, you can start with some of the books that cover the topic. Two such books are *Linux Programming Unleashed* by Kurt Wall (ISBN: 0-672-31607-2) and *Sams Teach Yourself Linux Programming in 24 Hours* by Warren Gay (ISBN: 0-672-31582-3).

PART

V

Configuring OpenLinux Network Servers

## CHAPTER 20

Installing and Configuring a Windows Network with Samba

In this chapter

OpenLinux as a Windows Network Server

One of the great success stories of open source software is Samba. Running on a Linux server, Samba looks like a Microsoft Windows NT file and print server to Windows 95/98 computers on the network. It does everything NT does, and many systems administrators think it does it better.

Whereas millions of Linux Web servers proved Linux's viability and reliability, Samba on Linux has been a secret success story. Offices around the world have Linux servers running Samba, and only a handful of key operators know the secret.

In today's offices, networking is essential. It wasn't always that way, but today, even a small office needs to be networked in order to share files, printers, faxes, email, the Internet, and much more.

The costs for networking can add hundreds of dollars to each computer system. Licensing fees alone can run thousands, if not tens of thousands, of dollars. For many, Samba and OpenLinux are the bargain that makes networking possible. No licensing fees or hidden charges are involved.

Using Linux and Samba does not even represent a compromise. Samba won a top award in January 1999 from *Windows NT Systems* magazine, a leading publication for Windows NT professionals, for its excellence in NT networking. (See the Samba Web site for details: www.samba.org.)

Samba is already one of the world's top networking programs, and Linux is one of the most stable operating systems available. It's an unbeatable combination.

If you're already sold, just jump ahead to the section on installing and configuring Samba. But if you want to know more about why Samba and Linux is more than just a good choice, read on. Here's a story about how Linux and Samba scored a top grade in a test that is tougher than most everyday office use.

They Put Samba to Work

A few years ago, a leading educator in the public school system in New York City called me. Steve Stoll was involved in an effort to set up a new kind of high school that would emphasize the use of computers in public education. This was before the World Wide Web was even a blip on anyone's screen.

He knew that I was a network systems engineer, and he wanted my advice. I was glad to help. We met a few times. The school they were planning still did not have its own building. It had a small budget for computers, with some of the big manufacturers showing interest in what was being done. Some computers would be donated, but networking was a big problem because the costs were prohibitive. They weren't sure what they were going to do. They decided to build a small network using commercial networking software that was going to cost thousands of dollars, even with the educational discount. In the beginning, they were only able to have one fully computerized classroom.

The Internet wasn't what it is today, but the students knew about services such as America OnLine and Prodigy and wanted access to them. The best they hoped to have in the school was one computer with a modem that could connect to a service.

Today, the Beacon School is a model computerized public school. A computer sits on every desk in every classroom. The library's research facilities are fully computerized. The students have full Internet access, and each student can post his own Web page. The success of the Beacon School within the limitations imposed by the New York City Public School system has made the school something of a celebrity in the ranks of educators.

Because I'd known about the early plans, I was a little surprised when I started hearing about this really successful school through other sources. Then one day a computer specialist at the United Nations Development Program started telling me about the things being done at the Beacon School and how it was being used as a model for other schools. The key to the school's success, he told me, was Linux.

I called Steve Stoll, and he confirmed that yes, the school was using Linux. Why don't you come over and look at what we've done, he suggested. So I went over and met with Chris Lehmann, the school's technical coordinator, and Danny Markovic, the systems administrator.

The school occupies a two-story building on the West Side of Manhattan, past the Lincoln Center near the Hudson River. Like any New York City public school, the student body is a rainbow mixture of youths from many backgrounds. Like the students in most any high school I've ever seen, the students at the Beacon School want only the best when it comes to facilities being provided by the school. They don't tolerate flakiness, and they'd be glad to suggest that the computer ate their homework—if the system had a reputation for instability.

Therefore, this is a tough laboratory for any computer system. As the song says, if you can make it here you can make it anywhere.

I met with Chris and Danny. Chris is a teacher and Danny a student at the school. They showed me what they are doing. The whole system supports about 700 students. The classrooms contain either Windows-based PCs or Macintoshes on the desktops, all tied together by a Linux-based network. The primary server is a standard PC from a major mail-order firm. Nothing special. It runs Samba for networking the Windows PCs and Netatalk for the Macintoshes, and it uses NFS for mounting two other Linux servers. Every classroom is wired for Ethernet, and the school has a Class C subnet and T1 connection that it obtained through a special grant.

The school uses imap on the Linux server for email so that no matter which computer a student is sitting at, he can read his email. Students can also access their email as well as their files from home.

The school uses the Linux server for maintaining two email discussion lists, one for students and the other for parents. Parents regularly get email notifications about what is happening at the school and all the important notices so that they can better participate in their children's education.

Part
V

Ch
20

The technical details aside, the Linux server has been a big success. The school had a different server until about two years ago. The decision to replace it with Linux wasn't taken lightly. This is not a place to be experimental. That belongs in the computer lab. Linux's reputation for reliability was a big factor in the decision.

Lehmann says that they've never regretted it. Linux has been a winner. And the price of Linux has been right, so they can give every student full network services from file and print services to email and the World Wide Web without breaking the school's tight budget. They couldn't do that before Linux. You can see the school's Web site at www.beaconschool.org (see Figure 20.1).

FIGURE 20.1
The Beacon School uses Linux to give students full intranet and Internet services.

So here's how you can get a network as good as any that money can buy.

How Samba Works

Samba is a networking software program that uses the *Server Message Block* (*SMB*) protocol on top of TCP/IP. SMB is the networking protocol built into Windows, and TCP/IP is the networking protocol used by Linux and the Internet.

The beauty of Samba is that it provides the means for Windows computers to talk to the Linux server without changing anything on the Windows computers or requiring any special software add-on for the Windows computers. Windows users don't have to know anything about Linux to use it. In fact, they won't even know that they are connecting to a non-Windows computer unless you tell them.

On a Windows network, the computers find each other by broadcasting their name over the network. When you open the Network Neighborhood icon on your desktop, you can see a list of the computers that are up and running and broadcasting their names.

Samba broadcasts the name of the Linux server in a way that you can see on a Windows network. When you see it in the Network Neighborhood, you can connect to the Linux computer running Samba.

When connected to the Linux server running Samba, Windows users can have a full range of file services, from a place to save their own files to public folders shared by multiple users.

Beside file services, the other primary use of a Samba server is printing services. Using Samba on Linux, you can easily share printers on a Windows network.

Network Terminology

Samba is started by running two programs: nmbd, a NetBIOS name server, and smbd, an SMB server that handles the file services and printer sharing.

Windows and Linux networking use some terms that you need to know:

- **NetBIOS**—The Network Basic Input/Output System (NetBIOS) is a network interface for IBM PCs. IBM originated it, and Microsoft uses it for networking Windows-based computers. NetBIOS networks are organized into workgroups. Basically, you name a workgroup and give each computer in the group a name, and then your computers can talk to each other using the NetBIOS name service. See Figure 20.2.

FIGURE 20.2
A NetBIOS Network.

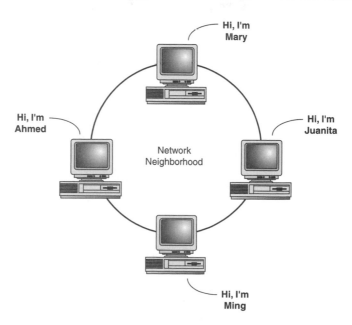

Part

V

Ch

20

■ **TCP/IP**—This is the network protocol used by Linux computers to talk to each other. It is also the network protocol for computers connecting on the Internet. Windows computers can also talk to Linux computers over TCP/IP connections, using programs like telnet or ftp. Samba runs NetBIOS on top of TCP/IP so that your Linux server looks like a Windows server for file and printer sharing. See Figure 20.3.

FIGURE 20.3
The Linux server and Windows workstation talk using TCP/IP.

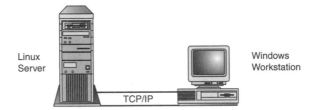

■ **SMB**—The Server Message Block is the protocol that implements Windows file and print sharing on a NetBIOS network. Microsoft's NT Server uses the SMB protocol for its networking services. See Figure 20.4.

FIGURE 20.4
Samba uses the SMB protocol over TCP/IP to create a NetBIOS network.

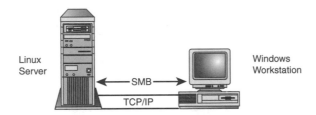

N O T E Microsoft recently changed the name of SMB to CIFS (Common Internet File System). CIFS is just the latest version of SMB and the two terms are often used interchangeably. ■

■ **File Shares**—A share is a resource that is on the SMB server and is available for the other computers in the workgroup to use. A file share is a directory on a disk and the files in it. See Figure 20.5.

■ **Printer Shares**—The A *printer share* is simply a printer that anyone on the network can use. A printer share in the smb.conf file might be named \\linux\hplaser. See Figure 20.5.

FIGURE 20.5
You can access
Samba file shares and
print shares through
the network.

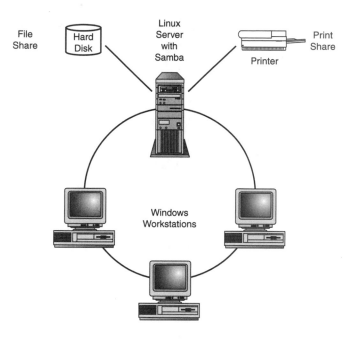

Installing Samba

OpenLinux 2.3 includes Samba version 2.0.5.

You can check the version of Samba on your system by checking the RPM database of installed software. The easiest way to do this is to open Kpackage, the KDE RPM package manager. On K Application Launcher, choose Utilities and select kpackage.

In Kpackage, select Find Package from the File menu or click on the spyglass icon. In Find Package, enter the word **samba**. You see something like Figure 20.6.

FIGURE 20.6
Kpackage displays the
Samba program infor-
mation.

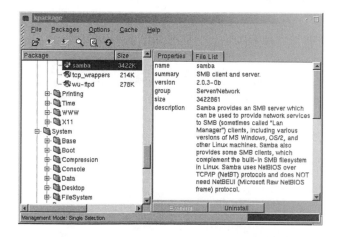

This shows you that Samba is installed, the version number, and other details about the Samba program. A look at the file list shows you all the files installed as a part of Samba and their locations on your system.

If Samba is not installed, you can install it from the OpenLinux CD included with this book. There are four files to install. For version 2.0.5, those files are

- samba-2.0.5-1.i386.rpm
- samba-doc-2.0.5-1.i386.rpm
- smbfs-2.0.5-1.i386.rpm
- swat-2.0.5-1.i386.rpm

Open the K File Manager and click once on each of the files. The K Package program will automatically start for each one. Click the Install button to install each updated package.

This installs samba and samba-doc, the program and documentation files. The file with the name that starts with *smbfs* installs the Samba mount and unmount programs, smbmount and smbumount. The filename that begins with swat installs the Samba Web configuration tool SWAT.

You'll next need to create the initial Samba configuration file. A sample file was installed as a part of Samba. You can copy the sample file and make it the starting basis for your new configuration.

Open a terminal window and, at the prompt, enter this command:

`cd /etc/samba.d`

Then copy the sample file:

`cp smb.conf.sample smb.conf`

Then you'll need to make a password file. To create a Samba password file from all the usernames already on your system, enter the following command:

`cat /etc/passwd ¦ mksmbpasswd > /etc/samba.d/smbpasswd`

Next you'll need to reset the Samba password for one of the Linux users added this way. Enter the following command:

`smbpasswd username`

For new users added later to your OpenLinux system, use the smbpasswd command with the -a flag to give them access using Samba. For example, to add user mary, you would enter the command:

`smbpasswd -a mary`

Then you are prompted for the new user's password. Don't forget to create an account for each new user in OpenLinux first.

After Samba has been installed, you'll need to start it. Enter the following command:

```
/etc/rc.d/init.d/samba start
```

Samba periodically updates itself by checking the configuration file for changes. The only change that won't be updated this way is a change in the NetBIOS name. If you want the change to be recognized immediately or if you have changed the NetBIOS name, you have to stop Samba and restart it. To stop Samba and restart it with one command, enter the following:

```
/etc/rc.d/init.d/samba restart
```

If you want Samba to start up automatically every time you start your OpenLinux system, use the COAS system administration tool for daemons. Make sure a check mark appears in front of the entry that says SMB server processes (samba). Then, the next time you start up your OpenLinux computer, Samba starts automatically.

Even though Samba is installed, it won't work correctly until you've configured it with SWAT.

Also Install SWAT, the Web-Based Configuration Tool

SWAT (the *Samba Web Administration Tools*) is the Web-based Samba configuration tool.

Before you use SWAT the first time, you'll need to check some configuration files. Use a text editor such as Kedit and open each file and check these configuration settings.

First, make sure that port 901 has been configured for SWAT. Open the file named services in the /etc directory. There is probably an entry that says

```
Swat      901/tcp
```

If it's there, you are OK. If it's not there, add it to the end of the file. This just says that SWAT can be accessed on port 901.

Next, check inetd. This is the port monitor. The ports that are to be monitored and the actions to be carried out when a request arrives at the designated port are configured in the inetd.conf file. You'll need to make sure that it is also correctly set up.

Open the inetd.conf file in the /etc directory with a text editor. Check for a line that starts with the word *swat*. If it's not there, put the following basic line into the file:

```
swat      stream      tcp      nowait      root      /usr/sbin/swat swat
```

If you are using TCP wrappers for network security, the line needs to look like this:

```
swat      stream      tcp      nowait      root      /usr/sbin/tcpd /usr/sbin/swat
```

Any time you make a change in the inetd.conf file, you need to restart it for the changes to go into effect. That's done with the following command:

```
killall -HUP inetd
```

Part

V

Ch

20

SWAT uses the *PAM* (*Plugable Authentication Module*) system, so you need to check the configuration of the PAM subsystem used by SWAT. Make sure you find a file named samba in the /etc/pam.d directory. It should have been created. This file needs the following two lines:

```
auth required /lib/security/pam_pwdb.so shadow nullok
account required /lib/security/pam_pwdb.so
```

If the file isn't there, create it and add the two lines.

Finally, an error in /etc/hosts.deny is added when the OpenLinux SWAT rpm is installed. Open the hosts.deny file in a text editor and change the SWAT line from

```
swat:ALL EXCEPT 127.0.0.2
```

to

```
swat:ALL EXCEPT 127.0.0.1
```

This line indicates that SWAT can run only from the Linux server. You are now ready to configure Samba using SWAT.

Configuring Samba

Follow three steps to get your Samba server running:

1. Set the global options.
2. Define the disk space and files to be shared.
3. Check the printers that are to be shared.

All this is set using SWAT.

You'll find all the Samba settings in a configuration file named smb.conf. You won't have to learn the exact syntax for this file—SWAT takes care of all that. SWAT is a Web-based configuration tool that helps you edit the file as well as monitor the Samba network.

Open a Web browser on your OpenLinux computer. You can use Netscape Navigator or the K File Manager. Use open location, and enter the following URL:

```
http://your-server's-name:901/
```

The 901 indicates the port defined in the services configuration file for accessing SWAT. When SWAT opens, you should see something that looks similar to Figure 20.7.

If you want to open SWAT in another computer on the network and you are using TCP wrappers, be sure to put the correct permissions in the hosts.allow and the hosts.deny file. You see a line for SWAT that includes the IP address of the computer you want to use to access SWAT.

FIGURE 20.7

The Samba configuration tool SWAT home page.

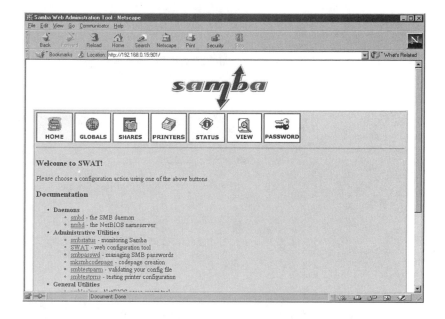

CAUTION

Be careful with allowing access to SWAT because it has complete control of your Samba network.

The SWAT home page has links to all the Samba documents. These are technical documents that are not generally easy to understand for a new user. They are designed to give systems administrators a reference guide.

The home page documentation shows a list of many of the utilities that are installed with Samba. It's not necessary to use or even know how to use everything installed with Samba in order to set up a Samba network. After you have your system up and running, however, you might want to spend some time looking over the documents. The more you know, the more you can get out of your network.

You'll find the three steps to getting the Samba server running on the SWAT pages labeled Globals, Shares, and Printers:

- **Globals**—Settings that are common for all resources
- **Shares**—Sets how disk space can be accessed by Windows users on the network
- **Printers**—Sets the printers available to Windows users on the network

Part

V

Ch

20

Configuring Samba's Global Settings

You'll find the basic options settings for Samba in the Global section of the configuration file. Click on the Globals button on the SWAT Web page to enter this section.

You see something similar to Figure 20.8.

FIGURE 20.8
Basic global settings for your Samba network.

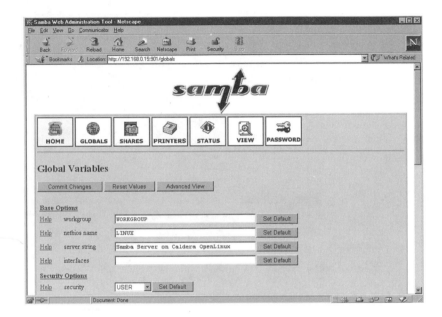

This page contains three buttons: Commit Changes, Reset Values, and Advanced View. Clicking on Commit Changes saves any changes you've made. If you do not see Commit Changes, you are not logged in as root, and you won't be able to make changes to the Samba configuration. Reset Values replaces any changes you've made with the original values in the current smb.conf file. Advanced View opens a page with all known options for Global settings.

The first time you configure Samba with SWAT, you have to restart the Samba nmbd and smbd servers before the changes go into effect. You can do that by entering the following command:

```
/etc/rc.d/init.d/samba restart
```

Or you can go to the Status page in SWAT and restart both servers.

Here are the basic settings in the Global settings and what they mean. After going over the basic settings, you'll find an explanation of some of the advanced settings. You don't need to do more than go over the basic settings, save your changes, and restart the servers in order to have your Samba network ready to run.

Base Options   This section defines the name of the workgroup and the name or names used by the server, and it lets you define multiple network cards for the Samba server, if they are installed on the system.

Workgroup   This is the Windows workgroup name for this server. In the Windows Network Neighborhood, browsing the Windows Network shows a list of workgroups. If the workgroup name is not entered correctly, the Windows workgroup cannot access the Samba server.

NetBIOS name   This is the name of the computer in the Windows workgroup. By default, Samba uses the first part of the DNS hostname of the computer. This is the normal setting, but you can make it anything you want.

Server string   This displays a comment next to the computer name when you browse the Network Neighborhood in Windows. It also appears in the print manager's comment box.

Interfaces   If your server has more than one network card, the interfaces option defines the multiple interfaces. The format is to enter IP address/netmask pairs. Say you have one network card with the IP address of 192.168.0.10 and a second card with the IP address of 192.168.0.56. You either enter **192.168.0.10/255.255.255.0** and **192.168.0.56/255.255.255.0**, or use the bit length for the netmask and enter **192.168.0.10/24** and **192.168.0.56/24**.

Security Options   This section sets the levels of security for accessing the Samba server, which can be simple security or complex levels of security depending on what you need.

Security   This is the security level that Samba uses. The default setting is USER. Before version 2.0 of Samba, the default was SHARE. Only use the SHARE setting if you want to allow users—such as a guest user—who can log in without a password. This is not generally a good idea. The USER level of security requires that the Windows computer user log in with a valid username and password. Encrypted passwords can also be used.

The SERVER level is like the USER setting, except that Samba uses a different Linux server or another Windows NT Server to validate the username and password.

Use the DOMAIN setting when a Windows NT Domain Controller validates security on your network. This mode requires that you use smbpasswd to add your Linux server to a Windows NT Domain. The Encrypt Passwords setting must be Yes. In this mode, Samba tries to validate the username and password by passing it to a Windows NT Domain Controller, in exactly the same way that a Windows NT Server does.

Encrypt Passwords   This setting controls whether encrypted passwords are used. Windows NT 4.0 with Service Pack 3 and above and Windows 98 both use encrypted passwords unless a registry entry is changed. For more information on using encrypted passwords in Samba, see the file ENCRYPTION.txt in the Samba documentation directory in /usr/docs. If you don't see a Samba directory, you haven't installed the documentation from the OpenLinux CD. You'll find it in the /Packages/RPMS directory.

Update encrypted If set to Yes, a user can log on with a plain text password, and his encrypted password in the smbpasswd file is updated automatically as he logs on. Use this option when you want to migrate from plain-text passwords to encrypted passwords without having to reenter everyone's passwords with smbpasswd. When all users have encrypted copies of their passwords in the smbpasswd file, turn this setting OFF. For this to work correctly, Encrypt Passwords must be set to NO while this one is set to Yes.

Guest account Guest accounts have always been a security problem on computer networks. If you don't need it, don't use it. If you *do* need it, the default setting here is Nobody. This is a guest account that's already created with limited rights and that can't print. Because the most common use of a guest account is sharing a network printer, the Nobody account doesn't serve the purpose. A common option is to use the ftp username that's already created for your system for anonymous ftp access. Its rights are already very limited, so it should be safe.

Hosts allow This option lists host computers that are permitted access to your server's file and print sharing. It improves security on the network. The default is for the field to be left blank, which means that any computer anywhere that can connect to the server has a right to access it. Usernames and passwords are still required, but restricting access through Hosts allow (or Hosts deny, the next setting) means that even if someone has gained access to a username and password that's not his, he can't get on the system unless he is sitting at a computer that's been given access rights.

You can specify the hosts by name or by IP number. Many conditional statements are accepted, such as INCLUDE and EXCEPT. See the smb.conf documentation for a full list. Here are some sample Host allow statements:

```
hosts allow = localhost, myhost.mynet.com
```

This allows access to all computers with hostnames that end in myhost.mynet.com.

```
hosts allow = localhost, 192.168. EXCEPT 192.168.0.66
```

This allows access to all computers with IP addresses that start with 192.168., except the computer with the IP address of 192.168.0.66.

```
hosts allow = localhost, tokijiro, kato
```

This restricts access to just the computers named tokijiro and kato.

Hosts deny This is the opposite of Hosts allow. It's a list of computers to be denied access to file and print services on your system.

Logging Options All actions on the server are logged. The standard logging is set to record only major events such as write failures or invalid logins. If you are having problems with your server, you can increase the logging level to get more information.

Log level This is a synonym for *debug level* and can be a number from 0 to 10. Level 0 logs error messages. If you are having problems with the system, you might want to use Level 3. The higher the log level, the bigger the file that's generated. Make this 0 unless you have a special need for more.

Max Log Size This sets the maximum size of the log files, in kilobytes. When the size is exceeded, Samba renames the log file, adding a .old extension, and starts a new log file. A size of 0 means no limit. The default is 5,000.

Tuning Options The socket options in this section can be adjusted to improve Samba's performance.

Socket Options These settings can be used to fine-tune Samba's network performance. Socket options control the networking layer of the operating system, which is the level at which the clients talk to the server. Any combination of the settings is permitted. Following are the socket options permitted in Samba:

- `SO_KEEPALIVE`—Enables keep connections alive, which detects lost connections and closes them.
- `SO_REUSEADDR`—Enables local address reuse.
- `SO_BROADCAST`—Enables permission to transmit broadcast messages.
- `TCP_NODELAY`—Forces TCP packets to be transmitted immediately. Can speed transmission of packets, but causes a greater load on the system because it disables TCP's built-in efficiency techniques. Don't use this if your Samba connections are on a wide area network or over the Internet.
- `IPTOS_LOWDELAY`—Enables IP packet delivery on a path with low delay.
- `IPTOS_THROUGHPUT`—Enables IP packet delivery on a path with high throughput.
- `SO_SNDBUF`—Sets the size of the output buffer.
- `SO_RCVBUF`—Sets the size of the input buffer.
- `SO_SNDLOWAT`—Sets minimum count for output.
- `SO_RCVLOWAT`—Sets minimum count for input.

The last four require a value, for example `SO_SNDBUF=8192`. There can't be spaces before or after the = sign.

The default setting is `TCP_NODELAY`. Some options you can try adding are `SO_KEEPALIVE`, `SO_SNDBUF=8192`, and `SO_RCVBUF=8192`. Depending on your network, these options might improve performance. The one socket option that makes the biggest performance improvement is `TCP_NODELAY` because Microsoft TCP/IP is slow in sending TCP acknowledgements. TCP sends a segment and then waits for acknowledgment (ACK). If ACK not received in a little while, the segment is re-sent. This setting cuts out the delay and essentially tells the Linux server to not wait for the acknowledgement before sending the next segment.

Part

V

Ch

20

Printing Options   This section sets the standard options for accessing printers set up on your Linux server.

Printing   This sets how printer status information is interpreted on your system, and also affects the default values for the `print` command and the other print related commands: `lpq`, `lppause`, `lpresume`, and `lprm`. For OpenLinux this needs to be set to `lprng`.

Browse Options   The section sets how the Samba server is seen in the network workgroup.

OS level   This sets the level Samba uses to advertise itself in the browse elections that are a part of Windows networking. The default is zero, which means that Samba loses elections to Windows machines. The browser election protocol selects a master browser on a Windows network. The browse list for the workgroup or NT domain is maintained on the master browser. The protocol is biased to favor computers running Windows NT Server and Workstation. It is possible for a Samba server to become the master browser. If you want to have Samba win browse elections, the OS level has to be equal to that of any other potential browsers in the workgroup or NT domain. If you want to make sure Samba wins all browser elections, set the value to a level greater than any other browser. The value for a Windows NT 4.0 Server is 33, Windows NT 3.51 Server is 32, Windows NT 4.0 Workstation is 17, Windows NT 3.51 Workstation is 16, Windows 95/98, and Windows for Workgroups is 1. Therefore, to win all browser elections set the OS level to 34. See BROWSING.txt in the Samba textdocs directory for more information.

Preferred master   If this is set to Yes, Samba advertises itself as the preferred master during browse elections. Set this to Yes only if Samba is being used as a domain master on the network. Usually this needs to be set to No.

CAUTION

Use this option with caution. If more than one computer on the network is set as master browser, broadcast wars will take place as each tries to declare its dominance, and your network will be tied up with the resulting broadcast traffic.

Local master   This option sets Samba to become a local master browser on a network subnet. The default setting is Yes. Unlike the preferred master setting, setting this to Yes doesn't mean that Samba becomes the local master browser on a subnet, just that it participates in elections for local master browser.

Domain master   This option sets Samba to become the domain master browser for its workgroup. Local master browsers that are in the same workgroup but on different subnets give Samba their local browse lists and then ask Samba for a complete copy of the browse list for the whole wide area network. If you set Samba to be the Domain master, you have to specify a WINS server for Samba to use.

WINS Options   WINS (*Windows Internet Name Service*) resolves hostnames into IP addresses on NetBIOS networks. WINS serves the same function as DNS (Domain Name Service) on a TCP/IP network. Samba can be set to use a WINS server, if you have one on your network, or it can be set up to act as a WINS server. It can also be set to not use WINS, which is the usual setting on small networks. In that case, the LMHOSTS file is used. The LMHOSTS (LanManager Hosts) file is similar to the Linux /etc/hosts file. For information on creating an LMHOSTS file, see the LMHOSTS.SAM sample file found in the Windows directory of all Windows 95/98 computers.

DNS proxy   This option is used when Samba acts as a WINS server. If a NetBIOS name has not been registered, Samba looks up the name on the DNS server. If you set this to Yes, Samba browsing and WINS services are blocked while a DNS lookup takes place, which can cause noticeable delays on the network. This is normally set to No.

WINS server   This sets the IP address or DNS name of the WINS server that Samba is to use for cross-subnet browsing. If WINS support (the next setting) is set to Yes, leave this blank or you'll receive an error.

WINS support   This setting controls whether Samba acts as a WINS server. Do not set this to Yes unless you have a multiple subnetted network and you want Samba to be your WINS server.

N O T E   Never have more than one WINS server on your network. ▪

Advanced Settings   If you click the Advanced View button, many more Samba options are listed. These options are used mostly for special purposes. You won't need to change any of them to set up a successful Samba network. Most users need to continue with setting up shares and printers. I explain many of the advanced settings later in this chapter.

Configuring Samba's Share Settings

Click the Shares button on the SWAT Web page to take the next step in getting the Samba server running. You see something similar to Figure 20.9.

Shares are the file services that are set up on the Samba server. This is where you define what users can access, from their own files in their own home directory to shared files and directories and shared CD-ROM drives.

Configuring Users' Home Directories   By default, two shares are already created: HOMES and PUBLIC. In the SWAT window, select HOMES and click Choose Share. This opens up the HOMES share and shows all its settings.

The Comment field normally says Home Directories, but it can be anything you want. Leave both the path field and the valid user fields blank.

FIGURE 20.9

Share settings for your Samba network.

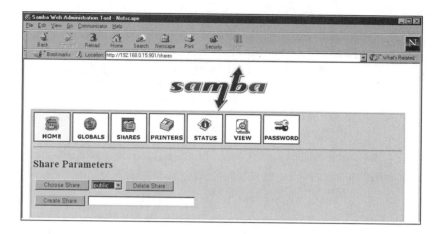

Set read-only to No, unless you don't want users to save their files. The create mask should be 0750.

Guest OK needs to be set to No. Only user should say No as well.

You can leave Hosts allow and Hosts deny blank, unless you know that you need to add names or IP addresses to be allowed or denied access. Normally, access is allowed to all: The field is left blank.

Browseable needs to be set to No, and Help should say Yes.

Save the settings by clicking on the Commit Changes button. Don't forget to stop the Samba daemons and restart them so that the changes go into effect.

Configuring a Public Directory   A public directory is used for saved files that all the users on the network can share. By default, a public directory share is already created for Samba. Make sure that you also find a directory named public in the /home directory on your Linux computer.

In the SWAT shares window, select PUBLIC and click Choose Share. This opens up the PUBLIC share and shows all its settings. If you want to see all the possible options, click the Advanced View button.

The Comment field can say anything you want. The default share that was created during installation says Public Stuff. The path field says /home/public.

The write list is the name of a file that has a list of users that are given read-write access to the public directory. If the connecting user is in this list, he has read and write access to the directory.

Set read-only to No, unless you want to give users more than just read-only access to files in the public directory.

Guest OK needs to be set to No, unless you've decided to allow guest logins.

You can leave Hosts allow and Hosts deny blank, unless you know that you need to add names or IP addresses to be allowed or denied access. Normally, access is allowed to all, which means the field is left blank.

Set Browseable and Help to Yes.

Save the settings by clicking the Commit Changes button. Don't forget to stop the Samba daemons and restart them so that the changes go into effect.

Sharing a Directory for Private Access   The HOME and PUBLIC shares might be all you need to get your Samba server running, but you can add many other shares.

One is a shared private directory. To create a shared private directory, first create the directory on the Linux system. For this example, the directory is named /home/private, but the directory can have any name and be placed anywhere on your system.

In the SWAT shares window in the Create Share field, enter a name for the new share. Call it private and click the Create Share button. This opens the settings for your PRIVATE share. You'll also need to be in the Advanced View, so click that button.

The comment field can say anything you want. The path should say /home/private (or whatever the pathname is for the directory you created).

In the field that sets Valid Users, enter the usernames of the users that are to have access to this private directory. It is a list, like this:

```
username1 username2 username3
```

The read-only setting should be No. The create mask needs to be 0765; Guest OK needs to say No.

Save the settings by clicking the Commit Changes button. Don't forget to stop the Samba daemons and restart them so that the changes go into effect.

Sharing a CD-ROM   You can make a CD-ROM drive on your Linux server shareable by everyone on the network. This is useful if you have a CD that contains data that everyone needs to access.

To create a shared CD-ROM drive, enter the name **cdrom** in the Create Share field of the SWAT shares window. Click the Create Share button. This opens the settings for your shared CD-ROM drive.

The comment field can say anything you want, such as CD-ROM. The path should say /mnt/cdrom.

Guest OK should say No.

The read-only setting and Browseable need to be set to Yes.

Save the settings by clicking the Commit Changes button. Don't forget to stop the Samba daemons and restart them so that the changes go into effect.

Configuring Samba's Printer Settings

After setting Shares, you can check the Printers setting. Click the Printers button on the SWAT Web page to enter this section.

You see something similar to Figure 20.10.

FIGURE 20.10

Printer settings for your Samba network.

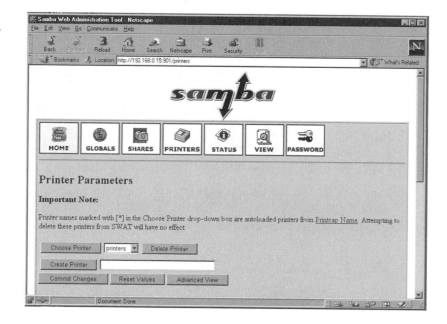

Normally, nothing needs to be done with the printers settings. From the drop-down menu, select Printers and click Choose Printer. The default settings are shown in Figure 20.11.

The default setup makes all printers that are set up on your Linux server available. The only time you need to make changes is if you don't want all printers to be accessible.

The default settings should say All Printers in the Comment field. The path should say /var/spool/samba.

Guest OK and Browseable should say No; Print OK and Available should say Yes; and Printing should say lprng.

Your Samba server is now all set up to run.

Make sure all the changes you've made in SWAT are saved, and make sure that you stopped smbd and nmbd and restarted them.

Next you'll have to set up the Windows computers to connect to the Samba server. I explain that procedure later in this chapter, after I explain some of Samba's Advanced options.

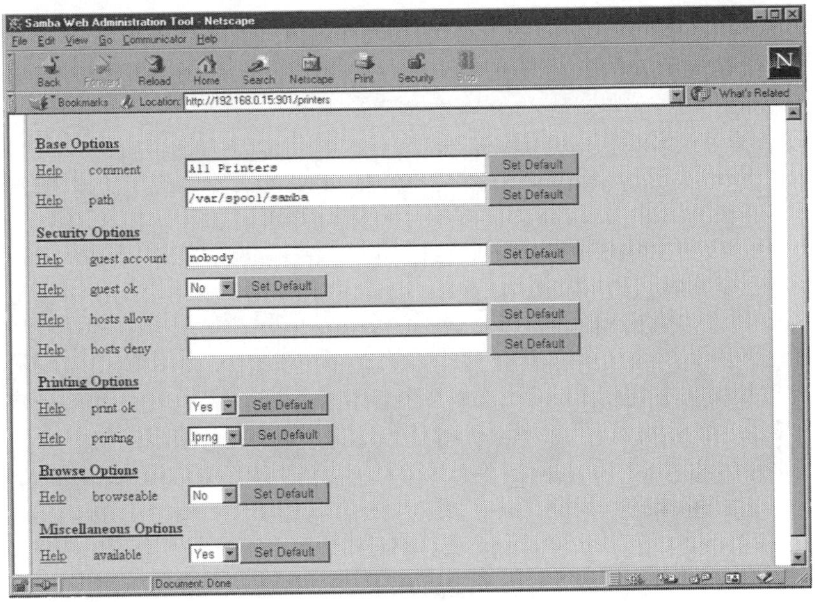

FIGURE 20.11
The default printer settings page in SWAT.

Setting Advanced Options

Beyond the basic settings, you can set many more options in Samba. None of them is necessary to get a system working, but some options might improve the performance of your system or be useful, especially if older computers are connected to your Samba server. On the Globals page of SWAT, select the Advanced View button. Here's a description, listed in order, of many of the options shown in the advanced view.

Base Options The advanced settings for base options adds the capability to list the Samba server with additional alias names in the workgroup's network neighborhood.

NetBIOS aliases This is a list of additional names by which the Samba server is known on the Windows browse list.

Security Options Security can be fine-tuned by putting additional limitations on access and passwords.

Use rhosts If this is set to Yes, it specifies that the .rhosts file in the user's home directory is read for the names of hosts and users who are allowed access without a password. Use of rhosts can be a major security hole, and should never be used, except by someone who is experienced and knows what he is doing.

Part
V
Ch
20

Min passwd length   This option sets the minimum password length.

Map to guest   This option sets what Samba is to do with user login requests that don't match a valid user. The three settings are

> **Never**—All login requests with an invalid password are rejected. This is the default.
>
> **Bad User**—Logins with an invalid password are rejected, but if someone is logging in with a username that is not valid, it is accepted and mapped to the guest account. All invalid user names are treated as a guest login.
>
> **Bad Password**—If someone logs in but enters the wrong password, he is automatically mapped to the guest account.

CAUTION

This option can cause problems because it means that any valid user who mistyped his password is silently logged in as a guest and will have no idea why he can't access his files. No error message is given to indicate that the password entered was wrong.

Null passwords   This option sets whether to allow access to accounts that have null passwords. Many processes run under usernames, like daemons that have null passwords. Enabling this can open a big security hole. Don't enable this unless you know what you are doing.

Password server   This option sets the name of a password server. Never point a Samba server at itself for password serving because this causes a loop and might lock up your Samba server. Use this if you don't want Samba to check the user database on the server on which it's running, but rather the user database on another Linux server.

SMB passwd file   This option sets the path to the encrypted smbpasswd file. In OpenLinux the default setting is /etc/samba.d/smbpasswd.

Hosts equiv   This option sets the name of a file that has a list of hosts that are allowed to log on without a password. The default setting is to leave the field blank, which disables this feature. I strongly recommend that you leave this at its default setting.

CAUTION

Using hosts equiv creates a major security hole and should only be used on networks with closed access that aren't in any way connected to any other networks.

Root directory   You can change the root directory from the default of /. This is sometimes done for added security. Changing the root directory requires that you mirror essential system files that are otherwise made inaccessible—such as the user database—or no one can log on.

Passwd program   This option sets the name of the program to use for setting passwords. The default is /usr/bin/passwd.

Username map   This option enables you to set a map of usernames. If users on your network have usernames on their Windows computers that are different from their usernames on the Linux server, a map file can be used so that only one name is necessary. Then the users can log in from Windows using their Windows name, and the map file is read to find their Linux user names and allow the login to continue. It's also useful for mapping multiple users to a single username so that they can share files more easily.

Password level   Linux passwords are case sensitive, but some Windows systems insist on converting passwords to all uppercase before sending them. The default setting of 0 tests whether passwords are all uppercase or all lowercase. If you use passwords that are mixed case, you'll need a higher level, which tests various case combinations. The higher the number, the more variations that are tested. Higher numbers, however, reduce network security and slow down password verification at login. Try to stick to all lowercase or all uppercase passwords on your Linux system.

Username level   Like the Password level setting, this sets the level of testing of the case used in user login names. The default setting of 0 tests passwords as either all uppercase or all lowercase. Settings and cautions are the same as for Password level settings.

Unix password sync   This option sets what Samba is to do when the encrypted Samba password has been changed with the smbpasswd command but the new password doesn't match the Linux password. The default is No—do nothing. If set to Yes, the command listed in the passwd program setting changes the Linux password so that it matches the Samba password.

Alternative permissions   Samba version 2.0 and higher do not use this option. Any settings here are ignored. In previous versions of Samba, it was used to set the DOS "read only" attribute for a file.

Revalidate   This setting is ignored unless the security level is set to SHARE. This sets whether Samba allows a user who has already been validated for one connection to a share (a file or printer resource) to connect to another share without being validated. The default setting is No. If set to Yes, the user is required to enter a username and password for each share being accessed.

Username   Multiple users can be listed here. If the list exists, Samba checks login passwords against the names in the list. Any login password that matches a name in the list is considered a valid login. This is a workaround for older Windows for Workgroups computers that don't correctly log in. If you aren't connecting WfW computers, don't use this setting.

Invalid users   This option lists users who are absolutely forbidden access.

Valid users   This option lists users who are allowed access to the network services. If this is left blank—as it usually is—any user entering a valid login name and password is allowed access. For additional security, put %s here. This is a variable that adds an additional restriction so that only a user whose username matches the name of the share, usually the home directory, can have access.

Admin users   This is a list of users who are given super-user access.

> **CAUTION**
>
> This is not normally a good idea for any reason. Anyone on this list can do anything on the system, just as if he were logged in as root. If you put any username in this list, you are asking for trouble.

Read list   This is a list of users who have read-only access, and it overrides any other settings. They cannot save files or write anything to the network server disks.

Write list   This is a list of users who have both read and write access. This overrides any other settings, even read-only settings.

Create mask   This sets the maximum permissions that a file created in Samba can have. The default setting is 0744.

Force create mode   This sets the minimum permissions that a file created in Samba can have. The default setting is 0000.

Directory mask   This sets the maximum permissions that a directory created in Samba can have. The default setting is 0744.

Force directory mode   This sets the minimum permissions that a directory created in Samba can have. The default setting is 0000.

Logging Options   The syslog option sets what Samba debug message is sent to the system logs. The timestamp on log entries can be turned off, to make the log file easier to read.

Syslog   This option sets the threshold for sending messages to syslog. Only messages with a debug level less than this value are sent to syslog. Setting options are 0–5. The default is 1, which sends error and warning messages.

Timestamp logs   Samba puts a time stamp on all log entries. This can be distracting if you are attempting to debug a problem. This setting allows time stamping to be turned off.

Protocol Options   This section sets the SMB protocol options. The default setup follows the setup design of a Windows NT Server. These settings are not usually changed because the purpose is to make the Linux server look like an NT server on the network.

Protocol   The SMB protocol has many generations of development. NT1 is the current version of the protocol. It's used by Windows NT, and is also known as CIFS. Normally, this option should not be changed from NT1.

Read raw   Raw reads allow reads of 65,535 bytes in one packet. This typically provides a major performance benefit.

Write raw   Raw writes allow writes of 65,535 bytes in one packet. This typically provides a major performance benefit. This option is normally set to Yes and almost never needs to be changed.

NT SMB support   This is a developer debugging option and should be left alone.

NT pipe support   This is a developer debugging option and should be left alone.

NT acl support   This is an experimental option and is off by default.

Announce version   This is the version number used by nmbd when announcing itself as a server. The default is 4.2. Do not change this.

Announce as   The valid options are NT, NT Server, NT Workstation, Win95, and WfW. This is used by nmbd when announcing itself to a network neighborhood browse list. Do not change this.

Max xmit   This option sets the maximum packet size that Samba negotiates. The default is 65,535, which is the maximum. In some cases you might find you get better performance with a smaller value. A value of less than 2,048 is likely to cause problems.

Name resolve order   This sets the order of the name services that Samba uses to resolve host names to IP addresses. The options are

> **lmhosts**—Looks up an IP address in the Samba lmhosts file.
>
> **host**—Does a standard hostname to IP address resolution, using the system /etc/hosts, NIS, or DNS lookups.
>
> **wins**—Queries a name with the IP address listed in the WINS server parameter. If no WINS server has been specified, this method is ignored.
>
> **bcast**—Does a broadcast on each of the known local interfaces listed in the interfaces parameter. This is the least reliable of the name resolution methods because it depends on the target host being on a locally connected subnet.

The default setting is lmhosts host wins bcast.

Time server   This option Sets whether Samba is to act as a time server. If set to Yes, all the Windows computers on your network can synchronize their time with the Samba server.

Tuning Options   Tuning the Samba server can improve performance. Be careful with changing options in this section. Changes should be tested first on a non-production server. A wrong setting can damage or destroy user files if the user is working on the server.

Change notify timeout   This option sets the frequency with which Samba checks a directory for changes. The default setting is once every 60 seconds. Anything more frequent can slow down overall performance.

Deadtime   This option sets the number of minutes of inactivity before a connection is considered dead and then disconnected. The deadtime takes effect only if the number of open files is zero. This is useful in preventing a large number of inactive connections from exhausting a server's resources. Windows automatically reconnects if needed, so most users never even notice the disconnection. Using this setting with a timeout of five minutes is recommended for most systems.

Getwd cache   When set to Yes, caching of the get working directory command is enabled. This can result in a significant performance improvement and should be set to Yes.

Keepalive   This sets the number of seconds between keepalive packets. If set to 0, no keepalive packets are sent. The socket option SO_KEEPALIVE can perform essentially the same function. Keepalive packets are not generally needed.

Lpq cache time   This sets how long lpq info is cached. The default is 10 seconds. Use a large value if your lpq command is very slow. A value of 0 disables caching completely.

Max disk size   This sets an upper limit on the reported size of disks. It does not limit the amount of data you can put on the disk. This option is primarily useful in working around bugs in some software that can't handle large disks (more than 1 gigabyte in size). The default setting is 0, which means no limit.

Read size   This sets the overlap of disk reads/writes with network reads/writes. If the amount of data being transferred is larger than this value, the server begins writing the data before it has received all the data. This overlapping improves system performance. It works best when the speeds of disk and network access are similar, having very little effect when the speed of one is much greater than the other. The default is 2,048. The optimal value varies between systems and can only be found by experimenting with your system. A value of more than 65,536 is useless.

Shared mem size   This option sets the size of the shared memory (in bytes) that Samba uses for file locking. The default size is one megabyte (1,048,576). If you have a large server with many files open simultaneously, you might need to increase this setting. If users are reporting file locking errors or if error messages appear in the log (saying something such as ERROR smb_shm_alloc : alloc of XX bytes failed), this setting might be too low.

Printing Options   On OpenLinux, set this to lpstat. This is a command that automatically generates a list of available printers.

Printer driver file   This option sets the location of the printer driver definition file that is used when serving drivers to Windows 95 clients. The default is /etc/samba.d/printers.def. For more details on setting up serving of printer drivers to Windows 95 clients, see the Samba document PRINTER_DRIVER.txt. On the version of OpenLinux included with this book, you can find it in the /usr/doc/samba-2.0.3/docs/textdocs/ directory. If you've upgraded to the version of Samba on your system, you need to find the textdocs directory for the version of Samba you are using.

Printer driver location   This option sets where to find the printer driver files for the automatic installation of drivers for Windows 95 machines. The default setting is blank. For details on setting this up, see the Samba document PRINTER_DRIVER.txt. This is in the /usr/doc/samba-2.0.3/docs/textdocs/ directory. If you've upgraded to the version of Samba on your system, you need to find the textdocs directory for the version of Samba you are using.

Filename Handling   Linux and Windows handle filenames very differently. Samba translates between the two systems so that Windows users see filenames in the way they would expect to find them. You can adjust these settings, but you have to set the defaults to make the best match of Linux and Windows.

Strip dot   This sets whether to strip trailing dots off Linux filenames. The default setting is No. Some CDs have filenames ending with a single dot. If you are having trouble reading filenames from a CD, try setting this to Yes.

Mangled stack   This parameter affects only DOS users or software that works in DOS mode and does not recognize long filenames. This parameter controls the number of mangled names that Samba is to cache. Long filenames are mangled to fit the DOS 8.3 name limit (see Figure 20.12). The *stack* is a list of recently mangled base names. Bigger values make it more likely that mangled names are successfully converted to correct long names, but large stack sizes slow directory access. Smaller stacks save memory in the server. It is not possible to guarantee absolutely correct long filenames, so be prepared for surprises.

FIGURE 20.12
A DOS listing of a directory on a Samba server. The short 8.3 format name on the left is a mangled form of the long name, which is shown on the right side of the directory listing.

Part
V

Ch
20

Client code page   This option sets the DOS code page that the clients accessing Samba are using. The choices are either 437 or 850. To determine which code page a Windows or DOS client is using, open a DOS command prompt and type the command **chcp**. This outputs the code page. The default for U.S. installations is code page 437. The default for Western Europe is code page 850.

Case sensitive   This sets whether filenames are case sensitive. The default is No, which is how DOS and Windows work.

Preserve case   This sets whether new filenames are created with the case sent by the user or whether they are forced to be the default case. The default is Yes, which preserves the case sent by the user.

Short preserve case   This sets whether new files that conform to the DOS 8.3 filename syntax are created all uppercase or whether they are forced to be the default case. The default setting is Yes, which creates filenames that are all in uppercase.

Mangle case   This sets whether names that have characters that aren't of the default case are mangled. If a DOS-compliant 8.3 filename has both uppercase and lowercase characters, such as Letter.txt, which has an uppercase L, mangling would force the name to be displayed in all uppercase letters. The default is No, which means that mixed case names aren't mangled.

Mangling char   This sets what character is used as the "magic" character in name mangling. The default is a tilde (~).

Hide dot files   This sets whether files starting with a dot appear as hidden files. The default setting is Yes.

Delete veto files   *Veto files* are hidden files. If this is set to Yes, when you attempt to delete a directory, Samba tries to delete any hidden files. If the hidden files can't be deleted, the directory can't be deleted. The normal setting is No.

Veto files   This lists files and directories that are neither visible nor accessible. Putting anything into this list degrades Samba's performance because Samba is forced to check all files and directories for a match as they are scanned. Normally this list is empty.

Hide files   This lists files or directories that are not visible but are accessible. Putting anything into this list degrades Samba's performance because Samba is forced to check all files and directories for a match as they are scanned. Normally, this list is empty.

Mangled names   This sets whether non-DOS names under Linux are to be mapped to DOS-compatible names (*mangled*) and made visible, or whether non-DOS names are to simply be ignored. The name mangling, if enabled, allows a file to be copied between Linux directories from Windows/DOS while retaining the long Linux filename. The default setting is Yes.

Mangled map   This is for those who want to directly map Linux filenames that are mangled to be viewable in DOS/Windows 3.x. Mangled names are not always usable. For example, on Linux the standard file extension for Web documents is .html, whereas for Windows it's .htm. The mangled extension can be forced to match. To map *html* to *htm*, you use `mangled map = (*.html *.htm)`.

Domain Options The Domain options are all experimental in the version of Samba that ships with OpenLinux 2.3. They are part of the unfinished Samba NT Domain Controller Code and might be removed in a later versions of Samba. Leave them all blank until the code is finished.

Logon Options If you are on a network that uses a Windows NT Primary Domain Controller, you can create a script to add users that have already been authenticated by the PDC.

Add user script Normally, all Samba users must be created first as users on your Linux server. For sites that use a Windows NT Primary Domain Controller to maintain their primary user database, creating Linux users and keeping the user list in sync with the Windows NT PDC is a big job. This option enables Samba to create Linux users on demand when a verified user accesses the Samba server. A script must be written that adds a user to your Linux server. This add user script is run as root, with any %u argument to be the username to create.

Delete user script This works the same way as the add user script, except that it deletes users in order to keep the Linux user database in sync with the Windows NT Primary Domain Controller.

Logon settings The different logon settings are used if Samba is set as a Windows 95 workgroup logon server. These settings are not used for Windows NT domains.

Configuring Windows 95/98/NT to Connect to a Samba Server

You can connect any Windows computer with an Ethernet connection to your Samba server. Make sure that the Windows computer has an Ethernet card and is connected to an Ethernet network. Then you need to configure the networking software.

Windows 95/98 Setup Follow these steps to install the networking software on a Windows 95/98 computer:

1. Insert the Windows 95/98 CD.
2. Click the My Computer icon on the desktop. When it opens, double-click the Control Panel icon.
3. In the Control Panel, double-click the Network icon.
4. Make sure that your Ethernet card is displayed. If not, exit the Network panel and double-click the Add Hardware icon. Follow the instructions to install the drivers for the Ethernet card. When that is properly installed, you're ready for the next step.
5. Click on the Identification tab (see Figure 20.13). Enter a Computer Name: the hostname for your computer. If you don't know the hostname, obtain it from your system administrator. The name you put here can be anything you want, but if you don't use the hostname, it can cause some unexpected conflicts.

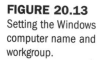

FIGURE 20.13

Setting the Windows computer name and workgroup.

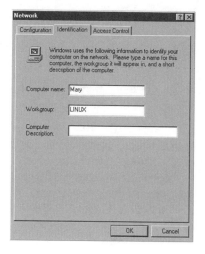

6. Enter the Workgroup name. Windows networks are organized around workgroups. If you don't know the workgroup name, obtain it from your system administrator. You can put anything you want in the Computer Description field to describe how the computer is used such as Graphics Department, or leave it blank. The description is displayed next to the computer's host name in the Network Neighborhood.

7. Click on the Configuration tab. You must install two components:

   ■ **Client for Microsoft Networks**—For your communication with the network

   ■ **TCP/IP**—The networking protocol for your computer's communication with the network

   If either of these is already installed, that's fine. Just follow the configuration steps to make sure they are properly configured for your Samba network. If other clients or protocols are installed, you don't need to worry about them. They don't interfere with the Samba network.

8. Add the Client for Microsoft Networks. Click the Add button and select Client. Click Add. In the pop-up window that opens, select Microsoft from the list in the left frame. Then, select Client for Microsoft Networks from the list that appears in the right frame. Click OK.

9. Add TCP/IP. Click the Add button and select Protocol. Click Add. In the pop-up window that opens, select Microsoft from the list in the left frame. Then, select TCP/IP from the list that appears in the right frame. Click OK.

10. Configure TCP/IP. Click the TCP/IP icon and then click the Properties button. You see something similar to Figure 20.14.

FIGURE 20.14
TCP/IP settings in Windows.

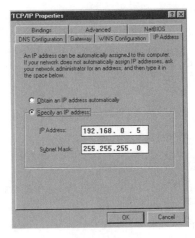

If your system is using a DHCP server for distributing IP addresses, leave this set to Obtain an IP address automatically. If your system is to be hard coded, check the Specify an IP address button and then enter the IP address and Subnet Mask for the computer. If you don't know these settings, obtain them from your network system administrator.

Your Internet service provider can assign IP addresses. If you are not directly connected to the Internet or if your system uses a firewall to connect to the Internet, you can use one of the reserved private IP addresses. The Class C reserved addresses for private networks are 192.168.0.0–192.168.255.255.

After entering the computer's IP address, select the tabs for any other settings that are necessary for your network. Usually this means setting the Gateway and DNS Configuration. If your network has a WINS server, you'll need to set that option here as well.

When the settings are complete, click OK and exit the network setup. Then you need to reboot your computer.

This finishes the installation of the networking software in Windows 95/98. The section "Connecting to the Samba Server" contains the rest of the steps for using the Samba network.

Windows NT Workstation Setup   Follow these steps to install the networking software on a Windows NT workstation computer:

1. Insert the Windows NT CD.
2. Click the My Computer icon on the desktop. When it opens, double-click the Control Panel icon.
3. In the Control Panel, double-click the Network icon.

Part
V

Ch
20

4. Click on the Adapter tab and make sure that your Ethernet card is displayed. If not, click the Add button. Select the driver that matches the adapter installed in your computer. Follow the instructions to install the drivers for the Ethernet card. When that is properly installed, you're ready for the next step.

5. Click on the Identification tab. Click the Change button and enter a Computer Name: the hostname for your computer. If you don't know the hostname, obtain it from your system administrator. The name here can be anything you want, but if you don't use the hostname it can cause some unexpected conflicts.

6. Enter the Workgroup name. Windows networks are organized around workgroups. If you don't know the workgroup name, get it from your system administrator. Click OK.

7. Click on the Services tab. Click the Add button. From the list, select NetBIOS Interface. Click OK.

8. To add TCP/IP, click on the Protocols tab. Click Add. In the pop-up window that opens, select TCP/IP Protocol from the list. Click OK.

9. To configure TCP/IP, click the TCP/IP Protocol icon and then click the Properties button. If your system is using a DHCP server for distributing IP addresses, leave this set to Obtain an IP from a DHCP server. If your system is to be hard coded, check the Specify an IP address button and then enter the IP address, Subnet Mask, and Default Gateway for the computer. If you don't know these settings, obtain them from your network system administrator.

After entering the computer's IP address, select the tabs for any other settings that are necessary for your network. Usually this means setting the DNS Configuration. If your network has a WINS server, you need to set that option here as well.

When you've finished with the settings, click OK and exit the network setup. Then you need to reboot your computer.

Connecting to the Samba Server

After networking is set up on your Windows computers, you can connect to the Samba server. Double-click the Network Neighborhood icon. You see the Samba server in the list of computers found on the network. Double-click on the icon for your Samba server. If your username and password on your Windows computer match the username and password on the Samba server, you should be given access.

You can map your Samba home directory to a Windows disk drive. Right-click the My Computer icon. Choose Map Network Drive. In the pop-up window that opens, the first field is the drive letter that is used. The first available drive letter is what is normally displayed. If you want a different drive, select the drive letter you want.

In the path field, type in the name of Samba server and your home directory. The format for this is *servername\directory*. Therefore, if your server name is Linux and your home directory, which uses your login name, is mary, the path is \\linux\mary. This is not the Linux path: It is the path that Windows sees when it connects to the Samba server.

If you check the Reconnect on logon box, the drive is mapped automatically every time you start up Windows.

Accessing Windows Computers from a Linux System

If you have Samba set up and running on your OpenLinux computer, you can use the utilities that come with it to access files and printers on a Windows-based computer that's been set up for file or printer sharing. Remember that Samba must be set up and working properly on your Linux computer before you can use any of these utilities. If you run into problems, first make sure that Samba is working correctly.

Using *smbmount*

You can use smbmount to mount a share from a Windows-based computer onto your Linux computer. The basic command is

```
smbmount //windows_computer_name/directory_name /mnt/mount_point
```

NOTE This uses forward slashes, not the DOS backslashes. Older versions required the DOS style backslashes. ■

```
smbmount //windows_computer_name/directory_name /mnt/mount_point -U username
```

This command adds the username if your Linux name is different than the username needed for the Windows computer.

Non-root users can use the smbumount command to unmount a mounted Windows share. The basic command is

```
smbumount /mnt/mount_point
```

Using *smbclient*

smbclient is an FTP-like utility for transferring files to and from a Windows computer. The Windows computer must have file sharing available.

You can use the program to send files to and receive files from a Windows computer.

The standard command to connect to a Windows computer is

```
smbclient \\windows_computer_name\share_name
```

Part
V

Ch
20

You are then prompted for your password. If everything works correctly, you are connected to the file share on the Windows computer. You see a prompt that looks like this:

```
smb: \>
```

If you type a question mark (?) at the prompt, a list of possible commands is shown. If you've used the standard command-line ftp program in Linux, this will look familiar. An `ls` or `dir` command displays a list of files. The `get` and `put` commands can be used to receive or send files.

Using *smbprint*

`smbprint` is a shell script that you can use to print to a printer connected to a Windows computer. This is useful if you are connected to a Windows-based network and need to print to a printer attached to a Windows-based PC.

You can find the procedure for setting up your Linux computer to print to a Windows computer in Chapter 8, "Installing and Configuring Printers."

After you have configured the printer on your OpenLinux computer, files can be printed in the usual way. Just designate which printer is to be the remote Windows printer. If you use `lpr` to print, the command is

```
lpr -Pprinter_name file_name
```

The printer name is the name of the printer in your printcap file. You can use COAS to see all the installed printers on your system.

## CHAPTER 21

Installing and Configuring NetWare Network Services

In this chapter

NetWare and OpenLinux

Novell NetWare (www.novell.com) is one of the top networking systems. It's found in many offices and offers many excellent features.

One of NetWare's strengths is its performance, especially when connecting an office of relatively slow PCs. This is, in part, because of the design of the NetWare IPX protocol. However, IPX is not the protocol used on the Internet; the Internet uses TCP/IP. The advantages of IPX have been diminished by the newer, faster, more powerful PCs now appearing on office desktops.

Novell has made a strategic shift away from IPX, and NetWare version 5 is based on TCP/IP, making it more compatible with Internet connectivity. However, because most installations of NetWare use either version 3.x or 4.x., connecting to a NetWare server from Linux using IPX remains an important option.

Former employees of Novell started Caldera Systems—the company that puts together the OpenLinux distribution—and they worked hard to make Linux and Novell work well together.

OpenLinux includes support for working with Novell NetWare 3.x and 4.x servers. You can work with these servers from any Linux command line, and your system looks like any other PC on the NetWare network.

You have to buy the OpenLinux package from Caldera Systems to get the software. It's included on a floppy disk in the box, but the version that ships with OpenLinux 2.2 is a beta version of the software. Download the latest version of the client from the Caldera Systems Web site; you can find the latest version of the NetWare client and administration utilities at www.calderasystems.com/doc/NetWare/linuxclient/index.html.

The NetWare client and utilities from Caldera Systems are not open source software. They are restricted, licensed software programs that are included with the regular OpenLinux 2.2 package from Caldera Systems.

The OpenLinux NetWare client provides basic NetWare support, including

- Automatic recognition of all NetWare servers, both NDS (4.x) and bindery (3.x and 4.x in bindery emulation)
- The capability to log in to multiple NDS trees simultaneously
- Printing and print queue management utilities
- NetWare broadcast message utilities

This chapter does not explain NetWare networking or what is involved in NetWare system administration; that is covered in a whole series of books available for purchase with the NetWare system. For reference, many good books are available on NetWare. This chapter is a guide to connecting to a NetWare server from your OpenLinux system—it does not detail the system administration tasks that can be performed from OpenLinux using the Caldera OpenLinux administration tools. This chapter provides a description of the tools and the commands needed to carry out the task. Only a NetWare systems administrator who knows the tasks involved should attempt to carry out administrative tasks from an OpenLinux computer.

One source for more in-depth information on NetWare networking is the book *Special Edition Using Netware 5.0* by Peter Kuo (ISBN: 0-7897-2056-6).

Installing the NetWare Client and Utilities

Install the NetWare client software from either the floppy disk that was included in the OpenLinux box or from the latest version downloaded from the Caldera Systems Web site. The filename of the package that was shipped with OpenLinux 2.2 is nwclient-4.2.0-col22-1.i386.rpm.

Insert the NetWare client floppy disk from Caldera Systems and mount it. You can use the floppy disk icon on the desktop if you've created it, or you can open a terminal window and enter the command **mount /mnt/floppy**. If you are using an update that you've downloaded from Caldera System's ftp site, you do not need to mount the floppy disk.

Next, start the K File Manager by clicking on the home folder icon on the K Panel. Use the arrow buttons to change directories and go to the floppy disk directory or the location of the update file. Click once on the file icon. Because it is an RPM package, this automatically starts Kpackage. When Kpackage opens, click the Install button to install the NetWare client package.

The NetWare utilities package is also on the floppy disk, and should be installed if you want to use any of the NetWare utilities. Updates are available on the Caldera Web site. The filename of the package that was shipped with OpenLinux 2.2 is nwutils-static-cl-1.1-17.i386.rpm.

The NetWare client automatically starts up each time you reboot your system. If you want it to start up immediately after you've installed it without rebooting your system, enter the following command:

```
/etc/rc.d/init.d/nwclient start
```

After nwclient has been started, the NetWare client administration utilities can be used.

Fixing a Linux IPX Problem

NetWare networks use the *IPX (Internetwork Packet Exchange)* protocol to "talk" with other computers on the network. TCP/IP is the default protocol used by Linux and the Internet; Appletalk is the protocol used on Macintosh networks.

In order for a Linux computer to talk to a computer on a NetWare network, it must use the IPX protocol. OpenLinux includes IPX, which is installed along with TCP/IP. The two do not conflict and can be used simultaneously on your OpenLinux computer.

There is a problem with the default installation of IPX in OpenLinux; the default installation sets IPX to autoconfigure for the network. The autoconfiguration is frequently wrong, and if you have a 3.x NetWare network, it almost never gets the frame type right. In addition, the autoconfiguration attempt will broadcast packets that can flood and overflow the network.

Make sure your OpenLinux computer is not connected to the network until you have disabled autoconfiguration, or you might cause problems on the NetWare network. On the OpenLinux system, use a text editor and edit the file named ipx in the /etc/sysconfig directory. Change the "AUTO" entry to off, and change the CONFIGURED entry to yes. Then, enter the frame type and network number for your network. The resulting changes in the file should look like this:

```
IPX_AUTO_INTERFACE=off
IPX_CONFIGURED=yes
IPX_FRAME=frame type
IPX_NETNUM=network number
```

The *frame type* is the frame type used on your network, with the most common types being 802.2, 802.3, and ether_ii. If you don't know the frame type or the network number, obtain them from your network administrator. To apply the new settings, stop and start IPX with these commands:

```
/etc/rd.d/init.d/ipx stop
/etc/rd.d/init.d/ipx start
```

Configuring the NetWare Client

The NetWare client has two settings that you can configure. Using a text editor, open the file named nwclient in the /etc/sysconfig/ directory. The first of the two options is

```
ONBOOT=yes
```

which indicates whether the NetWare client will be started automatically when the system starts. If the client is active, NetWare servers and trees appear under the /NetWare directory, and all NetWare utilities will function. The other option is

```
NWCLIENT_SINGLE_CONNECTION_TABLE=no
```

which keeps a separate record for each NetWare user. This means that if two different users are logged in to OpenLinux, each can log in to the same (or multiple) NetWare servers using different NetWare usernames. If this parameter is set to yes, all users will use a single connection record. This means that if two OpenLinux users attempt to log in to the same NetWare server, the first one to log in has his name in the connection record. The second user cannot log in to the NetWare server as himself, but he will have access to the NetWare server with the same access rights as the first user. This option should generally be avoided, although special situations occur in which it might be necessary to use it. If the option is set to yes, a big security hole is opened on your system.

After any configuration changes, the NetWare client needs to be stopped and restarted. To stop the NetWare client, enter the following command:

/etc/rc.d/init.d/nwclient stop

To restart the NetWare client, enter the following command:

/etc/rc.d/init.d/nwclient start

Using the NetWare Client and Utilities

Access to the NetWare servers on your network is in the /NetWare directory of your OpenLinux system.

In the /NetWare directory, you'll find two directories: NDS and Bindery. The NetWare 4.x servers are listed in the NDS directory. The NetWare 3.x (and 4.x in bindery emulation) servers are listed in the Bindery directory.

In the Bindery directory, there are subdirectories that are the Bindery servers on your network. Clicking on a subdirectory named for the server you want to access gives you access.

In the NDS directory are subdirectories named for the NDS directory trees available on your network. The name of each NDS directory tree is synonymous with the [Root] object in that directory tree.

Logging In

Before you can access the NetWare servers on your network, you have to log in to the server.

After you're logged in to a server, you can view any files and directories on that server, and you'll be capable of reading from and writing to files on the server, limited only by your access rights.

You have several options for logging in to a server or tree. Following are some of the commonly used methods. Open a terminal window and enter the commands in Table 21.1.

Table 21.1   NetWare Log In Commands

NetWare Client Command	What It Does
nwlogin NetWare_username	Logs you in to the nearest server.
nwlogin -t tree -u username	Logs you in to the NDS directory tree named in the tree parameter.
nwlogin -s server -u username	Logs you in to the particular server named in the server parameter.
nwlogout -s server	Logs you out of a NetWare server; this logs you off only the specified server.
nwlogout -t tree	Logs you out of an NDS directory tree; this logs you off only the specified tree.
nwlogout −a	Logs you off of all NetWare servers. ·

Part

V

Ch

21

Accessing the NetWare Servers

After logging in to a NetWare server, you can access files on the server just like any other files in your system. Depending on which directory you want to access, take one of the following actions:

- To access bindery servers, switch to the /NetWare/bindery directory. Each server's subdirectory includes directories that refer to disk volumes such as SYS or DATA. Clicking on a directory opens the directory for your access. Any files that you have rights to on those volumes will be accessible. You will also be capable of printing to the servers' print queues.

- To access NDS servers, change to the /NetWare/NDS directory. The name of each NDS Directory tree is synonymous with the [Root] object in that Directory tree. When you switch to an NDS directory tree, everything will be accessible through the directories that appear when you click on the directory names in the tree.

After you are logged in to a NetWare server, you can use the K File Manager to access the NetWare server drives, or you can open a terminal window and navigate the directories using the cd command.

Printing

The NetWare client enables you to print files directly to a NetWare print queue and specify how you want files to print.

To print a file, open a terminal window and enter the following command:

```
nwprint filename -s server_name -q print_queue_name
```

If your print job comes out with the "stair-step" look—meaning that the beginning of each line doesn't return to the beginning of the next line— the carriage return-line feed option needs to be added to the print command. In that case, use this command:

```
nwprint -c filename -s server_name -q print_queue_name
```

You can use the NetWare utilities to see the status of your print job. To view the print queue on a NetWare server, enter the following command at the prompt in a terminal window:

```
nwqstat -s server -q queue
```

You can also delete a print job from the print queue. First, look at what is in the print queue using the nwqstat command. See what the job number is for the print job you want to delete, and then enter the following command:

```
nwdelqjob -s server -q queue job_number
```

Using the Administrative Utilities

The utilities package has a whole set of tools that enable you to take care of many administration tasks on NetWare servers while working from your OpenLinux system. You need to be logged in as a user with supervisor rights on the NetWare server to use these utilities.

Administering Bindery Servers

NetWare 3.x servers store essential information—such as usernames and groups—in a database called the *bindery*. You can use the NetWare utilities to create, view, modify, and delete bindery objects such as users, groups, or print queues. Utilities are also provided to administer disk space quotas and file system trustees.

Following are NetWare client utilities for administering bindery servers.

The *nwbocreate* Command   To create a new NetWare bindery object, such as a user, group, or print queue, use the nwbocreate command.

To create a new user, enter the following command:

```
nwbocreate -s server_name -o user_name -t 1 -H home_directory
```

The server name needs the full Linux path, so it will be /NetWare/bindery/*server_name*. The username is the login name for the new user. There are three bindery object types: 1 is user, 2 is group, and 3 is print queue. The user's home directory also needs the full Linux path. A sample command to create a new user named Mary on a NetWare server named groucho is

```
nwbocreate -s /NetWare/bindery/groucho -o mary -t 1 -H
➥/NetWare/bindery/groucho/volumes/SYS/users/mary
```

To create a new group, enter the following command:

```
nwbocreate -s server_name -o group_name -t 2
```

To create a new print queue, enter the following command:

```
nwbocreate -s server_name -o print_queue_name -t 3
```

The *nwboprops* Command   To list the properties of a NetWare bindery object, enter the following command:

```
nwboprops -o object
```

Objects are resources and include the print queues, disk volumes, and users.

The *nwbpadd* Command   To add a value to a property of a NetWare bindery object, enter the following command:

```
nwbpadd -o path_to_bindery -p property_name -t property_type -v property_value
```

This works just like the nwbocreate command and requires the full Linux path. The property name can be one of the required properties or any of the optional properties. The possible types are SET, STRING, and SEGMENT. SET is used for adding a value to the property, STRING for entering new text for the property, and SEGMENT for indicating a hexadecimal value. Following is a sample command:

```
nwbpadd -o /NetWare/bindery/groucho/objects/mary -p NAME -t
➥STRING -v mary_smith
```

The *nwbpvalues* Command   To list all values of a property of a NetWare bindery object, enter the following command:

```
nwbpvalues -o path_to_bindery -p property_name
```

Use nwbpvalues to find the current property values for any object. A sample command to get the NAME property value is

```
nwbpvalues -o /NetWare/bindery/groucho/objects/mary -p NAME
```

The *nwbprm* Command   To remove a value from a property of a NetWare bindery object, enter the following command:

```
nwbprm -o path_to_bindery -p property_name -v property_value
```

The *nwborm* Command   To remove an object from the NetWare bindery, enter the following command:

```
nwborm -o path_to_bindery
```

A sample command to remove the user mary is

```
nwborm -o /NetWare/bindery/groucho/objects/mary
```

The *nwboaddtrust* Command   To give a NetWare bindery object rights to a NetWare directory, enter the following command:

```
nwboaddtrust -o path_to_bindery -p path -r [rights_mask]
```

The full Linux path is required. The rights mask uses the following NetWare settings:

> **R**—Read
>
> **W**—Write
>
> **C**—Create
>
> **E**—Erase
>
> **M**—Modify
>
> **F**—File Scan
>
> **A**—Access control

A sample command to give user mary rights to read, write, create, erase, modify, and scan files in the sales directory is

```
nwboaddtrust -o /NetWare/bindery/groucho/objects/mary -p
 /NetWare/bindery/groucho/volumes/DATA/groups/sales -r [RWCEMF]
```

The *nwboshowtrust* Command   To display a bindery object's rights to NetWare directories, enter the following command:

```
nwboshowtrust -o path_to_bindery -p path
```

For example, to see trustees of the sales directory, use the following command:

```
nwboshowtrust -p /NetWare/bindery/groucho/volumes/DATA/groups/sales
```

To see the trustees rights of the user mary, use the following command:

```
nwboaddtrust -o /NetWare/bindery/groucho/objects/mary
```

The *nwbosetspace* Command   To set a disk quota for a specific NetWare bindery directory, enter the following command:

```
nwbosetspace -d path_to_bindery quota_size
```

Following are the options for the size setting:

- -k—Size in kilobytes (KB)
- -m—Size in megabytes (MB)
- -b—Size in 4KB blocks

For example, to set the size limit on the sales directory of 750MB, use the following command:

```
nwbosetspace -d /NetWare/bindery/groucho/volumes/DATA/groups/sales -m 750
```

The *nwboshowspace* Command   To show the disk quota for a specific NetWare bindery directory, enter the following command:

```
nwboshowspace -d path_to_bindery
```

Administering NetWare Directory Services (NDS) Servers

NetWare 4.x and NetWare 5.x servers store usernames and groups in a distributed database used by NetWare Directory Services (NDS). The NetWare utilities include tools to administer an NDS directory by creating, viewing, modifying, and deleting objects and their attributes in NDS. NDS also provides utilities to administer disk space quotas and file system trustees. When creating a new NDS object such as a username, group, or print queue, you must specify values for some of its attributes. These attributes are called *mandatory attributes*, and they vary from object to object. Most objects don't have a mandatory attribute other than their Common Name. For example, when a User object is created, you must specify a value for both its Common Name—the name of the object in the Directory tree—and its Surname.

Following are the NetWare client utilities for administering NDS servers.

The *nwdsattrs* Command   To list attributes of an NDS object's class, enter the following command:

```
nwdsattrs -o path_to_NDS object
```

Part

V

Ch

21

The path is the full Linux path. A sample command to view the Organization object for MyCompany follows:

```
nwdsattrs -o /NetWare/NDS/NW-TREE/MyCompany
```

The *nwdsvalues* Command   To list the values of an NDS object's attribute, enter the following command:

```
nwdsvalues -o path_to_NDS_object -a attribute_name
```

For example, to view the fax attribute for user mary, use the following command:

```
nwdsvalues -o /NetWare/NDS/NW-TREE/MyCompany/SALES/mary -a fax
```

The *nwdsmodify* Command   To modify values of an NDS object's attribute, enter the following command:

```
nwdsmodify -o path_to_NDS_object -a attribute_name -v attribute
➥_value -s syntax -c operation
```

The possible operations are

   a—Add

   d—Delete

   r—Replace

For example, to modify the title attribute for user mary who has been promoted to vice president, use the following command:

```
nwdsmodify -o /NetWare/NDS/NW-TREE/MyCompany/SALES/mary
➥-a title -v VP -s Title -c r
```

The *nwdsrm* Command   To remove an NDS object from the tree, enter the following command:

```
nwdsrm -o path_to_NDS_object
```

For example, to remove the user joe, use the following command:

```
nwdsrm -o /NetWare/NDS/NW-TREE/MyCompany/SALES/joe
```

The *nwdsaddtrust* Command   To give a NetWare NDS object rights to a NetWare directory, enter the following command:

```
nwdsaddtrust -o path_to_NDS_object -p path -r [rights_mask]
```

The full Linux path is required. The rights mask uses the following NetWare settings:

   R—Read
   W—Write
   C—Create
   E—Erase

M—Modify

F—File Scan

A—Access control

A sample command to give user mary rights to read, write, create, erase, modify, and scan files in the sales directory follows:nwdsaddtrust -o /NetWare/NDS/NW-TREE/MyCompany/SALES/mary -p /NetWare/NDS/NW-TREE/MyCompany/DATA/groups/sales -r [RWCEMF]

The *nwdsshowtrust* Command   To display NetWare NDS object rights for NetWare directories, enter the following command:

```
nwdsshowtrust -o path_to_NDS_object -s server_name -p path
```

The trustees of the sales directory can be seen with this sample command:

```
nwdsshowtrust -p /NetWare/NDS/NW-TREE/MyCompany/DATA/groups/sales
 -s /NetWare/NDS/NW-TREE/MyCompany/HARPO
```

The trustee rights of user mary can be seen with this sample command:

```
nwdsshowtrust -o /NetWare/NDS/NW-TREE/MyCompany/SALES/mary -s
 /NetWare/NDS/NW-TREE/MyCompany/HARPO
```

The *nwdssetspace* Command   To set the disk quota for a specific NetWare NDS directory, enter the following command:

```
nwdssetspace -d path_to_bindery quota_size
```

Following are options for the size setting:

-   **-k**—Size in kilobytes (KB)

-   **-m**—Size in megabytes (MB)

-   **-b**—Size in 4K blocks

For example, to set a size limit on the sales directory of 750MB, use the following command:

```
nwdssetspace -d /NetWare/NDS/NW-TREE/MyCompany/harpo/DATA/groups/
sales -m 750
```

The *nwdsshowspace* Command   To show the disk quota for a specific NetWare NDS directory, enter the following command:

```
nwdsshowspace -d path_to_directory_service
```

For example, to see the size limit on the sales directory, use the following command:

```
nwdsshowspace -d /NetWare/NDS/NW-TREE/MyCompany/harpo/DATA/
groups/sales
```

Graphical NetWare Utilities

Graphical versions of some of the utilities are also available. You can use these from the K desktop by opening a terminal window and entering the command. Table 21.2 shows a list of the graphical NetWare utilities.

Part

V

Ch

21

Table 21.2   Graphical NetWare Utilities

Utility	Description
xnwprint	Prints to a NetWare print queue.
xnwdsadmin	An NDS properties administration tool.
xnwdscreate	Creates a new NDS object.
xnwdsrights	Views or grants an NDS object rights to a directory or file on a NetWare volume.
xnwdstrustees	Manages the NDS trustees of a NetWare directory or file.
xnwboadmin	Administers the properties of a NetWare bindery object.
xnwbocreate	Creates a new bindery object.
xnwborights	Grants a bindery object rights to a directory or file on a NetWare volume.
xnwbotrustees	Manages the trustees of a directory or file on a NetWare bindery server.
xnwmanageq	Views print jobs in a NetWare print queue and optionally deletes jobs in that queue.

Caldera NetWare for Linux

Caldera Systems produces a product that makes a Linux server look and act just like a Novell NetWare 4 server. The product is called NetWare for Linux, and you can download a free copy from the Caldera Systems Web site. The free copy is limited to three users. You can add additional users by purchasing license packs from Caldera Systems.

> **CAUTION**
>
> NetWare for Linux doesn't work on OpenLinux version 2.2. Caldera Systems first designed it to work with OpenLinux 1.2. The company says that it is "looking into" porting it to OpenLinux 2.2. In other words, when NetWare for Linux will be available for newer versions of OpenLinux is not yet known. However, it is a good product, and worth checking out by anyone looking to expand a NetWare network using Linux servers.

NetWare for Linux is not designed to work only on OpenLinux. You can use it on any Linux distribution using the Linux 2.0.3x kernel.

NetWare for Linux does not provide the full functionality of a NetWare server. You can use it to provide file, print, and directory services, but you cannot use NetWare NLMs with it. This product is best suited for expanding an existing NetWare network.

## CHAPTER 22

Installing and Configuring NFS

File Sharing Between Linux Computers

Sun Microsystems designed the Network File System for sharing files between UNIX computers. You can use NFS on OpenLinux to share files and directories from other Linux or UNIX computers on your network. You can even share files and directories from Windows 95 and Windows NT computers using NFS, though Samba is a better way to do this (for more information on Samba, see Chapter 20 on "Installing and Configuring a Windows Network with Samba.").

NFS is designed for sharing files on an *intranet*—an internal network—and not for file sharing across the Internet. Its design structure, especially its lack of necessary security features, makes it not at all suited for Internet use.

Better solutions for sharing files over the Internet are not only more secure but much faster than the relatively slow access provided by Linux NFS.

An NFS server is simply a computer that all the computers on a network can access. The NFS server has directories in which file systems from other computers are mounted. The computers that connect to the NFS server are called *NFS clients*. The clients can access directories on the NFS server without seeing any apparent difference between the actual files on the NFS server and files from another computer that have been mounted to a directory on the NFS server.

The standard OpenLinux installation includes everything you need for NFS services. To see which version of NFS is installed on your system, use the Kpackage Manager to search for NFS, or open a terminal window and enter the command rpm -q nfs.

By default, the NFS services are started automatically at boot on OpenLinux.

Using the NFS Client

Mounting an NFS volume is similar to mounting a floppy disk or CD-ROM. You can do this by entering a mount command, or you can include the file system information in the fstab file in the /etc directory for automatic mounting during your system's startup.

For more information, see the section in Chapter 3, "Configuring the KDE Desktop," that deals with mounting a CD-ROM drive.

Whichever way you choose to mount an NFS volume, you will need to create a directory on your system where it will be mounted. This is called the *mount point*. In the /mnt directory, make a directory that will be the NFS mount point.

The basic command for mounting a file system using NFS is

```
mount -t nfs nfs_server:nfs_volume /mnt/mount_point
```

This is the same mount command that's used for mounting other disks on your system. The -t option indicates that the type is NFS. It is not absolutely necessary to include the -t option because the mount program sees—because of the colon (:) in the command—that an NFS volume is being mounted. The nfs_server option must give the name of the server on your network, and the nfs_volume must be the name of the file directory that is being shared. Therefore, a sample mount command is

```
mount -t nfs kato:/shared_docs /mnt/docs
```

This NFS mounts the /shared_docs directory on the computer named kato on the /mnt/docs directory on your computer.

To see a list of directories available for NFS mounting on a server, use the following command:

```
showmount -e nfs_server
```

If you need to specify one of the many options for mounting, I'd advise using an entry in fstab for mounting. This not only simplifies the process, it means that the command options are entered once and then do not need to be reentered.

Adding an NFS Mount to Your Startup Configuration

You can automate NFS mounting by adding an entry into the fstab configuration file in the /etc directory. The fstab file contains all the mounts in your computer.

The easiest way to add an NFS mount to fstab is to use COAS (for more information on COAS see Chapter 5, "Configuring Your System with COAS."

Open a terminal window and enter this command:

```
coastool
```

In the COAS CLAM selection window, choose System Administration. In System Administration, select File system Administration. In the File System window, under the Action menu choose Mount NFS (shown in Figure 22.1).

In the Mount File System window, shown in Figure 22.2, enter the name of the drive you'll be mounting in the device name field. The directory field is for the name of the directory where you want the remote device mounted.

Click on the Options button to define the options. When the File System Options window opens, shown in Figure 22.3, you can check the options you want for this mount.

FIGURE 22.1
In COAS, the File System utility Action menu is accessed to add an NFS mount to your system.

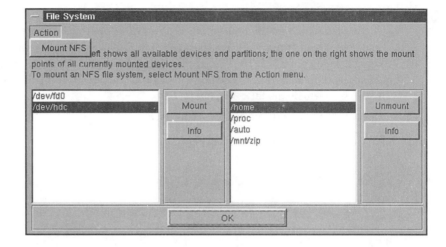

FIGURE 22.2
Define the NFS mount devices in the Mount File System window. If you want the device to be mounted every time you start up, make sure that Add to fstab is Yes.

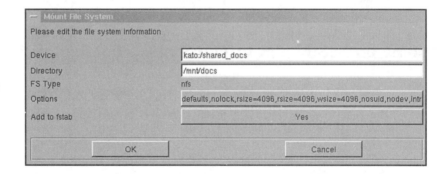

FIGURE 22.3
Use the File System Options window to configure NFS mount options.

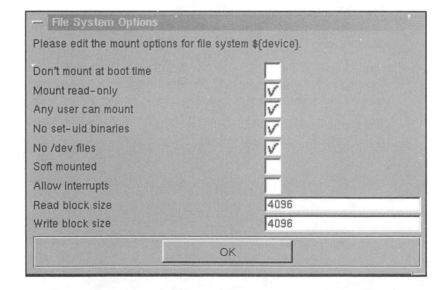

Table 22.1 lists the NFS mount options in COAS. The actual parameter name used in the fstab file is shown in the table in parentheses.

Table 22.1 NFS Mount Options

Option	How it's used
Don't mount at boot time (noauto)	Indicates that the volume is not automatically mounted. Mounting has to be done manually with a mount command, but all options are read from the fstab file and do not have to be entered with the mount command. Commonly used with disks such as CDs that can be changed.
Mount read-only (ro)	Mounts the system as read-only. Should be used for all mounted NFS volumes because of the security limitations of NFS.
Any user can mount (user)	Indicates that a user other than root can mount the volume. The default setting is that only root can mount.
No set-uid binaries (nosuid)	Does not allow set user ID or set group ID bits to be used. If it is used, the executed program behaves as though the owner of the file executed it. When the set-uid binary is owned by root, this can be a considerable security risk.
No /dev files (nodev)	Prevents access to device files in /dev. Generally a good security measure to add.
Soft mounted (soft)	If the server fails to respond, an error message is displayed and the connection isn't tried again. The default setting is hard mounted, which means that if the server doesn't respond, retry until it does respond.
Allow interrupts (intr)	Allows interruption of a request by using the Ctrl+C key combination. Useful when an NFS server has stopped responding. Check this unless you are using "Soft mounted" above.
Read block size (rsize=n)	Specifies the block size for read access. The default is 1,024. Other supported block sizes are 2,048, 4,096, and 8,192. A block size of 8,192 often improves the performance of an NFS mount.
Write block size (wsize=n)	Specifies the block size for write access. The details about rsize are the same for wsize.

Finally, make sure to click the button by Add to fstab in the Mount File System Window (see Figure 22.2). That way the system will be mounted every time your systems starts.

Using the NFS Server

OpenLinux can be used as an NFS server.

For NFS clicnts to mount an NFS file system, an NFS server must make the file system available. Usually, an NFS server does not make an entire disk partition available; usually, just a directory on the NFS server is made available for mounting.

The portmapper daemon controls access to NFS services. On OpenLinux, the portmapper uses the files hosts.allow and hosts.defy in the /etc directory for access control.

If you want other computers to be capable of mounting a directory from your system via NFS, you have to add a line in hosts.allow that indicates the IP address or domain of the computers to be granted access.

The portmap program will not attempt to look up a hostname or username, nor will it try to match NIS netgroups. This is done to avoid deadlocks that can seriously erode performance.

Here are some sample lines:

```
portmap : 192.168.30.69
portmap : 192.168.30.0/255.255.255.0
```

The first line allows NFS access to a specific computer. The second line allows NFS access to everyone in the 192.168.30.0 domain.

Setting up the Exports File

The exports file in the /etc directory determines which file systems are to be exported and what restrictions are placed on them. You can edit the exports configuration file with a text editor. Each file system that can be mounted is listed in exports on its own line, with any options listed next to it.

A sample line is

```
/home *.mycompany.com(rw)
```

This allows any users with a hostname in the mycompany.com domain to access the /home directory with read-write access.

Another sample shows some different options:

```
/opt mary.mycompany.com(ro) george.mycompany.com(ro)
```

This allows users on two computers, Mary and George, read-only access to /opt.

Table 22.2 lists some of the options in the exports file that are used to control access to NFS-mounted file systems.

Table 22.2   NFS Exports Options

Option	How it's used
insecure	Permits unauthenticated access from this host.
secure	Requires authentication from this host.
root_squash	A security feature that denies superusers special access rights.
no_root_squash	The opposite of the previous option: Superuser rights are not changed. This is the default setting.
ro	Mounts file system as read-only. This is the default setting.
rw	Mounts file system as read-write.
link_relative	Converts absolute symbolic links into relative links.
link_absolute	Leaves all symbolic links as they are. This is the default setting.
map_identity	The server should assume that the client uses the same uids and gids as found on the server. This is the default setting.
map_daemon	Tells the NFS server that the client and server do not have the same uids and gids. The ugidd daemon will then build a map of local and remote IDs.
all-squash	Maps all IDs to the anonymous user. Useful for exporting public directories.
no-all-squash	The opposite of the preceding option. This is the default setting.
noaccess	Excludes subdirectories from a client. Makes everything below the directory inaccessible to the client.

When the exports file has been created, NFS client can mount the NFS resource on your OpenLinux system.

Problems with NFS

NFS has many limitations, but security and speed are the two biggest.

The version of NFS included with OpenLinux 2.2 is not as robust as the NFS used by Sun and other UNIX systems. Many of the performance issues are expected to be answered with version 3 of Linux NFS.

Even version 3, however, cannot make NFS do things it was not designed to do. NFS does not support disk caching. In fact, the NFS specification requires that the server flush each block of data written to disk before it returns an acknowledgment so that no mounted NFS volume can take advantage of the speed boost offered by caching.

Security is a bigger problem. The NFS How-To included with OpenLinux includes a dire warning that many security risks are involved with using NFS. You should heed the warning. The ways to crack NFS are widely known, and crackers can easily use them to gain access to all of your files.

The loose security authentication used by NFS makes it easy to fool the system into seeing unauthorized users as authorized users. File transfers over an NFS network are not encrypted. Opening this over the Internet opens the network to having data intercepted and replaced. There are yet more security issues with NFS.

In a friendly environment, on a network that is not accessible from the Internet, NFS provides some wonderful functions, but the security difficulties make it generally not worth the effort on open systems on the Internet.

Generally, Samba provides much better performance with a high level of security, and is the preferred choice for file sharing on a Linux network. See Chapter 20 where I talk about Samba.

## CHAPTER 23

Installing and Configuring AppleTalk

Connecting Macintosh Computers to Your Linux Network Server

You can install AppleTalk networking on your Linux computer so that Macintosh computers can access the system to share disk file space and printers.

Netatalk is the server software that is used on your Linux system for this task. The Netatalk package supports AppleShare IP and classic AppleTalk protocols. With Netatalk, Macintosh computers can connect to your Linux network services—such as file and printer sharing—as if they were standard AppleTalk network services. The Netatalk suite was developed by the Research Systems UNIX Group at the University of Michigan (netatalk@umich.edu), which maintains and updates the software fairly regularly.

For Netatalk to work, you need TCP/IP networking up and running on your OpenLinux system. If you have Samba or any other networking software also installed on OpenLinux, it's not a problem. Netatalk does not in any way interfere with other networking protocols on your system.

N O T E An alternative way for Macintosh computers to access a Linux server is to use NFS. NFS client software on the Macintosh can be used to access Linux network resources. One of the most popular NFS clients for the Macintosh is Intragy Access, which includes NFS/Share. Intragy Access is a product of InterNetworking Systems, a division of Lucent Technologies, and can be found at www.ascend.com. For more information about setting up a Linux NFS server, see Chapter 22, "Installing and Configuring NFS."

Get the Program Files

OpenLinux includes AppleTalk support in its kernel. AppleTalk 0.18 for Linux NET4.0 is included as part of the standard installation of OpenLinux 2.2, but OpenLinux does not include the Netatalk suite. You need to download the source files and compile the program yourself. You can get Netatalk from the Netatalk home page at www.umich.edu/~rsug/netatalk/index.html.

Netatalk works with classic AppleTalk. There is also a version of the program that works with AppleShare IP. AppleShare IP requires that you have Mac OS 7.6 or higher.

Version 1.4 of Netatalk is the one most commonly used, even though it is beta software. It has much improved performance over version 1.3.3, while using much less memory. A version of the program with a set of patches by Adrian Sun that make Netatalk compatible with AppleShare IP is distributed as netatalk+asun.

A distribution that includes Adrian Sun's patches is put together by Anders Brownworth and should install without any problems on your OpenLinux system. You can find it on his Web page, along with the Linux Netatalk How-To, at thehamptons.com/anders/netatalk/. You'll find two versions: one that has shadow password support and one that doesn't. Pick the one that you want. If you are using the standard OpenLinux installation, get the version with shadow password support. These installation instructions are adapted from Anders Brownworth's instructions for installing Netatalk.

When you have the source code, you'll need to decompress and untar it with the following commands:

```
gzip netatalk-version_number_goes_here.tar.gz
tar xvf netatalk- version_number_goes_here.tar
```

Netatalk needs tcp wrappers as part of the installation. tcp wrappers are installed as part of your OpenLinux system, but the source files are not installed, and Netatalk needs the source files. From the OpenLinux CD, install the RPM package that starts with the name *tcp_wrappers-devel-. tcp wrappers* are used for security to authorize valid Netatalk connections. The tcp wrappers utility intercepts all requests to connect to your Linux server, checks to see whether the user is authorized to connect, and then allows valid users while blocking unauthorized users.

After that has been installed, enter the following command:

cp /usr/include/tcpd.h /usr/local/include

This puts a copy of tcpd.h into your Netatalk source include directory.

Compile and Install Netatalk

Now change to the directory with the Netatalk source files. For example, if you untarred version 1.4b2+asun2.1.1 of netatalk into the /tmp directory, you want to change to the /tmp/netatalk-1.4b2+asun2.1.1 directory.

In your Netatalk source directory, enter the following command:

make

This compiles the program.

To install Netatalk, make sure you are still in the Netatalk source directory, and enter the following command:

make install

This installs Netatalk into the /usr/local/atalk directory.

After you have installed the program files, you'll need to set up the services configuration. Add the following lines to your /etc/services file:

```
rtmp              1/ddp            # Routing Table Maintenance Protocol
nbp               2/ddp           # Name Binding Protocol
echo              4/ddp           # AppleTalk Echo Protocol
zip               6/ddp           # Zone Information Protocol
afpovertcp        548/tcp        # AFP over TCP
afpovertcp        548/udp
```

DDP is the AppleTalk Datagram Delivery Protocol. DDP is a protocol used on AppleTalk networks so that Macintoshes can "talk" to each other. The protocol for Linux and the Internet is TCP/IP. With Netatalk, TCP/IP packets and DDP packets are translated so that Macintoshes can talk to Linux servers.

Configuring Netatalk

Next, you need to copy some configuration files. Netatalk has five configuration files:

- **AppleVolumes.default**—The directories to share, plus optional names for directories. The default name is the last part of the pathname.

- **AppleVolumes.system**—Mapping of file extensions to extensions that Mac OS understands.

- **afpd.conf**—The configuration file for the AppleTalk file system daemon.

- **atalkd.conf**—This is the "classic AppleTalk" kernel interface. It links the AppleTalk module in the kernel and the functions of Netatalk. It even takes care of AppleTalk routing between multiple network cards.

- **papd.conf**—A daemon that makes Linux print queues available through AppleTalk. If this is left empty, it makes all entries in /etc/printcap available.

Probably none of the default settings need to be changed. For details on the options that can be changed in the Netatalk configuration files, see the Netatalk documentation. For the most part, though, the defaults never need to be changed, with the exception of the mapping information. See the section on AppleVolumes.system.

To set the configuration files with the default settings, copy the configuration files included with the Netatalk source. Enter the following command:

```
cp conf/atalkd.conf /usr/local/atalk/etc/
```

This is the configuration file for atalkd.

The next configuration file to be copied is afpd.conf. Enter the following command:

```
cp config/afpd.conf /usr/local/atalk/etc.
```

Now, add the mapping configuration files. Enter the following commands:

```
cp conf/AppleVolumes.default /usr/local/atalk/etc
cp conf/AppleVolumes.system /usr/local/atalk/etc
```

You might want to make some changes in the AppleVolumes.system configuration file. For example, add the following lines:

```
#
# volumes
~          Home
/music "Some Tunes"
#
# type / creator mappings
.txt      TEXT      MSWD
```

This causes two volumes to show up: one called Home, which is the user's home directory, and one called Some Tunes, which is the directory /music. The rest of the file is a listing of "dot extensions" to type / creator mappings.

A Mac file has two parts: a data fork and a resource fork. UNIX files are only one long list of bits. Therefore, if you have the file test.txt, created in UNIX, looking at it on the Mac reveals an Unknown Document icon unless there is an entry in the type / creator section of the AppleVolumes files.

The last line in the preceding example makes a file that ends in .txt show up as a Microsoft Word (MSWD) text (TEXT) document, and launches Word when it is double-clicked. (You actually register programs with Apple to have a an official creator mapping assigned.) The default list of type/creator mappings in the AppleVolumes.system file is probably adequate unless you plan to make many files in UNIX and use them on Macs. One possible reason for using a large type/creator map is if you plan to export the same directory to Windows clients via Samba and you want Mac users to double-click PC files to open them.

Ready to Start the Server

You are now ready to test the Netatalk server. Make sure you are still in the Netatalk source directory. Then enter the following command:

```
./rc.atalk.sysv start
```

If this doesn't work, make sure that you included the ./ at the beginning of the command. After a short time, this command starts up the Classic AppleTalk fileserver (atalkd) and AppleTalk IP (afpd). The AppleTalk fileserver takes the longest to start because it checks out the network before registering itself.

If everything seems to have started up without any error messages, go to a Mac and open the Chooser, under the Apple menu on the left-hand side. Click on AppleShare, and see whether your Netatalk server shows up. For ApplshareIP, you must click the ApplshareIP button and type your machine IP or hostname.

You then see a password prompt. You can only log in to the server with a non-root account that has a valid shell and a password of eight or fewer characters. Guest access is also permitted unless it has been specifically denied in afpd.conf. If you can login, you get a list of volumes that you can select and mount.

That's all there is to it. You now have the Netatalk server installed. It automatically starts up whenever you reboot the computer. You are ready to give Macintosh users on your network access to file and print services on your OpenLinux server.

## CHAPTER 24

Installing and Configuring a Dial-In Server and Fax Server

In this chapter

How to Let Users Call into Your System

You can set up a Linux server to accept incoming calls, which is one of the most requested features on a network. The rewards are great. You can allow users of an office network to dial into the system from home or from the road to retrieve files or read email. If your network has a full-time connection to the Internet, you can even use a dial-in server to access the Internet.

You can also set up a dial-in server on your home computer so you can dial into it from the office—or anywhere else—and retrieve the files you need.

The same software package that's used for setting up a dial-in server is also designed to act as a fax server to handle incoming faxes.

The features of the dial-in and fax servers are desirable, but setting up a server can be frustrating. The problems start with the great variations between brands and models of modems, and the problems seem to continue right up to finding out why someone from your office can't successfully dial into the network.

Setting up a dial-in server will make your system operate like a miniature Internet service provider, even if you aren't providing access to the Internet. You'll have many of the same headaches that ISPs face, and you'll find out why the successful ones have big technical support staffs.

In this chapter, you won't find instructions for setting up an ISP, so if that is your goal, you'll need to look elsewhere. This chapter outlines the steps for setting up a solidly functioning dial-in server with one to four modem connections that can serve a small to medium-sized office.

Getting the Right Modem

Before you can set up a dial-in server, you must have a working modem. Any external modem should work for a dial-in data server without too many problems.

Internal modems are generally cheaper and, therefore, more common. The so-called *winmodems* are the cheapest because essential parts have been left out. Winmodems make your system's CPU do the work that the modem should be doing, and they will not work for a dial-in server. The plug-and-play modems can cause some problems because you can't ensure they will have the same settings every time the system is started. The system BIOS assigns interrupts and even the serial port of plug-and-play modems during startup, which means that the serial port might not have the same settings every time. If the settings change for any reason, the dial-in server won't work.

If you are using an internal modem, get one that is sometimes called a *legacy modem*—it will work with older Windows 3.x and DOS systems. These modems probably aren't any different in price than the internal modems designed for Windows 95 systems. All the major modem manufacturers, such as 3Com, include legacy modems in their current line, but many dealers don't carry them. Legacy modems have jumpers on them that enable you to make hard settings.

The term *jumper* is used here to describe a means of changing port or IRQ assignments on a modem. This includes using switches as well as classic jumpers: removable connector devices used on pins on the modem card to enable or disable settings. Generally, the best solution is to use an external modem. External modems have the advantage of showing a series of LEDs, the lights that give information about the connection, which can be useful when debugging problems.

For a data dial-in server that isn't being used for faxes, any Hayes-compatible modem that works on your system should be capable of handling dial-in services. For fax services, you have to be more selective in the modem you choose. The fax services described in this chapter require that you have a Class 2 or 2.0 fax modem. This is the most reliable type of fax modem available. Essentially, the difference between Class 2/2.0 and Class 1 modems is that Class 2/2.0 modems do all the work, whereas Class 1 modems make the computer's CPU do much of the work while the modem acts mostly as a pass-through device.

Part
V

Ch
24

Set Up mgetty to Answer Incoming Calls

The mgetty program is used for dial-in services and for receiving faxes. According to the documentation for the program, the following modems are known to work for fax services using mgetty on a Linux computer:

- ZyXEL U1496
- MultiTech (various models)
- SupraFax v32bis
- GVC FM144/+
- TKR DM-24VF+ (Deltafax
- Zoom V.FAST 24K/28K

Other modems will work as well. Check the mgetty web site for an up-to-date list (`www.leo.org/~doerign/mgetty/`).

The mgetty program runs in the background on your computer and waits until a call comes into the modem. It answers the phone and then handles the modem-to-modem or modem-to-fax communications. For dial-in services, a PPP connection is established, and the user can then log in to your network. Users will have access to the network in a way that emulates access from their computer on the local area network. This means that dial-in access can pose a security risk to the network. If you have set up dial-in access, make sure that you have the level of security on your system that is expected on any network that can be accessed from the Internet.

To set up mgetty, you must be logged in as root.

The first thing to do is to make sure you have mgetty installed on your system. The full name of the program is mgetty+sendfax. These are two different programs, packaged together. Sendfax is a standalone program for sending fax files.

You can check whether it is installed on your system with Kpackage. Open Kpackage (from the K Application Starter, Utilities menu) and search for mgetty. The Kpackage Properties shows the package name as mgetty. The version that's installed with OpenLinux 2.2 is 1.1.8. You can click on the File List tab to see all the files that are included with mgetty+sendfax.

N O T E The package name is *mgetty*, and the program is *mgetty+sendfax*. It's a little confusing, I know. ■

You can also open a terminal window and enter the following command:

```
rpm -q mgetty
```

If Kpackage can't find mgetty, or you receive a response that says, `package mgetty is not installed`, you must install it from the OpenLinux CD.

To install the mgetty package, insert the OpenLinux CD and mount it:

```
mount /mnt/cdrom
```

Use the K File Manager (click on the home folder on the K Panel to access the File Manager) and use the arrow buttons to change to the Packages folder on the disk:

```
/mnt/cdrom/Packages/RPMS
```

In the packages folder, find the file with a name that begins with *mgetty*. On the OpenLinux 2.2 disk included with this book, the filename is mgetty-1.1.8.Jul27-2.i386.rpm. Click on the file's icon and the Kpackage installer automatically opens. Click the Install button to complete the installation.

After mgetty is installed, the next step is to configure the program. The following instructions describe how to set up mgetty for dial-in to a single modem. If you have more than one modem, the setup is the same for each additional modem, but you will have to make the changes necessary to reflect the different serial ports for each of the other modems.

The mgetty configuration file is in the mgetty+sendfax subdirectory in the /etc directory. Open the file mgetty.config in a text editor.

In the configuration file, find the port specific section. Here, you'll define your modem's serial port. The Linux serial ports are ttyS0, ttyS1, ttyS2, and ttyS3, which correspond to COM1, COM2, COM3, and COM4 on Windows systems.

Add a section for the serial port you are using for dial-in. This example uses the setting for ttyS1, which is the port most frequently used for modem communications. However, if that is not what you are using, change it to the port you are using by entering the following command:

```
port ttyS1
init-chat "" AT&F&C1&D2
speed 115200
```

This sets up the modem speed and the initialization string for the modem. Check the modem documentation for the correct initialization string for your modem. The port speed of 115,200bps is the standard speed setting for a v.90 or 56K modem.

You can change many other options in mgetty.config, but none of them are necessary for most dial-in servers. The mgetty documentation lists all the different configuration parameters that can be changed or added here.

Part
V
Ch
24

The next step is to enable AutoPPP. Close the mgetty.config file and open the login.config file. Find the line with /AutoPPP/ in it and delete the pound sign (#) at the beginning of the line. This uncomments the line, meaning that the configuration setting will be used. Edit the line so that it reads as follows:

```
/AutoPPP/ - @ /usr/sbin/pppd +pap login
```

Here's what this line means:

- **/AutoPPP/**—Enables AutoPPP
- **-**—Indicates that no user ID is set on the call
- **@**—Displays the caller's username with all "who" queries
- **/usr/sbin/pppd +pap**—Starts a PPP session with the Password Authentication Protocol (+pap) for logins
- **login**—Forces the use of the system password file for all PAP authentication

That's all that mgetty configuration requires. The next step is to tell mgetty what port to monitor. This is handled in the inittab file in the /etc directory. Open inittab in a text editor and add the following line:

```
S1:2345:respawn:/usr/sbin/mgetty ttyS1
```

This sets up mgetty to monitor port S1 (ttyS1). If your port is different, put the proper port number at the beginning of the line.

After this, you need to force initd to reread inittab to see the changes. Enter the following command:

```
/sbin/init q
```

This starts mgetty, and your system is now ready to accept incoming PAP authenticated PPP connections through /dev/ttyS1. PAP needs two things: a name and a "secret" password. The name is the user's login name. The user's password is the "secret" needed by PAP.

Windows 95/98 users can now dial in to your system using their login name and password.

Blocking Incoming Calls

You can prevent mgetty from accepting calls. Create an empty file in the /etc directory called nologin.ttyS1. If your modem is on a different port, change S1 to the port you are using. If mgetty detects an incoming call and sees this file, it will not answer the phone.

This can be useful any time you want to block incoming calls. For example, if you don't want calls to come in while you are doing maintenance on the system, you can simply add this file when you start, and delete it when you are finished. This has an added advantage, because if the call is never answered, the caller isn't charged for the connection.

You can write a script to run on a schedule, where cron puts this file into the /etc directory during certain hours or on certain days. This way, the file can be put into place during the day so a phone line can be used to accept voice calls; but at night, the file can be removed so that mgetty will answer incoming calls.

cron is a system for scheduling tasks. To create a schedule to block daytime-only modem access, create the file nologin.ttyS1.backup in the /etc directory:

```
touch /etc/nologin.ttyS1.backup
```

This creates a backup file that will be copied for the working file.

Then, open crontab in a terminal window using the following command:

```
crontab -e
```

Then add the following lines:

```
0 9 * * 1-5 /bin/cp /etc/nologin.ttyS1.backup /etc/nologin.ttyS1
0 17 * * 1-5 /bin/rm /etc/nologin.ttyS1
```

Save the file. The first line indicates that at 9 a.m. on Monday through Friday (1-5). The nologin.ttyS1 is put into place so that no modem logins will be accepted, thus freeing up the phone line for voice calls. The second line indicates that at 5 p.m. (17) the nologin.ttyS1 file is deleted, thus enabling acceptance of modem calls.

Using mgetty to Receive Faxes

You can also configure mgetty to accept incoming faxes. An mgetty fax server must be on a separate computer from a dial-in data server. mgetty will accept the faxes in the raw "G3" fax format. *G3* stands for *Group 3*, the CCITT standard for encoding images for fax transmission.

When you've received a fax, you'll need other programs to view or print the faxes. You can do this with the K Fax Viewer, which is part of the KDE desktop system on OpenLinux.

The setup of mgetty is similar. Edit the mgetty.config file in the mgetty+sendfax subdirectory in the /etc directory.

Go to the port specific section and define your fax modem's serial port. This example uses the setting for ttyS2, but if that is not what you are using, change it to the port that is in use:

```
port ttyS1
init-chat "" AT&F&C1&D2
speed 19200
modem-type cls2
```

This sets up the modem speed and the initialization string for the modem. Check the modem documentation for the correct initialization string for your particular modem. Typically, fax modems that are used on servers are slower than data modems because fax machines cannot use faster transfer rates. The slower fax modems will give you full service, but they are usually cheaper and have proven reliability. The port speed of 19,200bps is the standard speed setting for a fax modem. The modem class type options are

- **auto**—mgetty will detect the modem type (not desirable if you want to make sure that only fax calls are accepted).
- **c2.0**—Modem uses Class 2.0 fax mode. If your modem supports both Class 2 and 2.0, use this setting to force the modem to use 2.0. Class 2.0 works better because it has better standardization.
- **cls2**—Modem uses Class 2 fax mode; mgetty won't try class 2.0.

The next step is to tell mgetty what port to monitor. This is handled in the inittab file in the /etc directory. Open inittab in a text editor and add the following line:

```
S1:2345:respawn:/usr/sbin/mgetty ttyS1
```

This enables mgetty to monitor port S1 (ttyS1). If your port is different, put the proper port number at the beginning of the line.

After this, you need to force initd to reread inittab to see the changes. Enter the following command:

```
/sbin/init q
```

Faxes will be received and placed in the /var/spool/fax/incoming directory. You can view them with the K Fax Viewer, found under Graphics on the K Application Launcher.

The K Fax Viewer can do more than just view faxes. You can also use it to print faxes if you have a printer connected to your computer or if you have set up printing to a printer on a network.

The beauty of the K Fax Viewer is that it automatically converts fax G3 images from the many possible variations into a format that can be read and printed from your computer.

The raw fax files can be in different heights, widths, and resolutions. The K Fax Viewer can autodetect and correct all these variations, or you can manually adjust the settings.

The *GIMP* (*graphics image manipulation program*), which is installed as part of the standard OpenLinux, can also read fax G3 format files. You can open the fax files in GIMP and convert them into other formats for printing, or into a gif or jpeg format for use on Web pages or as email attachments. For more information on using GIMP, see Chapter 18, "Configuring and Running GIMP."

Using Sendfax

Sendfax is a basic fax sending program that is included with mgetty. It will send a single fax file of multiple pages to one fax number.

The first step is to create a file to fax. The fax file must end up in G3 format so that you can send it. The easiest way to do this is to use the GhostScript conversion tools. First, you must save the file in PostScript format. You can use WordPerfect to do this. WordPerfect can read most file formats, and it can save to a PostScript format.

After a file is in PostScript format, you must convert it to G3. GhostScript will do this. A typical command for using GhostScript to convert PostScript to G3 looks like this:

```
gs -sDEVICE=dfaxhigh -sOutputFile=/tmp/fax.g3.%d yourdocument.ps
```

This runs the GhostScript utility (gs) and converts the PostScript file named yourdocument.ps into a G3 document named fax.g3.

If you want to fax a graphic, open the file in GIMP and convert it to fax G3 format.

After you have created the file and converted it to G3 format, you are ready to send the fax. The command to send a fax follows:

```
sendfax -v -n phone_number fax_file
```

Watch closely the first few times you send a fax this way. If problems arise, it will lock up your modem so that you can't use it without rebooting the system.

After everything is set up, you should be able to start regularly sending faxes from your computer.

Installing and Configuring a Firewall

A Firewall Server for a High Level of Security

Firewalls have become popular as a frontline of defense against computer break-ins. Although nothing is foolproof, firewalls give a network a high level of security.

A firewall protects your network when it is connected to the Internet. A firewall device sits between your network and the Internet so that users on your network can get out, but intruders can't get in.

The term *firewall* comes from the construction industry. When apartment houses or offices are built, they are constructed with special walls that are resistant to fire. If a fire starts in one portion of the building, the firewall stops or slows the expansion of the fire into other parts of the building.

A network firewall stands in the way of an outside intruder. When you have an open connection to the Internet, that connection *out* means that there is also a way *into* the system. A firewall computer blocks the incoming connection and prevents it from "spreading" into the network.

The two primary approaches used to build firewalls today are *packet filtering* and *proxy servers*. Packet filtering systems allow or block connections based on the security policy defined for the system. Proxy servers sit, more or less transparently, between a user on a local area network and the Internet. Instead of talking to each other directly, each talks to a proxy. The proxy then allows or denies the connection.

A firewall server can serve multiple purposes. In fact, it is possible to set up a firewall server that is an Internet gateway, a network Name Server, and a firewall all rolled into one. The most secure firewall, however, is set up as a separate server that has what you can consider a DMZ between the firewall and the internal network. In the DMZ are servers that need to be reachable from the Internet such as Web servers and mail servers, which don't have critical files on them.

This chapter describes a packet filtering firewall for a small or home office. It can even be adapted to a medium-sized office, but it is not adequate for a complex network.

This firewall is based on the following design:

■ You have an Internet connection through a router. This can be an ISDN, DSL, cable modem, frame-relay, T1, or some other kind of connection through a router that is set up and maintained by your Internet service provider. This can also be a dial-up modem connection, although this chapter won't cover that setup.

■ A firewall server will be set up between the router and your local area network.

The equipment involved in this setup includes

- A working local area network connected through an Ethernet hub.
- A Linux computer with two Ethernet network cards. One is connected to the local area network by a cable going to the hub. The other is connected to the router by cable.
- A router connected to the Internet.

This is the basic setup for our firewall server (as shown in Figure 25.1). It will meet the needs of most small and some medium-sized networks. One variation on this configuration places servers that you need for public access outside the firewall.

FIGURE 25.1

Diagram of network with a firewall server.

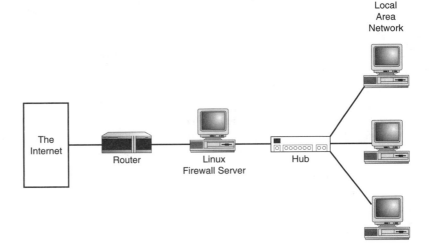

Outside the firewall, you might have a Web server and your mail server. These are servers to which you want to be able to connect from outside your local area network. You need to secure these servers on their own. They should not have sensitive files on them, and they should not be the company database or anything else that you want to protect. On the mail server, you can ensure a higher level of security by using encryption for email transmissions.

Such a network would look similar to the chart in Figure 25.2.

This adds the following equipment:

- A Web server
- A mail server
- An additional hub

This chapter deals with configuring the firewall server, which can be used for either type of network, and with configuring the computers on the local area network so they can connect to the Internet through the firewall server.

Part
V

Ch
25

FIGURE 25.2

Diagram of network with a firewall and Web and mail servers.

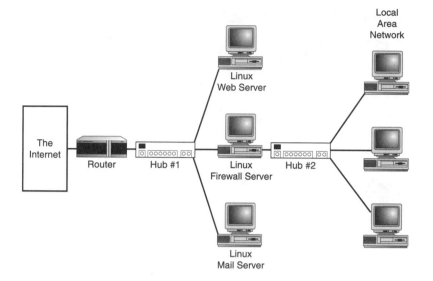

You do not need a fancy computer to set up a firewall server. The minimum computer required by OpenLinux 2.2 will work fine. Following is a list of the minimum hardware you need:

- A Pentium-compatible CPU
- 32MB of RAM
- 3.5-inch floppy drive
- CD-ROM drive
- 1GB hard drive
- A mouse (three-button mouse recommended) and a 4MB video card (8MB recommended)
- SVGA monitor
- Two Ethernet cards

First, install OpenLinux on the firewall server and make sure that it is working correctly.

Next, take these four steps for setting up the server:

1. Modify the OpenLinux kernel to enable IP forwarding and IP masquerading.
2. Configure IP forwarding and IP masquerading.
3. Configure the Ethernet cards in the firewall server.
4. Secure the firewall server.

The firewall server is ready to run. The final step is setting up the computers on the local network to connect through the firewall.

Step 1: Modify the OpenLinux Kernel to Enable IP Forwarding and IP Masquerading

The OpenLinux firewall server uses *IP forwarding* and *IP masquerading*. These are powerful software tools that allow a Linux server to operate like commercial firewalls and network routers. IP forwarding monitors network traffic and forwards packets or blocks them based on security rules that you define. IP masquerading, also known as address hiding, conceals the IP addresses of computers on the internal network when they are connecting to the Internet.

When a computer behind the Linux firewall accesses the Internet, it can operate as if it were directly connected to the Internet. It will appear to be a fully qualified Internet host, even though it does not have an official IP address.

This can be done because the Linux firewall server is a fully qualified host on the Internet. When a user connects to the Internet through the Linux firewall server, the firewall computer translates the requests from the local computer and sends them out to the Internet. The firewall server translates the replies and returns them to the computer on the local network.

Following is an example of what happens on your local area network when someone accesses the Web. In this example, the computer on your local network is named my_computer, and it has an internal network IP address of 192.168.1.25. This is one of the private network IP addresses that is not valid on the Internet, so any request coming from a computer with this IP address is rejected as invalid.

The firewall server is named Linux. It has a valid IP address. For this example, its IP address is 123.456.789.000.

1. Netscape is started on my_computer, and a request is made to read
   http://www.cnn.com (see Figure 25.3).
2. The request is checked with the DNS server. The DNS server returns the information that www.cnn.com is IP address 207.25.71.6 (see Figure 25.4).
3. Netscape proceeds to request a connection using that IP address (see Figure 25.5).
4. The request is passed through the firewall computer. When the firewall server sees the request, the network packets carrying the request are rewritten so that instead of coming from a computer with the IP address of 192.168.1.25, they appear to be coming from the firewall computer, which has a valid IP address (see Figure 25.6).

FIGURE 25.3
Step 1.

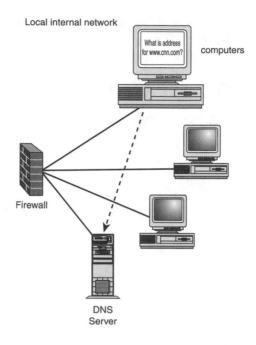

Local internal network

What is address for www.cnn.com?

computers

Firewall

DNS Server

FIGURE 25.4
Step 2.

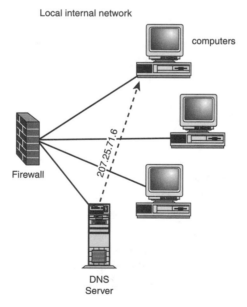

Local internal network

computers

207.25.71.6

Firewall

DNS Server

FIGURE 25.5
Step 3.

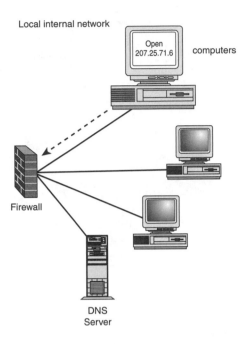

Local internal network

Open
207.25.71.6

computers

Firewall

DNS
Server

FIGURE 25.6
Step 4.

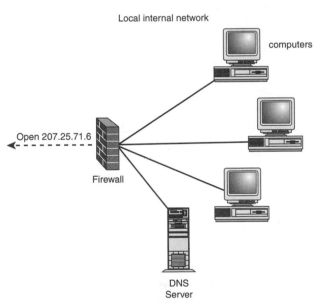

Local internal network

computers

Open 207.25.71.6

Firewall

DNS
Server

5. When the server at www.cnn.com sees the request, it sees that it is coming from a computer with the IP address of 123.456.789.000. It sees that the request is valid, and returns the requested Web page (see Figure 25.7).

FIGURE 25.7
Step 5.

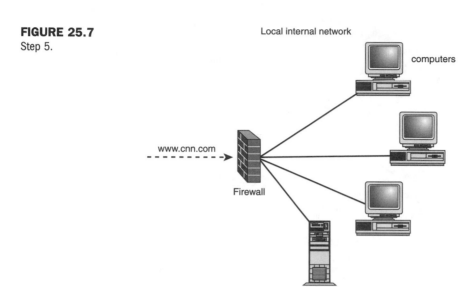

6. When the packets carrying the Web page from www.cnn.com return, they go back to the IP address of the firewall server. The firewall server receives the packets and sees that they are really intended for my_computer. The firewall computer translates the packets and passes them on to my_computer (see Figure 25.8).

FIGURE 25.8
Step 6.

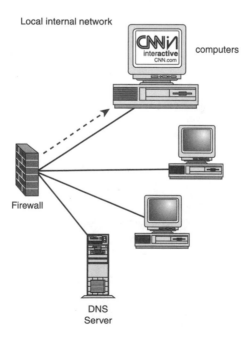

In this way, the computer on the local network has full access to the Internet without any computer on the Internet having access past the firewall server.

Building a New Firewall Kernel

The firewall functions are not built into the standard OpenLinux kernel. The only way to use OpenLinux for a firewall server is to rebuild the kernel so that it supports IP forwarding, IP chains, IP masquerading, IP firewalling, and all the other kernel modules used for this task.

Therefore, you must follow these steps to build a new firewall kernel:

1. Install the kernel sources from the OpenLinux installation CD. You need to add the following packages:

   - linux-source-common
   - linux-source-i386
   - glibc-devel
   - ncurses-devel

N O T E All the packages are included with this book's OpenLinux CD. Insert the disk into the CD drive and mount it. To mount the CD, open a terminal window and enter the following command:

`mount /mnt/cdrom`

Then open the K File Manager by clicking on the home folder on the K Panel. Use the arrow buttons to change to the /mnt/cdrom/Packages/RPMS directory. Find each of the RPM packages (the files with the names that begin with the names listed previously) and click the file icon. This opens the Kpackage utility. Click Install to complete the installation. ■

2. Configure the kernel. Change to the kernel source directory:

   `cd /usr/src/linux`

3. You have three different ways to start the kernel configuration program:

   - `make config`
   - `make menuconfig`
   - `make xconfig`

   The third option has a graphical interface and offers the most flexibility.

4. Many questions need to be answered for kernel configuration. Following are the options that must be included to enable all the firewall features. This list does not cover all the other options that must be included in order to have a functioning OpenLinux system; you must also include all the configuration options needed for your server's hardware and the installed network interfaces.

Part
V

Ch
25

Code Maturity Level Options

Prompt for development and/or incomplete code/drivers Yes. This allows the kernel to create the firewall modules and enable the option for port forwarding.

Loadable Module Support

Enable loadable module support Yes. This enables you to load modules such as network card device drivers and the firewall modules.

General Setup

Networking support Yes. This enables support for networking in the kernel.

Networking Options

Packet socket Yes. This enables you to use TCPDUMP to debug any problems. This is optional.

Kernel/User netlink socket Yes. This allows logging of firewall hits. This is optional.

Routing messages No. This has nothing to do with a network firewall.

Network firewalls Yes. This enables packet filtering with IP chains and is required for IP masquerading.

TCP/IP networking Yes. This enables the Internet's TCP/IP protocol.

IP: multicasting No. This is not used for a firewall.

IP: advanced router No. This is not needed for IP chains or IP masquerading.

IP: firewalling Yes. This *is* a firewall computer, after all!

IP: firewall packet netlink device Yes. This is useful for monitoring attacks on the firewall. This is optional.

IP: always defragment (required for masquerading) Yes. IP Masquerading does not work without this.

IP: masquerading Yes. This enables IP Masquerading.

IP: ICMP masquerading Yes. This masquerading is for TCP and UDP packets. This adds support for ICMP packets such as ping or the Windows 95 tracert program.

IP: masquerading special modules support Yes. This enables the option for later enabling external computers to connect to specified internal machines. This is an optional setting.

IP: ipautofw masq support (EXPERIMENTAL) No. ipautofw is a workaround to allow masquerading of protocols that are not yet supported by IP masquerading. Don't use it on a working firewall server.

IP: ipportfw masq support (EXPERIMENTAL) No. Port Forwarding is an addition to IP masquerading that is used to run a Web server behind the firewall computer. The code to support this is still under development.

IP: ip fwmark masq-forwarding support (EXPERIMENTAL) No. This enables you to specify different routes for packets with different firewalling mark (fwmark) values directly from IP chains. This is also under development, and is still experimental.

IP: optimize as router not host Yes. This optimizes the kernel for packet forwarding by turning off copy and checksum.

IP: GRE tunnels over IP No. *Tunneling* means encapsulating the data of one protocol type within another protocol and sending it over a channel that understands the encapsulating protocol. This tunnel driver implements Generic Routing Encapsulation. This is an optional setting.

IP: aliasing support No. This is not needed for a firewall computer.

IP: TCP syncookie support (not enabled per default) Yes. This provides protection against a denial-of-service attack known as *SYN flooding*.

Network Device Support

Network device support Yes. This must be enabled. This is the network sublayer.

Dummy net driver support Yes. This is a bit bucket device (traffic you send to this device goes into oblivion) that can also be used for debugging. It often comes in handy and won't enlarge the kernel.

File Systems

/proc filesystem support Yes. This is required to enable the Linux network forwarding system.

Show configuration as /proc/config No. This is being dropped from future releases of Linux.

> **N O T E** These are the options needed for the firewall server. Just make sure that all the other necessary options for your system are also selected. ■

Compiling and Installing the Kernel

After the kernel has been configured, it must be compiled. Use the following command to check on dependencies and make sure they are in place:

```
make dep
```

It's a good idea to run the following command next:

```
make clean
```

Then compile the kernel as follows:

```
make zImage
```

If make zImage ends without any error messages, you are ready to install the kernel. Give it a name that identifies it as being optimized for a firewall. A common choice in this case is to add masq to the standard name. Copy the new kernel to the /boot directory:

```
cp /usr/src/linux/arch/i386/boot/zImage /boot/vmlinuz-2.2.5-masq
```

Next, compile the modules. Preserve the working modules as follows:

```
mv /lib/modules/2.2.5 /lib/modules/2.2.5-current
```

Now compile the modules. Enter the following command:

```
make modules
```

If at the end there are no errors, the next step is

```
make modules_install
```

Now the modules have to be put in a directory that matches the name of the kernel so that the kernel can find them on startup. To do this, use the following example (this is only an example—make sure to use the proper filenames that you have on your system):

```
mv /lib/modules/2.2.5 /lib/modules/2.2.5-masq
mv /lib/modules/2.2.5-current /lib/modules/2.2.5
```

Now the new kernel and modules are installed. The last step starts with configuring LILO. Add an entry for the new kernel. Following is a sample configuration file, but yours probably looks different:

```
# general section
#
boot = /dev/hda1
install = /boot/boot.b
message = /boot/message
prompt

# wait 5 seconds (50 10ths) for user to select the entry to load
timeout = 50

#
# default entry
#

image = /boot/vmlinuz-2.2.5-masq
        label = linux
```

```
        root = /dev/hda1
        read-only

#

image = /boot/vmlinuz-2.2.5
        label = oldlinux
        root = /dev/hda1
        read-only
```

Test the new kernel by shutting down and rebooting the computer. When the computer comes back up, you can finish the configuration of the new modules. Change to the directory:

```
cd /etc/modules/2.2.5
```

This directory name needs to match the kernel version, so if your kernel version is not 2.2.5, put in the correct number. If you started out with version 2.2.5 and built a new kernel that is version 2.2.6, copy the 2.2.5 directory as follows:

```
cp -R /etc/modules/2.2.5 /etc/modules/2.2.6
```

This copies the file that lists the modules to be loaded on startup. If you installed OpenLinux with Lizard, you'll find the .default, .rootfs, default, and rootfs files in this directory. If you installed using LISA, you'll also find a file that starts with a timestamp and ends with .config.

In the /etc/modules/2.2.5 directory (or whatever version you are working with) are the files for loading modules on startup. When OpenLinux starts, it first looks for the timestamp file, and then for the hidden file named .default, and finally for the default file. So all you really need are the default and rootfs files. You can delete the two hidden files and the timestamp files if you want.

In the default file is a list of all the modules to load at boot time. If you have a module that needs to be loaded at boot, you can add it to the list. You have to put in the exact name, without the .o extension.

Some driver modules have settings that need to be passed when they are loaded. Do this by creating a file in the /etc/modules/options/ directory. The name of the file must match the name of the module, without the .o.

You are now finished building the new kernel.

Autostart the Firewall

Add a line to your startup script so that the firewall software starts every time you reboot.

Open the rc.local file in the /etc/rc.d directory and add the following two lines:

```
#rc.firewall script to start the firewall
/etc/rc.d/rc.firewall
```

Part

V

Ch

25

Step 2: Configure IP Forwarding and IP Masquerading

To start IP masquerading, you have to set a policy for the firewall's forwarding function. IP chains are used to turn on IP masquerading for the computers on the local network. The rc.firewall startup script is used to set the policies.

The startup script with the policies needs to be created. Use a text editor and create a file in the /etc/rc.d directory and name it rc.firewall. The following example, adapted from the *Linux IP Masquerade Mini How-To*, sets up the minimum necessary firewall policies (for stronger, more secure firewall policies, you need to consult the IP Masquerade and IP Chains documentation):

```
#!/bin/sh
#
# rc.firewall - Sets up minimum firewall policies using IP
Masquerade and IPCHAINS
#
# Load all required IP MASQ modules
#
# NOTE:  Only load the IP MASQ modules you need.  All current IP MASQ modules
#          are shown below but are commented out from loading.
# Needed to initially load modules
#
/sbin/depmod -a
# Supports the proper masquerading of FTP file transfers using the PORT method
#
/sbin/modprobe ip_masq_ftp
#
# Supports the masquerading of RealAudio over UDP.  Without this module,
#       RealAudio WILL function but in TCP mode.  This can cause a reduction
#       in sound quality
#
#/sbin/modprobe ip_masq_raudio
#
# Supports the masquerading of IRC DCC file transfers
#
#/sbin/modprobe ip_masq_irc
#
# Supports the masquerading of Quake and QuakeWorld by default.
This modules is
#   for multiple users behind the Linux MASQ server.  If you are going to play
#   Quake II and/or Quake I/II on other server ports, use the second example.
#
# Quake I / QuakeWorld (ports 26000 and 27000)
#/sbin/modprobe ip_masq_quake
#
# Quake I / QuakeWorld / and Quake II (ports 26000, 27000, 27910)
#/sbin/modprobe ports=ip_masq_quake 26000,27000,27910
#
```

```
# Supports the masquerading of the CuSeeme video conferencing software
#
#/sbin/modprobe ip_masq_cuseeme
#
#Supports the masquerading of the VDO-live video conferencing software
#
#/sbin/modprobe ip_masq_vdolive
#
#CRITICAL:  Enable IP forwarding since it is disabled by default since
#
#
#
echo "1" > /proc/sys/net/ipv4/ip_forward
#
# Dynamic IP users:
#
#   If you get your IP address dynamically from SLIP, PPP, or DHCP,
enable this following
#       option.  This enables dynamic-ip address hacking in IP MASQ,
 making the life
#       with Diald and similar programs much easier.
#
#echo "1" > /proc/sys/net/ipv4/ip_dynaddr
#
# MASQ timeouts
#
#   2 hrs timeout for TCP session timeouts
#  10 sec timeout for traffic after the TCP/IP "FIN" packet is received
#  60 sec timeout for UDP traffic (MASQ'ed ICQ users must enable a 30sec
 firewall timeout in ICQ itself)
#
ipchains -M -S 7200 10 60
#
# Enable simple IP forwarding and Masquerading
#
#  NOTE:  The following is an example for an internal
LAN address in the 192.168.0.x
#         network with a 255.255.255.0 or a "24" bit subnet mask.
#
#         Please change this network number and subnet mask to match
your internal LAN setup
#
ipchains -P forward DENY
ipchains -A forward -s 192.168.0.0/24 -j MASQ
#
# DHCP:  For people who receive their external IP address from
either DHCP or BOOTP
#         such as ADSL or Cablemodem users, it is necessary to use
the following
#         before the deny command.  The "bootp_client_net_if_name"
should be replaced
#         the name of the link that the DHCP/BOOTP server will
put an address on to?
```

```
#           This will be something like "eth0", "eth1", etc.
#
#           This example is currently commented out.
#
#
#ipchains -A input -j ACCEPT -w bootp_clients_net_if_name
-s 0/0 68 -d 0/0 67 -p udp
#
#
```

The script needs to be made executable. Enter the following command:

chmod 700 /etc/rc.d/rc.firewall

That's all there is to it. This gives you basic firewall protection. The firewall policies can be finely tuned so that individual policies are set for each individual computer on the network, allowing full access to some, limited access to others, and denying access to the rest.

Step 3:. Configure the Ethernet Cards in the Firewall Server

The firewall server has two Ethernet cards. The server uses the two cards to act as a bridge between the internal network and the external Internet.

Use COAS to configure your two Ethernet cards. One will have a private IP address that is from the subnet of your local area network. The usual practice is to use an address block in one of the 192.168.*.* subnets. For the examples used here, the local network subnet is in the 192.168.1.0 to 192.168.1.255 range. The gateway machine is usually the first address on the network, so the firewall server—which is also the gateway machine—has the IP address of 192.168.1.1.

In the Ethernet configuration in COAS, this is set up with the following parameters:

```
Device=eth0
IP address=192.168.1.1
Netmask=255.255.255.0
Broadcast address=192.168.1.255
```

Then the second Ethernet card needs to be configured. It has the IP address that your ISP has assigned it. The settings for the second adapter might look like this (with a different IP address, of course):

```
Device=eth1
IP address=123.456.789.000
Netmask=255.255.255.0
Broadcast address=123.456.789.255
```

Then you'll need to edit the network configuration file in the /etc/sysconfig directory. This enables forwarding and defines the gateway device. Add these lines to the /etc/sysconfig/network file (using your real IP address):

```
FORWARD_IPV4=true
GATEWAY=123.456.789.000
GATEWAYDEV=eth1
```

Step 4: Secure the Firewall Server

The firewall server needs all the standard security measures that are implemented on any computer on the Internet. Take special care with this because the firewall server is the most vulnerable computer on your network.

A good place to start is in Chapter 29, "Overview of Network Security."

Configuring the Computers on the Local Network

The computers on the local network all need to be configured to use the firewall server so that they can connect to the Internet.

Each computer on the local network needs to be set up with the TCP/IP network protocol. Each needs to be given a private network IP address, all within the same subnet. Be sure to include the DNS server information for your network. This can be the same DNS server the firewall machine is using. Then make the firewall server the gateway address.

To configure a Windows 95/98 computer, follow these instructions:

1. In the Control Panel, open the Network icon.
2. Select TCP/IP and click the Properties button.
3. On the IP Address tab, enter the IP address for the computer and the Subnet Mask, which is 255.255.255.0.
4. Select the Gateway tab. Add the IP address of the firewall server as the gateway. Be sure to click the Add button.
5. Select the DNS tab and enter a computer name. Because the computers don't have an official IP address, they are not part of an official domain. Avoid possible confusion that can be caused by putting a real domain name here. Put in something descriptive, such as **office**, which isn't a domain at all. It will be safe and won't cause any problems. Therefore, if you name the computer mary and put office as the domain, the full name of the computer is mary.office.
6. Click on OK and restart the computer.

Your computer is now capable of connecting to the Internet through the firewall server.

Part
V

Ch
25

## CHAPTER 26

Installing and Configuring the Apache Web Server

Apache, the Top Web Server in the World

If your company wants to be on the Internet, you have many alternatives. One of them is to operate your own Web server. Apache is the number one Web server software in the world—more than 57% of the Internet's Web servers use Apache to serve up their Web pages according to the Netcraft survey of Web servers (www.netcraft.com/survey/). These include many of the most active Web sites. The next closest Web server software is Microsoft's Internet Server, which is running on about 23% of the Web's servers.

Apache is the Web server software that IBM includes with many of the Web servers it sells, and it's included with every copy of OpenLinux. Like Linux, Apache is a free, open-source system.

The name comes from *A Patchy Server*. Apache was originally a series of patch files for the NCSA Web server software, one of the original Web server packages. The National Center for Supercomputer Applications was also where Mosaic, the first Web browser, was built.

Apache is included in almost every Linux distribution, and it is installed automatically with OpenLinux. The Web server is already running on your computer, and it is ready for use. If you want to see it, you can connect to it by opening a Web browser on any computer on your local network and entering the IP address of the computer running OpenLinux. Figure 26.1 shows the default Web page that is installed with the OpenLinux 2.2 Apache server.

FIGURE 26.1
The default home page on the Apache server running on OpenLinux 2.2.

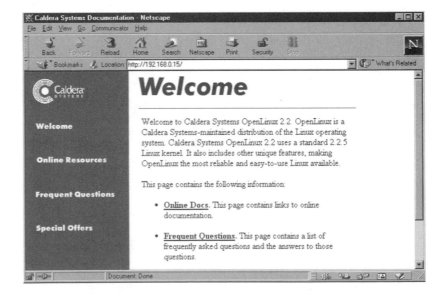

Apache is known for its reliability, performance, and complete set of features. Apache's features and strengths are really too numerous to list. Its domination on the World Wide Web should probably be enough to convince you to at least give it a try.

Apache isn't necessarily the server of choice for everyone. The version included with OpenLinux is suitable for setting up an information server, but it should not be used for setting up an E-commerce Web site.

Most Web sites are set up to be information servers: They are designed to provide information that a company, an organization, or an individual hopes will be widely read. There is no need for a higher level of security when transferring this type of Web page than that which is part of Apache.

Web sites that need to handle credit card transactions are another matter. The credit card number is transmitted across the Internet from the browser to the server. Anything transmitted across the Internet can, in theory, be intercepted by crackers using sophisticated tools. (This is not something that is casually done, and few Web transmissions are ever actually intercepted by unauthorized parties.)

Secure transactions involve using encryption so that even if someone intercepts the data they cannot decode it. The most common way to secure transactions is with the *SSL* protocol. *SSL* stands for *Secure Socket Layer*. It's a protocol developed by Netscape that uses a form of public key encryption. The Web browser uses a publicly available key to encrypt the data before sending it across the Internet. Only someone who has the private key can decode the resulting data.

Apache can handle SSL, but U.S. government security laws prevent the company from including the technology to do it with any shipping package. You *can* add SSL to your Apache server, but it requires some programming skills. Check the Apache home page (shown in Figure 26.2) at `www.apache.org` for links and information on adding SSL to your Apache Web server.

Part

V

Ch

26

Apache's only real downside is that it doesn't have any easy-to-use maintenance tools that have a Windows-based interface, or tools that can be accessed through a Web browser. Setup and maintenance of the server have to be done with command-line scripting tools. These tools, however, are not difficult to learn and use. They just can't be very difficult if millions of Web sites are using Apache!

An Apache project is working to develop a Web-based interface for maintaining an Apache server. One Web-based interface that's at a beta level of development is named Comanche, the Configuration Manager for Apache. The Comanche home page is at `comanche.com.dtu.dk/comanche/`. Also, the Apache GUI Project Web site at `gui.apache.org` has a complete list of all related developments.

FIGURE 26.2
Check out the Apache Web site for updates and complete information on running a Web server.

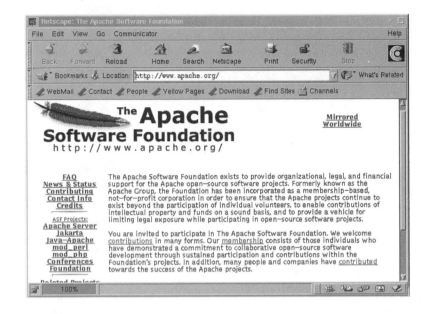

A graphical configuration tool that can be used now for Apache administration is Webmin. Webmin is a Web-based interface for system administration for Linux that can be used to set up user accounts, Apache, DNS, file sharing, and more. You can find Webmin on the Internet at www.webmin.com. Webmin is a good program and is useful for more than just administering a Web server. I use it on my own servers.

There are also two commercial programs for Apache administration and configuration: Stonghold can be found at www.c2.net/products/sh2/ and the Macintosh-only WebTen at www.tenon.com/products/webten/.

Configuring Apache

Apache's default configuration is a good starting point. Just make a few changes, and your Web server is ready to run.

The default directories for the Apache Web server are the following:

- **/home/httpd/cgi-bin**—This is the directory for CGI scripts and programs. The *Common Gateway Interface (CGI)* is the standard for communicating between HTTP (Web) servers and programs running on the server. Most gateway programs are scripts written in languages such as perl, although they can be compiled programs written in languages such as C++. This is how most of the sophisticated effects are done on the Web.

- **/home/httpd/html**—This is the directory for all the Web pages. The file named index.html in this directory is the Web page that automatically comes up if no other Web page is specified. This directory and any subdirectories are the parts of the server that are accessible to anyone connecting with a Web browser.
- **/var/log/httpd/apache/error_log**—This is a log file for errors.
- **/var/log/httpd/apache/access_log**—This is a log file for access to the Web server. Each file transfer is logged to this file.
- **/etc/httpd/apache/conf/**—This directory holds the Apache configuration files.

Apache is configured using three primary configuration files:

- **httpd.conf**—Basic system setup.
- **srm.conf**—Keeps track of where the Web server documents are located.
- **access.conf**—Who, what, when, and where access is allowed.

The following section covers some of the settings that you need to check before connecting your Apache Web server to the Internet.

Basic Server Configuration

The httpd.conf file sets the name of the server, the port under which it runs, where to find the other configuration files, and more.

Use a text editor to open the file httpd.conf in the /etc/httpd/apache/conf/ directory. The configuration file is structured with comments, followed by the actual configuration entries. The comments are preceded by a pound sign (#) and explain each configuration entry. Following is a sample of the first few entries in the default configuration file:

```
# This is the main server configuration file. See URL http://www.apache.org/
# for instructions.

# Do NOT simply read the instructions in here without understanding
# what they do, if you are unsure consult the online docs. You have been
# warned.

# Originally by Rob McCool

# Dynamic Shared Object (DSO) Support
#
# To be able to use the functionality of a module which was built as a DSO you
# have to place corresponding `LoadModule' lines at this location so the
# directives contained in it are actually available _before_ they are used.
# Please read the file README.DSO in the Apache 1.3 distribution for more
# details about the DSO mechanism and run `httpd -l' for the list of already
# built-in (statically linked and thus always available) modules in your httpd
# binary.
#
```

```
# Example:
# LoadModule foo_module libexec/mod_foo.so

# ServerType is either inetd, or standalone.

ServerType standalone

# If you are running from inetd, go to "ServerAdmin".

# Port: The port the standalone listens to. For ports < 1023, you will
# need httpd to be run as root initially.

Port 80
.
.
.
```

The following sections explain some of the configuration parameters.

CacheNegotiatedDocs

Proxy servers cache documents that are frequently requested on local networks. This results in less waiting for the user. The default setting for Apache asks proxy servers not to cache the documents they download. Uncommenting this option turns off this feature. To uncomment a line, delete the hash mark (#) at the beginning of the line.

ErrorLog

This is the name of the file into which Apache logs errors. The error log has a line for every time an error occurs when a Web browser tries to access a file on the server. The error log indicates the file requested and the error response.

Group

This indicates the user group for Apache. The default group is the nobody group, which has minimal permission rights.

HostnameLookups

This parameter sets the type of information saved in the access log file. If set to on, the hostname is looked up and saved in the log, rather than simply the IP address of the requester. Turning this on slows down the Web server, but makes the logs more useful. The default is off.

KeepAlive

This designates the number of keep-alive requests that the server accepts. A client Web browser uses a *keep-alive request* to download multiple documents within a single TCP connection.

KeepAliveTimeout

This parameter sets how long the server waits between document requests before dropping a connection. The default setting is 15 seconds.

MaxClient

This determines the maximum number of clients that can connect to your server at one time. If this limit is reached, new connections to the server are locked out. This prevents the server from being overloaded by requests.

Port

This parameter sets the port to which Apache listens for incoming connections. Port 80 is the default setting for all Web servers. If you change this port setting, you can run the Apache Web server so that only those who know the port number it is running on can access it. You can use this feature to set up a private Web page that isn't strictly private, but that can only be accessed by those who use the correct port number. If you set this port to 8080, for example, users have to access it by designating the port number. You do this by adding a colon and the port number to the Web site's URL. An example is www.my_company.com:8080.

ProxyRequests

If you want to use the Apache proxy server, set this option to on. You can use the Apache server as a proxy server when it is set up for that purpose on a gateway computer.

ServerAdmin

Set this to the email address of the person who administers your Web site. You must set this option.

ServerName

This is your server's hostname. This must be a valid DNS name that Internet Domain Name Servers can resolve.

ServerRoot

This names the directory in which configuration files and logs are kept for the server.

ServerType

This sets whether Apache is run standalone or through inetd. The default is standalone. This means that Apache will run on its own, rather than being started by inetd. There is no significant advantage to be gained by having Apache launched by inetd on a per-request basis.

Timeout

This parameter sets the number of seconds before a request to send or receive a document times out. The default setting of 400 is about 7 minutes. Adjusting this figure can improve performance.

TransferLog

This is the name of the file into which Apache logs requests for HTML files and CGI programs.

User

This sets the username for the Apache server. The default user is nobody. The nobody user has no permission rights to change anything on your system. This setting is used so that even if a cracker can break in as the Apache user, he is limited in any damage he can do.

The only options that you need to make sure to set are ServerAdmin and ServerName. The default settings for all the others stand as a good starting point. After you've run the server for a while, you can see whether any of the other settings need to be changed.

Server Resources Configuration

The srm.conf file sets which documents can be accessed on your Web server. Its structure is similar to the httpd.conf file.

The following sections describe some of the key configuration entries at which you need to look.

AccessFileName

This is the name of the file that has access control information for a given directory. It can be used to define access to a directory, and is usually set to .htaccess.

AddDescription

This parameter is used to add a description after a file named in a server generated index. The default setting is off.

DefaultIcon

This is the filename for a graphic, used for files that do not already have an icon defined.

DirectoryIndex

This parameter sets the default file to open on access, and is usually set to index.html. This is how you can enter a Web site name without designating a specific page on the site to open. If no html page is specifically requested, the default page displays.

DocumentRoot

This sets the default root directory for html files: /home/httpd/html.

IndexIgnore

This determines which directories and files to ignore when creating a directory listing. These are the files that you don't want people to see in the directory.

Redirect

This parameter sets a redirection for a URL that has been renamed or moved from your system. For example, the setting

```
Redirect 4sale.html http://www.another_server.com/4sale.html
```

redirects Web browsers' requests for the 4sale.html Web page to a page on another server.

UserDir

This sets the directory in which users can put personal Web files. The default setting is public_html, so users with accounts on the Web server can create a directory in their home directories called public_html and put HTML files there that they can retrieve from the Web server.

For example, if a user named Mary at my_company.com puts the 4sale.html file in the /home/mary/public_html directory, it can be accessed with the URL
```
www.my_company.com/~mary/4sale.html.
```

Security Configuration

The access.conf file sets permissions for who, what, when, and where files can be accessed.

The access.conf configuration file has a simple structure. There are opening and closing tags, with directives in between:

```
<Directory /directory path name>
Directive
Directive
</Directory>
```

The directives inside the opening and closing tags control how the directory's contents can be accessed. The opening tag lists the full pathname of the directory for which you are setting permissions. A sample entry in access.conf is

```
<Directory /home/httpd/html>
Options Includes
AllowOverrride All
order allow,deny
allow from all
</Directory>
```

The Options directive sets what can be done with files in the directory and its subdirectories. Following are the possible parameters:

- **None**—None of the options are allowed. This is the default setting for directories that only display html files and graphics.
- **Indexes**—If no index.html file is found, a directory listing is generated.
- **Includes**—Allows server-side includes, an HTML processing language for certain preset commands (such as getting the date a file was last modified).

> **CAUTION**
>
> It's generally not a good idea to use SSIs. They use extra server resources, forcing the server to read every line of html code for SSI commands. This can seriously slow down a busy server. SSIs can also open a small security hole in your system. Don't use them unless you know they are needed and you know how to secure their use.

- **FollowSymLinks**—Allows symbolic links to be followed. If this parameter is not included and you have files that are symbolic links, attempts to access them result in an error message.
- **ExecCGI**—Files in this directory are to be executed, not displayed.
- **MultiViews**—Content negotiated MultiViews are allowed.
- **All**—Selects all the options, except for MultiViews.

The AllowOverride directive sets the options that the directory's local access file (.htaccess) can override. The possible parameters are

- **All**—Allows the local access file to override all settings
- **AuthConfig**—Allows the local access file to include user authentication information
- **FileInfo**—Allows the local access file to add or change file description information
- **Indexes**—Allows the local access file to control how directory indexes are displayed
- **Limit**—Allows the local access file to control access to a subdirectory
- **Options**—Allows use of the Options directive in the local access file

The order directive enables you to set who can and cannot retrieve files from this directory. The default setting is all. The parameters are order, allow, and deny. The order directive sets the order in which the allow and deny directives are accessed. The parameters for deny and allow are either the word all, or an IP address or domain name. A sample entry is

```
order deny,allow
deny from all
allow from *.my_company.com
```

This restricts access to only those in your own domain.

If you have an open server but want to deny access to a certain domain, a sample entry is

```
order allow,deny
allow from all
deny from *.crackers.com
```

Managing the Web Server

Part
V
Ch
26

You'll want to know a few tasks to manage on your Web server and keep it running smoothly.

Starting and Stopping the Server

If you have the standard OpenLinux installation, the startup files are in the OpenLinux default location. If you installed Apache separately, the startup files might be in a different location, depending on how you did your installation.

To stop the Apache Web server, enter the following command:

/etc/rd.d/init.d/httpd stop

To start the server, enter

/etc/rd.d/init.d/httpd stop

NOTE You can start and stop the Web server only while logged in as root.

Apache Users and Groups

Web pages and directories are usually openly available to anyone who accesses the server. This is generally the goal of a Web server.

Sometimes, however, you want to restrict access to a certain user or group of users. The Apache Web server maintains a user database that is similar to the user access system used by Linux for controlling login access to the computer.

Local access control files are then used to restrict access to only designated users or groups.

To create a user for your Apache server, use the `htpasswd` command. The first time you create a user, you'll also need to create the password file by adding the `-c` parameter. The command is

```
htpasswd -c password_filename user_name
```

The filename must be in a directory that is accessible to the Apache server. The usual location is in the /etc/httpd/conf directory. Therefore, a sample command to create the password file and the first user is

```
htpasswd -c /etc/httpd/apache/conf/webusers mary
```

After you enter the command, you are prompted to enter a password for the user. The password is stored in an encrypted format. After you create the file, don't use the `-c` parameter to add users to the group. It forces the file to be deleted if it is there, and a new file is created. You can also use this command to modify the password of an existing user.

In addition to creating users, you can create groups. Groups simplify access control because you can put multiple users into a group and then give access to the group.

Create a groups file by using a text editor and putting a file in the same directory as the users file. You can call it whatever you want. In the groups file, put the name of the group and a colon, followed by the users in the group. For example, this is a sample entry to create the workshop group:

```
workshop: mary monica sekou
```

Configuring Access Control

With defined users and groups, you can make use of access control. You can do this with the .htaccess file, which is put in the directory to which you want to control access. To allow a directory to be restricted within a .htaccess file, first check that the access.conf file allows user authentication to be set up in a .htaccess file. This is controlled by the `AuthConfig` override. The access.conf file should include `AllowOverride AuthConfig` to allow the authentication directives to be used in a .htaccess file.

The format of the .htaccess file is similar to the access.conf security configuration file. No directory description is necessary because the access control is for the directory in which .htaccess is located. The directives are similar. Following are the main directives for .htaccess:

■ **AuthUserFile**—The full pathname of the user database file. The directive line, using the previous example, is

```
AuthGroupFile /etc/httpd/apache/conf/webusers
```

■ **AuthGroupFile**—The full pathname of the group file.

■ **AuthName**—Specifies a realm name. After a user has entered a valid username and password, any other resources within the same realm name can be accessed with the same username and password. This can be used to create two areas that share the same username and password.

■ **AuthType**—The protocol to be used for authentication. Basic is the only protocol recognized by all browsers.

■ **Require**—Limits access for users and groups. To restrict access to all users in the webusers password file, the directive is

```
require valid-user
```

Limit directory access to specific users by entering specific user names. This directive is

```
require user user_name1 user_name2 ...
```

Directory access can also be limited by group. This directive is

```
require group group_name1 group_name2 ...
```

order

The order directive works the same way it does in the access.conf file. See that entry for an explanation of how to use it.

This method of controlling access is relatively easy, but if it is used for a large number of users, the server can get bound up processing the user and group files. If you have a large user base that needs restricted access, look into the other user authentication options in Apache, particularly DBM.

Maintaining Logs

The Web server log files are very valuable. You can study or parse them to find out who is accessing the Web site, what they are accessing, and much more. Many sophisticated log analysis tools are available.

But log files never stop growing. The bigger the file, the harder it is to get information from it. Besides, left on their own, the log files can fill up the whole server.

For this reason, the log files need to be archived.

Because the Web server is constantly writing to the access log, you need a special program to archive the logs without disrupting the server's logging process. The `logrotate` command is used for this.

You can automate log rotation by adding a `TransferLog` entry to the httpd.conf file:

```
TransferLog "¦/usr/sbin/logrotate /directory_name/file_name time
```

The directory and filenames are the location to which the log files are to be moved. A time indicator is appended to the filename. The time parameter specifies in seconds how often to rotate the logs.

Getting an Internet Connection

After your Web server is set up, you'll need to connect it to the Internet before anyone can access it. A Web server needs a full-time connection, what is called 24x7: 24 hours a day, seven days a week.

The Web server cannot run on a dial-up connection like the ones used at home to connect to the Internet. There are other options.

Many ISPs enable you set up your Linux server at their site. This has the advantage that you have full access to a high-bandwidth connection, but your physical access to the Linux server is usually limited to certain hours (although access to change Web pages isn't limited).

This option saves the cost of installing a high-bandwidth connection to your office. The ISP's co-location charge can be half or less of the monthly charges for high-bandwidth connections.

The downside to co-location is that it doesn't provide a direct Internet connection to your office. If you want to have both Internet services for your office and a Web server for public access, you'll want a direct high-speed connection.

Many technologies are available for connecting to the Internet. You'll need to find an ISP that can tell you what options are available where you are located.

A dedicated leased line offers the highest possible bandwidth, at a premium price. The fastest is T3, which is extremely expensive. A T1 leased line is also very fast, and also expensive. DSL connections can match T1 speeds, but make sure it is symmetrical DSL. Only symmetrical DSL has equally fast incoming and outgoing speeds. Shared circuit connections use a dedicated circuit and share it among a number of users. This is a little like the freeway: Off-peak hours are great, but delays can occur during rush hour. Even so, rush hour on the freeway is still faster than maneuvering the local streets. This kind of shared high-speed connection is called *fractional T1*. The local streets are the slower connection options such as ISDN, and 56K Frame-Relay. They are still faster than standard home modem connections, but they can't give good performance for a busy Web server.

If you plan to build your business around your Web server, start with at least a T1 connection, especially if you expect to use your Web server for taking customer orders. Symmetrical DSL is also a good choice. You can start with a lower bandwidth and expand it, as needed, up to T1 speeds without having to add hardware.

If your needs are more limited, start with fractional T1 connection or symmetrical DSL. Both are good for entry-level servers or for any business that is using their Internet connection primarily for a Web server to share information about products or updates for customers. Both fractional T1 and symmetrical DSL are easy to upgrade as your needs expand.

Part

V

Ch

26

Installing and Configuring Mail Services

Setting Up a Mail Server

Email has become a preferred means of communication, with practically every office now using email for internal and external communications. For most offices, email is considered as essential as a phone service or an electrical service, and the email servers are expected to have the same level of reliability as those services.

Although email client programs on Windows computers have become more sophisticated and easier to use, mail servers can still be one of the most difficult type of servers to set up and maintain. Considering the difficulties, Linux has a particularly good track record for trouble-free email service.

One of the strengths of the Linux mail server is that it is based on open standards. This means that most user clients can be used with a Linux email server.

Successful email service requires that Mail User Agents (MUAs) be able to seamlessly send and retrieve mail from the server, and that the server's Mail Transport Agents (MTAs) seamlessly handle the mail flow.

MUAs, MTAs, and Mail Flow

MUAs are the email programs that you use every day like Outlook, Messenger, Pegasus Mail, or Eudora. *MTAs* are the mail server programs like Sendmail that actually handle sending and receiving the mail.

The standard mail flow looks something like this (any email program and mail server could be substituted for the programs used in this example):

You write a message in Pegasus Mail, a Mail User Agent. When you click on the Send button, the mail user agent connects with a server running Sendmail, the Mail Transport Agent. Each message includes an "envelope" with the recipient's name and address and the name and address of the sender. The mail transport agent delivers the mail to the mail server indicated by the address in the "envelope." On the other end, the MTA (mail server program) accepts the message and then delivers the mail to the mail spool and the MUA (email reader software) picks it up from the spool.

The standard OpenLinux installation supports both POP3 and IMAP4 for email client programs (MUAs), and it uses Sendmail as the default Mail Transport Agent. Sendmail is the backbone of about 75% of the email traffic on the Internet.

Sendmail basically performs two functions: sending and receiving mail. For this, it uses the Simple Mail Transfer Protocol (SMTP), a standard for transferring mail between Internet mail servers. Sendmail has always been free software, though a commercial version is now available with many additional features. One of the most popular features of the commercial edition is its easy-to-use configuration tool.

Sendmail has been around for about two decades. The original program was written by Eric Allman at the University of California at Berkeley. Allman still updates the code on the free version as well as the commercial edition.

The Web site for the free version of Sendmail that is included with OpenLinux is www.sendmail.org. The Web site for the commercial edition is www.sendmail.com.

POP3 and IMAP4 Email Clients

Most email clients use POP3 to access email. *POP3* stands for *Post Office Protocol version 3.* (POP is the original Internet email protocol.) Messages are stored on the server until the user logs on and downloads the mail. After the messages have been retrieved, they are usually deleted from the server.

POP3 is a proven technology. It is simple, and it works. Almost any email program can be used to retrieve POP3 messages from your OpenLinux mail server, which means that users can almost always use their favorite email program. Some of the most popular Windows-based email programs that support POP3 are Eudora, Pegasus Mail, Outlook Express, and Netscape Messenger.

However, POP3 has some limitations. Each email message is downloaded from the server and saved to the user's computer, which means that the message is saved to just one computer. So if the user also works from home, the message might be downloaded to the home computer and, therefore, not available on the office computer (or vice versa).

The *Interim Mail Access Protocol*, or *IMAP*, is a newer mail protocol that was designed to correct many of the limitations of POP3. IMAP version 4 on OpenLinux gives the mail server groupware-like functionality for email without the high per-user cost of groupware server licenses.

With IMAP4, the mail stays on the server. When a user logs in and accesses email, the email client connects to the server and reads the Inbox and folders on the mail server. When the user reads and then files or deletes the email, the messages stay on the server. This means that no matter whether the user is in the office, at home, or on the road, all current and filed email messages are available. This provides the greatest flexibility for users of the mail server.

Only about half of Windows-based email clients support IMAP, but the most popular ones do, including Outlook Express and Messenger. One nice feature of IMAP is that it doesn't matter if you switch email clients; as long as you use the IMAP protocol, all the mail is accessible. This means that if you use Eudora Pro on your computer at work to access email but you use Pine on your computer at home, you won't encounter any problems. If you use them both, you have access to all mail and folders in both.

Part
V

Ch
27

POP3 and IMAP4 on OpenLinux

Both POP3 and IMAP4 are installed in OpenLinux, and you usually need to do nothing more than allow users to access email using these protocols. Check the services file in the /etc directory and make sure that the following lines are not commented out:

TIP Lines beginning with a pound sign (#) are ignored as comments and not code. Therefore, when you want to have a line of code or a configuration line ignored, you can put a pound sign at the beginning of a line. That turns it into a comment. That way you don't lose the original code or configuration information. This is called *commenting out a line*.

```
pop3     110/tcp     pop3 # POP version 3
pop3     110/udp
.
.
.
imap2    143/tcp     imap    # Interim Mail Access Protocol
imap2    143/udp
```

That means that these services are available.

As long as users have an account on the Linux server, they can use their login name and password to access their email, either with POP3 or IMAP4. Users can even switch between protocols, but if they do, all messages retrieved by POP3 are removed from the server and won't be available when email is accessed using IMAP4.

The only setup for these services that you need to look at consists of the server's security measures. Make sure that the server has been completely secured.

Configuring Sendmail

The Mail Transport Agent for OpenLinux is Sendmail, which is the program at the core of the mail server.

Configuring Sendmail is one of the most difficult tasks on an OpenLinux computer and must be approached cautiously. To check that Sendmail is installed on your system and to see which version is installed, use Kpackage and search for Sendmail; or enter the following command:

```
rpm -qa sendmail | grep sendmail
```

This should show that both Sendmail and sendmail-cf are installed on your system. The version number for both programs included on the disk with this book is 8.9.1-4. The display should show:

```
sendmail-8.9.1-4
sendmail-cf-8.9.1-4
```

Sendmail handles the job of delivering, receiving, and routing mail messages using the Simple Mail Transport Protocol, or SMTP.

The primary configuration file for Sendmail—sendmail.cf—is in the /etc directory.

Sendmail's power and difficulty come from its great flexibility in handling mail. A look through the sendmail.cf file gives you an idea of both its possibilities and its difficulties. To see the contents of sendmail-cf, open a terminal window and enter the command:

```
less /etc/sendmail.cf
```

The configuration file is read when Sendmail is started.

The Sendmail configuration file should not be edited directly. Unless you've got years of experience, editing the file directly can be a nightmare. A program called M4 simplifies some of the most common configuration tasks for Sendmail. Even with the M4 utility, though, configuring Sendmail can be difficult.

The book to read for thorough configuration information is *Sendmail*, written by Sendmail's primary programmers, Eric Allman and Bryan Costales (O'Reilly & Associates; ISBN: 1565922220). The book is often referred to as the "bat book" because of the bat pictured on the cover. Reading this book is a requirement if you are going to run a full-production mail server using Sendmail. In the book, Allman admits, "The Sendmail program is difficult to configure and even more difficult to understand completely."

Another source of help on configuring Sendmail is the FAQ page at www.sendmail.org/faq/. It gives solutions to many of the common problems encountered in setting up Sendmail. You'll also find many other useful resources on the www.sendmail.org Web site.

Sendmail includes several sample configuration files with the default installation. No one ever creates a configuration from scratch. The sample files are copied and the copies are modified to build a working configuration.

Before doing any work on configuring Sendmail, you want to back up the default Sendmail configuration file in the /etc directory. Make copies of both sendmail.cf and sendmail.cw. The default configuration file that installs on OpenLinux sends and receives email using your machine's hostname and domain name as the return address.

The sendmail.cf file is the configuration file. The sendmail.cw file lists the domains that are to be accepted by Sendmail. The sendmail.cw can be empty if you define the domain in the sendmail.cf file. If Sendmail is handling mail for multiple hosts, the domain names of the hosts should be added to the sendmail.cw file.

If you are using Sendmail only to send and receive mail from your OpenLinux computer, you probably don't need to do anything to configure Sendmail; you can just start using the system as a basic mail server.

As you start using the mail server, you might find that you want to add or change certain features. Following is a description of a mail system at `my_company.com` that we've decided we want to change.

At `my_company.com`, we have 20 computers in the office, all running various flavors of Windows. The company has a mail server named zeus that runs Sendmail in the OpenLinux default configuration. The various Windows computers are set up with POP3 or IMAP4 email clients that access mail accounts on zeus. All email that goes out says it is coming from `zeus.my_company.com`.

This means that mail sent by Mary goes out with a return address of `mary@zeus.my_company.com`, user Monica's goes out with a return address of `monica@zeus.my_company.com`, and so on. Using a masquerading technique, you can change this so that zeus won't appear at all, and the return addresses sent with the email will be `mary@my_company.com`, `monica@my_company.com`, and so on.

Use the following steps to masquerade outgoing email so that it appears with only the domain name and not the host name:

1. Switch to the /usr/share/sendmail/cf/cf directory. In this directory are the sample M4 configuration files. These are the files that end with .mc. The file named generic-col2.2.mc is the file that was used to create the default sendmail.cf file on your system. Make a copy of this file and call it anything you want. For this example we'll use the following command:

   ```
   cp generic-col2.2.mc my_company.mc
   ```

2. Open the new file you've just created in a text editor. Add these two lines to the file, making sure to use the domain name you want to appear as the return address:

   ```
   MASQUERADE_AS(my_company.com)
   FEATURE(masquerade_envelope)
   ```

3. Enter the following command:

   ```
   m4 ../m4/cf.m4 my_company.mc > /etc/sendmail.cf
   ```

4. Stop Sendmail and restart it so that the change goes into effect. Enter the following two commands:

   ```
   /etc/rc.d/init.d/mta stop
   /etc/rc.d/init.d/mta start
   ```

Sendmail has now been configured, and all mail sent out by your server will show it as coming from `my_company.com`.

Just remember that Sendmail's complexity lies in its great flexibility, which means that the more you learn about it, the more you will be capable of doing with it.

## CHAPTER 28

Installing and Configuring an FTP Server

FTP Servers: The Second Most Popular Internet Servers

The File Transfer Protocol predates the World Wide Web, but it hasn't gone away. In fact, it's almost as common as the Web and is the second most popular Internet server type after Web servers because it's still the best way to move files from one computer to another. Many Web sites also have FTP servers that are linked for downloading files of many different types.

The WU-FTP server software is installed and running on every standard OpenLinux installation. This particular FTP server for UNIX systems was developed at Washington University, thus the *WU* in the name of the program. It is now maintained by an independent group that can be found at www.wu-ftpd.org. It is by far the most popular FTP server on the Internet, used on many anonymous FTP sites around the world.

This is because it has many special features for its anonymous FTP server in addition to extensive monitoring capabilities.

The FTP server in OpenLinux can be used for access by users with accounts on the system and for anonymous FTP. Users can access the server using an FTP client program on their computer, and then upload or download files from the server.

Anonymous FTP is popular because it provides a way for files to be made available publicly to anyone without an account on the server. Almost all Linux software is distributed this way, and many companies make support files, user documents, technical guides, and many other types of files available on anonymous FTP servers. These servers are a key component in most company customer support programs.

When a user logs in to the FTP server and provides a valid name and password, his full access rights are granted, making accessible the files and directories of that particular user. If a user logs in and enters the login name of anonymous, or ftp, he is given read-only access to the anonymous FTP directory. The user will not have access to—or even be capable of seeing—any other directories on the server.

Anonymous FTP Security and Chroot

When a user logs in to an FTP server as anonymous, a special command executes that hides everything on the system except the special FTP directory. This is what gives anonymous FTP its high level of security.

The special command is the chroot command, short for *change root*. As the name implies, this command makes it possible to make any directory appear to be the root directory.

When an anonymous FTP user enters a command to change directory, such as cd /pub, the user is actually changing to the /home/ftp/pub directory. The anonymous user never sees this because the chroot command masks out the rest of the system.

Because the rest of the system is not accessible, the user cannot run programs that are not in the /home/ftp directory. Even programs that are placed in the proper directories under /home/ftp can't run if they are linked with shared libraries that are outside the /home/ftp directory. Most Linux programs use shared libraries. Therefore, shared libraries have to be available under /home/ftp or programs that do not require shared libraries have to be used.

There are other limitations. For example, it is necessary to have an /etc directory with users and groups defined so that programs like ls will work. The ls command accesses user and group information to work.

The user and group files in the anonymous FTP directory are not actually used for logins. You should not add user or group information to them. The default user file created has root, bin, operator, ftp, and nobody defined. The user and group files do not include any password information and should not be changed unless you know what you are doing.

Files that are to be shared are usually placed in the /pub directory. Wherever they are placed, the actual file has to be put there. A link to the file from outside the restricted area won't work.

The default location for the anonymous FTP directory on your OpenLinux system is /home/ftp. When an anonymous user logs in to your FTP server, this directory looks like /(root). There are four default directories in /home/ftp: /bin, /etc, /lib, and /pub. Files for public downloading are placed in /pub. You can add any directories you want.

Any files that are put in /pub are publicly available for downloading. Anonymous users cannot put any files on the server; they can only download copies of files they find in the anonymous FTP /pub directory. Only someone who has been given the required rights can put files in this directory and make them available.

If you are logged in as root, copy the file into the /pub directory and change its permissions so that it is readable. You can also create a directory under /pub and copy files into that directory. Following is the procedure:

1. Copy the file to the FTP /pub directory:

   ```
   cp /home/support/update.file /home/ftp/pub/update.file
   ```

2. Make the file world readable:

   ```
   chmod a+r /home/ftp/pub/update.file
   ```

Now, anyone connecting to your FTP server can download this file.

You can also add a message that is displayed to anyone who logs in to the anonymous FTP server. Create a plain text file with your message and name it welcome.msg. Save it in the /home/ftp directory. When a user logs in anonymously, information about the FTP server and which version of WU-FTP is being run appears, followed by your message. These messages typically include special instructions, descriptions of the available files and their locations, or general greetings explaining the purpose of the FTP site.

The location and name of the message file is defined in the FTP server configuration file ftpaccess. Configuring the FTP server is explained later in this chapter.

Only the root user can create or modify the message file. To create the file, use a text editor to create the welcome.msg file. Here is a sample message:

```
Welcome to the My Company FTP site!
        ftp.my_company.com
            The local time is %T

        All transfers are logged.


Technical documents for our products can all be found in the /pub directory.

Can't find a file? -> mailto:support@my_company.comFor more information see
http://www.my_company.com/faq

This site is provided as a public service. For comments on this site, please
contact <%E>.
```

This message includes two "magic cookies": %T and %E. When these special characters are in the file, the FTP server converts them into predefined text. %T is the local time, and %E is the email address of the site's maintainer as defined in the ftpaccess configuration file. These two cookies and others are defined later in this chapter.

The welcome.msg file then must be placed in the /home/ftp directory. It should be owned by the root user and the root group.

The OpenLinux default setup of the FTP server puts basic security features into place, but you need to carefully go over all the settings before putting the server on the Internet.

In the default settings, the FTP server times out an inactive session after 15 minutes. Several configuration files are located in the /etc directory that control the FTP server. The following files are the key to your FTP server:

- **/etc/inetd.conf**—The settings here define how FTP connection requests are handled by the TCP Wrapper program.
- **/etc/hosts.allow and /etc/hosts.deny**—These are control files for the TCP wrapper program, which define who can access FTP services.
- **/etc/ftpusers**—Lists accounts on your OpenLinux system that are denied FTP access for security reasons. This is usually root.
- **/etc/ftpaccess**—Defines access rules. See the following.
- **/var/log/xferlog**—Log of all FTP file transfers.

The ftpaccess file is the key configuration file for the FTP server. The default ftpaccess configuration file installed on OpenLinux follows:

```
class    all    real,guest,anonymous   *

email root@localhost

loginfails 5

readme    README*    login
readme    README*    cwd=*

message /welcome.msg              login
message .message                  cwd=*

compress          yes           all
tar               yes           all
chmod         no              guest,anonymous
delete        no              guest,anonymous
overwrite         no              guest,anonymous
rename        no              guest,anonymous

log transfers anonymous,real inbound,outbound

shutdown /etc/shutmsg

passwd-check rfc822 warn
```

The following sections explain these parameters.

class

This defines a class of users. Failing to define a valid class for a host causes access to be denied. The class is given a name, all, and then members of the class are listed. There are three possible members of a class: anonymous, guest, and real. The anonymous keyword means that anonymous FTP access will be granted, the guest keyword means that users who are part of a special guest FTP group will have access, and the real keyword means FTP access will be granted to users with real accounts on the system. Setting up guest FTP accounts is a special job. You can find an introduction to the procedure at ftp://ftp.fni.com/pub/wu-ftpd/guest-howto.

email

This indicates the email address of the maintainer of the FTP server. Put the proper email address here. This address should be publicly displayed.

loginfails

This indicates the number of login failures before the FTP daemon shuts down the connection. The default value is 5.

readme

This parameter defines a file that notifies the user that it exists and when it was last modified any time he logs in or uses the change working directory command (cwd). README files usually contain important instructions for users about file contents, downloading, or installation instructions.

message

This parameter defines a file that is displayed to the user at login time or when the change working directory command is used. The message is displayed only once; otherwise, it can become a source of complaints. Messages can include *magic cookies* that replace the cookie with a specified text string. Following are the "magic cookies" for messages:

%T	local time
%C	current working directory
%E	the maintainer's email address as defined in ftpaccess
%R	remote hostname
%L	local hostname
%u	username as determined via RFC931 authentication
%U	username given at login time
%M	maximum allowed number of users in this class
%N	current number of users in this class

compress

Enables compression, as defined in the /etc/ftpconversions configuration file.

tar

This parameter enables tar capabilities, as defined in the /etc/ftpconversions configuration file.

chmod

This parameter enables or disables changing file permissions. If not indicated here, the default enables the function. The functions can be disabled by type: real, anonymous, and guest.

delete

This parameter enables or disables deleting files. If not indicated here, the default enables the function. The functions can be disabled by type: real, anonymous, and guest.

overwrite

This parameter enables or disables modifying files. If not indicated here, the default enables the function. The functions can be disabled by type: real, anonymous, and guest.

rename

This parameter enables or disables renaming files. If not indicated here, the default enables the function. The functions can be disabled by type: real, anonymous, and guest.

log transfers

This parameter enables logging of file transfers for either real or anonymous FTP users. Logging of transfers to the server (inbound) can be enabled separately from transfers from the server (outbound). You can specify logging by type: anonymous, guest, and real.

shutdown

If the indicated file exists, the server checks it regularly to see whether the server will be shut down. If a shutdown is planned, the user is notified, new connections are denied after a specified time before shutdown, and current connections are dropped at a specified time before shutdown.

passwd-check

This parameter defines the level and enforcement of password checking done by the server for anonymous FTP. Options for checking are none, trivial, and rfc822. The setting indicates that the password must be an rfc822-compliant address. If the address doesn't comply, the warn setting means that the user will be warned but then allowed to log in. The other enforcement option is enforce, which means that the user is warned and then logged out.

Part
V

Ch
28

Overview of Network Security

Basic Security

Security for computer systems and networks is a big topic. A chapter in a book cannot adequately cover everything necessary to understand and implement a full security plan for an office, big or small.

What you will find in this chapter is a practical guide to securing OpenLinux out of the box. This chapter covers about 80% of the possible security-related problems that come up. There are also pointers for further measures you can take.

Many fancy tools are available to help in securing your machines and network from unwanted attack: heavy-duty firewalls, security analysis tools, intrusion monitors, and more. These are often key to a successful security plan.

Successful security begins with the basics, however, starting with making sure that the computer itself is in a secure location.

Security is ultimately in the hands of the users. No matter what security measures might be in place, carelessness of individuals can compromise any or all security measures.

Users are generally uneducated in security issues and how to protect themselves. They need to be aware not only of the importance of security, but how it is implemented and what they can do to help protect the system: They need to know your security policies and procedures.

The first level of security is the password for accessing the system. Most passwords chosen by users are simple to remember, which usually means they are also easy to break.

To protect against crackers who are "sniffing" network traffic, passwords need to be impossible to guess. Don't let users choose their own passwords. Assign passwords that are a minimum of five characters long, and mix letters with numbers or symbols. Some excellent programs are available for generating passwords that are impossible to guess. Tom Van Vleck has created one of the best password generators I've found. It's a Java applet. You can run the program from his Web site at `www.best.com/~thvv/gpw.html`, or you can download the Java source, Java binaries, or C/C++ source from the same site.

For more information on passwords in Linux, see the Security How-To at the Linux Documentation Project at `sunsite.unc.edu/LDP/`.

N O T E If your system is part of a Windows-based network, consider using all lowercase letters in your passwords because the Windows system does not recognize the case of passwords and can send the wrong password if it depends on a mix of upper- and lowercase.

Reportedly, some military services use a simple technique of choosing two easy-to-remember but unrelated words and joining them with a symbol or number. An example of this kind of password is box9ever. You can use this technique to make up your own passwords. ■

For network administrators, security begins with applying what is known as the *principle of least privilege*: Users are never given more privilege than is necessary for them to do their job.

Ensuring least privilege requires that you identify what the user needs, determine the minimum set of privileges required to meet those needs, and then restrict the user's access to precisely those needs—and no more. The strictness that you use in applying this principle increases in direct proportion to the need you have for securing your system.

Following are some tips for basic security.

Tip #1 : Use File Permissions for Basic Security

File permissions are such a simple level of security that they sometimes are forgotten. File permissions determine who can and can't access files and directories on the system.

A user and a group own each file on the system. Every file has a set of nine switches that control who can read, write, or execute the file. User rights and group memberships control access to files and directories.

Review the section on file permissions in Chapter 7, "Using the Character Mode Terminal," and make sure that your files and directories are protected so that even legitimate users on the system can't go prying into other users' files.

Tip #2: Use Shadow Passwords

Make sure that your system is using shadow passwords. Linux passwords were originally saved in an encrypted format in the passwd file in the /etc directory. Shadow passwords are saved in a separate file named shadow in the /etc directory. Anyone who can log in to your system can read the passwd file, but no one except root can read the shadow file.

If shadow passwords are not used, the password information is kept in the passwd file. This password, while encrypted, is vulnerable because it is easy to decipher the real password. That's because the algorithm used for the encryption is widely known. Cracker programs that can decode these passwords are available on the Internet.

The problem is that you can't make the passwd file inaccessible. If you make it so that no one can read the file except root, no one except root can log in because this is the file in which all the user login information is kept. To solve this problem, the shadow system was introduced.

Shadow passwords work by storing the passwords in a separate file that only the system administrator can read. An encrypted password is no longer shown in the /etc/passwd file; rather, the password is represented by an asterisk (*).

No special maintenance or techniques are involved with using shadow passwords after they have been implemented.

Shadow passwords are installed by default as part of the standard installation, but you want to double-check this. To see whether shadow passwords are installed on your system, use the `list` command:

```
ls /etc/shadow
```

If you receive a message that no such file or directory exists, you need to install shadow passwords. You can use the `pwconv` tool to convert entries from the password file to the shadow file. Enter the command `pwconv`, and the passwords in the passwd file are converted into shadow passwords. The `pwck` utility checks the consistency of the passwd and shadow files and needs to be run periodically to ensure consistency.

Read the man documentation for `shadow` and `pwconv` for more information.

OpenLinux also includes Linux-PAM (Pluggable Authentication Modules) for password security, a system first developed by Sun Microsystems that supports high-level encryption routines like MD5. The Linux-PAM Web site is at `www.kernel.org/pub/linux/libs/pam/index.html`.

Tip #3: Get Security Updates

Caldera Systems regularly publishes security advisories. Sign up for the Caldera Systems Announce mail list. The advisories concern security vulnerabilities and how to fix them. Every advisory includes information on how to obtain an updated package that can fix the security hole. You can find a complete collection of the OpenLinux security advisories on the Caldera Systems Web site at `www.calderasystems.com/news/security/`.

NOTE To get on the security advisory list, send an email message to `majordomo@lists.calderasystems.com` with the command **subscribe Announce** in the body of the message. The subject of the message does not matter, so you can leave it blank.

In addition to getting all the security advisories, you'll receive announcements about Caldera products. These are infrequent, so you don't need to worry about being inundated with a lot of advertisements. You might even appreciate getting notices of new software from Caldera Systems.

There is more to system and network security than OpenLinux security issues, though. Keeping up-to-date on security can be a lot of work. Fortunately, many organizations specialize in providing users with bulletins and advice on Internet security. They are basically divided among government-sponsored groups, such as the Computer Emergency Response Team (CERT); university organizations, such as CERIAS; and vendors. All these organizations can help you protect your systems or deal with intrusions. Following is a listing of some of these organizations.

bugtraq   bugtraq is a mailing list for detailed discussions of system vulnerabilities. It generates a lot of email traffic. To subscribe, send an email message to `listserv@netspace.org` with the command `subscribe bugtraq` in the body of the message. The subject line doesn't matter.

CERT   The U.S. Department of Defense founded the U.S. Computer Emergency Response Team (CERT) in 1989 to protect the infrastructure of the Internet. It's located at Carnegie-Mellon University in Pittsburgh, Pennsylvania. CERT has a full-time staff that deals only with Internet security issues and is widely considered to be the most authoritative source on Internet security.

CERT has one of the largest mailing lists for security advisories. The CERT FTP archive contains a wide range of security programs, as well as every advisory and bulletin that CERT has issued.

Its Web site at `www.cert.org` is one of the best sources for security information. The team has a 24-hour hotline at (412) 268-7090. CERT advisories are posted on the Usenet newsgroup `comp.security.announce`. The ftp address is `ftp://info.cert.org`, and email is at `cert@cert.org`.

FIRST   The Forum of Incident and Response Security Teams, or FIRST, was founded in 1990. By the middle of 1997, FIRST comprised more than 60 incident response and security teams, which spanned the major global regions. You can find the current list of members at `www.first.org/team-info/`.

The FIRST membership consists of teams from a wide variety of organizations including educational institutions, commercial entities, vendors, government, and the military.

CERT redirects requests regarding security problems to the appropriate FIRST member so that FIRST can address the issue and provide resolution information to CERT for advisories or bulletins. The FIRST Web site is at `www.first.org`.

CIAC   The U.S. Department of Energy's Computer Incident Advisory Capability (CIAC) group was created in 1989 in response to the notorious Internet Worm. It primarily serves the Department of Energy from its Lawrence Livermore National Laboratory site. The Web site at `ciac.llnl.gov` offers advisories, security documents, and ftp links to many programs. There is also an email list for receiving security advisories.

CERIAS   The Center for Education and Research in Information Assurance and Security (CERIAS), located at Purdue University, is a leading university-based center for multidisciplinary research and education in areas of information security (computer security, network security, and communications security) and information assurance. The center grew out of the efforts of the Computer Operations, Audit, and Security Technology (COAST) project at Purdue, founded by Eugene Spafford. The COAST hot list and archives provide one of the most extensive collections of papers and tools for network security. The Web site is at `www.cerias.purdue.edu`.

advICE The advICE security database is designed for the security professional. It specializes in topics related to intrusion countermeasures. The material is broken down into the following categories: Educational Links, Books, FAQs, Introductory material, News, Discussion lists, and Notes. The Web site, referenced as Eight Little Green Men, is at www.8lgm.org.

Tip #4: Turn off Services that You Don't Need

As a multitasking system, Linux has a lot going on in the background. New users, in particular, are not aware of all the other activity taking place. The myriad of network services—email, Web servers, FTP, and other network services—are the most vulnerable parts of your system.

Turn off all the services that are not required for your machine to do the work it needs to do. Take a look at the services running on your system.

You can use the netstat command to list all services that are open and waiting for connections (as shown in Figure 29.1). Following is the command to list all TCP and UDP ports that are open:

```
netstat -atu
```

FIGURE 29.1

Output of netstat shows active Internet connections.

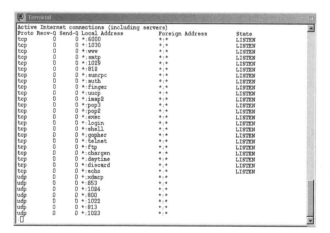

The listing shows a whole slew of services that are open and waiting for connections to your system, more than you might have guessed. Some are listed by names with which you might be familiar; others just list the port number.

This does not list all the services running on your system. To see the other services that are running, enter the following command:

```
ps -aux
netstat -atu
```

Whereas `netstat` shows you what ports are currently open and waiting for connections, `ps` shows you what is currently running, such as sendmail, httpd, and so on (as shown in Figure 29.2).

FIGURE 29.2
Output of `ps` shows active processes.

```
Terminal
USER        PID %CPU %MEM   VSZ  RSS TTY      STAT START   TIME COMMAND
root          1  0.1  0.7  1104  476 ?        S    04:43   0:03 init [5]
root          2  0.0  0.0     0    0 ?        SW   04:43   0:02 [kflushd]
root          3  0.0  0.0     0    0 ?        SW   04:43   0:00 [kpiod]
root          4  0.0  0.0     0    0 ?        SW   04:43   0:00 [kswapd]
root      10714  0.0  0.4  1072  300 ?        S    04:58   0:00 update (bdflush)
root      11299  0.0  0.9  1284  572 ?        S    04:59   0:00 syslogd
root      11367  0.0  1.1  1372  728 ?        S    04:59   0:00 klogd -k /boot/Sy
root      11387  0.0  0.8  1256  536 ?        S    04:59   0:00 inetd
bin       11391  0.0  0.6  1108  392 ?        S    04:59   0:00 rpc.portmap
root      13779  0.0  1.4  1572  888 ?        S    05:01   0:00 amd -F /etc/am.d/
root      13782  0.0  0.0     0    0 ?        SW   05:01   0:00 [rpciod]
root      13783  0.0  0.0     0    0 ?        SW   05:01   0:00 [lockd]
root      13796  0.0  0.9  1248  600 ?        S    05:01   0:00 cron
daemon    13802  0.0  0.8  1228  516 ?        S    05:01   0:00 atd
root      13808  0.0  1.6  1916 1068 ?        S    05:01   0:00 sendmail: accepti
root      13819  0.0  0.6  1092  396 ?        S    05:01   0:00 rpc.rstatd
root      13849  0.0  1.5  2280 1000 ?        S    05:01   0:00 httpd -f /etc/htt
nobody    13853  0.0  1.5  2292  992 ?        S    05:01   0:00 httpd -f /etc/htt
nobody    13854  0.0  1.5  2292  992 ?        S    05:01   0:00 httpd -f /etc/htt
root      13939  0.0  0.5  1076  376 tty1     S    05:02   0:00 /sbin/getty tty1
root      13940  0.0  0.5  1076  376 tty2     S    05:02   0:00 /sbin/getty tty2
root      13941  0.0  0.5  1076  376 tty3     S    05:02   0:00 /sbin/getty tty3
root      13942  0.0  0.5  1076  376 tty4     S    05:02   0:00 /sbin/getty tty4
root      13943  0.0  0.5  1076  376 tty5     S    05:02   0:00 /sbin/getty tty5
root      13944  0.0  0.5  1076  376 tty6     S    05:02   0:00 /sbin/getty tty6
root      13945  0.0  3.5  5444 2252 ?        S    05:02   0:00 /opt/kde/bin/kdm
root      13947  0.8  6.7 14660 4288 ?        S    05:02   0:12 /usr/X11R6/bin/X
root      13951  0.0  6.2  6356 3980 ?        S    05:02   0:00 -:0
root      13964  0.0  6.6  6136 4196 ?        S    05:03   0:01 kwm
root      13973  0.0  5.6  6132 3552 ?        S    05:03   0:00 /opt/kde/bin/kbgn
root      14005  0.0  8.1  7860 5188 ?        S    05:03   0:00 kfm
:
```

Several configuration files control what Linux runs, and how it runs. The Internet daemon, inetd, starts at boot time, looks for network connections, and—on request—launches the network service.

inetd has two configuration files in the /etc directory: the services file (which lists services by port number) and the inetd.conf file (which lists the services by name and then defines what program to run when the service is requested). The services listed in inetd.conf are services—such as telnet and ftp—that don't need to run continuously.

The services configuration file never needs to be changed. The inetd.conf is the file that controls what services can actually be accessed.

Look in inetd.conf and make sure that it lists only the services you need. Disable the rest and remove them.

Services that are enabled in the default OpenLinux setup but that are not needed for a desktop workstation include

- gopher
- exec
- talk
- ntalk
- pop2
- pop3

- imap
- uucp
- finger

Even ftp, telnet, shell, and login need to be disabled. These are all for remote connections to your system. If you need telnet and ftp services for remote connections, use secure shell connections (ssh) (see Tip #9).

Putting a pound sign (#) at the beginning of the line removes the service. After making any changes in inetd.conf, you must restart the inetd process for the changes to take effect. Enter the following command:

```
killall -HUP inetd
```

While working on the inetd.conf file, you might have noticed that every service starts with /usr/sbin/tcpd. This is the TCP Wrappers program (see Tip #8).

Tip #5: Monitor System Logs

Linux keeps an extensive set of logs of everything that takes place on your system. Experienced systems administrators make use of the logs for many aspects of their work. A lot of valuable information can be gathered from the logs. Logs tell you what's happening on your Linux system—everything from system errors to the details of what any user is doing on the system. System administrators track logs for reports of problems in the hardware as well as for signs of unwanted activity.

You can find the system logs in the /var/logs directory. The messages file contains all the system messages. You can sometimes detect people running port scanners when you see entries from one host trying to access multiple ports on your system.

Here's the kind of thing that shows up in the logs (this sample log has been modified to hide the hostname of the source system because they are probably innocent; it has been changed to host.noname.nodomain.none):

```
Apr 14 01:43:31 loot in.pop3d[27398]: refused connect from
➥host.noname.nodomain.none
Apr 14 01:43:32 loot in.imapd[27400]: refused connect from
➥host.noname.nodomain.none
Apr 14 01:43:33 loot in.pop3d[27401]: refused connect from
➥host.noname.nodomain.none
Apr 14 01:43:34 loot in.pop3d[27402]: refused connect from
➥host.noname.nodomain.none
```

This represents a scan of the POP3 and IMAP servers. (Other ports were scanned as well; this is just a sample listing.)

Scans seem to happen with some regularity, and if your system is basically secure, you don't need to worry about them. Watch your logs for login attempts, though. For example, if you see that a login by root occurred at a time when you know root didn't log in, your system might have been compromised. The emphasis here is on the word *"might."* Many processes are run as root, so make sure you understand the log correctly before you make any assumptions.

If you see a login listing in the logs for a user that doesn't match your list of known users, again your system might have been compromised. These are things to check in the logs that might indicate that there has been a break-in.

Tip #6: Check the User List for Unauthorized Users

This is another simple step in security that is often overlooked. If your system has been broken into, crackers often create an account for themselves. This is particularly true on big systems with hundreds or thousands of users, where one more user might be easily overlooked.

The user database on any Linux network server needs to be periodically checked, and not only for unauthorized user names. Users who are gone need to be removed. (The most frequent source of break-ins is a user who left with a grievance.)

In addition to setting up their own privileged account, crackers often install the *"Linux Root Kit."* This is a software package, easily available on the Internet, that replaces the login, ls, ps, netstat, tcpd, and other utilities with versions that can hide their activities. The replacement ls program hides the intruder's directories. The login program enables them log in as rewt, with full root privileges. The netstat program hides their connections. The "Linux Root Kit" is typically hidden in the home directory of the unauthorized user, though the replacement ls program hides the package itself.

So finding an unauthorized user can be a sign of an intrusion. If you've found an unauthorized user, try logging in as rewt. If you get an interesting response and aren't just rejected, your system has probably been compromised.

Tip #7: Make Special Backups for Security Purposes

If your system has been broken into, it can be a big job trying to trace the tracks of the intruder. In fact, it can be downright impossible.

If your system is set up with separate partitions for system files, your job will be easier. You can simply reformat the system partition, and a good backup will get the system working again.

Make a backup of the system directories after the initial installation. In addition, any time you update the system files, make a new backup. Don't overwrite the previous backup, though. When you start restoring because of a break-in, you can't be sure how far back you have to go because you don't know at what point the break-in occurred. It's probably not that far back, though. Most crackers aren't the patient type. They don't wait for months before using a vulnerability they've discovered (besides, who knows how long the vulnerability will stay open). On a well-monitored system, most break-ins are discovered within a day or two—a week at the most.

The backups of the system files for recovery from an unauthorized break-in should not be considered to be part of the regular backup rotation. Do them separately and keep them separate.

Tip #8: Use TCP Wrappers

When a service is requested from your computer, TCP wrappers (tcpd) check whether the connection is allowed, using rules you set up. TCP wrappers are installed as part of the standard OpenLinux setup.

The protected services are listed in the inetd.conf file in the /etc directory. Look for lines that include /usr/sbin/tcpd. These are the services that are using the TCP wrapper program. Following is a sample line from the inetd.conf file:

```
ftp     stream    tcp    nowait    root /usr/sbin/tcpd    in.ftpd -l -a
```

This shows that when a request is made to access the FTP server, the TCP wrapper program is started instead. The TCP wrapper checks whether the connection is legal on the basis of the rules set in the hosts.allow and hosts.deny files in the /etc directory. If the TCP wrapper determines that the connection is legal, the appropriate application server is started.

In this way, you can control access to your system's network services by configuring the hosts.allow and hosts.deny files.

For each service, you can specify a host, domain, or IP address range to allow or forbid.

The hosts.allow file is checked first, and the rules are checked from first to last. If a rule is found that allows the host, domain, or IP address of the connecting computer for the specified service, the connection request is allowed.

If the TCP wrapper program cannot find a rule allowing the connection, it checks the hosts.deny file for a rule specifically denying the request. The rules in the host.deny file are also checked from first to last. The first rule it finds that denies access to the specific connection causes the connection to be blocked.

If no rule is found denying the connection, it lets the service request go through. That can have serious implications. You might think that because the connection hasn't been specifically allowed, it is denied, but that's not the case. It must be specifically denied. That's why most hosts.deny files end with a rule entry that denies everything to everybody.

The format of the rules is the name of the service and a listing of the allowed host, domain, or IP addresses, separated by a colon (:). A sample hosts.allow file might look like this:

```
ALL : my_company.com .my_company.com
in.telnetd : 192.168.1
in.ftpd : ALL
```

This allows all connections for all services from my_company.com and *.my_company.com, it allows all computers with an IP address that is in the 192.168.1 subnet to connect by telnet, and it allows the world to use the server's FTP services.

A sample hosts.deny file might look like this:

```
ALL : ALL
```

This denies access to everyone, everywhere. That way, only those specified in hosts.allow can access network services on your system.

Tip #9: Use the Secure Shell (ssh)

If users on your network need to access the system using telnet or ftp, use the *"secure shell"* software that allows logins where the entire connection is encrypted. This requires special software on both the host and the client.

The ssh program was originally free, but now it is sold under a commercial license. It has many strong features and is worth checking out if you need a high level of security. The Web site for ssh is www.ssh.fi.

A free implementation of the ssh protocol is LSH, a GNU-licensed, open-source program. You can find it at www.linuxberg.com, a big repository of Linux software. The LSH implementation is under active development with the goal of having a free version of ssh that can provide end-to-end encryption and strong authentication for people who can't afford to use the commercial version of ssh.

LSH supports the basic operations, such as key exchange, encryption, compression, password authentication, and spawning of a remote shell (including a pty). However, it does not have all the features of the commercial program.

Tip #10: Use a One-Time Password System

Another way to secure remote connections is to use a one-time password system. When someone tries to log in, he must provide a unique password. A special calculator program produces the password for a single session. Because the password changes for the next login, even if a "sniffer" is used to capture the password, it is of no use to anyone.

Two of the best known of these systems come from Bellcore: SecureID and S/Key. SecureID uses a small device the size of a credit card that generates a password. When you log in to a network that is guarded by SecureID, you enter your own ID and then the password key that it generated. This is a commercial system that is used for access to systems that require strict security.

Bellcore's S/Key is a software-based freeware server system. You can find the latest version at MetaLab, at `metalab.unc.edu/metalab.shtml`. Look in the FTP archives in the /pub/linux/system/security directory. The file is called skey-2.2.tar.gz.

This also gives you a high level of security. The S/Key system is similar to the SecureID system. The user must enter his own password and a one-time password key to enter the system. After the key has been used once, it won't ever be used again.

Bellcore has a 30-day trial copy of a Windows-based S/Key client. This software means that Windows-based systems can log in to your Linux system running the S/Key server. You can download the software from Bellcore's Web site at `www.bellcore.com/SECURITY/skey.html`.

S/Key is not compatible with shadow passwords, and it will replace your original Linux login program. For these reasons, it is usually best to install it on a firewall computer that is only used for access from the world into your system.

Other Solutions

The subject of system and network security is vast and has filled many books. These tips will make your OpenLinux system more secure, but they do not guarantee absolute security. Some additional measures, that you can consider, follow. Whatever you decide to do, keep in mind that security is something that you'll always have to keep in mind as long as your system is connected to the Internet.

Tripwire

Tripwire is a utility that tracks changes in files and directories on your system. Any changes are noted. By using tripwire, you can quickly find where changes have been made on your system. It can even detect *"Trojan horses,"* files that crackers use to break into systems that have the same name as files commonly found on your computer and that appear to be the same in every way. Tripwire is free for noncommercial use. The Tripwire Web site is `www.tripwiresecurity.com`.

Nessus

Nessus is a free, open-sourced, and easy-to-use security auditing tool for Linux. It can perform up to 180 security checks on your network. When you run Nessus, it tests your system for holes that are well-known to crackers. If it finds one of the holes open on your system, it makes suggestions on how to close the hole. The Nessus Web site is www.nessus.org.

nmap

Because there are so many different ways to sneak into a system, one port scanner program such as Nessus is probably not enough. Another program that is similar to Nessus is nmap, which can find vulnerabilities that Nessus doesn't (just as Nessus can find vulnerabilities that nmap misses). You'll be surprised about the hidden entry ports that can be found on many systems. You can use nmap to find the vulnerable ports so that you can shut them down. The nmap Web site is www.insecure.org/nmap/.

Some Books to Check Out

Following is a list of some books that have more information on security:

Practical UNIX and Internet Security, 2nd Edition
Author: Simson Garfinkel and Gene Spafford
Publisher: O'Reilly & Associates
ISBN: 1565921488

Maximum Security, 2nd Edition
Author: Anonymous
Publisher: SAMS
ISBN: 0672313413

Internet Security Professional Reference, 2nd Edition
Author: Multiple Authors
Publisher: New Riders
ISBN: 156205760X

Internet Firewalls And Network Security, 2nd Edition
Author: Chris Hare
Publisher: New Riders
ISBN: 1562056328

Appendixes

Installing OpenLinux Using LISA

You can install OpenLinux using *LISA* (*Linux Installation and Administration*) , which is the nongraphical installation procedure used on older versions of OpenLinux.

Some Reasons to Use LISA Installation

You might need to use the LISA installation procedure for many reasons:

- You have a new video card not supported by XFree86.
- You have an older video terminal.
- You don't plan to use a windows environment or don't have standard equipment needed for it such as a mouse.
- You have hardware that requires special modules.
- You are upgrading a previous installation and don't want to reformat all of your disk partitions.

Steps for Installation

There are four steps for installation:

1. Obtaining hardware information
2. Preparing for installation
3. Creating installation floppy disks
4. Installing OpenLinux

Step 1: Obtaining Hardware Information

Before you can begin installation, you should collect as much information as possible about your computer. The standard OpenLinux installation uses Lizard (the Linux Installation Wizard), which can usually detect your hardware and install the proper drivers. If you haven't already looked at the Lizard installation process, check it out. This is the most advanced Linux installation tool you can get and if you can use it you should.

See Chapter 2, "Installing the Operating System," to learn about Lizard.

LISA has only a limited capability to detect computer hardware. If it fails to detect a particular component and you don't notice it during the installation process, LISA will not warn you that the installation is incomplete.

LISA requires that you know exactly what hardware you have in your system. After it does a simple probe, it will ask you if everything has been detected. There are many components that it will not detect and if you don't notice that something isn't detected (like a network card or a CD-ROM drive), the installation process will continue.

> **CAUTION**
>
> Make sure that LISA properly identifies your hard disks, CD-ROM drives, and network cards. Failure to recognize all of your hard disks can mean that necessary modules are not installed, making access to the disk impossible after installation is completed. Failure to recognize a CD-ROM drive can mean that installation will fail halfway through because everything will be set up but you can't install the software because it can't see the CD. Failure to recognize a network card will mean that after all the software is installed the network installation will not be possible.

To install using LISA, you should have a complete list of all the hardware on your computer so that at the appropriate point during installation you can make sure the drivers (called *modules*) are installed.

There are several ways to find out what hardware is installed in your computer.

- **From the computer seller or the documents that came with the new computer**—Sometimes the documents that come with a new computer give information about the hardware, but computer sellers often do not include this information. You can contact the seller and ask for complete documentation on the hardware inside the computer. Also, many computer sellers have Web sites that have more detailed information on the systems they sell. If you have an older system, it can be harder to obtain information from the seller.

- **Use Windows or DOS to obtain information**—If you have Windows or DOS installed on the computer, you can use its software tools for detecting hardware information.

- **Open up the computer and look inside**—Another way to find out what is installed in a computer is to open up the case and look at what is inside. This is only helpful if you are experienced with computer hardware. Someone who is experienced knows how to handle the components without damaging them and also knows how to read the necessary information from the cryptic markings and unmarked connectors found on most computer components.

Table A.1 provides a hardware checklist of what you should know before installing OpenLinux. Make a copy of this list and then write the answer in the column under "Your Computer."

Table A.1 Hardware Checklist		
Device	Information Needed	Your Computer
Disk drive controller	Type (IDE, SCSI) and model (SCSI only)	
Hard drive	Quantity, size, and order (first, second, so on)	
Memory	Amount in megabytes	
CD-ROM drive	Make and model	
Ethernet card	Make and model	
Mouse	Make, connector (serial, bus, or PS/2)	
Video card	Make and model	
Monitor	Make, model, maximum resolution, maximum horizontal and vertical refresh rates	
Modem	Make, model, serial port used	
Sound card	Make, model, I/O address, DMA channel, IRQ	
Printer	Type (HP, PostScript, and so on)	

Table A.2 provides a network information checklist. If you don't know the information, you should be able to obtain it from your network administrator.

Table A.2 Network Checklist	
Information Needed	Your Computer
Hostname for your computer	
Domain name of your network	
IP address assigned to your computer	
Network broadcast address for your network	
Netmask	
Gateway or router address	
Primary name server (DNS)	

Information Needed	Your Computer
Secondary name server (if you have a second DNS, but it's not necessary)	
Tertiary name server (if you have a third DNS, but it's not necessary)	

CAUTION

Make sure to get precise hardware information. Write down model numbers and all the related information. Double-check your list. An error can be disastrous. This is particularly true with video settings. If you use the wrong information for setting video modes, you can easily destroy your monitor. Take this warning seriously. I have seen monitors fry because of incorrect video settings.

Obtaining Hardware Information from Windows 95/98   If you have Windows 95/98 installed on your computer, you can use the Control Panel (seen in Figure A.1) to retrieve most of the hardware information you need. Follow these steps:

1. Open the system icon in the Control Panel. When the system properties panel opens (as seen in Figure A.1), it displays general system information.

2. Under computer information on this panel, you will find a description of the CPU in the computer, such as, Pentium II Processor. It also shows the amount of memory (RAM) on the computer in megabytes.

3. By clicking on the Device Manager tab, you can see all the components on the computer. You can print a report, including many details, if you have a printer attached to the computer. Click Print. Under Report Type, select All Devices and System Summary. Click OK and a full report is printed.

This produces a report with much of the information needed, but not all of it.

FIGURE A.1
The Control Panel. The Device Manager tab displays a list of hardware installed on the computer.

The Device Manager (seen in Figure A.2) displays a list of devices such as disk drives and network adapters. By going through the list and clicking the plus (+) sign, you can find information such as the make and model the device attached to the computer. For example, a click on the plus sign next to Mouse shows if you have a serial mouse or some other type of mouse.

FIGURE A.2

Devices listed in the Device Manager panel. By clicking the plus (+) sign, you can get a description of the particular device in your computer. For example, this figure shows the name and model of the display adapter.

For some devices, you want more than just the name description of the device. For modems, sound cards, video cards, and network cards you need additional information. For these devices you will want the interrupt, I/O port, DMA channel, and other connection information.

Select the device by name and click on Properties. Another information panel appears (as shown in Figure A.3):

- For the sound card, get the IRQ, I/O address, and DMA channel.
- For the modem, find the serial port.
- For the mouse, you'll want the port and the IRQ.
- For the network card, get the IRQ and the I/O address.

Obtaining Hardware Information from Windows NT   To obtain hardware information on a computer running Windows NT you need to run WinMSD (Windows NT Diagnostics):

1. Click Start, choose Run, and type in **WinMSD**, and then click OK.

2. Choose the Resources tab. You can write down the information, or if you have a printer connected, you can print the information. Click Print. Choose All Tabs and Summary. This prints a report that includes information on the CPU, the amount of memory, the disk drives, IRQ, I/O address, and DMA channels used by each device.

   Alternatively, you can click Devices in the Resources panel (as shown in Figure A.4) and select each individual device and get the details needed by clicking on Properties.

FIGURE A.3
Displaying resources used. This example shows that the modem is using COM3 serial port.

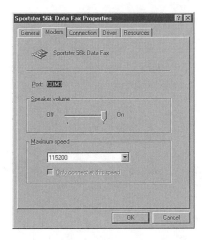

FIGURE A.4
Running Windows NT Diagnostics. Note that by displaying Devices on the Resource panel, you can pick each device and click on Properties to get more information. This example shows the properties of the sound card (auddrive).

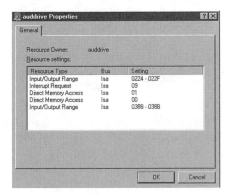

Getting Hardware Information from DOS In DOS, you can use the Microsoft Diagnostics program MSD. You can start MSD at the DOS prompt. Type **msd** and press Enter.

```
C:\> msd
```

A screen appears that shows the system device information. If a printer is connected to the computer, you can press Alt+F for a menu and press P to print. Choose Report All by pressing the spacebar. Use the Tab key to move the cursor to the OK button and then press Enter.

You can also use the Tab key to move between each device listed on the MSD screen or press the letter key that is highlighted for each device. Pressing the Enter key while a particular device is selected displays additional details about the device.

Step 2: Preparing for Installation

At this point, you should have decided how you want to use the computer.

See Chapter 1, "Preparing to Install OpenLinux," for information on the different ways to use OpenLinux if you aren't sure. You can also find information on hardware requirements.

You have three installation options:

- **Workstation**—Install OpenLinux on your hard disk with a single Linux partition and a Linux swap partition.
- **Multiboot system**—Install OpenLinux on its own partition on a computer that also uses another operating system, such as Windows 95/98.
- **Server**—Install OpenLinux on a single or multiple hard disks that have been partitioned for server-level operations.

For any installation, you should look at the section on partitioning in Chapter 2. Pay particular attention to formatting issues regarding the root partition. The Linux kernel has to be located below cylinder 1023 on the hard disk. Make sure that your setup meets this requirement, or Linux will not start.

If you are installing OpenLinux onto a workstation, you can go directly to Step 3. For server installations you should review the partitioning strategies discussed in Chapter 2. Then you can go to Step 3.

If you are upgrading OpenLinux or reinstalling the OpenLinux operating system, you should first make a backup if at all possible. Although you can install OpenLinux without reformatting your partitions, which should preserve user files if they are on a partition separate from system files, the unexpected can and will happen during installation. The only sure way to protect user files is to have a backup. Then you can go to Step 3.

If you want to install onto a multiboot system, you'll need to do a few things first.

First, install the other operating system, if it is not already on the computer's hard disk. Linux knows how to work with other operating systems, but no other operating system knows how to share with Linux.

If you want to use the Caldera Edition of PartitionMagic, it is included on the CD that comes with this book. Follow the procedures for setting up a dual-boot system using PartitionMagic as outlined in Chapter 2.

If you don't want to use PartitionMagic, you can use the fips program that is on the OpenLinux CD. Fips is a program that can safely split the hard disk without destroying anything on the disk. It works with Windows 95 or DOS formatted disks. It does not work with Windows 98 FAT32 or Windows NT NTFS formatted disks. The name fips stands for First nondestructive Interactive Partition Splitting program. The program is on the OpenLinux CD in the /col/tools/fips15 directory.

When Windows or DOS is installed on a hard disk, the usual procedure is to define the entire disk as a single partition in a DOS format. You can use fips to preserve the Windows or DOS partition, but it will take free, unused space and convert it into the Linux format.

Before using fips, make sure to back up the existing files. Then you should do a complete defragmentation of the hard disk. This gives fips more space to work with because it moves all the files together to one area of the disk. Windows has a utility called Disk Defragmenter that does this. Some versions of DOS have a program called DEFRAG.EXE or OPTIMIZE.EXE.

Fips comes with a README file and other documents that fully explain how to use it. If you are going to repartition your disk using fips, you should read these documents. Here's a summary of the steps to take to repartition your drive with fips:

1. **Boot your computer with DOS**—Windows 95 users need to choose Restart the Computer in MS-DOS Mode option found in Shut Down.

2. **Start the fips program**—The program is on the CD in the /col/tools/fips/fips-1.5 directory. Change to that directory and enter the command: **fips**.

3. **Follow the onscreen instructions**—Use the arrow keys to divide the space on the hard disk. Make sure the new partition you create is big enough for all the Linux files. See Chapter 2 for details on how much space is needed.

4. **Save the new partition information and exit fips**—Reboot the computer and make sure Windows or DOS runs properly. Run SCANDISK to confirm the integrity of the partition.

Step 3: Creating Installation Floppy Disks

To install OpenLinux using LISA, do not attempt to install OpenLinux by booting from the CD. If you do this, it will start the LIZARD installation process. You must start the LISA installation from a floppy boot disk. Thus, you need to create a boot disk and a modules disk to begin installation.

The boot disk starts the installation procedure. You might need the modules disks. The most common modules (drivers) are on the boot disk, but sometimes additional modules are needed. The most frequent reason for needing the modules disk is to get drivers for PCM-CIA cards or SCSI cards. On most systems, the modules disk is not used during installation.

To create the installation floppies, you must have a computer running Windows or DOS.

To Create Floppies from Windows   Make sure you have two blank, formatted floppy disks.

1. Insert the OpenLinux CD into the CD-ROM drive. The installation program should start. If it doesn't, run the SETUP program found in the WINSETUP directory of the CD.

2. On the main menu, choose Install Products. On the Install Options menu, choose Create Floppy Install Diskettes. The next screen, shown in Figure A.5, has the options for creating LISA installation disks.

FIGURE A.5
OpenLinux install options for creating LISA Install disks.

3. Take a formatted floppy disk, label it LISA Boot/Install, and put it in the floppy disk drive. Then, click Create Lisa Install diskette. When prompted, enter the drive letter of your floppy drive, usually A. The LISA Boot/Install disk is then built.

4. Repeat the same procedure to build the drivers disk, clicking instead on Create Lisa Modules Diskette. Label the disk LISA Modules.

To Create Floppies from DOS   You need two blank DOS-formatted floppy disks.

1. Boot the computer in DOS.

2. Insert the OpenLinux CD. Take a formatted floppy disk, label it LISA Boot/Install, and put it in the floppy disk drive.

3. At the DOS prompt type each of the following commands, followed by the Enter key:

```
d:
cd \col\launch\floppy
install
```

This starts the RAWRITE program, which prepares the floppy disk with the installation boot files. Remove the floppy disk.

4. Take another formatted floppy disk, label it LISA Modules, and put it in the floppy disk drive.

5. At the d: prompt type **modules** and press the Enter key. This starts the RAWRITE program again, which prepares the floppy with the modules files.

Step 4: Installing OpenLinux

Insert the disk labeled LISA Boot/Install and start your computer. If your computer is set to boot from the CD-ROM drive, do not insert the OpenLinux CD until it is needed. Otherwise, the LIZARD installation program will be started.

After a short pause, while boot information is being read from the floppy disk, a prompt appears. You can press the Enter key or wait a few seconds, and the LISA installation program automatically begins. During installation, you can maneuver between choices with the arrow keys. The Tab key moves from one item to another in the dialog box. At any time you can press the Esc key to cancel a selection. You can select Yes and No buttons by pressing the Y or N keys.

During installation you can view system messages by pressing left-Alt+F6 for kernel message and left-Alt+F8 for diagnostic messages. To return to the installation process, press left-Alt+F1.

Language Selection   To start the installation, choose the language to use during installation. In OpenLinux version 2.3 the languages available are English, Spanish, German, French, and Italian.

Keyboard Layout   Choose a keyboard layout. The keyboard maps match layouts used by country. This is only for installation. You also need to set a keyboard layout for the windows system when you configure X Window, the graphical system.

Using a Previously Saved Configuration   Do you want to use a previously saved configuration? If you created a configuration disk during a previous OpenLinux installation, you can use that disk here. The configuration disk primarily saves network information. It does not save hardware or partitioning information. On the first installation, when it asks about using a previously saved configuration the answer will always be No.

Change LISA Setup   You can change the LISA default settings. Unless you know what you are doing, you should not change any of the defaults:

- **Disable Plug and Play cards**—This option might be turned on if a plug-and-play card is causing problems during autoprobing and configuration. First time, leave it off.
- **Automatic network configuration with BOOTP**—This option is activated during network setup. BOOTP obtains network configuration information from a BOOTP server on your network. OpenLinux does not fully support BOOTP, and trying to use it here may fail. The best option is to not use BOOTP during installation.
- **Automatic network configuration with Netprobe**—Netprobe is a Caldera product similar to BOOTP that allows remote network configuration. Unless you are a network administrator who has configured a network to use Netprobe, leave it off.

Next, LISA begins the process of probing your computer system's hardware. You need to have your hardware list at hand to make sure all of your hardware is properly recognized. At this point, LISA is selecting drivers for your hard disk drives, CD-ROM drives, and network cards.

Hardware Found (IDE/ATAPI)   After probing your computer hardware, LISA displays a list of the IDE devices on your computer, usually the hard disk and CD-ROM drive. Note what the initial probe found and compare it to your list. If all hard disks, CD-ROM drives, and network cards in your computer were found, choose Yes and go to disk partitioning. Support for other devices such as sound cards is added after installation has been completed. The drivers being installed at this point are only for disk drives, CD-ROM drives, and network cards.

If hardware was missing, choose No and go to autoprobing.

Cautious Autoprobing   If you know precisely what hardware is missing from the list of hard disks, CD-ROM drives, and network cards, do not use autoprobing. Autoprobing can cause the computer to freeze. Instead, choose No and go to the Kernel Module Manager where you can choose the correct driver for your hardware.

Autoprobing attempts to detect hardware not found during the initial probe. If your system freezes during autoprobing, shut the computer off and restart installation.

After autoprobing, if all hardware is still not found, answer No to autoprobing again and go to the Kernel Module Manager.

Kernel Module Manager   The Kernel Module Manager lets you indicate precisely what hardware is installed in your computer. It will show you a list of all hardware supported by OpenLinux: the hardware drivers available in OpenLinux.

The module manager offers four choices:

- **Finish kernel module management**—This exits the Module Manager so that you can continue with the installation.
- **Analyze kernel modules**—This can be used to see what has already been found in your system and which drivers have been selected for that hardware.
- **Load kernel modules**—This displays a choice of drivers for CD-ROMs, SCSI adapters, and network cards. Choose from the list shown. You may have to remove the installation disk and insert the modules disk to load a driver not available on the installation disk. After a driver is selected, a window appears asking for parameters for the hardware such as IRQ and I/O settings. Enter the information for your hardware.
- **Remove kernel modules**—When a module is giving you problems or if autoprobing chose the wrong module, it can be removed here.

When you have selected all the hardware drivers, if you inserted the modules disk, make sure to remove it and reinsert the Boot/Install disk before proceeding to the next step. Then choose Finish kernel module management and continue to prepare the hard disk partition.

Change Partition Table   Now you can prepare the hard disk by partitioning the disk and formatting the partitions. Windows identifies most hard drives and partitions with a letter like C or D. Linux identifies these devices by using a subdirectory name.

All devices are found in the /dev directory. Linux uses the device drivers found in /dev for accessing the hard drives, floppy drives, CD-ROM drives, mouse devices, and other hardware devices on your computer. Hard disks and CD-ROMs can be either IDE or SCSI.

Each drive is identified with a set of letters and numbers. Floppy drives start with *fd*. IDE hard drives all start with *hd*. SCSI hard disks start with *sd*. Floppy drives are numbered. Hard drives are counted by letters. The first hard drive of either IDE or SCSI type is given the letter *a*, the second drive the letter *b*, and so on. Each drive is also broken down into four possible primary partitions. Partitions are divisions of the disk. You can use a hard disk as one big drive or divide it up into multiple partitions that can be used separately, almost like separate drives. Table A.3 shows some common device names in Linux.

Table A.3 Hardware Devices	
Floppy drive A	/dev/fd0
First IDE hard disk	/dev/hda
First SCSI hard disk	/dev/sda
First primary partition on first IDE hard disk	/dev/hda1
Second primary partition on first IDE hard disk	/dev/hda2
First primary partition on first SCSI hard disk	/dev/sda1

These device names are used for partitioning and formatting the hard disks during installation. They also are used for accessing the hard disks after Linux is installed.

If this is your first installation, you will need to select the hard disk to prepare with the Linux fdisk utility. If you have previously installed Linux, you may not need to partition the disk with fdisk, and you can move on to Installation Source Selection.

The Hard Disk Selection screen shows you a list of hard disks available on your computer. Select the disk you want to use for OpenLinux. Typically this is the disk identified as /dev/hda. If you have more than one hard disk, you will be given the chance to choose additional disks to partition after preparing the first hard drive.

Installing OpenLinux requires a minimum of two partitions. One is for the operating system and all the other files, the other is a swap partition. On multiuser systems, particularly network servers, it is a good idea to break down the partitions and not use just one big partition. For more information on partitioning strategies, see partitioning in Chapter 2.

Create a Swap Partition   The operating system uses a swap partition when it needs extra memory. This usually occurs when running large or multiple programs. That's why it's sometimes called *virtual memory*.

The swap partition should be at least 16 megabytes in size. Usually the swap partition is the same size as the amount of memory on the computer so that if you have 32 megabytes of RAM you would make your swap partition 32 megabytes. The maximum possible size of a swap partition is 128 megabytes. For more information on how to get the best performance from your swap partition, see the section on partitioning in Chapter 2.

These are the steps to create a swap partition with fdisk:

1. Type **p** to list the current partitions. Note what partitions exist. For example, if Windows or DOS is installed, it typically shows up as /dev/hda1.

2. Type **n** to create a new partition and press Enter.

3. Type **p** to create a primary partition. Type the number of the primary partition you are creating, usually the next available number after any partitions already installed. If there are no partitions on your disk, type the number **1**. If Windows is installed on /dev/hda1, you would type **2** here to create the second primary partition or /dev/hda2.

4. Specify the size of this partition. First, type the cylinder number where the partition will start (usually the first number shown in parentheses), and press Enter. Next, define the size of the swap partition by typing the plus sign (+) followed by the size in megabytes. Don't forget the plus sign. For a 32 megabyte swap partition, type **+32M** and press the Enter key.

5. Finally, mark the partition as swap space. Type the **t** and press Enter. Type the number of the partition you just created: for /dev/hda2, the number would be **2** and press Enter. Then enter the hex code for a swap partition: **82**.

Create the Linux Root Partition   The next step is to create the Linux root partition. If you are creating multiple partitions, see the section on partitioning in Chapter 2. You create multiple partitions in the same way as you create the root partition. You need to know what drives are on the system, how they are divided, and what the size of each partition is. These are the steps to create a Linux root partition with fdisk:

1. Type **p** to list the current partitions. Note what partitions exist.

2. Type **n** to create a new partition and press Enter.

3. Type **p** to create a primary partition. Type the number of the primary partition you are creating, usually the next available number after any partitions already installed. If /dev/hda1 is your swap partition, type **2** here to create the second primary partition or /dev/hda2.

4. Specify the size of this partition. First type the cylinder number where the partition starts, usually the first number shown in parentheses and press Enter. Next, define the size of the partition. You can do this by specifying the size in megabytes. For example, to create a 1 gigabyte partition type **+1024M**. Alternatively, you can choose the entire hard disk for the root partition by typing the last cylinder number displayed in parentheses. Fdisk automatically marks the new partition with hex code 83 for native Linux.

Saving the Changes   To save the new partition information, you must write the information to the disk. Type **w** at the command prompt and press Enter. You should see a message indicating that the partition table has been modified.

You now return to the Hard Disk Selection panel. Select No Further Hard Disk Changes. Some computers might prompt you to reboot the computer and restart the installation process. This is not normally necessary with new systems. On older systems, the computer might not properly read the new partition table. If you reboot, you will have to go through all the installation steps up to changing the partition table.

Configure Swap Space   The partition that is defined as the swap area should be highlighted in this panel. Select Continue and the swap space is formatted.

Installation Source Selection   This is where you indicate where the OpenLinux distribution disk is. Select CD-ROM and press Enter. The next panel shows a list of all possible CD-ROM drives. Your CD-ROM drive should be highlighted automatically. You may want to note the information that's displayed about your CD-ROM drive for your own records.

Make sure the OpenLinux CD is inserted in the drive and then press the Enter key to continue.

LISA then shows information about the CD that it found in the CD-ROM drive. If the information is correct, press Enter.

Create Root Partition   The next step is to select, mount, and format the root partition. The partition that's highlighted on the Selection panel should be the one you created earlier. Press Enter to continue. A warning is then displayed that formatting this partition erases all data. Because this is the root partition, you should format it. Not formatting to save system files from an earlier installation can create undesirable conflicts. Select Yes and continue. To the question about checking for defective sectors, you can safely say No.

After the root partition is formatted, LISA asks whether you want to create additional Linux partitions. If you have set up your system for multiple partitions, answer Yes; otherwise, say No and continue to select installation type.

If you are mounting multiple partitions and if the partition has been previously prepared with Linux ext2 format, LISA will warn you that it is a Linux format partition that does not need to be reformatted. For more information on the Linux file system, see Chapter 6, "Understanding and Using the OpenLinux File System." Reformatting causes all data on the partition to be lost. It is safe to say No to reformatting. You have to indicate the mount point for the additional partitions. For more information on mount points, see partitioning in Chapter 2.

Software Package Preselection   LISA next gives you several choices for selecting which software packages you should install. I recommend the standard system selection, unless you are an experienced OpenLinux user who knows a great deal about the different packages available. The standard system takes about 720 megabytes and includes the following:

- The KDE desktop
- Corel WordPerfect
- StarOffice
- Netscape Communicator
- The BRU backup and restore utility
- NetWare client and administrative utilities
- Apache Web server
- Sendmail
- News
- Majordomo
- Hundreds of games
- COAS for system administration
- Development tools

If you need software packages that are not included with the standard install, you can easily add them later. Choosing to install everything not only creates a bloated system, it could prove to be a security hole for an inexperienced user. Small or minimal installs should only be done when there is a specific need, and custom selection of individual software packages should not be attempted unless you are a highly experienced OpenLinux user. It's too easy to create a system that doesn't have everything that is needed for even a minimal working system by choosing wrongly in a custom installation.

Highlight your package selection choice and press Enter to continue.

Selecting the X-Server   Before the selected software packages are installed, LISA asks for X-Server information. The X-Server is a software server that handles windowing capabilities on a Linux computer. To have windowing on your computer, you need to install the appropriate X-Server software packages.

Because Linux is designed as a high-reliability modular system, the windowing system is separate from the core kernel. This gives Linux added stability because even if the windowing system were to fail, the core Linux system would continue to run. In fact, you can set up OpenLinux to run without a monitor or video card altogether. The Microsoft Windows system has windowing built into the kernel, which means that if the windowing system fails, the entire system fails. It also means that system performance is closely tied to the quality and speed of the video card. Linux's overall system performance is not affected by the video card.

In Linux, the windowing system is X Window, which was created by researchers at the Massachusetts Institute of Technology in collaboration with several leading computer manufacturers. The X Window server is XFree86, which is the X Window for the PC (the 86 refers to Intel's chip series ending with the numbers *86*). By default, LISA installs the VGA16 server. You should also select to install the SVGA server. You should then add the server for the video card in your computer. If you see the server for the video processor chip used by your card in the list, move the arrow key to highlight the server and then press the spacebar to select it. If it's not clear from the list, which shows only video chip types, you should do your best to determine the chip set for your video card. Otherwise, you'll have to install the X-Server for that chipset later before you can use it in the XFree86 setup. In that setup, you can choose the video card by make and model to get the exact settings for your card.

If you are using a commercially available X-windows server such as AcceleratedX or MetroX, all you need to choose at this point are the VGA16 and SVGA servers. Commercial X Window servers often have drivers for the latest models of the high-end video cards and sometimes also offer performance gains for certain types of use.

The VGA16 server is a basic 16-color server that is needed for almost any kind of X-Window setup. For higher resolution and more colors, if your video card is not one of those listed, the SVGA server may work. The VGA16 server is a generic server that works with almost any video card. When nothing else works, use it even though it has limited color and resolution capability.

Press Enter to continue. The software packages are now installed. This can take some time: 15 minutes to an hour depending on the speed of your system, the speed of your CD-ROM drive, and the number of software packages that you chose to install.

Hostname Entry   After all the software packages have been installed, LISA starts the network configuration. The first question requests the *fully qualified domain name* (*FQDN*) for your computer. This means the name of your computer plus its domain. If you are on a network, the network administrator assigns the hostname and the domain name. Obtain that information and enter it here. If your computer will be a Web server, it is common to use the hostname of www. If your computer is not on a network, give the computer whatever name you want, but include a nonexistent domain like the default domain name shown: .nodomain.nowhere. For example, a computer named HAL that is not on a network could be named here as hal.nodomain.nowhere.

Network Card Configuration

If you have a network card, enter Yes at the next panel. If you do not have a network card, select No and go on to Configuring the Clock.

If you have a network card, the device name is probably eth0. Like floppy drives, Ethernet cards are listed as devices and are numbered beginning with the number 0 and going up for each additional card. Linux sees the first Ethernet card as /dev/eth0.

The next panels ask for the IP address, network mask, broadcast address, and router/gateway address. If you don't know these, get them from your network administrator.

The next part of network configuration is entering the DNS name server information. If you have a name server, enter the IP address. Normally you will have a primary and a secondary name server. Some networks even use a third, tertiary name server. A name server matches names to IP addresses; a second or third server is used when the primary server is unavailable.

If your system uses NIS, get the configuration information from the system administrator and enter it in the last panel. Sun Microsystems created the Network Information System, which is usually found only on all-UNIX networks. If you are not using it, select Do Not Use NIS and press Enter to continue.

CMOS Time   The computer's hardware clock is set in the CMOS Time panel. Time settings are marked on files and in email sent from your computer. Most Internet servers use Greenwich Mean Time (GMT or UTC), but the BIOS on most PC system boards uses local time. This can mean that using GMT for OpenLinux may run into system conflicts. Your best choice is to use local time.

If your computer has both OpenLinux and Windows or DOS installed on it, you must choose local time; otherwise, time settings will get discombobulated every time you switch operating systems because those other operating systems recognize only local time.

Finally, you need to indicate your time zone.

Configure Mouse Type   Make sure you choose the correct mouse type. If you don't, your mouse won't respond properly when you set up X Window. Most new Pentium II and newer systems use the PS/2 mouse. If you have a PS/2 mouse, it doesn't matter what brand it is—Mouse Man, Microsoft, Logitech, Mouse Systems, or some other—you will select PS/2 mouse.

Select Printer Driver   At this point, you can select a printer driver for a printer attached to your computer or a printer on the network that you can access. If the printer you use is not on the list, sometimes a driver for a printer made by the same manufacturer will work. Some printers also emulate common printer languages such as Hewlett-Packard's HPCL, and choosing a Hewlett-Packard print driver works with those printers. You then are asked to indicate the port to which the printer is connected, often the first parallel port. This is listed as Parallel Port 0x3bc (/dev/lp0,6,0 (LPT1). The next question is about the default resolution for the printer. This is 600×600 for most laser printers sold today, older printers are 300×300. Last, select the default paper size for your printer.

Password for Root   The Password for root panel lets you set the password for the root directory, also sometimes called *superuser*. Because OpenLinux is designed to be a multiple-user system, regular user accounts cannot make changes to the basic system. They can only make changes on their own files. This is for both the security of the system and to protect other users from mistakes or abuse of the system by an individual user.

But, of course, you must make critical system changes. For this purpose, there is a superuser—root. The root user does system administration and configuration. For more information on root and user accounts, see Chapter 5, "Configuring Your System with COAS."

Type in a password and then retype it to confirm that it is typed correctly. Passwords should be six or more characters, can include letters or numbers but not punctuation, and are case-sensitive. The characters you type won't show onscreen so that someone looking at the video monitor can't read the password. Anyone who knows this password can do anything they want to your system, so be cautious with it, but make sure you don't forget this password. If you don't know the root password, you may be forced to reinstall the entire system.

Creating the First Account   Because the superuser can do anything, you should only login as root when necessary for system administration tasks. Usually you will log in as a regular user. The next step in the LISA installation process is to create the first user account. This is the account you normally will use.

LISA starts creating the first user account by asking for the user login name. It displays the name col (Caldera Open Linux). You should not use this name. It is a sample display only and using col would create a potential security hole on your system.

Typical user login names are the first name of the user (for example, mary); the initials for the first, middle, and last name of the user (mps); or the first name initial with the last name of the user (msmith). In the next panels, LISA asks for a User ID, the user group, home directory, and shell. None of these need to be changed unless you are a systems administrator and you know that you want to use something different than the default. For more information on user ID numbers and user groups see user administration in Chapter 5 on COAS.

In the panel asking for the user's full name, you can type in the full name of the user. This is the name that is displayed in messages sent from the user. The next panel is for entering a password for the new user. This works just like entering the password for root: You must type the password twice to confirm accuracy.

Configuring the LILO Boot Manager   The next step is to configure the LILO boot manager. *LILO* stands for the *LInux LOader*. When your computer starts, it will first load LILO. LILO then starts OpenLinux, or it can be used to choose another operating system if you have another one on your system.

The LILO configuration begins with a Boot Setup Analysis. LISA looks at the computer's primary hard disk to see whether any kind of boot manager is already installed. If you have Windows or DOS, that information should appear in the list that is displayed here. Press Enter to continue.

The next panel offers a list of possible ways to install the LILO boot manager. These are the options and what each means:

- **The Master Boot Record of the first hard disk**—Putting LILO on the MBR is the old-fashioned way of doing it. It works almost every time, but if you have Windows NT on the same hard disk, you can't use the MBR. Putting LILO on the MBR on a Windows NT computer makes it impossible to use NT. Windows NT users should consider using PartitionMagic or boot LILO from a floppy disk to start OpenLinux. Installing LILO on the MBR has generally gone out of favor. The preference is the next choice, in the Linux root partition.

- **The Linux root partition**—This leaves the Master Boot Record intact, and control is simply passed to LILO because the Linux partition is marked as the active partition. This also makes disk recovery easier because altering the MBR can potentially make the whole disk unusable if a problem arises.

- **Some other partition**—This works in the same way as the root partition. Some Linux professionals prefer to use the /boot partition, which they've set by fdisk to be below cylinder 1,023 so that they can be sure to not run into a common problem with the big multiple-gigabyte disks commonly found in computers today.

- **A floppy disk**—The main reason to use a floppy boot disk is when you don't want to change the way your computer normally boots. This is the case in computers that are also running Windows NT. Some high-security systems use a floppy disk for starting. In those systems, the floppy becomes the key for starting OpenLinux.

After you've selected where you want LILO installed, you are asked to select the boot image for LILO. Find the image with the name modular in it, use the arrow keys to get it highlighted, and press the Enter key to continue.

The next panel asks for a name for this boot option. You can leave the name linux. This name is used when you start up the computer. In this case, it means that you would type **linux** to start OpenLinux, though typically OpenLinux is the default system, and you won't have to type anything. If you have another operating system on the same computer, you would type in the name for that boot option in order for it to start. The typical name given to start Windows or DOS is dos. You can make it **win** if you prefer, just type in the word *win*.

If you need any boot parameters, you should enter them in the next panel. If anything appears by default, don't change it. If you aren't sure whether you need to add any parameters, you can add these later after installation. The only one I've ever regularly added is for memory over 64 megabytes. Versions of OpenLinux before 2.3 did not automatically recognize memory over 64 megabytes, so if you had 128 megabytes of memory, you had to add the parameter mem=128M. This is not necessary in version 2.3, which has calls to auto-register memory over 64 megabytes.

The next panel lets you select additional LILO entries. Pay careful attention here. If you fail to add additional boot images at this point you will not be able to access Windows or DOS on your computer if they are already installed. Then you have to edit the LILO configuration file and enter the precise information for accessing the other systems.

Look through the list and select any additional boot images you want such as DOS, for computers with Windows or DOS installed on them. The name you give this boot option is the name you type during startup if you want to boot to this operating system. When you've selected all the boot images you want to use, select No further entries to add to LILO and press Enter.

When the Install LILO as Configured panel is displayed, press Enter once more to install LILO.

Configure Daemon/Server Autostart   Now you are asked to indicate which services will be started when you boot Linux. Use the arrow keys to move between the choices. Use the spacebar to select or unselect a service. Unless you know what you are doing, you should leave the defaults that are shown.

You can alter the settings after installing OpenLinux by starting LISA and selecting or unselecting services at that time.

The final procedure is to choose an X11 Server. You'll see a list of the servers you selected earlier in the installation. If you are not sure what to choose, VGA16 will work with almost any video card available. You are given the option to set up the X Window server at this point. The safe choice is to select No and configure X Window after the installation of OpenLinux is completed and the Linux operating system is running.

Before the system restarts with the new Linux operating system, it offers to save the current configuration. This does not save hardware information, but saves network configuration information. It can save you some typing if you have to reinstall. If you want to do this, remove the Boot/Install disk and insert a blank formatted disk. Then select Yes and press the Enter key. After it's done writing to disk, remove the floppy, and mark it OpenLinux Configuration. This is not an emergency disk: It does not boot the system, and you cannot do a system recovery with the information on this disk.

That's it! You've finished installing OpenLinux. Restart the computer. Do not turn the computer off at this point, or you risk losing data from the install. You will probably want to go on to configuring the X Window system. You can find the steps to do in Appendix B, "XFree86 Configuration."

XFree86 Configuration

XFree86, the X Window system used by OpenLinux, is a PC-based windowing system based on the X Window system created by researchers at the Massachusetts Institute of Technology in collaboration with several leading computer manufacturers. X Window works differently than windowing on other computer systems because X Window is a base system that does not include a user interface with menus and scroll bars. The window manager provides these. In OpenLinux, the window manager is KDE, though KDE is more than just a window manager.

CAUTION

Be careful when setting the video card and monitor in XFree86. Using the wrong settings can cause serious damage to your video card or monitor. Do not "play" with the settings. Use only settings that come from the manufacturer of the equipment on your system. I cannot emphasize this enough. Ignore this warning at the risk of destroying your computer equipment.

For KDE to work, however, an X Window server must be running. That's where Xfree86 comes in.

Linux uses a Windows server so that it can give multiple users greater flexibility. By running an X Window server, you can have a Windows session from your computer running on a monitor that is connected through a network as well as on the monitor directly connected to your computer.

XFree86 is maintained by a team of developers who keep support up to date with all the new video cards available. Unfortunately, some limitations get in the way. Some manufacturers insist on keeping the programming interface to their video cards a secret so that users can't build a driver independently unless they pay a licensing fee and sign a confidentiality agreement.

This effectively prevents the XFree86 team from developing support for those cards. These manufacturers should then provide the support, but few do. In the case where no specific support is available for a video card, the SVGA server usually works.

You will need to run XFree86 configuration if you want to change your video setup or if you installed OpenLinux using LISA. To start the XFree86 configuration, you need to be logged in as root. If you have not logged in as root, you can "become" root by using the su command. Open a terminal window and enter:

`su -`

The su (substitute user) utility lets you become the root user if you know the password. Using the - (hyphen) parameter means that the home directory and environment variables are changed to those used by root.

To start the configuration program, type `XF86Setup` and press the Enter key. When typing in this command, remember that Linux is case sensitive.

In some cases, running XF86Setup after the initial install fails because of a security conflict. To fix that problem, use an editor to put the following line into the /etc/X11/xinit/xserverrc file:

```
HOST='hostname --fqdn'
```

Then change all instances of $HOSTNAME to $HOST.

You can also use the nongraphical, text-based configuration program xf86config, which requires a little more technical understanding of the setup process but covers essentially the same setup process. It is a good alternative if XF86Setup fails to work.

If you are asked whether to use the current XFree86 settings, select Yes and press the Enter key. Before XF86Setup can start, the computer must switch to graphics mode. This usually takes less than a minute. Press Enter to switch to graphics mode. The opening screen is shown in Figure B.1.

App B

FIGURE B.1
XFree86 setup.

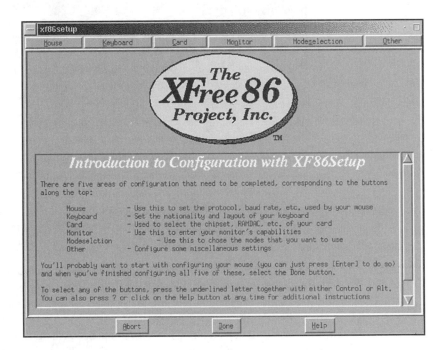

Configuring the Mouse

If you can already move your mouse around the screen, you can skip the mouse setup. If your mouse doesn't respond, you can use the arrow and Tab keys to move around.

Alt+M selects Mouse setup (shown in Figure B.2); you select the type of mouse. The device setting is the port to which your mouse is connected. A serial mouse that Windows identifies as connected to COM1 is connected to /dev/ttyS0 in Linux. The PS/2 connection is /dev/psaux.

FIGURE B.2

Mouse configuration.

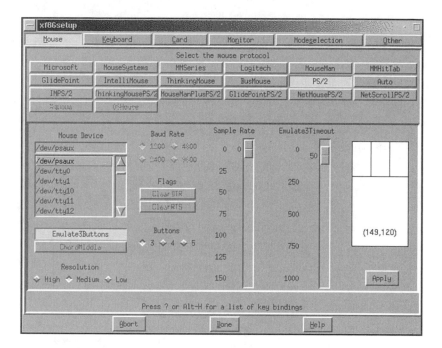

A dysfunctional mouse can be difficult to configure. All makes of PS/2 mouse devices work the same, but serial mouse devices are not the same, even within the same make. For example, sometimes a Logitech mouse won't work when configured as Logitech but will work if configured as Microsoft.

TIP Some Microsoft mouse devices are "smart": They won't respond until they receive a signal from Microsoft's Windows. Sometimes setting these mouse devices to MouseSystems makes them work.

A three-button mouse is preferred for all Linux systems because the systems make good use of the third button, for example in cut and paste operations. If you don't have a three-button mouse, you can set a two-button mouse to emulate three buttons. When it is turned on in the XFree86 setup, holding two buttons down at the same time emulates a third button.

The third button can be used for copying and pasting when working on a character mode terminal or on the KDE desktop. To use it, highlight an area that you want to copy by holding down the left mouse button. When the section to be copied is highlighted, move the mouse pointer to the location where you want to paste the highlighted text and press the third button, if you have one, or both buttons at the same time, if you have enabled three-button emulation. The highlighted section is pasted into the new location.

Pressing the letter a after making a change in the setup applies the change.

Configuring the Keyboard

With a working mouse, you can click on the Keyboard tab to change the keyboard settings (shown in Figure B.3.). The default setting is the U.S. English keyboard. If you want a different setting, you can select it here. Also, if you are using something other than the standard 101-key keyboard, you can change this setting.

FIGURE B.3
Keyboard configuration.

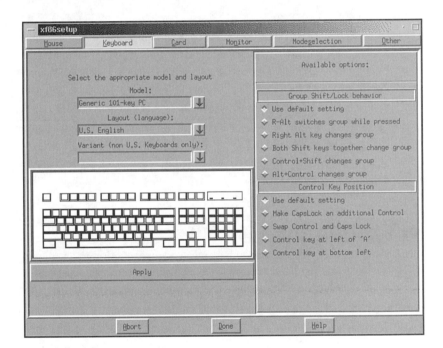

Configuring the Video Card

Selecting the Card tab opens the video card setup. Click on the Card List button to see a list of video card drivers that are included with OpenLinux (shown in Figure B.4). After you've selected the video card that matches the one in your computer, a message should appear on the bottom of the screen, saying, "That's probably all there is to configuring your card."

FIGURE B.4
Video card configuration. The card list shows video drivers by make and model.

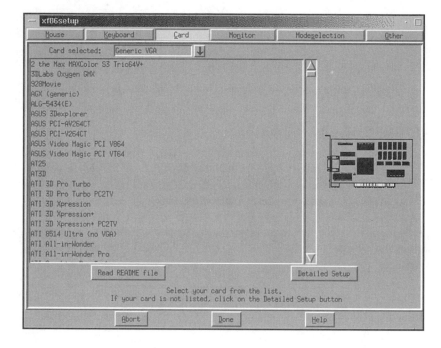

If you can't find the right driver for your card or if the driver you selected isn't responding correctly, choose the SVGA settings. The system will work, but it won't take advantage of the advanced capabilities of your video card.

Configuring the Monitor

After selecting the Monitor tab, you can begin configuring your monitor (shown in Figure B.5). You need to know your monitor's refresh rates. If you don't know, you need to pick one of the options shown. Picking the wrong refresh rate can be hazardous to your monitor's health. In fact, it's possible to fry a monitor this way.

Most new monitors are multifrequency, meaning they can display at a number of different refresh rates. Picking a refresh rate that is too high is dangerous. If you are not sure, pick Standard VGA.

> **CAUTION**
>
> Some people seem to think that because a higher refresh rate improves the graphics on a monitor, they can just pick it here to get better quality. However, if your monitor doesn't support that rate, you'll be in trouble. If you are lucky, your system will only freeze up, and you'll have to reboot. If you aren't lucky, you can cause irreparable damage. Be cautious.

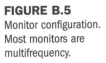

FIGURE B.5
Monitor configuration.
Most monitors are
multifrequency.

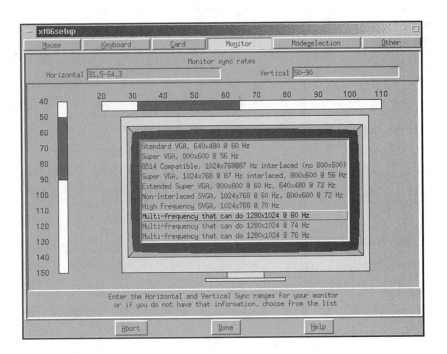

Laptops can be particularly difficult to configure. I needed to use a commercially developed X server rather than XFree86 to get my laptop to work. I obtained AcceleratedX from Xi Graphics (www.xig.com), which has drivers for most laptops and also most of the latest video cards.

Choosing Resolution Modes and Color Depth

The Mode selection tab enables you to select the resolution and color depth for your display (shown in Figure B6). The X server defaults to a basic 640×480 resolution. Unlike Windows 95, at this resolution X Window does not constrain the objects to the size of the window. This creates a situation in which objects on the screen seem to go beyond the screen where you can't see them or get to them, which is unworkable for most users.

You'll want to set a minimum resolution of 800×600. All video cards sold today have at least 4MB of memory, meaning that they can support a base resolution of 1024×768. The resolution and color depth your video card will support depends on the amount of video memory on the card. Eight-bit color displays a basic 256-color palette; 16-bit color displays more than 65,000 colors. True color is the name given to 24-bit color depth, which displays 16 million colors.

FIGURE B.6
Mode configuration.

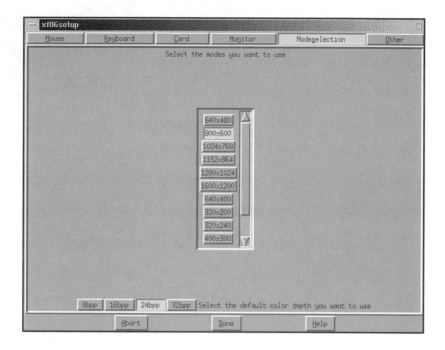

Configuring Other Settings

The last tab is for other settings. Do not change the defaults unless you know what you are doing. One of the defaults enables the server to be "killed" with the keyboard combination Ctrl+Alt+Backspace. This can be useful when you are having problems with the video display and need to exit X Window.

Click Done when you are finished with the setup. The XF86Setup program then tries out the new settings. If the results appear normal, you can click Save the configuration and exit. The configuration file is saved and made available for all users. If you are prompted with a question about creating a link to the X server setup, select Yes and press the Enter key.

The XF86Config File

The configuration file for the X server is a standard Linux configuration file that the XF86Setup normally creates. The file is named XF86Config and is in the /etc directory. It is a text file that you can edit using the Text Editor in the KDE desktop or with a terminal editor such as vi. For tips on using the vi text editor, see the section on vi in Chapter 7, "Using the Character Mode Terminal."

The configuration file is read each time the X server starts. Advanced users can perform some fine-tuning or troubleshooting by tweaking this configuration file.

The file is divided into four sections. The first section sets global options for the mouse, keyboard, and directory locations. This section almost never needs to be changed. The second section covers monitors, and the third section is for video cards. The last section, the screen section, puts it all together.

```
You can find a complete description of all the options in this file in the
manual page entry for XF86Config. To see this, typeman 5 XF86Config
```

Files Section

This section lists the files that X server uses. It shows the color and font files.

```
Section "Files"
    RgbPath      "/usr/X11R6/lib/X11/rgb"
    FontPath
"/usr/X11R6/lib/X11/fonts/misc/,/usr/X11R6/lib/X11/fonts/75dpi/:unscaled,/usr/X11
R6/lib/X11/fonts/100dpi/:unscaled,/usr/X11R6/lib/X11/fonts/Type1/,/usr/X11R6/lib/
X11/fonts/Speedo/,/usr/X11R6/lib/X11/fonts/75dpi/,/usr/X11R6/lib/X11/fonts/100dpi
/"
EndSection
```

The RgbPath is the location of the RGB color database. The FontPath lists each font type that is installed.

ServerFlags Section

Server flags are special options needed for the video card. You will rarely find a need to change this section. It corresponds to the Other setup panel in XF86Setup. For example, if you want to turn off the Ctrl+Alt+Backspace key combination to "kill" the X server, you put the word DontZap on its own line in this section.

```
Section "ServerFlags"
EndSection
```

Keyboard Section

This section specifies keyboard options such as key mapping:

```
Section "Keyboard"
    Protocol        "Standard"
    AutoRepeat      500 5
    LeftAlt         Meta
    RightAlt        Meta
    ScrollLock      Compose
    RightCtl        Control
    XkbKeycodes     "xfree86"
```

```
    XkbTypes          "default"
    XkbCompat         "default"
    XkbSymbols        "us(pc101)"
    XkbGeometry       "pc"
    XkbKeymap         "xfree86(us)"
    XkbRules          "xfree86"
    XkbModel          "pc101"
    XkbLayout         "us"
EndSection
```

The protocol is almost always Standard. The `AutoRepeat` rate is the delay before repeating the key at the rate specified after the delay time. The `Protocol` must be set to `Standard`; no other protocol is supported. Legacy UNIX programs use the `LeftAlt`, `RightAlt`, `ScrollLock`, and `RightCtl` settings, and they aren't used on standard Linux systems. The other settings are for the keyboard model, the keyboard layout, and the language layout to use.

Pointer Section

The Pointer section deals with the mouse or other pointing device:

```
Section "Pointer"
    Protocol          "PS/2"
    Device            "/dev/psaux"
    BaudRate          1200
    Emulate3Timeout 50
    Resolution        100
    Emulate3Buttons
EndSection
```

The `Protocol` specifies the type of mouse you are using. Common protocols are BusMouse, PS/2, IntelliMouse, Logitech, Microsoft, MouseMan, MouseSystems, and ThinkingMouse. The `Device` setting is the port used by the mouse: /dev/psaux is for the PS/2 mouse port, /dev/ttyS0 is COM1, and /dev/ttyS1 is COM2. The BaudRate setting is only used by the Logitech mouse.

The `Emulate3Timeout` is how close in time in milliseconds the two buttons must be pressed to be considered simultaneous. The default setting is 50. If you find that you can't get the two buttons pressed together, try setting this to 100 to give you a little more time. `Emulate3Buttons` enables a two-button mouse to emulate a three-button mouse. This adds extra functionality in OpenLinux.

Monitor Section

CAUTION

This is the most important section in the configuration file—and the most dangerous. Make changes at your own risk, and do not attempt them unless you are absolutely certain of what you are doing.

For each resolution, there is a `ModeLine` entry in the Monitor section. These lines describe the refresh vertical and horizontal refresh rates for your monitor:

```
Section "Monitor"
    Identifier      "Monitor"
    VendorName      "Make"
    ModelName       "Model"
    HorizSync       31.5-64.3
    VertRefresh     50-90
    ModeLine    "800x600"    60.66 800 864 928 1088 600 616 621 657 -hsync -vsync
EndSection
```

The `Identifier` is any name you want to give for the monitor. Normally this is a name you use to identify this monitor configuration. The `VendorName` is also any text you want. Normally it is the brand name of the monitor. The `ModelName` is any text you want. Normally this would be the model number of your monitor. None of these three settings has any configuration meaning.

The `HorizSync` setting is the horizontal sync range in kHz for your monitor. Obtain this information from the documentation with the monitor. The `VertRefresh` setting is the refresh rate in Hz for your monitor. Get this information from the documentation with the monitor. The `ModeLine` setting defines possible modes for the monitor. These settings are determined by a combination of resolution refresh rate as well as the dot clock frequency and timings. The VideoModes.doc file in the /usr/X11R6/doc/ directory describes in detail how to determine these values. It is much easier to let the XFree86 configuration software do this for you.

CAUTION

Wrong information or errors in any of the `HorizSync`, `VertRefresh`, or `ModeLine` settings can permanently damage the monitor.

Device Section

The Device section defines the system's video card. In addition to identifying the make and model of the video card, it also shows the chipset, video RAM, clock signals, and options for the card:

CAUTION

The clock signals are the only setting that can be difficult to figure out. The values must be listed in the proper order. A mistake here can blow your monitor.

```
Section "Device"
    Identifier        "Video Card"
    VendorName        "Make"
    BoardName         "Model"
    Chipset           "S3"
    VideoRam          4086
    Clocks            25.30 28.32 34.55 43.16 32.90 66.56 72.00 88.05 59.99
EndSection
```

The Identifier is the name you want to use to identify this video card configuration. The VendorName is any text you want. Normally it is the brand name of the video card. The BoardName is any text you want. Normally this would be the model number of your video card. None of these settings has any configuration meaning.

The Chipset identifies your video chipset. This is an optional entry since the X server will probe the hardware to determine the chipset. VideoRam is the amount of video memory on the video card. Clocks are the dot-clocks on the graphics board. The values are in MHz. The value number and order of this line is based on information stored internally in the video card. Do not edit this line. The X server will probe the board to get the correct settings.

Screen Section

The Screen section ties together the monitor and device entries to create the X desktop. The driver indicates the X server for this screen. The driver is probably one of the following: Accel, SVGA, VGA16, VGA2, or Mono. The Screen section also has a Display subsection for defining resolution settings.

```
Section "Screen"
    Driver            "Accel"
    Device            "Video Card"
    Monitor           "Monitor"
    DefaultColorDepth 8
    BlankTime         0
    SuspendTime       0
    OffTime           0
    SubSection "Display"
        Depth         8
        Modes         "800x600"
        ViewPort      0 0
    EndSubSection
    SubSection "Display"
        Depth         15
        Modes         "800x600"
    EndSubSection
    SubSection "Display"
        Depth         16
        Modes         "800x600"
        ViewPort      0 0
    EndSubSection
    SubSection "Display"
```

```
        Depth          24
        Modes          "800x600"
        ViewPort       0 0
    EndSubSection
    SubSection "Display"
        Depth          32
        Modes          "800x600"
        ViewPort       0 0
    EndSubSection
EndSection
```

Each screen section must begin with a driver entry. The possible driver names are Accel (for all accelerated X servers including S3, S3V, Mach8, Mach32, Mach64, 8514, P9000, AGX I128, TGA, 3Dlabs, and W32), Mono, SVGA, VGA2 (monochrome VGA), and VGA16.

The Device is the device name used in the Device section. The Monitor is the monitor name used in the Monitor section. The DefaultColorDepth is the color depth to use when Depth in the Display section is not specified.

Each subsection defines the settings for the different supported color depths. A setting of 8 allows 256 colors. A setting of 16 is for thousands of colors. A setting of 24 is for millions of colors. The modes setting is for resolution. The most common resolutions are 1024×768, 800×600, and 640×480. The ViewPort is with virtual windows, which are not enabled in the default OpenLinux setup. The setting of 0 0 indicates there is no virtual window.

The GNU General Public License

Version 2, June 1991

Copyright[copy] 1989, 1991 Free Software Foundation, Inc., 59 Temple Place, Suite 330, Boston, MA 02111-1307 USA

Everyone is permitted to copy and distribute verbatim copies of this license document, but changing it is not allowed.

Preamble

The licenses for most software are designed to take away your freedom to share and change it. By contrast, the GNU General Public License is intended to guarantee your freedom to share and change free software—to make sure the software is free for all its users. This General Public License applies to most of the Free Software Foundation's software and to any other program whose authors commit to using it. (Some other Free Software Foundation software is covered by the GNU Library General Public License instead.) You can apply it to your programs, too.

When we speak of free software, we are referring to freedom, not price. Our General Public Licenses are designed to make sure that you have the freedom to distribute copies of free software (and charge for this service if you wish), that you receive source code or can get it if you want it, that you can change the software or use pieces of it in new free programs, and that you know you can do these things.

To protect your rights, we need to make restrictions that forbid anyone to deny you these rights or to ask you to surrender the rights. These restrictions translate to certain responsibilities for you if you distribute copies of the software, or if you modify it.

For example, if you distribute copies of such a program, whether gratis or for a fee, you must give the recipients all the rights that you have. You must make sure that they, too, receive or can get the source code. And you must show them these terms so they know their rights.

We protect your rights with two steps: (1) copyright the software, and (2) offer you this license which gives you legal permission to copy, distribute, and/or modify the software.

Also, for each author's protection and ours, we want to make certain that everyone understands that there is no warranty for this free software. If the software is modified by someone else and passed on, we want its recipients to know that what they have is not the original, so that any problems introduced by others will not reflect on the original authors' reputations.

Finally, any free program is threatened constantly by software patents. We wish to avoid the danger that redistributors of a free program will individually obtain patent licenses, in effect making the program proprietary. To prevent this, we have made it clear that any patent must be licensed for everyone's free use or not licensed at all.

The precise terms and conditions for copying, distribution, and modification follow.

GNU GENERAL PUBLIC LICENSE TERMS AND CONDITIONS FOR COPYING, DISTRIBUTION, AND MODIFICATION

0. This License applies to any program or other work which contains a notice placed by the copyright holder saying it may be distributed under the terms of this General Public License. The "Program", below, refers to any such program or work, and a "work based on the Program" means either the Program or any derivative work under copyright law: that is to say, a work containing the Program or a portion of it, either verbatim or with modifications and/or translated into another language. (Hereinafter, translation is included without limitation in the term "modification.") Each licensee is addressed as "you."

Activities other than copying, distribution, and modification are not covered by this License; they are outside its scope. The act of running the Program is not restricted, and the output from the Program is covered only if its contents constitute a work based on the Program (independent of having been made by running the Program). Whether that is true depends on what the Program does.

1. You may copy and distribute verbatim copies of the Program's source code as you receive it, in any medium, provided that you conspicuously and appropriately publish on each copy an appropriate copyright notice and disclaimer of warranty; keep intact all the notices that refer to this License and to the absence of any warranty; and give any other recipients of the Program a copy of this License along with the Program.

You may charge a fee for the physical act of transferring a copy, and you may at your option offer warranty protection in exchange for a fee.

2. You may modify your copy or copies of the Program or any portion of it, thus forming a work based on the Program, and copy and distribute such modifications or work under the terms of Section 1 above, provided that you also meet all of these conditions:

a. You must cause the modified files to carry prominent notices stating that you changed the files and the date of any change.

b. You must cause any work that you distribute or publish, that in whole or in part contains or is derived from the Program or any part thereof, to be licensed as a whole at no charge to all third parties under the terms of this License.

c. If the modified program normally reads commands interactively when run, you must cause it, when started running for such interactive use in the most ordinary way, to print or display an announcement including an appropriate copyright notice and a notice that there is no warranty (or else, saying that you provide a warranty) and that users may redistribute the program under these conditions, and telling the user how to view a copy of this License. (Exception: if the Program itself is interactive but does not normally print such an announcement, your work based on the Program is not required to print an announcement.)

These requirements apply to the modified work as a whole. If identifiable sections of that work are not derived from the Program, and can be reasonably considered independent and separate works in themselves, then this License, and its terms, do not apply to those sections when you distribute them as separate works. But when you distribute the same sections as part of a whole which is a work based on the Program, the distribution of the whole must be on the terms of this License, whose permissions for other licensees extend to the entire whole, and thus to each and every part regardless of who wrote it.

Thus, it is not the intent of this section to claim rights or contest your rights to work written entirely by you; rather, the intent is to exercise the right to control the distribution of derivative or collective works based on the Program.

In addition, mere aggregation of another work not based on the Program with the Program (or with a work based on the Program) on a volume of a storage or distribution medium does not bring the other work under the scope of this License.

3. You may copy and distribute the Program (or a work based on it, under Section 2) in object code or executable form under the terms of Sections 1 and 2 above provided that you also do one of the following:

a. Accompany it with the complete corresponding machine-readable source code, which must be distributed under the terms of Sections 1 and 2 above on a medium customarily used for software interchange; or,

b. Accompany it with a written offer, valid for at least three years, to give any third party, for a charge no more than your cost of physically performing source distribution, a complete machine-readable copy of the corresponding source code, to be distributed under the terms of Sections 1 and 2 above on a medium customarily used for software interchange; or,

c. Accompany it with the information you received as to the offer to distribute corresponding source code. (This alternative is allowed only for noncommercial distribution and only if you received the program in object code or executable form with such an offer, in accord with Subsection b above.)

The source code for a work means the preferred form of the work for making modifications to it. For an executable work, complete source code means all the source code for all modules it contains, plus any associated interface definition files, plus the scripts used to control compilation and installation of the executable. However, as a special exception, the source code distributed need not include anything that is normally distributed (in either source or binary form) with the major components (compiler, kernel, and so on) of the operating system on which the executable runs, unless that component itself accompanies the executable.

If distribution of executable or object code is made by offering access to copy from a designated place, then offering equivalent access to copy the source code from the same place counts as distribution of the source code, even though third parties are not compelled to copy the source along with the object code.

4. You may not copy, modify, sublicense, or distribute the Program except as expressly provided under this License. Any attempt otherwise to copy, modify, sublicense or distribute the Program is void, and will automatically terminate your rights under this License. However, parties who have received copies, or rights, from you under this License will not have their licenses terminated so long as such parties remain in full compliance.

5. You are not required to accept this License, since you have not signed it. However, nothing else grants you permission to modify or distribute the Program or its derivative works. These actions are prohibited by law if you do not accept this License. Therefore, by modifying or distributing the Program (or any work based on the Program), you indicate your acceptance of this License to do so, and all its terms and conditions for copying, distributing or modifying the Program or works based on it.

6. Each time you redistribute the Program (or any work based on the Program), the recipient automatically receives a license from the original licensor to copy, distribute or modify the Program subject to these terms and conditions. You may not impose any further restrictions on the recipients' exercise of the rights granted herein. You are not responsible for enforcing compliance by third parties to this License.

7. If, as a consequence of a court judgment or allegation of patent infringement or for any other reason (not limited to patent issues), conditions are imposed on you (whether by court order, agreement or otherwise) that contradict the conditions of this License, they do not excuse you from the conditions of this License. If you cannot distribute so as to satisfy simultaneously your obligations under this License and any other pertinent obligations, then as a consequence you may not distribute the Program at all. For example, if a patent license would not permit royalty-free redistribution of the Program by all those who receive copies directly or indirectly through you, then the only way you could satisfy both it and this License would be to refrain entirely from distribution of the Program.

If any portion of this section is held invalid or unenforceable under any particular circumstance, the balance of the section is intended to apply and the section as a whole is intended to apply in other circumstances.

It is not the purpose of this section to induce you to infringe any patents or other property right claims or to contest validity of any such claims; this section has the sole purpose of protecting the integrity of the free software distribution system, which is implemented by public license practices. Many people have made generous contributions to the wide range of software distributed through that system in reliance on consistent application of that system; it is up to the author/donor to decide if he or she is willing to distribute software through any other system and a licensee cannot impose that choice.

This section is intended to make thoroughly clear what is believed to be a consequence of the rest of this License.

App
C

8. If the distribution and/or use of the Program is restricted in certain countries either by patents or by copyrighted interfaces, the original copyright holder who places the Program under this License may add an explicit geographical distribution limitation excluding those countries, so that distribution is permitted only in or among countries not thus excluded. In such case, this License incorporates the limitation as if written in the body of this License.

9. The Free Software Foundation may publish revised and/or new versions of the General Public License from time to time. Such new versions will be similar in spirit to the present version, but may differ in detail to address new problems or concerns.

   Each version is given a distinguishing version number. If the Program specifies a version number of this License which applies to it and "any later version," you have the option of following the terms and conditions either of that version or of any later version published by the Free Software Foundation. If the Program does not specify a version number of this License, you may choose any version ever published by the Free Software Foundation.

10. If you wish to incorporate parts of the Program into other free programs whose distribution conditions are different, write to the author to ask for permission. For software which is copyrighted by the Free Software Foundation, write to the Free Software Foundation; we sometimes make exceptions for this. Our decision will be guided by the two goals of preserving the free status of all derivatives of our free software and of promoting the sharing and reuse of software generally.

NO WARRANTY

11. BECAUSE THE PROGRAM IS LICENSED FREE OF CHARGE, THERE IS NO WARRANTY FOR THE PROGRAM, TO THE EXTENT PERMITTED BY APPLICABLE LAW. EXCEPT WHEN OTHERWISE STATED IN WRITING THE COPYRIGHT HOLDERS AND/OR OTHER PARTIES PROVIDE THE PROGRAM "AS IS" WITHOUT WARRANTY OF ANY KIND, EITHER EXPRESSED OR IMPLIED, INCLUDING, BUT NOT LIMITED TO, THE IMPLIED WARRANTIES OF MERCHANTABILITY AND FITNESS FOR A PARTICULAR PURPOSE. THE ENTIRE RISK AS TO THE QUALITY AND PERFORMANCE OF THE PROGRAM IS WITH YOU. SHOULD THE PROGRAM PROVE DEFECTIVE, YOU ASSUME THE COST OF ALL NECESSARY SERVICING, REPAIR, OR CORRECTION.

12. IN NO EVENT UNLESS REQUIRED BY APPLICABLE LAW OR AGREED TO IN WRITING WILL ANY COPYRIGHT HOLDER, OR ANY OTHER PARTY WHO MAY MODIFY AND/OR REDISTRIBUTE THE PROGRAM AS PERMITTED ABOVE, BE LIABLE TO YOU FOR DAMAGES, INCLUDING ANY GENERAL, SPECIAL, INCIDENTAL, OR CONSEQUENTIAL DAMAGES ARISING OUT OF THE USE OR INABILITY TO USE THE PROGRAM (INCLUDING BUT NOT LIMITED TO LOSS

OF DATA OR DATA BEING RENDERED INACCURATE OR LOSSES SUSTAINED BY YOU OR THIRD PARTIES OR A FAILURE OF THE PROGRAM TO OPERATE WITH ANY OTHER PROGRAMS), EVEN IF SUCH HOLDER OR OTHER PARTY HAS BEEN ADVISED OF THE POSSIBILITY OF SUCH DAMAGES.

END OF TERMS AND CONDITIONS

How to Apply These Terms to Your New Programs

If you develop a new program, and you want it to be of the greatest possible use to the public, the best way to achieve this is to make it free software which everyone can redistribute and change under these terms.

To do so, attach the following notices to the program. It is safest to attach them to the start of each source file to most effectively convey the exclusion of warranty; and each file should have at least the "copyright" line and a pointer to where the full notice is found.

```
<one line to give the program's name and a brief idea of what it does.>
➥ Copyright (C) <year> <name of author>
```

This program is free software; you can redistribute it and/or modify it under the terms of the GNU General Public License as published by the Free Software Foundation; either version 2 of the License, or (at your option) any later version.

This program is distributed in the hope that it will be useful, but WITHOUT ANY WARRANTY; without even the implied warranty of MERCHANTABILITY or FITNESS FOR A PARTICULAR PURPOSE. See the GNU General Public License for more details.

You should have received a copy of the GNU General Public License along with this program; if not, write to the Free Software Foundation, Inc., 59 Temple Place, Suite 330, Boston, MA 02111-1307 USA

Also add information on how to contact you by electronic and paper mail.

If the program is interactive, make it output a short notice like this when it starts in an interactive mode:

Gnomovision version 69, Copyright (C) year name of author
Gnomovision comes with ABSOLUTELY NO WARRANTY; for details type **show w**. This is free software, and you are welcome to redistribute it under certain conditions; type **show c** for details.

The hypothetical commands **show w** and **show c** should show the appropriate parts of the General Public License. Of course, the commands you use may be called something other than **show w** and **show c**; they could even be mouse clicks or menu items—whatever suits your program.

You should also get your employer (if you work as a programmer) or your school, if any, to sign a "copyright disclaimer" for the program, if necessary. Here is a sample; alter the names:

```
Yoyodyne, Inc., hereby disclaims all copyright interest in the
program `Gnomovision' (which makes passes at compilers) written by James Hacker.
<signature of Ty Coon>, 1 April 1989
Ty Coon, President of Vice
```

This General Public License does not permit incorporating your program into proprietary programs. If your program is a subroutine library, you may consider it more useful to permit linking proprietary applications with the library. If this is what you want to do, use the GNU Library General Public License instead of this License.

Finding Help

There are many ways to find additional help or information about OpenLinux. You can find help on your computer or on the World Wide Web. Other books and periodicals are available. In addition, Caldera Systems and other companies have support services.

Stay on top of security alerts and fixes at the OpenLinux security Web site at `www.calderasystems.com/news/security/index.html`.

Caldera Systems provides many ways to get support. If you have purchased the full OpenLinux package put together by Caldera Systems, you can get 90 days or five incidents of support for installation problems by email. Contact `support@calderasystems.com`.

If you bought a copy of OpenLinux packaged by a reseller, you will have to contact the reseller to see if it has installation support. Most don't.

The OpenLinux disk included with this book does not include installation support.

Caldera Systems has several fee-based support programs. If you are a business that demands that its computer system be up and running 24 hours a day, these support programs are a good idea. The fees are typical to what other operating systems charge for similar support services. For information, phone Caldera Systems at 888–GO–LINUX (888–465–4689). Some of this support, particularly installation and phone support, is provided by other companies, not Caldera Systems.

A number of other service providers also provide support for OpenLinux. The Caldera Systems Web page contains a list of Authorized Service Centers. Other service centers also provide quality support. You should ask around for recommendations.

Caldera Systems also has a free Web-based support site. The site is at `www.calderasystems.com/support/support.calderasystems.com`. Offered on the site are links to several sources of support information:

- **Support Knowledge Base**—A searchable support knowledge base provides answers that the Caldera Systems support staff have given to technical and service questions. This is the first place to look. Sometimes I've found that someone else has already asked my question, and the answer is here. The direct Web address is `support.calderasystems.com`.

- **Downloadable Files**—Check here regularly for package updates, bug fixes, and security patches. The Web address is `www.calderasystems.com/support/resources.html`; choose Caldera Systems Download Updates.

- **Technical Guides**—This includes online guides to OpenLinux, problem-solving guides, documents for specific program packages included with OpenLinux, and links to the entire Linux Documentation Project. The Web address is `www.calderasystems.com/support/resources.html`; choose Caldera Systems Technical Guides.

- **User-to-User Forums**—This contains information on how to join the OpenLinux users forum and other forums maintained by Caldera Systems. The OpenLinux users forum is one of the best Linux email discussion lists available on the Internet. It covers more than just OpenLinux. You'll find users of other Linux distributions there as well, because of the quality of the discussion. The direct Web address to get to this page is `www.calderasystems.com/support/forums.html`.

- **Education Services**—This provides links to a Caldera Systems OpenLinux training program. The direct Web address to this page is `www.calderasystems.com/education/`.

- **Support Programs**—This includes technical support options from Caldera Systems. The direct Web address to this page is `www.calderasystems.com/support/details.html`.

Online Documentation

All the OpenLinux technical guides and the How To documents from the Linux Documentation Project are on the OpenLinux installation CD. Use a Web browser to open the index.html file in the col/doc directory. Figure D.1 shows the guide page.

Documentation for all the software packages installed with OpenLinux can be found in the /usr/doc directory on your OpenLinux system.

FIGURE D.1
Installation manuals, Linux How To documents and FAQs are on the OpenLinux CD.

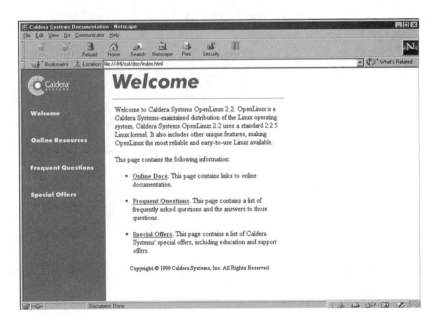

App

D

Man Pages

The original documentation for Linux was in the manual pages, usually called the "man" pages. These provide short explanations of how a particular program works.

Man pages have a wealth of information, but because programmers generally write them, they often assume a certain level of knowledge.

Linux old-timers swear by man pages. New users swear at them.

Man pages follow a common format so that once you learn how one works, all the others will be similar.

Access man pages at a terminal window. Type **xman &**, which opens the manual page browser. Using the **&** option runs the program in background. Click the Manual Page button. Select the Options button and choose Display Director. This displays an index of manual pages available.

You can also search for the manual for a particular program. Select Options and choose Search. Type the search string, which is the name of the program you want. Then press the Enter key. For example, typing in the name **samba** produces the manual page shown in Figure D.2.

FIGURE D.2

Manual page for Samba shows an explanation of the program.

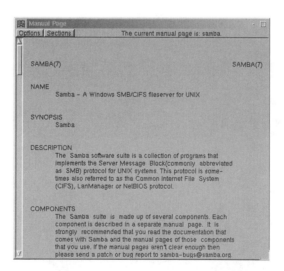

You can also type **man** and the name of a specific software package or command that you want. This displays the pages in the character terminal mode.

Help on the World Wide Web

You'll find many helpful Linux sites on the Web. It would take an entire book just to list them all. Here's some to get you started:

- **metalab.unc.edu/LDP/**—The Linux Documentation Project has all of the Guides, How-To documents, FAQs, Man Pages, and lots of other information about Linux. This is probably the single most important site for information related to Linux. It's the first place I check when I'm looking for Linux information.

- **www.freshmeat.net**—Freshmeat has a daily listing of what's new in the world of Linux. When I need to find a software package of any kind this is where I start my search. The is the second most useful Linux site after the LDP.

- **www.linux.org**—This is the Linux Online home page. It includes links to software, FAQs, the Linux Documentation Project, and much more. It attempts to be a clearinghouse for everything related to Linux. It has lots of links, but it can sometimes be difficult to sort through its long lists.

- **www.li.org**—Linux International has links to Linux resources. This is a well-organized site that is mainly oriented toward users who want to keep up-to-date on Linux development. Its White Papers pointers include a link to the "Practical Manager's Guide to Linux," which answers questions about Linux from a corporate point of view.

- **www.linuxhq.com**—LinuxHQ is a central resource for Linux kernel users and hackers; maintained by Linux kernel users and hackers. If you are just starting out, this is not the place to begin learning about the kernel. This site is intended for serious coders.

- **linuxpower.com**—Linuxpower is primarily a site for interviews and reviews. Reviews cover everything from new software to Linux trade shows.

- **www.linuxlinks.com**—Linux Links has lots of links related to Linux. It is well organized with helpful descriptions of the links. This is one of the most useful of the general Linux Web sites.

- **www.linuxresources.com**—Linux Resources is a resources page maintained by the Linux Journal. The Journal is a top Linux-oriented magazine. This Web site, however, can be difficult to decipher.

- **www.linuxnow.com**—Linux Now calls itself the most complete Linux reference on the Internet. You may have a little trouble figuring out the site, but it does seem to have one of the most comprehensive listings of Linux software. If you are searching for software for a specific task and you haven't found it elsewhere, you can probably find a link to it here.

App
D

- **www.linuxcare.com**—Linux Care has Linux information and service. It is maintained by a company that sells Linux service, including service for OpenLinux. It has some good links, but its knowledge base does not provide useful results.

- **www.linux.com**—Linux.com is maintained by VA Linux Systems, one of the biggest sellers of systems with Linux already installed. The Web site started in 1999 with limited resources. From the beginning it has one of the best searchable Linux knowledge bases.

- **www.linuxberg.com**—Linuxberg was started by the same folks who created the Tucows Web site listing Windows software. This site has a collection of software listings, but it some gaps. The listings don't always include some of the commonly used software in a given category. It has reviews of those packages that are included in its listings.

- **www.kde.org**—KDE is the home page for the K Desktop Environment.

- **www.apache.org**—The Apache home page for the Internet's most popular Web server.

- **www.samba.org**—This is the Samba home page for Samba networking software.

- **www.cs.utexas.edu/users/kharker/linux-laptop**—A Linux laptop site for notebook computer users. This is the most complete listing anywhere of the resources available for Linux on a notebook computer. It is indispensable if you plan to put Linux on your notebook.

Publications

Here's a list of Web-based magazines, news sources, books, and more:

- **www.linuxworld.com**—LinuxWorld is a Web-based Linux magazine. It has excellent articles on a wide range of topics. I check it regularly for new articles.

- **www.linuxjournal.com**—The Linux Journal is a popular printed magazine that was started in 1994. Each issue is packed with technically oriented articles. A limited number of articles are available on the Web. This is a magazine for hardcore Linux users.

- **www.linuxfocus.org**—Linux Focus is the only multilingual magazine on Linux. It is Web-based and available in English, French, German, Spanish, and Turkish. Arabic, Chinese, Dutch, Korean, Portuguese, and Russian editions are in development. Only a few issues have been published.

- **www.linuxgazette.com**—Linux Gazette is a Web-based publication published by Linux Journal. It can be difficult to click through the whole thing, and the site isn't searchable. The best way to approach this site is to visit it monthly and go through the current issue.

- **lwn.net/daily/**—Linux Daily News is like its name says: a daily listing of news reports about Linux. Any news report or announcement that mentions Linux is likely to find its way to a link on this site.

- **www.mcp.com**—Site for Linux books. Macmillan U.S.A. prints a wide variety of computer-related books, including this book.

- **slashdot.org**—Slashdot is a "News For Nerds" site filled with lively, often irreverent, discussion. It is definitely a site with a view. Check it occasionally, like you might check the daytime TV talk shows.

- **lwn.net**—Linux Weekly News has summaries of news reports related to Linux. The summaries include links to the full stories.

- **www.linuxtoday.com**—Linux Today is another Linux news summary site directed to business professionals. Its summaries are easy to read and are always short. Linux Today is a good way to quickly scan Linux-related news. You can also subscribe to its daily news summary, which is sent out by email. I find this the best way to stay up-to-date on Linux news. I'd recommend it to anyone who is working regularly with Linux.

App
D

Hardware Compatibility List

OpenLinux supports most Intel PC hardware. Some of the latest hardware options have only limited support, such as USB (Universal Serial Bus) devices. This is similar to the limitations in hardware support found in Windows NT.

OpenLinux runs on all Intel and Intel-compatible processors. It does not support as many peripherals and cards as Windows does. It is still necessary to consult the hardware compatibility list before choosing a new piece of hardware to add to an OpenLinux machine.

Linux was developed by its users. That includes the drivers that are necessary to make the hardware work. Only a handful of manufacturers write Linux drivers for their peripherals or cards. Some manufacturers that do not write Linux drivers have worked with Linux developers and provided the necessary information to write device drivers. Other companies maintain proprietary interfaces and drivers will not become available until the company writes one for Linux. If there is a peripheral or card that you want to use on your OpenLinux system that does not have a driver, make sure to let the manufacturer know that you need a Linux driver. Linux is growing in popularity and hardware manufacturers are hearing about it. Your request for a driver can help make Linux drivers a standard feature found with all new hardware.

The following tables show the hardware supported by OpenLinux 2.3. As new drivers are developed, they will be available in upgrades available from Caldera Systems. Be sure to check their Web site at `www.calderasystems.com/support/resources.html` for the availability of any updates.

Compatible Hardware

The following hardware is compatible with the Caldera OpenLinux release 2.3:

CPU	80386, 80486, Pentium, PentiumPro, Pentium II, and compatible processors
BUS	ISA, EISA, PCI, VL-Bus, AGP
RAM	32MB required (swap partition strongly recommended)

Disk Space Requirements

Following are the disk space requirements for Caldera OpenLinux 2.2:

Small	160MB
Recommended	580MB
Recommended + Commercial	780MB
Full	1.2GB

N O T E Allow for slightly more space than what is listed to allow for room in which to do work.

The recommended swap space size typically matches your RAM capacity. For example, if your machine has 64MB of RAM, a swap partition of 64MB should do. Installation can be initiated either from a 3 1/2-inch high-density disk drive or straight from the OpenLinux CD-ROM.

Compatible CD-ROM Drives

Table E.1 lists CD-ROM drives, and Table E.2 lists CD-ROM interface cards that are compatible with Caldera OpenLinux release 2.3.

> **NOTE** IDE/ATAPI CD-ROM drives are compatible and are covered on the IDE Drive Compatible list. ∎

Table E.1   Compatible CD-ROM Drives

Company	Model	Source	Module
Aztech	CDA268-01A	aztcd.c	aztcd.o
Conrad	TXC	aztcd.c	aztcd.o
Creative Labs	CD-200F (CD-200 not fully supported)	sbpcd.c	sbpcd.o
CyCDROM	CR520	aztcd.c	aztcd.o
	CR520ie	aztcd.c	aztcd.o
	CR540	aztcd.c	aztcd.o
	CR940ie	aztcd.c	aztcd.o
ECS-AT	Vertos 100	sbpcd.c	sbpcd.o
Funai	E2550UA	sbpcd.c	sbpcd.o
	MK4015	sbpcd.c	sbpcd.o
	2800F	sbpcd.c	sbpcd.o
Goldstar/Reveal	R420	gscd.c	gscd.o
IBM	External ISA drive	sbpcd.c	sbpcd.o
Kotubuki	See Panasonic		
Lasermate	CR328A	optcd.c	optcd.o
Longshine	LCS-7260	sbpcd.c	sbpcd.o
Matsushita	See Panasonic		

App
E

continues

Table E.1   Continued

Company	Model	Source	Module
Mitsumi	CRMC LU005S	mcd.c	mcd.o
	FX001S (single speed)	mcd.c	mcd.o
	FX001S (multisession)	mcdx.c	mcdx.o
	FX001D (double speed)	mcd.c	mcd.o
	FX001D (multisession)	mcdx.c	mcdx.o
Okano/Wearnes	CDD110	aztec.c	aztec.o
Optics Storage	DOLPHIN 8000 AT	optcd.c	optcd.o
Orchid	CDS-3110	aztcd.c	aztcd.o
Panasonic	CR-521	sbpcd.c	sbpcd.o
	CR-522	sbpcd.c	sbpcd.o
	CR-523	sbpcd.c	sbpcd.o
	CR-562	sbpcd.c	sbpcd.o
	CR-563	sbpcd.c	sbpcd.o
Philips/LMS	cm206 (w/ cm206 card)	cm206.c	cm206.o
Sanyo	CDR-H94A	sjcd.c	sjcd.o
Sony	CDU-31A (not auto-probed)	cdu31a.c	cdu31a.o
	CDU-33A (not auto-probed)	cdu31a.c	cdu31a.o
	CDU-510	sonycd535.c	sonycd535.o
	CDU-515	sonycd535.c	sonycd535.o
	CDU-531	sonycd535.c	sonycd535.o
	CDU-535	sonycd535.c	sonycd535.o
Teac	CD-55A	sbpcd.c	sbpcd.o

Table E.2	Compatible CD-ROM Interface Cards	
Company	Source	Module
ISP16	isp16.c	isp16.o
MAD16	isp16.c	isp16.o
Mozart	isp16.c	isp16.o

Most SCSI drives with a block size of 512 or 2048 bytes should work. You need a compatible SCSI controller card to use one of these drives.

N O T E Some CD-ROM drives are shipped with nonstandard SCSI adapters that might not be supported. ■

Most drives connected via IDE/ATAPI interfaces should work. A few of the vendors currently shipping compatible drives include Aztech, Mitsumi, NEC, Sony, Creative Labs, and Vertos. Some multiple CD changers such as the NEC CDR-251 and Sanyo's "nonstandard" 3-CD changer are supported as ATAPI drives and therefore do not have a special driver on the preceding list. A sample CD change program is included at the end of the following document:

```
/usr/src/linux/Documentation/cdrom/ide-cd
```

The CyCDROM 940i and 520ie drives, although connected to IDE interfaces, are not IDE devices; they use the Aztech driver.

Compatible Parallel Port Drives

Table E.3 contains a list of parallel port drives that are compatible with OpenLinux 2.3. Loading these drivers when compiled as modules requires the following steps:

1. Load the paride.o module using the **insmod** command.
2. Load the specific drivers for your hardware from the second table that follows.
3. Load the module that supplies the support required. The following table lists the available modules and the drives the modules support:

Module	Support offered
pd.o	IDE hard drives
pcd.o	ATAPI CD-ROM drives
pf.o	ATAPI hard drives
pt.o	ATAPI tape drives
pg.o	ATAPI generic drives (CD-R drives specifically)

Table E.3   Compatible Parallel Port Drives

Company	Model	Source	Module
Arista	ParaCD 525 (4/8 bit only)	arcd.c	arcd.o
ATEN	EH-100	aten.c	aten.o
Avatar	Shark	epat.c	epat.o
DataStor	Commuter adapter	comm.c	comm.o
	EP2000 adapter	dscd.c	dscd.o
Fidelity International Technology	TransDisk 2000	fit2.c	fit2.o
	TransDisk 3000	fit3.c	fit3.o
Freecom	Power CD (initialize with POWER-CD.SYS in DOS, then boot Linux with LOADLIN)	frpw.c	frpw.o
	IQ Cable	friq.c	friq.o
Hewlett-Packard	Tape drives (5GB & 8GB)	epat.c	epat.o
	7100 CD-RW	epat.c	epat.o
	7200 CD-RW	epat.c	epat.o
Imation	SuperDisk LS-120	epat.c	epat.o
KingByte Information Sys.	KBIC-951A adapter	kbic.c	kbic.o
	KBIC-917A adapter	kbic.c	kbic.o
KT Technology	PHd adapter	ktti.c	ktti.o
Maxell	SuperDisk LS-120	epat.c	epat.o
Microsolutions	Backpack CD-ROM	bpck.c	bpck.o
	Backpack PD/CD	bpck.c	bpck.o
	Backpack Hard Drives	bpck.c	bpck.o
	Backpack 8000t Tape Drives	bpck.c	bpck.o
OnSpec Electronics	90c20 adapter	on20.c	on20.o
	90c26 adapter	on26.c	on26.o

Company	Model	Source	Module
Shuttle	EPIA	epia.c	epia.o
Technologies	EPAT adapter	epat.c	epat.o
	EZ-135	epat.c	epat.o
	EZ-230	epat.c	epat.o
	SparQ	epat.c	epat.o

N O T E The Freecom Power CD listed in Table E.3 is a Mitsumi ATAPI drive. This drive includes a chip that implements IDE-over-parallel support. This chip requires special initialization that, due to copyright laws, cannot be included in the Linux driver. Therefore, the DOS driver POWER_CD.SYS must be loaded from DOS first, and then Linux can be booted (using a utility such as LOADLIN). ▓

Compatible Floppy Drives

The number of floppy drives that are *not* compatible with OpenLinux is so small that it is hardly even worth mentioning. Regardless, a few laptop drives require special boot/module parameters to get them working correctly. The HP Omnibook and the IBM L40SX Thinkpad are known to require additional parameters. These laptops are listed below, with the module information. The parameters needed and an explanation of how to use them can be found in the BootPrompt-HOWTO on the OpenLinux CD.

Company	Model	Source	Module
HP	Omnibook	floppy.c	floppy.o
IBM	L40SX ThinkPad	floppy.c	floppy.o

Compatible IDE Drives

Following is the list of IDE Drives that are compatible with OpenLinux 2.3.

IDE Hard Drives, CD-ROM Drives, and Tape Drives

Up to four IDE interfaces on one or more IRQs with up to eight disk/cdrom/tape/floppy drives are compatible with these drivers. OpenLinux, by default, ships with support for IDE hard drives on the first two controllers (two drives per controller—four drives total) and includes device files for up to four more devices without partitions. The only devices that can use partitions without creating new device files are the first four hard drives, connected to the first two IDE controllers only.

Basically, any IDE drive should be compatible with OpenLinux 2.2. This includes the UDMA drives found on all of the new PCs. This table shows the main IDE drivers included with OpenLinux 2.3.

Type	Source	Module
Hard Drives	ide.c	ide.o
CD-ROM Drives	ide-cd.c	ide-cd.o
Tape Drives	ide-tape.c	ide-tape.o

IDE Floppy (Removable) Drives

The following removable IDE devices are compatible with OpenLinux 2.3:

Company	Model	Source	Module
EASYSTOR	LS-120	ide-floppy.c	ide-floppy.o
Iomega	ZIP Drive	ide-floppy.c	ide-floppy.o

Compatible XT Hard Drive Controllers

The following XT Hard Drive controllers are compatible with OpenLinux 2.3:

Company	Model	Source	Module
DTC	5150CX	xd.c	xd.o
	5150X	xd.c	xd.o
OMTI	5520	xd.c	xd.o
Seagate	ST11M/R	xd.c	xd.o
	ST11R	xd.c	xd.o
Western Digital	WD1002-27X	xd.c	xd.o
	WD1002AWX1	xd.c	xd.o
	WD1004A27X	xd.c	xd.o
	WDXT-GEN2	xd.c	xd.o
XEBEC		xd.c	xd.o

Compatible SCSI Adapters

The following SCSI adapters are compatible with OpenLinux 2.3:

Company	Model	Source	Module
AMD	AM53C974	AM53C974.c	AM53C974.o
	AM79C974	AM53C974.c	AM53C974.o
Acard	AEC-671X	atp870u.c	atp870u.o
Adaptec	1502 (cannot be probed for)	aha152x.c	aha152x.o
	1520	aha152x.c	aha152x.o
	1522	aha152x.c	aha152x.o
	1535 (cannot be probed for)	aha1542.c	aha1542.o
	1542(A,CP,CF,?)	aha1542.c	aha1542.o
	1740	aha1740.c	aha1740.o
	274x	aic7xxx.c	aic7xxx.o
	274xT	aic7xxx.c	aic7xxx.o
	284x	aic7xxx.c	aic7xxx.o
	2910B	aic7xxx.c	aic7xxx.o
	2920 (PCI)	fdomain.c	fdomain.o
	2920C	aic7xxx.c	aic7xxx.o
	294x	aic7xxx.c	aic7xxx.o
	2940A	aic7xxx.c	aic7xxx.o
	2944	aic7xxx.c	aic7xxx.o
	2950x	aic7xxx.c	aic7xxx.o
	394x	aic7xxx.c	aic7xxx.o
	395x	aic7xxx.c	aic7xxx.o
	398x	aic7xxx.c	aic7xxx.o
	aic777x (motherboard)	aic7xxx.c	aic7xxx.o
	aic785x (motherboard)	aic7xxx.c	aic7xxx.o
	aic786x (7850 ultra)	aic7xxx.c	aic7xxx.o
	aic787x (motherboard)	aic7xxx.c	aic7xxx.o

App

E

continues

continued

Company	Model	Source	Module
	aic788x (motherboard)	aic7xxx.c	aic7xxx.o
	aic789x (motherboard)	aic7xxx.c	aic7xxx.o
	aic3860 (motherboard)	aic7xxx.c	aic7xxx.o
AdvanSys	ABP-510	advansys.c	advansys.o
	ABP-542	advansys.c	advansys.o
	ABP-742	advansys.c	advansys.o
	ABP-752	advansys.c	advansys.o
	ABP-842	advansys.c	advansys.o
	ABP-852	advansys.c	advansys.o
	ABP-920	advansys.c	advansys.o
	ABP-930	advansys.c	advansys.o
	ABP-930U	advansys.c	advansys.o
	ABP-930UA	advansys.c	advansys.o
	ABP-940	advansys.c	advansys.o
	ABP-940U	advansys.c	advansys.o
	ABP-940UW	advansys.c	advansys.o
	ABP-950	advansys.c	advansys.o
	ABP-960	advansys.c	advansys.o
	ABP-960U	advansys.c	advansys.o
	ABP-970	advansys.c	advansys.o
	ABP-970U	advansys.c	advansys.o
	ABP-980	advansys.c	advansys.o
	ABP-980U	advansys.c	advansys.o
	ABP-5140	advansys.c	advansys.o
	ABP-5142	advansys.c	advansys.o
	ABP-5150	advansys.c	advansys.o
Always	IN2000 (ISA)	in2000.c	in2000.o
AMI	MegaRAID	megaraid.c	megaraid.o
	FastDisk adapters (only true BusLogic clones)	BusLogic.c	BusLogic.o

Company	Model	Source	Module
BusLogic	BT-445C	BusLogic.c	BusLogic.o
	BT-445S	BusLogic.c	BusLogic.o
	BT-540CF	BusLogic.c	BusLogic.o
	BT-542B	BusLogic.c	BusLogic.o
	BT-542D	BusLogic.c	BusLogic.o
	BT-545C	BusLogic.c	BusLogic.o
	BT-545S	BusLogic.c	BusLogic.o
	BT-742A	BusLogic.c	BusLogic.o
	BT-747C	BusLogic.c	BusLogic.o
	BT-747D	BusLogic.c	BusLogic.o
	BT-747S	BusLogic.c	BusLogic.o
	BT-757C	BusLogic.c	BusLogic.o
	BT-757CD	BusLogic.c	BusLogic.o
	BT-757D	BusLogic.c	BusLogic.o
	BT-757S	BusLogic.c	BusLogic.o
	BT-946C	BusLogic.c	BusLogic.o
	BT-948	BusLogic.c	BusLogic.o
	BT-956C	BusLogic.c	BusLogic.o
	BT-956CD	BusLogic.c	BusLogic.o
	BT-958	BusLogic.c	BusLogic.o
	BT-958D	BusLogic.c	BusLogic.o
	Flashpoint LT (BT-930) Ultra SCSI-3	BusLogic.c	BusLogic.o
	Flashpoint LT (BT-930R) Ultra SCSI-3 w/ RAIDPlus	BusLogic.c	BusLogic.o
	Flashpoint LT (BT-920) Ultra SCSI-3 (BT-930 without BIOS)	BusLogic.c	BusLogic.o
	Flashpoint DL (BT-932) Dual Channel Ultra SCSI-3	BusLogic.c	BusLogic.o

App
E

continues

continued

Company	Model	Source	Module
	Flashpoint DL (BT-932R) Ultra SCSI-3 w/ RAIDPlus	BusLogic.c	BusLogic.o
	Flashpoint LW (BT-950) Wide Ultra SCSI-3	BusLogic.c	BusLogic.o
	Flashpoint LW (BT-950R) Wide Ultra SCSI-3 w/ RAIDPlus	BusLogic.c	BusLogic.o
	Flashpoint DW (BT-952) Dual Channel Wide Ultra SCSI-3	BusLogic.c	BusLogic.o
	Flashpoint DW (BT-952R) Dual Channel Wide Ultra SCSI-3 w/ RAIDPlus	BusLogic.c	BusLogic.o
Control Concepts	SCSI/IDE/SIO/PIO/ FDC cards	qlogicfas.c	qlogicfas.o
Dawicontrol	2974	tmscsim.c	tmscsim.o
DPT	EATA_PIO/DASD devices	eata_pio.c	eata_pio.o
	PM2011	eata_ dma.c eata.c	eata_dma.o eata.o
	PM2011B/9X	eata.c	eata.o
	PM2012A	eata.c	eata.o
	PM2012B	eata.c eata_ dma.c	eata.o eata_dma.o
	PM2021	eata_dma.c	eata_dma.o
	PM2021A/9X	eata.c	eata.o
	PM2022	eata_dma.c	eata_dma.o
	PM2022A/9X	eata.c	eata.o
	PM2024	eata_dma.c	eata_dma.o
	PM2041	eata_dma.c	eata_dma.o
	PM2042	eata_dma.c	eata_dma.o

Company	Model	Source	Module
	PM2044	eata_dma.c	eata_dma.o
	PM2122	eata_dma.c	eata_dma.o
	PM2122A/9X	eata.c	eata.o
	PM2124	eata_dma.c	eata_dma.o
	PM2144	eata_dma.c	eata_dma.o
	PM2322	eata_dma.c	eata_dma.o
	PM2322A/9X	eata.c	eata.o
	PM3021	eata.c eata_dma.c	eata.o eata_dma.o
	PM3122	eata_dma.c	eata_dma.o
	PM3222	eata.c eata_dma.c	eata.o eata_dma.o
	PM3224	eata.c eata_dma.c	eata.o eata_dma.o
	PM3222W	eata.c	eata.o
	PM3224W	eata.c	eata.o
	PM3332	eata_dma.c	eata_dma.o
	PM3334	eata_dma.c	eata_dma.o
DTC	3180	dtc.c	dtc.o
	3280	dtc.c	dtc.o
Future Domain	TMC-885	seagate.c	seagate.o
	TMC-950	seagate.c	seagate.o
	TMC-1610M	fdomain.c	fdomain.o
	TMC-1610MER	fdomain.c	fdomain.o
	TMC-1610MEX	fdomain.c	fdomain.o
	TMC-1650	fdomain.c	fdomain.o
	TMC-1660	fdomain.c	fdomain.o
	TMC-1670	fdomain.c	fdomain.o
	TMC-1680	fdomain.c	fdomain.o
	TMC-1800 based	fdomain.c	fdomain.o
	TMC-18C50 based	fdomain.c	fdomain.o
	TMC-18C30 based	fdomain.c	fdomain.o
	TMC-36C70 based	fdomain.c	fdomain.o
	TMC-3260 (PCI)	fdomain.c	fdomain.o

App

E

continues

continued

Company	Model	Source	Module
GVP	Series II SCSI	gvp11.c	gvp11.o
HP	4020i CD-R card	advansys.c	advansys.o
IBM	TMC-1680 based	fdomain.c	fdomain.o
ICP vortex Computersysteme GmbH	GDT3000/3020	gdth.c	gdth.o
	GDT3000A/3020A/3050A	gdth.c	gdth.o
	GDT3000B/3010A	gdth.c	gdth.o
	GDT2000/2020	gdth.c	gdth.o
	GDT6000/6020/6050	gdth.c	gdth.o
	GDT6000B/6010	gdth.c	gdth.o
	GDT6110/6510	gdth.c	gdth.o
	GDT6120/6520	gdth.c	gdth.o
	GDT6530	gdth.c	gdth.o
	GDT6550	gdth.c	gdth.o
	GDT6117/6517	gdth.c	gdth.o
	GDT6127/6527	gdth.c	gdth.o
	GDT6537	gdth.c	gdth.o
	GDT6557/6557-ECC	gdth.c	gdth.o
	GDT6115/6515	gdth.c	gdth.o
	GDT6125/6525	gdth.c	gdth.o
	GDT6535	gdth.c	gdth.o
	GDT6555/6555-ECC	gdth.c	gdth.o
	GDT6117RP/GDT6517RP	gdth.c	gdth.o
	GDT6127RP/GDT6527RP	gdth.c	gdth.o
	GDT6537RP	gdth.c	gdth.o
	GDT6557RP	gdth.c	gdth.o
	GDT6111RP/GDT6511RP	gdth.c	gdth.o
	GDT6121RP/GDT6521RP	gdth.c	gdth.o
	GDT6117RD/GDT6517RD	gdth.c	gdth.o
	GDT6127RD/GDT6527RD	gdth.c	gdth.o

Company	Model	Source	Module
	GDT6537RD	gdth.c	gdth.o
	GDT6557RD	gdth.c	gdth.o
	GDT6111RD/GDT6511RD	gdth.c	gdth.o
	GDT6121RD/GDT6521RD	gdth.c	gdth.o
	GDT6118RD/GDT6518RD	gdth.c	gdth.o
	GDT6538RD/GDT6638RD	gdth.c	gdth.o
	GDT6558RD/GDT6658RD	gdth.c	gdth.o
	GDT6111RP/GDT6511RP	gdth.c	gdth.o
Iomega	Jazz Jet PCI	advansys.c	advansys.o
	MatchMaker (par.port)	imm.c	imm.o
	PPA3 (parallel port Zip drive)	ppa.c	ppa.o
Initio	INI-910	i91uscsi.c	i91uscsi.o
	INI-9x00/UW	ini9100u.c	ini9100u.o
NCR	5380	g_NCR5380.c	g_NCR5380.o
	53c400 (no DMA)	g_NCR5380.c	g_NCR5380.o
	53c406a	NCR53c406a.c	NCR53c406a.o
	53c700 (chipset)	53c7,8xx.c	53c7,8xx.o
	53c700-66 (chipset)	53c7,8xx.c	53c7,8xx.o
	53c720 (chipset)	53c7,8xx.c	53c7,8xx.o
	53c810 (chipset)	ncr53c8xx.c 53c7,8xx.c	ncr53c8xx.o 53c7,8xx.o
	53c810A (chipset)	ncr53c8xx.c	ncr53c8xx.o
	53c815 (chipset)	ncr53c8xx.c	ncr53c8xx.o
	53c820 (chipset)	ncr53c8xx.c 53c7,8xx.c	ncr53c8xx.o 53c7,8xx.o
	53c825 (chipset)	ncr53c8xx.c	ncr53c8xx.o
	53c825A (chipset)	ncr53c8xx.c	ncr53c8xx.o
	53c860 (chipset)	ncr53c8xx.c	ncr53c8xx.o
	53c875 (chipset)	ncr53c8xx.c	ncr53c8xx.o
	53c876 (chipset)	ncr53c8xx.c	ncr53c8xx.o
	53c895 (chipset)	ncr53c8xx.c	ncr53c8xx.o

App

E

continues

continued

Company	Model	Source	Module
Perceptive Solutions	PCI-2000	pci2000.c	pci2000.o
	PCI-2000I	pci2000i.c	pci2000i.o
	PSI-240I	psi240i.c	psi240i.o
Pro Audio	Spectrum 16	pas16.c	pas16.o
	Studio 16	pas16.c	pas16.o
Qlogic	FastSCSI! (ISA VLB)	qlogicfas.c	qlogicfas.o
	IQ-PCI (no disconnect)	qlogicisp.c	qlogicisp.o
	IQ-PCI-10	qlogicisp.c	qlogicisp.o
	IQ-PCI-D	qlogicisp.c	qlogicisp.o
	PCI-Basic	AM53C974.c	AM53C974.o
Quantum	ISA-200S	fdomain.c	fdomain.o
	ISA-250MG	fdomain.c	fdomain.o
Seagate	ST01	seagate.c	seagate.o
	ST02	seagate.c	seagate.o
SIIG	i540 SpeedMaster	advansys.c	advansys.o
	i542 SpeedMaster	advansys.c	advansys.o
	Fast SCSI Pro PCI	advansys.c	advansys.o
TekRam	DC390	tmscsim.c	tmscsim.o
	DC390T	tmscsim.c	tmscsim.o
Trantor	T128	t128.c	t128.o
	T128F	t128.c	t128.o
	T130B	g_NCR5380.c	g_NCR5380.o
	T228	t128.c	t128.o
UltraStor	14F	u14-34f.c, ultrastor.c	u14-34f.o ultrastor.o
	24F	ultrastor.c	ultrastor.o
	34F	u14-34f.c ultrastor.c	u14-34f.o ultrastor.o

Company	Model	Source	Module
Western Digital	WD7000-FASST2	wd7000.c	wd7000.o
	WD7000-ASC	wd7000.c	wd7000.o
	WD7000-AX (ALPHA)	wd7000.c	wd7000.o
	WD7000-MX (ALPHA)	wd7000.c	wd7000.o
	WD7000-EX (ALPHA)	wd7000.c	wd7000.o

IDE-SCSI Devices

With the ide-scsi.o driver, you can use the Linux SCSI drivers instead of the native IDE ATAPI drivers. This supports ATAPI devices for which no native driver has been written (for example, an ATAPI PD-CD drive).

Compatible Serial Boards

These serial boards are compatible with OpenLinux 2.3:

Company	Model	Source	Module
Accent	Async	esp.c	esp.o
AST	FourPort	esp.c	esp.o
Comtrol	RocketPort	rocket.c	rocket.o
Cyclades	Cyclom-Y Boards	cyclades.c	cyclades.o
Cyclades	Cyclades-Z Boards	cyclades.c	cyclades.o
DigiBoard	EISA/Xem	epca.c	epca.o
	PC/Xe	pcxx.c epca.c	pcxx.o epca.o
	PC/Xem	epca.c	epca.o
	PC/Xeve	pcxx.c epca.c	pcxx.o epca.o
	PC/Xi	pcxx.c epca.c	pcxx.o epca.o
	PC/Xr	epca.c	epca.o
Hayes	ESP	esp.c	esp.o
Multi-tech	ISI Series	isicom.c	isicom.o
SDL Comm.	RISCom/8	riscom8.c	riscom8.o
Stallion	Brumby	istallion.c	istallion.o
	EasyIO	stallion.c	stallion.o
	EasyConnection 8/32	stallion.c	stallion.o
	EasyConnection 8/64	istallion.c	istallion.o
	ONboard	istallion.c	istallion.o
	Stallion	istallion.c	istallion.o
Specialix	IO8+ multiport	specialix.c	specialix.o

App

E

Compatible Mouse Pointing Devices

The following mouse pointing devices are compatible with OpenLinux 2.3:

Company	Model	Source	Module
ATI	XL	atixlmouse.c	atixlmouse.o
Logitech	Busmouse	busmouse.c	busmouse.o
Microsoft	Busmouse	msbusmouse.c	msbusmouse.o
PC110	Touchpad	pc110pad.c	pc110pad.o
ps/2	compatibles	pc_keyb.c	pc_keyb.o
QuickPort	C&ampT 82C710 mouse interfaces	qpmouse.c	qpmouse.o

Serial mouse devices are compatible with the generic serial port drivers in the Linux kernel. If the port is recognized, the mouse connected to it should be recognized as well.

N O T E Busmice are assumed to be running at IRQ 5, and PS/2 mouse devices are assumed to be running at IRQ 12. Any variations might mean that the mouse will not be recognized during by the Lizard installation program. You can continue with the installation and make the adjustments later, which can require expert knowledge to do. Or you can use the LISA installation method described in Appendix A, "Installing OpenLinux Using LISA." After installation, you can use the setserial utility to set the IRQ and I/O port for a bus mouse. For PS/2 mouse devices, you can use COAS and specifity the correct parameters for the IRQ and I/O port in the module that is loaded for the mouse. ■

Compatible Tape Drives

The following tape drives are compatible with OpenLinux 2.2. Most QIC-40, QIC-80, QIC-117, and QIC-3020 floppy tape drives are compatible with the ftape driver. The following is a list of drives mentioned by name in the ftape sources. There are no individual, per-drive drivers as with SCSI or Ethernet cards; all are covered under the same driver:

Company	Model	Source	Module
AIWA	CT-803	ftape	ftape.o
	td-S1600	ftape	ftape.o
Archive	31250Q (Escom)	ftape	ftape.o
	5580i	ftape	ftape.o
	S.Hornet (Ident./Escom)	ftape	ftape.o
	XL9250I (Conner/Escom)	ftape	ftape.o

Company	Model	Source	Module
Colorado	700	ftape	ftape.o
	1400	ftape	ftape.o
	DJ-10	ftape	ftape.o
	DJ-20	ftape	ftape.o
	FC-10	ftape	ftape.o
	FC-20	ftape	ftape.o
	T1000(HP)	ftape	ftape.o
	T3000(HP)	ftape	ftape.o
ComByte	DoublePlay	ftape	ftape.o
Conner	C250MQ	ftape	ftape.o
	C250MQT	ftape	ftape.o
	TSM420R	ftape	ftape.o
	TSM850R	ftape	ftape.o
	TSM1700R	ftape	ftape.o
	TST800R	ftape	ftape.o
	TST3200R	ftape	ftape.o
COREtape	QIC80	ftape	ftape.o
Exabyte	Eagle-96	ftape	ftape.o
	Eagle-tr3	ftape	ftape.o
Insight	80mb	ftape	ftape.o
Iomega	250	ftape	ftape.o
	700	ftape	ftape.o
	3200	ftape	ftape.o
	Ditto 800	ftape	ftape.o
	Ditto 2GB	ftape	ftape.o
Irwin	80SX	ftape	ftape.o
Jumbo	700	ftape	ftape.o
Mountain	FS8000	ftape	ftape.o
Pertec	MyTape 800	ftape	ftape.o
	MyTape 3200	ftape	ftape.o
Reveal	TB1400	ftape	ftape.o
Summit	SE 150	ftape	ftape.o
	SE 250	ftape	ftape.o

continues

App

E

continued

Company	Model	Source	Module
Teac	700	ftape	ftape.o
	800	ftape	ftape.o
	FT3010tr	ftape	ftape.o
Wangtek	3040F	ftape	ftape.o
	3080F	ftape	ftape.o
	3200	ftape	ftape.o

SCSI and IDE Tape Drives

There are no specific drivers for SCSI and IDE tape drives. Support for them is loaded along with the driver for the interface to which they are connected, so no special modules or drivers are required to use them. If the interface is up and running (SCSI or IDE), the drive connected to it is usable.

Video Cards Supported by XFree86 v 3.3.3.1

The following video cards are compatible with the XFree86 v 3.3.3.1 servers. At least one of the server packages provided in this XFree86 distribution supports most video cards currently on the market. Information about XFree86 supported hardware was extracted from the *XF86Setup* configuration utility that ships with XFree86 v 3.3.3.1. For additional information, refer to the Web pages at www.xfree86.org.

Company	Card	Server
2 the Max	MAXColor S3 Trio64V+	S3
3DLabs	Oxygen GMX	3DLabs
928Movie		S3
AGX (Generic)		AGX
ALG-5434 (E)		SVGA
ASUS	3Dexplorer	SVGA
	PCI-AV264CT	Mach64
	PCI-V264CT	Mach64
	VideoMagic PCI V864	S3
	VideoMagic PCI VT64	S3
AT25		SVGA
AT3D		SVGA

Company	Card	Server
ATI	3D Pro Turbo	Mach64
	3D Pro Turbo PC2TV	Mach64
	3D Xpression	Mach64
	3D Xpression+	Mach64
	3D Xpression+ PC2TV	Mach64
	8514 Ultra (no VGA)	Mach8
	All-in-Wonder	Mach64
	All-in-Wonder Pro	Mach64
	Graphics Pro Turbo	Mach64
	Graphics Pro Turbo with AT&ampT 20C408 RAMDAC	Mach64
	Graphics Pro Turbo with 68860 RAMDAC	Mach64
	Graphics Pro Turbo with 68860B RAMDAC	Mach64
	Graphics Pro Turbo with 68860C RAMDAC	Mach64
	Graphics Pro Turbo with 68875 RAMDAC	Mach64
	Graphics Pro Turbo with CH8398 RAMDAC	Mach64
	Graphics Pro Turbo with STG1702 RAMDAC	Mach64
	Graphics Pro Turbo with STG1703 RAMDAC	Mach64
	Graphics Pro Turbo with TLC34075 RAMDAC	Mach64
	Graphics Pro Turbo 1600	Mach64
	Graphics Ultra	Mach8
	Graphics Ultra Pro	Mach32
	Graphics Xpression w/ 68860 RAMDAC	Mach64
	Graphics Xpression w/ 68860B RAMDAC	Mach64
	Graphics Xpression w/ 68860C RAMDAC	Mach64
	Graphics Xpression w/ 68875 RAMDAC	Mach64

continues

App
E

continued

Company	Card	Server
	Graphics Xpression w/ AT&T 20C408 RAMDAC	Mach64
	Graphics Xpression w/ CH8398 RAMDAC	Mach64
	Graphics Xpression w/ Mach64 CT 264 CT)	Mach64
	Graphics Xpression w/ STG1702 RAMDAC	Mach64
	Graphics Xpression w/ STG1703 RAMDAC	Mach64
	Graphics Xpression w/ TLC34075 RAMDAC	Mach64
	Intel Maui MU440EX motherboard	Mach64
	Mach32	Mach32
	Mach64	Mach64
	Mach64 w/ 68860 RAMDAC	Mach64
	Mach64 w/ 68860B RAMDAC	Mach64
	Mach64 w/ 68860C RAMDAC	Mach64
	Mach64 w/ 68875 RAMDAC	Mach64
	Mach64 w/ Internal RAMDAC	Mach64
	Mach64 w/ STG1702 RAMDAC	Mach64
	Mach64 w/ STG1703 RAMDAC	Mach64
	Mach64 w/ TLC34075 RAMDAC	Mach64
	Mach64 3D RAGE II	Mach64
	Mach64 3D RAGE II+ DVD	Mach64
	Mach64 3D RAGE IIC	Mach64
	Mach64 3D RAGE Pro	Mach64
	Mach64 CT (264 CT), Internal RAMDAC	Mach64
	Mach64 GT (264 GT), aka 3D RAGE, Internal RAMDAC	Mach64
	Mach64 VT (264 VT), Internal RAMDAC	Mach64
	Mach64 w/ AT&T 20C408 RAMDAC	Mach64
	Mach64 w/ CH8398 RAMDAC	Mach64
	Mach64 w/ IBM RGB514 RAMDAC	Mach64

Company	Card	Server
	Pro Turbo+PC2TV, 3D RAGE II+DVD	Mach64
	Ultra Plus	Mach32
	Video Xpression	Mach64
	Video Xpression+	Mach64
	Win Boost	Mach64
	Win Boost w/ 68860 RAMDAC	Mach64
	Win Boost w/ 68860B RAMDAC	Mach64
	Win Boost w/ 68860C RAMDAC	Mach64
	Win Boost w/ 68875 RAMDAC	Mach64
	Win Boost w/ AT&T 20C408 RAMDAC	Mach64
	Win Boost w/ CH8398 RAMDAC	Mach64
	Win Boost w/ Mach64 CT (264CT)	Mach64
	Win Boost w/ STG1702 RAMDAC	Mach64
	Win Boost w/ STG1703 RAMDAC	Mach64
	Win Boost w/ TLC34075 RAMDAC	Mach64
	WinCharger	Mach64
	WinCharger w/ AT&ampT 20C408 RAMDAC	Mach64
	WinCharger w/ 68860 RAMDAC	Mach64
	WinCharger w/ 68860B RAMDAC	Mach64
	WinCharger w/ 68860C RAMDAC	Mach64
	WinCharger w/ 68875 RAMDAC	Mach64
	WinCharger w/ CH8398 RAMDAC	Mach64
	WinCharger w/ Mach64 CT (264CT)	Mach64
	WinCharger w/ STG1702 RAMDAC	Mach64
	WinCharger w/ STG1703 RAMDAC	Mach64
	WinCharger w/ TLC34075 RAMDAC	Mach64
	Win Turbo	Mach64
	WinTurbo w/ AT&ampT 20C408 RAMDAC	Mach64
	WinTurbo w/ 68860 RAMDAC	Mach64
	WinTurbo w/ 68860B RAMDAC	Mach64
	WinTurbo w/ 68860C RAMDAC	Mach64
	WinTurbo w/ 68875 RAMDAC	Mach64
	WinTurbo w/ CH8398 RAMDAC	Mach64

App

E

continues

continued

Company	Card	Server
	WinTurbo w/ Mach64 CT (264CT)	Mach64
	WinTurbo w/ STG1702 RAMDAC	Mach64
	WinTurbo w/ STG1703 RAMDAC	Mach64
	WinTurbo w/ TLC34075 RAMDAC	Mach64
	Wonder SVGA	SVGA
	Xpert 98	Mach64
	Xpert XL	Mach64
	Xpert@Play 98	Mach64
	Xpert@Play PCI and AGP, 3D RAGE Pro	Mach64
	Xpert@Work, 3D RAGE Pro	Mach64
ATrend	ATC-2165A	SVGA
AccelStar	Permedia II AGP	3DLabs
Actix	GE32+ 2MB	S3
	GE32i	S3
	GE64	S3
	ProStar	SVGA
	ProStar 64	SVGA
	Ultra	S3
Acumos	AVGA3	SVGA
Alliance	ProMotion 6422	SVGA
Ark Logic	ARK1000PV (Generic)	SVGA
	ARK1000VL (Generic)	SVGA
	ARK2000MT (Generic)	SVGA
	ARK2000PV (Generic)	SVGA
Avance Logic	2101	SVGA
	2228	SVGA
	2301	SVGA
	2302	SVGA
	2308	SVGA
	2401	SVGA
Binar Graphics	AnyView	SVGA
Boca	Vortex (Sierra RAMDAC)	AGX

Company	Card	Server
California Graphics	SunTracer 6000	SVGA
Canopus Co.	PowerWindow 3DV	SVGA
	Total-3D	VGA16
Cardex	Challenger (Pro)	SVGA
	Cobra	SVGA
	Trio64	S3
	Trio64Pro	S3
Chips & Technologies	CT64200	SVGA
	CT64300	SVGA
	CT65520	SVGA
	CT65525	SVGA
	CT65530	SVGA
	CT65535	SVGA
	CT65540	SVGA
	CT65545	SVGA
	CT65546	SVGA
	CT65548	SVGA
	CT65550	SVGA
	CT65554	SVGA
	CT65555	SVGA
	CT68554	SVGA
	CT69000	SVGA
Cirrus Logic	GD542x	SVGA
	GD543x	SVGA
	GD544x	SVGA
	GD5462	SVGA
	GD5464	SVGA
	GD5465	SVGA
	GD5480	SVGA
	GD62xx (Laptop)	SVGA
	GD64xx (Laptop)	SVGA
	GD754x (Laptop)	SVGA

continues

App
E

continued

Company	Card	Server
Colorgraphic	Dual Lightning	SVGA
Compaq	Armada 7380DMT	S3
	Armada 7730MT	S3
Creative Labs	3D Blaster PCI (Verite 1000)	SVGA
	Blaster Exxtreme	3DLabs
	Graphics Blaster 3D	SVGA
	Graphics Blaster Eclipse (OEM model CT6510)	SVGA
	Graphics Blaster MA201	SVGA
	Graphics Blaster MA202	SVGA
	Graphics Blaster MA302	SVGA
	Graphics Blaster MA334	SVGA
DFI-WG1000		SVGA
DFI-WG5000		SVGA
DFI-WG6000		SVGA
DSV3325		SVGA
DSV3326		S3
DataExpert	DSV3325	SVGA
	DSV3365	S3
Dell	S3 805	S3
	onboard ET4000	SVGA
Diamond	Edge 3D	SVGA
	Fire GL 1000	3DLabs
	Fire GL 1000 PRO	3DLabs
	Fire GL 3000	3DLabs
	Speedstar (Plus)	SVGA
	Speedstar 24	SVGA
	Speedstar 24X (not fully supported)	SVGA
	Speedstar 64	SVGA
	Speedstar A50	SVGA
	Speedstar HiColor	SVGA
	Speedstar Pro (not SE)	SVGA
	Speedstar Pro 1100	SVGA

Company	Card	Server
	Speedstar Pro SE (CLGD5430/5434)	SVGA
	Speedstar 64 Graphics 2000/2200	SVGA
	Stealth 24	S3
	Stealth 3D 2000	SVGA
	Stealth 3D 2000 Pro	SVGA
	Stealth 3D 3000	SVGA
	Stealth 3D 4000	SVGA
	Stealth 32	SVGA
	Stealth 64 DRAM SE	S3
	Stealth 64 DRAM w/ S3 SDAC	S3
	Stealth 64 DRAM w/ S3 Trio64	S3
	Stealth 64 VRAM	S3
	Stealth 64 Video VRAM (TI RAMDAC)	S3
	Stealth II S220	SVGA
	Stealth Pro	S3
	Stealth VRAM	S3
	Stealth Video 2500	SVGA
	Stealth Video DRAM	S3
	Stealth 64 Graphics 2001 series	SVGA
	Stealth 64 Graphics 2xx0 series (864 + SDAC)	S3
	Stealth 64 Graphics 2xx0 series (Trio64)	S3
	Stealth 64 Video 2001 series (2121/2201)	S3
	Stealth 64 Video 2120/2200	S3
	Stealth 64 3200	S3
	Stealth 64 Video 3240/3400 (IBM RAMDAC)	S3
	Stealth 64 Video 3240/3400 (TI RAMDAC)	S3
	Viper 330	SVGA
	Viper 550	SVGA
	Viper PCI 2MB	P9000

App

E

continues

continued

Company	Card	Server
	Viper Pro Video	SVGA
	Viper VLB 2MB	P9000
EIZO (VRAM)		AGX
ELSA	ERAZOR II	S3
	GLoria-4	S3
	GLoria-8	S3
	GLoria Synergy	3DLabs
	GLoria-L	3DLabs
	GLoria-L/MX	3DLabs
	GLoria-S	3DLabs
	GLoria-XL	3DLabs
	Victory ERAZOR	SVGA
	Victory 3D	SVGA
	Victory 3DX	SVGA
	Winner 1000/T2D	S3
	Winner 1000 R3D	SVGA
	Winner 1000AVI (AT&T 20C409 version)	S3
	Winner 1000AVI (SDAC version)	S3
	Winner 1000ISA	S3
	Winner 1000Pro w/ S3 SDAC	S3
	Winner 1000Pro w/ STG1700 or AT&T RAMDAC	S3
	Winner 1000Pro/X	S3
	Winner 1000TRIO	S3
	Winner 1000TRIO/V	S3
	Winner 1000TwinBus	S3
	Winner 1000VL	S3
	Winner 2000	S3
	Winner 2000 Office	3DLabs
	Winner 2000AVI	S3
	Winner 2000AVI/3D	SVGA
	Winner 2000PRO-2	S3

Company	Card	Server
	Winner 2000PRO-4	S3
	Winner 2000PRO/X-2	S3
	Winner 2000PRO/X-4	S3
	Winner 2000PRO/X-8	S3
	Winner 3000	SVGA
	Winner 3000-L-42	SVGA
	Winner 3000-M-22	SVGA
	Winner 3000-S	SVGA
Epson	CardPC (onboard)	SVGA
ET3000 (Generic)		SVGA
ET4000 (Generic)		SVGA
ET4000/W32i, W32p (Generic)		SVGA
ET4000/W32		SVGA
ET6000 (Generic)		SVGA
ET6100 (Generic)		SVGA
ExpertColor	DSV3325	SVGA
	DSV3365	S3
Generic VGA Compatible		VGA16
Genoa	5400	SVGA
	8500VL (-28)	SVGA
	8900 Phantom 32i	SVGA
	Phantom 64i w/ S3 SDAC	S3
	VideoBlitz III AV	S3
Hercules	Dynamite	W32
	Dynamite 128/Video	SVGA
	Dynamite Power	SVGA
	Dynamite Pro	SVGA
	Graphite HG210	AGX
	Graphite Power	AGX
	Graphite Pro	AGX
	Graphite Terminator 64	S3

App
E

continues

continued

Company	Card	Server
	Graphite Terminator 64/DRAM	S3
	Graphite Terminator Pro 64	S3
	Stingray	SVGA
	Stingray 64/V w/ ICS5342	SVGA
	Stingray 64/V w/ ZoomDAC	SVGA
	Stingray 128 3D	SVGA
	Stingray Pro	SVGA
	Stingray Pro/V	SVGA
	Terminator 3D/DX	SVGA
	Terminator 64/3D	SVGA
	Terminator 64/Video	S3
	Thriller3D	SVGA
Integral	Flashpoint	SVGA
Intel	5430	SVGA
Interay	PMC Viper	SVGA
JAX	8241	S3
Jaton	Video 58P	SVGA
	Video 70P	SVGA
Jazz Multimedia	G-Force 128	SVGA
LeadTek	WinFast 3D S600	SVGA
	WinFast 3D S680	SVGA
	WinFast S200	SVGA
	WinFast S430	S3
	WinFast S510	S3
	WinFast 2300	S3
MELCO	WGP-VG4S	SVGA
	WGP-VX8	SVGA
MSI	MS-4417	SVGA
Matrox	Comet	SVGA
	Marvel II	SVGA
	Millennium 2/4/8 MB	SVGA
	Millennium (MGA)	SVGA
	Millennium II 4/8/16 MB	SVGA

Company	Card	Server
	Millennium II AGP	SVGA
	Millennium G200 4/8/16 MB	SVGA
	Millennium G200 SD 4/8/16 MB	SVGA
	Mystique	SVGA
	Mystique G200 4/8/16 MB	SVGA
	Productiva G100 4/8 MB	SVGA
MediaGX		SVGA
MediaVision	Proaxcel 128	SVGA
Mirage	Z-128	SVGA
Miro	Crystal 10SD w/ GenDAC	S3
	Crystal 12SD	S3
	Crystal 16S	S3
	Crystal 20SD PCI w/ S3 SDAC	S3
	Crystal 20SD VLB w/ S3 SDAC (BIOS 3.xx)	S3
	Crystal 20SD w/ ICD2061A (BIOS 2.xx)	S3
	Crystal 20SD w/ ICS2494 (BIOS 1.xx)	S3
	Crystal 20SV	S3
	Crystal 22SD	S3
	Crystal 40SV	S3
	Crystal 80SV	S3
	Crystal 8S	S3
	Crystal DVD	SVGA
	Crystal VRX	SVGA
	MiroVideo 20TD	SVGA
	Video 20SV	S3
	MiroMedia 3D	SVGA
NeoMagic (Laptop/Notebook)		SVGA
Number Nine	FX Motion 331	S3
	FX Motion 332	SVGA
	FX Motion 531	S3

continues

App
E

continued

Company	Card	Server
	FX Motion 771	S3
	FX Vision 330	S3
	GXE Level 10/11/12	S3
	GXE Level 14/16	S3
	GXE64	S3
	GXE64 Pro	S3
	GXE64 w/ S3 Trio64	S3
	Imagine I-128 (2–8MB)	I128
	Imagine I-128 Series 2 (2–4MB)	I128
	Imagine I-128-T2R	I128
	Revolution 3D AGP (4–8MB SGRAM)	I128
	Visual 9FX Reality 332	SVGA
Oak	87 ISA (generic)	SVGA
	87 VLB (generic)	SVGA
	ISA card (generic)	SVGA
Ocean/Octek	AVGA-20	SVGA
	Combo-26	SVGA
	Combo-28	SVGA
	VL-VGA-26	SVGA
	VL-VGA-28	SVGA
	VL-VGA-1000	SVGA
Orchid	Celsius (AT&ampT RAMDAC)	AGX
	Celsius (Sierra RAMDAC)	AGX
	Fahrenheit 1280	S3
	Fahrenheit VA	S3
	Fahrenheit 1280+	S3
	Fahrenheit Video 3D	SVGA
	Kelvin 64	SVGA
	Kelvin 64 VLB Rev. A	SVGA
	Kelvin 64 VLB Rev. B	SVGA
	P9000 VLB	P9000

Company	Card	Server
Paradise	Accelerator Value	SVGA
Paradise/WD	90CXX	SVGA
PC-Chips	M567 Mainboard	SVGA
Pixelview	Combo TV 3D AGP (Prolink)	SVGA
	Combo TV Pro (Prolink)	SVGA
Rendition	Verite 1000	SVGA
	Verite 2x00	SVGA
Revolution	3D (T2R)	I128
RIVA	TNT	SVGA
	128	SVGA
S3	801/805 (Generic)	S3
	801/805 w/ AT&ampT 20C490 RAMDAC	S3
	801/805 w/ AT&ampT 20C490 RAMDAC and ICD2061A	S3
	801/805 w/ Chrontel 8391	S3
	801/805 w/ S3 GenDAC	S3
	801/805 w/ SC1148{2,3,4} RAMDAC	S3
	801/805 w/ SC1148{5,7,9} RAMDAC	S3
	864 (Generic)	S3
	864 w/ AT&ampT 20C498 or 21C498	S3
	864 w/ SDAC (86C716)	S3
	864 w/ STG1703	S3
	868 (Generic)	S3
	868 w/ AT&ampT 20C409	S3
	868 w/ AT&ampT 20C498 or 21C498	S3
	868 w/ SDAC (86C716)	S3
	86C260 (Generic)	SVGA
	86C280 (Generic)	SVGA
	86C325 (Generic)	SVGA
	86C357 (Generic)	SVGA
	86C365 (Trio3D) (not fully supported)	VGA16
	86C375 (Generic)	SVGA

App
E

continues

continued

Company	Card	Server
	86C385 (Generic)	SVGA
	86C391 (Savage3D) (not fully supported)	VGA16
	86C764 (Generic)	S3
	86C765 (Generic)	S3
	86C775 (Generic)	S3
	86C785 (Generic)	S3
	86C801 (Generic)	S3
	86C805 (Generic)	S3
	86C864 (Generic)	S3
	86C868 (Generic)	S3
	86C911 (Generic)	S3
	86C924 (Generic)	S3
	86C928 (Generic)	S3
	86C964 (Generic)	S3
	86C968 (Generic)	S3
	86C988 (Generic)	SVGA
	86CM65	S3
	911/924 (Generic)	S3
	924 w/ SC1148 DAC	S3
	928 (Generic)	S3
	964 (Generic)	S3
	968 (Generic)	S3
	Aurora64V+ (Generic)	S3
	Savage3D (Not fully supported)	VGA16
	Trio3D (not fully supported)	VGA16
	Trio32 (Generic)	S3
	Trio64 (Generic)	S3
	Trio64+ (Generic)	S3
	Trio64V2 (Generic)	S3
	Trio64V2/DX (Generic)	S3
	Trio64V2/GX (Generic)	S3

Company	Card	Server
	ViRGE	SVGA
	ViRGE (Generic)	SVGA
	ViRGE/DX (Generic)	SVGA
	ViRGE/GX (Generic)	SVGA
	ViRGE/GX2 (Generic)	SVGA
	ViRGE/MX (Generic)	SVGA
	ViRGE/MX+ (Generic)	SVGA
	ViRGE/VX (Generic)	SVGA
	Vision864 (Generic)	S3
	Vision868 (Generic)	S3
	Vision964 (Generic)	S3
	Vision968 (Generic)	S3
Sharp	9080	S3
	9090	S3
SNI	PC5H W32	SVGA
	Scenic W32	SVGA
SPEA	Mercury 64	S3
	Mirage	S3
SPEA/V7	Mercury	S3
	Mirage P64	S3
	Mirage P64 w/ S3 Trio64	S3
	Mirage VEGA Plus	SVGA
	ShowTime Plus	SVGA
STB	Horizon	SVGA
	Horizon Video	SVGA
	LightSpeed	SVGA
	LightSpeed 128	SVGA
	MVP-2	SVGA
	MVP-2 PCI	SVGA
	MVP-2X	SVGA
	MVP-4 PCI	SVGA
	MVP-4X	SVGA
	Nitro (64)	SVGA

App
E

continues

continued

Company	Card	Server
	Nitro 3D	SVGA
	Nitro 64 Video	SVGA
	nvidia 128	SVGA
	Pegasus	S3
	Powergraph 64	S3
	Powergraph 64 Video	S3
	Powergraph X-24	S3
	Powergraph 3D	SVGA
	Velocity 3D	SVGA
	Velocity 64 Video	S3
	Velocity 128	SVGA
SiS	3D PRO AGP	SVGA
	5597	SVGA
	5598	SVGA
	6326	SVGA
	SG86C201	SVGA
	SG86C205	SVGA
	SG86C215	SVGA
	SG86C225	SVGA
Sierra	Screaming 3D	SVGA
Sigma	Concorde	SVGA
	Legend	SVGA
Spider	Black Widow	AGX
	Black Widow Plus	AGX
	Tarantula 64	S3
	VLB Plus	SVGA
TechWorks	Thunderbolt	SVGA
	Ultimate 3D	SVGA
Toshiba	Tecra 540CDT	SVGA
	Tecra 550CDT	SVGA
	Tecra 750CDT	SVGA
	Tecra 750DVD	SVGA

Company	Card	Server
Trident	3DImage975 (Generic)	SVGA
	3DImage975 AGP (Generic)	SVGA
	3DImage985 AGP (Generic)	SVGA
	8900/9000 (Generic)	SVGA
	8900D (Generic)	SVGA
	Cyber9382 (Generic)	SVGA
	Cyber9385 (Generic)	SVGA
	Cyber9388 (Generic)	SVGA
	Cyber9397 (Generic)	SVGA
	TGUI9400CXi (Generic)	SVGA
	TGUI9420DGi (Generic)	SVGA
	TGUI9430DGi (Generic)	SVGA
	TGUI9440 (Generic)	SVGA
	TGUI9660 (Generic)	SVGA
	TGUI9680 (Generic)	SVGA
	TGUI9682 (Generic)	SVGA
	TGUI9685 (Generic)	SVGA
	TVGA8800BR (not fully supported)	VGA16
	TVGA8800CS (not fully supported)	VGA16
	TVGA9200CXr (Generic)	SVGA
Unsupported VGA compatible		VGA16
VI720		SVGA
VL-41		S3
VidTech	FastMax P20	S3
VideoLogic	GrafixStar 300	S3
	GrafixStar 400	S3
	GrafixStar 500	S3
	GrafixStar 550	SVGA
	GrafixStar 560 (PCI/AGP)	SVGA
	GrafixStar 600	SVGA
	GrafixStar 700	S3

App
E

continues

continued

Company	Card	Server
ViewTop PCI		SVGA
WD	90C24 (Laptop)	SVGA
	90C24A or 90C24A2 (Laptop)	SVGA
Weitek	P9100 (Generic)	SVGA
WinFast	3D S600	SVGA
	S200	SVGA
	S430	S3
	S510	S3
XGA-1 (ISA bus)		AGX
XGA-2 (ISA bus)		AGX

A few miscellaneous servers are available aside from the officially developed XFree86 servers. OpenLinux does not support these servers. One such server is the 3Dfx server offered at the Linux3D home page. This server boasts support for the following hardware:

- Voodoo Graphics
- Voodoo2
- Voodoo Rush

Please note that this is not a simple plug-and-go solution for 3Dfx support. You must follow the instructions on the Linux3D Web page to install this!

Another server for SiS chipsets is available at `www.suse.de/XSuSE/XSuSE_E.html`. This server supports the following chipsets:

- SiS 86c201
- SiS 86c202, SiS 86c205
- SiS 5597
- SiS 5598
- SiS 6326 AGP
- SiS 530
- SiS 620

An i740 server is available and has been successfully tested on the following video card:

- Real3D Starfighter AGP

Precision Insight has developed X servers for some graphics hardware not yet supported by XFree86. They have Neomagic and i740 X servers. These servers can be downloaded from their Web site at `www.precisioninsight.com/products.html`.

Compatible Network Cards

The following Ethernet, frame relay, token ring, and radio modem cards are compatible with OpenLinux 2.3:

Company	Model	Source	Module
3Com	Etherlink	3c501.c	3c501.o
	Etherlink II	3c503.c	3c503.o
	Etherlink Plus	3c505.c	3c505.o
	Etherlink II/16	3c503.c	3c503.o
	Etherlink 16	3c507.c	3c507.o
	Etherlink III (3c509)	3c509.c	3c509.o
	Etherlink III (3c579)	3c509.c	3c509.o
	Etherlink III (3c590)	3c59x.c	3c59x.o
	Fast Etherlink (3c590, 3c592, 3c595, 3c597)	3c59x.c	3c59x.o
	Fast Etherlink XL (3c900, 3c905, 3c905B)	3c59x.c	3c59x.o
	Corkscrew Etherlink XL (ISA)	3c515.c	3c515.o
	Tigon based (3c985)	acenic.c	acenic.o
Accton	EtherDuo PCI	tulip.c	tulip.o
	EN1207 (all three types)	tulip.c	tulip.o
Adaptec	ANA6901/C	tulip.c	tulip.o
	ANA6911/TX	tulip.c	tulip.o
Allied Telesis	AT1500	lance.c	lance.o
	AT1700 (ALPHA)	at1700.c	at1700.o
	LA100PCI-T	tulip.c	tulip.o
Alteon	AceNIC Gigabit	acenic.c	acenic.o

continues

App
E

Company	Model	Source	Module
AMD Lance	PCnet-ISA	lance.c	lance.o
	PCnet-ISA+	lance.c	lance.o
	PCnet-PCI	lance32.c	lance32.o
		pcnet32.c	pcnet32.o
	PCnet-PCI II	lance.c	lance.o
	PCnet-32	lance32.c	lance32.o
	PCnet-Fast	pcnet32.c	pcnet32.o
Ansel Com.	AC3200 EISA	ac3200.c	ac3200.o
AT-Lan-Tec/Realtek	RTL8002 (chip)	atp.c	atp.o
	RTL8012(chip)	atp.c	atp.o
Bay Networks	Netgear FX310 TX 10/100	tulip.c	tulip.o
	Netgear GA620	acenic.c	acenic.o
BOCA	AMD 79C960-based cards	lance.c	lance.o
Cabletron	E2100	e2100.c	e2100.o
CardBus	epic100.c	epic100.o	
C-NET	CNE-935	tulip.c	tulip.o
Cogent	EM100	tulip.c	tulip.o
	EM110	tulip.c	tulip.o
	EM400	tulip.c	tulip.o
	EM960	tulip.c	tulip.o
	EM964 Quartet	tulip.c	tulip.o
Compaq	Netelligent 10 (PCI)	tlan.c	tlan.o
	Netelligent 10/100 (PCI)	tlan.c	tlan.o
	Integrated NetFlex-3/P (PCI)	tlan.c	tlan.o
	NetFlex-3/P (PCI)	tlan.c	tlan.o
	ProLiant Netelligent 10/100 (PCI)	tlan.c	tlan.o
	Dual Port Netelligent 10/100 (PCI)	tlan.c	tlan.o

Company	Model	Source	Module
	Deskpro 4000 5233MMX (PCI)	tlan.c	tlan.o
	Netelligent 10 T2 (PCI)	tlan.c	tlan.o
	Netelligent 10/100 TX (PCI)	tlan.c	tlan.o
	Netelligent 10/100 TX UDP (PCI)	tlan.c	tlan.o
	Netelligent 10/100 TX w/ embedded UTP (PCI)	tlan.c	tlan.o
	Integrated Netelligent 10/100 TX (PCI)	tlan.c	tlan.o
	Integrated NetFlex-3/P (PCI)	tlan.c	tlan.o
	NetFlex-3/P (PCI)	tlan.c	tlan.o
	Dual Port Netelligent 10/100 TX (PCI)	tlan.c	tlan.o
Compex	Readylink ENET100-VG4 (EISA/PCI)	hp100.c	hp100.o
	Readylink 2000	ne.c	ne.o
	FreedomLine 100/VG (ISA, EISA, PCI)	hp100.c	hp100.o
Comtrol	Hostess SV-11	hostess_sv11.c	hostess_sv11.o
COSA	ISA adapter	cosa.c	cosa.o
Crystal Lan	CS8900	cs89x0.c	cs89x0.o
	CS8920	cs89x0.c	cs89x0.o
Danpex	EN-9400P3	tulip.c	tulip.o
D-Link	DE-530CT	tulip.c	tulip.o
	DE-600	de600.c	de600.o
	DE-620	de620.c	de620.o
	DFE500-Tx	tulip.c	tulip.o
	DFE-530TX	via-rhine.c	via-rhine.o

continues

App
E

Company	Model	Source	Module
DEC	DEPCA	depca.c	depca.o
	DE-100	depca.c	depca.o
	DE-101	depca.c	depca.o
	DE-200 Turbo	depca.c	depca.o
	DE-201 Turbo	depca.c	depca.o
	DE-202 Turbo (TP BNC)	depca.c	depca.o
	DE-203 Turbo (BNC)	ewrk3.c	ewrk3.o
	DE-204 Turbo (TP)	ewrk3.c	ewrk3.o
	DE-205 Turbo (TP BNC)	ewrk3.c	ewrk3.o
	DE-210	depca.c	depca.o
	DE-422 (EISA)	depca.c	depca.o
	DE-425 (TP BNC EISA)	de4x5.c	de4x5.o
	DE-434 (TP PCI)	de4x5.c	de4x5.o
	DE-435 (TP BNC AUI PCI)	de4x5.c	de4x5.o
	DE-450 (TP BNC AUI PCI)	de4x5.c	de4x5.o
	DE-500 10/100	de4x5.c	de4x5.o
	EtherWORKS	depca.c	depca.o
	EtherWORKS III	ewrk3.c	ewrk3.o
	EtherWORKS 10 (PCI)	tulip.c	tulip.o
	EtherWORKS 10/100 (PCI)	tulip.c	tulip.o
	QSILVER	tulip.c	tulip.o
	DEC chips 21040/ 21041/21140/21142/ 21143	tulip.c	tulip.o
	DEC chips 21040 (no SROM)/21041A/ 21140A	de4x5.c	de4x5.o
Digi	RightSwitch SE/x	dgrs.c	dgrs.o
Essential	RoadRunner HIPPI	rrunner.c	rrunner.o

Company	Model	Source	Module
Fujitsu	FMV-181	fmv18x.c	fmv18x.o
	FMV-181A	at1700.c	at1700.o
	FMV-182	fmv18x.c	fmv18x.o
	FMV-182A	at1700.c	at1700.o
	FMV-183	fmv18x.c	fmv18x.o
	FMV-183A	at1700.c	at1700.o
	FMV-184	fmv18x.c	fmv18x.o
	FMV-184A	at1700.c	at1700.o
Hewlett-Packard	100VG-AnyLan	hp100.c	hp100.o
	27248B (Cascade)	hp100.c	hp100.o
	AMD 79C960 based cards)	lance.c	lance.o
	HP300	hplance.c	hplance.o
	J2405A	lance.c	lance.o
	J2577 (Cascade)	hp100.c	hp100.o
	J2577 (REVA Cascade)	hp100.c	hp100.o
	J2573 (Cascade)	hp100.c	hp100.o
	J2573 (REVA Cascade)	hp100.c	hp100.o
	J2585[AB]	hp100.c	hp100.o
	J2970	hp100.c	hp100.o
	J2973	hp100.c	hp100.o
	PC-Lan	hp.c	hp.o
	PC-Lan Plus	hp-plus.c	hp-plus.o
IBM	ThinkPad (built-in network interface)	znet.c	znet.o
ICL	EtherTeam 16i	eth16i.c	eth16i.o
	EtherTeam32 (EISA)	eth16i.c	eth16i.o
Intel	EtherExpress Pro/10	eepro.c	eepro.o
	EtherExpress Pro/10 (PCI)	eep10pci.c	eep10pci.o
	EtherExpress Pro/100B	eepro100.c	eepro100.o

App

E

continues

Company	Model	Source	Module
	EtherExpress 16	eexpress.c	eexpress.o
	Other i82557 based cards	eepro100.c	eepro100.o
Kingston	DEC 21x4x-based cards	de4x5.c	de4x5.o
	AMD 79C960-based cards	lance.c	lance.o
	EtherX KNE100TX	tulip.c	tulip.o
	EtherX KNT40T	tulip.c	tulip.o
KTI	ET32P2	ne.c	ne.o
Linksys	AMD 79C960-based cards	lance.c	lance.o
	DEC 21x4x-based cards	de4x5.c	de4x5.o
	EtherPCI	tulip.c	tulip.o
Mylex	LNE390	lne390.c	lne390.o
NE1000	ne.c	ne.o	
NE1500	lance.c	lance.o	
NE2000	ne.c	ne.o	
NE2100	lance.c	lance.o	
	ni65.c	ni65.o	
NE2500	lance.c	lance.o	
NE3210	ne3210.c	ne3210.o	
NetVin	NV5000	ne.c	ne.o
NI5210	ni52.c	ni52.o	
NI6510	ni65.c	ni65.o	
Olicom	OC-2325	tlan.c	tlan.o
	OC-2183	tlan.c	tlan.o
	OC-2326	tlan.c	tlan.o
Packet Engine	"Yellowfin" G-NIC	yellowfin.c	yellowfin.o
Pure Data	PDI8023-8	wd.c	wd.o
	PDUC8023	wd.c	wd.o
	PDI8023-16	wd.c	wd.o
Racal-Interlan	ES3210 (EISA)	es3210.c	es3210.o
	NI5010	ni5010.c	ni5010.o

Company	Model	Source	Module
Realtek	8029	ne.c	ne.o
	RTL8129/8139 Fast Ethernet	rtl8139.c	rtl8139.o
RedCreek Communications	PCI cards	rcpci45.c	rcpc145.o
Schneider & Koch	G16	sk_g16.c	sk_g16.o
SEEQ	8005 based cards	seeq8005.c	seeq8005.o
SMC	83c790 chips	smc-ultra32.c	smc-ultra32.o
	8432	de4x5.c	de4x5.o
	8432BT	tulip.c	tulip.o
	9000 Series	smc9194.c	smc9194.o
	9332 (w/ new SROM)	de4x5.c	de4x5.o
	Ultra	smc-ultra.c	smc-ultra.o
	EtherEZ (ISA)	smc-ultra.c	smc-ultra.o
	EtherPower 10 (PCI)	tulip.c	tulip.o
	EtherPower 10/100 (PCI)	tulip.c	tulip.o
	Ultra32 EISA	smc-ultra32.c	smc-ultra32.o
	EtherPower II	epic100.c	epic100.o
Surecom	EP-320X	tulip.c	tulip.c
	NE34	ne.c	ne.o
Thomas Conrad	TC 5048	tulip.c	tulip.c
VIA	86c100A Rhine-II (PCI)	via-rhine.c	via-rhine.o
	82C926 Amazon	ne.c	ne.o
Winbond	89C940	ne.c	ne.o
Western Digital	WD8003	wd.c	wd.o
	WD8013	wd.c	wd.o
Zenith	Z-Note	znet.c	znet.o
Zynx	ZX312 EtherAction	tulip.c	tulip.o
	ZX314	tulip.c	tulip.o
	ZX315 EtherArray	tulip.c	tulip.o
	ZX316 10/100 4 port	de4x5.c	de4x5.o
	ZX342/344/345/346/348/351	tulip.c	tulip.o

App

E

ARCnet Cards

The following ARCnet cards are compatible with OpenLinux 2.3. To use the module, load arc-net.o and then the card-specific module.

Company	Model	Source	Module
ARCnet	ARCnet RIM I	arc-rimi.c	arc-rimi.o
	ARCnet card w/ memory mapped COM90xx chipset	com90xx.c	com90xx.o
	ARCnet card w/ COM20020 chipset	com20020.c	com20020.o
	ARCnet card w/ IO mapped COM90xx chipset	com90io.c	com90io.o

Supported Frame Relay Cards

The following frame relay interface cards are compatible with OpenLinux 2.3. The cards can be configured using the dlcicfg and fradcfg utilities. These utilities are available at `ftp://ftp.invlogic.com/pub/linux`:

Company	Model	Source	Module
Sangoma	S502A	sdla.c	sdla.o
	S502E	sdla.c	sdla.o
	S507	sdla.c	sdla.o
	S508	sdla.c	sdla.o

FDDI Cards

Company	Model	Source	Module
DEC	FDDIcontroller (EISA/PCI)	defxx.c	

Supported Radio Modem/Network Cards

The following radio modem cards are compatible with OpenLinux 2.3:

Company	Model	Source	Module
AT&T	GIS Wavelan	wavelan.c	wavelan.o
Baycom	par96	baycom.c	baycom.o
	par97	baycom.c	baycom.o
	picpar	baycom.c	baycom.o
	ser12	baycom.c	baycom.o
Creative Labs	SoundBlaster	sm.c	sm.o
	SoundBlaster (HF FSK)	hfmodem	hfmodem.o
Gracilis	PackeTwin	pt.c	pt.o
Ottawa Amateur Radio Club	PI	pi2.c	pi2.o
	PI2	pi2.c	pi2.o
WSS	WSS (half duplex)	sm.c	sm.o
z8530 SCC		scc.c	scc.o

Supported Token Ring Cards

Company	Model	Source	Module
IBM	Any non-DMA cards	ibmtr.c	ibmtr.o
PCMCIA	The PCMCIA-HOWTO lists all supported PCMCIA	devices.	

App

E

Compatible iRDA devices

The following Infrared (iRDA) Devices are compatible with OpenLinux 2.3:

Company	Model	Source	Module
ACTiSYS	IR-220L (dongle)	actisys.c	actisys.o
ACTiSYS	IR-220L+ (dongle)	actisys.c	actisys.o
Extended Systems	JetEye PC	esi.c	esi.o
Tekram	IrMate IR-210B (dongle)	tekram.c	tekram.o

continues

Company	Model	Source	Module
Sharp	Universal Infrared Communications Controller (UIRCC)	uircc.c	uircc.o
Winbond	W83977Af Super IO chip	w83977af.c	w83977af.o
National Semiconductor	PC87108 chip	pc87108.c	pc87108.o

Unsupported Hardware

The following list is not necessarily complete, but it includes some of the hardware known not to work with Caldera OpenLinux release 2.3 out of the box. Some of it might work with the use of additional software from other vendors or kernel patches. Check the Linux user groups and discussion lists for tips and updates on making these peripheral devices work.

- "WinModems" (modems made specifically for Windows systems)
- "WinPrinters" (printers made specifically for Windows systems)

Running Linux on Specific Notebook Models

For details on setup of Linux on a notebook computer, see Kenneth Harker's Linux on Laptops Web site at www.cs.utexas.edu/users/kharker/linux-laptop/. It includes small How-To style documents that describe setup and configuration of Linux on specific notebooks. If you do not see a specific notebook brand or model listed, no one has taken the time to document the specifics of installing or running Linux for that machine.

Linux PCMCIA Supported Device List

A list of PCMCIA cards supported by Linux is maintained by David Hinds. The list can be obtained on the Web at ftp://hyper.stanford.edu/pub/pcmcia/. If the PCMCIA card you have is not listed as supported, then do not expect it to work with Linux.

Index

Other Related Titles

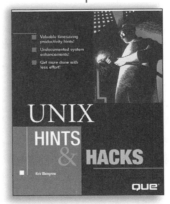

What's On the CD-ROM?

The CD-ROM included with this book contains Caldera's OpenLinux 2.3, which is freely available from Caldera's FTP site. This software includes

- KDE 1.1.1
- Netscape Communicator 4.61
- LIZARD, the graphical installation wizard

The following are commercial upgrades that are also available on the included CD-ROM:

- PartitionMagic, Caldera Edition
- BootMagic, Caldera Edition

The following are available in Caldera's commercial package of OpenLinux 2.3:

- BRU
- StarOffice 5.1
- WordPerfect 8
- ApplixWare 4.4.2

OpenLinux Support

Caldera Systems, Inc. does not provide support for the software accompanying this book.

Fee-based support for OpenLinux is available at 1-800-850-7779.

If you encounter problems with the content of this book or defects in the CD, please visit our Web site at www.mcp.com/support.